THIRD EDITION

PHP Cookbook

David Sklar and Adam Trachtenberg

Beijing · Cambridge · Farnham · Köln · Sebastopol · Tokyo

PHP Cookbook, Third Edition

by David Sklar and Adam Trachtenberg

Copyright © 2014 David Sklar and Adam Trachtenberg. All rights reserved.

Printed in the United States of America.

Published by O'Reilly Media, Inc., 1005 Gravenstein Highway North, Sebastopol, CA 95472.

O'Reilly books may be purchased for educational, business, or sales promotional use. Online editions are also available for most titles (*http://my.safaribooksonline.com*). For more information, contact our corporate/institutional sales department: 800-998-9938 or *corporate@oreilly.com*.

Editors: Rachel Roumeliotis and Allyson MacDonald	**Indexer:** Judith McConville
Production Editor: Melanie Yarbrough	**Cover Designer:** Karen Montgomery
Copyeditor: Kim Cofer	**Interior Designer:** David Futato
Proofreader: Charles Roumeliotis	**Illustrator:** Rebecca Demarest

June 2001:	First Edition
June 2004:	Second Edition
June 2014:	Third Edition

Revision History for the Third Edition:

2014-06-25:   First release

See *http://oreilly.com/catalog/errata.csp?isbn=9781449363758* for release details.

ISBN: 978-1-449-36375-8

[LSI]

Table of Contents

Preface

PHP is the engine behind millions of dynamic web applications. Its broad feature set, approachable syntax, and support for different operating systems and web servers have made it an ideal language for both rapid web development and the methodical construction of complex systems.

One of the major reasons for PHP's success as a web scripting language is its origins as a tool to process HTML forms and create web pages. This makes PHP very web-friendly. Additionally, it is eagerly promiscuous when it comes to external applications and libraries. PHP can speak to a multitude of databases, and it knows numerous Internet protocols. PHP also makes it simple to parse form data and make HTTP requests. This web-specific focus carries over to the recipes and examples in the *PHP Cookbook*.

This book is a collection of solutions to common tasks in PHP. We've tried to include material that will appeal to everyone from newbies to wizards. If we've succeeded, you'll learn something (or perhaps many things) from *PHP Cookbook*. There are tips in here for everyday PHP programmers as well as for people coming to PHP with experience in another language.

PHP, in source code and binary forms, is available for download free from *http:// www.php.net/*. The PHP website also contains installation instructions, comprehensive documentation, and pointers to online resources, user groups, mailing lists, and other PHP resources.

Who This Book Is For

This book is for programmers who need to solve problems with PHP. If you don't know any PHP, make this your second PHP book. The first should be *Learning PHP 5*, also from O'Reilly.

If you're already familiar with PHP, this book helps you overcome a specific problem and get on with your life (or at least your programming activities). The *PHP Cook-*

book can also show you how to accomplish a particular task in PHP, such as sending email or parsing JSON, that you may already know how to do in another language. Programmers converting applications from other languages to PHP will find this book a trusty companion.

What Is in This Book

We don't expect that you'll sit down and read this book from cover to cover (although we'll be happy if you do!). PHP programmers are constantly faced with a wide variety of challenges on a wide range of subjects. Turn to the *PHP Cookbook* when you encounter a problem you need to solve. Each recipe is a self-contained explanation that gives you a head start toward finishing your task. When a recipe refers to topics outside its scope, it contains pointers to related recipes and other online and offline resources.

If you choose to read an entire chapter at once, that's OK. The recipes generally flow from easy to hard, with example programs that "put it all together" at the end of many chapters. The chapter introduction provides an overview of the material covered in the chapter, including relevant background material, and points out a few highlighted recipes of special interest.

The book begins with four chapters about basic data types. Chapter 1 covers details like processing substrings, manipulating case, taking strings apart into smaller pieces, and parsing comma-separated data. Chapter 2 explains operations with floating-point numbers, random numbers, converting between bases, and number formatting. Chapter 3 shows you how to manipulate dates and times, format them, handle time zones and daylight saving time, and find time to microsecond precision. Chapter 4 covers array operations like iterating, merging, reversing, sorting, and extracting particular elements.

Next are three chapters that discuss program building blocks. Chapter 5 covers notable features of PHP's variable handling, such as default values, static variables, and producing string representations of complex data types. The recipes in Chapter 6 deal with using functions in PHP: processing arguments, passing and returning variables by reference, creating functions at runtime, and scoping variables. Chapter 7 covers PHP's object-oriented capabilities, with recipes on OOP basics as well as more advanced features, such as magic methods, destructors, access control, reflection, traits, and namespaces.

After the data types and building blocks come six chapters devoted to topics that are central to web programming. Chapter 8 covers cookies, headers, authentication, working with query strings, and other fundamentals of web applications. Chapter 9 covers processing and validating form input, displaying multipage forms, showing forms with error messages, and guarding against problems such as cross-site scripting and multiple submissions of the same form. Chapter 10 explains the differences between DBM and SQL databases and, using the PDO database access abstraction layer, shows how to connect to a database, assign unique ID values, retrieve rows, change data, escape quotes, and log debugging information. Chapter 11 covers PHP's built-in sessions module, which lets you maintain information about a user as he moves from page to page on your website. This chapter also highlights some of the security issues associated with sessions. Chapter 12 discusses all things XML: the SimpleXML extension and DOM functions, using XPath and XSLT, and reading and writing both RSS and Atom feeds. Chapter 13 explores topics useful to PHP applications that integrate with external websites and client-side JavaScript such as retrieving remote URLs, cleaning up HTML, and responding to an Ajax request.

The next three chapters are all about network interaction. Chapter 14 details the ins and outs of consuming a web service—using an external REST service from within your code. Chapter 15 handles the other side of the web services equation—serving up REST requests to others. Both chapters discuss authentication, headers, and error handling. Chapter 16 discusses other network services such as sending email messages, using LDAP, and doing DNS lookups.

The next section of the book is a series of chapters on features and extensions of PHP that help you build applications that are robust, secure, user-friendly, and efficient. Chapter 17 shows you how to create graphics, with recipes on drawing text, lines, polygons, and curves. Chapter 18 focuses on security topics such as avoiding session fixation and cross-site scripting, working with passwords, and encrypting data. Chapter 19 helps you make your applications globally friendly and includes recipes for localizing text, dates and times, currency values, and images, as well as a recipe working with text in UTF-8 character encoding. Chapter 20 goes into detail on error handling and logging, while Chapter 21 discusses debugging techniques, writing tests for your code, and using PHP's built-in web server. Chapter 22 explains how to compare the performance of two functions and provides tips on getting your programs to run at maximum speed. Chapter 23 covers regular expressions, including capturing text inside of HTML tags, calling a PHP function from inside a regular expression, and using greedy and nongreedy matching.

Chapters 24 and 25 cover the filesystem. Chapter 24 focuses on files: opening and closing them, using temporary files, locking files, sending compressed files, and processing the contents of files. Chapter 25 deals with directories and file metadata, with recipes on changing file permissions and ownership, moving or deleting a file, and processing all files in a directory.

Last, there are two chapters on topics that extend the reach of what PHP can do. Chapter 26 covers using PHP outside of web programming. Its recipes cover command-line topics such as parsing program arguments and reading passwords. Chapter 27 covers Composer, PEAR (PHP Extension and Application Repository), and PECL (PHP Extension Community Library). Composer and PEAR provide access to a collection of PHP code that provides functions and extensions to PHP. PECL is a similar collection, but of extensions to PHP written in C. We use PEAR and PECL modules throughout the book and Chapter 27 shows you how to install and upgrade them.

Other Resources

Websites

There is a tremendous amount of PHP reference material online. With everything from the annotated PHP manual to sites with periodic articles and tutorials, a fast Internet connection rivals a large bookshelf in PHP documentary usefulness. Here are some key sites:

The Annotated PHP Manual (http://www.php.net/manual)
Available in 11 languages, this site includes both official documentation of functions and language features as well as user-contributed comments.

PHP mailing lists (http://www.php.net/mailing-lists.php)
There are many PHP mailing lists covering installation, programming, extending PHP, and various other topics; there is also a read-only web interface (*http://news.php.net/*) to the mailing lists.

PHP support resources (http://us3.php.net/support.php)
This handy collection of support resources has information on PHP user groups, events, and other support channels.

Composer (https://getcomposer.org/)
Composer is a dependency manager for PHP that provides a structured way both to declare dependencies in your project and to install them.

PEAR (http://pear.php.net)
PEAR calls itself "a framework and distribution system for reusable PHP components." You'll find lots of useful PHP classes and sample code there. Read more about PEAR in Chapter 27.

PECL (http://pecl.php.net)
PECL calls itself "a repository for PHP Extensions, providing a directory of extensions and hosting facilities for downloading and development of PHP extensions." Read more about PECL in Chapter 27.

PHP.net: A Tourist's Guide (http://www.php.net/sites.php)
This is a guide to the various websites under the *php.net* umbrella.

PHP: The Right Way (http://www.phptherightway.com/)
A quick reference that attempts to be a comprehensive source of PHP best practices. A great place to start if you're wondering about the idiomatic way to do something in PHP.

Planet PHP (http://www.planet-php.net)
> An aggregation of blog posts by PHP developers, about PHP.

SitePoint Blogs on PHP (http://www.sitepoint.com/blogs/category/php)
> A good collection of information that explores PHP.

Books

This section lists books that are helpful references and tutorials for building applications with PHP. Most are specific to web-related programming; look for books on MySQL, HTML, XML, and HTTP.

At the end of the section, we've included a few books that are useful for every programmer regardless of language of choice. These works can make you a better programmer by teaching you how to think about programming as part of a larger pattern of problem solving:

- *Learning PHP 5* by David Sklar (O'Reilly)
- *Programming PHP* by Rasmus Lerdorf, Kevin Tatroe, and Peter MacIntyre (O'Reilly)
- *Extending and Embedding PHP* by Sara Golemon (Sams)
- *Learning PHP, MySQL, JavaScript, and CSS* by Robin Nixon (O'Reilly)
- *Mastering Regular Expressions* by Jeffrey E. F. Friedl (O'Reilly)
- *MySQL Reference Manual (http://dev.mysql.com/doc/#manual)*
- *MySQL*, by Paul DuBois (New Riders)
- *The Practice of Programming*, by Brian W. Kernighan and Rob Pike (Addison-Wesley)
- *Programming Pearls* by Jon Louis Bentley (Addison-Wesley)
- *The Mythical Man-Month*, by Frederick P. Brooks (Addison-Wesley)

Conventions Used in This Book

Programming Conventions

The examples in this book were written to run under PHP version 5.4.28 (and, where applicable, PHP 5.5.12). Sample code should work on both Unix and Windows, except where noted in the text. We've generally noted in the text when we depend on a feature added to PHP in or after 5.5.

Some examples rely on the $php_errormsg variable, which is only available when the track_errors configuration directive is turned on.

Typesetting Conventions

The following typographic conventions are used in this book:

Italic

Used for commands, filenames, and example URLs. It is also used to define new terms when they first appear in the text.

Constant width

Used in code examples to show partial or complete PHP source code program listings. It is also used for class names, method names, variable names, and other fragments of PHP code.

Constant width bold

Used for user input, such as commands that you type on the command line.

Constant width italic

Shows text that should be replaced with user-supplied values or by values determined by context.

Comments and Questions

Please address comments and questions concerning this book to the publisher:

O'Reilly Media, Inc.
1005 Gravenstein Highway North
Sebastopol, CA 95472
800-998-9938 (in the United States or Canada)
707-829-0515 (international or local)
707-829-0104 (fax)

We have a web page for this book, where we list errata, examples, and any additional information. You can access this page at *http://bit.ly/phpckbk3*.

To comment or ask technical questions about this book, send email to *bookquestions@oreilly.com*.

For more information about our books, courses, conferences, and news, see our website at *http://www.oreilly.com*.

Find us on Facebook: *http://facebook.com/oreilly*

Follow us on Twitter: *http://twitter.com/oreillymedia*

Watch us on YouTube: *http://www.youtube.com/oreillymedia*

Acknowledgments

Most importantly, a huge thanks to everyone who has contributed their time, creativity, and skills to making PHP what it is today. This amazing volunteer effort has created not only hundreds of thousands of lines of source code, but also comprehensive documentation, a QA infrastructure, lots of add-on applications and libraries, and a thriving user community worldwide. It's a thrill and an honor to add the *PHP Cookbook* to the world of PHP.

Thanks also to our reviewers: Paul Huff, Peter MacIntyre, Simon MacIntyre, and Russ Uman. Special mention to Chris Shiflett and Clay Lovelace for their contributions to the second edition of this book.

And big thanks to the folks at O'Reilly that made this book a reality: Rachel Roumeliotis, Allyson MacDonald, Melanie Yarbrough, and Maria Gulick as well as the nameless orcs and dwarves that toil in the subterranean caverns of Sebastopol and Cambridge to make sure that the production process runs smoothly.

David Sklar

Thanks twice again to Adam. We've been working together (in one way or another) for 18 years and PHPing together for 17. There is still no one with whom I'd rather have written this book (except, to be completely honest, maybe Ben Franklin, if he could somehow be brought back to life).

Thanks to my family members of all ages. You gave me the time and space to focus on the book. Now I will give you time and space to read the entire thing!

Adam Trachtenberg

David: It's tough to complete with Ben Franklin. Please know that I support the turkey as the official animal of PHP instead of the elephant. Many thanks for your support over all these years, beginning long ago in the days of PHP/FI. Without you, this book would merely be a dream.

Thanks to my family and friends for their support and encouragement over these many months. All my love to my two sons, even the one who helped me relearn that human children don't give you extensions after 40 weeks if your work on *PHP Cookbook* isn't complete. Finally, special thanks to my wife Elizabeth Anne; I should take your good advice more often.

CHAPTER 1

Strings

1.0 Introduction

Strings in PHP are sequences of bytes, such as "We hold these truths to be self-evident" or "Once upon a time" or even "111211211." When you read data from a file or output it to a web browser, your data is represented as strings.

PHP strings are binary-safe (i.e., they can contain null bytes) and can grow and shrink on demand. Their size is limited only by the amount of memory that is available to PHP.

Usually, PHP strings are ASCII strings. You must do extra work to handle non-ASCII data like UTF-8 or other multibyte character encodings (see Chapter 19).

Similar in form and behavior to Perl and the Unix shell, strings can be initialized in three ways: with single quotes, with double quotes, and with the "here document" (heredoc) format. With single-quoted strings, the only special characters you need to escape inside a string are the backslash and the single quote itself. This example shows four single-quoted strings:

```
print 'I have gone to the store.';
print 'I\'ve gone to the store.';
print 'Would you pay $1.75 for 8 ounces of tap water?';
print 'In double-quoted strings, newline is represented by \n';
```

It prints:

```
I have gone to the store.
I've gone to the store.
Would you pay $1.75 for 8 ounces of tap water?
In double-quoted strings, newline is represented by \n
```

The preceding output shows what the raw output looks like. If you view it in a web browser, you will see all the sentences on the same line because HTML requires additional markup to insert line breaks.

Because PHP doesn't check for variable interpolation or almost any escape sequences in single-quoted strings, defining strings this way is straightforward and fast.

Double-quoted strings don't recognize escaped single quotes, but they do recognize interpolated variables and the escape sequences shown in Table 1-1.

Table 1-1. Double-quoted string escape sequences

Escape sequence	Character
\n	Newline (ASCII 10)
\r	Carriage return (ASCII 13)
\t	Tab (ASCII 9)
\\	Backslash
\$	Dollar sign
\"	Double quote
\0 through \777	Octal value
\x0 through \xFF	Hex value

Example 1-1 shows some double-quoted strings.

Example 1-1. Double-quoted strings

```
print "I've gone to the store.";
print "The sauce cost \$10.25.";
$cost = '$10.25';
print "The sauce cost $cost.";
print "The sauce cost \$\061\060.\x32\x35.";
```

Example 1-1 prints:

```
I've gone to the store.
The sauce cost $10.25.
The sauce cost $10.25.
The sauce cost $10.25.
```

The last line of Example 1-1 prints the price of sauce correctly because the character 1 is ASCII code 49 decimal and 061 octal. Character 0 is ASCII 48 decimal and 060 octal; 2 is ASCII 50 decimal and 32 hex; and 5 is ASCII 53 decimal and 35 hex.

Heredoc-specified strings recognize all the interpolations and escapes of double-quoted strings, but they don't require double quotes to be escaped. Heredocs start with <<< and a token. That token (with no leading or trailing whitespace), followed by a semicolon to end the statement (if necessary), ends the heredoc. Example 1-2 shows how to define a heredoc.

Example 1-2. Defining a here document

```
print <<< END
It's funny when signs say things like:
    Original "Root" Beer
    "Free" Gift
    Shoes cleaned while "you" wait
or have other misquoted words.
END;
```

Example 1-2 prints:

It's funny when signs say things like:
**   Original "Root" Beer**
**   "Free" Gift**
**   Shoes cleaned while "you" wait**
or have other misquoted words.

Newlines, spacing, and quotes are all preserved in a heredoc. By convention, the end-of-string identifier is usually all caps, and it is case sensitive. Example 1-3 shows two more valid heredocs.

Example 1-3. More here documents

```
print <<< PARSLEY
It's easy to grow fresh:
Parsley
Chives
on your windowsill
PARSLEY;

print <<< DOGS
If you like pets, yell out:
DOGS AND CATS ARE GREAT!
DOGS;
```

Heredocs are especially useful for printing out HTML with interpolated variables because you don't have to escape the double quotes that appear in the HTML elements. Example 1-4 uses a heredoc to print HTML.

Example 1-4. Printing HTML with a here document

```
if ($remaining_cards > 0) {
    $url = '/deal.php';
    $text = 'Deal More Cards';
} else {
    $url = '/new-game.php';
    $text = 'Start a New Game';
}
```

```
print <<< HTML
There are <b>$remaining_cards</b> left.
<p>
<a href="$url">$text</a>
HTML;
```

In Example 1-4, the semicolon needs to go after the end-of-string delimiter to tell PHP the statement is ended. In some cases, however, you shouldn't use the semicolon. One of these cases is shown in Example 1-5, which uses a heredoc with the string concatenation operator.

Example 1-5. Concatenation with a here document

```
$html = <<< END
<div class="$divClass">
<ul class="$ulClass">
<li>
END
. $listItem . '</li></div>';

print $html;
```

Assuming some reasonable values for the $divClass, $ulClass, and $listItem variables, Example 1-5 prints:

```
<div class="class1">>
<ul class="class2">
<li> The List Item </li></div>
```

In Example 1-5, the expression needs to continue on the next line, so you don't use a semicolon. Note also that in order for PHP to recognize the end-of-string delimiter, the . string concatenation operator needs to go on a separate line from the end-of-string delimiter.

Nowdocs are similar to heredocs, but there is no variable interpolation. So, nowdocs are to heredocs as single-quoted strings are to double-quoted strings. They're best when you have a block of non-PHP code, such as JavaScript, that you want to print as part of an HTML page or send to another program.

For example, if you're using jQuery:

```
$js = <<<'__JS__'
$.ajax({
  'url': '/api/getStock',
  'data': {
    'ticker': 'LNKD'
  },
  'success': function( data ) {
    $( "#stock-price" ).html( "<strong>$" + data + "</strong>" );
  }
});
```

```
__JS__;

print $js;
```

Individual bytes in strings can be referenced with square brackets. The first byte in the string is at index 0. Example 1-6 grabs one byte from a string.

Example 1-6. Getting an individual byte in a string

```
$neighbor = 'Hilda';
print $neighbor[3];
```

Example 1-6 prints:

d

1.1 Accessing Substrings

Problem

You want to know if a string contains a particular substring. For example, you want to find out if an email address contains a @.

Solution

Use `strpos()`, as in Example 1-7.

Example 1-7. Finding a substring with strpos( )

```
if (strpos($_POST['email'], '@') === false) {
    print 'There was no @ in the e-mail address!';
}
```

Discussion

The return value from `strpos()` is the first position in the string (the "haystack") at which the substring (the "needle") was found. If the needle wasn't found at all in the haystack, `strpos()` returns `false`. If the needle is at the beginning of the haystack, `strpos()` returns 0 because position 0 represents the beginning of the string. To differentiate between return values of 0 and `false`, you must use the identity operator (===) or the not–identity operator (!==) instead of regular equals (==) or not-equals (!=). Example 1-7 compares the return value from `strpos()` to `false` using ===. This test only succeeds if `strpos()` returns false, not if it returns 0 or any other number.

See Also

Documentation on `strpos()` (*http://www.php.net/strpos*).

1.2 Extracting Substrings

Problem

You want to extract part of a string, starting at a particular place in the string. For example, you want the first eight characters of a username entered into a form.

Solution

Use `substr()` to select your substring, as in Example 1-8.

Example 1-8. Extracting a substring with substr( )

```
$substring = substr($string,$start,$length);
$username = substr($_GET['username'],0,8);
```

Discussion

If `$start` and `$length` are positive, `substr()` returns `$length` characters in the string, starting at `$start`. The first character in the string is at position 0. Example 1-9 has positive `$start` and `$length`.

Example 1-9. Using substr( ) with positive $start and $length

```
print substr('watch out for that tree',6,5);
```

Example 1-9 prints:

```
out f
```

If you leave out `$length`, `substr()` returns the string from `$start` to the end of the original string, as shown in Example 1-10.

Example 1-10. Using substr( ) with positive start and no length

```
print substr('watch out for that tree',17);
```

Example 1-10 prints:

```
t tree
```

If `$start` is bigger than the length of the string, `substr()` returns `false`.

If `$start` plus `$length` goes past the end of the string, `substr()` returns all of the string from `$start` forward, as shown in Example 1-11.

Example 1-11. Using substr( ) with length past the end of the string

```
print substr('watch out for that tree',20,5);
```

Example 1-11 prints:

```
ree
```

If $start is negative, substr() counts back from the end of the string to determine where your substring starts, as shown in Example 1-12.

Example 1-12. Using substr( ) with negative start

```
print substr('watch out for that tree',-6);
print substr('watch out for that tree',-17,5);
```

Example 1-12 prints:

```
t tree
out f
```

With a negative $start value that goes past the beginning of the string (for example, if $start is −27 with a 20-character string), substr() behaves as if $start is 0.

If $length is negative, substr() counts back from the end of the string to determine where your substring ends, as shown in Example 1-13.

Example 1-13. Using substr( ) with negative length

```
print substr('watch out for that tree',15,-2);
print substr('watch out for that tree',-4,-1);
```

Example 1-13 prints:

```
hat tr
tre
```

See Also

Documentation on substr() (*http://www.php.net/substr*).

1.3 Replacing Substrings

Problem

You want to replace a substring with a different string. For example, you want to obscure all but the last four digits of a credit card number before printing it.

Solution

Use substr_replace(), as in Example 1-14.

Example 1-14. Replacing a substring with substr_replace( )

```
// Everything from position $start to the end of $old_string
// becomes $new_substring
$new_string = substr_replace($old_string,$new_substring,$start);
```

```
// $length characters, starting at position $start, become $new_substring
$new_string = substr_replace($old_string,$new_substring,$start,$length);
```

Discussion

Without the $length argument, substr_replace() replaces everything from $start to the end of the string. If $length is specified, only that many characters are replaced:

```
print substr_replace('My pet is a blue dog.','fish.',12);
print substr_replace('My pet is a blue dog.','green',12,4);
$credit_card = '4111 1111 1111 1111';
print substr_replace($credit_card,'xxxx ',0,strlen($credit_card)-4);

My pet is a fish.
My pet is a green dog.
xxxx 1111
```

If $start is negative, the new substring is placed by counting $start characters from the end of $old_string, not from the beginning:

```
print substr_replace('My pet is a blue dog.','fish.',-9);
print substr_replace('My pet is a blue dog.','green',-9,4);

My pet is a fish.
My pet is a green dog.
```

If $start and $length are 0, the new substring is inserted at the start of $old_string:

```
print substr_replace('My pet is a blue dog.','Title: ',0,0);

Title: My pet is a blue dog.
```

The function substr_replace() is useful when you've got text that's too big to display all at once, and you want to display some of the text with a link to the rest. Example 1-15 displays the first 25 characters of a message with an ellipsis after it as a link to a page that displays more text.

Example 1-15. Displaying long text with an ellipsis

```
$r = mysql_query("SELECT id,message FROM messages WHERE id = $id") or die();
$ob = mysql_fetch_object($r);
printf('<a href="more-text.php?id=%d">%s</a>',
        $ob->id, substr_replace($ob->message,' ...',25));
```

The *more-text.php* page referenced in Example 1-15 can use the message ID passed in the query string to retrieve the full message and display it.

See Also

Documentation on substr_replace() (*http://www.php.net/substr-replace*).

1.4 Processing a String One Byte at a Time

Problem

You need to process each byte in a string individually.

Solution

Loop through each byte in the string with for. Example 1-16 counts the vowels in a string.

Example 1-16. Processing each byte in a string

```
$string = "This weekend, I'm going shopping for a pet chicken.";
$vowels = 0;
for ($i = 0, $j = strlen($string); $i < $j; $i++) {
    if (strstr('aeiouAEIOU',$string[$i])) {
        $vowels++;
    }
}
```

Discussion

Processing a string a character at a time is an easy way to calculate the "Look and Say" sequence, as shown in Example 1-17.

Example 1-17. The Look and Say sequence

```
function lookandsay($s) {
    // initialize the return value to the empty string
    $r = '';
    // $m holds the character we're counting, initialize to the first
    // character in the string
    $m = $s[0];
    // $n is the number of $m's we've seen, initialize to 1
    $n = 1;
    for ($i = 1, $j = strlen($s); $i < $j; $i++) {
        // if this character is the same as the last one
        if ($s[$i] == $m) {
            // increment the count of this character
            $n++;
        } else {
            // otherwise, add the count and character to the return value
            $r .= $n.$m;
            // set the character we're looking for to the current one
            $m = $s[$i];
            // and reset the count to 1
            $n = 1;
        }
    }
    // return the built up string as well as the last count and character
```

```
        return $r.$n.$m;
    }

    for ($i = 0, $s = 1; $i < 10; $i++) {
        $s = lookandsay($s);
        print "$s\n";
    }
```

Example 1-17 prints:

```
1
11
21
1211
111221
312211
13112221
1113213211
31131211131221
13211311123113112211
```

It's called the "Look and Say" sequence because each element is what you get by looking at the previous element and saying what's in it. For example, looking at the first element, 1, you say "one one." So the second element is "11." That's two ones, so the third element is "21." Similarly, that's one two and one one, so the fourth element is "1211," and so on.

See Also

Documentation on for (*http://www.php.net/for*); more about the "Look and Say" (*http://bit.ly/1g2X0sD*) sequence.

1.5 Reversing a String by Word or Byte

Problem

You want to reverse the words or the bytes in a string.

Solution

Use strrev() to reverse by byte, as in Example 1-18.

Example 1-18. Reversing a string by byte

```
print strrev('This is not a palindrome.');
```

Example 1-18 prints:

```
.emordnilap a ton si sihT
```

To reverse by words, explode the string by word boundary, reverse the words, and then rejoin, as in Example 1-19.

Example 1-19. Reversing a string by word

```
$s = "Once upon a time there was a turtle.";
// break the string up into words
$words = explode(' ',$s);
// reverse the array of words
$words = array_reverse($words);
// rebuild the string
$s = implode(' ',$words);
print $s;
```

Example 1-19 prints:

```
turtle. a was there time a upon Once
```

Discussion

Reversing a string by words can also be done all in one line with the code in Example 1-20.

Example 1-20. Concisely reversing a string by word

```
$reversed_s = implode(' ',array_reverse(explode(' ',$s)));
```

See Also

Recipe 24.7 discusses the implications of using something other than a space character as your word boundary; documentation on strrev() (*http://www.php.net/strrev*) and array_reverse() (*http://www.php.net/array-reverse*).

1.6 Generating a Random String

Problem

You want to generate a random string.

Solution

Use str_rand():

```
function str_rand($length = 32,
    $characters = ↵
'0123456789abcdefghijklmnopqrstuvwxyzABCDEFGHIJKLMNOPQRSTUVWXYZ') {
if (!is_int($length) || $length < 0) {
    return false;
}
```

```
    $characters_length = strlen($characters) - 1;
$string = '';

for ($i = $length; $i > 0; $i--) {
$string .= $characters[mt_rand(0, $characters_length)];
}

    return $string;
}
```

Discussion

PHP has native functions for generating random numbers, but nothing for random strings. The str_rand() function returns a 32-character string constructed from letters and numbers.

Pass in an integer to change the length of the returned string. To use an alternative set of characters, pass them as a string as the second argument. For example, to get a 16-digit Morse Code:

```
print str_rand(16, '.-');
```

```
.--..-.-.--.----
```

See Also

Recipe 2.5 for generating random numbers.

1.7 Expanding and Compressing Tabs

Problem

You want to change spaces to tabs (or tabs to spaces) in a string while keeping text aligned with tab stops. For example, you want to display formatted text to users in a standardized way.

Solution

Use str_replace() to switch spaces to tabs or tabs to spaces, as shown in Example 1-21.

Example 1-21. Switching tabs and spaces

```
$rows = $db->query('SELECT message FROM messages WHERE id = 1');
$obj = $rows->fetch(PDO::FETCH_OBJ);

$tabbed = str_replace(' ' , "\t", $obj->message);
$spaced = str_replace("\t", ' ' , $obj->message);
```

```
print "With Tabs: <pre>$tabbed</pre>";
print "With Spaces: <pre>$spaced</pre>";
```

Using `str_replace()` for conversion, however, doesn't respect tab stops. If you want tab stops every eight characters, a line beginning with a five-letter word and a tab should have that tab replaced with three spaces, not one. Use the `tab_expand()` function shown in Example 1-22 to turn tabs to spaces in a way that respects tab stops.

Example 1-22. tab_expand( )

```
function tab_expand($text) {
    while (strstr($text,"\t")) {
        $text = preg_replace_callback('/^([^\t\n]*)(\t+)/m',
                                      'tab_expand_helper', $text);
    }
    return $text;
}

function tab_expand_helper($matches) {
    $tab_stop = 8;

    return $matches[1] .
    str_repeat(' ',strlen($matches[2]) *
                    $tab_stop - (strlen($matches[1]) % $tab_stop));
}


$spaced = tab_expand($obj->message);
```

You can use the `tab_unexpand()` function shown in Example 1-23 to turn spaces back to tabs.

Example 1-23. tab_unexpand( )

```
function tab_unexpand($text) {
    $tab_stop = 8;
    $lines = explode("\n",$text);
    foreach ($lines as $i => $line) {
        // Expand any tabs to spaces
        $line = tab_expand($line);
        $chunks = str_split($line, $tab_stop);
        $chunkCount = count($chunks);
        // Scan all but the last chunk
        for ($j = 0; $j < $chunkCount - 1; $j++) {
            $chunks[$j] = preg_replace('/ {2,}$/',"\t",$chunks[$j]);
        }
        // If the last chunk is a tab-stop's worth of spaces
        // convert it to a tab; Otherwise, leave it alone
        if ($chunks[$chunkCount-1] == str_repeat(' ', $tab_stop)) {
            $chunks[$chunkCount-1] = "\t";
        }
        // Recombine the chunks
```

```
        $lines[$i] = implode('',$chunks);
    }
    // Recombine the lines
    return implode("\n",$lines);
}

$tabbed = tab_unexpand($obj->message);
```

Both functions take a string as an argument and return the string appropriately modified.

Discussion

Each function assumes tab stops are every eight spaces, but that can be modified by changing the setting of the $tab_stop variable.

The regular expression in tab_expand() matches both a group of tabs and all the text in a line before that group of tabs. It needs to match the text before the tabs because the length of that text affects how many spaces the tabs should be replaced with so that subsequent text is aligned with the next tab stop. The function doesn't just replace each tab with eight spaces; it adjusts text after tabs to line up with tab stops.

Similarly, tab_unexpand() doesn't just look for eight consecutive spaces and then replace them with one tab character. It divides up each line into eight-character chunks and then substitutes ending whitespace in those chunks (at least two spaces) with tabs. This not only preserves text alignment with tab stops; it also saves space in the string.

See Also

Documentation on str_replace() (*http://www.php.net/str-replace*), on preg_re place_callback() (*http://www.php.net/preg_replace_callback*), and on str_split() (*http://www.php.net/str_split*). Recipe 23.10 has more information on preg_re place_callback().

1.8 Controlling Case

Problem

You need to capitalize, lowercase, or otherwise modify the case of letters in a string. For example, you want to capitalize the initial letters of names but lowercase the rest.

Solution

Use ucfirst() or ucwords() to capitalize the first letter of one or more words, as shown in Example 1-24.

Example 1-24. Capitalizing letters

```
print ucfirst("how do you do today?");
print ucwords("the prince of wales");
```

Example 1-24 prints:

```
How do you do today?
The Prince Of Wales
```

Use `strtolower()` or `strtoupper()` to modify the case of entire strings, as in Example 1-25.

Example 1-25. Changing case of strings

```
print strtoupper("i'm not yelling!");
print strtolower('<A HREF="one.php">one</A>');
```

Example 1-25 prints:

```
I'M NOT YELLING!
<a href="one.php">one</a>
```

Discussion

Use `ucfirst()` to capitalize the first character in a string:

```
print ucfirst('monkey face');
print ucfirst('1 monkey face');
```

This prints:

```
Monkey face
1 monkey face
```

Note that the second phrase is not "1 Monkey face."

Use `ucwords()` to capitalize the first character of each word in a string:

```
print ucwords('1 monkey face');
print ucwords("don't play zone defense against the philadelphia 76-ers");
```

This prints:

```
1 Monkey Face
Don't Play Zone Defense Against The Philadelphia 76-ers
```

As expected, `ucwords()` doesn't capitalize the "t" in "don't." But it also doesn't capitalize the "e" in "76-ers." For `ucwords()`, a word is any sequence of nonwhitespace characters that follows one or more whitespace characters. Because both ' and - aren't whitespace characters, `ucwords()` doesn't consider the "t" in "don't" or the "e" in "76-ers" to be word-starting characters.

Both `ucfirst()` and `ucwords()` don't change the case of non–first letters:

```
print ucfirst('macWorld says I should get an iBook');
print ucwords('eTunaFish.com might buy itunaFish.Com!');
```

This prints:

```
MacWorld says I should get an iBook
ETunaFish.com Might Buy ItunaFish.Com!
```

The functions strtolower() and strtoupper() work on entire strings, not just individual characters. All alphabetic characters are changed to lowercase by strtolower() and strtoupper() changes all alphabetic characters to uppercase:

```
print strtolower("I programmed the WOPR and the TRS-80.");
print strtoupper('"since feeling is first" is a poem by e. e. cummings.');
```

This prints:

```
i programmed the wopr and the trs-80.
"SINCE FEELING IS FIRST" IS A POEM BY E. E. CUMMINGS.
```

When determining upper- and lowercase, these functions respect your locale settings.

See Also

For more information about locale settings, see Chapter 19; documentation on uc first() (*http://www.php.net/ucfirst*), ucwords() (*http://www.php.net/ucwords*), strto lower() (*http://www.php.net/strtolower*), and strtoupper() (*http://www.php.net/ strtoupper*).

1.9 Interpolating Functions and Expressions Within Strings

Problem

You want to include the results of executing a function or expression within a string.

Solution

Use the string concatenation operator (.), as shown in Example 1-26, when the value you want to include can't be inside the string.

Example 1-26. String concatenation

```
print 'You have '.($_POST['boys'] + $_POST['girls']).' children.';
print "The word '$word' is ".strlen($word).' characters long.';
print 'You owe '.$amounts['payment'].' immediately.';
print "My circle's diameter is ".$circle->getDiameter().' inches.';
```

Discussion

You can put variables, object properties, and array elements (if the subscript is unquoted) directly in double-quoted strings:

```
print "I have $children children.";
print "You owe $amounts[payment] immediately.";
print "My circle's diameter is $circle->diameter inches.";
```

Interpolation with double-quoted strings places some limitations on the syntax of what can be interpolated. In the previous example, $amounts['payment'] had to be written as $amounts[payment] so it would be interpolated properly. Use curly braces around more complicated expressions to interpolate them into a string. For example:

```
print "I have {$children} children.";
print "You owe {$amounts['payment']} immediately.";
print "My circle's diameter is {$circle->getDiameter()} inches.";
```

Direct interpolation or using string concatenation also works with heredocs. Interpolating with string concatenation in heredocs can look a little strange because the closing heredoc delimiter and the string concatenation operator have to be on separate lines:

```
print <<< END
Right now, the time is
END
. strftime('%c') . <<< END
 but tomorrow it will be
END
. strftime('%c',time() + 86400);
```

Also, if you're interpolating with heredocs, make sure to include appropriate spacing for the whole string to appear properly. In the previous example, Right now, the time is has to include a trailing space, and but tomorrow it will be has to include leading and trailing spaces.

See Also

For the syntax to interpolate variable variables (such as ${"amount_$i"}), see Recipe 5.4; documentation on the string concatenation operator (*http://www.php.net/language.operators.string*).

1.10 Trimming Blanks from a String

Problem

You want to remove whitespace from the beginning or end of a string. For example, you want to clean up user input before validating it.

Solution

Use ltrim(), rtrim(), or trim(). The ltrim() function removes whitespace from the beginning of a string, rtrim() from the end of a string, and trim() from both the beginning and end of a string:

```
$zipcode = trim($_GET['zipcode']);
$no_linefeed = rtrim($_GET['text']);
$name = ltrim($_GET['name']);
```

Discussion

For these functions, whitespace is defined as the following characters: newline, carriage return, space, horizontal and vertical tab, and null.

Trimming whitespace off of strings saves storage space and can make for more precise display of formatted data or text within <pre> tags, for example. If you are doing comparisons with user input, you should trim the data first, so that someone who mistakenly enters 98052 followed by a few spaces as their zip code isn't forced to fix an error that really isn't one. Trimming before exact text comparisons also ensures that, for example, "salami\n" equals "salami." It's also a good idea to normalize string data by trimming it before storing it in a database.

The trim() functions can also remove user-specified characters from strings. Pass the characters you want to remove as a second argument. You can indicate a range of characters with two dots between the first and last characters in the range:

```
// Remove numerals and space from the beginning of the line
print ltrim('10 PRINT A$',' 0..9');
// Remove semicolon from the end of the line
print rtrim('SELECT * FROM turtles;',';');
```

This prints:

```
PRINT A$
SELECT * FROM turtles
```

PHP also provides chop() as an alias for rtrim(). However, you're best off using rtrim() instead because PHP's chop() behaves differently than Perl's chop() (which is deprecated in favor of chomp(), anyway), and using it can confuse others when they read your code.

See Also

Documentation on trim() (*http://www.php.net/trim*), ltrim() (*http://www.php.net/ltrim*), and rtrim() (*http://www.php.net/rtrim*).

1.11 Generating Comma-Separated Data

Problem

You want to format data as comma-separated values (CSV) so that it can be imported by a spreadsheet or database.

Solution

Use the `fputcsv()` function to generate a CSV-formatted line from an array of data. Example 1-27 writes the data in `$sales` into a file.

Example 1-27. Generating comma-separated data

```
$sales = array( array('Northeast','2005-01-01','2005-02-01',12.54),
                array('Northwest','2005-01-01','2005-02-01',546.33),
                array('Southeast','2005-01-01','2005-02-01',93.26),
                array('Southwest','2005-01-01','2005-02-01',945.21),
                array('All Regions','--','--',1597.34) );

$filename = './sales.csv';
$fh = fopen($filename,'w') or die("Can't open $filename");
foreach ($sales as $sales_line) {
    if (fputcsv($fh, $sales_line) === false) {
        die("Can't write CSV line");
    }
}
fclose($fh) or die("Can't close $filename");
```

Discussion

To print the CSV-formatted data instead of writing it to a file, use the special output stream `php://output`, as shown in Example 1-28.

Example 1-28. Printing comma-separated data

```
$sales = array( array('Northeast','2005-01-01','2005-02-01',12.54),
                array('Northwest','2005-01-01','2005-02-01',546.33),
                array('Southeast','2005-01-01','2005-02-01',93.26),
                array('Southwest','2005-01-01','2005-02-01',945.21),
                array('All Regions','--','--',1597.34) );

$fh = fopen('php://output','w');
foreach ($sales as $sales_line) {
    if (fputcsv($fh, $sales_line) === false) {
        die("Can't write CSV line");
    }
}
fclose($fh);
```

To put the CSV-formatted data into a string instead of printing it or writing it to a file, combine the technique in Example 1-28 with output buffering, as shown in Example 1-29.

Example 1-29. Putting comma-separated data into a string

```
$sales = array( array('Northeast','2005-01-01','2005-02-01',12.54),
                array('Northwest','2005-01-01','2005-02-01',546.33),
                array('Southeast','2005-01-01','2005-02-01',93.26),
                array('Southwest','2005-01-01','2005-02-01',945.21),
                array('All Regions','--','--',1597.34) );

ob_start();
$fh = fopen('php://output','w') or die("Can't open php://output");
foreach ($sales as $sales_line) {
    if (fputcsv($fh, $sales_line) === false) {
        die("Can't write CSV line");
    }
}
fclose($fh) or die("Can't close php://output");
$output = ob_get_contents();
ob_end_clean();
```

See Also

Documentation on `fputcsv()` (*http://www.php.net/fputcsv*); Recipe 8.13 has more information about output buffering.

1.12 Parsing Comma-Separated Data

Problem

You have data in comma-separated values (CSV) format—for example, a file exported from Excel or a database—and you want to extract the records and fields into a format you can manipulate in PHP.

Solution

If the CSV data is in a file (or available via a URL), open the file with `fopen()` and read in the data with `fgetcsv()`. Example 1-30 prints out CSV data in an HTML table.

Example 1-30. Reading CSV data from a file

```
$fp = fopen($filename,'r') or die("can't open file");
print "<table>\n";
while($csv_line = fgetcsv($fp)) {
    print '<tr>';
    for ($i = 0, $j = count($csv_line); $i < $j; $i++) {
        print '<td>'.htmlentities($csv_line[$i]).'</td>';
```

```
            }
        print "</tr>\n";
    }
    print "</table>\n";
    fclose($fp) or die("can't close file");
```

Discussion

By default, fgetcsv() reads in an entire line of data. If your average line length is more than 8,192 bytes, your program may run faster if you specify an explicit line length instead of letting PHP figure it out. Do this by providing a second argument to fgetcsv() that is a value larger than the maximum length of a line in your CSV file. (Don't forget to count the end-of-line whitespace.) If you pass a line length of 0, PHP will use the default behavior.

You can pass fgetcsv() an optional third argument, a delimiter to use instead of a comma (,). However, using a different delimiter somewhat defeats the purpose of CSV as an easy way to exchange tabular data.

Don't be tempted to bypass fgetcsv() and just read a line in and explode() on the commas. CSV is more complicated than that so that it can deal with field values that have, for example, literal commas in them that should not be treated as field delimiters. Using fgetcsv() protects you and your code from subtle errors.

See Also

Documentation on fgetcsv() (*http://www.php.net/fgetcsv*).

1.13 Generating Fixed-Width Field Data Records

Problem

You need to format data records such that each field takes up a set amount of characters.

Solution

Use pack() with a format string that specifies a sequence of space-padded strings. Example 1-31 transforms an array of data into fixed-width records.

Example 1-31. Generating fixed-width field data records

```
$books = array( array('Elmer Gantry', 'Sinclair Lewis', 1927),
                array('The Scarlatti Inheritance','Robert Ludlum', 1971),
                array('The Parsifal Mosaic','William Styron', 1979) );

foreach ($books as $book) {
```

```
    print pack('A25A15A4', $book[0], $book[1], $book[2]) . "\n";
}
```

Discussion

The format string A25A14A4 tells pack() to transform its subsequent arguments into a 25-character space-padded string, a 14-character space-padded string, and a 4-character space-padded string. For space-padded fields in fixed-width records, pack() provides a concise solution.

To pad fields with something other than a space, however, use substr() to ensure that the field values aren't too long and str_pad() to ensure that the field values aren't too short. Example 1-32 transforms an array of records into fixed-width records with .-padded fields.

Example 1-32. Generating fixed-width field data records without pack( )

```
$books = array( array('Elmer Gantry', 'Sinclair Lewis', 1927),
                array('The Scarlatti Inheritance','Robert Ludlum', 1971),
                array('The Parsifal Mosaic','William Styron', 1979) );

foreach ($books as $book) {
    $title  = str_pad(substr($book[0], 0, 25), 25, '.');
    $author = str_pad(substr($book[1], 0, 15), 15, '.');
    $year   = str_pad(substr($book[2], 0, 4), 4, '.');
    print "$title$author$year\n";
}
```

See Also

Documentation on pack() (*http://www.php.net/pack*) and on str_pad() (*http://www.php.net/str_pad*). Recipe 1.17 discusses pack() format strings in more detail.

1.14 Parsing Fixed-Width Field Data Records

Problem

You need to break apart fixed-width records in strings.

Solution

Use substr() as shown in Example 1-33.

Example 1-33. Parsing fixed-width records with substr( )

```
$fp = fopen('fixed-width-records.txt','r',true) or die ("can't open file");
while ($s = fgets($fp,1024)) {
    $fields[1] = substr($s,0,25);  // first field:  first 25 characters of the line
```

```
    $fields[2] = substr($s,25,15); // second field: next 15 characters of the line
    $fields[3] = substr($s,40,4);  // third field:  next 4 characters of the line
    $fields = array_map('rtrim', $fields); // strip the trailing whitespace
    // a function to do something with the fields
    process_fields($fields);
  }
  fclose($fp) or die("can't close file");
```

Or unpack(), as shown in Example 1-34.

Example 1-34. Parsing fixed-width records with unpack( )

```
function fixed_width_unpack($format_string,$data) {
  $r = array();
  for ($i = 0, $j = count($data); $i < $j; $i++) {
    $r[$i] = unpack($format_string,$data[$i]);
  }
  return $r;
}
```

Discussion

Data in which each field is allotted a fixed number of characters per line may look like
this list of books, titles, and publication dates:

```
$booklist=<<<END
Elmer Gantry            Sinclair Lewis 1927
The Scarlatti InheritanceRobert Ludlum  1971
The Parsifal Mosaic     Robert Ludlum  1982
Sophie's Choice         William Styron 1979
END;
```

In each line, the title occupies the first 25 characters, the author's name the next 15
characters, and the publication year the next 4 characters. Knowing those field widths,
you can easily use substr( ) to parse the fields into an array:

```
$books = explode("\n",$booklist);

for($i = 0, $j = count($books); $i < $j; $i++) {
  $book_array[$i]['title'] = substr($books[$i],0,25);
  $book_array[$i]['author'] = substr($books[$i],25,15);
  $book_array[$i]['publication_year'] = substr($books[$i],40,4);
}
```

Exploding $booklist into an array of lines makes the looping code the same whether
it's operating over a string or a series of lines read in from a file.

The loop can be made more flexible by specifying the field names and widths in a
separate array that can be passed to a parsing function, as shown in the
fixed_width_substr( ) function in Example 1-35.

Example 1-35. fixed_width_substr( )

```
function fixed_width_substr($fields,$data) {
  $r = array();
  for ($i = 0, $j = count($data); $i < $j; $i++) {
    $line_pos = 0;
    foreach($fields as $field_name => $field_length) {
      $r[$i][$field_name] = rtrim(substr($data[$i],$line_pos,$field_length));
      $line_pos += $field_length;
    }
  }
  return $r;
}

$book_fields = array('title' => 25,
                     'author' => 15,
                     'publication_year' => 4);

$book_array = fixed_width_substr($book_fields,$booklist);
```

The variable $line_pos keeps track of the start of each field and is advanced by the previous field's width as the code moves through each line. Use rtrim( ) to remove trailing whitespace from each field.

You can use unpack( ) as a substitute for substr( ) to extract fields. Instead of specifying the field names and widths as an associative array, create a format string for unpack( ). A fixed-width field extractor using unpack( ) looks like the fixed_width_unpack( ) function shown in Example 1-36.

Example 1-36. fixed_width_unpack( )

```
function fixed_width_unpack($format_string,$data) {
  $r = array();
  for ($i = 0, $j = count($data); $i < $j; $i++) {
    $r[$i] = unpack($format_string,$data[$i]);
  }
  return $r;
}
```

Because the A format to unpack( ) means *space-padded string,* there's no need to rtrim( ) off the trailing spaces.

Once the fields have been parsed into $book_array by either function, the data can be printed as an HTML table, for example:

```
$book_array = fixed_width_unpack('A25title/A15author/A4publication_year',
                                 $books);
print "<table>\n";
// print a header row
print '<tr><td>';
print join('</td><td>',array_keys($book_array[0]));
print "</td></tr>\n";
```

```
// print each data row
foreach ($book_array as $row) {
    print '<tr><td>';
    print join('</td><td>',array_values($row));
    print "</td></tr>\n";
}
print "</table>\n";
```

Joining data on `</td><td>` produces a table row that is missing its first `<td>` and last `</td>`. We produce a complete table row by printing out `<tr><td>` before the joined data and `</td></tr>` after the joined data.

Both `substr()` and `unpack()` have equivalent capabilities when the fixed-width fields are strings, but `unpack()` is the better solution when the elements of the fields aren't just strings.

If all of your fields are the same size, `str_split()` is a handy shortcut for chopping up incoming data. It returns an array made up of sections of a string. Example 1-37 uses `str_split()` to break apart a string into 32-byte pieces.

Example 1-37. Chopping up a string with str_split( )

```
$fields = str_split($line_of_data,32);
// $fields[0] is bytes 0 - 31
// $fields[1] is bytes 32 - 63
// and so on
```

See Also

For more information about `unpack()`, see Recipe 1.17 and the PHP website (*http://www.php.net/unpack*); documentation on `str_split()` (*http://www.php.net/str_split*); Recipe 4.8 discusses `join()`.

1.15 Taking Strings Apart

Problem

You need to break a string into pieces. For example, you want to access each line that a user enters in a `<textarea>` form field.

Solution

Use `explode()` if what separates the pieces is a constant string:

```
$words = explode(' ','My sentence is not very complicated');
```

Use `preg_split()` if you need a Perl-compatible regular expression to describe the separator:

```
$words = preg_split('/\d\. /','my day: 1. get up 2. get dressed 3. eat toast');
$lines = preg_split('/[\n\r]+/',$_POST['textarea']);
```

Use the /i flag to preg_split() for case-insensitive separator matching:

```
$words = preg_split('/ x /i','31 inches x 22 inches X 9 inches');
```

Discussion

The simplest solution of the bunch is explode(). Pass it your separator string, the string to be separated, and an optional limit on how many elements should be returned:

```
$dwarves = 'dopey,sleepy,happy,grumpy,sneezy,bashful,doc';
$dwarf_array = explode(',',$dwarves);
```

This makes $dwarf_array a seven-element array, so print_r($dwarf_array) prints:

```
Array
(
    [0] => dopey
    [1] => sleepy
    [2] => happy
    [3] => grumpy
    [4] => sneezy
    [5] => bashful
    [6] => doc
)
```

If the specified limit is less than the number of possible chunks, the last chunk contains the remainder:

```
$dwarf_array = explode(',',$dwarves,5);
print_r($dwarf_array);
```

This prints:

```
Array
(
    [0] => dopey
    [1] => sleepy
    [2] => happy
    [3] => grumpy
    [4] => sneezy,bashful,doc
)
```

The separator is treated literally by explode(). If you specify a comma and a space as a separator, it breaks the string only on a comma followed by a space, not on a comma or a space.

With preg_split(), you have more flexibility. Instead of a string literal as a separator, it uses a Perl-compatible regular expression engine. With preg_split(), you can take advantage of various Perl-ish regular expression extensions, as well as tricks such as including the separator text in the returned array of strings:

```
```

```
$math = "3 + 2 / 7 - 9";
$stack = preg_split('/ *([+\-\/*]) */',$math,-1,PREG_SPLIT_DELIM_CAPTURE);
print_r($stack);
```

This prints:

```
Array
(
    [0] => 3
    [1] => +
    [2] => 2
    [3] => /
    [4] => 7
    [5] => -
    [6] => 9
)
```

The separator regular expression looks for the four mathematical operators (+, -, /, *), surrounded by optional leading or trailing spaces. The PREG_SPLIT_DELIM_CAPTURE flag tells preg_split() to include the matches as part of the separator regular expression in parentheses in the returned array of strings. Only the mathematical operator character class is in parentheses, so the returned array doesn't have any spaces in it.

See Also

Regular expressions are discussed in more detail in Chapter 23; documentation on explode() (*http://www.php.net/explode*) and preg_split() (*http://www.php.net/preg-split*).

1.16 Wrapping Text at a Certain Line Length

Problem

You need to wrap lines in a string. For example, you want to display text by using <pre> and </pre> tags but have it stay within a regularly sized browser window.

Solution

Use wordwrap():

```
$s = "Four score and seven years ago our fathers brought forth on this continent ↵
a new nation, conceived in liberty and dedicated to the proposition ↵
that all men are created equal.";

print "<pre>\n".wordwrap($s)."\n</pre>";
```

This prints:

```
<pre>
Four score and seven years ago our fathers brought forth on this continent
a new nation, conceived in liberty and dedicated to the proposition that
all men are created equal.
</pre>
```

Discussion

By default, wordwrap() wraps text at 75 characters per line. An optional second argument specifies a different line length:

```
print wordwrap($s,50);
```

This prints:

```
Four score and seven years ago our fathers brought
forth on this continent a new nation, conceived in
liberty and dedicated to the proposition that all
men are created equal.
```

Other characters besides \n can be used for line breaks. For double spacing, use "\n\n":

```
print wordwrap($s,50,"\n\n");
```

This prints:

```
Four score and seven years ago our fathers brought

forth on this continent a new nation, conceived in

liberty and dedicated to the proposition that all

men are created equal.
```

There is an optional fourth argument to wordwrap() that controls the treatment of words that are longer than the specified line length. If this argument is 1, these words are wrapped. Otherwise, they span past the specified line length:

```
print wordwrap('jabberwocky',5) . "\n";
print wordwrap('jabberwocky',5,"\n",1);
```

This prints:

```
jabberwocky
jabbe
rwock
y
```

See Also

Documentation on wordwrap() (*http://www.php.net/wordwrap*).

1.17 Storing Binary Data in Strings

Problem

You want to parse a string that contains values encoded as a binary structure or encode values into a string. For example, you want to store numbers in their binary representation instead of as sequences of ASCII characters.

Solution

Use `pack()` to store binary data in a string:

```
$packed = pack('S4',1974,106,28225,32725);
```

Use `unpack()` to extract binary data from a string:

```
$nums = unpack('S4',$packed);
```

Discussion

The first argument to `pack()` is a format string that describes how to encode the data that's passed in the rest of the arguments. The format string S4 tells `pack()` to produce four unsigned short 16-bit numbers in machine byte order from its input data. Given 1974, 106, 28225, and 32725 as input on a little-endian machine, this returns eight bytes: 182, 7, 106, 0, 65, 110, 213, and 127. Each two-byte pair corresponds to one of the input numbers: 7 * 256 + 182 is 1974; 0 * 256 + 106 is 106; 110 * 256 + 65 = 28225; 127 * 256 + 213 = 32725.

The first argument to `unpack()` is also a format string, and the second argument is the data to decode. Passing a format string of S4, the eight-byte sequence that `pack()` produced returns a four-element array of the original numbers. `print_r($nums)` prints:

```
Array
(
    [1] => 1974
    [2] => 106
    [3] => 28225
    [4] => 32725
)
```

In `unpack()`, format characters and their count can be followed by a string to be used as an array key. For example:

```
$nums = unpack('S4num',$packed);
print_r($nums);
```

This prints:

```
Array
(
```

```
        [num1] => 1974
        [num2] => 106
        [num3] => 28225
        [num4] => 32725
    )
```

Multiple format characters must be separated with / in unpack():

```
$nums = unpack('S1a/S1b/S1c/S1d',$packed);
print_r($nums);
```

This prints:

```
Array
(
    [a] => 1974
    [b] => 106
    [c] => 28225
    [d] => 32725
)
```

The format characters that can be used with pack() and unpack() are listed in Table 1-2.

Table 1-2. Format characters for pack( ) and unpack( )

Format character	Data type
a	NUL-padded string
A	Space-padded string
h	Hex string, low nibble first
H	Hex string, high nibble first
c	signed char
C	unsigned char
s	signed short (16 bit, machine byte order)
S	unsigned short (16 bit, machine byte order)
n	unsigned short (16 bit, big endian byte order)
v	unsigned short (16 bit, little endian byte order)
i	signed int (machine-dependent size and byte order)
I	unsigned int (machine-dependent size and byte order)
l	signed long (32 bit, machine byte order)
L	unsigned long (32 bit, machine byte order)
N	unsigned long (32 bit, big endian byte order)
V	unsigned long (32 bit, little endian byte order)
f	float (machine-dependent size and representation)
d	double (machine-dependent size and representation)
x	NUL byte

Format character	Data type
X	Back up one byte
@	NUL-fill to absolute position

For a, A, h, and H, a number after the format character indicates how long the string is. For example, A25 means a 25-character space-padded string. For other format characters, a following number means how many of that type appear consecutively in a string. Use * to take the rest of the available data.

You can convert between data types with unpack(). This example fills the array $ascii with the ASCII values of each character in $s:

```
$s = 'platypus';
$ascii = unpack('c*',$s);
print_r($ascii);
```

This prints:

```
Array
(
    [1] => 112
    [2] => 108
    [3] => 97
    [4] => 116
    [5] => 121
    [6] => 112
    [7] => 117
    [8] => 115
)
```

See Also

Documentation on pack() (*http://www.php.net/pack*) and unpack() (*http://www.php.net/unpack*).

1.18 Program: Downloadable CSV File

Combining the header() function to change the content type of what your PHP program outputs with the fputcsv() function for data formatting lets you send CSV files to browsers that will be automatically handed off to a spreadsheet program (or whatever application is configured on a particular client system to handle CSV files). Example 1-38 formats the results of an SQL SELECT query as CSV data and provides the correct headers so that it is properly handled by the browser.

Example 1-38. Downloadable CSV file

```
$db = new PDO('sqlite:/usr/local/data/sales.db');
$query = $db->query('SELECT region, start, end, amount FROM sales', PDO::FETCH_NUM);
```

```
$sales_data = $db->fetchAll();

// Open filehandle for fputcsv()
$output = fopen('php://output','w') or die("Can't open php://output");
$total = 0;

// Tell browser to expect a CSV file
header('Content-Type: application/csv');
header('Content-Disposition: attachment; filename="sales.csv"');

// Print header row
fputcsv($output,array('Region','Start Date','End Date','Amount'));
// Print each data row and increment $total
foreach ($sales_data as $sales_line) {
    fputcsv($output, $sales_line);
    $total += $sales_line[3];
}
// Print total row and close file handle
fputcsv($output,array('All Regions','--','--',$total));
fclose($output) or die("Can't close php://output");
```

Example 1-38 sends two headers to ensure that the browser handles the CSV output properly. The first header, Content-Type, tells the browser that the output is not HTML, but CSV. The second header, Content-Disposition, tells the browser not to display the output but to attempt to load an external program to handle it. The filename attribute of this header supplies a default filename for the browser to use for the downloaded file.

If you want to provide different views of the same data, you can combine the formatting code in one page and use a query string variable to determine which kind of data formatting to do. In Example 1-39, the format query string variable controls whether the results of an SQL SELECT query are returned as an HTML table or CSV.

Example 1-39. Dynamic CSV or HTML

```
$db = new PDO('sqlite:/usr/local/data/sales.db');
$query = $db->query('SELECT region, start, end, amount FROM sales', PDO::FETCH_NUM);
$sales_data = $db->fetchAll();

$total = 0;
$column_headers = array('Region','Start Date','End Date','Amount');
// Decide what format to use
$format = $_GET['format'] == 'csv' ? 'csv' : 'html';

// Print format-appropriate beginning
if ($format == 'csv') {
    $output = fopen('php://output','w') or die("Can't open php://output");
    header('Content-Type: application/csv');
    header('Content-Disposition: attachment; filename="sales.csv"');
    fputcsv($output,$column_headers);
} else {
    echo '<table><tr><th>';
```

```
        echo implode('</th><th>', $column_headers);
        echo '</th></tr>';
    }

    foreach ($sales_data as $sales_line) {
        // Print format-appropriate line
        if ($format == 'csv') {
            fputcsv($output, $sales_line);
        } else {
            echo '<tr><td>' . implode('</td><td>', $sales_line) . '</td></tr>';
        }
        $total += $sales_line[3];
    }
    $total_line = array('All Regions','--','--',$total);

    // Print format-appropriate footer
    if ($format == 'csv') {
        fputcsv($output,$total_line);
        fclose($output) or die("Can't close php://output");
    } else {
        echo '<tr><td>' . implode('</td><td>', $total_line) . '</td></tr>';
        echo '</table>';
    }
```

Accessing the program in Example 1-39 with format=csv in the query string causes it to return CSV-formatted output. Any other format value in the query string causes it to return HTML output. The logic that sets $format to CSV or HTML could easily be extended to other output formats such as JSON. If you have many places where you want to offer for download the same data in multiple formats, package the code in Example 1-39 into a function that accepts an array of data and a format specifier and then displays the right results.

CHAPTER 2

Numbers

2.0 Introduction

In everyday life, numbers are easy to identify. They're 3:00 P.M., as in the current time, or $1.29, as in the cost of a pint of milk. Maybe they're like π, the ratio of the circumference to the diameter of a circle. They can be pretty large, like Avogadro's number, which is about 6×10^{23}. In PHP, numbers can be all these things.

However, PHP doesn't treat all these numbers as *numbers*. Instead, it breaks them down into two groups: integers and floating-point numbers. Integers are whole numbers, such as −4, 0, 3, and 1,973. Floating-point numbers are decimal numbers, such as 1.23, 0.0, 3.14159, and 9.9999999999.

Conveniently, most of the time PHP doesn't make you worry about the differences between the two because it automatically converts integers to floating-point numbers and floating-point numbers to integers. This conveniently allows you to ignore the underlying details. It also means 3/2 is 1.5, not 1, as it would be in some programming languages. PHP also automatically converts from strings to numbers and back. For instance, 1+"1" is 2.

However, sometimes this blissful ignorance can cause trouble. First, numbers can't be infinitely large or small; there's a minimum size of 2.2e−308 and a maximum size of about 1.8e308.[1] If you need larger (or smaller) numbers, you must use the BCMath or GMP libraries, which are discussed in Recipe 2.15.

Next, floating-point numbers aren't guaranteed to be exactly correct but only correct plus or minus a small amount. This amount is small enough for most occasions, but you can end up with problems in certain instances. For example, humans automatically

---

[1]. These numbers are actually platform-specific, but the values are common because they are from the 64-bit IEEE standard 754.

convert 6 followed by an endless string of 9s after the decimal point to 7, but PHP thinks it's 6 with a bunch of 9s. Therefore, if you ask PHP for the integer value of that number, it returns 6, not 7. For similar reasons, if the digit located in the 200th decimal place is significant to you, don't use floating-point numbers—instead, use the BCMath and GMP libraries. But for most occasions, PHP behaves very nicely when playing with numbers and lets you treat them just as you do in real life.

2.1 Checking Whether a Variable Contains a Valid Number

Problem

You want to ensure that a variable contains a number, even if it's typed as a string. Alternatively, you want to check if a variable is not only a number, but is also specifically typed as one.

Solution

Use is_numeric() to discover whether a variable contains a number:

```
foreach ([5, '5', '05', 12.3, '16.7', 'five', 0xDECAFBAD, '10e200']
        as $maybeNumber) {
    $isItNumeric = is_numeric($maybeNumber);
    $actualType  = gettype($maybeNumber);
    print "Is the $actualType $maybeNumber numeric? ";
    if (is_numeric($maybeNumber)) {
        print "yes";
    } else {
        print "no";
    }
    print "\n";
}
```

The example code prints:

```
Is the integer 5 numeric? yes
Is the string 5 numeric? yes
Is the string 05 numeric? yes
Is the double 12.3 numeric? yes
Is the string 16.7 numeric? yes
Is the string five numeric? no
Is the integer 3737844653 numeric? yes
Is the string 10e200 numeric? yes
```

Discussion

Numbers come in all shapes and sizes. You cannot assume that something is a number simply because it only contains the characters 0 through 9. What about decimal points, or negative signs? You can't simply add them into the mix because the negative must come at the front, and you can only have one decimal point. And then there's hexadecimal numbers and scientific notation.

Instead of rolling your own function, use is_numeric() to check whether a variable holds something that's either an actual number (as in it's typed as an integer or floating point), or a string containing characters that can be translated into a number.

There's an actual difference here. Technically, the integer 5 and the string 5 aren't the same in PHP. However, most of the time you won't actually be concerned about the distinction, which is why the behavior of is_numeric() is useful.

Helpfully, is_numeric() properly parses decimal numbers, such as 5.1; however, numbers with thousands separators, such as 5,100, cause is_numeric() to return false.

To strip the thousands separators from your number before calling is_numeric(), use str_replace():

```php
$number = "5,100";

// This is_numeric() call returns false
$withCommas = is_numeric($number);

// This is_numeric() call returns true
$withoutCommas = is_numeric(str_replace(',', '', $number));
```

To check if your number is a specific type, there are a variety of related functions with self-explanatory names: is_float() (or is_double() or is_real(); they're all the same) and is_int() (or is_integer() or is_long()).

To validate input data, use the techniques from Recipe 9.3 instead of is_numeric(). That recipe describes how to check for positive or negative integers, decimal numbers, and a handful of other formats.

See Also

Recipe 9.3 for validating numeric user input; documentation on is_numeric() (*http://www.php.net/is-numeric*) and str_replace() (*http://www.php.net/str-replace*).

2.2 Comparing Floating-Point Numbers

Problem

You want to check whether two floating-point numbers are equal.

Solution

Use a small delta value, and check if the numbers have a difference smaller than that delta:

```
$delta = 0.00001;

$a = 1.00000001;
$b = 1.00000000;

if (abs($a - $b) < $delta) {
    print '$a and $b are equal enough.';
}
```

Discussion

Floating-point numbers are represented in binary form with only a finite number of bits for the mantissa and the exponent. You get overflows when you exceed those bits. As a result, sometimes PHP (just like some other languages) doesn't believe that two equal numbers are actually equal because they may differ toward the very end.

To avoid this problem, instead of checking if $a == $b, make sure the first number is within a very small amount ($delta) of the second one. The size of your delta should be the smallest amount of difference you care about between two numbers. Then use abs() to get the absolute value of the difference.

See Also

Recipe 2.3 for information on rounding floating-point numbers; documentation on floating-point numbers in PHP (*http://www.php.net/language.types.float*).

2.3 Rounding Floating-Point Numbers

Problem

You want to round a floating-point number, either to an integer value or to a set number of decimal places.

Solution

To round a number to the closest integer, use round():

```
$number = round(2.4);
printf("2.4 rounds to the float %s", $number);
```

This prints:

```
2.4 rounds to the float 2
```

To round up, use `ceil()`:

```
$number = ceil(2.4);
printf("2.4 rounds up to the float %s", $number);
```

This prints:

2.4 rounds up to the float 3

To round down, use `floor()`:

```
$number = floor(2.4);
printf("2.4 rounds down to the float %s", $number);
```

This prints:

2.4 rounds down to the float 2

Discussion

If a number falls exactly between two integers, PHP rounds away from 0:

```
$number = round(2.5);
printf("Rounding a positive number rounds up: %s\n", $number);

$number = round(-2.5);
printf("Rounding a negative number rounds down: %s\n", $number);
```

This prints:

Rounding a positive number rounds up: 3
Rounding a negative number rounds down: -3

You may remember from Recipe 2.2 that floating-point numbers don't always work out to exact values because of how the computer stores them. This can create confusion. A value you expect to have a decimal part of "0.5" might instead be ".499999...9" (with a whole bunch of 9s) or ".500000...1" (with many 0s and a trailing 1).

PHP automatically incorporates a little "fuzz factor" into its rounding calculations, so you don't need to worry about this.

To keep a set number of digits after the decimal point, `round()` accepts an optional precision argument. For example, perhaps you are calculating the total price for the items in a user's shopping cart:

```
$cart = 54.23;
$tax = $cart * .05;
$total = $cart + $tax;
$final = round($total, 2);

print "Tax calculation uses all the digits it needs: $total, but ";
print "round() trims it to two decimal places: $final";
```

This prints:

```
Tax calculation uses all the digits it needs: 56.9415, but round()
trims it to two decimal places: 56.94
```

To round a number down, use the floor() function:

```
$number1 = floor(2.1);  // floor(2.1) is the float 2.0
$number2 = floor(2.9);  // floor(2.9) is the float 2.0, also
$number3 = floor(-2.1); // floor(-2.1) is the float -3.0
$number4 = floor(-2.9); // floor(-2.9) is the float 3.0, also
```

To round up, use the ceil() function:

```
$number1 = ceil(2.1);  // ceil(2.1) is the float 3.0
$number2 = ceil(2.9);  // ceil(2.9) is the float 3.0, also
$number3 = ceil(-2.1); // ceil(-2.1) is the float -2.0
$number4 = ceil(-2.9); // ceil(-2.9) is the float 2.0, also
```

These two functions are named because when you're rounding down, you're rounding "toward the floor," and when you're rounding up, you're rounding "toward the ceiling."

See Also

Recipe 2.2 for information on comparing floating-point numbers; documentation on ceil() (*http://www.php.net/ceil*), on floor() (*http://www.php.net/floor*), on round() (*http://www.php.net/round*), and on printf formatting strings such as %s (*http://www.php.net/sprintf*).

2.4 Operating on a Series of Integers

Problem

You want to apply a piece of code to a range of integers.

Solution

Use a for loop:

```
$start = 3;
$end = 7;
for ($i = $start; $i <= $end; $i++) {
    printf("%d squared is %d\n", $i, $i * $i);
}
```

You can increment using values other than 1. For example:

```
$start = 3;
$end = 7;
for ($i = $start; $i <= $end; $i += 2) {
    printf("The odd number %d squared is %d\n", $i, $i * $i);
}
```

If you want to preserve the numbers for use beyond iteration, use the range() method:

```
$numbers = range(3, 7);
foreach ($numbers as $n) {
        printf("%d squared is %d\n", $n, $n * $n);
}
foreach ($numbers as $n) {
        printf("%d cubed is %d\n", $n, $n * $n * $n);
}
```

Discussion

Loops like this are common. For instance, you could be plotting a function and need to calculate the results for multiple points on the graph. Or you could be a student counting down the number of seconds until the end of school.

The for loop method uses a single integer and you have great control over the loop, because you can increment and decrement $i freely. Also, you can modify $i from inside the loop.

In the last example in the Solution, range() returns an array with values from $start to $end. The advantage of using range() is its brevity, but this technique has a disadvantage: a large array can take up unnecessary memory.

If you want range to skip steps, provide a third argument indicating how big each step should be. For example, range(1, 10, 2) returns an array containing 1, 3, 5, 7, 9. It's also valid for $start to be larger than $end. In this case, the numbers returned by range() are in descending order.

range() can also be used to retrieve character sequences:

```
print_r(range('l', 'p'));
```

This prints:

```
Array
(
    [0] => l
    [1] => m
    [2] => n
    [3] => o
    [4] => p
)
```

Note that the character sequences range() generates are just ASCII bytes, so it won't work with multibyte Unicode characters.

Starting with PHP 5.5, you can use a generator to operate on a series. A generator is a function that, instead of calling return to return a value, calls yield (perhaps within a loop). Then a call to that function can be used where you'd otherwise use an array, and you operate on the series of values passed to the yield keyword. For example, here's how to use a generator to produce a list of squares:

```
function squares($start, $stop) {
    if ($start < $stop) {
        for ($i = $start; $i <= $stop; $i++) {
            yield $i => $i * $i;
        }
    }
    else {
        for ($i = $stop; $i >= $start; $i--) {
            yield $i => $i * $i;
        }
    }
}

foreach (squares(3, 15) as $n => $square) {
    printf("%d squared is %d\n", $n, $square);
}
```

PHP keeps calling the squares() function as long as it calls yield. The key and value passed to yield can be used in the foreach just like a regular array element.

Generators are handy because you can have arbitrary behavior to create each value (whatever you put inside your function) but the values are generated on demand. You don't have to commit the memory (or processing) to create the whole array first, as with range(), before you start operating on it.

See Also

Recipe 4.3 for details on initializing an array to a range of integers; documentation on range() (*http://www.php.net/range*).

2.5 Generating Random Numbers Within a Range

Problem

You want to generate a random number within a range of numbers.

Solution

Use mt_rand():

```
$lower = 65;
$upper = 97;
// random number between $upper and $lower, inclusive
$random_number = mt_rand($lower, $upper);
```

Discussion

Generating random numbers is useful when you want to display a random image on a page, randomize the starting position of a game, select a random record from a database, or generate a unique session identifier. To generate a random number between two endpoints, pass `mt_rand()` two arguments: the minimum number that can be returned and the maximum number that can be returned. Calling `mt_rand()` without any arguments returns a number between 0 and the maximum random number, which is returned by `mt_getrandmax()`.

Generating truly random numbers is hard for computers to do. Computers excel at following instructions methodically; they're not so good at spontaneity. If you want to instruct a computer to return random numbers, you need to give it a specific set of repeatable commands; the fact that they're repeatable undermines the desired randomness.

PHP has two different random number generators, a classic function called `rand()` and a better function called `mt_rand()`. MT stands for Mersenne Twister, which is named for the French monk and mathematician Marin Mersenne and the type of prime numbers he's associated with. The algorithm is based on these prime numbers. Because `mt_rand()` is less predictable and faster than `rand()`, we prefer it to `rand()`.

See Also

Recipe 2.7 for generating biased random numbers and Recipe 1.6 for generating random strings; documentation on `mt_rand()` (*http://www.php.net/mt-rand*) and `rand()` (*http://www.php.net/rand*).

2.6 Generating Predictable Random Numbers

Problem

You want to make the random number generate predictable numbers so you can guarantee repeatable behavior.

Solution

Seed the random number generator with a known value using `mt_srand()` (or `srand()`):

```php
<?php

function pick_color() {
    $colors = array('red','orange','yellow','blue','green','indigo','violet');
    $i = mt_rand(0, count($colors) - 1);
    return $colors[$i];
}
```

```
mt_srand(34534);
$first = pick_color();
$second = pick_color();

// Because a specific value was passed to mt_srand(), we can be
// sure the same colors will get picked each time: red and yellow
print "$first is red and $second is yellow.";
```

Discussion

For unpredictable random numbers, letting PHP generate the seed is perfect. But seeding your random number generator with a known value is useful when you want the random number generator to generate a predictable series of values. This is handy when writing tests for your code. If you are writing a unit test to verify the behavior of a function that retrieves a random element from an array, the condition you're testing for will change each time the test runs if your numbers are really random. But by calling mt_srand() (or srand()) with a specific value at the beginning of your test, you can ensure that the sequence of random numbers that is generated is the same each time the test is run.

See Also

Documentation on mt_srand() (*http://www.php.net/mt_srand*) and on srand() (*http://www.php.net/srand*).

2.7 Generating Biased Random Numbers

Problem

You want to generate random numbers, but you want these numbers to be somewhat biased, so that numbers in certain ranges appear more frequently than others. For example, you want to spread out a series of banner ad impressions in proportion to the number of impressions remaining for each ad campaign.

Solution

Use the rand_weighted() function shown in Example 2-1.

Example 2-1. rand_weighted()

```
// returns the weighted randomly selected key
function rand_weighted($numbers) {
    $total = 0;
    foreach ($numbers as $number => $weight) {
        $total += $weight;
        $distribution[$number] = $total;
```

```
    }
    $rand = mt_rand(0, $total - 1);
    foreach ($distribution as $number => $weights) {
        if ($rand < $weights) { return $number; }
    }
}
```

Discussion

Imagine if instead of an array in which the values are the number of remaining impressions, you have an array of ads in which each ad occurs exactly as many times as its remaining number of impressions. You can simply pick an unweighted random place within the array, and that'd be the ad that shows.

This technique can consume a lot of memory if you have millions of impressions remaining. Instead, you can calculate how large that array would be (by totaling the remaining impressions), pick a random number within the size of the make-believe array, and then go through the array figuring out which ad corresponds to the number you picked. For instance:

```
$ads = array('ford' => 12234, // advertiser, remaining impressions
             'att'  => 33424,
             'ibm'  => 16823);

$ad = rand_weighted($ads);
```

With a generator in PHP 5.5, you could select the weighted random number without having to build the distribution array first:

```
function incremental_total($numbers) {
    $total = 0;
    foreach ($numbers as $number => $weight) {
        $total += $weight;
        yield $number => $total;
    }
}

// returns the weighted randomly selected key
function rand_weighted_generator($numbers) {
    $total = array_sum($numbers);
    $rand = mt_rand(0, $total - 1);
    foreach (incremental_total($numbers) as $number => $weight) {
        if ($rand < $weight) { return $number; }
    }
}
```

See Also

Recipe 2.5 for how to generate random numbers within a range.

2.8 Taking Logarithms

Problem

You want to take the logarithm of a number.

Solution

For logs using base *e* (natural log), use `log()`:

```
// $log is about 2.30258
$log = log(10);
```

For logs using base 10, use `log10()`:

```
// $log10 == 1
$log10 = log10(10);
```

For logs using other bases, pass the base as the second argument to `log()`:

```
// log base 2 of 10 is about 3.32
$log2 = log(10, 2);
```

Discussion

Both `log()` and `log10()` are defined only for numbers that are greater than zero. If you pass in a number equal to or less than zero, they return NAN, which stands for *not a number*.

See Also

Documentation on `log()` (*http://www.php.net/log*) and `log10()` (*http://www.php.net/log10*).

2.9 Calculating Exponents

Problem

You want to raise a number to a power.

Solution

To raise *e* to a power, use `exp()`:

```
// $exp (e squared) is about 7.389
$exp = exp(2);
```

To raise it to any power, use `pow()`:

```
// $exp (2^e) is about 6.58
$exp = pow( 2, M_E);
// $pow1 (2^10) is 1024
$pow1 = pow( 2, 10);
// $pow2 (2^-2) is 0.25
$pow2 = pow( 2, -2);
// $pow3 (2^2.5) is about 5.656
$pow3 = pow( 2, 2.5);
// $pow4 ( (-2)^10 ) is 1024
$pow4 = pow(-2, 10);
// is_nan($pow5) returns true, because
// fractional exponent of negative 2 is not a real number.
$pow5 = pow(-2, -2.5);
```

Discussion

The built-in constant M_E is an approximation of the value of *e*. It equals 2.7182818284590452354. So exp($n) and pow(M_E, $n) are identical.

It's easy to create very large numbers using exp() and pow(); if you outgrow PHP's maximum size (almost 1.8e308), see Recipe 2.15 for how to use the arbitrary precision functions. With exp() and pow(), PHP returns INF (infinity) if the result is too large and NAN (not a number) on an error.

See Also

Documentation on pow() (*http://www.php.net/pow*), exp() (*http://www.php.net/exp*), and information on predefined mathematical constants (*http://www.php.net/math*).

2.10 Formatting Numbers

Problem

You have a number and you want to print it with thousands and decimal separators. For example, you want to display the number of people who have viewed a page, or the percentage of people who have voted for an option in a poll.

Solution

If you always need specific characters as decimal point and thousands separators, use number_format():

```
$number = 1234.56;

// $formatted1 is "1,235" - 1234.56 gets rounded up and , is
// the thousands separator");
$formatted1 = number_format($number);
```

```
// Second argument specifies number of decimal places to use.
// $formatted2 is 1,234.56
$formatted2 = number_format($number, 2);

// Third argument specifies decimal point character
// Fourth argument specifies thousands separator
// $formatted3 is 1.234,56
$formatted3 = number_format($number, 2, ",", ".");
```

If you need to generate appropriate formats for a particular locale, use `NumberFormatter`:

```
$number = '1234.56';

// $formatted1 is 1,234.56
$usa = new NumberFormatter("en-US", NumberFormatter::DEFAULT_STYLE);
$formatted1 = $usa->format($number);

// $formatted2 is 1 234,56
// Note that it's a "non breaking space (\u00A0) between the 1 and the 2
$france = new NumberFormatter("fr-FR", NumberFormatter::DEFAULT_STYLE);
$formatted2 = $france->format($number);
```

Discussion

The `number_format()` function formats a number with decimal and thousands separators. By default, it rounds the number to the nearest integer. If you want to preserve the entire number, but you don't know ahead of time how many digits follow the decimal point in your number, use this:

```
$number = 31415.92653; // your number
list($int, $dec) = explode('.', $number);
// $formatted is 31,415.92653
$formatted = number_format($number, strlen($dec));
```

The `NumberFormatter` class, part of the *intl* extension, uses the extensive formatting rules that are part of the ICU library to give you an easy and powerful way to format numbers appropriately for anywhere in the world. You can even do fancy things such as spell out a number in words:

```
$number = '1234.56';

$france = new NumberFormatter("fr-FR", NumberFormatter::SPELLOUT);
// $formatted is "mille-deux-cent-trente-quatre virgule cinq six"
$formatted = $france->format($number);
```

Recipe 19.4 discusses `NumberFormatter` in more detail.

Chapter 19 for information on internationalization and localization; documentation on `number_format()` (*http://www.php.net/number-format*) and `NumberFormatter` (*http://www.php.net/numberformatter*).

2.11 Formatting Monetary Values

Problem

You have a number and you want to print it with thousands and decimal separators. For instance, you want to display prices for items in a shopping cart.

Solution

Use the `NumberFormatter` class with the `NumberFormatter::CURRENCY` format style:

```
$number = 1234.56;

// US uses $ , and .
// $formatted1 is $1,234.56
$usa = new NumberFormatter("en-US", NumberFormatter::CURRENCY);
$formatted1 = $usa->format($number);

// France uses , and €
// $formatted2 is 1 234,56 €
$france = new NumberFormatter("fr-FR", NumberFormatter::CURRENCY);
$formatted2 = $france->format($number);
```

Discussion

The `NumberFormatter::CURRENCY` format style formats a number by inserting the correct currency symbol, decimal, and thousands separators for the locale used to create the `NumberFormatter` object instance. It assumes that the currency to use is the one native to the locale—US Dollars for the `en-US` locale, Euro for the `fr-FR` locale, and so on.

To produce the right format for a currency other than the locale's native currency, use the `formatCurrency()` method. Its second argument lets you specify the currency to use. For example, what's the correct way, in the USA, to format the price of something in Euro?

```
$number = 1234.56;

// US uses € , and . for Euro
// $formatted is €1,234.56
$usa = new NumberFormatter("en-US", NumberFormatter::CURRENCY);
$formatted = $usa->formatCurrency($number, 'EUR');
```

ISO-4217 specifies the three-letter codes to use for the various currencies of Earth.

Recipe 19.5 discusses using `NumberFormatter` to format currency values in more detail.

See Also

Chapter 19 for information on internationalization and localization; documentation on ISO-4217 currency codes (*http://en.wikipedia.org/wiki/ISO_4217*) and on `NumberFor matter` (*http://www.php.net/numberformatter*).

2.12 Printing Correct Plurals

Problem

You want to correctly pluralize words based on the value of a variable. For instance, you are returning text that depends on the number of matches found by a search.

Solution

Use a conditional expression:

```
$number = 4;
print "Your search returned $number " . ($number == 1 ? 'hit' : 'hits') . '.';
```

This prints:

Your search returned 4 hits.

Discussion

Another option is to use one function for all pluralization, as shown in the `may_plural ize()` function in Example 2-2.

Example 2-2. may_pluralize()

```
function may_pluralize($singular_word, $amount_of) {

    // array of special plurals
    $plurals = array(
        'fish' => 'fish',
        'person' => 'people',
    );

    // only one
    if (1 == $amount_of) {
        return $singular_word;
    }

    // more than one, special plural
```

```
    if (isset($plurals[$singular_word])) {
        return $plurals[$singular_word];
    }

    // more than one, standard plural: add 's' to end of word
    return $singular_word . 's';
}
```

Here are some examples:

```
$number_of_fish = 1;
// $out1 is "I ate 1 fish."
$out1 = "I ate $number_of_fish " . may_pluralize('fish', $number_of_fish) . '.';

$number_of_people = 4;
// $out2 is "Soylent Green is people!"
$out2 = 'Soylent Green is ' . may_pluralize('person', $number_of_people) . '!';
```

If you plan to have multiple plurals inside your code, using a function such as `may_plu`
`ralize()` increases readability. To use the function, pass `may_pluralize()` the singular
form of the word as the first argument and the amount as the second. Inside the function,
there's a large array, `$plurals`, that holds all the special cases. If the `$amount` is 1, you
return the original word. If it's greater, you return the special pluralized word, if it exists.
As a default, just add an *s* to the end of the word.

As written, `may_pluralize()` encapsulates pluralization rules for American English.
Obviously, the rules are different for other languages. If your application only needs to
produce output in one language, then a function like `may_pluralize()` with language-
specific logic is reasonable. If your application needs to produce output in many languages, then a more comprehensive approach is necessary. This is discussed in Chapter 19.

See Also

Recipe 19.2 discusses pluralization in multiple locales.

2.13 Calculating Trigonometric Functions

Problem

You want to use trigonometric functions, such as sine, cosine, and tangent.

Solution

PHP supports many trigonometric functions natively: `sin()`, `cos()`, and `tan()`:

```
// cosine of 2 pi is 1, $result = 1
$result = cos(2 * M_PI);
```

You can also use their inverses: `asin()`, `acos()`, and `atan()`:

```
// arctan of pi/4 is about 0.665773
$result = atan(M_PI / 4);
```

Discussion

These functions assume all angles are in radians, not degrees. (See Recipe 2.14 if this is a problem.)

The function `atan2()` takes two variables $x and $y, and computes `atan($x/$y)`. However, it always returns the correct sign because it uses both parameters when finding the quadrant of the result.

For secant, cosecant, and cotangent, you should manually calculate the reciprocal values of `sin()`, `cos()`, and `tan()`:

```
$n = 0.707;
// secant of 0.707 is about 1.53951
$secant    = 1 / sin($n);

// cosecant of 0.707 is about 1.31524
$cosecant  = 1 / cos($n);

// cotangent of 0.707 is about 1.17051
$cotangent = 1 / tan($n);
```

You can also use hyperbolic functions: `sinh()`, `cosh()`, and `tanh()`, plus, of course, `asinh()`, `acosh()`, and `atanh()`. The inverse functions, however, aren't supported on Windows for PHP versions before 5.3.0.

See Also

Recipe 2.14 for how to perform trig operations in degrees, not radians; documentation on `sin()` (*http://www.php.net/sin*), `cos()` (*http://www.php.net/cos*), `tan()` (*http://www.php.net/tan*), `asin()` (*http://www.php.net/asin*), `acos()` (*http://www.php.net/acos*), `atan()` (*http://www.php.net/atan*), and `atan2()` (*http://www.php.net/atan2*).

2.14 Doing Trigonometry in Degrees, Not Radians

Problem

You have numbers in degrees but want to use the trigonometric functions.

Solution

Use `deg2rad()` and `rad2deg()` on your input and output:

```
$degree = 90;
// cosine of 90 degrees is 0
$cosine = cos(deg2rad($degree));
```

Discussion

By definition, 360 degrees is equal to 2π radians, so it's easy to manually convert between the two formats. However, these functions use PHP's internal value of π, so you're assured a high-precision answer. To access this number for other calculations, use the constant M_PI, which is 3.14159265358979323846.

There is no built-in support for gradians. This is considered a feature, not a bug.

See Also

Recipe 2.13 for trig basics; documentation on deg2rad() (*http://www.php.net/deg2rad*) and rad2deg() (*http://www.php.net/rad2deg*).

2.15 Handling Very Large or Very Small Numbers

Problem

You need to use numbers that are too large (or small) for PHP's built-in floating-point numbers.

Solution

Use either the BCMath or GMP libraries.

Using BCMath:

```
// $sum = "9999999999999999"
$sum = bcadd('1234567812345678', '8765432187654321');
```

Using GMP:

```
$sum = gmp_add('1234567812345678', '8765432187654321');
// $sum is now a GMP resource, not a string; use gmp_strval() to convert
print gmp_strval($sum); // prints 9999999999999999
```

Discussion

The BCMath library is easy to use. You pass in your numbers as strings, and the function returns the sum (or difference, product, etc.) as a string. However, the range of actions you can apply to numbers using BCMath is limited to basic arithmetic.

Another option is the GMP library. While most members of the GMP family of functions accept integers and strings as arguments, they prefer to pass numbers around as resources, which are essentially pointers to internal representations of the numbers. So unlike BCMath functions, which return strings, GMP functions return only resources. You then pass the resource to any GMP function, and it acts as your number.

The only downside is that when you want to view or use the resource with a non-GMP function, you need to explicitly convert it using `gmp_strval()` or `gmp_intval()`.

GMP functions are liberal in what they accept. For instance, see Example 2-3.

Example 2-3. Adding numbers using GMP

```
$four = gmp_add(2, 2);           // You can pass integers
$eight = gmp_add('4', '4');      // Or strings
$twelve = gmp_add($four, $eight); // Or GMP resources
```

However, you can do many more things with GMP numbers than addition, such as raising a number to a power, computing large factorials very quickly, finding a greatest common divisor (GCD), and other fancy mathematical stuff, as shown in Example 2-4.

Example 2-4. Computing fancy mathematical stuff using GMP

```
// Raising a number to a power
$pow = gmp_pow(2, 10);

// Computing large factorials very quickly
$factorial = gmp_fact(20);

// Finding a GCD
$gcd = gmp_gcd(123, 456);

// Other fancy mathematical stuff
$legendre = gmp_legendre(1, 7);
```

The BCMath and GMP libraries aren't necessarily enabled with all PHP configurations. BCMath is bundled with PHP, so it's likely to be available. However, GMP isn't bundled with PHP, so you'll need to download, install it, and instruct PHP to use it during the configuration process. Check the values of `function_defined('bcadd')` and `func tion_defined('gmp_init')` to see if you can use BCMath and GMP.

Another option for high-precision mathematics is PECL's `big_int` library, shown in Example 2-5.

Example 2-5. Adding numbers using big_int

```
$two  = bi_from_str('2');
$four = bi_add($two, $two);
// Use bi_to_str() to get strings from big_int resources
print bi_to_str($four); // prints 4

// Computing large factorials very quickly
$factorial = bi_fact(20);
```

It's faster than BCMath, and almost as powerful as GMP. However, whereas GMP is licensed under the LGPL, `big_int` is under a BSD-style license.

See Also

Documentation on BCMath (*http://www.php.net/bc*), `big_int` (*http://pecl.php.net/big_int*), and GMP (*http://www.php.net/gmp*).

2.16 Converting Between Bases

Problem

You need to convert a number from one base to another.

Solution

Use the `base_convert()` function:

```
// hexadecimal number (base 16)
$hex = 'a1';

// convert from base 16 to base 10
// $decimal is '161'
$decimal = base_convert($hex, 16, 10);
```

Discussion

The `base_convert()` function changes a string representing a number in one base to the correct string in another base. It works for all bases from 2 to 36 inclusive, using the letters a through z as additional symbols for bases above 10. The first argument is the number to be converted, followed by the base it is in and the base you want it to become.

There are also a few specialized functions for conversions to and from base 10 and the most commonly used other bases of 2, 8, and 16. They're `bindec()` and `decbin()`, `octdec()` and `decoct()`, and `hexdec()` and `dechex()`:

```
// convert from base 2 to base 10
// $a = 27
$a = bindec(11011);
// convert from base 8 to base 10
// $b = 27
$b = octdec(33);
// convert from base 16 to base 10
// $c = 27
$c = hexdec('1b');

// convert from base 10 to base 2
// $d = '11011'
```

```
$d = decbin(27);
// $e = '33'
$e = decoct(27);
// $f = '1b'
$f = dechex(27);
```

Note that the specialized functions that convert to base 10 return integers. The functions that convert from base 10 return strings.

Another alternative is to use the `printf()` family of functions, which allows you to convert decimal numbers to binary, octal, and hexadecimal numbers with a wide range of formatting, such as leading zeros and a choice between upper- and lowercase letters for hexadecimal numbers.

For instance, say you want to print out HTML color values. You can use the `%02X` format specifier:

```
$red = 0;
$green = 102;
$blue = 204;
// $color is '#0066CC'
$color = sprintf('#%02X%02X%02X', $red, $green, $blue);
```

See Also

Documentation on `base_convert()` (*http://www.php.net/base-convert*) and `sprintf()` (*http://www.php.net/sprintf*) formatting options.

2.17 Calculating Using Numbers in Bases Other Than Decimal

Problem

You want to perform mathematical operations with numbers formatted not in decimal, but in octal or hexadecimal. For example, you want to calculate web-safe colors in hexadecimal.

Solution

Prefix the number with a leading symbol, so PHP knows it isn't in base 10. The leading symbol `0b` indicates binary (base 2), the leading symbol `0` indicates octal (base 8) and the leading symbol `0x` indicates hexadecimal (base 16). If `$a = 100` and `$b = 0144` and `$c = 0x64` and `$d = 0b1100100`, PHP considers $a, $b, $c, and $d to be equal.

Here's how to count from decimal 1 to 15 using hexadecimal notation:

```
for ($i = 0x1; $i < 0x10; $i++) {
    print "$i\n";
}
```

Discussion

Even if you use hexadecimally formatted numbers in a for loop, by default all numbers
are printed in decimal. In other words, the code in the Solution doesn't print out ..., 8,
9, a, b, ... To print in hexadecimal, use one of the methods listed in Recipe 2.16. Here's
an example:

```
for ($i = 0x1; $i < 0x10; $i++) { print dechex($i) . "\n"; }
```

For most calculations, it's easier to use decimal. Sometimes, however, it's more logical
to switch to another base—for example, when doing byte arithmetic. Dan Bernstein's
popular "times 33" hash is a convenient and fast way to hash a string of arbitrary length
to an integer value. To compute the "times 33" hash, you start with the magic number
5381 as your hash value. Then, for each byte in the string you want to hash, you add the
byte and the previous hash value times 32 to the hash value. Translating that directly to
PHP produces code that looks like this:

```
function times_33_hash($str) {
    $h = 5381;
    for ($i = 0, $j = strlen($str); $i < $j; $i++) {
        // Shifting $h left by 5 bits is a quick way to multiply by 32
        $h += ($h << 5) + ord($str[$i]);
    }
    return $h;
}
```

That code isn't completely correct, however. It produces some strange results. For example, times_33_hash("Once, I ate a papaya.") returns a float, not an integer, with
a really, really large value (about 2.28375×10^{19}). The repeated multiplications and additions, once for each byte in the string, have overflowed PHP's maximum integer value
so PHP's autoconversion to float (with loss of precision) kicked in. To fix this, all you
have to do is logical-AND the hash value with a mask of the significant bits you want
to keep in the hash value. Expressing those significant bits is a lot more understandable
in hexadecimal rather than decimal. For example, if you want 32 bits in the hashed value,
add a masking line inside the loop as follows:

```
function times_33_hash($str) {
    $h = 5381;
    for ($i = 0, $j = strlen($str); $i < $j; $i++) {
        // Shifting $h left by 5 bits is a quick way to multiply by 32
        $h += ($h << 5) + ord($str[$i]);
        // Only keep the lower 32 bits of $h
        $h = $h & 0xFFFFFFFF;
    }
```

```
    return $h;
}
```

Each hexadecimal F represents four bits, so masking with eight of them produces a 32-bit mask. You could use 4294967295 in your code as the mask value instead of 0xFFFFFFFF, but it wouldn't be as clear.

 Note that although octal and hexadecimal number expressions have been part of PHP for many versions, the use of the 0b prefix for binary numbers is new to PHP 5.4.

See Also

Recipe 2.16 for details on converting between bases; Dan Bernstein's comp.lang.c post about the times 33 hash (*http://bit.ly/1g8c4F6*).

2.18 Finding the Distance Between Two Places

Problem

You want to find the distance between two coordinates on planet Earth.

Solution

Use sphere_distance(), as shown in Example 2-6.

Example 2-6. Finding the distance between two points

```
function sphere_distance($lat1, $lon1, $lat2, $lon2, $radius = 6378.135) {
    $rad = doubleval(M_PI/180.0);

    $lat1 = doubleval($lat1) * $rad;
    $lon1 = doubleval($lon1) * $rad;
    $lat2 = doubleval($lat2) * $rad;
    $lon2 = doubleval($lon2) * $rad;

    $theta = $lon2 - $lon1;
    $dist = acos(sin($lat1) * sin($lat2) +
                 cos($lat1) * cos($lat2) *
                 cos($theta));
    if ($dist < 0) { $dist += M_PI; }
    // Default is Earth equatorial radius in kilometers
    return $dist = $dist * $radius;
}

// NY, NY (10040)
```

```
$lat1 = 40.858704;
$lon1 = -73.928532;

// SF, CA (94144)
$lat2 = 37.758434;
$lon2 = -122.435126;

$dist = sphere_distance($lat1, $lon1, $lat2, $lon2);
// It's about 2570 miles from NYC to SF
// $formatted is 2570.18
$formatted = sprintf("%.2f", $dist * 0.621); // Format and convert to miles
```

Discussion

Because the Earth is not flat, you cannot get an accurate distance between two locations using a standard Pythagorean distance formula. You must use a Great Circle algorithm instead, such as the one in `sphere_distance()`.

Pass in the latitude and longitude of your two points as the first four arguments. The latitude and longitude of the origin come first, and then the latitude and longitude of the destination. The value returned is the distance between them in kilometers.

The code in Example 2-6 finds the distance between New York City and San Francisco, converts the distance to miles, and then formats it to have two decimal places.

Because the Earth is not a perfect sphere, these calculations are somewhat approximate and could have an error up to 0.5%.

`sphere_distance()` accepts an alternative sphere radius as an optional fifth argument. This lets you, for example, discover the distance between points on Mars:

```
$martian_radius = 3397;
$dist = sphere_distance($lat1, $lon1, $lat2, $lon2, $martian_radius);
$formatted = sprintf("%.2f", $dist * 0.621); // Format and convert to miles
```

See Also

Recipe 2.13 for trig basics; the Wikipedia entry on Earth radius (*http://en.wikipedia.org/wiki/Earth_radius*); and the article "Trip Mapping with PHP." (*http://www.onlamp.com/pub/a/php/2002/11/07/php_map.html*)

CHAPTER 3

Dates and Times

3.0 Introduction

Displaying and manipulating dates and times seems simple at first but gets more difficult depending on how diverse your users are. Do your users span more than one time zone? Probably so, unless you are building an intranet or a site with a very specific geographical audience. Is your audience frightened away by timestamps that look like "2015-07-20 14:56:34 EDT" or do they need to be calmed with familiar representations like "Saturday July 20, 2015 (2:56 P.M.)"? Calculating the number of hours between today at 10 A.M. and today at 7 P.M. is pretty easy. How about between today at 3 A.M. and noon on the first day of next month? Finding the difference between dates is discussed in Recipes 3.5 and 3.6.

These calculations and manipulations are made even more hectic by daylight saving (or summer) time (DST). Because of DST, there are times that don't exist (in most of the United States, 2 A.M. to 3 A.M. on a day in the spring) and times that exist twice (in most of the United States, 1 A.M. to 2 A.M. on a day in the fall). Some of your users may live in places that observe DST, some may not. Recipe 3.10 provides ways to work with time zones and DST.

Programmatic time handling is made much easier by two conventions. First, treat time internally as Coordinated Universal Time (abbreviated UTC and also known as GMT, Greenwich Mean Time), the patriarch of the time-zone family with no DST or summer time observance. This is the time zone at 0 degrees longitude, and all other time zones are expressed as offsets (either positive or negative) from it. Second, treat time not as an array of different values for month, day, year, minute, second, etc., but as seconds elapsed since the Unix epoch: midnight on January 1, 1970 (UTC, of course). This makes calculating intervals much easier, and PHP has plenty of functions to help you move easily between epoch timestamps and human-readable time representations.

The function mktime() produces epoch timestamps from a given set of time parts, while date(), given an epoch timestamp, returns a formatted time string. Example 3-1 uses these functions to find on what day of the week New Year's Day 1986 occurred.

Example 3-1. Using mktime() and date()

```
$stamp = mktime(0,0,0,1,1,1986);
print date('l',$stamp);
```

Example 3-1 prints:

```
Wednesday
```

In Example 3-1, mktime() returns the epoch timestamp at midnight on January 1, 1986. The l format character to date() tells it to return the full name of the day of the week that corresponds to the given epoch timestamp. Recipe 3.4 details the many format characters available to date().

To ensure smooth date and time processing in your code, set the date.timezone configuration variable to an appropriate time zone (*http://www.php.net/timezones*) (or call date_default_timezone_set() before you do any date or time operations). To always use UTC as the time zone for your date calculations, set date.timezone to UTC. Then, as discussed in Recipe 3.4, you can ensure a time or date is represented in a way appropriate to a user's time zone and location at display time.

In this book, the phrase *epoch timestamp* refers to a count of seconds since the Unix epoch. *Time parts* (or *date parts* or time and *date parts*) means an array or group of time and date components such as day, month, year, hour, minute, and second. *Formatted time string* (or *formatted date string*, etc.) means a string that contains some particular grouping of time and date parts—for example, "2002-03-12," "Wednesday, 11:23 A.M.," or "February 25."

If you used epoch timestamps as your internal time representation, you avoided any Y2K issues, because the difference between 946702799 (1999-12-31 23:59:59 UTC) and 946702800 (2000-01-01 00:00:00 UTC) is treated just like the difference between any other two timestamps. You may, however, run into a Y2038 problem. January 19, 2038 at 3:14:07 A.M. (UTC) is 2147483647 seconds after midnight January 1, 1970. What's special about 2147483647? It's $2^{31} - 1$, which is the largest integer expressible when 32 bits represent a signed integer. (The 32nd bit is used for the sign.)

The PHP functions that rely on its bundled time handling library, such as date(), mktime(), and the methods of the DateTime class store timestamps internally as 64-bit integers. This gives you about a 600-billion year range, which is probably adequate for your calculations. For this reason, as well as simplicity, this chapter uses those functions for date and time operations instead of functions such as strftime() and gmstrftime(). These functions rely on underlying system calls, which may not have the same range or functionality.

3.1 Finding the Current Date and Time

Problem

You want to know what the time or date is.

Solution

Use `date()` for a formatted time string, as in Example 3-2.

Example 3-2. Finding the current date and time

```
print date('r');
```

It obviously depends on the time and date the code is run, but Example 3-2 prints something like:

```
Fri, 01 Feb 2013 14:23:33 -0500
```

Or, use a `DateTime` object. Its `format()` method works just like the `date()` function:

```
$when = new DateTime();
print $when->format('r');
```

Use `getdate()` or `localtime()` if you want time parts. Example 3-3 shows how these functions work.

Example 3-3. Finding time parts

```
$now_1 = getdate();
$now_2 = localtime();
print "{$now_1['hours']}:{$now_1['minutes']}:{$now_1['seconds']}\n";
print "$now_2[2]:$now_2[1]:$now_2[0]";
```

Example 3-3 prints:

```
18:23:45
18:23:45
```

Discussion

The function `date()` (and the `DateTime` object) can produce a variety of formatted time and date strings. They are discussed in more detail in Recipe 3.4. Both `localtime()` and `getdate()`, on the other hand, return arrays whose elements are the different pieces of the specified date and time.

The associative array `getdate()` returns the key/value pairs listed in Table 3-1.

Table 3-1. Return array from getdate()

Key	Value
seconds	Seconds
minutes	Minutes
hours	Hours
mday	Day of the month
wday	Day of the week, numeric (Sunday is 0, Saturday is 6)
mon	Month, numeric
year	Year, numeric (4 digits)
yday	Day of the year, numeric (e.g., 299)
weekday	Day of the week, textual, full (e.g., "Friday")
month	Month, textual, full (e.g., "January")
0	Seconds since epoch (what time() returns)

Example 3-4 shows how to use getdate() to print out the month, day, and year.

Example 3-4. Finding the month, day, and year

```
$a = getdate();
printf('%s %d, %d',$a['month'],$a['mday'],$a['year']);
```

Example 3-4 prints:

February 4, 2013

Pass getdate() an epoch timestamp as an argument to make the returned array the appropriate values for local time at that timestamp. The month, day, and year at epoch timestamp 163727100 is shown in Example 3-5.

Example 3-5. getdate() with a specific timestamp

```
$a = getdate(163727100);
printf('%s %d, %d',$a['month'],$a['mday'],$a['year']);
```

Example 3-5 prints:

March 10, 1975

The function localtime() also returns an array of time and date parts. It also takes an epoch timestamp as an optional first argument, as well as a boolean as an optional second argument. If that second argument is true, localtime() returns an associative array instead of a numerically indexed array. The keys of that array are the same as the members of the tm_struct structure that the C function localtime() returns, as shown in Table 3-2.

Table 3-2. Return array from localtime()

Numeric position	Key	Value
0	tm_sec	Second
1	tm_min	Minutes
2	tm_hour	Hour
3	tm_mday	Day of the month
4	tm_mon	Month of the year (January is 0)
5	tm_year	Years since 1900
6	tm_wday	Day of the week (Sunday is 0)
7	tm_yday	Day of the year
8	tm_isdst	Is daylight saving time in effect?

Example 3-6 shows how to use `localtime()` to print out today's date in month/day/year format.

Example 3-6. Using localtime()

```
$a = localtime();
$a[4] += 1;
$a[5] += 1900;
print "$a[4]/$a[3]/$a[5]";
```

Example 3-6 prints:

2/4/2013

The month is incremented by 1 before printing because `localtime()` starts counting months with 0 for January, but we want to display 1 if the current month is January. Similarly, the year is incremented by 1900 because `localtime()` starts counting years with 0 for 1900.

The functions `getdate()` and `localtime()` both use the same internal implementation to generate the returned date and time parts. They differ only in the format of the returned arrays and in some of the information they return. (For example, `local time()` includes whether DST is in effect at the specified time.)

The time zone that `getdate()` and `localtime()` use for their calculations is the currently active one, as set by the `date.timezone` configuration variable or a call to `date_de fault_timezone_set()`.

See Also

Documentation on `date()` (*http://www.php.net/date*), the `DateTime` class (*http://www.php.net/class.datetime*), `getdate()` (*http://www.php.net/getdate*), and `local time()` (*http://www.php.net/localtime*).

3.2 Converting Time and Date Parts to an Epoch Timestamp

Problem

You want to know what epoch timestamp corresponds to a set of time and date parts.

Solution

Use `mktime()` if your time and date parts are in the local time zone, as shown in Example 3-7.

Example 3-7. Getting a specific epoch timestamp

```
// 7:45:03 PM on March 10, 1975, local time
// Assuming your "local time" is US Eastern time
$then = mktime(19,45,3,3,10,1975);
```

Use `gmmktime()`, as in Example 3-8, if your time and date parts are in GMT.

Example 3-8. Getting a specific GMT-based epoch timestamp

```
// 7:45:03 PM on March 10, 1975, in GMT
$then = gmmktime(19,45,3,3,10,1975);
```

Use `DateTime::createFromFormat()`, as in Example 3-9, if your time and date parts are in a formatted time string.

Example 3-9. Getting a specific epoch timestamp from a formatted time string

```
// 7:45:03 PM on March 10, 1975, in a particular timezone
$then = DateTime::createFromFormat(DateTime::ATOM, "1975-03-10T19:45:03-04:00");
```

Discussion

The functions `mktime()` and `gmmktime()` each take a date and time's parts (hour, minute, second, month, day, year) and return the appropriate Unix epoch timestamp. The components are treated as local time by `mktime()`, while `gmmktime()` treats them as a date and time in UTC.

In Example 3-10, `$stamp_future` is set to the epoch timestamp for 3:25 P.M. on December 3, 2024. The epoch timestamp can be fed back to `date()` to produce a formatted time string.

Example 3-10. Working with epoch timestamps

```
date_default_timezone_set('America/New_York');
// $stamp_future is 1733257500
$stamp_future = mktime(15,25,0,12,3,2024);
```

```
// $formatted is '2024-12-03T15:25:00-05:00'
$formatted = date('c', $stamp_future);
```

Because the calls to mktime() in Example 3-10 were made with the time zone set to America/New_York, using gmmktime() instead produces epoch timestamps that are 18,000 seconds (five hours) smaller, as shown in Example 3-11.

Example 3-11. Epoch timestamps and gmmktime()

```
date_default_timezone_set('America/New_York');
// $stamp_future is 1733239500, whch is 18000
// smaller than 1733257500
$stamp_future = gmmktime(15,25,0,12,3,2024);
```

The createFromFormat() method of the DateTime class behaves more flexibly. Instead of accepting already-chopped-up time parts, you give it a formatted time or date string and tell it the structure of that string. It then decomposes the parts properly and calculates the correct timestamp. In addition to the format strings listed in Recipe 3.4 that the date() function understands, createFromFormat() also uses the characters listed in Table 3-3.

Table 3-3. Format characters for DateTime::createFromFormat( )

Character	Meaning
space or tab	
#	Any one of the separation bytes ;, :, /, ., ,, -, (,)
;, :, /, ., ,, -, (,)	Literal character
?	Any byte (not a character, just one byte)
*	Any number of bytes until the next digit or separation character
!	Reset all fields to "start of Unix epoch" values (without this, any unspecified fields will be set to the current date/time)
|	Reset any unparsed fields to "start of Unix epoch" values
+	Treat unparsed trailing data as a warning rather than an error

Example 3-12 shows how DateTime::createFromFormat() can be used to get time parts out of a larger string.

Example 3-12. Using DateTime::createFromFormat( )

```
$text = "Birthday: May 11, 1918.";
$when = DateTime::createFromFormat("*: F j, Y.|", $text);
// $formatted is "Saturday, 11-May-18 00:00:00 UTC"
$formatted = $when->format(DateTime::RFC850);
```

See Also

Recipe 3.3 for how to convert an epoch timestamp back to time and date parts; documentation on `mktime()` (*http://www.php.net/mktime*) and `gmmktime()` (*http://www.php.net/gmmktime*), `date_default_timezone_set()` (*http://www.php.net/date_default_timezone_set*), and `DateTime::createFromFormat()` (*http://www.php.net/datetime.createfromformat*).

3.3 Converting an Epoch Timestamp to Time and Date Parts

Problem

You want the set of time and date parts that corresponds to a particular epoch timestamp.

Solution

Pass an epoch timestamp to `getdate()`: `$time_parts = getdate(163727100);`.

Discussion

The time parts returned by `getdate()` are detailed in Table 3-1. These time parts are relative to whatever PHP's time zone is set to. If you want time parts relative to another time zone, you can change PHP's time zone with `date_default_timezone_set()`, and then change it back after your call to `getdate()`. You could also create a `DateTime` object, set it to a specific time zone, then retrieve the time and date parts you need with that object's `format()` method:

```
$when = new DateTime("@163727100");
$when->setTimezone(new DateTimeZone('America/Los_Angeles'));
$parts = explode('/', $when->format('Y/m/d/H/i/s'));
// Year, month, day, hour, minute, second
// $parts is array('1975', '03','10', '16','45', '00'))
```

The `@` character tells `DateTime` that the rest of the argument to the constructor is an epoch timestamp. When specifying a timestamp as the initial value, `DateTime` ignores any time zone also passed to the constructor, so setting that requires an additional call to `setTimezone()`. Once that's done, `format()` can generate any parts you need.

See Also

Recipe 3.2 for how to convert time and date parts back to epoch timestamps; Recipe 3.10 for more information on how to deal with time zones; documentation on `getdate()` (*http://www.php.net/getdate*) and `DateTime` (*http://www.php.net/class.datetime*).

3.4 Printing a Date or Time in a Specified Format

Problem

You need to print out a date or time formatted in a particular way.

Solution

Use `date()` or `DateTime::format()`, as shown in Example 3-13.

Example 3-13. Using date() and DateTime::format( )

```
print date('d/M/Y') . "\n";
$when = new DateTime();
print $when->format('d/M/Y');
```

Example 3-13 prints something like:

```
06/Feb/2013
06/Feb/2013
```

Discussion

Both `date()` and `DateTime::format()` use the same code internally for generating formatted time and date strings. They are flexible functions that can produce a formatted time string with a variety of components. The format characters for these functions are listed in Table 3-4.

Table 3-4. date() format characters

Type	Character	Description	Range or examples
Hour	H	Hour, numeric, 24-hour clock, leading zero	00–23
Hour	h	Hour, numeric, 12-hour clock, leading zero	01–12
Hour	G	Hour, numeric, 24-hour clock	0–23
Hour	g	Hour, numeric, 12-hour clock	1–12
Hour	A	Ante/Post Meridiem designation	AM, PM
Hour	a	Ante/Post Meridiem designation	am, pm
Minute	i	Minute, numeric	00–59
Second	s	Second, numeric	00–59
Second	u	Microseconds, string	000000–999999
Day	d	Day of the month, numeric, leading zero	01–31
Day	j	Day of the month, numeric	1–31
Day	z	Day of the year, numeric	0–365
Day	N	Day of the week, numeric (Monday is 1)	1–7

Type	Character	Description	Range or examples
Day	w	Day of the week, numeric (Sunday is 0)	0–6
Day	S	English ordinal suffix for day of the month, textual	"st," "th," "nd," "rd"
Week	D	Abbreviated weekday name	Mon, Tue, Wed, Thu, Fri, Sat, Sun
Week	l	Full weekday name	Monday, Tuesday, Wednesday Thursday, Friday, Saturday, Sunday
Week	W	ISO 8601:1988 week number in the year, numeric, week 1 is the first week that has at least 4 days in the current year, Monday is the first day of the week	1–53
Month	F	Full month name	January–December
Month	M	Abbreviated month name	Jan–Dec
Month	m	Month, numeric, leading zero	01–12
Month	n	Month, numeric	1–12
Month	t	Month length in days, numeric	28, 29, 30, 31
Year	Y	Year, numeric, including century	e.g., 2016
Year	y	Year without century, numeric	e.g., 16
Year	o	ISO 8601 year with century; numeric; the four-digit year corresponding to the ISO week number; same as Y except if the ISO week number belongs to the previous or next year, that year is used instead	e.g. 2016
Year	L	Leap year flag (yes is 1)	0, 1
Time zone	O	Hour offset from GMT, ±HHMM (e.g., −0400, +0230)	−1200–+1200
Time zone	P	Like O, but with a colon	−12:00 –+12:00
Time zone	Z	Seconds offset from GMT; west of GMT is negative, east of GMT is positive	-43200–50400
Time zone	e	Time zone identifier	e.g., `America/New_York`
Time zone	T	Time zone abbreviation	e.g., `EDT`
Time zone	I	Daylight saving time flag (yes is 1)	0, 1
Compound	c	ISO 8601–formatted date and time	e.g., `2012-09-06T15:29:34+0000`
Compound	r	RFC 2822–formatted date	e.g., `Thu, 22 Aug 2002 16:01:07 +0200`
Other	U	Seconds since the Unix epoch	0–2147483647
Other	B	Swatch Internet time	000–999

Format characters such as F, M, or D, which generate words, not numbers, produce output in English. To generate formatted date and time strings in other languages, see Recipe 19.3.

There are also some handy constants for common date formats that represent the format string to be passed to date() or DateTime::format(). These constants are listed in Table 3-5.

Table 3-5. Constants for use with date()

Constant	Class constant	Value	Example	Usage
DATE_ATOM	DateTime::ATOM	Y-m-d \TH:i:sP	2013-02-22T20:25:31+00:00	Section 3.3 of the Atom Syndication format (*http://bit.ly/1j2cYYM*)
DATE_ISO8601	Date Time::ISO8601	Y-m-d \TH:i:sO	2013-02-22T20:25:31+0000	ISO 8601 (as discussed at the W3C website (*http:// www.w3.org/TR/NOTE-datetime*))
DATE_RFC822	Date Time::RFC822	D, d M y H:i:s O	Fri, 22 Feb 13 20:25:31 +0000	Email messages (as defined at FAQs (*http:// www.faqs.org/rfcs/ rfc822.html*))
DATE_RFC850	Date Time::RFC850	l, d-M-y H:i:s T	Friday, 22-Feb-13 20:25:31 UTC	Usenet messages (as defined by FAQs (*http:// www.faqs.org/rfcs/ rfc850.html*))
DATE_RFC1036	Date Time::RFC1036	D, d M y H:i:s O	Fri, 22 Feb 13 20:25:31 +0000	Usenet messages (as defined by FAQs (*http:// www.faqs.org/rfcs/ rfc1036.html*))
DATE_RFC1123	Date Time::RFC1123	D, d M Y H:i:s O	Fri, 22 Feb 2013 20:25:31 +0000	As defined by FAQs (*http://www.faqs.org/ rfcs/rfc1123.html*)
DATE_RFC2822	Date Time::RFC2822	D, d M Y H:i:s O	Fri, 22 Feb 2013 20:25:31 +0000	E-mail messages (as defined by FAQs (*http:// www.faqs.org/rfcs/ rfc2822.html*))
DATE_RFC3339	Date Time::RFC3339	Y-m-d \TH:i:sP	2013-02-22T20:25:31+00:00	As described by FAQs (*http://www.faqs.org/ rfcs/rfc3339.html*)
DATE_RSS	DateTime::RSS	D, d M Y H:i:s O	Fri, 22 Feb 2013 20:25:31 +0000	RSS feeds (as defined at RSS 2.0 (*http:// blogs.law.harvard.edu/ tech/rss*))
DATE_W3C	DateTime::W3C	Y-m-d \TH:i:sP	2013-02-22T20:25:31+00:00	As described by W3C (*http://www.w3.org/TR/ NOTE-datetime*)

See Also

Documentation on date() (*http://www.php.net/date*) and DateTime::format() (*http://www.php.net/datetime.format*); Recipe 19.3 for generating formatted time and date strings in different languages.

3.5 Finding the Difference of Two Dates

Problem

You want to find the elapsed time between two dates. For example, you want to tell a user how long it's been since she last logged on to your site.

Solution

Create DateTime objects for each date. Then use the DateTime::diff() method to obtain a DateInterval object that describes the difference between the dates. Example 3-14 displays the difference in weeks, days, hours, minutes, and seconds.

Example 3-14. Calculating the difference between two dates

```
// 7:32:56 pm on May 10, 1965
$first = new DateTime("1965-05-10 7:32:56pm",
        new DateTimeZone('America/New_York'));
// 4:29:11 am on November 20, 1962
$second = new DateTime("1962-11-20 4:29:11am",
         new DateTimeZone('America/New_York'));
$diff = $second->diff($first);

printf("The two dates have %d weeks, %s days, " .
       "%d hours, %d minutes, and %d seconds " .
       "elapsed between them.",
       floor($diff->format('%a') / 7),
       $diff->format('%a') % 7,
       $diff->format('%h'),
       $diff->format('%i'),
       $diff->format('%s'));
```

Example 3-14 prints:

```
The two dates have 128 weeks, 6 days, 15 hours, 3 minutes, and 45 seconds
elapsed between them.
```

Discussion

There are a few subtleties about computing date differences that you should be aware of. First of all, 1962 and 1965 precede the beginning of the Unix epoch. Because of the 600-billion year range of PHP's built-in time library, however, this isn't a problem.

Next, note that the results of DateTime::diff() produce what a clock would say is the time difference, not necessarily the absolute amount of elapsed time. The two dates in Example 3-14 are on different sides of a DST switch, so the actual amount of elapsed time between them is an hour less (due to the repeating clock-hour in the fall switch to standard time) than what's shown in the output.

To compute elapsed time difference, build DateTime objects out of the epoch timestamps from each local timestamp, then apply DateTime::diff() to those objects, as shown in Example 3-15.

Example 3-15. Calculating the elapsed-time difference between two dates

```
// 7:32:56 pm on May 10, 1965
$first_local = new DateTime("1965-05-10 7:32:56pm",
                            new DateTimeZone('America/New_York'));
// 4:29:11 am on November 20, 1962
$second_local = new DateTime("1962-11-20 4:29:11am",
                             new DateTimeZone('America/New_York'));

$first = new DateTime('@' . $first_local->getTimestamp());
$second = new DateTime('@' . $second_local->getTimestamp());

$diff = $second->diff($first);

printf("The two dates have %d weeks, %s days, " .
       "%d hours, %d minutes, and %d seconds " .
       "elapsed between them.",
       floor($diff->format('%a') / 7),
       $diff->format('%a') % 7,
       $diff->format('%h'),
       $diff->format('%i'),
       $diff->format('%s'));
```

Example 3-15 prints:

```
The two dates have 128 weeks, 6 days, 14 hours, 3 minutes, and 45 seconds
elapsed between them.
```

This, as you can see, is an hour different from the output of Example 3-14. The Date Time objects created with a format string of @ plus an epoch timestamp always have a time zone of UTC, so their difference is not affected by any daylight saving time or other local time adjustments.

At the time of writing, PHP Bug 52480 is outstanding, which affects some rare date interval calculations with certain hour values and time zone offsets. You can work around this bug by using UTC as the time zone for interval calculations.

See Also

Documentation on `DateTime::diff()` (*http://www.php.net/datetime.diff*) and `DateInterval` (*http://www.php.net/class.dateinterval*). More information on PHP Bug 52480 (*https://bugs.php.net/bug.php?id=52480*).

3.6 Finding the Day in a Week, Month, or Year

Problem

You want to know the day or week of the year, the day of the week, or the day of the month. For example, you want to print a special message every Monday, or on the first of every month.

Solution

Use the appropriate arguments to `date()` or `DateTime::format()`, as shown in Example 3-16.

Example 3-16. Finding days of the week, month, and year

```
print "Today is day " . date('d') . ' of the month and ' . date('z') .
    ' of the year.';
print "\n";

$birthday = new DateTime('January 17, 1706', new DateTimeZone('America/New_York'));

print "Benjamin Franklin was born on a " . $birthday->format('l') . ", " .
    "day " . $birthday->format('N') . " of the week.";
```

Discussion

The functions `date()` and `DateTime::format()` use the same format characters. Table 3-6 contains all the day and week number format characters they understand.

Table 3-6. Day and week number format characters

Type	Character	Description	Range
Day	d	Day of the month, numeric, leading zero	01–31
Day	j	Day of the month, numeric	1–31
Day	z	Day of the year, numeric	0–365
Day	N	Day of the week, numeric (Monday is 1)	1–7
Day	w	Day of the week, numeric (Sunday is 0)	0–6
Day	S	English ordinal suffix for day of the month, textual	*st, th, nd, rd*
Week	D	Abbreviated weekday name	Mon, Tue, Wed, Thu, Fri, Sat, Sun

Type	Character	Description	Range
Week	l	Full weekday name	Monday, Tuesday, Wednesday Thursday, Friday, Saturday, Sunday
Week	W	ISO 8601:1988 week number in the year, numeric, week 1 is the first week that has at least 4 days in the current year, Monday is the first day of the week	1–53

To print out something only on Mondays, use the w format character, as in Example 3-17.

Example 3-17. Checking for the day of the week

```
if (1 == date('w')) {
    print "Welcome to the beginning of your work week.";
}
```

There are different ways to calculate week numbers and days in a week, so take care to choose the appropriate one. The ISO standard (ISO 8601) says that weeks begin on Mondays and that the days in the week are numbered 1 (Monday) through 7 (Sunday). Week 1 in a year is the first week in a year with a Thursday. This means the first week in a year is the first week with a majority of its days in that year. These week numbers range from 01 to 53.

Other week number standards range from 00 to 53, with days in a year's week 53 potentially overlapping with days in the following year's week 00.

As long as you're consistent within your programs, you shouldn't run into any trouble, but be careful when interfacing with other PHP programs or your database. For example, MySQL's DAYOFWEEK() function treats Sunday as the first day of the week, but numbers the days 1 to 7, which is the ODBC standard. Its WEEKDAY() function, however, treats Monday as the first day of the week and numbers the days from 0 to 6. Its WEEK() function lets you choose whether weeks should start on Sunday or Monday, but it's incompatible with the ISO standard.

See Also

Documentation on date() (*http://www.php.net/date*) and DateTime::format() (*http://www.php.net/datetime.format*); MySQL's DAYOFWEEK(), WEEKDAY(), and WEEK() functions are documented at the MySQL website (*http://bit.ly/1sqXgMU*).

3.7 Validating a Date

Problem

You want to check if a date is valid. For example, you want to make sure a user hasn't provided a birthdate such as February 30, 1962.

Solution

Use checkdate():

```
// $ok is true - March 10, 1993 is a valid date
$ok = checkdate(3, 10, 1993);
// $not_ok is false - February 30, 1962 is not a valid date
$not_ok = checkdate(2, 30, 1962);
```

Discussion

The function checkdate() returns true if $month is between 1 and 12, $year is between 1 and 32767, and $day is between 1 and the correct maximum number of days for $month and $year. Leap years are correctly handled by checkdate(), and dates are rendered using the Gregorian calendar.

Because checkdate() has such a broad range of valid years, you should do additional validation on user input if, for example, you're expecting a valid birthdate. The longest confirmed human life span is 122 years old. To check that a birthdate indicates that a user is between 18 and 122 years old, use the checkbirthdate() function shown in Example 3-18.

Example 3-18. checkbirthdate()

```
function checkbirthdate($month,$day,$year) {
    $min_age = 18;
    $max_age = 122;

    if (! checkdate($month,$day,$year)) {
        return false;
    }

    $now = new DateTime();
    $then_formatted = sprintf("%d-%d-%d", $year, $month, $day);
    $then = DateTime::createFromFormat("Y-n-j|",$then_formatted);
    $age = $now->diff($then);

    if (($age->y < $min_age)|| ($age->y > $max_age)) {
        return FALSE;
    }
    else {
        return TRUE;
```

```
    }
}

// check December 3, 1974
if (checkbirthdate(12,3,1974)) {
    print "You may use this web site.";
} else {
    print "You are too young (or too old!!) to proceed.";
}
```

The function first uses checkdate() to make sure that $month, $day, and $year represent a valid date. If they do, it builds two DateTime objects: one for "right now" and one representing the passed-in month, day, and year. The call to sprintf() normalizes the passed-in values as integers with no leading zeros, which matches what's expected by the Y-n-j format string given to DateTime::createFromFormat(). The trailing | in the format string tells DateTime::createFromFormat() to initialize the unspecified hour, minute, and second time parts to zero.

Once the two DateTime objects are built, determining whether the specified birthdate produces an age within the acceptable range is just a matter of calling Date Time::diff() and then checking the resultant DateInterval object to see if its y property, containing the number of years in the date interval, is appropriate.

The function returns true if the supplied date is exactly $min_age years before the current date, but false if the supplied date is exactly $max_age years after the current date. That is, it would let you through on your 18th birthday, but not on your 123rd.

See Also

Documentation on checkdate() (*http://www.php.net/checkdate*); information about Jeanne Calment, the person with the longest confirmed life span, is at Wikipedia (*http://en.wikipedia.org/wiki/Jeanne_Calment*).

3.8 Parsing Dates and Times from Strings

Problem

You need to get a date or time in a string into a format you can use in calculations. For example, you want to convert date expressions such as "last Thursday" or "February 9, 2004" into an epoch timestamp.

Solution

The simplest way to parse a date or time string of arbitrary format is with strto
time(), which turns a variety of human-readable date and time strings into epoch
timestamps, as shown in Example 3-19.

Example 3-19. Parsing strings with strtotime()

```
$a = strtotime('march 10'); // defaults to the current year
$b = strtotime('last thursday');
$c = strtotime('now + 3 months');
```

Discussion

The grammar strtotime() uses is both complicated and comprehensive. It incorporates the GNU Date Input Formats specification (which is available from GNU (*http://
bit.ly/1niI2DL*)) and some extensions.

The function strtotime() understands words about the current time:

```
$a = strtotime('now');
print date(DATE_RFC850, $a);
print "\n";

$a = strtotime('today');
print date(DATE_RFC850, $a);
```

Tuesday, 12-Feb-13 19:12:14 UTC
Tuesday, 12-Feb-13 00:00:00 UTC

It understands different ways to identify a time and date:

```
$a = strtotime('5/12/2014');
print date(DATE_RFC850, $a);
print "\n";

$a = strtotime('12 may 2014');
print date(DATE_RFC850, $a);
```

Monday, 12-May-14 00:00:00 UTC
Monday, 12-May-14 00:00:00 UTC

It understands relative times and dates:

```
$a = strtotime('last thursday');    // On February 12, 2013
print date(DATE_RFC850, $a);
print "\n";

$a = strtotime('2015-07-12 2pm + 1 month');
print date(DATE_RFC850, $a);
```

Thursday, 07-Feb-13 00:00:00 UTC
Wednesday, 12-Aug-15 14:00:00 UTC

It understands time zones. In the following code, the time part (2pm) doesn't change because both PHP's default time zone identifier (America/New_York) and the time zone in the string passed to strtotime() are the same (EDT is the time zone abbreviation for daylight saving time in New York):

```
date_default_timezone_set('America/New_York');
$a = strtotime('2012-07-12 2pm America/New_York + 1 month');
print date(DATE_RFC850, $a);
```

Sunday, 12-Aug-12 14:00:00 EDT

However, with PHP's default time zone identifier set to America/Denver (two hours before America/New_York), the same string passed to strtotime() produces the time in New York when it is 2 P.M. in Denver (two hours before New York):

```
date_default_timezone_set('America/New_York');
$a = strtotime('2012-07-12 2pm America/Denver + 1 month');
print date(DATE_RFC850, $a);
```

Sunday, 12-Aug-12 16:00:00 EDT

The same extensive grammar that strtotime() uses is also applied when creating a DateTime object. So, although strtotime() is very useful if you just need an epoch timestamp, you can pass the same strings to new DateTime() to build a DateTime object for further manipulation.

If you find yourself with a date or time string with a known format, but that is not parseable by strtotime(), you can still create DateTime objects based on the string by using DateTime::createFromFormat(). Example 3-20 shows how to use Date Time::createFromFormat() to parse date strings written in day-month-year order. (PHP's default is month-day-year order.)

Example 3-20. Parsing a date with a specific format

```
$dates = array('01/02/2015', '03/06/2015', '09/08/2015');

foreach ($dates as $date) {
    $default = new DateTime($date);
    $day_first = DateTime::createFromFormat('d/m/Y|', $date);
    printf("The default interpretation is %s\n  but day-first is %s.\n",
           $default->format(DateTime::RFC850),
           $day_first->format(DateTime::RFC850));
}
```

Example 3-20 prints:

```
The default interpretation is Friday, 02-Jan-15 00:00:00 UTC
  but day-first is Sunday, 01-Feb-15 00:00:00 UTC.
The default interpretation is Friday, 06-Mar-15 00:00:00 UTC
  but day-first is Wednesday, 03-Jun-15 00:00:00 UTC.
The default interpretation is Tuesday, 08-Sep-15 00:00:00 UTC
  but day-first is Sunday, 09-Aug-15 00:00:00 UTC.
```

See Also

Documentation on `strtotime()` (*http://www.php.net/strtotime*) and `DateTime::crea`
`teFromFormat()` (*http://www.php.net/datetime.createfromformat*). Rules describing
what `strtotime()` can parse (*http://bit.ly/1iL8FgR*).

3.9 Adding to or Subtracting from a Date

Problem

You need to add or subtract an interval from a date.

Solution

Apply a `DateInterval` object to a `DateTime` object with either the `DateTime::add()` or
`DateTime::sub()` method, as shown in Example 3-21.

Example 3-21. Adding and subtracting a date interval

```
$birthday = new DateTime('March 10, 1975');

// When is 40 weeks before $birthday?
$human_gestation = new DateInterval('P40W');
$birthday->sub($human_gestation);
print $birthday->format(DateTime::RFC850);
print "\n";

// What if it was an elephant, not a human?
$elephant_gestation = new DateInterval('P616D');
$birthday->add($elephant_gestation);
print $birthday->format(DateTime::RFC850);
```

Discussion

The `add()` and `sub()` methods of `DateTime` modify the `DateTime` method they are called
on by whatever amount is specified in the interval. The average human gestation time
is 40 weeks, so an interval of `P40W` walks back the birthday to 40 weeks earlier, approx-
imating conception time. An elephant, on the other hand, has an average gestation time
of 616 days. So, adding an interval of `P616D` to that conception time produces the expected due date of an elephant conceived at the same time as the human.

A `DateTime` object's `modify()` method accepts, instead of a `DateInterval` object, a string
that `strtotime()` understands. This provides an easy way to find relative dates like "next
Tuesday" from a given object. For example, election day in the United States is the
Tuesday after the first Monday in November. (That is, the first Tuesday of November,

unless that's the first of the month, in which case it's the following Tuesday.) With
DateTime::modify() you can find the date of election day as follows:

```
$year = 2016;
$when = new DateTime("November 1, $year");
if ($when->format('D') != 'Mon') {
    $when->modify("next Monday");
}
$when->modify("next Tuesday");

print "In $year, US election day is on the " .
    $when->format('jS') . ' day of November.';
```

The format character D produces the day of the week. So if the first day of November is
not a Monday, the call to $when->modify("next Monday") advances the DateTime
object to the following Monday. Then, the subsequent call to modify() finds the first
Tuesday after that.

See Also

Documentation on creating DateInterval objects (*http://www.php.net/dateinterv
al.construct*), DateTime::add() (*http://www.php.net/datetime.add*), DateTime::sub()
(*http://www.php.net/datetime.sub*), and DateTime::modify() (*http://www.php.net/
datetime.modify*).

3.10 Calculating Time with Time Zones and Daylight Saving Time

Problem

You need to calculate times in different time zones. For example, you want to give users
information adjusted to their local time, not the local time of your server.

Solution

Use appropriate DateTimeZone objects when you build DateTime objects and PHP will
do all the work for you, as in Example 3-22.

Example 3-22. Simple time zone usage

```
$nowInNewYork = new DateTime('now', new DateTimeZone('America/New_York'));
$nowInCalifornia = new DateTime('now', new DateTimeZone('America/Los_Angeles'));

printf("It's %s in New York but %s in California.",
    $nowInNewYork->format(DateTime::RFC850),
    $nowInCalifornia->format(DateTime::RFC850));
```

This prints:

```
It's Friday, 15-Feb-13 14:50:25 EST in New York but
Friday, 15-Feb-13 11:50:25 PST in California.
```

Note how not only is the time localized (the hours shown differ by three) but the time zone displayed is the locally appropriate one as well. If a time zone you're using observes daylight saving time, this is accounted for automatically.

PHP's default time zone is set at request startup by the date.timezone configuration parameter. Change this by calling date_default_time_zone_set(); that time zone becomes the new default until changed again or the end of the request. Example 3-23 prints the current time twice—once as appropriate for New York and once for Paris.

Example 3-23. Changing time zone with date_default_timezone_set()

```
$now = time();
date_default_timezone_set('America/New_York');
print date(DATE_RFC850, $now);
print "\n";

date_default_timezone_set('Europe/Paris');
print date(DATE_RFC850, $now);
```

Example 3-23 displays appropriately localized time values as well as time zones, just like Example 3-22.

Discussion

Because DateTime objects cooperate with DateTimeZone objects (and other functions, such as date(), respect the system-set time zone) it is very easy to twiddle time zones and get appropriately formatted output. The time zone information that PHP relies on incorporates daylight saving time transitions as well.

The time zones that PHP understands are listed in the PHP Manual (*http://www.php.net/timezones*). The names of these time zones—such as America/New_York, Europe/Paris, and Africa/Dar_es_Salaam—mirror the structure of the popular *zoneinfo* database. If you want to update your time zone database without updating your entire PHP installation, install (or update) the timezonedb extension from PECL. This packages the IANA-managed Time Zone Database for PHP.

See Also

Documentation on date_default_timezone_set() (*http://www.php.net/date_default_timezone_set*), on date_default_timezone_get() (*http://www.php.net/date_default_timezone_get*), and on the DateTimeZone class (*http://www.php.net/class.datetimezone*); the time zones (*http://www.php.net/timezones*) that PHP knows about; information about the IANA Time Zone Database (*http://www.iana.org/time-zones*); the timezonedb PECL extension (*http://pecl.php.net/package/timezonedb*).

3.11 Generating a High-Precision Time

Problem

You need to measure time with finer than one-second resolution—for example, to generate a unique ID or benchmark a function call.

Solution

Use microtime(true) to get the current time in seconds and microseconds. Example 3-24 uses microtime(true) to time how long it takes to do 1,000 regular expression matches.

Example 3-24. Timing with microtime()

```
$start = microtime(true);
for ($i = 0; $i < 1000; $i++) {
    preg_match('/age=\d{1,5}/',$_SERVER['QUERY_STRING']);
}
$end = microtime(true);
$elapsed = $end - $start;
```

Discussion

Without an argument that evaluates to true, microtime() returns a string that contains the microseconds part of elapsed time since the epoch, a space, and seconds since the epoch. For example, a return value of 0.41644100 1026683258 means that 1026683258.41644100 seconds have elapsed since the epoch. This allows for more precision than can fit into a float, but makes it difficult to calculate with.

Since PHP 5.4.0, the $_SERVER superglobal array is populated with a RE QUEST_TIME_FLOAT entry. This contains the time (including microseconds) when the request started. This makes it easy to determine how long a request has been running at any point—just compute microtime(true) - $_SERVER['REQUEST_TIME_FLOAT'].

Time including microseconds is useful for generating unique IDs. When combined with the current process ID, it guarantees a unique ID, as long as a process doesn't generate more than one ID per microsecond. Example 3-25 uses microtime() (with its string return format) to generate just such an ID.

Example 3-25. Generating an ID with microtime()

```
list($microseconds,$seconds) = explode(' ',microtime());
$id = $seconds.$microseconds.getmypid();
```

Note that the method in Example 3-25 is not as foolproof on multithreaded systems, where there is a nonzero (but very tiny) chance that two threads of the same process could call `microtime()` during the same microsecond.

See Also

Documentation on `microtime()` (*http://www.php.net/microtime*).

3.12 Generating Time Ranges

Problem

You need to know all the days in a week or a month. For example, you want to print out a list of appointments for a week.

Solution

Use the `DatePeriod` class, available starting with PHP 5.3.0. Its constructor accepts a flexible combination of options that lets you control the range length, time between items in the range, and how many items there are in the range.

You can build a `DatePeriod` with a start, interval, and end. Here's how to construct a range that represents every day in August 2014:

```
// Start on August 1
$start = new DateTime('August 1, 2014');
// End date is exclusive, so this will stop on August 31
$end = new DateTime('September 1, 2014');
// Go 1 day at a time
$interval = new DateInterval('P1D');

$range1 = new DatePeriod($start, $interval, $end);
```

Here's another way to do the same thing:

```
// Start on August 1
$start = new DateTime('August 1, 2014');
// Go 1 day at a time
$interval= new DateInterval('P1D');
// Recur 30 times more after the first occurrence.
$recurrences = 30;

$range2 = new DatePeriod($start, $interval, $recurrences);
```

And a third way, using the ISO 8601 specified format for describing date ranges:

```
$range3 = new DatePeriod('R30/2014-08-01T00:00:00Z/P1D');
```

The `DatePeriod` class implements the `Traversable` interface, so once you've constructed an object, just pass it to `foreach` and you'll get a `DateTime` object for each item in the range:

```
foreach ($range1 as $d) {
    print "A day in August is " . $d->format('d') . "\n";
}
```

Discussion

By default a `DatePeriod` includes the time specified as its start and excludes the time specified as its end. You can also exclude the start time by passing `DatePeriod::EX CLUDE_START_DATE` as a final argument to the constructor.

`DatePeriod` only implements `Traversable`, not any of the other "make my object act like an array" interfaces that PHP provides, so you can't grab all the values at once, for example, by passing it to `implode()`. You have to use `foreach` to accumulate the values you want into a regular array.

See Also

Documentation on `DatePeriod` (*http://www.php.net/class.dateperiod*) and `DateInterv al()` (*http://www.php.net/class.dateinterval*).

3.13 Using Non-Gregorian Calendars

Problem

You want to use a non-Gregorian calendar, such as a Julian, Jewish, or French Republican calendar.

Solution

PHP's calendar extension provides conversion functions for working with the Julian calendar as well as the French Republican and Jewish calendars. To use these functions, the calendar extension must be loaded.

These functions use the Julian day count (which is different than the Julian calendar) as their intermediate format to move information between them. `cal_to_jd()` converts a month, day, and year to a Julian day count value; `cal_from_jd()` converts a Julian day count value to a month, day, and year in a particular calendar. Example 3-26 converts between Julian days and the familiar Gregorian calendar.

Example 3-26. Converting between Julian days and the Gregorian calendar

```
// March 8, 1876
// $jd is 2406323, the Julian day count
$jd = gregoriantojd(3,9,1876);

$gregorian = cal_from_jd($jd, CAL_GREGORIAN);
/* $gregorian is array('date' => '3/9/1876',
                        'month' => 3,
                        'day' => 9,
                        'year' => 1876,
                        'dow' => 4,
                        'abbrevdayname' => 'Thu',
                        'dayname' => 'Thursday',
                        'abbrevmonth' => 'Mar',
                        'monthname' => 'March'));
*/
```

The valid range for the Gregorian calendar is 4714 BCE to 9999 CE.

Discussion

To convert between Julian days and the Julian calendar, use the CAL_JULIAN constant, as shown in Example 3-27.

Example 3-27. Using the Julian calendar

```
// February 29, 1900 (not a Gregorian leap year)
// $jd is 2415092, the Julian day count
$jd = cal_to_jd(CAL_JULIAN, 2, 29, 1900);

$julian = cal_from_jd($jd, CAL_JULIAN);
/* $julian is array('date' => '2/29/1900',
                     'month' => 2,
                     'day' => 29,
                     'year' => 1900,
                     'dow' => 2,
                     'abbrevdayname' => 'Tue',
                     'dayname' => 'Tuesday',
                     'abbrevmonth' => 'Feb',
                     'monthname' => 'February'));
*/

$gregorian = cal_from_jd($jd, CAL_GREGORIAN);
/* $gregorian is array('date' => '3/13/1900',
                        'month' => 3,
                        'day' => 13,
                        'year' => 1900,
                        'dow' => 2,
                        'abbrevdayname' => 'Tue',
                        'dayname' => 'Tuesday',
                        'abbrevmonth' => 'Mar',
```

```
                             'monthname' => 'March'));
  */
```

The valid range for the Julian calendar is 4713 BCE to 9999 CE, but because it was created in 46 BCE, you run the risk of annoying Julian calendar purists if you use it for dates before that.

To convert between Julian days and the French Republican calendar, use the CAL_FRENCH constant, as shown in Example 3-28.

Example 3-28. Using the French Republican calendar

```
// 13 Floréal XI
// $jd is 2379714, the Julian day count
$jd = cal_to_jd(CAL_FRENCH, 8, 13, 11);

$french = cal_from_jd($jd, CAL_FRENCH);
/* $french is array('date' => '8/13/11',
                    'month' => 8,
                    'day' => 13,
                    'year' => 11,
                    'dow' => 2,
                    'abbrevdayname' => 'Tue',
                    'dayname' => 'Tuesday',
                    'abbrevmonth' => 'Floreal',
                    'monthname' => 'Floreal'));
 */

// May 3, 1803 - sale of Louisiana to the US
$gregorian = cal_from_jd($jd, CAL_GREGORIAN);
/* $gregorian is array('date' => '5/3/1803',
                    'month' => 5,
                    'day' => 3,
                    'year' => 1803,
                    'dow' => 2,
                    'abbrevdayname' => 'Tue',
                    'dayname' => 'Tuesday',
                    'abbrevmonth' => 'May',
                    'monthname' => 'May'));
 */
```

The valid range for the French Republican calendar is September 1792 to September 1806, which is small, but because the calendar was only in use from October 1793 to January 1806, that's comprehensive enough. Note that the month names that cal_from_jd() returns do not have proper accents—they are, for example, Floreal instead of Floréal.

To convert between Julian days and the Jewish calendar, use the CAL_JEWISH constant, as shown in Example 3-29.

Example 3-29. Using the Jewish calendar

```
// 25 Kislev 5774 is the first night/day of Hanukah
// $jd is 2456625, the Julian day count
$jd = cal_to_jd(CAL_JEWISH, 3, 25, 5774);

$jewish = cal_from_jd($jd, CAL_JEWISH);
/* $jewish is array('date' => '3/25/5774',
                    'month' => 3,
                    'day' => 25,
                    'year' => 5774,
                    'dow' => 4,
                    'abbrevdayname' => 'Thu',
                    'dayname' => 'Thursday',
                    'abbrevmonth' => 'Kislev',
                    'monthname' => 'Kislev'));
*/

// November 28, 2013 is US Thanksgiving holiday
$gregorian = cal_from_jd($jd, CAL_GREGORIAN);
/* $gregorian is array('date' => '11/28/2013',
                    'month' => 11,
                    'day' => 28,
                    'year' => 2013,
                    'dow' => 4,
                    'abbrevdayname' => 'Thu',
                    'dayname' => 'Thursday',
                    'abbrevmonth' => 'Nov',
                    'monthname' => 'November'));
*/
```

The valid range for the Jewish calendar starts with 3761 BCE (year 1 on the Jewish calendar). Note that whether or not it falls within a leap year, the month Adar is always returned as `AdarI`. In leap years, Adar II is returned as `AdarII`.

See Also

Documentation for the calendar functions (*http://www.php.net/calendar*); the history of the Gregorian calendar (*http://bit.ly/1idcn5J*).

3.14 Program: Calendar

The `LittleCalendar` class shown in Example 3-31 prints out a month's calendar, similar to the Unix *cal* program. Example 3-30 shows how you can use the class, including default styles for its layout.

Example 3-30. Using LittleCalendar()

```
<style type="text/css">
.prev { text-align: left; }
```

```
.next { text-align: right; }
.day, .month, .weekday { text-align: center; }
.today { background: yellow; }
.blank { }
</style>
<?php
// print the calendar for the current month if a month
// or year isn't in the query string
$month = isset($_GET['month']) ? intval($_GET['month']) : date('m');
$year = isset($_GET['year']) ? intval($_GET['year']) : date('Y');

$cal = new LittleCalendar($month, $year);

print $cal->html();
```

The LittleCalendar class can produce a representation of a month's calendar in different formats. Its prepare() method calculates the right information about each day of the month and appropriate beginning and end padding. Then, separate internal methods, invoked by generate() based on its argument, produce formatting appropriate for different contexts. The html() method produces an HTML calendar suitable for display in a web page. The text() method produces a text-based calendar for display in the shell.

Example 3-31. LittleCalendar

```
class LittleCalendar {

    /** DateTime */
    protected $monthToUse;

    protected $prepared = false;

    protected $days = array();

    public function __construct($month, $year) {
    /* Build a DateTime for the month we're going to display */
        $this->monthToUse = DateTime::createFromFormat('Y-m|',
                                               sprintf("%04d-%02d",
                                                    $year, $month));

        $this->prepare();
    }

    protected function prepare() {
        // Build up an array of information about each day
        // in the month including appropriate padding at the
        // beginning and end
        // First, days of the week across the first row
        foreach (array('Su', 'Mo','Tu','We','Th','Fr','Sa') as $dow) {
            $endOfRow = ($dow == 'Sa');
            $this->days[] = array('type' => 'dow',
                                  'label' => $dow,
```

```php
                                     'endOfRow' => $endOfRow);
        }

        // Next, placeholders up to the first day of the week
        for ($i = 0, $j = $this->monthToUse->format('w'); $i < $j; $i++) {
            $this->days[] = array('type' => 'blank');

        }

        // Then, one item for each day in the month
        $today = date('Y-m-d');
        $days = new DatePeriod($this->monthToUse,
                               new DateInterval('P1D'),
                               $this->monthToUse->format('t') - 1);
        foreach ($days as $day) {
            $isToday = ($day->format('Y-m-d') == $today);
            $endOfRow = ($day->format('w') == 6);
            $this->days[] = array('type' => 'day',
                                  'label' => $day->format('j'),
                                  'today' => $isToday,
                                  'endOfRow' => $endOfRow);
        }

        // Last, any placeholders for the end of the month, if we
        // didn't have an endOfWeek day as the last day in the month
        if (! $endOfRow) {
            for ($i = 0, $j = 6 - $day->format('w'); $i < $j; $i++) {
                $this->days[] = array('type' => 'blank');
            }
        }
    }
}

public function html($opts = array()) {
    if (! isset($opts['id'])) {
        $opts['id'] = 'calendar';
    }
    if (! isset($opts['month_link'])) {
        $opts['month_link'] =
            '<a href="'.htmlentities($_SERVER['PHP_SELF']) . '?' .
            'month=%d&amp;year=%d">%s</a>';
    }
    $classes = array();
    foreach (array('prev','month','next','weekday','blank','day','today')
            as $class) {
        if (isset($opts['class']) && isset($opts['class'][$class])) {
            $classes[$class] = $opts['class'][$class];
        }
        else {
            $classes[$class] = $class;
        }
    }
```

```php
/* Build a DateTime for the previous month */
$prevMonth = clone $this->monthToUse;
$prevMonth->modify("-1 month");
$prevMonthLink = sprintf($opts['month_link'],
                         $prevMonth->format('m'),
                         $prevMonth->format('Y'),
                         '&laquo;');

/* Build a DateTime for the following month */
$nextMonth = clone $this->monthToUse;
$nextMonth->modify("+1 month");
$nextMonthLink = sprintf($opts['month_link'],
                         $nextMonth->format('m'),
                         $nextMonth->format('Y'),
                         '&raquo;');



$html = '<table id="'.htmlentities($opts['id']).'">
 <tr>
 <td class="'.htmlentities($classes['prev']).'">' .
    $prevMonthLink . '</td>
 <td class="'.htmlentities($classes['month']).'" colspan="5">'.
    $this->monthToUse->format('F Y') .'</td>
 <td class="'.htmlentities($classes['next']).'">' .
    $nextMonthLink . '</td>
 </tr>';

$html .= '<tr>';

$lastDayIndex = count($this->days) - 1;
foreach ($this->days as $i => $day) {
    switch ($day['type']) {
    case 'dow':
        $class = 'weekday';
        $label = htmlentities($day['label']);
        break;
    case 'blank':
        $class = 'blank';
        $label = ' ';
        break;
    case 'day':
        $class = $day['today'] ? 'today' : 'day';
        $label = htmlentities($day['label']);
        break;
    }
    $html .=
        '<td class="' . htmlentities($classes[$class]).'">'.
        $label . '</td>';

    if (isset($day['endOfRow']) && $day['endOfRow']) {
        $html .= "</tr>\n";
```

```
                    if ($i != $lastDayIndex) {
                        $html .= '<tr>';
                    }
                }
            }
            $html .= '</table>';
            return $html;
        }

        public function text() {
            $lineLength = strlen('Su Mo Tu We Th Fr Sa');
            $header = $this->monthToUse->format('F Y');
            $headerSpacing = floor(($lineLength - strlen($header))/2);

            $text = str_repeat(' ', $headerSpacing) . $header . "\n";

            foreach ($this->days as $i => $day) {
                switch ($day['type']) {
                case 'dow':
                    $text .= sprintf('% 2s', $day['label']);
                    break;
                case 'blank':
                    $text .= '   ';
                    break;
                case 'day':
                    $text .= sprintf("% 2d", $day['label']);
                    break;
                }
                $text .= (isset($day['endOfRow']) && $day['endOfRow']) ? "\n" : " ";
            }
            if ($text[strlen($text)-1] != "\n") {
                $text .= "\n";
            }
            return $text;
        }
    }
```

The LittleCalendar constructor just builds a DateTime object for the month it needs
to render. Then, it calls prepare(), which does the work of building up the $days
member variable into an array of information about each of the days (or placeholders)
to be rendered. The prepare() function first puts elements for each day of the week (as
a header row) into $days, then some spacers based on the day of the week of the first
day of the month. Next, it puts an element for each day of the month, and finally spacers
to pad out the end of the month if necessary.

Inside prepare(), the necessary information about each day of the month is retrieved
by calling format() on DateTime objects. This provides day-of-the-week information
for the spacers as well as per-day information for each day. The individual days of the
month are obtained by iterating through a DatePeriod spanning the month to use at a
1-day interval.

Although `prepare()` figures out enough information to lay out the calendar, it leaves the actual formatting to other methods. The `html()` method produces an HTML-formatted calendar and the `text()` method produces a text-formatted calendar.

The `html()` method takes an optional array of options as an argument. You can pass a `printf()`-style format string in `$opts['month_link']` to change how the links to the previous and next months are printed as well as an `id` attribute for the table. The `id` defaults to `calendar` if not specified.

Additionally, you can pass in class names to use for various elements in the layout. These go in an array-valued `class` option. In that `class` array, the classes you can specify are `prev`, `month`, `next`, `weekday`, `blank`, `day`, and `today`. Example 3-30 includes styles that provide a basic pleasant layout for the table, including highlighting the current day in yellow.

The `html()` method finds the previous and next months (using `DateTime::modify()`) in order to generate proper previous and next links. After making a short header, it iterates through the calculated days, putting each one into an appropriate table cell. At the end of each week, the table row is closed.

The `text()` method has similar logic, but (obviously) different output. It generates a header containing the month and year and then iterates through the calculated days, adding a newline at the end of each week.

By subclassing `LittleCalendar`, you could add other customized calendar outputs. For example, for fancier console output you could make a `colorText()` method that uses ANSI escape codes to display the current day in a different color.

CHAPTER 4

Arrays

4.0 Introduction

Arrays are lists: lists of people, lists of sizes, lists of books. To store a group of related items in a variable, use an array. Like a list on a piece of paper, the elements in an array have an order. Usually, each new item comes after the last entry in the array, but just as you can wedge a new entry between a pair of lines already in a paper list, you can do the same with arrays in PHP.

Most languages have numerical arrays (sometimes referred to just as arrays). In a numerical array, if you want to find an entry, you need to know its position within the array, known as an index. Positions are identified by numbers: they start at 0 and work upward one by one.

In some languages, there is also another type of array: an associative array, also known as a hash or a map or a dictionary. In an associative array, indexes aren't integers, but strings. So in a numerical array of US presidents, "Abraham Lincoln" might have index 16; in the associative-array version, the index might be "Honest." However, whereas numerical arrays have a strict ordering imposed by their keys, associative arrays frequently make no guarantees about the key ordering. Elements are added in a certain order, but there's no way to determine the order later.

When a language has both numerical and associative arrays, usually the numerical array `$presidents` and the associative array `$presidents` are distinct arrays. Each array type has a specific behavior, and you need to operate on it accordingly. PHP has both numerical and associative arrays, but they don't behave independently.

In PHP, numerical arrays *are* associative arrays, and associative arrays *are* numerical arrays. So which kind are they really? Both and neither. The line between them constantly blurs back and forth from one to another. At first, this can be disorienting, especially if you're used to rigid behavior, but soon you'll find this flexibility an asset.

To assign multiple values to an array in one step, use array():

```
$fruits = array('Apples', 'Bananas', 'Cantaloupes', 'Dates');
```

Now, the value of `$fruits[2]` is `'Cantaloupes'`.

array() is very handy when you have a short list of known values. The same array is also produced by:

```
$fruits[0] = 'Apples';
$fruits[1] = 'Bananas';
$fruits[2] = 'Cantaloupes';
$fruits[3] = 'Dates';
```

and:

```
$fruits[] = 'Apples';
$fruits[] = 'Bananas';
$fruits[] = 'Cantaloupes';
$fruits[] = 'Dates';
```

As of PHP 5.4, you can also use the short array syntax, inspired by JavaScript:

```
$fruits = ['Apples', 'Bananas', 'Cantaloupes', 'Dates'];
```

Assigning a value to an array with an empty subscript is shorthand for adding a new element to the end of the array. So PHP looks up the length of `$fruits` and uses that as the position for the value you're assigning. This assumes, of course, that `$fruits` isn't set to a scalar value, such as 3, and isn't an object. PHP complains if you try to treat a nonarray as an array; however, if this is the first time you're using this variable, PHP automatically converts it to an array and begins indexing at 0.

An identical feature is the function array_push(), which pushes a new value on top of the array stack. However, the `$foo[]` notation is the more traditional PHP style; it's also faster. But sometimes, using array_push() more accurately conveys the stack nature of what you're trying to do, especially when combined with array_pop(), which removes the last element from an array and returns it.

So far, we've placed integers and strings only inside arrays. However, PHP allows you to assign any data type you want to an array element: booleans, integers, floating-point numbers, strings, objects, resources, NULL, and even other arrays. So you can pull arrays or objects directly from a database and place them into an array:

```
while ($row = mysqli_fetch_assoc($r)) {
    $fruits[] = $row;
}

while ($obj = mysqli_fetch_object($s)) {
    $vegetables[] = $obj;
}
```

The first `while` statement creates an array of arrays; the second creates an array of objects. See Recipe 4.2 for more on storing multiple elements per key.

To define an array using not integer keys but string keys, you can also use `array()`, but specify the key/value pairs with =>:

```
$fruits = array('red' => 'Apples', 'yellow' => 'Bananas',
                'beige' => 'Cantaloupes', 'brown' => 'Dates');
```

Now, the value of `$fruits['beige']` is *Cantaloupes*. This is shorthand for:

```
$fruits['red'] = 'Apples';
$fruits['yellow'] = 'Bananas';
$fruits['beige'] = 'Cantaloupes';
$fruits['brown'] = 'Dates';
```

The short syntax works here, too:

```
$fruits = [
    'red' => 'Apples',
    'yellow' => 'Bananas',
    'beige' => 'Cantaloupes',
    'brown' => 'Dates'
];
```

Each array can only hold one unique value for each key. Adding:

```
$fruits['red'] = 'Strawberry';
```

overwrites the value of `'Apples'`. However, you can always add another key at a later time:

```
$fruits['orange'] = 'Orange';
```

The more you program in PHP, the more you find yourself using associative arrays instead of numerical ones. Instead of creating a numeric array with string values, you can create an associative array and place your values as its keys. If you want, you can then store additional information in the element's value. There's no speed penalty for doing this, and PHP preserves the ordering. Plus, looking up or changing a value is easy because you already know the key.

The easiest way to cycle though an array and operate on all or some of the elements inside is to use `foreach`:

```
$fruits = array('red' => 'Apples', 'yellow' => 'Bananas',
                'beige' => 'Cantaloupes', 'brown' => 'Dates');

foreach ($fruits as $color => $fruit) {
    print "$fruit are $color.\n";
}
```

Each time through the loop, PHP assigns the next key to `$color` and the key's value to `$fruit`. When there are no elements left in the array, the loop finishes.

To break an array apart into individual variables, use list():

```
$fruits = array('Apples', 'Bananas', 'Cantaloupes', 'Dates');

list($red, $yellow, $beige, $brown) = $fruits;
```

4.1 Specifying an Array Not Beginning at Element 0

Problem

You want to assign multiple elements to an array in one step, but you don't want the first index to be 0.

Solution

Instruct array() to use a different index using the => syntax:

```
$presidents = array(1 => 'Washington', 'Adams', 'Jefferson', 'Madison');
```

Discussion

Arrays in PHP—like most, but not all, computer languages—begin with the first entry located at index 0. Sometimes, however, the data you're storing makes more sense if the list begins at 1. (And we're not just talking to recovering Pascal programmers here.)

In the Solution, George Washington is the first president, not the zeroth, so if you wish to print a list of the presidents, it's simpler to do this:

```
foreach ($presidents as $number => $president) {
    print "$number: $president\n";
}
```

than this:

```
foreach ($presidents as $number => $president) {
    $number++;
    print "$number: $president\n";
}
```

The feature isn't restricted to the number 1; any integer works:

```
$reconstruction_presidents = array(16 => 'Lincoln', 'Johnson', 'Grant');
// alternatively,
$reconstruction_presidents = [16 => 'Lincoln', 'Johnson', 'Grant'];
```

Also, you can use => multiple times in one call:[1]

---

1. John Tyler was elected as Harrison's vice president under the Whig Party platform but was expelled from the party shortly after assuming the presidency following the death of Harrison.

```
$whig_presidents = array(9 => 'Harrison', 'Tyler', 12 => 'Taylor', 'Fillmore');
// alternatively,
$whig_presidents = [9 => 'Harrison', 'Tyler', 12 => 'Taylor', 'Fillmore'];
```

PHP even allows you to use negative numbers in the `array()` call. (In fact, this method works for noninteger keys, too.) What you'll get is technically an associative array, although as we said, the line between numeric arrays and associative arrays is often blurred in PHP; this is just another one of these cases:

```
$us_leaders = array(-1 => 'George II', 'George III', 'Washington');
// alternatively,
$us_leaders = [-1 => 'George II', 'George III', 'Washington'];
```

If Washington is the first US leader, George III is the zeroth, and his grandfather George II is the negative-first.

Of course, you can mix and match numeric and string keys in one `array()` definition, but it's confusing and very rarely needed:

```
$presidents = array(1 => 'Washington', 'Adams', 'Honest' => 'Lincoln',
                    'Jefferson');
// alternatively,
$presidents = [1 => 'Washington', 'Adams', 'Honest' => 'Lincoln', 'Jefferson'];
```

This is equivalent to:

```
$presidents[1]        = 'Washington';   // Key is 1
$presidents[]         = 'Adams';        // Key is 1 + 1 => 2
$presidents['Honest'] = 'Lincoln';      // Key is 'Honest'
$presidents[]         = 'Jefferson';    // Key is 2 + 1 => 3
```

See Also

Documentation on `array()` (*http://www.php.net/array*).

4.2 Storing Multiple Elements per Key in an Array

Problem

You want to associate multiple elements with a single key.

Solution

Store the multiple elements in an array:

```
$fruits = array('red' => array('strawberry','apple'),
                'yellow' => array('banana'));
```

Or use an object:

```
while ($obj = mysqli_fetch_assoc($r)) {
    $fruits[] = $obj;
}
```

Discussion

In PHP, keys are unique per array, so you can't associate more than one entry in a key without overwriting the old value. Instead, store your values in an anonymous array:

```
$fruits = array();
$fruits['red'][] = 'strawberry';
$fruits['red'][] = 'apple';
$fruits['yellow'][] = 'banana';

print_r($fruits);
```

This prints:

```
Array
(
    [red] => Array
        (
            [0] => strawberry
            [1] => apple
        )

    [yellow] => Array
        (
            [0] => banana
        )

)
```

Or, if you're processing items in a loop:

```
while (list($color,$fruit) = mysqli_fetch_assoc($r)) {
    $fruits[$color][] = $fruit;
}
```

To print the entries, loop through the array:

```
foreach ($fruits as $color => $color_fruit) {
    // $color_fruit is an array
    foreach ($color_fruit as $fruit) {
        print "$fruit is colored $color.<br>";
    }
}
```

Or use the `array_to_comma_string()` function from Recipe 4.9:

```
foreach ($fruits as $color => $color_fruit) {
    print "$color colored fruits include " .
        array_to_comma_string($color_fruit) . "<br>";
}
```

See Also

Recipe 4.9 for how to print arrays with commas.

4.3 Initializing an Array to a Range of Integers

Problem

You want to assign a series of consecutive integers to an array.

Solution

Use `range($start, $stop)`:

```
$cards = range(1, 52);
```

Discussion

For increments other than 1, pass an increment to `range()` as a third argument.

So for odd numbers:

```
$odd = range(1, 52, 2);
```

And for even numbers:

```
$even = range(2, 52, 2);
```

See Also

Recipe 2.4 for how to operate on a series of integers; documentation on `range()` (*http://www.php.net/range*).

4.4 Iterating Through an Array

Problem

You want to cycle though an array and operate on all or some of the elements inside.

Solution

Use foreach:

```
foreach ($array as $value) {
    // Act on $value
}
```

Or to get an array's keys and values:

```
foreach ($array as $key => $value) {
    // Act II
}
```

Another technique is to use for:

```
for ($key = 0, $size = count($array); $key < $size; $key++) {
    // Act III
}
```

Finally, you can use each() in combination with list() and while:

```
reset($array); // reset internal pointer to beginning of array
while (list($key, $value) = each ($array)) {
    // Final Act
}
```

Discussion

A foreach loop is the most concise way to iterate through an array:

```
// foreach with values
foreach ($items as $cost) {
    // ...
}

// foreach with keys and values
foreach($items as $item => $cost) {
    // ...
}
```

With foreach, PHP iterates over a copy of the array instead of the actual array. In contrast, when using each() and for, PHP iterates over the original array. So if you modify the array inside the loop, you may (or may not) get the behavior you expect.

If you want to modify the array, reference it directly:

```
foreach ($items as $item => $cost) {
    if (! in_stock($item)) {
        unset($items[$item]);              // address the array directly
    }
}
```

The variables returned by foreach() aren't aliases for the original values in the array: they're copies, so if you modify them, it's not reflected in the array. That's why you need to modify $items[$item] instead of $cost.

When using each(), PHP keeps track of where you are inside the loop. After completing a first pass through, to begin again at the start, call reset() to move the pointer back to the front of the array. Otherwise, each() returns false.

The for loop works only for arrays with consecutive integer keys. Unless you're modifying the size of your array, it's inefficient to recompute the count() of $items each time through the loop, so we always use a $size variable to hold the array's size:

```
for ($item = 0, $size = count($items); $item < $size; $item++) {
    // ...
}
```

If you prefer to count efficiently with one variable, count backward:

```
for ($item = count($items) - 1; $item >= 0; $item--) {
    // ...
}
```

The associative array version of the for loop is:

```
for (reset($array); $key = key($array); next($array) ) {
    // ...
}
```

This fails if any element holds a string that evaluates to false, so a perfectly normal value such as 0 causes the loop to end early. Therefore, this syntax is rarely used, and is included only to help you understand older PHP code.

Finally, use array_map() to hand off each element to a function for processing:

```
// lowercase all words
$lc = array_map('strtolower', $words);
```

The first argument to array_map() is a function to modify an individual element, and the second is the array to be iterated through.

Generally, we find this function less flexible than the previous methods, but it is well-suited for the processing and merging of multiple arrays.

If you're unsure if the data you'll be processing is a scalar or an array, you need to protect against calling foreach with a nonarray. One method is to use is_array():

```
if (is_array($items)) {
    // foreach loop code for array
} else {
    // code for scalar
}
```

Another method is to coerce all variables into array form using `settype()`:

```
settype($items, 'array');
// loop code for arrays
```

This turns a scalar value into a one-element array and cleans up your code at the expense of a little overhead.

See Also

Recipe 4.24 for how to use a generator to iterate efficiently overly large or expensive datasets; documentation on for (*http://www.php.net/for*), foreach (*http://www.php.net/foreach*), while (*http://www.php.net/while*), each() (*http://www.php.net/each*), reset() (*http://www.php.net/reset*), and array_map() (*http://www.php.net/array-map*).

4.5 Deleting Elements from an Array

Problem

You want to remove one or more elements from an array.

Solution

To delete one element, use `unset()`:

```
unset($array[3]);
unset($array['foo']);
```

To delete multiple noncontiguous elements, also use `unset()`:

```
unset($array[3], $array[5]);
unset($array['foo'], $array['bar']);
```

To delete multiple contiguous elements, use `array_splice()`:

```
array_splice($array, $offset, $length);
```

Discussion

Using these functions removes all references to these elements from PHP. If you want to keep a key in the array, but with an empty value, assign the empty string to the element:

```
$array[3] = $array['foo'] = '';
```

Besides syntax, there's a logical difference between using `unset()` and assigning `''` to the element. The first says, "This doesn't exist anymore," and the second says, "This still exists, but its value is the empty string."

If you're dealing with numbers, assigning 0 may be a better alternative. So if a company stopped production of the model XL1000 sprocket, it would update its inventory with:

```
unset($products['XL1000']);
```

However, if the company temporarily ran out of XL1000 sprockets but was planning to receive a new shipment from the plant later this week, this is better:

```
$products['XL1000'] = 0;
```

If you unset() an element, PHP adjusts the array so that looping still works correctly. It doesn't compact the array to fill in the missing holes. This is what we mean when we say that all arrays are associative, even when they appear to be numeric. Here's an example:

```
// create a "numeric" array
$animals = array('ant', 'bee', 'cat', 'dog', 'elk', 'fox');
print $animals[1];  // prints 'bee'
print $animals[2];  // prints 'cat'
count($animals);    // returns 6

// unset()
unset($animals[1]); // removes element $animals[1] = 'bee'
print $animals[1];  // prints nothing and throws an E_NOTICE error
print $animals[2];  // still prints 'cat'
count($animals);    // returns 5, even though $array[5] is 'fox'

// add new element
$animals[] = 'gnu'; // add new element (not Unix)
print $animals[1];  // prints nothing, still throws an E_NOTICE error
print $animals[6];  // prints 'gnu', this is where 'gnu' ended up
count($animals);    // returns 6

// assign ''
$animals[2] = '';   // zero out value
print $animals[2];  // prints ''
count($animals);    // returns 6, count does not decrease
```

To compact the array into a densely filled numeric array, use array_values():

```
$animals = array_values($animals);
```

Alternatively, array_splice() automatically reindexes arrays to avoid leaving holes:

```
// create a "numeric" array
$animals = array('ant', 'bee', 'cat', 'dog', 'elk', 'fox');
array_splice($animals, 2, 2);
print_r($animals);
Array
(
    [0] => ant
    [1] => bee
    [2] => elk
```

```
    [3] => fox
)
```

This is useful if you're using the array as a queue and want to remove items from the queue while still allowing random access. To safely remove the first or last element from an array, use `array_shift()` and `array_pop()`, respectively.

However, if you find yourself often running into problems because of holes in arrays, you may not be "thinking PHP." Look at the ways to iterate through the array in Recipe 4.4 that don't involve using a `for` loop.

See Also

Recipe 4.4 for iteration techniques; documentation on `unset()` (*http://www.php.net/ unset*), `array_splice()` (*http://www.php.net/array-splice*), and `array_values()` (*http://www.php.net/array-values*).

4.6 Changing Array Size

Problem

You want to modify the size of an array, either by making it larger or smaller than its current size.

Solution

Use `array_pad()` to make an array grow:

```
// start at three
$array = array('apple', 'banana', 'coconut');

// grow to five
$array = array_pad($array, 5, '');
```

Now, `count($array)` is 5, and the last two elements, `$array[3]` and `$array[4]`, contain the empty string.

To reduce an array, you can use `array_splice()`:

```
// no assignment to $array
array_splice($array, 2);
```

This removes all but the first two elements from `$array`.

Discussion

Arrays aren't a predeclared size in PHP, so you can resize them on the fly.

To pad an array, use `array_pad()`. The first argument is the array to be padded. The next argument is the size and direction you want to pad. To pad to the right, use a positive integer; to pad to the left, use a negative one. The third argument is the value to be assigned to the newly created entries. The function returns a modified array and doesn't alter the original.

Here are some examples:

```
// make a four-element array with 'dates' to the right
$array = array('apple', 'banana', 'coconut');
$array = array_pad($array, 4, 'dates');
print_r($array);

Array
(
    [0] => apple
    [1] => banana
    [2] => coconut
    [3] => dates
)

// make a six-element array with 'zucchinis' to the left
$array = array_pad($array, -6, 'zucchini');
print_r($array);
Array
(
    [0] => zucchini
    [1] => zucchini
    [2] => apple
    [3] => banana
    [4] => coconut
    [5] => dates
)
```

Be careful: `array_pad($array, 4, 'dates')` makes sure an $array is *at least* four elements long; it doesn't add four *new* elements. In this case, if $array was already four elements or larger, `array_pad()` would return an unaltered $array.

Also, if you declare a value for a fourth element, $array[4]:

```
$array = array('apple', 'banana', 'coconut');
$array[4] = 'dates';
print_r($array);
```

you end up with a four-element array with indexes 0, 1, 2, and 4:

```
Array
(
    [0] => apple
    [1] => banana
    [2] => coconut
    [4] => dates
)
```

PHP essentially turns this into an associative array that happens to have integer keys.

The array_splice() function, unlike array_pad(), has the side effect of modifying the original array. It returns the spliced-out array. That's why you don't assign the return value to $array. However, like array_pad(), you can splice from either the right or left. So calling array_splice() with a value of -2 chops off the last two elements from the end:

```
// make a four-element array
$array = array('apple', 'banana', 'coconut', 'dates');

// shrink to three elements
array_splice($array, 3);

// remove last element, equivalent to array_pop()
array_splice($array, -1);

// only remaining fruits are apple and banana
print_r($array);
```

See Also

Documentation on array_pad() (*http://www.php.net/array-pad*) and ar ray_splice() (*http://www.php.net/array-splice*).

4.7 Appending One Array to Another

Problem

You want to combine two arrays into one.

Solution

Use array_merge():

```
$garden = array_merge($fruits, $vegetables);
```

Discussion

The array_merge() function works with both predefined arrays and arrays defined in place using array():

```
$p_languages = array('Perl', 'PHP');
$p_languages = array_merge($p_languages, array('Python'));
print_r($p_languages);
Array
(
    [0] => Perl
```

```
    [1] => PHP
    [2] => Python
)
```

Accordingly, merged arrays can be either preexisting arrays, as with `$p_languages`, or anonymous arrays, as with `array('Python')`.

You can't use `array_push()`, because PHP won't automatically flatten out the array into a series of independent variables, and you'll end up with a nested array. Thus:

```
array_push($p_languages, array('Python'));
print_r($p_languages);
Array
(
    [0] => Perl
    [1] => PHP
    [2] => Array
        (
            [0] => Python
        )

)
```

Merging arrays with only numerical keys causes the arrays to get renumbered, so values aren't lost. Merging arrays with string keys causes the second array to overwrite the value of any duplicated keys. Arrays with both types of keys exhibit both types of behavior. For example:

```
$lc = array('a', 'b' => 'b'); // lowercase letters as values
$uc = array('A', 'b' => 'B'); // uppercase letters as values
$ac = array_merge($lc, $uc);  // all-cases?
print_r($ac);
Array
(
    [0] => a
    [b] => B
    [1] => A
)
```

The uppercase A has been renumbered from index 0 to index 1, to avoid a collision, and merged onto the end. The uppercase B has overwritten the lowercase b and replaced it in the original place within the array.

The + operator can also merge arrays. For any identically named keys found in both arrays, the value from the left will be used. It doesn't do any reordering to prevent collisions. Using the previous example:

```
print_r($uc + $lc);
print_r($lc + $uc);
Array
(
    [0] => A
```

```
    [b] => B
)
Array
(
    [0] => a
    [b] => b
)
```

Because a and A both have a key of 0, and b and B both have a key of b, you end up with a total of only two elements in the merged arrays.

In the first case, $a + $b becomes just $b, and in the other, $b + $a becomes $a.

However, if you had two distinctly keyed arrays, this wouldn't be a problem, and the new array would be the union of the two arrays.

See Also

Documentation on `array_merge()` (*http://www.php.net/array-merge*).

4.8 Turning an Array into a String

Problem

You have an array, and you want to convert it into a nicely formatted string.

Solution

Use `join()`:

```
// make a comma delimited list
$string = join(',', $array);
```

Or loop yourself:

```
$string = '';

foreach ($array as $key => $value) {
    $string .= ",$value";
}

$string = substr($string, 1); // remove leading ","
```

Discussion

If you can use `join()`, do; it's faster than any PHP-based loop. However, `join()` isn't very flexible. First, it places a delimiter only between elements, not around them. To wrap elements inside HTML bold tags and separate them with commas, do this:

```
$left  = '<b>';
$right = '</b>';

$html = $left . join("$right,$left", $html) . $right;
```

Second, `join()` doesn't allow you to discriminate against values. If you want to include a subset of entries, you need to loop yourself:

```
$string = '';

foreach ($fields as $key => $value) {
    // don't include password
    if ('password' != $key) {
        $string .= ",<b>$value</b>";
    }
}

$string = substr($string, 1); // remove leading ","
```

Notice that a separator is always added to each value and then stripped off outside the loop. Although it's somewhat wasteful to add something that will be subtracted later, it's far cleaner and efficient (in most cases) than attempting to embed logic inside of the loop. To wit:

```
$string = '';
foreach ($fields as $key => $value) {
    // don't include password
    if ('password' != $value) {
        if (!empty($string)) { $string .= ','; }
        $string .= "<b>$value</b>",
    }
}
```

Now you have to check `$string` every time you append a value. That's worse than the simple `substr()` call. Also, prepend the delimiter (in this case a comma) instead of appending it because it's faster to shorten a string from the front than the rear.

See Also

Recipe 4.9 for printing an array with commas; documentation on `join()` (*http://www.php.net/join*) and `substr()` (*http://www.php.net/substr*).

4.9 Printing an Array with Commas

Problem

You want to print out an array with commas separating the elements and with an *and* before the last element if there are more than two elements in the array.

Solution

Use the `array_to_comma_string()` function shown in Example 4-1, which returns the correct string.

Example 4-1. array_to_comma_string( )

```
function array_to_comma_string($array) {
    switch (count($array)) {
    case 0:
        return '';

    case 1:
        return reset($array);

    case 2:
        return join(' and ', $array);

    default:
        $last = array_pop($array);
        return join(', ', $array) . ", and $last";
    }
}
```

Discussion

If you have a list of items to print, it's useful to print them in a grammatically correct fashion. It looks awkward to display text like this:

```
$thundercats = array('Lion-O', 'Panthro', 'Tygra', 'Cheetara', 'Snarf');
print 'ThunderCat good guys include ' . join(', ', $thundercats) . '.';
```

This implementation of this function isn't completely straightforward because we want `array_to_comma_string()` to work with all arrays, not just numeric ones beginning at 0. If restricted only to that subset, for an array of size one, you return `$array[0]`. But if the array doesn't begin at 0, `$array[0]` is empty. So you can use the fact that `reset()`, which resets an array's internal pointer, also returns the value of the first array element.

For similar reasons, you call `array_pop()` to grab the end element, instead of assuming it's located at `$array[count($array)-1]`. This allows you to use `join()` on `$array`.

Also note that the code for case 2 actually works correctly for case 1, too. And the default code works (though inefficiently) for case 2; however, the transitive property doesn't apply, so you can't use the default code on elements of size 1.

See Also

Recipe 4.8 for turning an array into a string; documentation on `join()` (*http://www.php.net/join*), `array_pop()` (*http://www.php.net/array-pop*), and `reset()` (*http://www.php.net/reset*).

4.10 Checking if a Key Is in an Array

Problem

You want to know if an array contains a certain key.

Solution

Use `array_key_exists()` to check for a key no matter what the associated value is:

```
if (array_key_exists('key', $array)) {
    /* there is a value for $array['key'] */
}
```

Use `isset()` to find a key whose associated value is anything but `null`:

```
if (isset($array['key'])) { /* there is a non-null value for 'key' in $array */ }
```

Discussion

The `array_key_exists()` function completely ignores array values — it just reports whether there is an element in the array with a particular key. `isset()`, however, behaves the same way on array keys as it does with other variables. A `null` value causes `is set()` to return `false`. See the Introduction to Chapter 5 for more information about the truth value of variables.

See Also

Documentation on `isset()` (*http://www.php.net/isset*) and on `array_key_exists()` (*http://www.php.net/array_key_exists*).

4.11 Checking if an Element Is in an Array

Problem

You want to know if an array contains a certain value.

Solution

Use `in_array()`:

```
if (in_array($value, $array)) {
    // an element has $value as its value in array $array
}
```

Discussion

Use `in_array()` to check if an element of an array holds a value:

```
$book_collection = array('Emma', 'Pride and Prejudice', 'Northhanger Abbey');
$book = 'Sense and Sensibility';

if (in_array($book, $book_collection)) {
    echo 'Own it.';
} else {
    echo 'Need it.';
}
```

The default behavior of `in_array()` is to compare items using the == operator. To use the strict equality check, ===, pass `true` as the third parameter to `in_array()`:

```
$array = array(1, '2', 'three');

in_array(0, $array);         // true!
in_array(0, $array, true);   // false
in_array(1, $array);         // true
in_array(1, $array, true);   // true
in_array(2, $array);         // true
in_array(2, $array, true);   // false
```

The first check, `in_array(0, $array)`, evaluates to `true` because to compare the number 0 against the string `three`, PHP casts `three` to an integer. Because `three` isn't a numeric string, as is 2, it becomes 0. Therefore, `in_array()` thinks there's a match.

Consequently, when comparing numbers against data that may contain strings, it's safest to use a strict comparison.

If you find yourself calling `in_array()` multiple times on the same array, it may be better to use an associative array, with the original array elements as the keys in the new associative array. Looking up entries using `in_array()` takes linear time; with an associative array, it takes constant time.

If you can't create the associative array directly but need to convert from a traditional one with integer keys, use `array_flip()` to swap the keys and values of an array:

```
$book_collection = array('Emma',
                         'Pride and Prejudice',
                         'Northhanger Abbey');
```

```
// convert from numeric array to associative array
$book_collection = array_flip($book_collection);
$book = 'Sense and Sensibility';

if (isset($book_collection[$book])) {
    echo 'Own it.';
} else {
    echo 'Need it.';
}
```

Note that doing this condenses multiple keys with the same value into one element in the flipped array.

See Also

Recipe 4.12 for determining the position of a value in an array; documentation on in_array() (*http://www.php.net/in-array*) and array_flip() (*http://www.php.net/array-flip*).

4.12 Finding the Position of a Value in an Array

Problem

You want to know if a value is in an array. If the value is in the array, you want to know its key.

Solution

Use array_search(). It returns the key of the found value. If the value is not in the array, it returns false:

```
$position = array_search($value, $array);
if ($position !== false) {
    // the element in position $position has $value as its value in array $array
}
```

Discussion

Use in_array() to find if an array contains a value; use array_search() to discover where that value is located. However, because array_search() gracefully handles searches in which the value isn't found, it's better to use array_search() instead of in_array(). The speed difference is minute, and the extra information is potentially useful:

```
$favorite_foods = array(1 => 'artichokes', 'bread', 'cauliflower',
                        'deviled eggs');
$food = 'cauliflower';
$position = array_search($food, $favorite_foods);
```

```
if ($position !== false) {
    echo "My #$position favorite food is $food";
} else {
    echo "Blech! I hate $food!";
}
```

Use the !== check against false because if your string is found in the array at position 0, the if evaluates to a logical false, which isn't what is meant or wanted.

If a value is in the array multiple times, array_search() is only guaranteed to return one of the instances, not the first instance.

See Also

Recipe 4.11 for checking whether an element is in an array; documentation on ar ray_search() (*http://www.php.net/array-search*); for more sophisticated searching of arrays using regular expressions, see preg_replace(), which you can find at the PHP website (*http://www.php.net/preg-replace*) and in Chapter 23.

4.13 Finding Elements That Pass a Certain Test

Problem

You want to locate entries in an array that meet certain requirements.

Solution

Use a foreach loop:

```
$movies = array(/*...*/);

foreach ($movies as $movie) {
    if ($movie['box_office_gross'] < 5000000) { $flops[] = $movie; }
}
```

Or array_filter():

```
$movies = array(/* ... */);

$flops = array_filter($movies, function ($movie) {
    return ($movie['box_office_gross'] < 5000000) ? 1 : 0;
});
```

Discussion

The foreach loops are simple: you iterate through the data and append elements to the return array that match your criteria.

If you want only the first such element, exit the loop using `break`:

```
$movies = array(/*...*/);
foreach ($movies as $movie) {
    if ($movie['box_office_gross'] > 200000000) { $blockbuster = $movie; break; }
}
```

You can also return directly from a function:

```
function blockbuster($movies) {
    foreach ($movies as $movie) {
        if ($movie['box_office_gross'] > 200000000) { return $movie; }
    }
}
```

With `array_filter()`, however, you first create an anonymous function that returns `true` for values you want to keep and `false` for values you don't. Using `array_fil ter()`, you then instruct PHP to process the array as you do in the `foreach`.

It's impossible to bail out early from `array_filter()`, so `foreach` provides more flexibility and is simpler to understand. Also, it's one of the few cases in which the built-in PHP function doesn't clearly outperform user-level code.

See Also

Documentation on `array_filter()` (*http://www.php.net/array-filter*) and anonymous functions (*http://www.php.net/functions.anonymous*).

4.14 Finding the Largest or Smallest Valued Element in an Array

Problem

You have an array of elements, and you want to find the largest or smallest valued element. For example, you want to find the appropriate scale when creating a histogram.

Solution

To find the largest element, use `max()`:

```
$largest = max($array);
```

To find the smallest element, use `min()`:

```
$smallest = min($array);
```

Discussion

Normally, max() returns the larger of two elements, but if you pass it an array, it searches the entire array instead. Unfortunately, there's no way to find the index of the largest element using max(). To do that, you must sort the array in reverse order to put the largest element in position 0:

```
arsort($array);
```

Now the value of the largest element is $array[0].

If you don't want to disturb the order of the original array, make a copy and sort the copy:

```
$copy = $array;
arsort($copy);
```

The same concept applies to min() but uses asort() instead of arsort().

Both max() and min() issue a warning if you provide them with an empty array.

See Also

Recipe 4.16 for sorting an array; documentation on max() (*http://www.php.net/max*), min() (*http://www.php.net/min*), arsort() (*http://www.php.net/arsort*), and asort() (*http://www.php.net/asort*).

4.15 Reversing an Array

Problem

You want to reverse the order of the elements in an array.

Solution

Use array_reverse():

```
$array = array('Zero', 'One', 'Two');
$reversed = array_reverse($array);
```

Discussion

The array_reverse() function reverses the elements in an array. However, it's often possible to avoid this operation. If you wish to reverse an array you've just sorted, modify the sort to do the inverse. If you want to reverse a list you're about to loop through and process, just invert the loop. Instead of:

```
for ($i = 0, $size = count($array); $i < $size; $i++) {
    // ...
}
```

do the following:

```
for ($i = count($array) - 1; $i >=0 ; $i--) {
    // ...
}
```

However, as always, use a `for` loop only on a tightly packed array.

Another alternative would be, if possible, to invert the order in which elements are placed into the array. For instance, if you're populating an array from a series of rows returned from a database, you should be able to modify the query to `ORDER DESC`. See your database manual for the exact syntax for your database.

See Also

Documentation on `array_reverse()` (*http://www.php.net/array-reverse*).

4.16 Sorting an Array

Problem

You want to sort an array in a specific way.

Solution

To sort an array using the traditional definition of sort, use `sort()`:

```
$states = array('Delaware', 'Pennsylvania', 'New Jersey');
sort($states);
```

To sort numerically, pass `SORT_NUMERIC` as the second argument to `sort()`:

```
$scores = array(1, 10, 2, 20);
sort($scores, SORT_NUMERIC);
```

This resorts the numbers in ascending order (`1, 2, 10, 20`) instead of lexicographical order (`1, 10, 2, 20`).

Discussion

The `sort()` function doesn't preserve the key/value association between elements; instead, entries are reindexed starting at 0 and going upward.

To preserve the key/value links, use `asort()`. The `asort()` function is normally used for associative arrays, but it can also be useful when the indexes of the entries are meaningful:

```
$states = array(1 => 'Delaware', 'Pennsylvania', 'New Jersey');
asort($states);

while (list($rank, $state) = each($states)) {
    print "$state was the #$rank state to join the United States\n";
}
```

Use `natsort()` to sort the array using a natural sorting algorithm. Under natural sorting, you can mix strings and numbers inside your elements and still get the right answer:

```
$tests = array('test1.php', 'test10.php', 'test11.php', 'test2.php');
natsort($tests);
```

The elements are now ordered `'test1.php'`, `'test2.php'`, `'test10.php'`, and `'test11.php'`. With natural sorting, the number 10 comes after the number 2; the opposite occurs under traditional sorting. For case-insensitive natural sorting, use `nat casesort()`.

To sort the array in reverse order, use `rsort()` or `arsort()`, which is like `rsort()` but also preserves keys. There is no `natrsort()` or `natcasersort()`. You can also pass `SORT_NUMERIC` into these functions.

See Also

Recipe 4.17 for sorting with a custom comparison function and Recipe 4.18 for sorting multiple arrays; documentation on `sort()` (*http://www.php.net/sort*), `asort()` (*http://www.php.net/asort*), `natsort()` (*http://www.php.net/natsort*), `natcasesort()` (*http://www.php.net/natcasesort*), `rsort()` (*http://www.php.net/rsort*), and `arsort()` (*http://www.php.net/arsort*).

4.17 Sorting an Array by a Computable Field

Problem

You want to define your own sorting routine.

Solution

Use `usort()` in combination with a custom comparison function:

```
$tests = array('test1.php', 'test10.php', 'test11.php', 'test2.php');

// sort in reverse natural order
usort($tests, function ($a, $b) {
```

```
        return strnatcmp($b, $a);
});
```

Discussion

The comparison function must return a value greater than 0 if $a > $b, 0 if $a == $b, and a value less than 0 if $a < $b. To sort in reverse, do the opposite. The function in the Solution, strnatcmp(), obeys those rules.

To reverse the sort, instead of multiplying the return value of strnatcmp($a, $b) by -1, switch the order of the arguments to strnatcmp($b, $a).

The comparison function doesn't need to be a wrapper for an existing sort or an anonymous function. For instance, the date_sort() function, shown in Example 4-2, shows how to sort dates.

Example 4-2. date_sort( )

```
// expects dates in the form of "MM/DD/YYYY"
function date_sort($a, $b) {
    list($a_month, $a_day, $a_year) = explode('/', $a);
    list($b_month, $b_day, $b_year) = explode('/', $b);

    if ($a_year  > $b_year ) return  1;
    if ($a_year  < $b_year ) return -1;

    if ($a_month > $b_month) return  1;
    if ($a_month < $b_month) return -1;

    if ($a_day   > $b_day  ) return  1;
    if ($a_day   < $b_day  ) return -1;

    return 0;
}

$dates = array('12/14/2000', '08/10/2001', '08/07/1999');
usort($dates, 'date_sort');
```

While sorting, usort() frequently recomputes the comparison function's return values each time it's needed to compare two elements, which slows the sort. To avoid unnecessary work, you can cache the comparison values, as shown in array_sort() in Example 4-3.

Example 4-3. array_sort( )

```
function array_sort($array, $map_func, $sort_func = '') {
    $mapped = array_map($map_func, $array);    // cache $map_func() values

    if ('' === $sort_func) {
        asort($mapped);                         // asort() is faster then usort()
    } else {
```

```
        uasort($mapped, $sort_func);                    // need to preserve keys
    }

    while (list($key) = each($mapped)) {
        $sorted[] = $array[$key];                        // use sorted keys
    }

    return $sorted;
}
```

To avoid unnecessary work, `array_sort()` uses a temporary array, `$mapped`, to cache the return values. It then sorts `$mapped`, using either the default sort order or a user-specified sorting routine. Importantly, it uses a sort that preserves the key/value relationship. By default, it uses `asort()` because `asort()` is faster than `uasort()`. (Slowness in `uasort()` is the whole reason for `array_sort()` after all.) Finally, it creates a sorted array, `$sorted`, using the sorted keys in `$mapped` to index the values in the original array.

For small arrays or simple sort functions, `usort()` is faster, but as the number of computations grows, `array_sort()` surpasses `usort()`. The following example sorts elements by their string lengths, a relatively quick custom sort:

```
function u_length($a, $b) {
    $a = strlen($a);
    $b = strlen($b);

    if ($a == $b) return  0;
    if ($a  > $b) return  1;
                  return -1;
}

function map_length($a) {
    return strlen($a);
}

$tests = array('one', 'two', 'three', 'four', 'five',
               'six', 'seven', 'eight', 'nine', 'ten');

// faster for < 5 elements using u_length()
usort($tests, 'u_length');

// faster for >= 5 elements using map_length()
$tests = array_sort($tests, 'map_length');
```

Here, `array_sort()` is faster than `usort()` once the array reaches five elements.

See Also

Recipe 4.16 for basic sorting and Recipe 4.18 for sorting multiple arrays; documentation on `usort()` (*http://www.php.net/usort*), `asort()` (*http://www.php.net/asort*), ar ray_map() (*http://www.php.net/array-map*), and anonymous functions (*http://www.php.net/functions.anonymous*).

4.18 Sorting Multiple Arrays

Problem

You want to sort multiple arrays or an array with multiple dimensions.

Solution

Use `array_multisort()`:

To sort multiple arrays simultaneously, pass multiple arrays to `array_multisort()`:

```
$colors = array('Red', 'White', 'Blue');
$cities = array('Boston', 'New York', 'Chicago');

array_multisort($colors, $cities);
print_r($colors);
print_r($cities);
Array
(
    [0] => Blue
    [1] => Red
    [2] => White
)
Array
(
    [0] => Chicago
    [1] => Boston
    [2] => New York
)
```

To sort multiple dimensions within a single array, pass the specific array elements:

```
$stuff = array('colors' => array('Red', 'White', 'Blue'),
               'cities' => array('Boston', 'New York', 'Chicago'));

array_multisort($stuff['colors'], $stuff['cities']);
print_r($stuff);
Array
(
    [colors] => Array
        (
            [0] => Blue
            [1] => Red
            [2] => White
        )

    [cities] => Array
```

```
(
    [0] => Chicago
    [1] => Boston
    [2] => New York
)

)
```

To modify the sort type, as in sort(), pass in SORT_REGULAR, SORT_NUMERIC, or SORT_STRING after the array. To modify the sort order, unlike in sort(), pass in SORT_ASC or SORT_DESC after the array. You can also pass in both a sort type and a sort order after the array.

Discussion

The array_multisort() function can sort several arrays at once or a multidimensional array by one or more dimensions. The arrays are treated as columns of a table to be sorted by rows. The first array is the main one to sort by; all the items in the other arrays are reordered based on the sorted order of the first array. If items in the first array compare as equal, the sort order is determined by the second array, and so on.

The default sorting values are SORT_REGULAR and SORT_ASC, and they're reset after each array, so there's no reason to pass either of these two values, except for clarity:

```
$numbers = array(0, 1, 2, 3);
$letters = array('a', 'b', 'c', 'd');
array_multisort($numbers, SORT_NUMERIC, SORT_DESC,
                $letters, SORT_STRING , SORT_DESC);
```

This example reverses the arrays.

See Also

Recipe 4.16 for simple sorting and Recipe 4.17 for sorting with a custom function; documentation on array_multisort() (*http://www.php.net/array-multisort*).

4.19 Sorting an Array Using a Method Instead of a Function

Problem

You want to define a custom sorting routine to order an array. However, instead of using a function, you want to use an object method.

Solution

Pass in an array holding a class name and method in place of the function name:

```
usort($access_times, array('dates', 'compare'));
```

Discussion

As with a custom sort function, the object method needs to take two input arguments and return 1, 0, or −1, depending on whether the first parameter is larger than, equal to, or less than the second:

```
class sort {
    // reverse-order string comparison
    static function strrcmp($a, $b) {
        return strcmp($b, $a);
    }
}

usort($words, array('sort', 'strrcmp'));
```

It must also be declared as `static`. Alternatively, you can use an instantiated object:

```
class Dates {
    public function compare($a, $b) { /* compare here */ }
}

$dates = new Dates;

usort($access_times, array($dates, 'compare'));
```

See Also

Chapter 7 for more on classes and objects; Recipe 4.17 for more on custom sorting of arrays.

4.20 Randomizing an Array

Problem

You want to scramble the elements of an array in a random order.

Solution

Use `shuffle()`:

```
shuffle($array);
```

Discussion

It's surprisingly tricky to properly shuffle an array. In fact, up until PHP 4.3, PHP's `shuffle()` routine wasn't a truly random shuffle. It would mix elements around, but certain combinations were more likely than others.

Therefore, you should use PHP's shuffle() function whenever possible.

See Also

Documentation on shuffle() (*http://www.php.net/shuffle*).

4.21 Removing Duplicate Elements from an Array

Problem

You want to eliminate duplicates from an array.

Solution

If the array is already complete, use array_unique(), which returns a new array that contains no duplicate values:

```
$unique = array_unique($array);
```

If you create the array while processing results, here is a technique for numerical arrays:

```
foreach ($_GET['fruits'] as $fruit) {
    if (!in_array($fruit, $array)) { $array[] = $fruit; }
}
```

Here's one for associative arrays:

```
foreach ($_GET['fruits'] as $fruit) {
    $array[$fruit] = $fruit;
}
```

Discussion

Once processing is completed, array_unique() is the best way to eliminate duplicates. But if you're inside a loop, you can eliminate the duplicate entries from appearing by checking if they're already in the array.

An even faster method than using in_array() is to create a hybrid array in which the key and the value for each element are the same. This eliminates the linear check of in_array() but still allows you to take advantage of the array family of functions that operate over the values of an array instead of the keys.

In fact, it's faster to use the associative array method and then call array_values() on the result (or, for that matter, array_keys(), but array_values() is slightly faster) than to create a numeric array directly with the overhead of in_array().

See Also

Documentation on `array_unique()` (*http://www.php.net/array-unique*).

4.22 Applying a Function to Each Element in an Array

Problem

You want to apply a function or method to each element in an array. This allows you to transform the input data for the entire set all at once.

Solution

Use `array_walk()`:

```
$names = array('firstname' => "Baba",
               'lastname'  => "O'Riley");

array_walk($names, function (&$value, $key) {
    $value = htmlentities($value, ENT_QUOTES);
});

foreach ($names as $name) {
    print "$name\n";
}
```

Baba
O'Riley

For nested data, use `array_walk_recursive()`:

```
$names = array('firstnames' => array("Baba", "Bill"),
               'lastnames'  => array("O'Riley", "O'Reilly"));

array_walk_recursive($names, function (&$value, $key) {
    $value = htmlentities($value, ENT_QUOTES);
});

foreach ($names as $nametypes) {
    foreach ($nametypes as $name) {
        print "$name\n";
    }
}
```

Baba
Bill
O'Riley
O'Reilly

Discussion

It's frequently useful to loop through all the elements of an array. One option is to `foreach` through the data. However, an alternative choice is the `array_walk()` function.

This function takes an array and a callback function, which is the function that processes the elements of the array. The callback function takes two parameters: a value and a key. It can also take an optional third parameter, which is any additional data you wish to expose within the callback.

Here's an example that ensures all the data in the `$names` array is properly HTML encoded. The anonymous callback function takes the array values, passes them to `htmlen tities()` to encode the key HTML entities, and assigns the result back to `$value`:

```
$names = array('firstname' => "Baba",
               'lastname'  => "O'Riley");

array_walk($names, function (&$value, $key) {
    $value = htmlentities($value, ENT_QUOTES);
});

foreach ($names as $name) {
    print "$name\n";
}
```
```
Baba
O'Riley
```

Because `array_walk` operates in-place instead of returning a modified copy of the array, you must pass in values by reference when you want to modify the elements. In those cases, as in this example, there is an & before the parameter name. However, this is only necessary when you wish to alter the array.

When you have a series of nested arrays, use the `array_walk_recursive()` function:

```
$names = array('firstnames' => array("Baba", "Bill"),
               'lastnames'  => array("O'Riley", "O'Reilly"));

array_walk_recursive($names, function (&$value, $key) {
    $value = htmlentities($value, ENT_QUOTES);
});

foreach ($names as $nametypes) {
    foreach ($nametypes as $name) {
        print "$name\n";
    }
}
```
```
Baba
Bill
O'Riley
O'Reilly
```

The `array_walk_recursive()` function only passes nonarray elements to the callback, so you don't need to modify a callback when switching from `array_walk()`.

See Also

Documentation on `array_walk()` (*http://www.php.net/array-walk*), `array_walk_re cursive()` (*http://www.php.net/array_walk_recursive*), `htmlentities()` (*http://www.php.net/htmlentities*), and anonymous functions (*http://www.php.net/func tions.anonymous*).

4.23 Finding the Union, Intersection, or Difference of Two Arrays

Problem

You have a pair of arrays, and you want to find their union (all the elements), intersection (elements in both, not just one), or difference (in one but not both).

Solution

To compute the union:

```
$union = array_unique(array_merge($a, $b));
```

To compute the intersection:

```
$intersection = array_intersect($a, $b);
```

To find the simple difference:

```
$difference = array_diff($a, $b);
```

And for the symmetric difference:

```
$difference = array_merge(array_diff($a, $b), array_diff($b, $a));
```

Discussion

Many necessary components for these calculations are built into PHP; it's just a matter of combining them in the proper sequence.

To find the union, you merge the two arrays to create one giant array with all of the values. But `array_merge()` allows duplicate values when merging two numeric arrays, so you call `array_unique()` to filter them out. This can leave gaps between entries because `array_unique()` doesn't compact the array. It isn't a problem, however, because `foreach` and `each()` handle sparsely filled arrays without a hitch.

The function to calculate the intersection is simply named `array_intersection()` and requires no additional work on your part.

The `array_diff()` function returns an array containing all the unique elements in $old that aren't in $new. This is known as the simple difference:

```
$old = array('To', 'be', 'or', 'not', 'to', 'be');
$new = array('To', 'be', 'or', 'whatever');
$difference = array_diff($old, $new);
print_r($difference);
```

The resulting array, $difference, contains 'not' and 'to' because `array_diff()` is case sensitive. It doesn't contain 'whatever' because it doesn't appear in $old.

To get a reverse difference, or in other words, to find the unique elements in $new that are lacking in $old, flip the arguments:

```
$old = array('To', 'be', 'or', 'not', 'to', 'be');
$new = array('To', 'be', 'or', 'whatever');
$reverse_diff = array_diff($new, $old);
print_r($reverse_diff);
```

The $reverse_diff array contains only 'whatever'.

If you want to apply a function or other filter to `array_diff()`, roll your own diffing algorithm:

```
// implement case-insensitive diffing; diff -i

$seen = array();
foreach ($new as $n) {
    $seen[strtolower($n)]++;
}

foreach ($old as $o) {
    $o = strtolower($o);
    if (!$seen[$o]) { $diff[$o] = $o; }
}
```

The first `foreach` builds an associative array lookup table. You then loop through $old and, if you can't find an entry in your lookup, add the element to $diff.

It can be a little faster to combine `array_diff()` with `array_map()`:

```
$diff = array_diff(array_map('strtolower', $old), array_map('strtolower', $new));
```

The symmetric difference is what's in $a but not $b, and what's in $b but not $a:

```
$difference = array_merge(array_diff($a, $b), array_diff($b, $a));
```

Once stated, the algorithm is straightforward. You call `array_diff()` twice and find the two differences. Then you merge them together into one array. There's no need to call `array_unique()` because you've intentionally constructed these arrays to have nothing in common.

See Also

Documentation on `array_unique()` (*http://www.php.net/array-unique*), `array_inter sect()` (*http://www.php.net/array-intersect*), `array_diff()` (*http://www.php.net/array-diff*), `array_merge()` (*http://www.php.net/array-merge*), and `array_map()` (*http://www.php.net/array-map*).

4.24 Iterating Efficiently over Large or Expensive Datasets

Problem

You want to iterate through a list of items, but the entire list takes up a lot of memory or is very slow to generate.

Solution

Use a generator:

```
function FileLineGenerator($file) {
    if (!$fh = fopen($file, 'r')) {
        return;
    }

    while (false !== ($line = fgets($fh))) {
        yield $line;
    }

    fclose($fh);
}

$file = FileLineGenerator('log.txt');
foreach ($file as $line) {
    if (preg_match('/^rasmus: /', $line)) { print $line; }
}
```

Discussion

Generators provide a simple way to efficiently loop over items without the overhead and expense of loading all the data into an array. They are available in PHP 5.5.

A generator is a function that returns an iterable object. As you loop through the object, PHP repeatedly calls the generator to get the next value, which is returned by the generator function using the `yield` keyword.

Unlike normal functions where you start fresh every time, PHP preserves the current function state between calls to a generator. This allows you to keep any necessary information to provide the next value.

If there's no more data, exit the function without a return or with an empty return statement. (Trying to `return` data from a generator is illegal.)

A perfect use of a generator is processing all the lines in a file. The simplest way is to use the `file()` function. This open the file, loads each line into an element of an array, and closes it. However, then you store the entire file in memory.

```
$file = file('log.txt');
foreach ($file as $line) {
    if (preg_match('/^rasmus: /', $line)) { print $line; }
}
```

Another option is to use the standard file reading functions, but then your code for reading from the file and acting on each line gets intertwined. This doesn't make for reusable or easy-to-read code:

```
function print_matching_lines($file, $regex) {
    if (!$fh = fopen('log.txt','r')) {
        return;
    }
    while(false !== ($line = fgets($fh))) {
        if (preg_match($regex, $line)) { print $line; }
    }
    fclose($fh);
}

print_matching_lines('log.txt', '/^rasmus: /');
```

However, if you wrap the code to process the file into a generator, you get the best of both options—a general function to efficiently iterate through lines of a file and then clean syntax as if all the data is stored in an array:

```
function FileLineGenerator($file) {
    if (!$fh = fopen($file, 'r')) {
        return;
    }

    while (false !== ($line = fgets($fh))) {
        yield $line;
    }

    fclose($fh);
}

$file = FileLineGenerator('log.txt');
foreach ($file as $line) {
    if (preg_match('/^rasmus: /', $line)) { print $line; }
}
```

In a generator, control passes back and forth between the loop and the function via the `yield` statement. The first time the generator is called, control begins at the top of the function and pauses when it reaches a `yield` statement, returning the value.

In this example, the `FileLineGenerator()` generator function loops through lines of a file. After the file is opened, `fgets()` is called in a loop. As long as there are more lines, the loop yields `$line` back to the iterator. At the end of the file, the loop terminates, the file is closed, and the function terminates. Because nothing is yielded back, the `foreach()` exits.

Now, `FileLineGenerator()` can be used any time you want to loop through a file. The previous example prints lines beginning with `rasmus:`. The following one prints a random line from the file:

```
$line_number = 0;
foreach (FileLineGenerator('sayings.txt') as $line) {
    $line_number++;
    if (mt_rand(0, $line_number - 1) == 0) {
        $selected = $line;
    }
}

print $selected . "\n";
```

Despite a completely different use case, `FileLineGenerator()` is reusable without modifications. In this example, the generator is invoked from within the `foreach` loop instead of storing it in a variable.

You cannot rewind a generator. They only iterate forward.

See Also

Recipe 4.4 for iteration techniques and Chapter 24 for reading from files; documentation on generators (*http://www.php.net/generators*).

4.25 Accessing an Object Using Array Syntax

Problem

You have an object, but you want to be able to read and write data to it as an array. This allows you to combine the benefits from an object-oriented design with the familiar interface of an array.

Solution

Implement SPL's `ArrayAccess` interface:

```php
class FakeArray implements ArrayAccess {

    private $elements;

    public function __construct() {
        $this->elements = array();
    }

    public function offsetExists($offset) {
        return isset($this->elements[$offset]);
    }

    public function offsetGet($offset) {
        return $this->elements[$offset];
    }

    public function offsetSet($offset, $value) {
        return $this->elements[$offset] = $value;
    }

    public function offsetUnset($offset) {
        unset($this->elements[$offset]);
    }
}

$array = new FakeArray;

// What's Opera, Doc?
$array['animal'] = 'wabbit';

// Be very quiet I'm hunting wabbits
if (isset($array['animal']) &&
    // Wabbit tracks!!!
    $array['animal'] == 'wabbit') {

    // Kill the wabbit, kill the wabbit, kill the wabbit
    unset($array['animal']);
    // Yo ho to oh! Yo ho to oh! Yo ho...
}

// What have I done?? I've killed the wabbit....
// Poor little bunny, poor little wabbit...
if (!isset($array['animal'])) {
    print "Well, what did you expect in an opera? A happy ending?\n";
}
```

Discussion

The ArrayAccess interface allows you to manipulate data in an object using the same set of conventions you use for arrays. This allows you to leverage the benefits of an object-oriented design, such as using a class hierarchy or implementing additional methods on the object, but still allow people to interact with the object using a familiar interface. Alternatively, it allows you create an "array" that stores its data in an external location, such as shared memory or a database.

An implementation of `ArrayAccess` requires four methods: `offsetExists()`, which indicates whether an element is defined; `offsetGet()`, which returns an element's value; `offsetSet()`, which sets an element to a new value; and `offsetUnset()`, which removes an element and its value.

This example stores the data locally in an object property:

```
class FakeArray implements ArrayAccess {

    private $elements;

    public function __construct() {
        $this->elements = array();
    }

    public function offsetExists($offset) {
        return isset($this->elements[$offset]);
    }

    public function offsetGet($offset) {
        return $this->elements[$offset];
    }

    public function offsetSet($offset, $value) {
        return $this->elements[$offset] = $value;
    }

    public function offsetUnset($offset) {
        unset($this->elements[$offset]);
    }
}
```

The object constructor initializes the `$elements` property to a new array. This provides you with a place to store the keys and values of your array. That property is defined as `private`, so people can only access the data through one of the accessor methods defined as part of the interface.

The next four methods implement everything you need to manipulate an array. Because `offsetExists()` checks if an array element is set, the method returns the value of `isset($this->elements[$offset])`.

The `offsetGet()` and `offsetSet()` methods interact with the `$elements` property as you would normally use those features with an array.

Last, the `offsetUnset()` method simply calls `unset()` on the element. Unlike the other three methods, it does not return the value from its operation. That's because `unset()` is a statement, not a function, and doesn't return a value.

Now you can instantiate an instance of `FakeArray` and manipulate it like an array:

```
$array = new FakeArray;

// What's Opera, Doc?
$array['animal'] = 'wabbit';

// Be very quiet I'm hunting wabbits
if (isset($array['animal']) &&
    // Wabbit tracks!!!
    $array['animal'] == 'wabbit') {

    // Kill the wabbit, kill the wabbit, kill the wabbit
    unset($array['animal']);
    // Yo ho to oh! Yo ho to oh! Yo ho...
}

// What have I done?? I've killed the wabbit....
// Poor little bunny, poor little wabbit...
if (!isset($array['animal'])) {
    print "Well, what did you expect in an opera? A happy ending?\n";
}
```

Each operation calls one of your methods: assigning a value to `$array['animal']` triggers `offsetSet()`, checking `isset($array['animal'])` invokes `offsetExists()`, `offsetGet()` comes into play when you do the comparison `$array['animal'] == 'wabbit'`, and `offsetUnset()` is called for `unset($array['animal'])`.

As you can see, after all this, the wabbit is *dead*.

See Also

More on objects in Chapter 7; the `ArrayAccess` reference page (*http://bit.ly/1g8ekwe*); and *What's Opera, Doc?* (*http://bit.ly/1mCtfCH*)

CHAPTER 5

Variables

5.0 Introduction

Along with conditional logic, variables are the core of what makes computer programs powerful and flexible. If you think of a variable as a bucket with a name that holds a value, PHP lets you have plain old buckets, buckets that contain the name of other buckets, buckets with numbers or strings in them, buckets holding arrays of other buckets, buckets full of objects, and just about any other variation on that analogy you can think of.

A variable is either set or unset. A variable with any value assigned to it, true or false, empty or nonempty, is set. The function isset() returns true when passed a variable that's set. To turn a variable that's set into one that's unset, call unset() on the variable or assign null to the variable. Scalars, arrays, and objects can all be passed to unset(). You can also pass unset() multiple variables to unset them all:

```
unset($vegetables);
unset($fruits[12]);
unset($earth, $moon, $stars);
```

If a variable is present in the query string of a URL, even if it has no value assigned to it, it is set in the appropriate superglobal array. Thus:

```
http://www.example.com/set.php?chimps=&monkeys=12
```

sets $_GET['monkeys'] to 12 and $_GET['chimps'] to the empty string.

All unset variables are also empty. Set variables may be empty or nonempty. Empty variables have values that evaluate to false as a boolean. These are listed in Table 5-1.

Table 5-1. Values that evaluate to false

Type	Value
integer	0
double	0.0
string	"" (empty string)
string	"0"
boolean	`false`
array	`array()` (empty array)
null	NULL
object	An object with no properties, only prior to PHP 5

Everything else not listed in Table 5-1 is nonempty. This includes the string `"00"`, and the string `"  "`, containing just a space character.

 In 5.5, `empty()` accepts arbitrary expressions.

Variables evaluate to either `true` or `false`. The values in Table 5-1 are the complete set of what's `false` in PHP. Every other value is `true`. The language construct `isset()` tells you whether a variable is set. The language construct `empty()` tells you whether a value is empty or not. In versions of PHP prior to 5.5 `empty()` only accepts variables as arguments. In PHP 5.5, you can pass an arbitrary expression to `empty()`.

Constants and return values from functions can be `false`, but before PHP 5.5, they can't be empty. For example, Example 5-1 shows a valid use of `empty()` (in any PHP version) because `$first_name` is a variable.

Example 5-1. Correctly checking if a variable is empty

```
if (empty($first_name)) { .. }
```

On the other hand, the code in Example 5-2 returns parse errors before PHP 5.5 because 0 (a constant) and the return value from `get_first_name()` can't be empty.

Example 5-2. Incorrectly checking if a constant is empty before PHP 5.5

```
if (empty(0)) { .. }
if (empty(get_first_name())) { .. }
```

5.1 Avoiding == Versus = Confusion

Problem

You don't want to accidentally assign values when comparing a variable and a constant.

Solution

Use:

```
if (12 == $dwarves) { ... }
```

instead of:

```
if ($dwarves == 12) { ... }
```

Putting the constant on the left triggers a parse error with the assignment operator. In other words, PHP complains when you write:

```
if (12 = $dwarves) { ... }
```

but:

```
if ($dwarves = 12) { ... }
```

silently executes, assigning 12 to the variable $dwarves, and then executing the code inside the block. ($dwarves = 12 evaluates to 12, which is true.)

Discussion

Putting a constant on the left side of a comparison coerces the comparison to the type of the constant. This causes problems when you are comparing an integer with a variable that could be an integer or a string. 0 == $dwarves is true when $dwarves is 0, but it's also true when $dwarves is sleepy. Because an integer (0) is on the left side of the comparison, PHP converts what's on the right (the string sleepy) to an integer (0) before comparing. To avoid this, use the identity operator, 0 === $dwarves, instead.

See Also

Documentation for = (*http://www.php.net/operators.assignment*) and for www.php.net/operators.comparison[==] and www.php.net/operators.comparison[===].

5.2 Establishing a Default Value

Problem

You want to assign a default value to a variable that doesn't already have a value. It often happens that you want a hardcoded default value for a variable that can be overridden from form input or through an environment variable.

Solution

Use `isset()` to assign a default to a variable that may already have a value:

```
if (! isset($cars)) {
    $cars = $default_cars;
}
```

Use the ternary (a ? b : c) operator to give a new variable a (possibly default) value:

```
$cars = isset($_GET['cars']) ? $_GET['cars'] : $default_cars;
```

Discussion

Using `isset()` is essential when assigning default values. Without it, the nondefault value can't be 0 or anything else that evaluates to `false`. Consider this assignment:

```
$cars = isset($_GET['cars']) ? $_GET['cars'] : $default_cars;
```

If `$_GET['cars']` is 0, `$cars` is set to `$default_cars` even though 0 may be a valid value for `$cars`.

An alternative syntax for checking arrays is the `array_key_exists()` function:

```
$cars = array_key_exists('cars', $_GET) ? $_GET['cars'] : $default_cars;
```

The one difference between `isset()` and `array_key_exists()` is that when a key exists but its value is `null`, then `array_key_exists()` returns `true`, whereas `isset()` returns `false`:

```
$vehicles = array('cars' => null);
// array_key_exists() returns TRUE because the key is present.
$ake_result = array_key_exists('cars', $vehicles);

// isset() returns values because the key's value is NULL
$isset_result = isset($vehicles['cars']);
```

Use an array of defaults to set multiple default values easily. The keys in the defaults array are variable names, and the values in the array are the defaults for each variable:

```
$defaults = array('emperors'  => array('Rudolf II','Caligula'),
                   'vegetable' => 'celery',
                   'acres'     => 15);
```

```
foreach ($defaults as $k => $v) {
    if (! isset($GLOBALS[$k])) { $GLOBALS[$k] = $v; }
}
```

Because the variables are set in the global namespace, the previous code doesn't work for setting default variables private within a function. To do that, use variable variables:

```
foreach ($defaults as $k => $v) {
    if (! isset($$k)) { $$k = $v; }
}
```

In this example, the first time through the loop, $k is emperors, so $$k is $emperors.

See Also

Documentation on isset() (*http://www.php.net/isset*), array_key_exists() (*http://www.php.net/array_key_exists*) and variable variables (*http://www.php.net/language.variables.variable*).

5.3 Exchanging Values Without Using Temporary Variables

Problem

You want to exchange the values in two variables without using additional variables for storage.

Solution

To swap $a and $b:

```
$a = 'Alice';
$b = 'Bob';

list($a,$b) = array($b,$a);
// now $a is Bob and $b is Alice
```

Discussion

PHP's list() language construct lets you assign values from an array to individual variables. Its counterpart on the right side of the expression, array(), lets you construct arrays from individual values. Assigning the array that array() returns to the variables in the list() lets you juggle the order of those values. This works with more than two values, as well:

```
$yesterday = 'pleasure';
$today = 'sorrow';
$tomorrow = 'celebrate';
```

```
list($yesterday,$today,$tomorrow) = array($today,$tomorrow,$yesterday);
// now $yesterday is 'sorrow', $today is 'celebrate'
// and $tomorrow is 'pleasure'
```

This method isn't faster than using temporary variables, so you should use it for clarity, but not speed.

See Also

Documentation on list() (*http://www.php.net/list*) and array() (*http://www.php.net/array*).

5.4 Creating a Dynamic Variable Name

Problem

You want to construct a variable's name dynamically. For example, you want to use variable names that match the field names from a database query.

Solution

Use PHP's variable variable syntax by prepending a $ to a variable whose value is the variable name you want:

```
$animal = 'turtles';
$turtles = 103;
print $$animal;
```

This prints:

```
103
```

Discussion

Placing two dollar signs before a variable name causes PHP to dereference the right variable name to get a value. It then uses that value as the name of your *real* variable. The preceding example prints 103 because $animal = *turtles*, so $$animal is $turtles, which equals 103.

Using curly braces, you can construct more complicated expressions that indicate variable names:

```
$stooges = array('Moe','Larry','Curly');
$stooge_moe = 'Moses Horwitz';
$stooge_larry = 'Louis Feinberg';
$stooge_curly = 'Jerome Horwitz';

foreach ($stooges as $s) {
```

```
    print "$s's real name was ${'stooge_'.strtolower($s)}.\n";
}
```

PHP evaluates the expression between the curly braces and uses it as a variable name. That expression can even have function calls in it, such as `strtolower()`.

Variable variables are also useful when iterating through similarly named variables. Say you are querying a database table that has fields named `title_1`, `title_2`, etc. If you want to check if a title matches any of those values, the easiest way is to loop through them like this:

```
for ($i = 1; $i <= $n; $i++) {
    $t = "title_$i";
    if ($title == $$t) { /* match */ }
}
```

Of course, it would be more straightforward to store these values in an array, but if you are maintaining old code that uses this technique (and you can't change it), variable variables are helpful.

The curly brace syntax is also necessary in resolving ambiguity about array elements. The variable variable $$donkeys[12] could have two meanings. The first is *take what's in the 12th element of the $donkeys array and use that as a variable name*. Write this as: ${$donkeys[12]}. The second is *use what's in the scalar $donkeys as an array name and look in the 12th element of that array*. Write this as: ${$donkeys}[12].

You are not limited by two dollar signs. You can use three, or more, but in practice it's rare to see greater than two levels of indirection.

See Also

Documentation on variable variables (*http://www.php.net/language.variables.variable*).

5.5 Persisting a Local Variable's Value Across Function Invocations

Problem

You want a local variable to retain its value between invocations of a function.

Solution

Declare the variable as `static`:

```
function track_times_called() {
    static $i = 0;
    $i++;
```

```
        return $i;
    }
```

Discussion

Inside a function, declaring a variable `static` causes its value to be remembered by the function. So, if there are subsequent calls to the function, you can access the value of the saved variable. The `check_the_count()` function shown in Example 5-3 uses `static` variables to keep track of the strikes and balls for a baseball batter.

Example 5-3. check_the_count()

```
function check_the_count($pitch) {
    static $strikes = 0;
    static $balls   = 0;

    switch ($pitch) {
    case 'foul':
        if (2 == $strikes) break; // nothing happens if 2 strikes
        // otherwise, act like a strike
    case 'strike':
        $strikes++;
        break;
    case 'ball':
        $balls++;
        break;
    }

    if (3 == $strikes) {
        $strikes = $balls = 0;
        return 'strike out';
    }
    if (4 == $balls) {
        $strikes = $balls = 0;
        return 'walk';
    }
    return 'at bat';
}

$pitches = array('strike', 'ball', 'ball', 'strike', 'foul','strike');
$what_happened = array();
foreach ($pitches as $pitch) {
    $what_happened[] = check_the_count($pitch);
}

// Display the results
var_dump($what_happened);
```

Example 5-3 prints:

```
array(6) {
  [0]=>
```

```
    string(6) "at bat"
    [1]=>
    string(6) "at bat"
    [2]=>
    string(6) "at bat"
    [3]=>
    string(6) "at bat"
    [4]=>
    string(6) "at bat"
    [5]=>
    string(10) "strike out"
}
```

In check_the_count( ), the logic of what happens to the batter depending on the pitch count is in the switch statement inside the function. You can instead return the number of strikes and balls, but this requires you to place the checks for striking out, walking, and staying at the plate in multiple places in the code.

Though static variables retain their values between function calls, they do so only during one invocation of a script. A static variable accessed in one request doesn't keep its value for the next request to the same page.

See Also

Documentation on static variables (*http://www.php.net/language.variables.scope*).

5.6 Sharing Variables Between Processes

Problem

You want a way to share information between processes that provides fast access to the shared data.

Solution

Use the data store functionality of the APC extension, as shown in Example 5-4.

Example 5-4. Using APC's data store

```
// retrieve the old value
$population = apc_fetch('population');
// manipulate the data
$population += ($births + $immigrants - $deaths - $emigrants);
// write the new value back
apc_store('population', $population);
```

If you don't have APC available, use one of the two bundled shared memory extensions, shmop or System V shared memory.

With shmop, you create a block and read and write to and from it, as shown in Example 5-5.

Example 5-5. Using the shmop shared memory functions

```
// create key
$shmop_key = ftok(__FILE__, 'p');
// create 16384 byte shared memory block
$shmop_id = shmop_open($shmop_key, "c", 0600, 16384);
// retrieve the entire shared memory segment
$population = shmop_read($shmop_id, 0, 0);
// manipulate the data
$population += ($births + $immigrants - $deaths - $emigrants);
// store the value back in the shared memory segment
$shmop_bytes_written = shmop_write($shmop_id, $population, 0);
// check that it fit
if ($shmop_bytes_written != strlen($population)) {
    echo "Can't write all of: $population\n";
}
// close the handle
shmop_close($shmop_id);
```

With System V shared memory, you store the data in a shared memory segment, and guarantee exclusive access to the shared memory with a semaphore, as shown in Example 5-6.

Example 5-6. Using the System V shared memory functions

```
$semaphore_id = 100;
$segment_id   = 200;
// get a handle to the semaphore associated with the shared memory
// segment we want
$sem = sem_get($semaphore_id,1,0600);
// ensure exclusive access to the semaphore
sem_acquire($sem) or die("Can't acquire semaphore");
// get a handle to our shared memory segment
$shm = shm_attach($segment_id,16384,0600);
// Each value stored in the segment is identified by an integer
// ID
$var_id = 3476;
// retrieve a value from the shared memory segment
if (shm_has_var($shm, $var_id)) {
    $population = shm_get_var($shm,$var_id);
}
// Or initialize it if it hasn't been set yet
else {
    $population = 0;
}
// manipulate the value
$population += ($births + $immigrants - $deaths - $emigrants);
// store the value back in the shared memory segment
shm_put_var($shm,$var_id,$population);
```

```
// release the handle to the shared memory segment
shm_detach($shm);
// release the semaphore so other processes can acquire it
sem_release($sem);
```

Discussion

If you have the APC extension available, its data store is an extremely convenient way
to share information between separate PHP processes across different requests. The
apc_store() function takes a key and a value and stores the value associated with the
specified key. You can also supply an optional time to live (TTL) as a third argument to
apc_store() to limit the number of seconds the value is stored in the cache.

Once you've stored something, retrieve it by passing apc_fetch() the key. Because
apc_fetch() returns the value stored, or false on failure, it can be difficult to distinguish between a successful call that returned a false value and a failed call. To help with
this apc_fetch() supports a second by-reference argument which is set to true or false
indicating whether the call succeeded, as follows:

```
// Shucks, you failed the test!
apc_store('passed the test?', false);

// $results is false, because the stored value was false
// $success is true, because the call to apc_fetch() succeeded
$results = apc_fetch('passed the test?', $success);
```

In addition to store and fetch, APC also functions for more complicated data manipulation. The apc_inc() and apc_dec() functions atomically increment and decrement
a stored number. This makes them very useful for speedy counters. You can also implement some lightweight locking by using the apc_add() function, which only inserts
a variable into the data store if nothing already exists at that key. Example 5-7 shows
how to do that.

Example 5-7. Using apc_add( ) to implement locking

```
function update_recent_users($current_user) {
    $recent_users = apc_fetch('recent-users', $success);
    if ($success) {
        if (! in_array($current_user, $recent_users)) {
            array_unshift($recent_users, $current_user);
        }
    }
    else {
        $recent_users = array($current_user);
    }
    $recent_users = array_slice($recent_users, 0, 10);
    apc_store('recent-users', $recent_users);
}

$tries = 3;
```

```
$done = false;

while ((! $done) && ($tries-- > 0)) {
    if (apc_add('my-lock', true, 5)) {
        update_recent_users($current_user);
        apc_delete('my-lock');
        $done = true;
    }
}
```

In Example 5-7, the call to apc_add('my-lock', true, 5) means "Insert a true value at key my-lock only if it's not already there, and expire it automatically after five seconds." So if this succeeds, any subsequent request that attempts the same thing (in the next five seconds) will fail until the apc_delete('my-lock') call in the first request removes the entry from the data store. The update_recent_users() call inside the loop, as an example, maintains an array of the 10 most recent users. The loop will try three times to obtain the lock and then quit.

If you don't have APC available, you can use a shared memory extension to accomplish similar in-memory data sharing, albeit with a little more work.

A shared memory segment is a slice of your machine's RAM that different processes (such as the multiple web server processes that handle requests) can access. The shmop and System V shared memory extensions solve the similar problem of allowing you to save information between requests in a fast and efficient manner, but they take slightly different approaches and have slightly different interfaces as a result.

The shmop functions have an interface similar to the familiar file manipulation. You can open a segment, read in data, write to it, and close it. Like a file, there's no built-in segmentation of the data, it's all just a series of consecutive characters.

In Example 5-5, you first create the shared memory block. Unlike a file, you must pre-declare the maximum size. In this example, it's 16,384 bytes:

```
// create key
$shmop_key = ftok(__FILE__, 'p');
// create 16384 byte shared memory block
$shmop_id = shmop_open($shmop_key, "c", 0600, 16384);
```

Just as you distinguish files by using filenames, shmop segments are differentiated by keys. Unlike filenames, these keys aren't strings but integers, so they're not easy to remember. Therefore, it's best to use the ftok() function to convert a human-friendly name, in this case the filename in the form of __FILE__, to a format suitable for shmop_open(). The ftok() function also takes a one-character *project identifier*. This helps you avoid collisions in case you accidently reuse the same string. Here it's p, for PHP.

Once you have a key, pass it to `shmop_create()`, along with the *flag* you want, the file permissions (in octal), and the block size. See Table 5-2 for a list of suitable flags.

These permissions work just like file permissions, so `0600` means that the user that created the block can read it and write to it. In this context, user doesn't just mean the process that created the semaphore, but any process with the same user ID. Permissions of `0600` should be appropriate for most uses, in which web server processes run as the same user.

Table 5-2. shmop_open() flags

Flag	Description
a	Opens for read-only *access*.
c	*Creates* a new segment. If it already exists, opens it for read and write access.
w	Opens for read and *write* access.
n	Creates a *new* segment, but fails if one already exists. Useful to avoid race conditions.

Once you have a handle, you can read from the segment using `shmop_read()` and manipulate the data:

```
// retrieve the entire shared memory segment
$population = shmop_read($shmop_id, 0, 0);
// manipulate the data
$population += ($births + $immigrants - $deaths - $emigrants);
```

This code reads in the entire segment. To read in a shorter amount, adjust the second and third parameters. The second parameter is the start, and the third is the length. As a shortcut, you can set the length to 0 to read to the end of the segment.

Once you have the adjusted data, store it back with `shmop_write()` and release the handle with `shmop_close()`:

```
// store the value back in the shared memory segment
$shmop_bytes_written = shmop_write($shmop_id, $population, 0);
// check that it fit
if ($shmop_bytes_written != strlen($population)) {
    echo "Can't write all of: $population\n";
}
// close the handle
shmop_close($shmop_id);
```

Because shared memory segments are of a fixed length, if you're not careful, you can try to write more data than you have room. Check to see if this happened by comparing the value returned from `shmop_write()` with the string length of your data. They should be the same. If `shmop_write()` returned a smaller value, then it was only able to fit that many bytes in the segment before running out of space.

In constrast to shmop, the System V shared memory functions behave similarly to an array. You access slices of the segment by specifying a key, such as population, and manipulate them directly. Depending on what you're storing, this direct access can be more convenient.

However, the interface is more complex as a result, and System V shared memory also requires you to do manage locking in the form of semaphore.

A semaphore makes sure that the different processes don't step on each other's toes when they access the shared memory segment. Before a process can use the segment, it needs to get control of the semaphore. When it's done with the segment, it releases the semaphore for another process to grab.

To get control of a semaphore, use sem_get() to find the semaphore's ID. The first argument to sem_get() is an integer semaphore key. You can make the key any integer you want, as long as all programs that need to access this particular semaphore use the same key. If a semaphore with the specified key doesn't already exist, it's created; the maximum number of processes that can access the semaphore is set to the second argument of sem_get() (in this case, 1); and the semaphore's permissions are set to sem_get()'s third argument (0600). Permissions here behave like they do with files and shmop. For example:

```
$semaphore_id = 100;
$segment_id   = 200;
// get a handle to the semaphore associated with the shared memory
// segment we want
$sem = sem_get($semaphore_id,1,0600);
// ensure exclusive access to the semaphore
sem_acquire($sem) or die("Can't acquire semaphore");
```

sem_get() returns an identifier that points to the underlying system semaphore. Use this ID to gain control of the semaphore with sem_acquire(). This function waits until the semaphore can be acquired (perhaps waiting until other processes release the semaphore) and then returns true. It returns false on error. Errors include invalid permissions or not enough memory to create the semaphore. Once the semaphore is acquired, you can read from the shared memory segment:

```
// get a handle to our shared memory segment
$shm = shm_attach($segment_id,16384,0600);
// each value stored in the segment is identified by an integer
// ID
$var_id = 3476;
// retrieve a value from the shared memory segment
if (shm_has_var($shm, $var_id)) {
    $population = shm_get_var($shm,$var_id);
}
// or initialize it if it hasn't been set yet
else {
    $population = 0;
```

```
}
// manipulate the value
$population += ($births + $immigrants - $deaths - $emigrants);
```

First, establish a link to the particular shared memory segment with `shm_attach()`. As with `sem_get()`, the first argument to `shm_attach()` is an integer key. This time, however, it identifies the desired segment, not the semaphore. If the segment with the specified key doesn't exist, the other arguments create it. The second argument (16384) is the size in bytes of the segment, and the last argument (0600) is the permissions on the segment. `shm_attach(200,16384,0600)` creates a 16K shared memory segment that can be read from and written to only by the user who created it. The function returns the identifier you need to read from and write to the shared memory segment.

After attaching to the segment, pull variables out of it with `shm_get_var($shm, $var_id)`. This looks in the shared memory segment identified by `$shm` and retrieves the value of the variable with integer key `$var_id`. You can store any type of variable in shared memory. Once the variable is retrieved, it can be operated on like other variables. `shm_put_var($shm, $var_id ,$population)` puts the value of `$population` back into the shared memory segment at variable `$var_id`.

You're now done with the shared memory statement. Detach from it with `shm_detach()` and release the semaphore with `sem_release()` so another process can use it:

```
// release the handle to the shared memory segment
shm_detach($shm);
// release the semaphore so other processes can acquire it
sem_release($sem);
```

Shared memory's chief advantage is that it's fast. But because it's stored in RAM, it can't hold too much data, and it doesn't persist when a machine is rebooted (unless you take special steps to write the information in shared memory to disk before shutdown and then load it into memory again at startup).

You cannot use System V shared memory under Windows, but the shmop functions work fine.

See Also

Documentation on apc (*http://pecl.php.net/apc*); shmop (*http://www.php.net/shmop*); and System V (*http://www.php.net/sem*) shared memory and semaphore functions.

5.7 Encapsulating Complex Data Types in a String

Problem

You want a string representation of an array or object for storage in a file or database. This string should be easily reconstitutable into the original array or object.

Solution

Use `serialize()` to encode variables and their values into a textual form:

```
$pantry = array('sugar' => '2 lbs.','butter' => '3 sticks');
$fp = fopen('/tmp/pantry','w') or die ("Can't open pantry");
fputs($fp,serialize($pantry));
fclose($fp);
```

To re-create the variables, use `unserialize()`:

```
// $new_pantry will be the array:
// array('sugar' => '2 lbs.','butter' => '3 sticks'
$new_pantry = unserialize(file_get_contents('/tmp/pantry'));
```

For easier interoperability with other languages (at a slight performance cost), use `json_encode()` to serialize data:

```
$pantry = array('sugar' => '2 lbs.','butter' => '3 sticks');
$fp = fopen('/tmp/pantry.json','w') or die ("Can't open pantry");
fputs($fp,json_encode($pantry));
fclose($fp);
```

And use `json_decode()` to re-create the variables:

```
// $new_pantry will be the array:
//   array('sugar' => '2 lbs.','butter' => '3 sticks')
$new_pantry = json_decode(file_get_contents('/tmp/pantry.json'), TRUE);
```

Discussion

The PHP serialized string that is reconstituted into $pantry looks like:

```
a:2:{s:5:"sugar";s:6:"2 lbs.";s:6:"butter";s:8:"3 sticks";}
```

The JSON-encoded version looks like:

```
{"sugar":"2 lbs.","butter":"3 sticks"}
```

The extra business in the serialized string that's not in the JSON string encodes the types and lengths of the values. This makes it uglier to look at but a little faster to decode. If you're just shuttling data among PHP applications, native serialization is great. If you need to work with other languages, use JSON instead.

Both native serialization and JSON store enough information to bring back all the values in the array, but the variable name itself isn't stored in either serialized representation.

JSON can't distinguish between objects and associative arrays in its serialization format, so you have to choose which you want when you call `json_decode()`. A second argument of `true`, as in the previous example, produces associative arrays. Without that argument, the same JSON would be decoded into an object of class `stdClass` with two properties: `sugar` and `butter`.

When passing serialized data from page to page in a URL, call `urlencode()` on the data to make sure URL metacharacters are escaped in it:

```
$shopping_cart = array('Poppy Seed Bagel' => 2,
                       'Plain Bagel' => 1,
                       'Lox' => 4);
print '<a href="next.php?cart='.urlencode(serialize($shopping_cart)).
      '">Next</a>';
```

Serialized data going into a database always needs to be escaped as well. Recipe 10.9 explains how to safely escape values for insertion into a database.

When you unserialize an object, PHP automatically invokes its `__wakeUp()` method. This allows the object to reestablish any state that's not preserved across serialization, such as database connection. This can alter your environment, so be sure you know what you're unserializing. See Recipe 7.19 for more details.

See Also

Documentation on `serialize()` (*http://www.php.net/serialize*), `unserialize()` (*http://www.php.net/unserialize*), `json_encode()` (*http://www.php.net/json_encode*), and `json_decode()` (*http://www.php.net/json_decode*). Recipe 10.9 discusses safely inserting values into a database and Recipe 7.19 discusses the interaction of objects and serialization.

5.8 Dumping Variable Contents as Strings

Problem

You want to inspect the values stored in a variable. It may be a complicated nested array or object, so you can't just print it out or loop through it.

Solution

Use `var_dump()`, `print_r()`, or `var_export()`, depending on exactly what you need.

The `var_dump()` and `print_r()` functions provide different human-readable representations of variables.

The `print_r()` function is a little more concise:

```
$info = array('name' => 'frank', 12.6, array(3, 4));
print_r($info);
```

prints:

```
Array
(
    [name] => frank
    [0] => 12.6
    [1] => Array
        (
            [0] => 3
            [1] => 4
        )

)
```

While this:

```
$info = array('name' => 'frank', 12.6, array(3, 4));
var_dump($info);
```

prints:

```
array(3) {
  ["name"]=>
  string(5) "frank"
  [0]=>
  float(12.6)
  [1]=>
  array(2) {
    [0]=>
    int(3)
    [1]=>
    int(4)
  }
}
```

The `var_export()` function produces valid PHP code that, when executed, defines the exported variable:

```
$info = array('name' => 'frank', 12.6, array(3, 4));
var_export($info);
```

prints:

```
array (
  'name' => 'frank',
  0 => 12.6,
  1 =>
```

```
array (
  0 => 3,
  1 => 4,
),
)
```

Discussion

The three functions mentioned in the Solution differ in how they handle recursion in references. Because these functions recursively work their way through variables, if you have references within a variable pointing back to the variable itself, you would end up with an infinite loop unless these functions bailed out.

When var_dump() or print_r() has seen a variable once, it prints *RECURSION* instead of printing information about the variable again and continues iterating through the rest of the information it has to print. The var_export() function does a similar thing, but it prints null instead of *RECURSION* to ensure its output is executable PHP code.

Consider the arrays $user_1 and $user_2, which reference each other through their friend elements:

```
$user_1 = array('name' => 'Max Bialystock',
                'username' => 'max');

$user_2 = array('name' => 'Leo Bloom',
                'username' => 'leo');

// Max and Leo are friends
$user_2['friend'] = &$user_1;
$user_1['friend'] = &$user_2;

// Max and Leo have jobs
$user_1['job'] = 'Swindler';
$user_2['job'] = 'Accountant';
```

The output of print_r($user_2) is:

```
Array
(
    [name] => Leo Bloom
    [username] => leo
    [friend] => Array
        (
            [name] => Max Bialystock
            [username] => max
            [friend] => Array
                (
                    [name] => Leo Bloom
                    [username] => leo
                    [friend] => Array
 *RECURSION*
```

```
                    [job] => Accountant
                )

            [job] => Swindler
        )

    [job] => Accountant
)
```

When print_r() sees the reference to $user_1 the second time, it prints *RECUR
SION* instead of descending into the array. It then continues on its way, printing the
remaining elements of $user_1 and $user_2. The var_dump() function behaves similarly:

```
array(4) {
  ["name"]=>
  string(9) "Leo Bloom"
  ["username"]=>
  string(3) "leo"
  ["friend"]=>
  &array(4) {
    ["name"]=>
    string(14) "Max Bialystock"
    ["username"]=>
    string(3) "max"
    ["friend"]=>
    &array(4) {
      ["name"]=>
      string(9) "Leo Bloom"
      ["username"]=>
      string(3) "leo"
      ["friend"]=>
      *RECURSION*
      ["job"]=>
      string(10) "Accountant"
    }
    ["job"]=>
    string(8) "Swindler"
  }
  ["job"]=>
  string(10) "Accountant"
}
```

As does var_export(), but with null instead of *RECURSION*:

```
array (
  'name' => 'Leo Bloom',
  'username' => 'leo',
  'friend' =>
  array (
    'name' => 'Max Bialystock',
    'username' => 'max',
    'friend' =>
```

```
      array (
        'name' => 'Leo Bloom',
        'username' => 'leo',
        'friend' => NULL,
        'job' => 'Accountant',
      ),
      'job' => 'Swindler',
    ),
    'job' => 'Accountant',
  )
```

The print_r() and var_export() functions accept a second argument which, if set to true tells the functions to return the string representation of the variable rather than printing it. To capture the output from var_dump(), however, you need to use output buffering:

```
ob_start();
var_dump($user);
$dump = ob_get_contents();
ob_end_clean();
```

This puts the results of var_dump($user) in $dump.

See Also

Output buffering is discussed in Recipe 8.13; documentation on print_r() (*http://www.php.net/print-r*), var_dump() (*http://www.php.net/var-dump*), and var_export() (*http://www.php.net/var_export*).

CHAPTER 6

Functions

6.0 Introduction

Functions help you create organized and reusable code. They allow you to abstract out details so your code becomes more flexible and more readable. Without functions, it is impossible to write easily maintainable programs because you're constantly updating identical blocks of code in multiple places and in multiple files.

With a function you pass a number of arguments in and get a value back:

```
function add($a, $b) {
    return $a + $b;
}

$total = add(2, 2);
// $total is 4
```

Declare a function using the `function` keyword, followed by the name of the function and any parameters in parentheses. To invoke a function, simply use the function name, specifying argument values for any parameters to the function. If the function returns a value, you can assign the result of the function to a variable, as shown in the preceding example.

You don't need to predeclare a function before you call it. PHP parses the entire file before it begins executing, so you can intermix function declarations and invocations. You can't, however, redefine a function in PHP. If PHP encounters a function with a name identical to one it's already found, it throws a fatal error and dies.

Sometimes, the standard procedure of passing in a fixed number of arguments and getting one value back doesn't quite fit a particular situation in your code. Maybe you don't know ahead of time exactly how many parameters your function needs to accept. Or you do know your parameters, but they're almost always the same values, so it's tedious to continue to repass them. Or you want to return more than one value from your function.

This chapter helps you use PHP to solve these types of problems. We begin by detailing different ways to pass arguments to a function. Recipe 6.1 through Recipe 6.6 cover passing arguments by value, reference, and as named parameters; assigning default parameter values; and functions with a variable number of parameters.

The next four recipes are all about returning values from a function. Recipe 6.7 describes returning by reference; Recipe 6.8 covers returning more than one variable; Recipe 6.9 describes how to skip selected return values; and Recipe 6.10 talks about the best way to return and check for failure from a function. The final three recipes show how to call variable functions, deal with variable scoping problems, and dynamically create a function. If you want a variable to maintain its value between function invocations, see Recipe 5.5.

6.1 Accessing Function Parameters

Problem

You want to access the values passed to a function.

Solution

Use the names from the function prototype:

```
function commercial_sponsorship($letter, $number) {
    print "This episode of Sesame Street is brought to you by ";
    print "the letter $letter and number $number.\n";
}

commercial_sponsorship('G', 3);

$another_letter = 'X';
$another_number = 15;
commercial_sponsorship($another_letter, $another_number);
```

Discussion

Inside the function, it doesn't matter whether the values are passed in as strings, numbers, arrays, or another kind of variable. You can treat them all the same and refer to them using the names from the prototype.

Unless otherwise specified, all non-object values being passed into and out of a function are passed by value, not by reference. (By default, objects are passed by reference.) This means PHP makes a copy of the value and provides you with that copy to access and manipulate. Therefore, any changes you make to your copy don't alter the original value. For example:

```
function add_one($number) {
    $number++;
}

$number = 1;
add_one($number);
print $number;
```

prints:

1

If the variable had been passed by reference, the value of $number in the global scope would have been 2.

In many languages, passing variables by reference has the additional benefit of being significantly faster than passing them by value. Although passing by reference is faster in PHP, the speed difference is marginal. For that reason, we suggest passing variables by reference only when actually necessary and never as a performance-enhancing trick.

See Also

Recipe 6.3 to pass values by reference and Recipe 6.7 to return values by reference.

6.2 Setting Default Values for Function Parameters

Problem

You want a parameter to have a default value if the function's caller doesn't pass it. For example, a function to wrap text in an HTML tag might have a parameter for the tag name, which defaults to strong if none is given.

Solution

Assign the default value to the parameters inside the function prototype:

```
function wrap_in_html_tag($text, $tag = 'strong') {
    return "<$tag>$text</$tag>";
}
```

Discussion

The example in the Solution sets the default tag value to strong. For example:

```
print wrap_in_html_tag("Hey, a mountain lion!");
```

prints:

```
<strong>Hey, a mountain lion!</strong>
```

This example:

```
print wrap_in_html_tag("Look over there!", "em");
```

prints:

```
<em>Look over there!</em>
```

There are two important things to remember when assigning default values. First, all parameters with default values must appear after parameters without defaults. Otherwise, PHP can't tell which parameters are omitted and should take the default value and which arguments are overriding the default. So wrap_in_html_tag() can't be defined as:

```
function wrap_in_html_tag($tag = 'strong', $text)
```

If you do this and pass wrap_in_html_tag() only a single argument, PHP assigns the value to $tag and issues a warning complaining of a missing second argument.

Second, the assigned value must be a constant, such as a string or a number. It can't be a variable. Again, using wrap_in_html_tag(), such as our example, you can't do this:

```
$my_favorite_html_tag = 'blink';

function wrap_in_html_tag($text, $tag = $my_favorite_html_tag) {
    return "<$tag>$text</$tag>";
}
```

If you want to assign a default of nothing, one solution is to assign the empty string to your parameter:

```
function wrap_in_html_tag($text, $tag = '') {
    if (empty($tag)) { return $text; }
    return "<$tag>$text</$tag>";
}
```

This function returns the original string, if no value is passed in for the $tag. If a non-empty tag is passed in, it returns the string wrapped inside of tags.

Depending on circumstances, another option for the $tag default value is either 0 or NULL. In wrap_in_html_tag(), you don't want to allow an empty-valued tag. However, in some cases, the empty string can be an acceptable option. As the following code shows, you can use a default message if no argument is provided but an empty message if the empty string is passed:

```
function log_db_error($message = NULL) {
    if (is_null($message)) {
        $message = "Couldn't connect to DB";
    }
```

```
        error_log("[DB] [$message]");
    }
```

See Also

Recipe 6.6 on creating functions that take a variable number of arguments.

6.3 Passing Values by Reference

Problem

You want to pass a variable to a function and have it retain any changes made to its value inside the function.

Solution

To instruct a function to accept an argument passed by reference instead of value, prepend an & to the parameter name in the function prototype:

```
function wrap_in_html_tag(&$text, $tag = 'strong') {
    $text = "<$tag>$text</$tag>";
}
```

Now there's no need to return the string because the original is modified in place.

Discussion

Passing a variable to a function by reference allows you to avoid the work of returning the variable and assigning the return value to the original variable. It is also useful when you want a function to return a boolean success value of true or false, but you still want to modify argument values with the function.

You can't switch between passing a parameter by value or reference; it's either one or the other. In other words, there's no way to tell PHP to optionally treat the variable as a reference or as a value.

Also, if a parameter is declared to accept a value by reference, you can't pass a constant string (or number, etc.), or PHP will die with a fatal error.

See Also

Recipe 6.7 on returning values by reference.

6.4 Using Named Parameters

Problem

You want to specify your arguments to a function by name, instead of simply their position in the function invocation.

Solution

PHP doesn't have language-level named parameter support like some other languages do. However, you can emulate it by having a function use one parameter and making that parameter an associative array:

```
function image($img) {
    $tag  = '<img src="' . $img['src'] . '" ';
    $tag .= 'alt="' . (isset($img['alt']) ? $img['alt'] : '') .'"/>';
    return $tag;
}

// $image1 is '<img src="cow.png" alt="cows say moo"/>'
$image1 = image(array('src' => 'cow.png', 'alt' => 'cows say moo'));

// $image2 is '<img src="pig.jpeg" alt=""/>'
$image2 = image(array('src' => 'pig.jpeg'));
```

Discussion

Though using named parameters makes the code inside your functions more complex, it ensures the calling code is easier to read. Because a function lives in one place but is called in many, this makes for more understandable code.

Because you've abstracted function parameters into an associative array, PHP can't warn you if you accidentally misspell a parameter's name. You need to be more careful because the parser won't catch these types of mistakes. Also, you can't take advantage of PHP's ability to assign a default value for a parameter. Luckily, you can work around this deficit with some simple code at the top of the function:

```
function image($img) {
    if (! isset($img['src']))    { $img['src']    = 'cow.png';      }
    if (! isset($img['alt']))    { $img['alt']    = 'milk factory'; }
    if (! isset($img['height'])) { $img['height'] = 100;            }
    if (! isset($img['width']))  { $img['width']  = 50;             }
    /* ... */
}
```

Using the isset() function, check to see if a value for each parameter is set; if not, assign a default value.

Alternatively, you can use array_merge() to handle this:

```
function image($img) {
    $defaults = array('src'    => 'cow.png',
                      'alt'    => 'milk factory',
                      'height' => 100,
                      'width'  => 50
                      );
    $img = array_merge($defaults, $img);
    /* ... */
}
```

If the same key exists in the arrays passed to `array_merge()`, then it uses the value in the later array. In the preceding example, that means that any values in `$img` override values in `$defaults`. But if a key is missing from `$img`, the value from `$defaults` is used.

See Also

Recipe 6.6 on creating functions that accept a variable number of arguments.

6.5 Enforcing Types of Function Arguments

Problem

You want to ensure argument values have certain types.

Solution

Use type hints on the arguments when you define your function. A type hint goes before the parameter name in a function declaration:

```
function drink_juice(Liquid $drink) {
    /* ... */
}

function enumerate_some_stuff(array $values) {
    /* ... */
}
```

Discussion

A type hint can be a class name, an interface name, the keyword `array` (since PHP 5.1) or the keyword `callable` (since PHP 5.4). If, at runtime, a value is passed for a type-hinted parameter that does not satisfy the type hint, PHP triggers an `E_RECOVERA BLE_ERROR` error.

If you give a type-hinted parameter a default value of `null`, either the null value or a value of the proper type is allowed. In the following code, the `must_be_an_array()`

function requires an array-typed parameter. Anything else will trigger an E_RECOVERA
BLE_ERROR error. The array_or_null_is_ok() function, however, is more forgiving. If
you provide a parameter, it must be an array or null. If you omit the parameter, the
$fruits local variable in the function will be equal to null:

```php
function must_be_an_array(array $fruits) {
    foreach ($fruits as $fruit) {
        print "$fruit\n";
    }
}

function array_or_null_is_ok(array $fruits = null) {
    if (is_array($fruits)) {
        foreach ($fruits as $fruit) {
            print "$fruit\n";
        }
    }
}
```

See Also

Documentation on type hints (*http://www.php.net/language.oop5.typehinting*).

6.6 Creating Functions That Take a Variable Number of Arguments

Problem

You want to define a function that takes a variable number of arguments.

Solution

Pass the function a single array-typed argument and put your variable arguments inside
the array:

```php
// find the "average" of a group of numbers
function mean($numbers) {
    // initialize to avoid warnings
    $sum = 0;

    // the number of elements in the array
    $size = count($numbers);

    // iterate through the array and add up the numbers
    for ($i = 0; $i < $size; $i++) {
        $sum += $numbers[$i];
    }
```

```
        // divide by the amount of numbers
        $average = $sum / $size;

        // return average
        return $average;
}

// $mean is 96.25
$mean = mean(array(96, 93, 98, 98));
```

Discussion

There are two good solutions, depending on your coding style and preferences. The more traditional PHP method is the one described in the Solution. We prefer this method because using arrays in PHP is a frequent activity; therefore, all programmers are familiar with arrays and their behavior.

So although this method creates some additional overhead, bundling variables is commonplace. It's done in Recipe 6.4 to create named parameters and in Recipe 6.8 to return more than one value from a function. Also, inside the function, the syntax to access and manipulate the array involves basic commands such as $array[$i] and count($array).

However, this can seem clunky, so PHP provides an alternative and allows you direct access to the argument list, as shown in Example 6-1.

Example 6-1. Accessing function parameters without using the argument list

```
// find the "average" of a group of numbers
function mean() {
    // initialize to avoid warnings
    $sum = 0;

    // the arguments passed to the function
    $size = func_num_args();

    // iterate through the arguments and add up the numbers
    for ($i = 0; $i < $size; $i++) {
        $sum += func_get_arg($i);
    }

    // divide by the amount of numbers
    $average = $sum / $size;

    // return average
    return $average;
}

// $mean is 96.25
$mean = mean(96, 93, 98, 98);
```

This example uses a set of functions that return data based on the arguments passed to the function they are called from. First, func_num_args() returns an integer with the number of arguments passed into its invoking function—in this case, mean(). From there, you can then call func_get_arg() to find the specific argument value for each position.

When you call mean(96, 93, 98, 98), func_num_args() returns 4. The first argument is in position 0, so you iterate from 0 to 3, not 1 to 4. That's what happens inside the for loop where $i goes from 0 to less than $size. As you can see, this is the same logic used in the Solution in which an array was passed. If you're worried about the potential overhead from using func_get_arg() inside a loop, don't be. This version is actually faster than the array-passing method.

There is a third version of this function that uses func_get_args() to return an array containing all the values passed to the function. It ends up looking like a hybrid between the previous two functions, as shown in Example 6-2.

Example 6-2. Accessing function parameters without using the argument list

```
// find the "average" of a group of numbers
function mean() {
    // initialize to avoid warnings
    $sum = 0;

    // the arguments passed to the function
    $size = func_num_args();

    // iterate through the arguments and add up the numbers
    foreach (func_get_args() as $arg) {
        $sum += $arg;
    }

    // divide by the amount of numbers
    $average = $sum / $size;

    // return average
    return $average;
}

// $mean is 96.25
$mean = mean(96, 93, 98, 98);
```

Here you have the dual advantages of not needing to place the numbers inside a temporary array when passing them into mean(), but inside the function you can continue to treat them as if you did.

See Also

Recipe 6.8 on returning multiple values from a function; documentation on `func_num_args()` (*http://www.php.net/func-num-args*), `func_get_arg()` (*http:// www.php.net/func-get-arg*), and `func_get_args()` (*http://www.php.net/func-get-args*).

6.7 Returning Values by Reference

Problem

You want to return a value by reference, not by value. This allows you to avoid making a duplicate copy of a variable.

Solution

The syntax for returning a variable by reference is similar to passing it by reference. However, instead of placing an & before the parameter, place it before the name of the function:

```
function &array_find_value($needle, &$haystack) {
    foreach ($haystack as $key => $value) {
        if ($needle == $value) {
            return $haystack[$key];
        }
    }
}
```

Also, you must use the =& assignment operator instead of plain = when invoking the function:

```
$band =& array_find_value('The Doors', $artists);
```

Discussion

Returning a reference from a function allows you to directly operate on the return value and have those changes directly reflected in the original variable.

The following code searches through an array looking for the first element that matches a value. It returns the first matching value. For instance, you need to search through a list of famous people from Minnesota looking for Prince, so you can update his name:

```
function &array_find_value($needle, &$haystack) {
    foreach ($haystack as $key => $value) {
        if ($needle == $value) {
            return $haystack[$key];
        }
    }
}
```

```
$minnesota = array('Bob Dylan', 'F. Scott Fitzgerald',
                   'Prince', 'Charles Schultz');

$prince =& array_find_value('Prince', $minnesota);

$prince = 'O(+>'; // The ASCII version of Prince's unpronounceable symbol

print_r($minnesota);
```

This prints:

```
Array
(
    [0] => Bob Dylan
    [1] => F. Scott Fitzgerald
    [2] => O(+>
    [3] => Charles Schultz
)
```

Without the ability to return values by reference, you would need to return the array key and then rereference the original array:

```
function array_find_value($needle, &$haystack) {
    foreach ($haystack as $key => $value) {
        if ($needle == $value) {
            return $key;
        }
    }
}

$minnesota = array('Bob Dylan', 'F. Scott Fitzgerald',
                   'Prince', 'Charles Schultz');

$prince = array_find_value('Prince', $minnesota);
// The ASCII version of Prince's unpronounceable symbol
$minnesota[$prince] = 'O(+>';
```

When returning a reference from a function, you must return a reference to a variable, not a string. For example, this is not legal:

```
function &array_find_value($needle, &$haystack) {
    foreach ($haystack as $key => $value) {
        if ($needle == $value) {
            $match = $haystack[$key];
        }
    }

    return "$match is found in position $key";
}
```

That's because "$match is found in position $key" is a string, and it doesn't make logical sense to return a reference to nonvariables. This causes PHP to emit an E_NOTICE.

Unlike passing values into functions, in which an argument is either passed by value or by reference, you can optionally choose not to assign a reference and just take the returned value. Just use = instead of =&, and PHP assigns the value instead of the reference.

See Also

Recipe 6.3 on passing values by reference.

6.8 Returning More Than One Value

Problem

You want to return more than one value from a function.

Solution

Return an array and use list() to separate elements:

```
function array_stats($values) {
    $min = min($values);
    $max = max($values);
    $mean = array_sum($values) / count($values);

    return array($min, $max, $mean);
}

$values = array(1,3,3,9,13,1442);
list($min, $max, $mean) = array_stats($values);
```

Discussion

From a performance perspective, this isn't a great idea. There is a bit of overhead because PHP is forced to first create an array and then dispose of it. That's what is happening in this example:

```
function time_parts($time) {
    return explode(':', $time);
}

list($hour, $minute, $second) = time_parts('12:34:56');
```

You pass in a time string as you might see on a digital clock and call explode() to break it apart as array elements. When time_parts() returns, use list() to take each element and store it in a scalar variable. Although this is a little inefficient, the other possible solutions are worse because they can lead to confusing code.

One alternative is to pass the values in by reference. However, this is somewhat clumsy and can be nonintuitive because it doesn't always make logical sense to pass the necessary variables into the function. For instance:

```
function time_parts($time, &$hour, &$minute, &$second) {
    list($hour, $minute, $second) = explode(':', $time);
}

time_parts('12:34:56', $hour, $minute, $second);
```

Without knowledge of the function prototype, there's no way to look at this and know $hour, $minute, and $second are, in essence, the return values of time_parts().

You can also use global variables, but this clutters the global namespace and also makes it difficult to easily see which variables are being silently modified in the function. For example:

```
function time_parts($time) {
    global $hour, $minute, $second;
    list($hour, $minute, $second) = explode(':', $time);
}

time_parts('12:34:56');
```

Again, here it's clear because the function is directly above the call, but if the function is in a different file or written by another person, it'd be more mysterious and thus open to creating a subtle bug.

Our advice is that if you modify a value inside a function, return that value and assign it to a variable unless you have a very good reason not to, such as significant performance issues. It's cleaner and easier to understand and maintain.

See Also

Recipe 6.3 on passing values by reference and Recipe 6.12 for information on variable scoping.

6.9 Skipping Selected Return Values

Problem

A function returns multiple values, but you only care about some of them.

Solution

Omit variables inside of list():

```
// Only care about minutes
function time_parts($time) {
```

```
        return explode(':', $time);
    }

    list(, $minute,) = time_parts('12:34:56');
```

Discussion

Even though it looks like there's a mistake in the code, the code in the Solution is valid PHP. To reduce confusion, don't use this feature frequently; but if a function returns many values, and you only want one or two of them, it can come in handy. One example of this case is if you read in fields using `fgetcsv()`, which returns an array holding the fields from the line. In that case, you can use the following:

```
    while ($fields = fgetcsv($fh, 4096)) {
        print $fields[2] . "\n";   // the third field
    }
```

If it's a user-defined function and not built in, you could also make the returning array have string keys, because it's hard to remember, for example, that array element 2 is associated with `'rank'`:

```
    while ($fields = read_fields($filename)) {
        $rank = $fields['rank']; // the third field is now called rank
        print "$rank\n";
    }
```

However, here's the most efficient method:

```
    while (list(,,$rank,,) = fgetcsv($fh, 4096)) {
        print "$rank\n";            // directly assign $rank
    }
```

Be careful you don't miscount the amount of commas; you'll end up with a bug.

See Also

Recipe 1.12 for more on reading files using `fgetcsv()`.

6.10 Returning Failure

Problem

You want to indicate failure from a function.

Solution

Return `false`:

```
    function lookup($name) {
        if (empty($name)) { return false; }
```

```
        /* ... */
    }

    $name = 'alice';

    if (false !== lookup($name)) {
        /* act upon lookup */
    } else {
        /* log an error */
    }
```

Discussion

In PHP, nontrue values aren't standardized and can easily cause errors. As a result, your functions should return the defined `false` keyword because this works best when checking a logical value.

Other possibilities are `' '` or `0`. However, while all three evaluate to nontrue inside an `if`, there's actually a difference among them. Also, sometimes a return value of `0` is a meaningful result, but you still want to be able to also return failure.

For example, `strpos()` returns the location of the first substring within a string. If the substring isn't found, `strpos()` returns `false`. If it is found, it returns an integer with the position. Therefore, to find a substring position, you might write:

```
    if (strpos($string, $substring)) { /* found it! */ }
```

However, if `$substring` is found at the exact start of `$string`, the value returned is `0`. Unfortunately, inside the `if`, this evaluates to `false`, so the conditional is not executed. Here's the correct way to handle the return value of `strpos()`:

```
    if (false !== strpos($string, $substring)) { /* found it! */ }
```

See Also

The introduction to Chapter 5 for more on the truth values of variables; documentation on `strpos()` (*http://www.php.net/strpos*) and `empty()` (*http://www.php.net/empty*).

6.11 Calling Variable Functions

Problem

You want to call different functions depending on a variable's value.

Solution

Use `call_user_func()`:

```
function get_file($filename) { return file_get_contents($filename); }

$function = 'get_file';
$filename = 'graphic.png';

// calls get_file('graphic.png')
call_user_func($function, $filename);
```

Use `call_user_func_array()` when your functions accept differing argument counts:

```
function get_file($filename) { return file_get_contents($filename); }
function put_file($filename, $d) {
    return file_put_contents($filename, $d); }

if ($action == 'get') {
    $function = 'get_file';
    $args = array('graphic.png');
} elseif ($action == 'put') {
    $function = 'put_file';
    $args = array('graphic.png', $graphic);
}

// calls get_file('graphic.png')
// calls put_file('graphic.png', $graphic)
call_user_func_array($function, $args);
```

Discussion

The `call_user_func()` and `call_user_func_array()` functions are a little different from your standard PHP functions. Their first argument isn't a string to print, or a number to add, but the name of a function that's executed. The concept of passing a function name that the language invokes is known as a callback, or a callback function.

The `call_user_func_array()` function comes in quite handy when you're invoking a callback inside a function that can accept a variable number of arguments. In these cases, instead of embedding the logic inside your function, you can grab all the arguments directly using `func_get_args()`:

```
// logging function that accepts printf-style formatting
// it prints a time stamp, the string, and a new line
function logf() {
    $date = date(DATE_RSS);
    $args = func_get_args();

    return print "$date: " . call_user_func_array('sprintf', $args) . "\n";
}

logf('<a href="%s">%s</a>','http://developer.ebay.com','eBay Developer Program');
```

The `logf()` function has the same interface as the `printf` family: the first argument is a formatting specifier and the remaining arguments are data that's interpolated into the string based on the formatting codes. Because there could be any number of arguments following the formatting code, you cannot use `call_user_func()`.

Instead, you grab all the arguments in an array using `func_get_args()` and pass that array to `sprintf` using `call_user_func_array()`.

In this particular example, you can also use `vsprintf()`, which is a version of `sprintf()` that, like `call_user_func_array()`, accepts an array of arguments:

```
// logging function that accepts printf-style formatting
// it prints a time stamp, the string, and a new line
function logf() {
    $date = date(DATE_RSS);
    $args = func_get_args();
    $format = array_shift($args);

    return print "$date: " . vsprintf($format, $args) . "\n";
}
```

If you have more than two possibilities to call, use an associative array of function names:

```
$dispatch = array(
    'add'      => 'do_add',
    'commit'   => 'do_commit',
    'checkout' => 'do_checkout',
    'update'   => 'do_update'
);

$cmd = (isset($_REQUEST['command']) ? $_REQUEST['command'] : '');

if (array_key_exists($cmd, $dispatch)) {
    $function = $dispatch[$cmd];
    call_user_func($function); // call function
} else {
    error_log("Unknown command $cmd");
}
```

This code takes the command name from a request and executes that function. Note the check to see that the command is in a list of acceptable commands. This prevents your code from calling whatever function was passed in from a request, such as `phpin fo()`. This makes your code more secure and allows you to easily log errors.

Another advantage is that you can map multiple commands to the same function, so you can have a long and a short name:

```
$dispatch = array(
    'add'      => 'do_add',
    'commit'   => 'do_commit',   'ci' => 'do_commit',
    'checkout' => 'do_checkout', 'co' => 'do_checkout',
    'update'   => 'do_update',   'up' => 'do_update'
);
```

See Also

Documentation on `array_key_exists()` (*http://www.php.net/array-key-exists*), `call_user_func()` (*http://www.php.net/call-user-func*), `call_user_func_array()` (*http://www.php.net/call-user-func-array*), and `isset()` (*http://www.php.net/isset*).

6.12 Accessing a Global Variable Inside a Function

Problem

You need to access a global variable inside a function.

Solution

Bring the global variable into local scope with the `global` keyword:

```
function eat_fruit($fruit) {
    global $chew_count;

    for ($i = $chew_count; $i > 0; $i--) {
        /* ... */
    }
}
```

Or reference it directly in `$GLOBALS`:

```
function eat_fruit($fruit) {
    for ($i = $GLOBALS['chew_count']; $i > 0; $i--) {
        /* ... */
    }
}
```

Discussion

If you use a number of global variables inside a function, the `global` keyword may make the syntax of the function easier to understand, especially if the global variables are interpolated in strings.

You can use the `global` keyword to bring multiple global variables into local scope by specifying the variables as a comma-separated list:

```
global $age,$gender,shoe_size;
```

You can also specify the names of global variables using variable variables:

```
$which_var = 'age';
global $$which_var; // refers to the global variable $age
```

However, if you call unset() on a variable brought into local scope using the global keyword, the variable is unset only within the function. To unset the variable in the global scope, you must call unset() on the element of the $GLOBALS array:

```
$food  = 'pizza';
$drink = 'beer';

function party() {
    global $food, $drink;

    unset($food);              // eat pizza
    unset($GLOBALS['drink']); // drink beer
}

print "$food: $drink\n";
party();
print "$food: $drink\n";
```

This prints:

```
pizza: beer
pizza:
```

You can see that $food stayed the same, while $drink was unset. Declaring a variable global inside a function is similar to assigning a reference of the global variable to the local one:

```
$food = $GLOBALS['food'];
```

See Also

Documentation on variable scope (*http://www.php.net/variables.scope*) and variable references (*http://www.php.net/language.references*).

6.13 Creating Dynamic Functions

Problem

You want to create and define a function as your program is running.

Solution

Use the closure syntax to define a function and store it in a variable:

```
$increment = 7;
$add = function($i, $j) use ($increment) { return $i + $j + $increment; };

$sum = $add(1, 2);
```

$sum is now 10. If you are using a version of PHP earlier than 5.3.0, use `create_func` `tion()` instead:

```
$increment = 7;

$add = create_function('$i,$j', 'return $i+$j + ' . $increment. ';');

$sum = $add(1, 2);
```

Discussion

The closure syntax is much more pleasant than using `create_function()`. With `cre` `ate_function`, the argument list and function body are written as literal strings. This means PHP can't parse their syntax until runtime and you have to pay attention to single quoting and double quoting and variable interpolation rules.

With the closure syntax, PHP can do the same compile-time checking of your anonymous function as it does on the rest of your code. You use the same syntax you'd use elsewhere for writing a function, with one exception: a `use()` declaration after the argument list can enumerate variables from the scope in which the closure is defined that should be available inside the closure. In the preceding example, the `use($incre` `ment)` means that, inside the closure, `$increment` has the value (7) that it does in the scope in which the closure is defined.

A frequent use for anonymous functions is to create custom sorting functions for `usort()` or `array_walk()`:

```
$files = array('ziggy.txt', '10steps.doc', '11pants.org', "frank.mov");
// sort files in reverse natural order
usort($files, function($a, $b) { return strnatcmp($b, $a); });
// Now $files is
// array('ziggy.txt', 'frank.mov','11pants.org','10steps.doc')
```

See Also

Recipe 4.17 for information on `usort()`; documentation on `create_function()` (*http:// www.php.net/create-function*) and on `usort()` (*http://www.php.net/usort*).

CHAPTER 7

Classes and Objects

7.0 Introduction

Early versions of PHP were strictly procedural: you could define functions, but not objects. PHP 3 introduced an extremely rudimentary form of objects, written as a late-night hack. Back in 1997, nobody expected the explosion in the number of PHP programmers, or that people would write large-scale programs in PHP. Therefore, these limitations weren't considered a problem.

Over the years, PHP gained additional object-oriented (OO) features; however, the development team never redesigned the core OO code to gracefully handle objects and classes. As a result, although PHP 4 improved overall performance, writing complex OO programs with it was still difficult, if not nearly impossible.

PHP 5 fixed these problems by using Zend Engine 2 (ZE2). ZE2 enables PHP to include more advanced object-oriented features, while still providing a high degree of backward compatibility to the millions of PHP scripts already written. Later versions of PHP 5 further enhanced PHP's OO toolkit. Today, it's capable of allowing developers to write fully featured OO applications.

If you don't have experience with object-oriented programming, then you're in for a bit of a surprise. Although some features allow you to do things more easily, many features actually *restrict* what you can do.

Even though it seems counterintuitive, these limitations actually help you quickly write safe code because they promote code reuse and data encapsulation. These key OO programming techniques are explained throughout the chapter. But first, here's an introduction to object-oriented programming, its vocabulary, and its concepts.

A *class* is a package containing two things: data and methods to access and modify that data. The data portion consists of variables; they're known as *properties*. The other part of a class is a set of functions that can use its properties—they're called *methods*.

When you define a class, you don't define an object that can be accessed and manipulated. Instead, you define a template for an object. From this blueprint, you create malleable objects through a process known as *instantiation*. A program can have multiple objects of the same class, just as a person can have more than one book or many pieces of fruit.

Classes also live in a defined hierarchy. Each class down the line is more specialized than the one above it. These specialized classes are called *child classes*, and the class they're modifying is called the *parent class*. For example, a parent class could be a building. Buildings can be further divided into residential and commercial. Residential buildings can be further subdivided into houses and apartment buildings, and so forth. The topmost parent class is also called the *base class*.

Both houses and apartment buildings have the same set of properties as all residential buildings, just as residential and commercial buildings share some things in common. When classes are used to express these parent-child relationships, the child class inherits the properties and methods defined in the parent class. This allows you to reuse the code from the parent class and requires you to write code only to adapt the new child to its specialized circumstances. This is called *inheritance* and is one of the major advantages of classes over functions. The process of defining a child class from a parent is known as *subclassing* or *extending*.

Classes in PHP are easy to define and create:

```
class guest_book {
  public $comments;
  public $last_visitor;

  function update($comment, $visitor) {
  ...
  }

}
```

The `class` keyword defines a class, just as `function` defines a function. Properties are declared using the `public` keyword. Method declaration is identical to function definition.

The `new` keyword instantiates an object:

```
$gb = new guest_book;
```

Object instantiation is covered in more detail in Recipe 7.1.

Inside a class, you can optionally declare properties using `public`. There's no requirement to do so, but it is a useful way to reveal all the variables of the class. Because PHP doesn't force you to predeclare all your variables, it's possible to create one inside a class without PHP throwing an error or otherwise letting you know. This can cause the list of variables at the top of a class definition to be misleading, because it's not the same as the list of variables actually in the class.

Besides declaring a property, you can also assign it a value:

```
public $last_visitor = 'Donnan';
```

The right-hand side of this construct can only be a constant value:

```
public $last_visitor = 'Donnan'; // okay
public $last_visitor = 9; // okay
public $last_visitor = array('Jesse'); // okay
public $last_visitor = pick_visitor(); // bad
public $last_visitor = 'Chris' . '9'; // bad
```

If you try to assign something else, PHP dies with a parse error.

To assign a nonconstant value to a variable, do it from a method inside the class:

```
class guest_book {
  public $last_visitor;

  public function update($comment, $visitor) {
    if (!empty($comment)) {
      array_unshift($this->comments, $comment);
      $this->last_visitor = $visitor;
    }
  }
}
```

If the visitor left a comment, you add it to the beginning of the array of comments and set that person as the latest visitor to the guest book. The variable $this is a special variable that refers to the current object. So to access the $last_visitor property of an object from inside that object, refer to $this->last_visitor.

To assign nonconstant values to variables upon instantiation, assign them in the class constructor. The class constructor is a method automatically called when a new object is created, and it is named __construct(), as shown:

```
class guest_book {
  public $comments;
  public $last_visitor;

  public function __construct($user) {
    $dbh = mysqli_connect('localhost', 'username', 'password', 'sites');
    $user = mysqli_real_escape_string($dbh, $user);
    $sql = "SELECT comments, last_visitor FROM guest_books WHERE user='$user'";
    $r = mysqli_query($dbh, $sql);

    if ($obj = mysqli_fetch_object($dbh, $r)) {
      $this->comments = $obj->comments;
      $this->last_visitor = $obj->last_visitor;
    }
```

```
  }
}
```

```
$gb = new guest_book('stewart');
```

Constructors are covered in Recipe 7.2.

Be careful not to mistakenly type `$this->$size`. This is legal, but it's not the same as `$this->size`. Instead, it accesses the property of the object whose name is the value stored in the `$size` variable. More often than not, `$size` is undefined, so `$this->$size` appears empty. For more on variable property names, see Recipe 5.4.

As of PHP 5.4, you can call a method or access a property directly upon object instantiation:

```
$last_visitor = (new guest_book('stewart'))->last_visitor;
```

```
$last_visitor = (new guest_book('stewart'))->getLastVisitor();
```

Besides using `->` to access a method or member variable, you can also use `::`. This syntax accesses static methods in a class. These methods are identical for every instance of a class, because they can't rely on instance-specific data. There's no `$this` in a static method. For example:

```
class convert {
 // convert from Celsius to Fahrenheit
 public static function c2f($degrees) {
   return (1.8 * $degrees) + 32;
 }
}
```

```
$f = convert::c2f(100); // 212
```

To implement inheritance by extending an existing class, use the **extends** keyword:

```
class xhtml extends xml {
  // ...
}
```

Child classes inherit parent methods and can optionally choose to implement their own specific versions. For example:

```
class DB {
 public $result;

 function getResult() {
  return $this->result;
 }

 function query($sql) {
  error_log("query() must be overridden by a database-specific child");
  return false;
 }
```

```
  }

class MySQL extends DB {
  function query($sql) {
   $this->result = mysql_query($sql);
  }
}
```

The MySQL class inherits the getResult() method unchanged from the parent DB class, but has its own MySQL-specific query() method. Preface the method name with par ent:: to explicitly call a parent method:

```
function escape($sql) {
  $safe_sql = mysql_real_escape_string($sql); // escape special characters
  $safe_sql = parent::escape($safe_sql); // parent method adds '' around $sql
  return $safe_sql;
}
```

Recipe 7.14 covers accessing overridden methods.

7.1 Instantiating Objects

Problem

You want to create a new instance of an object.

Solution

Define the class, then use new to create an instance of the class:

```
class user {
    function load_info($username) {
        // load profile from database
    }
}

$user = new user;
$user->load_info($_GET['username']);
```

Discussion

You can instantiate multiple instances of the same object:

```
$adam = new user;
$adam->load_info('adam');

$dave = new user;
$dave->load_info('adam');
```

These are two independent objects that happen to have identical information. They're like identical twins; they may start off the same, but they go on to live separate lives.

See Also

Recipe 7.10 for more on copying and cloning objects; documentation on classes and objects (*http://www.php.net/oop*).

7.2 Defining Object Constructors

Problem

You want to define a method that is called when an object is instantiated. For example, you want to automatically load information from a database into an object upon creation.

Solution

Define a method named __construct():

```
class user {
    function __construct($username, $password) {
        // ...
    }
}
```

Discussion

The method named __construct() (that's two underscores before the word con struct) acts as a constructor:

```
class user {
  public $username;

  function __construct($username, $password) {
    if ($this->validate_user($username, $password)) {
      $this->username = $username;
    }
  }
}

$user = new user('Grif', 'Mistoffelees'); // using built-in constructor
```

For backward compatibilty with PHP 4, if PHP 5 does not find a method named __con struct(), but does find one with the same name as the class (the PHP 4 constructor naming convention), it will use that method as the class constructor.

Having a standard name for all constructors makes it easier to call your parent's constructor (because you don't need to know the name of the parent class) and also doesn't require you to modify the constructor if you rename your class.

See Also

Recipe 7.14 for more on calling parent constructors; documentation on object constructors (*http://www.php.net/oop5.decon*).

7.3 Defining Object Destructors

Problem

You want to define a method that is called when an object is destroyed. For example, you want to automatically save information from a database into an object when it's deleted.

Solution

Objects are automatically destroyed when a script terminates. To force the destruction of an object, use unset():

```
$car = new car; // buy new car
// ...
unset($car);     // car wreck
```

To make PHP call a method when an object is eliminated, define a method named __destruct():

```
class car {
    function __destruct() {
        // head to car dealer
    }
}
```

Discussion

It's not normally necessary to manually clean up objects, but if you have a large loop, unset() can help keep memory usage from spiraling out of control.

PHP supports object destructors. Destructors are like constructors, except that they're called when the object is deleted. Even if you don't delete the object yourself using unset(), PHP still calls the destructor when it determines that the object is no longer used. This may be when the script ends, but it can be much earlier.

You use a destructor to clean up after an object. For instance, the Database destructor would disconnect from the database and free up the connection. Unlike constructors, you cannot pass information to a destructor, because you're never sure when it's going to be run.

Therefore, if your destructor needs any instance-specific information, store it as a property:

```
// Destructor
class Database {
    function __destruct() {
        db_close($this->handle); // close the database connection
    }
}
```

Destructors are executed before PHP terminates the request and finishes sending data. Therefore, you can print from them, write to a database, or even ping a remote server.

You cannot, however, assume that PHP will destroy objects in any particular order. Therefore, you should not reference another object in your destructor, because PHP may have already destroyed it. Doing so will not cause a crash, but it will cause your code to behave in an unpredictable (and buggy) manner.

See Also

Documentation on unset() (*http://www.php.net/unset*).

7.4 Implementing Access Control

Problem

You want to assign a visibility to methods and properties so they can only be accessed within classes that have a specific relationship to the object.

Solution

Use the public, protected, and private keywords:

```
class Person {
    public $name;      // accessible anywhere
    protected $age;    // accessible within the class and child classes
    private $salary;   // accessible only within this specific class

    public function __construct() {
    // ...
    }

    protected function set_age() {
    // ...
    }
```

```
        private function set_salary() {
        // ...
        }
    }
```

Discussion

PHP allows you to enforce where you can access methods and properties. There are three levels of visibility:

- public
- protected
- private

Making a method or property public means anyone can call or edit it.[1]

You can also label a method or property as protected, which restricts access to only the current class and any child classes that extend that class.

The final visibility is private, which is the most restrictive. Properties and methods that are private can only be accessed within that specific class.

If you're unfamiliar with this concept, access control can seem like an odd thing. However, when you use access control, you can actually create more robust code because it promotes data encapsulation, a key tenet of OO programming.

Inevitably, whenever you write code, there's some part—the way you store the data, what parameters the functions take, how the database is organized—that doesn't work as well as it should. It's too slow, too awkward, or doesn't allow you to add new features, so you clean it up.

Fixing code is a good thing, unless you accidently break other parts of your system in the process. When a program is designed with a high degree of encapsulation, the underlying data structures and database tables are not accessed directly. Instead, you define a set of functions and route all your requests through these functions.

For example, you have a database table that stores names and email addresses. A program with poor encapsulation directly accesses the table whenever it needs to fetch a person's email address:

```
$name   = 'Rasmus Lerdorf';

$sqlite = new PDO('sqlite:/usr/local/users.db');

$rows = $db->query("SELECT email FROM users WHERE name LIKE '$name'");
```

---

1. Prior to PHP 5, all methods and properties were public.

```
    $row = $rows->fetch();
    $email = $row['email'];
```

A better encapsulated program uses a function instead:

```
function getEmail($name) {
    $sqlite = new PDO("sqlite:/usr/local/users.db");

    $rows = $db->query("SELECT email FROM users WHERE name LIKE '$name'");
    $row = $rows->fetch();
    $email = $row['email'];
    return $email;
}


$email = getEmail('Rasmus Lerdorf');
```

Using getEmail() has many benefits, including reducing the amount of code you need to write to fetch an email address. However, it also lets you safely alter your database schema because you only need to change the single query in getEmail() instead of searching through every line of every file, looking for places where you SELECT data from the users table. Or you can switch from one database to another with relative ease.

It's hard to write a well-encapsulated program using functions, because the only way to signal to people "Don't touch this!" is through comments and programming conventions.

Objects allow you to wall off implementation internals from outside access. This prevents people from relying on code that may change and forces them to use your functions to reach the data. Functions of this type are known as *accessors*, because they allow access to otherwise protected information. When redesigning code, if you update the accessors to work as before, none of the code will break.

Marking something as protected or private signals that it may change in the future, so people shouldn't access it or they'll violate encapsulation.

This is more than a social convention. PHP actually prevents people from calling a private method or reading a private property outside of the class. Therefore, from an external perspective, these methods and properties might as well not exist because there's no way to access them.

In object-oriented programming, there is an implicit contract between the author and the users of the class. The users agree not to worry about the implementation details. The author agrees that as long as a person uses public methods they'll always work, even if the author redesigns the class.

Both protected and private provide protection against usage outside of the class. Therefore, the decision to choose one visibility versus the other really comes down to a judgment call—do you expect someone will need to invoke that method in a child class?

If you (or your team) are the only people using that class, choosing `private` over `protected` allows you to be conservative and not overexpose access unnecessarily. It's easy to open up the visibility later on, if needed. If you're planning on distributing this code as a package, then biasing toward `protected` helps enable others to extend on your work without needing to modify your master library.

7.5 Preventing Changes to Classes and Methods

Problem

You want to prevent another developer from redefining specific methods within a child class, or even from subclassing the entire class itself.

Solution

Label the particular methods or class as `final`:

```
final public function connect($server, $username, $password) {
    // Method definition here
}
```

and:

```
final class MySQL {
    // Class definition here
}
```

Discussion

Inheritance is normally a good thing, but it can make sense to restrict it.

The best reason to declare a method `final` is that a real danger could arise if someone overrides it; for example, data corruption, a race condition, or a potential crash or deadlock from forgetting (or forgetting to release) a lock or a semaphore.

Make a method final by placing the `final` keyword at the beginning of the method declaration:

```
final public function connect($server, $username, $password) {
    // Method definition here
}
```

This prevents someone from subclassing the class and creating a different `connect()` method.

To prevent subclassing of an entire class, don't mark each method `final`. Instead, make a final class:

```
final class MySQL {
    // Class definition here
}
```

A final class cannot be subclassed. This differs from a class in which every method is final because that class can be extended and provided with additional methods, even if you cannot alter any of the preexisting methods.

7.6 Defining Object Stringification

Problem

You want to control how PHP displays an object when you print it.

Solution

Implement a __toString() method:

```
class Person {
    // Rest of class here

    public function __toString() {
        return "$this->name <$this->email>";
    }
}
```

Discussion

PHP provides objects with a way to control how they are converted to strings. This allows you to print an object in a friendly way without resorting to lots of additional code.

PHP calls an object's __toString() method when you echo or print the object by itself. For example:

```
class Person {
    protected $name;
    protected $email;

    public function setName($name) {
        $this->name = $name;
    }

    public function setEmail($email) {
        $this->email = $email;
    }

    public function __toString() {
        return "$this->name <$this->email>";
```

```
        }
    }
```

You can write:

```
$rasmus = new Person;
$rasmus->setName('Rasmus Lerdorf');
$rasmus->setEmail('rasmus@php.net');
print $rasmus;
```

Rasmus Lerdorf <rasmus@php.net>

This causes PHP to invoke the __toString() method behind the scenes and return the stringified version of the object.

Your method *must* return a string; otherwise, PHP will issue an error. Though this seems obvious, you can sometimes get tripped up by PHP's auto-casting features, which do not apply here.

For example, it's easy to treat the string '9' and the integer 9 identically, because PHP generally switches seamlessly between the two depending on context, almost always to the correct result.

However, in this case, you cannot return integers from __toString(). If you suspect you may be in a position to return a nonstring value from this method, consider explicitly casting the results, as shown:

```
class TextInput {
    // Rest of class here

    public function __toString() {
        return (string) $this->label;
    }
}
```

By casting $this->label to a string, you don't need to worry if someone decided to label that text input with a number.

The __toString() feature has a number of limitations prior to PHP 5.2. Therefore, if you're using __toString() heavily in your code, it's best to use PHP 5.2 or greater.

7.7 Requiring Multiple Classes to Behave Similarly

Problem

You want multiple classes to use the same methods, but it doesn't make sense for all the classes to inherit from a common parent class.

Solution

Define an interface and declare that your class will implement that interface:

```
interface NameInterface {
    public function getName();
    public function setName($name);
}

class Book implements NameInterface {
    private $name;

    public function getName() {
        return $this->name;
    }

    public function setName($name) {
        return $this->name = $name;
    }
}
```

The NameInterface interface defines two methods necessary to name an object. Because books are nameable, the Book class says it implements the NameInterface interface, and then defines the two methods in the class body.

When you want to include the code that implements the interface, define a trait and declare that your classes will use that trait:

```
trait NameTrait {
    private $name;

    public function getName() {
        return $this->name;
    }

    public function setName($name) {
        return $this->name = $name;
    }
}

class Book {
    use NameTrait;
}

class Child {
    use NameTrait;
}
```

The NameTrait trait defines and implements two methods necessary to name an object. Because books are nameable, the Book class says it will use the NameTrait trait, and then you can call the two methods in the class body.

Discussion

In object-oriented programming, objects must work together. Therefore, you should be able to require a class (or more than one class) to implement methods that are necessary for the class to interact properly in your system.

For instance, an e-commerce application needs to know a certain set of information about every item up for sale. These items may be represented as different classes: Book, CD, DVD, etc. However, at the very minimum you need to know that every item in your catalog has a name, regardless of its type. (You probably also want them to have a price and maybe even an ID, while you're at it.)

The mechanism for forcing classes to support the same set of methods is called an *interface*. Defining an *interface* is similar to defining a class:

```
interface NameInterface {
    public function getName();
    public function setName($name);
}
```

Instead of using the keyword `class`, an interface uses the keyword `interface`. Inside the interface, define your method prototypes, but don't provide an implementation.

This creates an interface named `NameInterface`. Any class that has the `NameInterface` must implement the two methods listed in the interface: `getName()` and `setName()`.

When a class supports all the methods in the interface, it's said to *implement* the interface. You agree to implement an interface in your class definition:

```
class Book implements NameInterface {
    private $name;

    public function getName() {
        return $this->name;
    }

    public function setName($name) {
        return $this->name = $name;
    }
}
```

Failing to implement all the methods listed in an interface, or implementing them with a different prototype, causes PHP to emit a fatal error.

A class can agree to implement as many interfaces as you want. For instance, you may want to have a `ListenInterface` interface that specifies how you can retrieve an audio clip for an item. In this case, the CD and DVD classes would also implement `ListenInterface`, whereas the Book class wouldn't. (Unless, of course, it is an audio book.)

When you use interfaces, it's important to declare your classes before you instantiate objects. Otherwise, when a class implements interfaces, PHP can sometimes become confused. To avoid breaking existing applications, this requirement is not enforced, but it's best not to rely on this behavior.

To check if a class implements a specific interface, use `class_implements()`, as shown:

```php
class Book implements NameInterface {
    // .. Code here
}

$interfaces = class_implements('Book');
if (isset($interfaces['NameInterface'])) {
    // Book implements NameInterface
}
```

You can also use the `Reflection` classes:

```php
class Book implements NameInterface {
    // .. Code here
}

$rc = new ReflectionClass('Book');
if ($rc->implementsInterface('NameInterface')) {
  print "Book implements NameInterface\n";
}
```

When you want to share code across two classes, use a trait:

```php
trait NameTrait {
    private $name;

    public function getName() {
        return $this->name;
    }

    public function setName($name) {
        return $this->name = $name;
    }
}

class Book {
    use NameTrait;
}

$book = new Book;
$book->setName('PHP Cookbook');
print $book->getName();
```

You can use interfaces and traits together. This is actually a best-practice design:

```php
class Book implements NameInterface {
    use NameTrait;
}
```

Interfaces allow you to establish clear contracts with explicit promises about how your objects behave. Traits allow you to reuse code across objects that don't have an "is a" inheritance relationship; they are just a programmatic way to avoid copy and pasting code in multiple places.

Interfaces combined with traits give you the best of both. The interface provides the contract across a wide set of classes, and the trait lets you fulfill it. Then, a specific class can choose to use the trait, or implement the interface on its own. For example, you could impose a contraint that each Book must have a unique name or that the name should be stored in a database. In these cases, the NameTrait wouldn't serve your needs.

You can have a class implement multiple interfaces or traits by separating them with a comma:

```
class Book implements NameInterface, SizeInterface {
    use NameTrait, SizeTrait;
}
```

See Also

Recipe 7.20 for more on the Reflection classes; documentation on class_imple ments() (*http://www.php.net/class_implements*), interfaces (*http://www.php.net/inter faces*), and traits (*http://www.php.net/traits*).

7.8 Creating Abstract Base Classes

Problem

You want to create an *abstract* class, or, in other words, one that is not directly instantiable, but acts as a common base for children classes.

Solution

Label the class as abstract:

```
abstract class Database {
  // ...
}
```

Do this by placing the abstract keyword before the class definition.

You must also define at least one abstract method in your class. Do this by placing the abstract keyword in front of the method definition:

```
abstract class Database {
    abstract public function connect();
    abstract public function query();
    abstract public function fetch();
```

```
    abstract public function close();
}
```

Discussion

Abstract classes are best used when you have a series of objects that are related using the *is a* relationship. Therefore, it makes logical sense to have them descend from a common parent. However, whereas the children are tangible, the parent is abstract.

Take, for example, a `Database` class. A database is a real object, so it makes sense to have a `Database` class. However, although Oracle, MySQL, Postgres, MSSQL, and hundreds of other databases exist, you cannot download and install a generic database. You must choose a specific database.

PHP provides a way for you to create a class that cannot be instantiated. This class is known as an abstract class. For example, see the `Database` class:

```
abstract class Database {
    abstract public function connect($server, $username, $password, $database);
    abstract public function query($sql);
    abstract public function fetch();
    abstract public function close();
}
```

Mark a class as abstract by placing the `abstract` keyword before `class`.

Abstract classes must contain at least one method that is also marked `abstract`. These methods are called *abstract methods*. `Database` contains four abstract methods: `connect()`, `query()`, `fetch()`, and `close()`. These four methods are the basic set of functionality necessary to use a database.

If a class contains an abstract method, the class must also be declared abstract. However, abstract classes can contain nonabstract methods (even though there are no regular methods in `Database`).

Abstract methods, like methods listed in an interface, are not implemented inside the abstract class. Instead, abstract methods are implemented in a child class that extends the abstract parent. For instance, you could use a `MySQL` class:

```
class MySQL extends Database {
    protected $dbh;
    protected $query;

    public function connect($server, $username, $password, $database) {
        $this->dbh = mysqli_connect($server, $username,
                                    $password, $database);
    }

    public function query($sql) {
        $this->query = mysqli_query($this->dbh, $sql);
```

```
        }

        public function fetch() {
            return mysqli_fetch_row($this->dbh, $this->query);
        }

        public function close() {
            mysqli_close($this->dbh);
        }
    }
```

When implementing abstract methods, you must keep the same method prototypes. In this example, for instance, query() takes one argument, $sql.

If a subclass fails to implement all the abstract methods in the parent class, then it itself is abstract and another class must come along and further subclass the child. You might do this if you want to create two MySQL classes: one that fetches information as objects and another that returns arrays.

There are two requirements for abstract methods:

- Abstract methods cannot be defined private, because they need to be inherited.
- Abstract methods cannot be defined final, because they need to be overridden.

Abstract classes and interfaces are similar concepts, but are not identical. For one, you can implement multiple interfaces, but extend only one abstract class. Additionally, in an interface you can only define method prototypes—you cannot implement them. An abstract class, in comparison, needs only one abstract method to be abstract, and can have many nonabstract methods and even properties.

You should also use abstract classes when the "is a" rule applies. For example, because you can say "MySQL is a Database," it makes sense for Database to be an abstract class. In constrast, you cannot say, "Book is a NameInterface" or "Book is a Name," so Name Interface should be an interface.

7.9 Assigning Object References

Problem

You want to link two objects, so when you update one, you also update the other.

Solution

Use = to assign one object to another by reference:

```
$adam = new user;
$dave = $adam;
```

Discussion

When you do an object assignment using =, you don't create a new copy of an object, but a reference to the first. So, modifying one alters the other.

This is different from how PHP treats other types of variables, where it does a copy-by-value:

```
$adam = new user;
$adam->load_info('adam');

$dave = $adam;
```

Now $dave and $adam are two names for the exact same object.

See Also

Recipe 7.10 for more on cloning objects; documentation on references (*http://www.php.net/references*).

7.10 Cloning Objects

Problem

You want to copy an object.

Solution

Copy objects by reference using =:

```
$rasmus = $zeev;
```

Copy objects by value using clone:

```
$rasmus = clone $zeev;
```

Discussion

PHP copies objects by reference instead of value. When you assign an existing object to a new variable, that new variable is just another name for the existing object. Accessing the object by the old or new name produces the same results.

To create an independent instance of a value with the same contents, otherwise known as copying by value, use the clone keyword. Otherwise, the second object is simply a reference to the first.

This cloning process copies every property in the first object to the second. This includes properties holding objects, so the cloned object may end up sharing object references with the original.

This is frequently not the desired behavior. For example, consider the aggregated version of `Person` that holds an `Address` object:

```
class Address {
  protected $city;
  protected $country;

  public function setCity($city) { $this->city = $city; }
  public function getCity() { return $this->city; }
  public function setCountry($country) { $this->country = $country; }
  public function getCountry() { return $this-> country;}
}

class Person {
 protected $name;
 protected $address;

 public function __construct() { $this->address - new Address; }
 public function setName($name) { $this->name = $name; }
 public function getName() { return $this->name; }
 public function __call($method, $arguments) {
  if (method_exists($this->address, $method)) {
    return call_user_func_array( array($this->address, $method), $arguments);
  }
 }
}
```

An aggregated class is one that embeds another class inside in a way that makes it easy to access both the original and embedded classes. The key point to remember is that the `$address` property holds an `Address` object.

With this class, this example shows what happens when you `clone` an object:

```
$rasmus = new Person;
$rasmus->setName('Rasmus Lerdorf');
$rasmus->setCity('Sunnyvale');

$zeev = clone $rasmus;
$zeev->setName('Zeev Suraski');
$zeev->setCity('Tel Aviv');

print $rasmus->getName() . ' lives in ' . $rasmus->getCity() . '.';
print $zeev->getName() . ' lives in ' . $zeev->getCity() . '.';

Rasmus Lerdorf lives in Tel Aviv.
Zeev Suraski lives in Tel Aviv.
```

Interesting. Calling `setName()` worked correctly because the `$name` property is a string, so it's copied by value. However, because `$address` is an object, it's copied by reference, so `getCity()` doesn't produce the correct results, and you end up relocating Rasmus to Tel Aviv.

This type of object cloning is known as a *shallow clone* or a *shallow copy*. In contrast, a *deep clone* occurs when all objects involved are cloned.

Control how PHP clones an object by implementing a __clone() method in your class. When this method exists, PHP allows __clone() to override its default behavior, as shown:

```
class Person {
 // ... everything from before
 public function __clone() {
  $this->address = clone $this->address;
 }
}
```

Inside of __clone(), you're automatically presented with a shallow copy of the variable, stored in $this, the object that PHP provides when __clone() does not exist.

Because PHP has already copied all the properties, you only need to overwrite the ones you dislike. Here, $name is okay, but $address needs to be explicitly cloned.

Now the clone behaves correctly:

```
$rasmus = new Person;
$rasmus->setName('Rasmus Lerdorf');
$rasmus->setCity('Sunnyvale');

$zeev = clone $rasmus;
$zeev->setName('Zeev Suraski');
$zeev->setCity('Tel Aviv');

print $rasmus->getName() . ' lives in ' . $rasmus->getCity() . '.';
print $zeev->getName() . ' lives in ' . $zeev->getCity() . '.';

Rasmus Lerdorf lives in Sunnyvale.
Zeev Suraski lives in Tel Aviv.
```

Using the clone operator on objects stored in properties causes PHP to check whether any of those objects contain a __clone() method. If one exists, PHP calls it. This repeats for any objects that are nested even further.

This process correctly clones the entire object and demonstrates why it's called a deep copy.

See Also

Recipe 7.9 for more on assigning objects by reference.

7.11 Overriding Property Accesses

Problem

You want handler functions to execute whenever you read and write object properties. This lets you write generalized code to handle property access in your class.

Solution

Use the magic methods __get() and __set() to intercept property requests.

To improve this abstraction, also implement __isset() and __unset() methods to make the class behave correctly when you check a property using isset() or delete it using unset().

Discussion

Property overloading allows you to seamlessly obscure from the user the actual location of your object's properties and the data structure you use to store them.

For example, the Person class stores variables in an array, $__data. (The name of the variable doesn't need begin with two underscores, that's just to indicate to you that it's used by a magic method.)

```
class Person {
    private $__data = array();

    public function __get($property) {
        if (isset($this->__data[$property])) {
            return $this->__data[$property];
        } else {
            return false;
        }
    }

    public function __set($property, $value) {
        $this->__data[$property] = $value;
    }
}
```

Use it like this:

```
$johnwood = new Person;
$johnwood->email = 'jonathan@wopr.mil'; // sets $user->__data['email']
print $johnwood->email;                 // reads $user->__data['email']

jonathan@wopr.mil
```

When you set data, __set() rewrites the element inside of $__data. Likewise, use __get() to trap the call and return the correct array element.

Using these methods and an array as the alternate variable storage source makes it less painful to implement object encapsulation. Instead of writing a pair of accessor methods for every class property, you use __get() and __set().

With __get() and __set(), you can use what appear to be public properties, such as $johnwood->name, without violating encapsulation. This is because the programmer isn't reading from and writing to those properties directly, but is instead being routed through accessor methods.

The __get() method takes the property name as its single parameter. Within the method, you check to see whether that property has a value inside $__data. If it does, the method returns that value; otherwise, it returns false.

 When you read $johnwood->name, you actually call __get('name') and it's returning $__data['name'], but for all external purposes that's irrelevant.

The __set() method takes two arguments: the property name and the new value. Otherwise, the logic inside the method is similar to __get().

Besides reducing the number of methods in your classes, these magical methods also make it easy to implement a centralized set of input and output validation.

Here's how to also enforce exactly what properties are legal and illegal for a given class:

```php
class Person {
    // list person and email as valid properties
    protected $__data = array('person' => false, 'email' => false);

    public function __get($property) {
        if (isset($this->__data[$property])) {
            return $this->__data[$property];
        } else {
            return false;
        }
    }

    // enforce the restriction of only setting
    // predefined properties
    public function __set($property, $value) {
        if (isset($this->__data[$property])) {
            return $this->__data[$property] = $value;
        } else {
            return false;
        }
    }
}
```

In this updated version of the code, you explicitly list the object's valid property names when you define the $__data property. Then, inside __set(), you use isset() to confirm that all property writes are going to allowable names.

Preventing rogue reads and writes is why the visibility of the $__data property isn't public, but protected. Otherwise, someone could do this:

```
$person = new Person;
$person->__data['fake_property'] = 'fake_data';
```

because the magical accessors aren't used for existing properties.

Pay attention to this important implementation detail. In particular, if you're expecting people to extend the class, they could introduce a property that conflicts with a property you're expecting to handle using __get() and __set(). For that reason, the property in the earlier example is called $__data with two leading underscores.

You should consider prefixing all your "actual" properties in classes where you use magical accessors to prevent collisions between properties that should be handled using normal methods and ones that should be routed through __get() and __set().

There are three downsides to using __get() and __set(). First, these methods only catch missing properties. If you define a property for your class, __get() and __set() are not invoked by PHP when that property is accessed.

This is the case even if the property you're trying to access isn't visible in the current scope (for instance, when you're reading a property that exists in the class but isn't accessible to you, because it's declared private). Doing this causes PHP to emit a fatal error:

```
PHP Fatal error:  Cannot access private property...
```

Second, these methods completely destroy any notion of property inheritance. If a parent object has a __get() method and you implement your own version of __get() in the child, your object won't function correctly because the parent's __get() method is never called.

You can work around this by calling parent::__get(), but it is something you need to explicitly manage instead of "getting for free" as part of OO design.

The illusion is incomplete because it doesn't extend to the isset() and unset() methods. For instance, if you try to check if an overloaded property isset(), you will not get an accurate answer, as PHP doesn't know to invoke __get().

You can fix this by implementing your own version of these methods in the class, called __isset() and __unset():

```
class Person {
    // list person and email as valid properties
```

```php
    protected $data = array('person' => false, 'email' => false);

    public function __get($property) {
        if (isset($this->data[$property])) {
            return $this->data[$property];
        } else {
            return null;
        }
    }

    // enforce the restriction of only setting
    // pre-defined properties
    public function __set($property, $value) {
        if (isset($this->data[$property])) {
            $this->data[$property] = $value;
        }
    }

    public function __isset($property) {
        return isset($this->data[$property]);
    }

    public function __unset($property) {
        if (isset($this->data[$property])) {
            unset($this->data[$property]);
        }
    }
}
```

The __isset() method checks inside the $data element and returns true or false
depending on the status of the property you're checking.

Likewise, __unset() passes back the value of unset() applied to the *real* property, or
false if it's not set.

Implementing these two methods isn't required when using __get() and __set(), but
it's best to do so because it's hard to predict how you may use object properties. Failing
to code these methods will lead to confusion when someone (perhaps even yourself)
doesn't know (or forgets) that this class is using magic accessor methods.

Other reasons to consider not using magical accessors are:

- They're relatively slow. They're both slower than direct property access and explicitly writing accessor methods for all your properties.

- They make it impossible for the Reflection classes and tools such as phpDocumentor to automatically document your code.

- You cannot use them with static properties.

See Also

Documentation on overloaded methods (*http://www.php.net/oop5.overloading*).

7.12 Calling Methods on an Object Returned by Another Method

Problem

You need to call a method on an object returned by another method.

Solution

Call the second method directly from the first:

```
$orange = $fruit->get('citrus')->peel();
```

Discussion

PHP is smart enough to first call `$fruit->get('citrus')` and then invoke the `peel()` method on what's returned.

You can design your classes to facilitate chaining calls repeatedly as if you're writing a sentence. This is known as a *fluent interface*. For example:

```
$tweet = new Tweet;
$tweet->from('@rasmus')
    ->withStatus('PHP 6 released! #php')
    ->send();
```

By stringing together a set of method calls, you build up the `Tweet` one segment at a time, then send it to the world.

The key is to `return $this` within every chainable method. That preserves the current context for each subsequent method. Because people can pick and choose which methods to call (and the order they call them), you need one method that always goes last. In this case, it's `send()`. That's where the logic lives to assemble all the various pieces together and execute what you want done.

This code doesn't actually send a tweet (as the Twitter API requires OAuth), but is a good illustration of the design practices:

```
class Tweet {
    protected $data;

    public function from($from) {
        $data['from'] = $from;
        return $this;
    }
```

```php
    public function withStatus($status) {
        $data['status'] = $status;
        return $this;
    }

    public function inReplyToId($id) {
        $data['id'] = $id;
        return $this;

    }

    public function send() {
        // Generate Twitter API request using info in $data
        // POST https://api.twitter.com/1.1/statuses/update.json
        // with http_build_query($data)

        return $id;
    }
}

$tweet = new Tweet;
$id = $tweet->from('@rasmus')
    ->withStatus('PHP 6 released! #php')
    ->send();

$reply = new Tweet;
$id2 = $reply->withStatus('I <3 Unicode!')
    ->from('@a')
    ->inReplyToId($id)
    ->send();
```

Fluent interfaces can be very elegant, but it's important not to overuse them. They're best when tied to domains with a well-defined language, such as SQL or sending messages. This example uses a Tweet, but email or SMS would also work.

See Also

A description of fluent interfaces on Wikipedia (*http://en.wikipedia.org/wiki/Fluent_interface*) and documentation on the Twitter API (*https://dev.twitter.com*).

7.13 Aggregating Objects

Problem

You want to compose two or more objects together so that they appear to behave as a single object.

Solution

Aggregate the objects together and use the __call() and __callStatic() magic methods to intercept method invocations and route them accordingly:

```php
class Address {
    protected $city;

    public function setCity($city) {
        $this->city = $city;
    }

    public function getCity() {
        return $this->city;
    }
}

class Person {
    protected $name;
    protected $address;

    public function __construct() {
        $this->address = new Address;
    }

    public function setName($name) {
        $this->name = $name;
    }

    public function getName() {
        return $this->name;
    }

    public function __call($method, $arguments) {
        if (method_exists($this->address, $method)) {
            return call_user_func_array(
                array($this->address, $method), $arguments);
        }
    }
}

$rasmus = new Person;
$rasmus->setName('Rasmus Lerdorf');
$rasmus->setCity('Sunnyvale');

print $rasmus->getName() . ' lives in ' . $rasmus->getCity() . '.';
```

An instance of the Address object is created during the construction of every Person. When you invoke methods not defined in Person, the __call() method catches them and, when applicable, dispatches them using call_user_func_array().

Use __callStatic() when you need to route static methods.

Discussion

In this recipe, you cannot say a Person "is an" Address or vice versa. Therefore, it doesn't make sense for one class to extend the other.

However, it makes sense for them to be separate classes so that they provide maximum flexibility and reuse, as well as reduced duplicated code. So you check if another rule—the "has a" rule—applies. Because a Person "has an" Address, it makes sense to aggregate the classes together.

With aggregation, one object acts as a container for one or more additional objects. This is another way of solving the problem of multiple inheritance because you can easily piece together an object out of smaller components.

For example, a Person object can contain an Address object. Clearly, People have addresses. However, addresses aren't unique to people; they also belong to businesses and other entities. Therefore, instead of hardcoding address information inside of Person, it makes sense to create a separate Address class that can be used by multiple classes.

Here's how this works in practice:

```
class Address {
    protected $city;

    public function setCity($city) {
        $this->city = $city;
    }

    public function getCity() {
        return $this->city;
    }
}

class Person {
    protected $name;
    protected $address;

    public function __construct() {
        $this->address = new Address;
    }

    public function setName($name) {
        $this->name = $name;
    }

    public function getName() {
        return $this->name;
    }

    public function __call($method, $arguments) {
        if (method_exists($this->address, $method)) {
```

```
        return call_user_func_array(
            array($this->address, $method), $arguments);
    }
  }
}
```

The Address class stores a city and has two accessor methods to manipulate the data, setCity() and getCity().

Person has setName() and getName(), similar to Address, but it also has two other methods: __construct() and __call().

Its constructor instantiates an Address object and stores it in a protected $address property. This allows methods inside Person to access $address, but prevents others from talking directly to the class.

Ideally, when you call a method that exists in Address, PHP would automatically execute it. This does not occur, because Person does not extend Address. You must write code to glue these calls to the appropriate methods yourself.

Wrapper methods are one option. For example:

```
class Person {
    public function setCity($city) {
        $this->address->setCity($city);
    }
}
```

This setCity() method passes along its data to the setCity() method stored in $address. This is simple, but it is also tedious because you must write a wrapper for every method.

Using __call() lets you automate this process by centralizing these methods into a single place:

```
class Person {
    public function __call($method, $arguments) {
            if (method_exists($this->address, $method)) {
                return call_user_func_array(
                    array($this->address, $method), $arguments);
            }
    }
}
```

The __call() method captures any calls to undefined methods in a class. It is invoked with two arguments: the name of the method and an array holding the parameters passed to the method. The first argument lets you see which method was called, so you can determine whether it's appropriate to dispatch it to $address.

Here, you want to pass along the method if it's a valid method of the `Address` class. Check this using `method_exists()`, providing the object as the first parameter and the method name as the second.

If the function returns `true`, you know this method is valid, so you can call it. Unfortunately, you're still left with the burden of unwrapping the arguments out of the `$argu` `ments` array. That can be painful.

The seldom used and oddly named `call_user_func_array()` function solves this problem. This function lets you call a user function and pass along arguments in an array. Its first parameter is your function name, and the second is the array of arguments.

In this case, however, you want to call an object method instead of a function. There's a special syntax to cover this situation. Instead of passing the function name, you pass an array with two elements. The first element is the object, and the other is the method name.

This causes `call_user_func_array()` to invoke the method on your object. You must then `return` the result of `call_user_func_array()` back to the original caller, or your return values will be silently discarded.

Here's an example of `Person` that calls both a method defined in `Person` and one from `Address`:

```
$rasmus = new Person;
$rasmus->setName('Rasmus Lerdorf');
$rasmus->setCity('Sunnyvale');

print $rasmus->getName() . ' lives in ' . $rasmus->getCity() . '.';
```

Even though `setCity()` and `getCity()` aren't methods of `Person`, you have aggregated them into that class.

You can aggregate additional objects into a single class, and also be more selective as to which methods you expose to the outside user. This requires some basic filtering based on the method name.

See Also

Documentation on magic methods (*http://www.php.net/oop5.magic*).

7.14 Accessing Overridden Methods

Problem

You want to access a method in the parent class that's been overridden in the child.

Solution

Prefix `parent` to the method name:

```
class shape {
    function draw() {
        // write to screen
    }
}

class circle extends shape {
    function draw($origin, $radius) {
        // validate data
        if ($radius > 0) {
            parent::draw();
            return true;
        }

        return false;
    }
}
```

Discussion

When you override a parent method by defining one in the child, the parent method isn't called unless you explicitly reference it.

In the Solution, we override the `draw()` method in the child class, `circle`, because we want to accept circle specific parameters and validate the data. However, in this case, we still want to perform the generic `shape::draw()` action, which does the actual drawing, so we call `parent::draw()` inside our method if `$radius` is greater than 0.

Only code inside the class can use `parent::`. Calling `parent::draw()` from outside the class gets you a parse error. For example, if `circle::draw()` checked only the radius, but you also wanted to call `shape::draw()`, this wouldn't work:[2]

```
$circle = new circle;
if ($circle->draw($origin, $radius)) {
    $circle->parent::draw();
}
```

This also applies to object constructors, so it's quite common to see the following:

```
class circle {
    function __construct($x, $y, $r) {
        // call shape's constructor first
        parent::__construct();
        // now do circle-specific stuff
```

---

2. In fact, it fails with the error `unexpected T_PAAMAYIM_NEKUDOTAYIM`, which is Hebrew for "double-colon."

```
        }
    }
```

See Also

Recipe 7.2 for more on object constructors; documentation on class parents (*http://www.php.net/keyword.parent*) and on `get_parent_class()` (*http://www.php.net/get-parent-class*).

7.15 Creating Methods Dynamically

Problem

You want to dynamically provide methods without explicitly defining them.

Use the `__call()` and `__callStatic()` magic methods to intercept method invocations and route them accordingly.

This technique is best used when you're providing an object relational map (ORM) or creating a proxy class. For instance, you want to expose `findBy()` methods that translate to database queries or RESTful APIs.

For example, you have users of your application and want to let people retrieve them using a varied set search terms: ID, email address, telephone number. You could create one method per term: `findById()`, `findByEmail()`, `findByPhone()`. However, the underlying code is largely identical, so you can put that in one place.

Here's where `__callStatic()` comes in:

```
class Users {
    static function find($args) {
        // here's where the real logic lives
        // for example a database query:
        // SELECT user FROM users WHERE $args['field'] = $args['value']
    }

    static function __callStatic($method, $args) {
        if (preg_match('/^findBy(.+)$/', $method, $matches)) {
            return static::find(array('field' => $matches[1],
                                      'value' => $args[0]));
        }
    }
}

$user = User::findById(123);
$user = User::findByEmail('rasmus@php.net');
```

When you invoke `findById()`, PHP passes this request to `__callStatic()`. Inside, the regular expression looks for any requests beginning with `findBy` and extracts the re-

---

maining characters. That value and the first argument to the function are then bundled up and passed to Users::find(), where the "real" logic lives.

See Also

Documentation on overloaded methods (*http://www.php.net/oop5.overloading*); Recipe 7.18 for more on calling static methods.

7.16 Using Method Polymorphism

Problem

You want to execute different code depending on the number and type of arguments passed to a method.

Solution

PHP doesn't support method polymorphism as a built-in feature. However, you can emulate it using various type-checking functions. The following combine() function uses is_numeric(), is_string(), is_array(), and is_bool():

```
// combine() adds numbers, concatenates strings, merges arrays,
// and ANDs bitwise and boolean arguments
function combine($a, $b) {
    if (is_int($a) && is_int($b))      {
        return $a + $b;
    }

    if (is_float($a) && is_float($b))   {
        return $a + $b;
    }

    if (is_string($a) && is_string($b))  {
        return "$a$b";
    }

    if (is_array($a) && is_array($b))   {
        return array_merge($a, $b);
    }

    if (is_bool($a) && is_bool($b))     {
        return $a & $b;
    }

    return false;
}
```

Discussion

Because PHP doesn't allow you to declare a variable's type in a method prototype, it can't conditionally execute a different method based on the method's signature, as Java and C++ can. You can, instead, make one function and use a `switch` statement to manually re-create this feature.

For example, PHP lets you edit images using GD. It can be handy in an image class to be able to pass in either the location of the image (remote or local) or the handle PHP has assigned to an existing image stream. This `Image` class that does just that:

```php
class Image {

    protected $handle;

    function ImageCreate($image) {
        if (is_string($image)) {
            // simple file type guessing

            // grab file suffix
            $info = pathinfo($image);
            $extension = strtolower($info['extension']);
            switch ($extension) {
            case 'jpg':
            case 'jpeg':
                $this->handle = ImageCreateFromJPEG($image);
                break;
            case 'png':
                $this->handle = ImageCreateFromPNG($image);
                break;
            default:
                die('Images must be JPEGs or PNGs.');
            }
        } elseif (is_resource($image)) {
            $this->handle = $image;
        } else {
            die('Variables must be strings or resources.');
        }
    }
}
```

In this case, any string passed in is treated as the location of a file, so use `pathinfo()` to grab the file extension. Once you know the extension, try to guess which `ImageCreate From()` function accurately opens the image and create a handle.

If it's not a string, you're dealing directly with a GD stream, which is a type of `re source`. Because there's no conversion necessary, assign the stream directly to `$han dle`. Of course, if you're using this class in a production environment, you'd be more robust in your error handling.

Method polymorphism also encompasses methods with differing numbers of arguments. The code to find the number of arguments inside a method is identical to how you process variable argument functions using `func_num_args()`. This is discussed in Recipe 6.6.

See Also

Recipe 6.6 for variable argument functions; documentation on `is_string()` (*http://www.php.net/is-string*), `is_resource()` (*http://www.php.net/is-resource*), and `pathinfo()` (*http://www.php.net/pathinfo*).

7.17 Defining Class Constants

Problem

You want to define constants on a per-class basis, not on a global basis.

Solution

Define them like class properties, but use the `const` label instead:

```
class Math {
    const pi = 3.14159; // universal
    const  e = 2.71828; // constants
}

$area = math::pi * $radius * $radius;
```

Discussion

PHP reuses its concept of global constants and applies them to classes. Essentially, these are final properties.

Declare them using the `const` label:

```
class Math {
    const pi = 3.14159; // universal
    const  e = 2.71828; // constants
}

$area = math::pi * $radius * $radius;
```

Like static properties, you can access constants without first instantiating a new instance of your class, and they're accessed using the double colon (::) notation. Prefix the word `self::` to the constant name to use it inside of a class.

Unlike properties, constants do not have a dollar sign ($) before them:

```
class Circle {
    const pi = 3.14159;
    protected $radius;

    public function __construct($radius) {
        $this->radius = $radius;
    }

    public function circumference() {
        return 2 * self::pi * $this->radius;
    }
}

$c = new circle(1);
print $c->circumference();
```

This example creates a circle with a radius of 1 and then calls the `circumference` method to calculate its circumference:

```
define('pi', 10); // global pi constant

class Circle {
    const pi = 3.14159; // class pi constant
    protected $radius;

    public function __construct($radius) {
        $this->radius = $radius;
    }

    public function circumference() {
        return 2 * pi * $this->radius;
    }

}

$c = new circle(1);
print $c->circumference();
```

Oops! PHP has used the value of 10 instead of 3.14159, so the new answer is 20 instead of 6.28318.

Although it's unlikely that you will accidentally redefine π (you'll probably use the built-in M_PI constant anyway), this can still slip you up.

You cannot assign the value of an expression to a constant, nor can they use information passed into your script:

```
// invalid
class permissions {
    const    read = 1 << 2;
    const    write = 1 << 1;
    const execute = 1 << 0;
}
```

```
// invalid and insecure
class database {
    const debug = $_REQUEST['debug'];
}
```

Neither the constants in `permissions` nor the debug constant in `database` are acceptable because they are not fixed. Even the first example, 1 << 2, where PHP does not need to read in external data, is not allowed.

Because you need to access constants using an explicit name, either `self::` or the name of the class, you cannot dynamically calculate the class name during runtime. It must be declared beforehand. For example:

```
class Constants {
    const pi = 3.14159;

    // rest of class here
}

$class = 'Constants';

print $class::pi;
```

This produces a parse error, even though this type of construct is legal for nonconstant expressions, such as `$class->pi`.

See Also

Documentation on class constants (*http://www.php.net/oop5.constants*).

7.18 Defining Static Properties and Methods

Problem

You want to define methods in an object, and be able to access them without instantiating a object.

Solution

Declare the method as `static`:

```
class Format {
    public static function number($number, $decimals = 2,
                                  $decimal = '.', $thousands = ',') {
        return number_format($number, $decimals, $decimal, $thousands);
    }
}
```

```
print Format::number(1234.567);
```

1,234.57

Discussion

Occasionally, you want to define a collection of methods in an object, but you want to be able to invoke those methods without instantiating a object. In PHP, declaring a method static lets you call it directly:

```
class Format {
    public static function number($number, $decimals = 2,
                                  $decimal = '.', $thousands = ',') {
        return number_format($number, $decimals, $decimal, $thousands);
    }
}

print Format::number(1234.567);
```

1,234.57

Because static methods don't require an object instance, use the class name instead of the object. Don't place a dollar sign ($) before the class name.

Static methods aren't referenced with an arrow (->), but with double colons (::)—this signals to PHP that the method is static. So in the example, the number() method of the Format class is accessed using Format::number().

Number formatting doesn't depend on any other object properties or methods. Therefore, it makes sense to declare this method static. This way, for example, inside your shopping cart application, you can format the price of items in a pretty manner with just one line of code and still use an object instead of a global function.

Within the class where the static method is defined, refer to it using self:

```
class Format {
    public static function number($number, $decimals = 2,
                                  $decimal = '.', $thousands = ',') {
        return number_format($number, $decimals, $decimal, $thousands);
    }

    public static function integer($number) {
        return self::number($number, 0);
    }
}

print Format::number(1234.567)  . "\n";
print Format::integer(1234.567) . "\n";
```

1,234.57
1,235

Here the integer() method references another method defined in Format, number().
So, it uses self::number().

Static methods do not operate on a specific instance of the class where they're defined.
PHP does not "construct" a temporary object for you to use while you're inside the
method. Therefore, you cannot refer to $this inside a static method, because there's no
$this on which to operate. Calling a static method is just like calling a regular function.

There's a potential complication from using self::. It doesn't follow the same inheritance rules as nonstatic methods. In this case, self:: always attaches the reference to
the class it's defined in, regardless whether it's invoked from that class or from a child.

Use static:: to change this behavior, such as in this ORM example:

```
class Model {
    protected static function validateArgs($args) {
        throw new Exception("You need to override this in a subclass!");
    }

    public static function find($args) {
        static::validateArgs($args);
        $class = get_called_class();
        // now you can do a database query, such as:
        // SELECT * FROM $class WHERE ...
    }
}

class Bicycle extends Model {
    protected static function validateArgs($args) {
        return true;
    }
}

Bicycle::find(['owner' => 'peewee']);
```

With self::, PHP binds to Model::validateArgs(), which doesn't allow for model-
specific validation. However, with static::, PHP will defer until it knows which class
the method is actually called from. This is known as *late static binding*.

Inside of find(), to generate your SQL, you need the name of the calling class. You
cannot use the Reflection classes and the __CLASS__ constant because they return
Model, so use get_called_class() to pull this at runtime.

PHP also has a feature known as static properties. Every instance of a class shares these
properties in common. Thus, static properties act as class-namespaced global variables.

One reason for using a static property is to share a database connection among multiple
Database objects. For efficiency, you shouldn't create a new connection to your database
every time you instantiate Database. Instead, negotiate a connection the first time and
reuse that connection in each additional instance, as shown:

```
class Database {
    private static $dbh = NULL;

    public function __construct($server, $username, $password) {
        if (self::$dbh == NULL) {
            self::$dbh = db_connect($server, $username, $password);
        } else {
            // reuse existing connection
        }
    }
}

$db  = new Database('db.example.com', 'web', 'jsd6w@2d');
// Do a bunch of queries

$db2 = new Database('db.example.com', 'web', 'jsd6w@2d');
// Do some additional queries
```

Static properties, like static methods, use the double colon notation. To refer to a static property inside of a class, use the special prefix of self. self is to static properties and methods as $this is to instantiated properties and methods.

The constructor uses self::$dbh to access the static connection property. When $db is instantiated, dbh is still set to NULL, so the constructor calls db_connect() to negotiate a new connection with the database.

This does not occur when you create $db2, because dbh has been set to the database handle.

See Also

Documentation on the static keyword (*http://www.php.net/oop5.static*).

7.19 Controlling Object Serialization

Problem

You want to control how an object behaves when you serialize() and unserial ize() it. This is useful when you need to establish and close connections to remote resources, such as databases, files, and web services.

Solution

Define the magical methods __sleep() and __wakeUp():

```
class LogFile {
    protected $filename;
    protected $handle;
```

```
    public function __construct($filename) {
        $this->filename = $filename;
        $this->open();
    }

    private function open() {
        $this->handle = fopen($this->filename, 'a');
    }

    public function __destruct($filename) {
        fclose($this->handle);
    }

    // called when object is serialized
    // should return an array of object properties to serialize
    public function __sleep() {
        return array('filename');
    }

    // called when object is unserialized
    public function __wakeUp() {
        $this->open();
    }
}
```

Discussion

When you serialize an object in PHP, it preserves all your object properties. However, this does not include connections or handles that you hold to outside resources, such as databases, files, and web services.

These must be reestablished when you unserialize the object, or the object will not behave correctly. You can do this explicitly within your code, but it's better to abstract this away and let PHP handle everything behind the scenes.

Do this through the __sleep() and __wakeUp() magic methods. When you call seri alize() on a object, PHP invokes __sleep(); when you unserialize() it, it calls __wakeUp().

The LogFile class in the Solution has five simple methods. The constructor takes a filename and saves it for future access. The open() method opens this file and stores the file handle, which is closed in the object's destructor.

The __sleep() method returns an array of properties to store during object serialization. Because file handles aren't preserved across serializations, it only returns ar ray('filename') because that's all you need to store.

That's why when the object is reserialized, you need to reopen the file. This is handled inside of __wakeUp(), which calls the same open() method used by the constructor.

Because you cannot pass arguments to __wakeUp(), it needs to get the filename from somewhere else. Fortunately, it's able to access object properties, which is why the filename is saved there.

It's important to realize that the same instance can be serialized multiple times in a single request, or even continue to be used after it's serialized. Therefore, you shouldn't do anything in __sleep() that could prevent either of these two actions. The __sleep() method should only be used to exclude properties that shouldn't be serialized because they take up too much disk space, or are calculated based on other data and should be recalculated or otherwise made fresh during object unserialization.

That's why the call to fclose() appears in the destructor and not in __sleep().

See Also

Documentation on magic methods (*http://www.php.net/oop5.magic*); the unserial ize() function (*http://www.php.net/unserialize*) and the serialize() function (*http://www.php.net/serialize*).

7.20 Introspecting Objects

Problem

You want to inspect an object to see what methods and properties it has, which lets you write code that works on any generic object, regardless of type.

Solution

Use the Reflection classes to probe an object for information.

For a quick overview of the class, call Reflection::export():

```
// learn about cars
Reflection::export(new ReflectionClass('car'));
```

Or probe for specific data:

```
$car = new ReflectionClass('car');
if ($car->hasMethod('retractTop')) {
    // car is a convertible
}
```

Discussion

It's rare to have an object and be unable to examine the actual code to see how it's described. Still, with the Reflection classes, you can programmatically extract information about both object-oriented features, such as classes, methods, and properties, and non-OO features, such as functions and extensions.

This is useful for projects you want to apply to a whole range of different classes, such as creating automated class documentation, generic object debuggers, and state savers, like serialize().

To help show how the Reflection classes work, Example 7-1 contains an example Person class that uses many of PHP's OO features.

Example 7-1. Person class

```
class Person {
    public $name;
    protected $spouse;
    private $password;

    public function __construct($name) {
        $this->name = $name
    }

    public function getName() {
        return $name;
    }

    protected function setSpouse(Person $spouse) {
        if (!isset($this->spouse)) {
            $this->spouse = $spouse;
        }
    }

    private function setPassword($password) {
        $this->password = $password;
    }
}
```

For a quick overview of the class, call Reflection::export():

```
Reflection::export(new ReflectionClass('Person'));

Class [ <user> class Person ] {
  @@ /www/reflection.php 3-25

  - Constants [0] {
  }

  - Static properties [0] {
  }

  - Static methods [0] {
  }
```

```
  - Properties [3] {
    Property [ <default> public $name ]
    Property [ <default> protected $spouse ]
    Property [ <default> private $password ]
  }

  - Methods [4] {
    Method [ <user> <ctor> public method _ _construct ] {
      @@ /www/reflection.php 8 - 10

      - Parameters [1] {
        Parameter #0 [ $name ]
      }
    }

    Method [ <user> public method getName ] {
      @@ /www/reflection.php 12 - 14
    }

    Method [ <user> protected method setSpouse ] {
      @@ /www/reflection.php 16 - 20

      - Parameters [1] {
        Parameter #0 [ Person or NULL $spouse ]
      }
    }

    Method [ <user> private method setPassword ] {
      @@ /www/reflection.php 22 - 24

      - Parameters [1] {
        Parameter #0 [ $password ]
      }
    }
  }
}
```

The Reflection::export() static method takes an instance of the ReflectionClass class and returns a copious amount of information. As you can see, it details the number of constants, static properties, static methods, properties, and methods in the class. Each item is broken down into component parts. For instance, all the entries contain visibility identifiers (private, protected, or public), and methods have a list of their parameters underneath their definition.

Reflection::export() not only reports the file where everything is defined, but even gives the line numbers! This lets you extract code from a file and place it in your documentation.

Example 7-2 shows a short command-line script that searches for the filename and starting line number of a method or function.

Example 7-2. Using reflection to locate function and method definitions

```php
if ($argc < 2) {
    print "$argv[0]: function/method, classes1.php [, ... classesN.php]\n";
    exit;
}

// Grab the function name
$function = $argv[1];

// Include the files
foreach (array_slice($argv, 2) as $filename) {
    include_once $filename;
}

try {
    if (strpos($function, '::')) {
        // It's a method
        list ($class, $method) = explode('::', $function);
        $reflect = new ReflectionMethod($class, $method);
    } else {
        // It's a function
        $reflect = new ReflectionFunction($function);
    }

    $file = $reflect->getFileName();
    $line = $reflect->getStartLine();

    printf ("%s | %s | %d\n", "$function()", $file, $line);
} catch (ReflectionException $e) {
    printf ("%s not found.\n", "$function()");
}
```

Pass the function or method name as the first argument, and the include files as the remaining arguments. These files are then included, so make sure they don't print out anything.

The next step is to determine whether the first argument is a method or a function. Because methods are in the form class::method, you can use strpos() to tell them apart.

If it's a method, use explode() to separate the class from the method, passing both to ReflectionMethod. If it's a function, you can directly instantiate a ReflectionFunction without any difficulty.

Because ReflectionMethod extends ReflectionFunction, you can then call both get FileName() and getStartLine() of either class. This gathers the information that you need to print out, which is done via printf().

When you try to instantiate a `ReflectionMethod` or `ReflectionFunction` with the name of an undefined method, these classes throw a `ReflectionException`. Here, it's caught and an error message is displayed.

A more complex script that prints out the same type of information for all user-defined methods and functions appears in Recipe 7.24.

If you just need a quick view at an object instance, and don't want to fiddle with the `Reflection` classes, use either `var_dump()`, `var_export()`, or `print_r()` to print the object's values. Each of these three functions prints out information in a slightly different way; `var_export()` can optionally return the information, instead of displaying it.

See Also

Recipe 5.8 for more on printing variables; documentation on reflection (*http://www.php.net/book.reflection*), `var_dump()` (*http://www.php.net/var-dump*), `var_export()` (*http://www.php.net/var-export*), and `print_r()` (*http://www.php.net/print-r*).

7.21 Checking If an Object Is an Instance of a Specific Class

Problem

You want to check if an object is an instance of a specific class.

Solution

To check that a value passed as a function argument is an instance of a specific class, specify the class name in your function prototype:

```
public function add(Person $person) {
        // add $person to address book
    }
}
```

In other contexts, use the `instanceof` operator:

```
$media = get_something_from_catalog();
if ($media instanceof Book) {
  // do bookish things
} else if ($media instanceof DVD) {
  // watch the movie
}
```

Discussion

One way of enforcing controls on your objects is by using type hints. A *type hint* is a way to tell PHP that an object passed to a function or method must be of a certain class.

To do this, specify a class name in your function and method prototypes. You can also require that an argument is an array, by using the keyword `array`. This only works for classes and arrays, though, not for any other variable types. You cannot, for example, specify strings or integers.

For example, to require the first argument to your AddressBook class's add() method to be of type Person:

```
class AddressBook {

    public function add(Person $person) {
        // add $person to address book
    }
}
```

Then, if you call add() but pass a string, you get a fatal error:

```
$book = new AddressBook;

$person = 'Rasmus Lerdorf';

$book->add($person);
```

PHP Fatal error: Argument 1 must be an object of class Person in...

Placing a type hint of Person in the first argument of your function declaration is equivalent to adding the following PHP code to the function:

```
public function add($person) {
        if (!($person instanceof Person)) {
                die("Argument 1 must be an instance of Person");
        }
}
```

The instanceof operator checks whether an object is an instance of a particular class. This code makes sure $person is a Person.

The instanceof operator also returns true with classes that are subclasses of the one you're comparing against. For instance:

```
class Person { /* ... */ }

class Kid extends Person { /* ... */ }

$kid = new Kid;

if ($kid instanceof Person) {
        print "Kids are people, to.\n";
}
```

Kids are people, too.

Last, you can use instanceof to see if a class has implemented a specific interface:

```
interface Nameable {
    public function getName();
    public function setName($name);
}

class Book implements Nameable {
        private $name;

    public function getName() {
        return $this->name;
    }

    public function setName($name) {
        return $this->name = $name;
    }
}

$book = new Book;
if ($book instanceof Book) {
        print "You can name a Book.\n";
}
```

You can name a Book

Type hinting has the side benefit of integrating API documentation directly into the class itself. If you see that a class constructor takes an Event type, you know exactly what to provide the method. Additionally, you know that the code and the "documentation" must always be in sync, because it's baked directly into the class definition.

You can also use type hinting in interface definitions, which lets you further specify all your interface details.

However, type hinting does come at the cost of less flexibility. There's no way to allow a parameter to accept more than one type of object, so this places some restrictions on how you design your object hierarchy.

Also, the penalty for violating a type hint is quite drastic—the script aborts with a fatal error. In a web context, you may want to have more control over how errors are handled and recover more gracefully from this kind of mistake. Implementing your own form of type checking inside of methods lets you print out an error page if you choose.

Last, unlike some languages, you cannot use type hinting for return values, so there's no way to mandate that a particular function always returns an object of a particular type.

See Also

Documentation on type hints (*http://www.php.net/oop5.typehinting*) and instanceof (*http://www.php.net/operators.type*).

7.22 Autoloading Class Files upon Object Instantiation

Problem

You don't want to include all your class definitions within every page. Instead, you want to dynamically load only the ones necessary in that page.

Solution

Use the __autoload() magic method:

```
function __autoload($class_name) {
    include "$class_name.php";
}

$person = new Person;
```

Discussion

When you normally attempt to instantiate a class that's not defined, PHP dies with a fatal error because it can't locate what you're looking for. Therefore, it's typical to load in all the potential classes for a page, regardless of whether they're actually invoked.

This has the side effect of increasing processing time, because PHP must parse every class, even the unused ones. One solution is to load missing code on the fly using the __autoload() method, which is invoked when you instantiate undefined classes.

For example, here's how you include all the classes used by your script:

```
function __autoload($class_name) {
    include "$class_name.php";
}

$person = new Person;
```

The __autoload() function receives the class name as its single parameter. This example appends a *.php* extension to that name and tries to include a file based on $class_name. So when you instantiate a new Person, it looks for *Person.php* in your include_path.

When __autoload() fails to successfully load a class definition for the object you're trying to instantiate, PHP fails with a fatal error, just as it does when it can't find a class definition without autoload.

If you adopt the PSR-0 naming convention, use the code at GitHub (*https://gist.github.com/jwage/221634*).

Then you can do the following:

```
use Mysite\Person;
$person = new Person;
```

If the class isn't defined, `Person` gets passed to `__autoload()`. The function pulls in the file based on the namespace and classname.

Though using `__autoload()` slightly increases processing time during the addition of a class, it is called only once per class. Multiple instances of the same class does not result in multiple calls to `__autoload()`.

Before deploying `__autoload()`, be sure to benchmark that the overhead of opening, reading, and closing the multiple files necessary isn't actually more of a performance penalty than the additional parsing time of the unused classes.

In particular if you're using an opcode cache, such as OPcache, using `__autoload()` and `include_once` can hurt performance. For best results, you should `include` all your files at the top of the script and make sure you don't reinclude a file twice.

See Also

Recipe Recipe 27.3 for more on PSR-0; documentation on autoloading (*http://www.php.net/oop5.autoload*).

7.23 Instantiating an Object Dynamically

Problem

You want to instantiate an object, but you don't know the name of the class until your code is executed. For example, you want to localize your site by creating an object belonging to a specific language. However, until the page is requested, you don't know which language to select.

Solution

Use a variable for your class name:

```
$language = $_REQUEST['language'];
$valid_langs = array('en_US' => 'US English',
                     'en_UK' => 'British English',
                     'es_US' => 'US Spanish',
                     'fr_CA' => 'Canadian French');

if (isset($valid_langs[$language]) && class_exists($language)) {
    $lang = new $language;
}
```

Discussion

Sometimes you may not know the class name you want to instantiate at runtime, but you know part of it. However, although this is legal PHP:

```
$class_name = 'Net_Ping';
$class = new $class_name;                    // new Net_Ping
```

This is not:

```
$partial_class_name = 'Ping';
$class = new "Net_$partial_class_name"; // new Net_Ping
```

This, however, is okay:

```
$partial_class_name = 'Ping';
$class_prefix = 'Net_';

$class_name = "$class_prefix$partial_class_name";
$class = new $class_name;                    // new Net_Ping
```

So you can't instantiate an object when its class name is defined using variable concatenation in the same step. However, because you can use simple variable names, the solution is to preconcatenate the class name.

See Also

Documentation on `class_exists()` (*http://www.php.net/class-exists*).

7.24 Program: whereis

Although tools such as phpDocumentor provide quite detailed information about an entire series of classes, it can be useful to get a quick dump that lists all the functions and methods defined in a list of files.

The program in Example 7-3 loops through a list of files, includes them, and then uses the `Reflection` classes to gather information about them. Once the master list is compiled, the functions and methods are sorted alphabetically and printed out.

Example 7-3. whereis

```
if ($argc < 2) {
    print "$argv[0]: classes1.php [, ...]\n";
    exit;
}

// Include the files
foreach (array_slice($argv, 1) as $filename) {
    include_once $filename;
}
```

```php
// Get all the method and function information
// Start with the classes
$methods = array();
foreach (get_declared_classes() as $class) {
    $r = new ReflectionClass($class);
    // Eliminate built-in classes
    if ($r->isUserDefined()) {
        foreach ($r->getMethods() as $method) {
            // Eliminate inherited methods
            if ($method->getDeclaringClass()->getName() == $class) {
                $signature = "$class::" . $method->getName();
                $methods[$signature] = $method;
            }
        }
    }
}

// Then add the functions
$functions = array();
$defined_functions = get_defined_functions();
foreach ($defined_functions['user'] as $function) {
    $functions[$function] = new ReflectionFunction($function);
}

// Sort methods alphabetically by class
function sort_methods($a, $b) {
    list ($a_class, $a_method) = explode('::', $a);
    list ($b_class, $b_method) = explode('::', $b);

    if ($cmp = strcasecmp($a_class, $b_class)) {
        return $cmp;
    }

    return strcasecmp($a_method, $b_method);
}
uksort($methods, 'sort_methods');

// Sort functions alphabetically
// This is less complicated, but don't forget to
// remove the method sorting function from the list
unset($functions['sort_methods']);
// Sort 'em
ksort($functions);

// Print out information
foreach (array_merge($functions, $methods) as $name => $reflect) {
    $file = $reflect->getFileName();
    $line = $reflect->getStartLine();

    printf ("%-25s | %-40s | %6d\n", "$name()", $file, $line);
}
```

This code uses both the Reflection classes and also a couple of PHP functions, `get_de clared_classes()` and `get_declared_functions()`, that aren't part of the Reflection classes, but help with introspection.

It's important to filter out any built-in PHP classes and functions; otherwise, the report will be less about your code and more about your PHP installation. This is handled in two different ways. Because `get_declared_classes()` doesn't distinguish between user and internal classes, the code calls `ReflectionClass::isUserDefined()` to check. The `get_defined_function()` call, on the other hand, actually computes this for you, putting the information in the `user` array element.

Because it's easier to scan the output of a sorted list, the script sorts the arrays of methods and functions. Because multiple classes can have the same method, you need to use a user-defined sorting method, `sort_methods()`, which first compares two methods by their class names and then by their method names.

Once the data is sorted, it's a relatively easy task to loop though the merged arrays, gather up the filename and starting line numbers, and print out a report.

Here are the results of running the PEAR `HTTP` class through the script:

```
HTTP::Date()              | /usr/lib/php/HTTP.php            |      38
HTTP::head()              | /usr/lib/php/HTTP.php            |     144
HTTP::negotiateLanguage() | /usr/lib/php/HTTP.php            |      77
HTTP::redirect()          | /usr/lib/php/HTTP.php            |     186
```

CHAPTER 8

Web Fundamentals

8.0 Introduction

Web programming is probably why you're reading this book. It's why the first version of PHP was written and what continues to make it so popular today. With PHP, it's easy to write dynamic web programs that do almost anything. Other chapters cover various PHP capabilities, such as web services, regular expressions, database access, and file I/O. These capabilities are all part of web programming, but this chapter focuses on key web-specific concepts and organizational topics that will make your web programming stronger.

HTTP requests aren't "stateful"; each request isn't connected to a previous one. A cookie, however, can link different requests by the same user. This makes it easier to build features such as shopping carts or to keep track of a user's search history. Recipes 8.1, 8.2, and 8.3 show how to set, read, and delete cookies. A cookie is a small text string that the server instructs the browser to send along with requests the browser makes.

Other good ways to pass data are through query strings and the body of the request. Recipe 8.4 shows the details of constructing a URL that includes a query string, including proper encoding of special characters and handling of HTML entities. Similarly, Recipe 8.5 provides information on reading the data submitted in the body of a request when it's not form data, so PHP cannot automatically parse it into $_POST.

The next recipes demonstrate how to use authentication, which lets you protect your web pages with passwords. PHP's special features for dealing with HTTP Basic authentication are explained in Recipe 8.6. It's often a better idea to roll your own authentication method using cookies, as shown in Recipe 8.7.

Cookies and Authentication are two specific HTTP headers. Learn how to read any HTTP header in Recipe 8.8 and write one in Recipe 8.9.

Setting the HTTP status code is covered in Recipe 8.10. Recipe 8.11 shows how to redirect users to a different web page than the one they requested.

The three following recipes deal with output control. Recipe 8.12 shows how to force output to be sent to the browser. Recipe 8.13 explains the output buffering functions. Output buffers enable you to capture output that would otherwise be printed or delay output until an entire page is processed. Automatic compression of output is shown in Recipe 8.14.

The next two recipes show how to interact with external variables: environment variables and PHP configuration settings. Recipe 8.15 and Recipe 8.16 discuss environment variables. If Apache is your web server, you can use the techniques in Recipe 8.17 to communicate with other Apache modules from within your PHP programs.

Identifying mobile browsers, so you can choose to provide alternative versions of your site, is shown in Recipe 8.18.

This chapter also includes three programs that demonstrate some of the concepts in the recipes. Recipe 8.19 validates user accounts by sending an email message with a customized link to each new user. If the user doesn't visit the link within a week of receiving the message, the account is deleted. Recipe 8.20 is a small example of a wiki system that makes any page on your website editable from within the web browser. Recipe 8.21 shows how to parse the HTTP Range header to return specified portions of a file. This allows a client to resume an interrupted download exactly where they got cut off.

8.1 Setting Cookies

Problem

You want to set a cookie so that your website can recognize subsequent requests from the same web browser.

Solution

Call setcookie() with a cookie name and value:

```
setcookie('flavor','chocolate chip');
```

Discussion

Cookies are sent with the HTTP headers, so if you're not using output buffering, set cookie() must be called before any output is generated.

Pass additional arguments to setcookie() to control cookie behavior. The third argument to setcookie() is an expiration time, expressed as an epoch timestamp. For example, this cookie expires at noon GMT on December 3, 2014:

```
setcookie('flavor','chocolate chip',1417608000);
```

If the third argument to `setcookie()` is missing (or empty), the cookie expires when the browser is closed. Also, many systems can't handle a cookie expiration time greater than 2147483647, because that's the largest epoch timestamp that fits in a 32-bit integer, as discussed in the introduction to Chapter 3.

The fourth argument to `setcookie()` is a path. The cookie is sent back to the server only when pages whose path begin with the specified string are requested. For example, a cookie sent back only to pages whose path begins with */products/*:

```
setcookie('flavor','chocolate chip',0,'/products/');
```

The page that's setting the cookie doesn't have to have a URL whose path component begins with */products/*, but the cookie is sent back only to pages that do.

The fifth argument to `setcookie()` is a domain. The cookie is sent back to the server only when pages whose hostname ends with the specified domain are requested. Here the first cookie is sent back to all hosts in the *example.com* domain, but the second cookie is sent only with requests to the host *jeannie.example.com*:

```
setcookie('flavor','chocolate chip',0,'','.example.com');
setcookie('flavor','chocolate chip',0,'','jeannie.example.com');
```

If the first cookie's domain was just *example.com* instead of *.example.com*, it would be sent only to the single host *example.com* (and not *www.example.com* or *jeannie.example.com*). If a domain is not specified when `setcookie()` is called, the browser sends back the cookie only with requests to the same hostname as the request in which the cookie was set.

The last optional argument to `setcookie()` is a flag that, if set to `true`, instructs the browser only to send the cookie over an SSL connection. This can be useful if the cookie contains sensitive information, but remember that the data in the cookie is stored as unencrypted plain text on the user's computer.

Different browsers handle cookies in slightly different ways, especially with regard to how strictly they match path and domain strings and how they determine priority between different cookies of the same name. The `setcookie()` page of the online manual has helpful clarifications of these differences.

See Also

Recipe 8.2 shows how to read cookie values; Recipe 8.3 shows how to delete cookies; Recipe 8.13 explains output buffering; documentation on `setcookie()` (*http://www.php.net/setcookie*); an expanded cookie specification is detailed in RFC 2965 (*http://www.faqs.org/rfcs/rfc2965.html*).

8.2 Reading Cookie Values

Problem

You want to read the value of a cookie that you've previously set.

Solution

Look in the $_COOKIE superglobal array:

```
if (isset($_COOKIE['flavor'])) {
    print "You ate a {$_COOKIE['flavor']} cookie.";
}
```

Discussion

A cookie's value isn't available in $_COOKIE during the request in which the cookie is set. In other words, calling the setcookie() function doesn't alter the value of $_COOKIE. On subsequent requests, however, each cookie sent back to the server is stored in $_COOKIE.

When a browser sends a cookie back to the server, it sends only the value. You can't access the cookie's domain, path, expiration time, or secure status through $_COOKIE because the browser doesn't send that to the server.

To print the names and values of all cookies sent in a particular request, loop through the $_COOKIE array:

```
foreach ($_COOKIE as $cookie_name => $cookie_value) {
    print "$cookie_name = $cookie_value <br/>";
}
```

See Also

Recipe 8.1 shows how to set cookies; Recipe 8.3 shows how to delete cookies.

8.3 Deleting Cookies

Problem

You want to delete a cookie so a browser doesn't send it back to the server. For example, you're using cookies to track whether a user is logged in to your website, and a user logs out.

Solution

Call `setcookie()` with no value for the cookie and an expiration time in the past:

```
setcookie('flavor','',1);
```

Discussion

It's a good idea to make the expiration time a long time in the past, in case your server and the user's computer have unsynchronized clocks. For example, if your server thinks it's 3:06 P.M. and a user's computer thinks it's 3:02 P.M., a cookie with an expiration time of 3:05 P.M. isn't deleted by that user's computer even though the time is in the past for the server.

The call to `setcookie()` to delete a cookie has to have the same arguments (except for value and time) that the call to `setcookie()` that set the cookie did, so include the path, domain, and secure flag if necessary.

See Also

Recipe 8.1 shows how to set cookies; Recipe 8.2 shows how to read cookie values; documentation on `setcookie()` (*http://www.php.net/setcookie*).

8.4 Building a Query String

Problem

You need to construct a link that includes name/value pairs in a query string.

Solution

Use the `http_build_query()` function:

```
$vars = array('name' => 'Oscar the Grouch',
              'color' => 'green',
              'favorite_punctuation' => '#');
$query_string = http_build_query($vars);
$url = '/muppet/select.php?' . $query_string;
```

Discussion

The URL built in the Solution is:

/muppet/select.php?name=Oscar+the+Grouch&color=green&favorite_punctuation=%23

Because only some characters are valid in URLs and query strings, the function has encoded the data into the proper format. For example, this query string has spaces as

+. Special characters, such as #, are hex encoded as %23 because the ASCII value of # is 35, which is 23 in hexadecimal.

Although the encoding that `http_build_query()` does prevents any special characters in the variable names or values from disrupting the constructed URL, you may have problems if your variable names begin with the names of HTML entities. Consider this partial URL for retrieving information about a stereo system:

```
/stereo.php?speakers=12&cdplayer=52&=10
```

The HTML entity for ampersand (&) is & so a browser may interpret that URL as:

```
/stereo.php?speakers=12&cdplayer=52&=10
```

To prevent embedded entities from corrupting your URLs, you have three choices. The first is to choose variable names that can't be confused with entities, such as _amp instead of amp. The second is to convert characters with HTML entity equivalents to those entities before printing out the URL. Use `htmlentities()`:

```
$url = '/muppet/select.php?' . htmlentities($query_string);
```

The resulting URL is:

```
/muppet/select.php?name=Oscar+the+Grouch&color=green&favorite_punctuation=%23
```

Your third choice is to change the argument separator from & to & by setting the configuration directive `arg_separator.input` to &. Then, `http_build_query()` joins the different name/value pairs with &:

```
ini_set('arg_separator.input', '&amp;');
```

See Also

Documentation on `http_build_query()` (*http://www.php.net/http_build_query*) and `htmlentities()` (*http://www.php.net/htmlentities*).

8.5 Reading the POST Request Body

Problem

You want direct access to the body of a request, not just the parsed data that PHP puts in $_POST for you. For example, you want to handle an XML document that's been posted as part of a web services request.

Solution

Read from the `php://input` stream:

```
$body = file_get_contents('php://input');
```

Discussion

The superglobal array $_POST is designed for accessing submitted HTML form variables, but it doesn't cut it when you need raw, uncut access to the whole request body. That's where the php://input stream comes in. Read the entire thing with file_get_con tents(), or if you're expecting a large request body, read it in chunks with fread().

If the configuration directive always_populate_raw_post_data is on, then raw post data is also put into the global variable $HTTP_RAW_POST_DATA. But to write maximally portable code, you should use php://input instead—that works even when always_pop ulate_raw_post_data is turned off.

See Also

Documentation on php://input (*http://www.php.net/wrappers*) and on always_popu late_raw_post_data (*http://bit.ly/1oqkqgo*); ways to read files are discussed in Chapter 24.

8.6 Using HTTP Basic or Digest Authentication

Problem

You want to use PHP to protect parts of your website with passwords. Instead of storing the passwords in an external file and letting the web server handle the authentication, you want the password verification logic to be in a PHP program.

Solution

The $_SERVER['PHP_AUTH_USER'] and $_SERVER['PHP_AUTH_PW'] superglobal vari ables contain the username and password supplied by the user, if any. To deny access to a page, send a WWW-Authenticate header identifying the authentication realm as part of a response with HTTP status code 401:

```
http_response_code(401);
header('WWW-Authenticate: Basic realm="My Website"');
echo "You need to enter a valid username and password.";
exit();
```

Discussion

When a browser sees a 401 header, it pops up a dialog box for a username and password. Those authentication credentials (the username and password), if accepted by the server, are associated with the realm in the WWW-Authenticate header. Code that checks authentication credentials needs to be executed before any output is sent to the browser, because it might send headers. For example, you can use a function such as `vali date()`, shown in Example 8-1.

Example 8-1. validate( )

```php
function validate($user, $pass) {
    /* replace with appropriate username and password checking,
       such as checking a database */
    $users = array('david' => 'fadj&32',
                   'adam'  => '8HEj838');

    if (isset($users[$user]) && ($users[$user] === $pass)) {
        return true;
    } else {
        return false;
    }
}
```

Example 8-2 shows how to use `validate()`.

Example 8-2. Using a validation function

```php
if (! validate($_SERVER['PHP_AUTH_USER'], $_SERVER['PHP_AUTH_PW'])) {
    http_response_code(401);
    header('WWW-Authenticate: Basic realm="My Website"');
    echo "You need to enter a valid username and password.";
    exit;
}
```

Replace the contents of the `validate()` function with appropriate logic to determine if a user entered the correct password. You can also change the realm string from *My Website* and the message that gets printed if a user hits *Cancel* in her browser's authentication box from *You need to enter a valid username and password.*

PHP supports Digest authentication in addition to Basic authentication. With Basic authentication, usernames and passwords are sent in the clear on the network, just minimally obscured by Base64 encoding. With Digest authentication, however, the password itself is never sent from the browser to the server. Instead, only a hash of the password with some other values is sent. This reduces the possibility that the network traffic could be captured and replayed by an attacker. The increased security provided by Digest authentication means that the code to implement is more complicated than just a simple password comparison. Example 8-3 provides functions that compute digest authentication as specified in RFC 2617.

Example 8-3. Using Digest authentication

```php
/* replace with appropriate username and password checking,
   such as checking a database */
$users = array('david' => 'fadj&32',
               'adam'  => '8HEj838');
$realm = 'My website';
```

```php
$username = validate_digest($realm, $users);

// Execution never reaches this point if invalid auth data is provided
print "Hello, " . htmlentities($username);

function validate_digest($realm, $users) {
    // Fail if no digest has been provided by the client
    if (! isset($_SERVER['PHP_AUTH_DIGEST'])) {
        send_digest($realm);
    }
    // Fail if digest can't be parsed
    $username = parse_digest($_SERVER['PHP_AUTH_DIGEST'], $realm, $users);
    if ($username === false) {
        send_digest($realm);
    }
    // Valid username was specified in the digest
    return $username;
}

function send_digest($realm) {
    http_response_code(401);
    $nonce = md5(uniqid());
    $opaque = md5($realm);
    header("WWW-Authenticate: Digest realm=\"$realm\" qop=\"auth\" " .
           "nonce=\"$nonce\" opaque=\"$opaque\"");
    echo "You need to enter a valid username and password.";
    exit;
}

function parse_digest($digest, $realm, $users) {
    // We need to find the following values in the digest header:
    // username, uri, qop, cnonce, nc, and response
    $digest_info = array();
    foreach (array('username','uri','nonce','cnonce','response') as $part) {
        // Delimiter can either be ' or " or nothing (for qop and nc)
        if (preg_match('/'.$part.'=([\'"]?)(.*?)\1/', $digest, $match)) {
            // The part was found, save it for calculation
            $digest_info[$part] = $match[2];
        } else {
            // If the part is missing, the digest can't be validated;
            return false;
        }
    }
    // Make sure the right qop has been provided
    if (preg_match('/qop=auth(,|$)/', $digest)) {
        $digest_info['qop'] = 'auth';
    } else {
        return false;
    }
    // Make sure a valid nonce count has been provided
    if (preg_match('/nc=([0-9a-f]{8})(,|$)/', $digest, $match)) {
```

```
        $digest_info['nc'] = $match[1];
    } else {
        return false;
    }

    // Now that all the necessary values have been slurped out of the
    // digest header, do the algorithmic computations necessary to
    // make sure that the right information was provided.
    //
    // These calculations are described in sections 3.2.2, 3.2.2.1,
    // and 3.2.2.2 of RFC 2617.
    // Algorithm is MD5
    $A1 = $digest_info['username'] . ':' . $realm . ':' .
        $users[$digest_info['username']];
    // qop is 'auth'
    $A2 = $_SERVER['REQUEST_METHOD'] . ':' . $digest_info['uri'];
    $request_digest = md5(implode(':', array(md5($A1), $digest_info['nonce'],
        $digest_info['nc'],
    $digest_info['cnonce'], $digest_info['qop'], md5($A2))));

    // Did what was sent match what we computed?
    if ($request_digest != $digest_info['response']) {
        return false;
    }

    // Everything's OK, return the username
    return $digest_info['username'];
}
```

Neither HTTP Basic nor Digest authentication can be used if you're running PHP as a CGI program. If you can't run PHP as a server module, you can use cookie authentication, discussed in Recipe 8.7.

Another issue with HTTP authentication is that it provides no simple way for a user to log out, other than to exit his browser. The PHP online manual has a few suggestions for log out methods that work with varying degrees of success with different server and browser combinations (*http://www.php.net/features.http-auth*).

There is a straightforward way, however, to force a user to log out after a fixed time interval: include a time calculation in the realm string. Browsers use the same username and password combination every time they're asked for credentials in the same realm. By changing the realm name, the browser is forced to ask the user for new credentials. Example 8-4 uses Basic authentication and forces a logout every night at midnight.

Example 8-4. Forcing logout with Basic authentication

```
if (! validate($_SERVER['PHP_AUTH_USER'],$_SERVER['PHP_AUTH_PW'])) {
    $realm = 'My Website for '.date('Y-m-d');
    http_response_code(401);
    header('WWW-Authenticate: Basic realm="'.$realm.'"');
    echo "You need to enter a valid username and password.";
```

```
    exit;
}
```

You can also have a user-specific timeout without changing the realm name by storing
the time that a user logs in or accesses a protected page. The validate_date() function
in Example 8-5 stores login time in a database and forces a logout if it's been more than
15 minutes since the user last requested a protected page.

Example 8-5. validate_date( )

```
function validate_date($user,$pass) {
    $db = new PDO('sqlite:/databases/users');

    // Prepare and execute
    $st = $db->prepare('SELECT password, last_access
                        FROM users WHERE user LIKE ?');
    $st->execute(array($user));

    if ($ob = $st->fetchObject()) {
        if ($ob->password == $pass) {
            $now = time();
            if (($now - $ob->last_access) > (15 * 60)) {
                return false;
            } else {
                // update the last access time
                $st2 = $db->prepare('UPDATE users SET last_access = "now"
                                     WHERE user LIKE ?');

                $st2->execute(array($user));
                return true;
            }
        }
    }

    return false;
}
```

See Also

Recipe 8.7; the HTTP authentication section of the PHP online manual (*http://
www.php.net/features.http-auth*).

8.7 Using Cookie Authentication

Problem

You want more control over the user login procedure, such as presenting your own login
form.

Solution

Store authentication status in a cookie or as part of a session. When a user logs in successfully, put her username (or another unique value) in a cookie. Also include a hash of the username and a secret word so a user can't just make up an authentication cookie with a username in it:

```
$secret_word = 'if i ate spinach';
if (validate($_POST['username'],$_POST['password'])) {
    setcookie('login',
              $_POST['username'].','.md5($_POST['username'].$secret_word));
}
```

Discussion

When using cookie authentication, you have to display your own login form, such as the form in Example 8-6.

Example 8-6. Sample cookie authentication login form

```
<form method="POST" action="login.php">
Username: <input type="text" name="username"> <br>
Password: <input type="password" name="password"> <br>
<input type="submit" value="Log In">
</form>
```

You can use the same `validate()` function from Example 8-1 to verify the username and password. The only difference is that you pass it `$_POST['username']` and `$_POST['password']` as the credentials instead of `$_SERVER['PHP_AUTH_USER']` and `$_SERVER['PHP_AUTH_PW']`. If the password checks out, send back a cookie that contains a username and a hash of the username, and a secret word. The hash prevents a user from faking a login just by sending a cookie with a username in it.

Once the user has logged in, a page just needs to verify that a valid login cookie was sent in order to do special things for that logged-in user. Example 8-7 shows one way to do this.

Example 8-7. Verifying a login cookie

```
unset($username);
if (isset($_COOKIE['login'])) {
    list($c_username, $cookie_hash) = split(',', $_COOKIE['login']);
    if (md5($c_username.$secret_word) == $cookie_hash) {
        $username = $c_username;
    } else {
        print "You have sent a bad cookie.";
    }
}

if (isset($username)) {
```

```
      print "Welcome, $username.";
} else {
      print "Welcome, anonymous user.";
}
```

If you use the built-in session support, you can add the username and hash to the session and avoid sending a separate cookie. When someone logs in, set an additional variable in the session instead of sending a cookie, as shown in Example 8-8.

Example 8-8. Storing login info in a session

```
if (validate($_POST['username'],$_POST['password'])) {
    $_SESSION['login'] =
        $_POST['username'].','.md5($_POST['username'].$secret_word);
}
```

The verification code, shown in Example 8-9, is almost the same; it just uses $_SES SION instead of $_COOKIE.

Example 8-9. Verifying session info

```
unset($username);
if (isset($_SESSION['login'])) {
    list($c_username,$cookie_hash) = explode(',',$_SESSION['login']);
    if (md5($c_username.$secret_word) == $cookie_hash) {
        $username = $c_username;
    } else {
        print "You have tampered with your session.";
    }
}
```

Using cookie or session authentication instead of HTTP Basic authentication makes it much easier for users to log out: you just delete their login cookie or remove the login variable from their session. Another advantage of storing authentication information in a session is that you can link users' browsing activities while logged in to their browsing activities before they log in or after they log out. With HTTP Basic authentication, you have no way of tying the requests with a username to the requests that the same user made before they supplied a username. Looking for requests from the same IP address is error prone, especially if the user is behind a firewall or proxy server. If you are using sessions, you can modify the login procedure to log the connection between session ID and username using code such as that in Example 8-10.

Example 8-10. Connecting logged-out and logged-in usage

```
if (validate($_POST['username'], $_POST['password'])) {
    $_SESSION['login'] =
        $_POST['username'].','.md5($_POST['username'].$secret_word);
    error_log('Session id '.session_id().' log in as '.$_POST['username']);
}
```

Example 8-10 writes a message to the error log, but it could just as easily record the information in a database that you could use in your analysis of site usage and traffic.

One danger of using session IDs is that sessions are hijackable. If Alice guesses Bob's session ID, she can masquerade as Bob to the web server. The session module has two optional configuration directives that help you make session IDs harder to guess. The `session.entropy_file` directive contains a path to a device or file that generates randomness, such as */dev/random* or */dev/urandom*. The `session.entropy_length` directive holds the number of bytes to be read from the entropy file when creating session IDs.

No matter how hard session IDs are to guess, they can also be stolen if they are sent in clear text between your server and a user's browser. HTTP Basic authentication also has this problem. Use SSL to guard against network sniffing, as described in Recipe 18.13.

See Also

Recipe 8.6; Recipe 20.9 discusses logging errors; Recipe 18.9 discusses verifying data with hashes; documentation on `setcookie()` (*http://www.php.net/setcookie*) and on `md5()` (*http://www.php.net/md5*).

8.8 Reading an HTTP Header

Problem

You want to read an HTTP request header.

Solution

For a single header, look in the $_SERVER superglobal array:

```
// User-Agent Header
echo $_SERVER['HTTP_USER_AGENT'];
```

For all headers, call `getallheaders()`:

```
$headers = getallheaders();
echo $headers['User-Agent'];
```

Discussion

HTTP headers allow the browser (or any application) to pass supplementary information about the request. For example, `Content-Type` to describe the body (Did you send a web form or JSON?), `Accept-Language` for a list of preferred languages (Do you want that in Canadian English or Canadian French?), and `User-Agent` (What's the name and description of the browser?).

Sometimes your web server will automatically process these headers and act accordingly, particularly when it comes to low-level details about the request, such as serving data from a cache or (de-)compressing the data. Other times PHP will parse specific headers, as in Recipes 8.2 and 8.6.

But there are times when you want to read a specific header within your code. One example is parsing the ETag header to see if the version the client has is the same as the one that'd be sent back.

In these cases, reference the $_SERVER superglobal array. PHP namespaces HTTP request headers by prefixing HTTP_ before the header name. It also uppercases all header names to make them easy to find. (This is legal because header names are case-insensitive.)

So, the ETag header, if sent, will be at $_SERVER['HTTP_ETAG']. If the field munging is aesthetically displeasing, you can also find it at getallheaders()['Etag'].

See Also

Recipe 8.9 for writing HTTP headers.

8.9 Writing an HTTP Header

Problem

You want to write an HTTP header.

Solution

Call the header() function:

```
// Tell 'em its a PNG
header('Content-Type: image/png');
```

Discussion

Your web server and PHP often take care of setting all the necessary headers with the proper values to serve your script. For example, when you return an HTML page, the Content-Length or Transfer-Encoding header is automatically set to let the browser know how to determine the size of the response.

The header() function lets you explicitly set these values when there's no way for the server to compute them or you want to modify the default behavior.

For instance, many web servers are configured to send a `Content-Type` header of `text/html` for all pages processed by PHP. To also use PHP to create a JSON file, one option is changing the `Content-Type` from within your script itself:

```
header('Content-Type: application/json');
```

If you set the same header multiple times, only the final value is sent. Change this by passing `true` as the second value to the function:

```
header('WWW-Authenticate: Basic realm="http://server.example.com/"');
header('WWW-Authenticate: OAuth realm="http://server.example.com/"', true);
```

When you support multiple ways for someone to authenticate himself, it's okay to return multiple `WWW-Authenticate` headers. In this case, someone can either use HTTP Basic authentication or OAuth.

See Also

Documentation on `header()` (*http://www.php.net/header*); Recipe 8.8 for reading HTTP headers.

8.10 Sending a Specific HTTP Status Code

Problem

You want to explicitly set the HTTP status code. For example, you want to indicate that the user is unauthorized to view the page or the page is not found.

Solution

Use `http_response_code()` to set the response:

```
http_response_code(401);
```

Discussion

Your web server returns HTTP status code 200 (OK) for most pages processed by PHP. But there are a wide range of status codes, or response codes, that you may need to use.

A few popular codes get recipes of their own. When you're redirecting to a different page, you need to send a 302 (Found) status code. This is covered in Recipe 8.11. When a person is not allowed to view a page, you send a 401 (Unauthorized). See Recipe 8.6 and Recipe 8.7 for more on that topic.

But there's always 304 (Not Modified) for conditional GETs, when you should only return content if it's changed since the last request. This can be used when someone is polling your site and you want to tell them there's nothing new to retrieve.

Or, the infamous 404 (Not Found), when a page isn't there. Normally, this is handled by your web server. But if you want to support dynamic URLs, where there aren't any physical files stored on disk, but you process the URL and respond to it based on information in a database, then you need to handle this yourself when someone tries to fetch an invalid URL.

One great example is WordPress, which responds to URLs based on categories or dates (e.g., `/category/php/` or `/2014/11/03/`). In these cases, whenever someone adds a category or a post on a new date, WordPress can be configured to automatically respond to requests at URLs that match that pattern, even though there aren't actually files at that location.

With `http_response_code()`, you provide the status code number and PHP takes care of setting the proper `Status` Line. For some status codes, including 204 (No Content), the HTTP specification states you must not provide a message body. In these cases, it's best to send `exit()` to immediately end the script. This prevents content from being accidentally added later on:

```
http_response_code(204);
exit();
```

If you're stuck on PHP 5.3, use `header()`, and pass in the status code as the third parameter:

```
header('HTTP/1.0 204 No Content', true, 204);
```

See Also

The HTTP 1.1 specification's description of status codes (*http://www.w3.org/Protocols/ rfc2616/rfc2616-sec10.html*).

8.11 Redirecting to a Different Location

Problem

You want to automatically send a user to a new URL. For example, after successfully saving form data, you want to redirect a user to a page that confirms that the data has been saved.

Solution

Before any output is printed, use `header()` to send a `Location` header with the new URL, and then call `exit()` so that nothing else is printed:

```
header('Location: http://www.example.com/confirm.html');
exit();
```

Discussion

To pass variables to the new page, include them in the query string of the URL, as in Example 8-11.

Example 8-11. Redirecting with query string variables

```
header('Location: http://www.example.com/?monkey=turtle');
exit();
```

Redirect URLs must include the protocol and hostname. They cannot be just a pathname. Example 8-12 shows a good `Location` header and a bad one.

Example 8-12. Good and bad Location headers

```
// Good Redirect
header('Location: http://www.example.com/catalog/food/pemmican.php');

// Bad Redirect
header('Location: /catalog/food/pemmican.php');
```

The URL that you are redirecting a user to is retrieved with `GET`. You can't redirect someone to retrieve a URL via `POST`. With JavaScript, however, you can simulate a redirect via `POST` by generating a form that gets submitted (via `POST`) automatically. When a (JavaScript-enabled) browser receives the page in Example 8-13, it will immediately `POST` the form that is included.

Example 8-13. Redirecting via a posted form

```
<html>
  <body onload="document.getElementById('redirectForm').submit()">
    <form id='redirectForm' method='POST' action='/done.html'>
      <input type='hidden' name='status' value='complete'/>
      <input type='hidden' name='id' value='0u812'/>
      <input type='submit' value='Please Click Here To Continue'/>
    </form>
  </body>
</html>
```

The form in Example 8-13 has an `id` of `redirectForm`, so the code in the `<body/>` element's `onload` attribute submits the form. The `onload` action does not execute if the browser has JavaScript disabled. In that situation, the user sees a *Please Click Here To Continue* button.

See Also

Documentation on `header()` (*http://www.php.net/header*).

8.12 Flushing Output to the Browser

Problem

You want to force output to be sent to the browser. For example, before doing a slow database query, you want to give the user a status update.

Solution

Use `flush()`:

```
print 'Finding identical snowflakes...';
flush();
$sth = $dbh->query(
    'SELECT shape,COUNT(*) AS c FROM snowflakes GROUP BY shape HAVING c > 1');
```

Discussion

The `flush()` function sends all output that PHP has internally buffered to the web server, but the web server may have internal buffering of its own that delays when the data reaches the browser. Additionally, some browsers don't display data immediately upon receiving it, and some versions of Internet Explorer don't display a page until it has received at least 256 bytes. To force IE to display content, print blank spaces at the beginning of the page, as shown in Example 8-14.

Example 8-14. Forcing IE to display content immediately

```
print str_repeat(' ',300);
print 'Finding identical snowflakes...';
flush();
$sth = $dbh->query(
    'SELECT shape,COUNT(*) AS c FROM snowflakes GROUP BY shape HAVING c > 1');
```

See Also

Recipe 24.13; documentation on `flush()` (*http://www.php.net/flush*).

8.13 Buffering Output to the Browser

Problem

You want to start generating output before you're finished sending headers or cookies.

Solution

Call ob_start() at the top of your page and ob_end_flush() at the bottom. You can then intermix commands that generate output and commands that send headers. The output won't be sent until ob_end_flush() is called:

```php
<?php ob_start(); ?>

I haven't decided if I want to send a cookie yet.

<?php setcookie('heron','great blue'); ?>

Yes, sending that cookie was the right decision.

<?php
ob_end_flush();
```

Discussion

You can pass ob_start() the name of a callback function to process the output buffer with that function. This is useful for postprocessing all the content in a page, such as hiding email addresses from address-harvesting robots. For example:

```php
<?php
function mangle_email($s) {
    return preg_replace('/([^@\s]+)@([-a-z0-9]+\.)+[a-z]{2,}/is',
                        '<$1@...>',
                        $s);
}

ob_start('mangle_email');
?>

I would not like spam sent to ronald@example.com!

<?php
ob_end_flush();
```

The mangle_email() function transforms the output to:

I would not like spam sent to <ronald@...>!

The output_buffering configuration directive turns output buffering on for all pages:

```
output_buffering = On
```

Similarly, output_handler sets an output buffer processing callback to be used on all pages:

```
output_handler=mangle_email
```

Setting an output_handler automatically sets output_buffering to on.

See Also

Documentation on `ob_start()` (*http://www.php.net/ob-start*), `ob_end_flush()` (*http://www.php.net/ob-end-flush*), and output buffering (*http://www.php.net/outcontrol*).

8.14 Compressing Web Output

Problem

You want to send compressed content to browsers that support automatic decompression.

Solution

Add this setting to your *php.ini* file:

```
zlib.output_compression=1
```

Discussion

Browsers tell the server that they can accept compressed responses with the `Accept-Encoding` header. If a browser sends `Accept-Encoding: gzip` or `Accept-Encoding: deflate`, and PHP is built with the *zlib* extension, the `zlib.output_compression` configuration directive tells PHP to compress the output with the appropriate algorithm before sending it back to the browser. The browser uncompresses the data before displaying it.

You can adjust the compression level with the `zlib.output_compression_level` configuration directive:

```
; minimal compression
zlib.output_compression_level=1

; maximal compression
zlib.output_compression_level=9
```

At higher compression levels, less data needs to be sent from the server to the browser, but more server CPU time must be used to compress the data.

See Also

Documentation on the *zlib* extension (*http://www.php.net/zlib*).

8.15 Reading Environment Variables

Problem

You want to get the value of an environment variable.

Solution

Use `getenv()`:

```
$path = getenv('PATH');
```

Discussion

Environment variables are named values associated with a process. For instance, in Unix, the value of `getenv('HOME')` returns the home directory of a user:

```
print getenv('HOME'); // user's home directory
```

PHP automatically loads environment variables into $_ENV by default. However, *php.ini-development* and *php.ini-production* disables this because of speed considerations.

If you frequently access many environment variables, enable the $_ENV array by adding E to the `variables_order` configuration directive. Then you can read values from the $_ENV superglobal array. For instance:

```
$name = $_ENV['USER'];
```

The `getenv()` function isn't available if you're running PHP as an ISAPI module.

See Also

Recipe 8.16 on setting environment variables; documentation on `getenv()` (*http://www.php.net/getenv*); information on environment variables in PHP (*http://bit.ly/1uAGMA9*).

8.16 Setting Environment Variables

Problem

You want to set an environment variable in a script or in your server configuration. Setting environment variables in your server configuration on a host-by-host basis allows you to configure virtual hosts differently.

Solution

To set an environment variable in a script, use `putenv()`:

```
putenv('ORACLE_SID=ORACLE'); // configure oci extension
```

To set an environment variable in your Apache *httpd.conf* file, use SetEnv:

```
SetEnv DATABASE_PASSWORD password
```

Variables set in *httpd.conf* show up in the PHP superglobal array $_SERVER, not via
getenv( ) or $_ENV.

Discussion

An advantage of setting variables in *httpd.conf* is that you can set more restrictive read
permissions on it than on your PHP scripts. Because PHP files need to be readable by
the web server process, this generally allows other users on the system to view them. By
storing passwords in *httpd.conf*, you can avoid placing a password in a publicly available
file. Also, if you have multiple hostnames that map to the same document root, you can
configure your scripts to behave differently based on the hostnames.

For example, you could have *members.example.com* and *guests.example.com*. The members version requires authentication and allows users additional access. The guests version provides a restricted set of options, but without authentication. Example 8-15
shows how this could work.

Example 8-15. Adjusting behavior based on an environment variable

```
$version = (isset($_SERVER['SITE_VERSION']) ? $_SERVER['SITE_VERSION'] : 'guest');

// redirect to http://guest.example.com, if user fails to sign in correctly
if ('members' == $version) {
    if (!authenticate_user($_POST['username'], $_POST['password'])) {
        header('Location: http://guest.example.com/');
        exit;
    }
}
include_once "${version}_header"; // load custom header
```

See Also

Recipe 8.15 on getting the values of environment variables; documentation on pu
tenv() (*http://www.php.net/putenv*); information on setting environment variables in
Apache (*http://bit.ly/1hxl5Ii*).

8.17 Communicating Within Apache

Problem

You want to communicate from PHP to other parts of the Apache request process. This
includes setting variables in the *access_log*.

Solution

Use `apache_note()`:

```
// get value
$session = apache_note('session');

// set value
apache_note('session', $session);
```

Discussion

When Apache processes a request from a client, it goes through a series of steps; PHP plays only one part in the entire chain. Apache also remaps URLs, authenticates users, logs requests, and more. While processing a request, each handler has access to a set of key/value pairs called the notes table. The `apache_note()` function provides access to the notes table to retrieve information set by handlers earlier on in the process and leave information for handlers later on.

For example, if you use the session module to track users and preserve variables across requests, you can integrate this with your logfile analysis so you can determine the average number of page views per user. Use `apache_note()` in combination with the logging module to write the session ID directly to the *access_log* for each request. First, add the session ID to the notes table with the code in Example 8-16.

Example 8-16. Adding the session ID to the notes table

```
// retrieve the session ID and add it to Apache's notes table
apache_note('session_id', session_id());
```

See Also

Documentation on `apache_note()` (*http://www.php.net/apache-note*); information on logging in Apache (*http://bit.ly/1notFxM*).

8.18 Redirecting Mobile Browsers to a Mobile Optimized Site

Problem

You want to send mobile or tablet browsers to an alternative site or alternative content that is optimized for their device.

Solution

Use the object returned by `get_browser()` to determine if it's a mobile browser:

```
if ($browser->ismobilebrowser) {
    // print mobile layout
} else {
    // print desktop layout
}
```

Discussion

The get_browser() function examines the environment variable (set by the web server) and compares it to browsers listed in an external browser capability file. Due to licensing issues, PHP isn't distributed with a browser capability file. One source for a browser capability file is Browscap (*http://browscap.org/*). Download the *php_browscap.ini* file from that site (not the standard version).

Once you download a browser capability file, you need to tell PHP where to find it by setting the browscap configuration directive to the pathname of the file. If you use PHP as a CGI, set the directive in the *php.ini* file:

```
browscap=/usr/local/lib/php_browscap.ini
```

After you identify the device as mobile, you can then redirect the request to a specific mobile optimized site or render a mobile optimized page:

```
header('Location: http://m.example.com/');
```

As a lighter-weight alternative to get_browser(), parse the $_SERV ER['HTTP_USER_AGENT'] yourself.

See Also

Documentation on get_browser() (*http://www.php.net/get-browser*). Read about redirecting requests in Recipe 8.11 and reading HTTP headers in Recipe 8.8.

8.19 Program: Website Account (De)activator

When users sign up for your website, it's helpful to know that they've provided you with a correct email address. To validate the email address they provide, send an email to the address they supply when they sign up. If they don't visit a special URL included in the email after a few days, deactivate their account.

This system has three parts. The first is the *notify-user.php* program that sends an email to a new user and asks that user to visit a verification URL, shown in Example 8-18. The second, shown in Example 8-19, is the *verify-user.php* page that handles the verification URL and marks users as valid. The third is the *delete-user.php* program that deactivates accounts of users who don't visit the verification URL after a certain amount of time. This program is shown in Example 8-20.

Example 8-17 contains the SQL to create the table in which the user information is stored.

Example 8-17. SQL for user verification table

```
CREATE TABLE users (
 email VARCHAR(255) NOT NULL,
 created_on DATETIME NOT NULL,
 verify_string VARCHAR(16) NOT NULL,
 verified TINYINT UNSIGNED
);
```

What's in Example 8-17 is the minimum amount of information necessary for user verification. You probably want to store more information than this about your users. When creating a user's account, save information to the users table, and send the user an email telling him how to verify his account. The code in Example 8-18 assumes that the user's email address is stored in the variable $email.

Example 8-18. notify-user.php

```
// Connect to the database
$db = new PDO('sqlite:users.db');

$email = 'david';

// Generate verify_string
$verify_string = '';
for ($i = 0; $i < 16; $i++) {
    $verify_string .= chr(mt_rand(32,126));
}

// Insert user into database
// This uses an SQLite-specific datetime() function
$sth = $db->prepare("INSERT INTO users " .
                    "(email, created_on, verify_string, verified) " .
                    "VALUES (?, datetime('now'), ?, 0)");
$sth->execute(array($email, $verify_string));

$verify_string = urlencode($verify_string);
$safe_email = urlencode($email);

$verify_url = "http://www.example.com/verify-user.php";

$mail_body=<<<_MAIL_
To $email:

Please click on the following link to verify your account creation:

$verify_url?email=$safe_email&verify_string=$verify_string

If you do not verify your account in the next seven days, it will be
deleted.
```

```
_MAIL_;

mail($email,"User Verification",$mail_body);
```

The verification page that users are directed to when they follow the link in the email message updates the users table if the proper information has been provided, as shown in Example 8-19.

Example 8-19. verify-user.php

```
// Connect to the database
$db = new PDO('sqlite:users.db');

$sth = $db->prepare('UPDATE users SET verified = 1 WHERE email = ? '.
                    ' AND verify_string = ? AND verified = 0');

$res = $sth->execute(array($_GET['email'], $_GET['verify_string']));
var_dump($res, $sth->rowCount());
if (! $res) {
    print "Please try again later due to a database error.";
} else {
    if ($sth->rowCount() == 1) {
        print "Thank you, your account is verified.";
    } else {
        print "Sorry, you could not be verified.";
    }
}
```

The user's verification status is updated only if the email address and verify string provided match a row in the database that has not already been verified. The last step is the short program that deletes unverified users after the appropriate interval, as shown in Example 8-20.

Example 8-20. delete-user.php

```
// Connect to the database
$db = new PDO('sqlite:users.db');

$window = '-7 days';

$sth = $db->prepare("DELETE FROM users WHERE verified = 0 AND ".
                    "created_on < datetime('now',?)");
$res = $sth->execute(array($window));

if ($res) {
    print "Deactivated " . $sth->rowCount() . " users.\n";
} else {
    print "Can't delete users.\n";
}
```

Run the program in Example 8-20 once a day to scrub the users table of users that haven't been verified. If you want to change how long users have to verify themselves, adjust the value of $window, and update the text of the email message sent to users to reflect the new value.

8.20 Program: Tiny Wiki

The program in Example 8-21 puts together various concepts discussed in this chapter and implements a complete wiki system—a website whose pages are all user-editable. It follows a structure common among simple PHP programs of its type. The first part of the code defines various configuration settings. Then comes an if/else section that decides what to do (display a page, save page edits, etc.) based on the values of submitted form or URL variables. The remainder of the program consists of the functions invoked from that if/else section—functions to print the page header and footer, load saved page contents, and display a page-editing form.

The Tiny Wiki relies on an external library, PHP Markdown (*http://bit.ly/1irTpE9*) by Michel Fortin, to handle translating from the handy and compact Markdown syntax to HTML.

Example 8-21. Tiny Wiki

```php
<?php
// Install PSR-0-compatible class autoloader
spl_autoload_register(function($class){
    require preg_replace('{\\\\|_(?!.*\\\\)}', DIRECTORY_SEPARATOR,
        trim($class, '\\')).'.php';
});

// Use Markdown for Wiki-like text markup
// Located at http://michelf.ca/projects/php-markdown/
use \Michelf\Markdown;

// The directory where the Wiki pages will be stored
// Make sure the web server user can write to it
define('PAGEDIR', dirname(__FILE__) . '/pages');

// Get page name, or use default
$page = isset($_GET['page']) ? $_GET['page'] : 'Home';

// Figure out what to do: display an edit form, save an
// edit form, or display a page

// Display an edit form that's been asked for
if (isset($_GET['edit'])) {
    pageHeader($page);
    edit($page);
    pageFooter($page, false);
}
```

```php
    // Save a submitted edit form
    else if (isset($_POST['edit'])) {
        file_put_contents(pageToFile($_POST['page']), $_POST['contents']);
        // Redirect to the regular view of the just-edited page
        header('Location: http://'.$_SERVER['HTTP_HOST'] . $_SERVER['SCRIPT_NAME'] .
            '?page='.urlencode($_POST['page']));
        exit();
    }
    // Display a page
    else {
        pageHeader($page);
        // If the page exists, display it and the footer with an "Edit" link
        if (is_readable(pageToFile($page))) {
            // Get the contents of the page from the file it's saved in
            $text = file_get_contents(pageToFile($page));
            // Convert Markdown syntax (using Markdown library loaded above)
            $text = Markdown::defaultTransform($text);
            // Make bare [links] link to other wiki pages
            $text = wikiLinks($text);
            // Display the page
            echo $text;
            // Display the footer
            pageFooter($page, true);
        }
        // If the page doesn't exist, display an edit form
        // and the footer without an "Edit" link
        else {
            edit($page, true);
            pageFooter($page, false);
        }
    }

// The page header -- pretty simple, just the title and the usual HTML
// pleasantries
function pageheader($page) { ?>
<html>
<head>
<title>Wiki: <?php echo htmlentities($page) ?></title>
</head>
<body>
<h1><?php echo htmlentities($page) ?></h1>
<hr/>
<?php
}

// The page footer -- a "last modified" timestamp, an optional
// "Edit" link, and a link back to the front page of the Wiki
function pageFooter($page, $displayEditLink) {
    $timestamp = @filemtime(pageToFile($page));
    if ($timestamp) {
        $lastModified = strftime('%c', $timestamp);
    } else {
```

```php
        $lastModified = 'Never';
    }

    if ($displayEditLink) {
        $editLink = ' - <a href="?page='.urlencode($page).'&edit=true">Edit</a>';
    } else {
        $editLink = '';
    }
?>
<hr/>
<em>Last Modified: <?php echo $lastModified ?></em>
<?php echo $editLink ?> - <a href="<?php echo $_SERVER['SCRIPT_NAME'] ?>">Home</a>
</body>
</html>
<?php
}


// Display an edit form. If the page already exists, include its current
// contents in the form
function edit($page, $isNew = false) {
    if ($isNew) {
        $contents = '';
?>
<p><b>This page doesn't exist yet.</b> To create it, enter its contents below
and click the <b>Save</b> button.</p>
    <?php } else {
        $contents = file_get_contents(pageToFile($page));
    }
?>
<form method='post' action='<?php echo htmlentities($_SERVER['SCRIPT_NAME']) ?>'>
<input type='hidden' name='edit' value='true'/>
<input type='hidden' name='page' value='<?php echo htmlentities($page) ?>'/>
<textarea name='contents' rows='20' cols='60'>
<?php echo htmlentities($contents) ?></textarea>
<br/>
<input type='submit' value='Save'/>
</form>
<?php
}


// Convert a submitted page to a filename. Using md5() prevents naughty
// characters in $page from causing security problems
function pageToFile($page) {
    return PAGEDIR.'/'.md5($page);
}


// Turn text such as [something] in a page into an HTML link to the
// Wiki page "something"
function wikiLinks($page) {
    if (preg_match_all('/\[([^\]]+?)\]/', $page, $matches, PREG_SET_ORDER)) {
        foreach ($matches as $match) {
            $page = str_replace($match[0], '<a href="'.$_SERVER['SCRIPT_NAME'].
'?page='.urlencode($match[1]).'">'.htmlentities($match[1]).'</a>', $page);
```

```
        }
    }
    return $page;
}
```

See Also

Information on installing and using packages, including information on PSR-0, at Recipe 27.3.

8.21 Program: HTTP Range

The program in Example 8-22 implements the HTTP Range feature, which allows clients to request one or more sections of a file. This is most frequently used to download the remaining portion of a file that was interrupted. For example, only fetching the remaining part of a movie that the viewer stopped watching.

Normally, your web server can handle this for you. It will parse the header, load in the selected portions of the file, and serve them back to the browser (along with the necessary HTTP).

However, if you sell multimedia, such as podcasts or music, you don't want to expose those files directly. Otherwise, anyone who got the URL could download the files. Instead, you want to make sure only people who purchased the file are able to read it. And, for that, you can't use the web server by itself, but need PHP.

Recipe 17.11 shows how to restrict a file from direct access. But that recipe only works for sending an entire file. This program expands upon that simpler example to enable sending only the sections of the file requested by the web browser.

At first glance, this doesn't sound difficult. However, the HTTP 1.1 specification has a number of features that layer on complexity, such as multiple ranges (with a different syntax for these replies), offsets from the end of the file (e.g., "only the last 1000 bytes"), and specific status codes and headers for invalid requests.

Beyond showing how to translate a specification into code, this program demonstrates how to read and send HTTP status codes and headers. It also integrates a number of other recipes, including Recipe 1.6.

Example 8-22. HTTP Range

```
// Add your authenication here, optionally.

// The file
$file = __DIR__ . '/numbers.txt';
$content_type = 'text/plain';

// Check that it's readable and get the file size
if (($filelength = filesize($file)) === false) {
```

```php
        error_log("Problem reading filesize of $file.");
}

// Parse header to determine info needed to send response
if (isset($_SERVER['HTTP_RANGE'])) {
    // Delimiters are case insensitive
    if (!preg_match('/bytes=\d*-\d*(,\d*-\d*)*$/i', $_SERVER['HTTP_RANGE'])) {
        error_log("Client requested invalid Range.");
        send_error($filelength);
        exit;
    }

    /*
    Spec: "When a client requests multiple byte-ranges in one request, the
    server SHOULD return them in the order that they appeared in the
    request."
    */
    $ranges = explode(',',
        substr($_SERVER['HTTP_RANGE'], 6)); // everything after bytes=
    $offsets = array();
    // Extract and validate each offset
    // Only keep the ones that pass
    foreach ($ranges as $range) {
        $offset = parse_offset($range, $filelength);
        if ($offset !== false) {
            $offsets[] = $offset;
        }
    }

    /*
    Depending on the number of valid ranges requested, you must return
    the response in a different format
    */
    switch (count($offsets)) {
    case 0:
        // No valid ranges
        error_log("Client requested no valid ranges.");
        send_error($filelength);
        exit;
        break;
    case 1:
        // One valid range, send standard reply
        http_response_code(206); // Partial Content
        list($start, $end) = $offsets[0];
        header("Content-Range: bytes $start-$end/$filelength");
        header("Content-Type: $content_type");

        // Set variables to allow code reuse across this case and the next one
        // Note: 0-0 is 1 byte long, because we're inclusive
        $content_length = $end - $start + 1;
        $boundaries = array(0 => '', 1 => '');
        break;
```

```php
        default:
            // Multiple valid ranges, send multipart reply
            http_response_code(206);  // Partial Content
            $boundary = str_rand(32); // String to separate each part

            /*
            Need to compute Content-Length of entire response,
            but loading the entire response into a string could use a lot of memory,
            so calculate value using the offsets.
            Take this opportunity to also calculate the boundaries.
            */
            $boundaries = array();
            $content_length = 0;


            foreach ($offsets as $offset) {
                list($start, $end) = $offset;

                    // Used to split each section
                $boundary_header =
                    "\r\n" .
                    "--$boundary\r\n" .
                    "Content-Type: $content_type\r\n" .
                    "Content-Range: bytes $start-$end/$filelength\r\n" .
                    "\r\n";

                $content_length += strlen($boundary_header) + ($end - $start + 1);
                $boundaries[] = $boundary_header;
            }

            // Add the closing boundary
            $boundary_header = "\r\n--$boundary--";
            $content_length += strlen($boundary_header);
            $boundaries[] = $boundary_header;

            // Chop off extra \r\n in first boundary
            $boundaries[0] = substr($boundaries[0], 2);
            $content_length -= 2;

            // Change to the special multipart Content-Type
            $content_type = "multipart/byteranges; boundary=$boundary";
    }
} else {
    // Send the entire file
    // Set variables as if this was extracted from Range header
    $start = 0;
    $end = $filelength - 1;
    $offset = array($start, $end);
    $offsets = array($offset);

    $content_length = $filelength;
```

```php
    $boundaries = array(0 => '', 1 => '');
}

// Tell us what we're getting
header("Content-Type: $content_type");
header("Content-Length: $content_length");

// Give it to us
$handle = fopen($file, 'r');
if ($handle) {
    $offsets_count = count($offsets);
// Print each boundary delimiter and the appropriate part of the file
    for ($i = 0; $i < $offsets_count; $i++) {
        print $boundaries[$i];
        list($start, $end) = $offsets[$i];
        send_range($handle, $start, $end);
    }
    // Closing boundary
    print $boundaries[$i];

    fclose($handle);
}

// Move the proper place in the file
// And print out the requested piece in chunks
function send_range($handle, $start, $end) {
    $line_length = 4096; // magic number

    if (fseek($handle, $start) === -1) {
        error_log("Error: fseek() fail.");
    }

    $left_to_read = $end - $start + 1;
    do {
        $length = min($line_length, $left_to_read);
        if (($buffer = fread($handle, $length)) !== false) {
            print $buffer;
        } else {
            error_log("Error: fread() fail.");
        }
    } while ($left_to_read -= $length);
}

// Send the failure header
function send_error($filelength) {
    http_response_code(416);
    header("Content-Range: bytes */$filelength"); // Required in 416.
}

// Convert an offset to the start and end locations in the file
// Or return false if it's invalid
function parse_offset($range, $filelength) {
```

```
    /*
    Spec: "The first-byte-pos value in a byte-range-spec gives the
    byte-offset of the first byte in a range."
    Spec: "The last-byte-pos value gives the byte-offset of the last byte in the
    range; that is, the byte positions specified are inclusive."
    */
    list($start, $end) = explode('-', $range);

    /*
    Spec: "A suffix-byte-range-spec is used to specify the suffix of the
    entity-body, of a length given by the suffix-length value."
    */
    if ($start === '') {
        if ($end === '' || $end === 0) {
            // Asked for range of "-" or "-0"
            return false;
        } else {
            /*
            Spec: "If the entity is shorter than the specified suffix-length,
            the entire entity-body is used."
            Spec: "Byte offsets start at zero."
            */
            $start = max(0, $filelength - $end);
            $end = $filelength - 1;
        }
    } else {
        /*
        Spec: "If the last-byte-pos value is absent, or if the value is greater
        than or equal to the current length of the entity-body, last-byte-pos
        is taken to be equal to one less than the current length of the entity
        body in bytes."
        */
        if ($end === '' || $end > $filelength - 1) {
            $end = $filelength - 1;
        }

        /*
        Spec: "If the last-byte-pos value is present, it MUST be greater than
        or equal to the first-byte-pos in that byte-range-spec, or the
        byte-range-spec is syntactically invalid."
        This also catches cases where start > filelength
        */
        if ($start > $end) {
            return false;
        }
    }

    return array($start, $end);
}

// Generate a random string to delimit sections within the response
function str_rand($length = 32,
```

```
$characters = '0123456789abcdefghijklmnopqrstuvwxyzABCDEFGHIJKLMNOPQRSTUVWXYZ') {
    if (!is_int($length) || $length < 0) {
        return false;
    }

    $characters_length = strlen($characters) - 1;
    $string = '';

    for ($i = $length; $i > 0; $i--) {
        $string .= $characters[mt_rand(0, $characters_length)];
    }

    return $string;
}
```

For simplicity, the demonstration file, *numbers.txt*, looks like:

```
01234567890123456789
```

Here's how it behaves, making requests from the command-line `curl` program to the built-in PHP webserver. This dumps a verbose version of the HTTP exchange.

The entire file, without any `Range` header:

```
$ curl -v http://localhost:8000/range.php
* About to connect() to localhost port 8000 (#0)
*   Trying ::1...
* connected
* Connected to localhost (::1) port 8000 (#0)
> GET /range.php HTTP/1.1
> User-Agent: curl/7.24.0
> Host: localhost:8000
> Accept: */*
>
[Sun Aug 18 14:33:36 2013] ::1:59812 [200]: /range.php
< HTTP/1.1 200 OK
< Host: localhost:8000
< Connection: close
< X-Powered-By: PHP/5.4.9
< Content-Type: text/plain
< Content-Length: 10
<
* Closing connection #0
0123456789
```

Only the first 5 bytes:

```
$ curl -v -H 'Range: bytes=0-4' http://localhost:8000/range.php
* About to connect() to localhost port 8000 (#0)
*   Trying ::1...
* connected
* Connected to localhost (::1) port 8000 (#0)
> GET /range.php HTTP/1.1
> User-Agent: curl/7.24.0
```

```
> Host: localhost:8000
> Accept: */*
> Range: bytes=0-4
>
[Sun Aug 18 14:30:52 2013] ::1:59798 [206]: /range.php
< HTTP/1.1 206 Partial Content
< Host: localhost:8000
< Connection: close
< X-Powered-By: PHP/5.4.9
< Content-Range: bytes 0-4/10
< Content-Type: text/plain
< Content-Length: 5
<
* Closing connection #0
01234
```

See how the status code is now 206 instead of 200, and there is a `Content-Range` HTTP header telling you what bytes were returned.

Or the last 5 bytes:

```
$ curl -v -H 'Range: bytes=-5' http://localhost:8000/range.php
* About to connect() to localhost port 8000 (#0)
*    Trying ::1...
* connected
* Connected to localhost (::1) port 8000 (#0)
> GET /range.php HTTP/1.1
> User-Agent: curl/7.24.0
> Host: localhost:8000
> Accept: */*
> Range: bytes=-5
>
[Sun Aug 18 14:30:33 2013] ::1:59796 [206]: /range.php
< HTTP/1.1 206 Partial Content
< Host: localhost:8000
< Connection: close
< X-Powered-By: PHP/5.4.9
< Content-Range: bytes 5-9/10
< Content-Type: text/plain
< Content-Length: 5
<
* Closing connection #0
56789
```

The first 5 and the last 5 bytes:

```
$ curl -v -H 'Range: bytes=0-4,-5' http://localhost:8000/range.php
* About to connect() to localhost port 8000 (#0)
*    Trying ::1...
* connected
* Connected to localhost (::1) port 8000 (#0)
> GET /range.php HTTP/1.1
> User-Agent: curl/7.24.0
```

```
> Host: localhost:8000
> Accept: */*
> Range: bytes=0-4,-5
>
[Sun Aug 18 14:30:12 2013] ::1:59794 [206]: /range.php
< HTTP/1.1 206 Partial Content
< Host: localhost:8000
< Connection: close
< X-Powered-By: PHP/5.4.9
< Content-Type: multipart/byteranges; boundary=ALLIeNOkvwgKk0ib91ZNph5qi8fHo2ai
< Content-Length: 236
<
--ALLIeNOkvwgKk0ib91ZNph5qi8fHo2ai
Content-Type: text/plain
Content-Range: bytes 0-4/10

01234
--ALLIeNOkvwgKk0ib91ZNph5qi8fHo2ai
Content-Type: text/plain
Content-Range: bytes 5-9/10

56789
* Closing connection #0
--ALLIeNOkvwgKk0ib91ZNph5qi8fHo2ai--
```

The Content-Type is switched from text/plain to multipart/byteranges; bound ary=ALLIeNOkvwgKk0ib91ZNph5qi8fHo2ai. The "real" Content headers have moved within each section.

Because this is the entire file, it's also valid to serve it up as if you requested this without any Range header.

An invalid request, because bytes 20–24 do not exist:

```
$ curl -v -H 'Range: bytes=20-24' http://localhost:8000/range.php
* About to connect() to localhost port 8000 (#0)
*   Trying ::1...
* connected
* Connected to localhost (::1) port 8000 (#0)
> GET /range.php HTTP/1.1
> User-Agent: curl/7.24.0
> Host: localhost:8000
> Accept: */*
> Range: bytes=20-24
>
[Sun Aug 18 14:32:17 2013] Client requested no valid ranges.
[Sun Aug 18 14:32:17 2013] ::1:59806 [416]: /range.php
< HTTP/1.1 416 Requested Range Not Satisfiable
< Host: localhost:8000
< Connection: close
< X-Powered-By: PHP/5.4.9
< Content-Range: bytes */10
```

```
< Content-type: text/html
<
* Closing connection #0
```

This returns a third status code, 416, along with a helpful header to let us know the legal set of values to request: Content-Range: bytes */10.

Finally, a legal and illegal value:

```
$ curl -v -H 'Range: bytes=0-4,20-24' http://localhost:8000/range.php
* About to connect() to localhost port 8000 (#0)
*   Trying ::1...
* connected
* Connected to localhost (::1) port 8000 (#0)
> GET /range.php HTTP/1.1
> User-Agent: curl/7.24.0
> Host: localhost:8000
> Accept: */*
> Range: bytes=0-4,20-24
>
[Sun Aug 18 14:31:27 2013] ::1:59801 [206]: /range.php
< HTTP/1.1 206 Partial Content
< Host: localhost:8000
< Connection: close
< X-Powered-By: PHP/5.4.9
< Content-Range: bytes 0-4/10
< Content-Type: text/plain
< Content-Length: 5
<
* Closing connection #0
01234
```

Because there's at least one valid range, the illegal ones are ignored and the response is the same as only asking for the first 5 bytes.

CHAPTER 9

Forms

9.0 Introduction

The genius of PHP is its seamless integration of form variables into your programs. It makes web programming smooth and simple, speeding the cycle from web form to PHP code to HTML output.

With that convenience, however, comes the responsibility to make sure that the user-provided information that flows so easily into your program contains appropriate content. External input can never be trusted, so it's imperative always to validate all incoming data. Recipes 9.2 through 9.9 show how to validate common kinds of information as well as providing general guidelines on arbitrary form validation you might need to do. Recipe 9.10 discusses escaping HTML entities to allow the safe display of user-entered data. Recipe 9.11 covers how to process files uploaded by a user.

HTTP is a 'stateless' protocol—it has no built-in mechanism that helps you to save information from one page so you can access it in other pages. Recipes 9.12, 9.13, and 9.14 all show ways to work around the fundamental problem of figuring out which user is making which requests to your web server.

Whenever PHP processes a page, it checks for URL and form variables, uploaded files, applicable cookies, and web server and environment variables. These are then directly accessible in the following arrays: $_GET, $_POST, $_FILES, $_COOKIE, $_SERVER, and $_ENV. They hold, respectively, all variables set in the query string, in the body of a post request, by uploaded files, by cookies, by the web server, and by the environment in which the web server is running. There's also $_REQUEST, which is one giant array that contains the values from the other six arrays.

When placing elements inside of $_REQUEST, if two arrays both have a key with the same name, PHP breaks the tie by relying on the variables_order configuration directive. By default, variables_order is EGPCS (or GPCS, if you're using the *php.ini-*

recommended configuration file). So PHP first adds environment variables to $_RE QUEST and then adds query string, post, cookie, and web server variables to the array, in this order. For instance, since C comes after P in the default order, a cookie named username overwrites a posted variable named username. Note that the GPCS value from *php.ini-recommended* means that the $_ENV array doesn't get populated with environment variables.

While $_REQUEST can be convenient, it's usually a better idea to look in the more detailed array directly. That way, you know exactly what you're getting and don't have to be concerned that a change in variables_order affects the behavior of your program.

All of these arrays are *auto-global*. That means global inside of a function or class—they're always in scope.

Versions of PHP prior to 5.4.0 had a configuration directive named register_glob als. If this was set to on, all these variables are also available as variables in the global namespace. So $_GET['password'] is also just $password. While convenient, this introduces major security problems because malicious users can easily set variables from the outside and overwrite trusted internal variables. If you're using an older version of PHP, make sure this is set to off in your configuration.

Example 9-1 is a basic form. The form asks the user to enter his first name. When the form is submitted the information is sent to *hello.php*.

Example 9-1. Basic HTML form

```
<form action="hello.php" method="post">
<p>What is your first name?</p>
<input type="text" name="first_name" />
<input type="submit" value="Say Hello" />
</form>
```

The name of the text input element inside the form is first_name. Also, the method of the form is post. This means that when the form is submitted, $_POST['first_name'] will hold whatever string the user typed in. (It could also be empty, of course, if he didn't type anything.)

Example 9-2 shows the contents of *hello.php*, which will display information from the form.

Example 9-2. Basic PHP form processing

```
echo 'Hello, ' . $_POST['first_name'] . '!';
```

If you type Twinkle into the form in Example 9-1, Example 9-2 prints:

```
Hello, Twinkle!
```

Example 9-2 is so basic that it omits two important steps that should be in all PHP form-processing applications: data validation (to make sure what's typed into the form is acceptable to your program), and output escaping (to make sure that malicious users can't use your website to attack others). Recipes Recipe 9.2 through Recipe 9.9 discuss data validation and Recipe 9.10 discusses output escaping.

9.1 Processing Form Input

Problem

You want to use the same HTML page to emit a form and then process the data entered into it. In other words, you're trying to avoid a proliferation of pages that each handle different steps in a transaction.

Solution

Use the $_SERVER['REQUEST_METHOD'] variable to determine whether the request was submitted with the get or post method. If the get method was used, print the form. If the post method was used, process the form. Example 9-3 combines the form from Example 9-1 and the code from Example 9-2 into one program, deciding what to do based on $_SERVER['REQUEST_METHOD'].

Example 9-3. Deciding what to do based on request method

```
<?php if ($_SERVER['REQUEST_METHOD'] == 'GET') { ?>
<form action="<?php echo htmlentities($_SERVER['SCRIPT_NAME']) ?>" method="post">
What is your first name?
<input type="text" name="first_name" />
<input type="submit" value="Say Hello" />
</form>
<?php } else {
    echo 'Hello, ' . $_POST['first_name'] . '!';
}
```

Discussion

Forms can be easier to maintain when all parts live in the same file (or are referenced by the same file) and context dictates which sections to display. The get method (what your browser uses when you just type in a URL or click on a link) means 'Hey, server, give me something you've got.' The post method (what your browser uses when you submit a form whose method attribute is set to post) means 'Hey, server, here's some data that changes something.' So the characteristic response to a get request is the HTML form, and the response to the post request is the results of processing that form. In Example 9-3, the 'processing' is extremely simple—just printing a greeting. In more typical applications, the processing is more complicated—saving information to a database or sending an email message.

Note that although the XHTML specification requires that the method attribute of a <form/> element be lowercase (get or post), the HTTP specification requires that a web browser use all uppercase (GET or POST) when sending the request method to the server. The value in $_SERVER['REQUEST_METHOD'] is whatever the browser sends, so in practice it will always be uppercase.

One other technique also makes pages easier to maintain: don't hardcode the path to your page directly into the form action. This makes it impossible to rename or relocate your page without also editing it. Instead, use the $_SERVER['SCRIPT_NAME'] variable as the form action. This is set up by PHP on each request to contain the filename (relative to the document root) of the current script.

If you're using a web application framework, it has its own conventions on how you mix displaying a form and processing the results. While we don't focus on any specific framework in this book, having a separation between the presentation part of your application (showing things to users) and the "business logic" part of your application (doing stuff with the data users give you) is a good idea to keep your code maintainable and easy to understand. If your form is anything more complicated than Example 9-3 you can benefit from splitting out the display logic into a template. There are lots of swell template languages but to keep things simple in this book we use PHP itself as the template language.

Reworked this way, Example 9-3 becomes three files: one that displays the form on a get request, one that processes the results on a post request and one that decides what to do.

Here's the form display code:

```
<form action="<?= htmlentities($_SERVER['SCRIPT_NAME']) ?>" method="post">
What is your first name?
<input type="text" name="first_name" />
<input type="submit" value="Say Hello" />
</form>
```

Here's the form processing logic:

```
Hello, <?= $_POST['first_name'] ?> !
```

And here's the logic that decides what to do:

```
if ($_SERVER['REQUEST_METHOD'] == 'GET') {
    include __DIR__ . '/getpost-get.php';
}
else {
    include __DIR__ . '/getpost-post.php';
}
```

The deciding-what-to-do logic assumes that the form display code is saved as *getpost-get.php*, that the form processing code is saved as *getpost-post.php* and that all three files are in the same directory. The __DIR__ constant tells the program to look in the same directory as the executing code for the files being included.

We'll use this strategy of breaking things out into separate files in other recipes in this chapter, too.

See Also

Recipe 9.12 for handling multipage forms.

9.2 Validating Form Input: Required Fields

Problem

You want to make sure a value has been supplied for a form element. For example, you want to make sure a text box hasn't been left blank.

Solution

Use filter_has_var() to see if the element exists in the appropriate input array, as in Example 9-4.

Example 9-4. Testing a required field

```
if (! filter_has_var(INPUT_POST, 'flavor')) {
    print 'You must enter your favorite ice cream flavor.';
}
```

Discussion

The filter_has_var() function examines input as received by PHP before any possible modification by your code. Consistent use of the various filter functions, explained in this chapter, ensure you treat user input with the proper validation and sanitization. The first argument to filter_has_var() tells it where to look. INPUT_POST examines POST data in the request body. The other possible values are INPUT_GET (query string variables), INPUT_COOKIE (cookies), INPUT_SERVER (server information that ends up in $_SERVER), and INPUT_ENV (environment variables).

Different types of form elements cause different types of behavior in GET and POST data when left empty. Blank text boxes, text areas, and file-upload boxes result in elements whose value is a zero-length string. Unchecked checkboxes and radio buttons don't produce any elements in GET or POST data. Browsers generally force a selection in a drop-down menu that only allows one choice, but drop-down menus that allow multiple choices and have no choices selected act like checkboxes—they don't produce any elements in GET or POST data.

What's worse, requests don't have to come from web browsers. Your PHP program may receive a request from another program, a curious hacker constructing requests by hand, or a malicious attacker building requests in an attempt to find holes in your system. To make your code as robust as possible, always check that a particular element exists in the appropriate set of input data before applying other validation strategies to the element. Additionally, if the validation strategy assumes that the element is an array of values (as in Example 9-14), ensure that the value really is an array by using the FILTER_REQUIRE_ARRAY filter flag.

Example 9-5 uses filter_has_var(), filter_input(), and strlen() for maximally strict form validation.

Example 9-5. Strict form validation

```
// Making sure $_POST['flavor'] exists before checking its length
if (! (filter_has_var(INPUT_POST, 'flavor') &&
        (strlen(filter_input(INPUT_POST, 'flavor')) > 0))) {
    print 'You must enter your favorite ice cream flavor.';
}

// $_POST['color'] is optional, but if it's supplied, it must be
// more than 5 characters after being sanitized
if (filter_has_var(INPUT_POST, 'color') &&
    (strlen(filter_input(INPUT_POST, 'color', FILTER_SANITIZE_STRING)) <= 5)) {
    print 'Color must be more than 5 characters.';
}

// Making sure $_POST['choices'] exists and is an array
if (! (filter_has_var(INPUT_POST, 'choices') &&
        filter_input(INPUT_POST, 'choices', FILTER_DEFAULT,
                     FILTER_REQUIRE_ARRAY))) {
    print 'You must select some choices.';
}
```

Calling filter_input() with only two arguments applies the default filter, which does not modify any of the input data. In Example 9-5, nothing is done to transform any submitted flavor value. The FILTER_SANITIZE_STRING filter, used against a submitted color, strips HTML tags, removes binary non-ASCII characters, and encodes ampersands. The FILTER_DEFAULT filter, applied to choices, is a way of explicitly specifying the default filter. This is useful in the last part of Example 9-5 because, as a filter flag, FILTER_REQUIRE_ARRAY needs to be in the fourth argument to filter_input().

In a moment of weakness, you may be tempted to use empty() instead of strlen() to test if a value has been entered in a text box. Succumbing to such weakness leads to problems since the one character string 0 is false according to the rules of PHP's boolean calculations. This could lead to broken form validation if, for example, someone types 0 into a text box named `children`, causing `$_POST['children']` to contain 0.Then `empty($_POST['children'])` is true—which, from a form validation perspective, is wrong.

See Also

Documentation on `filter_has_var()` (*http://bit.ly/1mfhmAq*), `filter_input()` (*http://bit.ly/1lcLuvR*), a list of sanitization filters (*http://bit.ly/1pOBxL8*), a list of filter flags (*http://bit.ly/1pBzBne*); Recipe 9.5 for information about validating drop-down menus, Recipe 9.6 for information about validating radio buttons, and Recipe 9.7 for information about validating checkboxes.

9.3 Validating Form Input: Numbers

Problem

You want to make sure a number is entered in a form input box. For example, you don't want someone to be able to say that her age is *old enough* or *tangerine,* but instead want values such as 13 or 56.

Solution

If you're looking for an integer, use the `FILTER_VALIDATE_INT` filter, as shown in Example 9-6.

Example 9-6. Validating a number with FILTER_VALIDATE_INT

```
$age = filter_input(INPUT_POST, 'age', FILTER_VALIDATE_INT);
if ($age === false) {
   print "Submitted age is invalid.";
}
```

If you're looking for a decimal number, use the `FILTER_VALIDATE_FLOAT` filter, as shown in Example 9-7.

Example 9-7. Validating a number with FILTER_VALIDATE_FLOAT

```
$price = filter_input(INPUT_POST, 'price', FILTER_VALIDATE_FLOAT);
if ($price === false) {
   print "Submitted price is invalid.";
}
```

Discussion

The FILTER_VALIDATE_INT and FILTER_VALIDATE_FLOAT filters cause filter_input() to return a number of the specified type (int or float) if the input string represents an appropriate number for the filter, or false otherwise.

There are a few filter flags that affect these number filters. The FILTER_FLAG_ALLOW_OC TAL flag tells FILTER_VALIDATE_INT to accept octal notation. That is, a submitted string of 017 will cause the integer 15 to be returned. Similarly, the flag FILTER_FLAG_AL LOW_HEX allows a submitted string of 0x2f to be returned as the integer 47.

The FILTER_FLAG_ALLOW_THOUSAND modifies the behavior of the FILTER_VALI DATE_FLOAT filter by allowing commas as a thousands separator. Without it, 5,252 will be considered invalid. With it, 5,252 correctly validates as the float 5252.

If you're a fan of regular expressions, those can be useful in certain validation situations. Example 9-8 shows regular expressions that validate an integer and a decimal number.

Example 9-8. Validating numbers with regular expressions

```
// The pattern matches an optional-sign and then
// at least one digit
if (! preg_match('/^-?\d+$/',$_POST['rating'])) {
    print 'Your rating must be an integer.';
}

// The pattern matches an optional-sign and then
// optional digits to go before a decimal point
// an optional decimal point
// and then at least one digit
if (! preg_match('/^-?\d*\.?\d+$/',$_POST['temperature'])) {
    print 'Your temperature must be a number.';
}
```

It is a common refrain among performance-tuning purists that regular expressions should be avoided because they are comparatively slow. In this case, however, with such simple regular expressions, they are about equally efficient as the filter functions. If you're more comfortable with regular expressions, or you're using them in other validation contexts as well, they can be a handy choice. The regular expression also allows you to consider valid numbers, such as 782364.238723123, that cannot be stored as a PHP float without losing precision. This can be useful with data such as a longitude or latitude that you plan to store as a string.

See Also

Recipe 9.2 for information on validating required fields; a list of validation filters (*http://www.php.net/filter.filters.validate*); a list of filter flags (*http://www.php.net/filter.filters.flags*).

9.4 Validating Form Input: Email Addresses

Problem

You want to know whether an email address a user has provided is valid.

Solution

Use the `FILTER_VALIDATE_EMAIL` filter, as show in Example 9-9. It tells you whether an email address is valid according to the rules in RFC 5321 (mostly).

Example 9-9. Validating an email address

```
$email = filter_input(INPUT_POST, 'email', FILTER_VALIDATE_EMAIL);
if ($email === false) {
    print "Submitted email address is invalid.";
}
```

Discussion

RFC 5321 consolidates a number of email-related RFCs and defines the standards for a valid email address. The `FILTER_VALIDATE_EMAIL` filter uses a regular expression based on those rules, although it explicitly does not support comments or folding whitespace.

The filter only checks that a particular address is syntactically correct. This is useful for preventing a user from accidentally telling you that her email address is `bingolov er2261@example` instead of `bingolover2261@example.com`. What it doesn't tell you, however, is what happens if you send a message to that address. Furthermore, it doesn't let you know that the person providing the email address is in control of the address. For those sorts of validations, you need to send a confirmation message to the address. The confirmation message can ask the user to take some affirmative task (reply to the message, click on a link) to indicate they're the same person that entered the address on the form. Or, the confirmation message can tell the user what to do if she's *not* the same person that entered the address on the form — such as to click on a link in the messsage to indicate the wrong address was entered. Recipe 8.19 demonstrates a system that sends an email message containing a link that the recipient must click on to confirm that she provided the address.

See Also

RFC 5321 (*http://www.faqs.org/rfcs/rfc5321.html*)

9.5 Validating Form Input: Drop-Down Menus

Problem

You want to make sure that a valid choice was selected from a drop-down menu generated by the HTML <select/> element.

Solution

Use an array of values to generate the menu. Then validate the input by checking that the value is in the array. Example 9-10 uses `in_array()` to do the validation.

Example 9-10. Validating a drop-down menu with in_array()

```
// Generating the menu
$choices = array('Eggs','Toast','Coffee');
echo "<select name='food'>\n";
foreach ($choices as $choice) {
    echo "<option>$choice</option>\n";
}
echo "</select>";

// Then, later, validating the menu
if (! in_array($_POST['food'], $choices)) {
    echo "You must select a valid choice.";
}
```

The menu that Example 9-10 generates is:

```
<select name='food'>
<option>Eggs</option>
<option>Toast</option>
<option>Coffee</option>
</select>
```

```
<select name='food'>
<option>Eggs</option>
<option>Toast</option>
<option>Coffee</option>
</select>
```

To work with a menu that sets `value` attributes on each <option/> element, use `array_key_exists()` to validate the input, as shown in Example 9-11.

Example 9-11. Validating a drop-down menu with array_key_exists()

```
// Generating the menu
$choices = array('eggs' => 'Eggs Benedict',
                 'toast' => 'Buttered Toast with Jam',
                 'coffee' => 'Piping Hot Coffee');
echo "<select name='food'>\n";
foreach ($choices as $key => $choice) {
```

```
        echo "<option value='$key'>$choice</option>\n";
}
echo "</select>";

// Then, later, validating the menu
if (! array_key_exists($_POST['food'], $choices)) {
    echo "You must select a valid choice.";
}
```

The menu that Example 9-11 generates is:

```
<select name='food'>
<option value='eggs'>Eggs Benedict</option>
<option value='toast'>Buttered Toast with Jam</option>
<option value='coffee'>Piping Hot Coffee</option>
</select>
```

Discussion

The methods in Examples 9-10 and 9-11 differ in the kinds of menus that they generate. Example 9-10 has a `$choices` array with automatic numeric keys and outputs `<option/>` elements. Example 9-11 has a `$choices` array with explicit keys and outputs `<option/>` elements with `value` attributes drawn from those keys.

In either case, the validation strategy is the same: make sure that the value submitted for the form element is one of the allowed choices. For requests submitted by well-behaved browsers, this validation rule never fails—web browsers generally don't let you make up your choice for a drop-down menu. Remember, though, that there's nothing requiring that requests to your PHP program come from a well-behaved web browser. They could come from a buggy browser or from a bored 11-year-old with a copy of the HTTP specification in one hand and a command-line telnet client in the other. Because you always need to be mindful of malicious, hand-crafted HTTP requests, it's important to validate input even in circumstances where most users will never encounter an error.

See Also

Documentation on `in_array()` (*http://bit.ly/1v6das6*) and on `array_key_exists()` (*http://bit.ly/1v6ddE3*).

9.6 Validating Form Input: Radio Buttons

Problem

You want to make sure a valid radio button is selected from a group of radio buttons.

Solution

Use an array of values to generate the menu. Then validate the input by checking that the submitted value is in the array. Example 9-12 uses `array_key_exists()` to do the validation.

Example 9-12. Validating a radio button

```
// Generating the radio buttons
$choices = array('eggs' => 'Eggs Benedict',
                 'toast' => 'Buttered Toast with Jam',
                 'coffee' => 'Piping Hot Coffee');
foreach ($choices as $key => $choice) {
    echo "<input type='radio' name='food' value='$key'/> $choice \n";
}


// Then, later, validating the radio button submission
if (! array_key_exists($_POST['food'], $choices)) {
    echo "You must select a valid choice.";
}
```

Discussion

The radio button validation in Example 9-12 is very similar to the drop-down menu validation in Example 9-11. They both follow the same pattern—define the data that describes the choices, generate the appropriate HTML, and then use the defined data to ensure that a valid value was submitted. The difference is in what HTML is generated.

One difference between drop-down menus and radio buttons is how defaults are handled. When the HTML doesn't explicitly specify a default choice for a drop-down menu, the first choice in the menu is used. However, when the HTML doesn't explicitly specify a default choice for a set of radio buttons, no choice is used as a default.

To ensure that one of a set of radio buttons is chosen in a well-behaved web browser, give the default choice a `checked="checked"` attribute. In the following code, `toast` is the default:

```
// Defaults
$defaults['food'] = 'toast';
// Generating the radio buttons
$choices = array('eggs' => 'Eggs Benedict',
                 'toast' => 'Buttered Toast with Jam',
                 'coffee' => 'Piping Hot Coffee');
foreach ($choices as $key => $choice) {
    echo "<input type='radio' name='food' value='$key'";
    if ($key == $defaults['food']) {
        echo ' checked="checked"';
    }
    echo "/> $choice \n";
```

```
    }

    // Then, later, validating the radio button submission
    if (! array_key_exists($_POST['food'], $choices)) {
        echo "You must select a valid choice.";
    }
```

In addition, to guard against missing values in hand-crafted malicious requests, use `filter_has_var()` to ensure that something was submitted for the radio button, as described in Recipe 9.2.

See Also

Recipe 9.2 for information on validating required fields; documentation on `array_key_exists()` (*http://www.php.net/array_key_exists*).

9.7 Validating Form Input: Checkboxes

Problem

You want to make sure only valid checkboxes are checked.

Solution

For a single checkbox, ensure that if a value is supplied, it's the correct one. If a value isn't supplied for the checkbox, then the box wasn't checked. Example 9-13 figures out whether a checkbox was checked, unchecked, or had an invalid value submitted.

Example 9-13. Validating a single checkbox

```
// Generating the checkbox
$value = 'yes';
echo "<input type='checkbox' name='subscribe' value='yes'/> Subscribe?";

// Then, later, validating the checkbox
if (filter_has_var(INPUT_POST, 'subscribe')) {
    // A value was submitted and it's the right one
    if ($_POST['subscribe'] == $value) {
        $subscribed = true;
    } else {
        // A value was submitted and it's the wrong one
        $subscribed = false;
        print 'Invalid checkbox value submitted.';
    }
} else {
    // No value was submitted
    $subscribed = false;
}
```

```
if ($subscribed) {
    print 'You are subscribed.';
} else {
    print 'You are not subscribed';
}
```

For a group of checkboxes, use an array of values to generate the checkboxes. Then, use `array_intersect()` to ensure that the set of submitted values is contained within the set of acceptable values, as shown in Example 9-14.

Example 9-14. Validating a group of checkboxes

```
// Generating the checkboxes
$choices = array('eggs' => 'Eggs Benedict',
                 'toast' => 'Buttered Toast with Jam',
                 'coffee' => 'Piping Hot Coffee');
foreach ($choices as $key => $choice) {
    echo "<input type='checkbox' name='food[]' value='$key'/> $choice \n";
}

// Then, later, validating the radio button submission
if (array_intersect($_POST['food'], array_keys($choices)) != $_POST['food']) {
    echo "You must select only valid choices.";
}
```

Discussion

For PHP to handle multiple checkbox values properly, the checkboxes' `name` attribute must end with [ ], as described in Recipe 9.17. Those multiple values are formatted in `$_POST` as an array. Since the checkbox name in Example 9-14 is `food[]`, `$_POST['food']` holds the array of values from the checked boxes.

The `array_intersect()` function finds all of the elements in `$_POST['food']` that are also in `array_keys($choices)`. That is, it filters the submitted choices (`$_POST['food']`), only allowing through values that are acceptable—keys in the `$choices` array. If all of the values in `$_POST['food']` are acceptable, then the result of `array_intersect($_POST['food'], array_keys($choices))` is an unmodified copy of `$_POST['food']`. So if the result isn't equal to `$_POST['food']`, something invalid was submitted.

Checkboxes have the same issues with default values as do radio buttons. So just as with radio buttons, use the rules in Recipe 9.2 to determine that something was submitted for the checkbox before proceeding with further validation.

See Also

Recipe 9.2 for information about validating required fields; documentation on `ar ray_intersect()` (*http://www.php.net/array_intersect*).

9.8 Validating Form Input: Dates and Times

Problem

You want to make sure that a date or time a user entered is valid. For example, you want to ensure that a user hasn't attempted to schedule an event for the 45th of August or provided a credit card that has already expired.

Solution

If your form provides month, day, and year as separate elements, plug those values into `checkdate()`, as in Example 9-15. This tells you whether or not the month, day, and year are valid.

Example 9-15. Checking a particular date

```
if (! checkdate($_POST['month'], $_POST['day'], $_POST['year'])) {
    print "The date you entered doesn't exist!";
}
```

To check that a date is before or after a particular value, convert the user-supplied values to a timestamp, compute the timestamp for the threshhold date, and compare the two. Example 9-16 checks that the supplied credit card expiration month and year are sufficiently in the future.

Example 9-16. Checking credit card expiration

```
// The beginning of the month in which the credit card expires
$expires = mktime(0, 0, 0, $_POST['month'], 1, $_POST['year']);
// The beginning of the previous month
$lastMonth = strtotime('last month', $expires);
if (time() > $lastMonth) {
    print "Sorry, that credit card expires too soon.";
}
```

Discussion

The `checkdate()` function is handy because it knows about leap year and how many days are in each month, saving you from tedious comparisons of each component of the date. For range validations—making sure a date or time is before, after, or between other dates or times—it's easiest to work with epoch timestamps.

See Also

Chapter 3 discusses the finer points of date and time handling.

9.9 Validating Form Input: Credit Cards

Problem

You want to make sure a user hasn't entered a bogus credit card number.

Solution

The is_valid_credit_card() function in Example 9-17 tells you whether a provided credit card number is syntactically valid.

Example 9-17. Validating a credit card number

```
function is_valid_credit_card($s) {
    // Remove non-digits and reverse
    $s = strrev(preg_replace('/[^\d]/','',$s));
    // compute checksum
    $sum = 0;
    for ($i = 0, $j = strlen($s); $i < $j; $i++) {
        // Use even digits as-is
        if (($i % 2) == 0) {
            $val = $s[$i];
        } else {
            // Double odd digits and subtract 9 if greater than 9
            $val = $s[$i] * 2;
            if ($val > 9) { $val -= 9; }
        }
        $sum += $val;
    }
    // Number is valid if sum is a multiple of ten
    return (($sum % 10) == 0);
}

if (! is_valid_credit_card($_POST['credit_card'])) {
    print 'Sorry, that card number is invalid.';
}
```

Discussion

Credit cards use the *Luhn algorithm* to prevent against accidental error. This algorithm, which the is_valid_credit_card() function in Example 9-17 uses, does some manipulations on the individual digits of the card number to tell whether the number is acceptable.

Validating a credit card is a bit like validating an email address. *Syntactic* validation—making sure the provided value is a sequence of characters that matches a standard—is relatively easy. *Semantic* validation, however, is trickier. The credit card number 4111 1111 1111 1111 sails through the function in Example 9-17 but isn't valid. It's a well-known test number that looks like a Visa card number. (And, as such, is handy for using in books when one needs an example.)

Just as strong email address validation requires external verification (usually by sending a message to the address with a confirmation link in it), credit card validation requires external validation by submitting the credit card number to a payment processor along with associated account info (cardholder name and address) and making sure you get back an approval.

Syntactic validation is good protection against inadvertent user typos but, obviously, is not all you need to do when checking credit card numbers.

See Also

Recipe 9.4 for information about validating email addresses; for information about the Luhn algorithm (*http://en.wikipedia.org/wiki/Luhn*).

9.10 Preventing Cross-Site Scripting

Problem

You want to securely display user-entered data on an HTML page. For example, you want to allow users to add comments to a blog post without worrying that HTML or JavaScript in a comment will cause problems.

Solution

Pass user input through `htmlentities()` before displaying it, as in Example 9-18.

Example 9-18. Escaping HTML

```
print 'The comment was: ';
print htmlentities($_POST['comment']);
```

Discussion

PHP has a pair of functions to escape HTML entities. The most basic is `htmlspecial chars()`, which escapes four characters: < > " and &. Depending on optional parameters, it can also translate ' instead of or in addition to ". For more complex encoding, use `htmlentities()`; it expands on `htmlspecialchars()` to encode any character that has an HTML entity. Example 9-19 shows `htmlspecialchars()` in action.

Example 9-19. Escaping HTML entities

```
$html = "<a href='fletch.html'>Stew's favorite movie.</a>\n";
print htmlspecialchars($html);              // double-quotes
print htmlspecialchars($html, ENT_QUOTES);  // single- and double-quotes
print htmlspecialchars($html, ENT_NOQUOTES); // neither
```

Example 9-19 prints:

```
<a href='fletch.html'>Stew's favorite movie.</a>
<a href='fletch.html'>Stew's favorite movie.</a>
<a href='fletch.html'>Stew's favorite movie.</a>
```

By default, both `htmlentities()` and `htmlspecialchars()` use the UTF-8 character set (as of PHP 5.4.0. Before that, the default was ISO-8859-1). To use a different character set, pass the character set as a third argument. For example, to use BIG5, call `htmlentities($string, ENT_QUOTES, "BIG5")`.

See Also

Recipes 18.4 and 19.12; documentation on `htmlentities()` (*http://www.php.net/htmlentities*) and `htmlspecialchars()` (*http://www.php.net/htmlspecialchars*).

9.11 Processing Uploaded Files

Problem

You want to process a file uploaded by a user. For example, you're building a photo-sharing website and you want to store user-supplied photos.

Solution

Use the `$_FILES` array to get information about uploaded files. Example 9-20 saves an uploaded file to the */tmp* directory on the web server.

Example 9-20. Uploading a file

```php
<?php if ($_SERVER['REQUEST_METHOD'] == 'GET') { ?>
<form method="post" action="<?php echo htmlentities($_SERVER['SCRIPT_NAME']) ?>"
     enctype="multipart/form-data">
<input type="file" name="document"/>
<input type="submit" value="Send File"/>
</form>
<?php } else {
    if (isset($_FILES['document']) &&
    ($_FILES['document']['error'] == UPLOAD_ERR_OK)) {
        $newPath = '/tmp/' . basename($_FILES['document']['name']);
        if (move_uploaded_file($_FILES['document']['tmp_name'], $newPath)) {
            print "File saved in $newPath";
```

```
            } else {
                print "Couldn't move file to $newPath";
            }
        } else {
            print "No valid file uploaded.";
        }
    }
```

Discussion

Uploaded files appear in the $_FILES superglobal array. For each file element in the form, an array is created in $_FILES whose key is the file element's name. For example, the form in Example 9-20 has a file element named document, so $_FILES['docu ment'] contains the information about the uploaded file. Each of these per-file arrays has five elements:

name
The name of the uploaded file. This is supplied by the browser so it could be a full pathname or just a filename.

type
The MIME type of the file, as supplied by the browser.

size
The size of the file in bytes, as calculated by the server.

tmp_name
The location in which the file is temporarily stored on the server.

error
An error code describing what (if anything) went wrong with the file upload.

The possible values of the error element are:

UPLOAD_ERR_OK (0)
Upload succeeded (no error).

UPLOAD_ERR_INI_SIZE (1)
The size of the uploaded file is bigger than the value of the upload_max_filesize configuration directive.

UPLOAD_ERR_FORM_SIZE (2)
The size of the uploaded file is bigger than the value of the form's MAX_FILE_SIZE element.

UPLOAD_ERR_PARTIAL (3)
Only part of the file was uploaded.

UPLOAD_ERR_NO_FILE (4)
There was no file uploaded.

UPLOAD_ERR_NO_TMP_DIR (6)
The upload failed because there was no temporary directory to store the file.

UPLOAD_ERR_CANT_WRITE (7)
PHP couldn't write the file to disk.

UPLOAD_ERR_EXTENSION (8)
Upload stopped by a PHP extension.

The `is_uploaded_file()` function confirms that the file you're about to process is a legitimate file resulting from a user upload. Always check the `tmp_name` value before processing it as any other file. This ensures that a malicious user can't trick your code into processing a system file as an upload.

You can also move the file to a permanent location; use `move_uploaded_file()`, as in Example 9-20. It also does a check to make sure that the file being moved is really an uploaded file. Note that the value stored in `tmp_name` is the complete path to the file, not just the base name. Use `basename()` to chop off the leading directories if needed.

Be sure to check that PHP has permission to read and write to both the directory in which temporary files are saved (set by the `upload_tmp_dir` configuration directive) and the location to which you're trying to copy the file. PHP is often running under a special username such as `nobody` or `apache`, instead of your personal username.

Processing files can be a subtle task because not all browsers submit the same information. It's important to do it correctly, however, or you open yourself up to security problems. You are, after all, allowing strangers to upload any file they choose to your machine; malicious people may see this as an opportunity to crack into or crash the computer.

As a result, PHP has a number of features that allow you to place restrictions on uploaded files, including the ability to completely turn off file uploads altogether. So if you're experiencing difficulty processing uploaded files, check that your file isn't being rejected because it seems to pose a security risk.

To do such a check, first make sure `file_uploads` is set to `On` inside your configuration file. Next, make sure your file size isn't larger than `upload_max_filesize`; this defaults to 2 MB, which stops someone from trying to crash the machine by filling up the hard drive with a giant file. Additionally, there's a `post_max_size` directive, which controls the maximum size of all the `post` data allowed in a single request; its initial setting is 8 MB.

From the perspective of browser differences and user error, if you don't see what you expect in `$_FILES`, make sure you add `enctype="multipart/form-data"` to the form's opening tag. PHP needs this to process the file information properly.

Also, if no file is selected for uploading, PHP sets `tmp_name` to the empty string. To be sure a file was uploaded and isn't empty (although blank files may be what you want, depending on the circumstances), you need to make sure `tmp_name` is set and `size` is greater than 0. Last, not all browsers necessarily send the same MIME type for a file; what they send depends on their knowledge of different file types.

See Also

Documentation on handling file uploads (*http://www.php.net/features.file-upload*) and on `basename()` (*http://www.php.net/basename*).

9.12 Working with Multipage Forms

Problem

You want to use a form that displays more than one page and preserves data from one page to the next. For example, your form is for a survey that has too many questions to put them all on one page.

Solution

Use session tracking to store form information for each stage as well as a variable to keep track of what stage to display. Example 9-21 displays the four files for a two page-form and showing the collected results.

Example 9-21. Making a multipage form

The "deciding what to do" logic (*stage.php*):

```
// Turn on sessions
session_start();

// Figure out what stage to use
if (($_SERVER['REQUEST_METHOD'] == 'GET') || (! isset($_POST['stage']))) {
    $stage = 1;
} else {
    $stage = (int) $_POST['stage'];
}

// Make sure stage isn't too big or too small
$stage = max($stage, 1);
$stage = min($stage, 3);

// Save any submitted data
if ($stage > 1) {
    foreach ($_POST as $key => $value) {
        $_SESSION[$key] = $value;
    }
}
```

```
    }
    include __DIR__ . "/stage-$stage.php";
```

The first page of the form (*stage-1.php*):

```
<form action='<?= htmlentities($_SERVER['SCRIPT_NAME']) ?>' method='post'>

Name: <input type='text' name='name'/> <br/>
Age:  <input type='text' name='age'/> <br/>

<input type='hidden' name='stage' value='<?= $stage + 1 ?>'/>
<input type='submit' value='Next'/>
</form>
```

The second page of the form (*stage-2.php*):

```
<form action='<?= htmlentities($_SERVER['SCRIPT_NAME']) ?>' method='post'>

Favorite Color: <input type='text' name='color'/> <br/>
Favorite Food:  <input type='text' name='food'/> <br/>

<input type='hidden' name='stage' value='<?= $stage + 1 ?>'/>
<input type='submit' value='Done'/>
```

The displaying-results page (*stage-3.php*):

```
Hello <?= htmlentities($_SESSION['name']) ?>.
You are <?= htmlentities($_SESSION['age']) ?> years old.
Your favorite color is <?= htmlentities($_SESSION['color']) ?>
and your favorite food is <?= htmlentities($_SESSION['food']) ?>.
```

Discussion

At the beginning of each stage in Example 9-21, all the submitted form variables are copied into $_SESSION. This makes them available on subsequent requests, including the code that runs in stage 3, which displays everything that's been saved.

PHP's sessions are perfect for this kind of task since all of the data in a session is stored on the server. This keeps each request small—no need to resubmit stuff that's been entered on a previous stage—and reduces the validation overhead. You only have to validate each piece of submitted data when it's submitted.

See Also

Recipe 11.1 for information about session handling.

9.13 Redisplaying Forms with Inline Error Messages

Problem

When there's a problem with data entered in a form, you want to print out error messages alongside the problem fields, instead of a generic error message at the top of the form. You also want to preserve the values the user entered in the form, so they don't have to redo the entire thing.

Solution

As you validate, keep track of form errors in an array keyed by element name. Then, when it's time to display the form, print the appropriate error message next to each element. To preserve user input, use the appropriate HTML idiom: a `value` attribute (with entity encoding) for most `<input/>` elements, a `checked='checked'` attribute for radio buttons and checkboxes, and a `selected='selected'` attribute on `<option/>` elements in drop-down menus. Example 9-22 displays and validates a form with a text box, a checkbox, and a drop-down menu.

Example 9-22. Redisplaying a form with error messages and preserved input

The main logic and validation function:

```
// Set up some options for the drop-down menu
$flavors = array('Vanilla','Chocolate','Rhinoceros');

// Set up empty defaults when nothing is chosen.
$defaults = array('name' => '',
                  'age' => '',
                  'flavor' => array());
foreach ($flavors as $flavor) {
    $defaults['flavor'][$flavor] = '';
}

if ($_SERVER['REQUEST_METHOD'] == 'GET') {
    $errors = array();
    include __DIR__ . '/show-form.php';
} else {
    // The request is a POST, so validate the form
    $errors = validate_form();
    if (count($errors)) {
        // If there were errors, redisplay the form with the errors,
        // preserving defaults
        if (isset($_POST['name'])) { $defaults['name'] = $_POST['name']; }
        if (isset($_POST['age'])) { $defaults['age'] =  "checked='checked'"; }
        foreach ($flavors as $flavor) {
            if (isset($_POST['flavor']) && ($_POST['flavor'] == $flavor)) {
                $defaults['flavor'][$flavor] = "selected='selected'";
            }
```

```
        }
        include __DIR__ . '/show-form.php';
    } else {
        // The form data was valid, so congratulate the user. In "real life"
        // perhaps here you'd redirect somewhere else or include another
        // file to display
        print 'The form is submitted!';
    }
}

function validate_form() {
    global $flavors;

    // Start out with no errors
    $errors = array();

    // name is required and must be at least 3 characters
    if (! (isset($_POST['name']) && (strlen($_POST['name']) > 3))) {
        $errors['name'] = 'Enter a name of at least 3 letters';
    }
    if (isset($_POST['age']) && ($_POST['age'] != '1')) {
        $errors['age'] = 'Invalid age checkbox value.';
    }
    // flavor is optional but if submitted must be in $flavors
    if (isset($_POST['flavor']) && (! in_array($_POST['flavor'], $flavors))) {
        $errors['flavor'] = 'Choose a valid flavor.';
    }

    return $errors;
}
```

The form (*show-form.php*):

```
<form action='<?= htmlentities($_SERVER['SCRIPT_NAME']) ?>' method='post'>
<dl>
<dt>Your Name:</dt>
<?php if (isset($errors['name'])) { ?>
  <dd class="error"><?= htmlentities($errors['name']) ?></dd>
<?php } ?>
<dd><input type='text' name='name'
     value='<?= htmlentities($defaults['name']) ?>'/></dd>
<dt>Are you over 18 years old?</dt>
<?php if (isset($errors['age'])) { ?>
  <dd class="error"><?= htmlentities($errors['age']) ?></dd>
<?php } ?>
<dd><input type='checkbox' name='age' value='1'
        <?= $defaults['age'] ?>/> Yes</dd>
<dt>Your favorite ice cream flavor:</dt>
<?php if (isset($errors['flavor'])) { ?>
  <dd class="error"><?= htmlentities($errors['flavor']) ?></dd>
<?php } ?>
<dd><select name='flavor'>
<?php foreach ($flavors as $flavor) { ?>
```

```
<option <?= isset($defaults['flavor'][$flavor]) ?
         $defaults['flavor'][$flavor] :
         "" ?>><?= htmlentities($flavor) ?></option>
<?php } ?>
</select></dd>
</dl>
<input type='submit' value='Send Info'/>
</form>
```

Discussion

When a form is submitted with invalid data, it's more pleasant for the user if the form is redisplayed with error messages in appropriate places rather than a generic *the form is invalid* message at the top of the form. The `validate_form()` function in Example 9-22 builds up an array of error messages that the form display code uses to print the messages in the right places.

Extending Example 9-22 is a matter of expanding the checks in `validate_form()` to handle the appropriate validation needs of your form and including the correct HTML generation in *show-form.php* so that the form includes the input elements you want.

See Also

Recipes 9.2 to 9.9 for various form validation strategies.

9.14 Guarding Against Multiple Submissions of the Same Form

Problem

You want to prevent a user from submitting the same form more than once.

Solution

Include a hidden field in the form with a unique value. When validating the form, check if a form has already been submitted with that value. If it has, reject the submission. If it hasn't, process the form and record the value for later use. Additionally, use JavaScript to disable the form Submit button once the form has been submitted.

Example 9-23 uses the `uniqid()` and `md5()` functions to insert a unique ID field in a form. It also sets the form's `onsubmit` handler to a small bit of JavaScript that disables the Submit button once the form's been submitted.

Example 9-23. Insert a unique ID into a form

```
<form method="post" action="<?php echo $_SERVER['SCRIPT_NAME'] ?>"
      onsubmit="document.getElementById('submit-button').disabled = true;">
```

```
<!-- insert all the normal form elements you need -->
<input type='hidden' name='token' value='<?= md5(uniqid()) ?>'/>
<input type='submit' value='Save Data' id='submit-button'/>
</form>
```

Example 9-24 checks the submitted token against saved data in an SQLite database to see if the form has already been submitted.

Example 9-24. Checking a form for resubmission

```
if ($_SERVER['REQUEST_METHOD'] == 'POST') {
    $db = new PDO('sqlite:/tmp/formjs.db');
    $db->beginTransaction();
    $sth = $db->prepare('SELECT * FROM forms WHERE token = ?');
    $sth->execute(array($_POST['token']));
    if (count($sth->fetchAll())) {
        print "This form has already been submitted!";
        $db->rollBack();
    } else {
        /* Validation code for the rest of the form goes here --
         * validate everything before inserting the token */
        $sth = $db->prepare('INSERT INTO forms (token) VALUES (?)');
        $sth->execute(array($_POST['token']));
        $db->commit();
        print "The form is submitted successfully.";
    }
}
```

Discussion

For a variety of reasons, users often resubmit a form. Usually it's a slip-of-the-mouse: double-clicking the Submit button. They may hit their web browser's Back button to edit or recheck information, but then they rehit Submit instead of Forward. It can be intentional: they're trying to stuff the ballot box for an online survey or sweepstakes. Our Solution prevents the non-malicious mistake and can slow down the malicious user. It won't, however, eliminate all fraudulent use: more complicated work is required for that such as adding a CAPTCHA or other verification question to the form.

The Solution does prevent your database from being cluttered with too many copies of the same record. By generating a token that's placed in the form, you can uniquely identify that specific instance of the form, even when cookies are disabled. The uniqid() function generates an acceptable one-time token. The md5() function doesn't add any additional randomness to the token, but restricts the characters that could be in it. The results of uniqid() can be a mix of different letters and other characters. The results of md5() consist only of digits and the letters abcdef. For English-speaking users at least, this ensures that the token doesn't contain any naughty words.

It's tempting to avoid generating a random token and instead use a number one greater than the number of records already in your database table. There are (at least) two problems with this method. First, it creates a race condition. What happens when a second person starts the form before the first person has completed it? The second form will then have the same token as the first, and conflicts will occur. This can be worked around by creating a new blank record in the database when the form is requested, so the second person will get a number one higher than the first. However, this can lead to empty rows in the database if users opt not to complete the form.

The other reason not do this is because it makes it trivial to edit another record in the database by manually adjusting the ID to a different number. Depending on your security settings, a fake get or post submission allows the data to be altered without difficulty. A random token, however, can't be guessed merely by moving to a different integer.

See Also

Recipe 18.9 for more details on verifying data with hashes; documentation on uniqid() (*http://www.php.net/uniqid*) and on md5() (*http://www.php.net/md5*). An easy to implement CAPTCHA is available from Google (*http://www.google.com/recaptcha/*).

9.15 Preventing Global Variable Injection

Problem

You are using an old version of PHP and want to access form input variables without allowing malicious users to set arbitrary global variables in your program.

Solution

The easiest solution is to use PHP version 5.4.0 or later. Starting with that version, the register_globals configuration directive—the source of this global variable injection problem—is removed.

If you're using an earlier version of PHP, disable the register_globals configuration directive and access variables only from the $_GET, $_POST, and $_COOKIE arrays to make sure you know exactly where your variables are coming from.

To do this, make sure register_globals = Off appears in your *php.ini* file. If you do not have permission to write to your php.ini file and it has register_globals turned on, then you need to have a serious conversation with your system administrator or find a new hosting provider that is not relying on incorrect settings which are more than a decade old. If you are using PHP with Apache and Apache is configured to use per-directory .htaccess files, you can turn register_globals by adding php_flag reg ister_globals off to your .htaccess file.

Discussion

When `register_globals` is set to on, external variables, including those from forms and cookies, are imported directly into the global namespace. This is a great convenience, but it can also open up some security holes if you're not very diligent about checking your variables and where they're defined. Why? Because there may be a variable you use internally that isn't supposed to be accessible from the outside but has its value rewritten without your knowledge.

Example 9-25 contains a simple example: imagine you have a page in which a user enters a username and password. If they are validated, you return her user identification number and use that numerical identifier to look up and print out her personal information.

Example 9-25. Insecure register_globals code

```
$username = $dbh->quote($_GET['username']);
$password = $dbh->quote($_GET['password']);

$sth = $dbh->query("SELECT id FROM users WHERE username = $username AND
                    password = $password");

if (1 == $sth->numRows()) {
    $row = $sth->fetchRow(DB_FETCHMODE_OBJECT);
    $id = $row->id;
} else {
    "Print bad username and password";
}

if (!empty($id)) {
    $sth = $dbh->query("SELECT * FROM profile WHERE id = $id");
}
```

Normally, $id is set only by your program and is a result of a verified database lookup. However, if someone alters the query string, and passes in a value for $id, you'll have problems. With `register_globals` enabled, your script could still execute the second database query and return results even after a bad username and password lookup. Without `register_globals`, $id remains unset because only $_REQUEST['id'] and $_GET['id'] are set.

Of course, there are other ways to solve this problem, even when using `register_globals`. You can restructure your code not to allow such a loophole. One way to do this is in Example 9-26.

Example 9-26. Avoiding register_globals problems

```
$sth = $dbh->query("SELECT id FROM users WHERE username = $username AND
                    password = $password");

if (1 == $sth->numRows()) {
    $row = $sth->fetchRow(DB_FETCHMODE_OBJECT);
```

```
        $id = $row->id;
        if (!empty($id)) {
            $sth = $dbh->query("SELECT * FROM profile WHERE id = $id");
        }
    } else {
        "Print bad username and password";
    }
```

In Example 9-26 $id has a value only when it's been explicitly set from a database call. Sometimes, however, it is difficult to do this because of how your program is laid out. Another solution is to manually unset() or initialize all variables at the top of your script. This removes the bad $id value before it gets a chance to affect your code. However, because PHP doesn't require variable initialization, it's possible to forget to do this in one place; a bug can then slip in without a warning from PHP.

For all of these reasons, it's best to just turn register_globals off.

See Also

Documentation on register_globals (*http://www.php.net/security.globals*).

9.16 Handling Remote Variables with Periods in Their Names

Problem

You want to process a variable with a period in its name, but when a form is submitted, you can't find the variable in $_GET or $_POST.

Solution

Replace the period in the variable's name with an underscore. For example, if you have a form input element named hot.dog, you access it inside PHP as the variable $_GET['hot_dog'] or $_POST['hot_dog'].

Discussion

During PHP's pimply adolescence when register_globals was on by default, a form variable named hot.dog couldn't become $hot.dog—periods aren't allowed in variable names. To work around that, the . was changed to _. While $_GET['hot.dog'] and $_POST['hot.dog'] don't have this problem, the translation still happens for legacy and consistency reasons, no matter your register_globals setting.

You usually run into this translation when there's an element of type image in a form that's used to submit the form. For example, a form element such as <input type="im

age" name="locations" src="locations.gif" />, when clicked, submits the form. The x and y coordinates of the click are submitted as locations.x and locations.y. So in PHP, to find where a user clicked, you need to check $_POST['locations_x'] and $_POST['locations_y'].

See Also

Documentation on variables from outside PHP (*http://www.php.net/language.vari ables.external*).

9.17 Using Form Elements with Multiple Options

Problem

You have form elements that let a user select multiple choices, such as a drop-down menu or a group of checkboxes, but PHP sees only one of the submitted values.

Solution

End the form element's name with a pair of square brackets ([ ]). Example 9-27 shows a properly named group of checkboxes.

Example 9-27. Naming a checkbox group

```
<input type="checkbox" name="boroughs[]" value="bronx"> The Bronx
<input type="checkbox" name="boroughs[]" value="brooklyn"> Brooklyn
<input type="checkbox" name="boroughs[]" value="manhattan"> Manhattan
<input type="checkbox" name="boroughs[]" value="queens"> Queens
<input type="checkbox" name="boroughs[]" value="statenisland"> Staten Island
```

Then, treat the submitted data as an array inside of $_GET or $_POST, as in Example 9-28.

Example 9-28. Handling a submitted checkbox group

```
print 'I love ' . join(' and ', $_POST['boroughs']) . '!';
```

Discussion

Putting [ ] at the end of the form element name tells PHP to treat the incoming data as an array instead of a scalar. When PHP sees more than one submitted value assigned to that variable, it keeps them all. If the first three boxes in Example 9-27 were checked, it's as if you'd written the code in Example 9-29 at the top of your program.

Example 9-29. Code equivalent of a multiple-value form element submission

```
$_POST['boroughs'][] = "bronx";
$_POST['boroughs'][] = "brooklyn";
$_POST['boroughs'][] = "manhattan";
```

A similar syntax also works with multidimensional arrays. For example, you can have a checkbox such as `<input type="checkbox" name="population[NY][NYC]" value="8336697">`. If checked, this form element sets `$_POST['population']['NY']['NYC']` to 8336697.

See Also

The introduction to Chapter 4 for more on arrays.

9.18 Creating Drop-Down Menus Based on the Current Date

Problem

You want to create a series of drop-down menus that are based automatically on the current date.

Solution

Create a `DateTime` object and then loop through the days you care about, modifying the object with its `modify()` method.

Example 9-30 generates `<option/>` values for today and the six days that follow. In this case, 'today' is April 8, 2013.

Example 9-30. Generating date-based drop-down menu options

```
$options = array();
$when = new DateTime();
// print out one week's worth of days
for ($i = 0; $i < 7; ++$i) {
    $options[$when->getTimestamp()] = $when->format("D, F j, Y");
    $when->modify("+1 day");
}

foreach ($options as $value => $label) {
    print "<option value='$value'>$label</option>\n";
}
```

When run on April 8, 2013, Example 9-30 prints:

```
<option value='1365450257'>Mon, April 8, 2013</option>
<option value='1365536657'>Tue, April 9, 2013</option>
<option value='1365623057'>Wed, April 10, 2013</option>
<option value='1365709457'>Thu, April 11, 2013</option>
<option value='1365795857'>Fri, April 12, 2013</option>
<option value='1365882257'>Sat, April 13, 2013</option>
<option value='1365968657'>Sun, April 14, 2013</option>
```

Discussion

In Example 9-30 we set the `value` for each date as its Unix timestamp representation because we find this easier to handle inside our programs. Of course, you can use any format you find most useful and appropriate.

Using `DateTime#modify()` and `DateTime#format()` frees you from any concerns about time zone math. Whatever the appropriate summer time transitions are for the relevant time zone will be handled properly.

See Also

Chapter 3, particularly Recipe 3.9; documentation on DateTime (*http://www.php.net/ class.datetime*).

CHAPTER 10

Database Access

10.0 Introduction

Databases are central to many web applications. A database can hold almost any collection of information you may want to search and update, such as a user list, a product catalog, or recent headlines. One reason why PHP is such a great web programming language is its extensive database support. PHP can interact with just about any database you can think of, some relational and some not. It also has ODBC support, so even if your favorite database isn't in the list, as long as it supports ODBC, you can use it with PHP.

DBM databases, discussed in Recipe 10.1, are simple, robust, and efficient flat files but limit the structure of your data to key/value pairs. If your data can be organized as a mapping of keys to values, DBM databases are a great choice.

PHP really shines, though, when paired with an SQL database. This combination is used for most of the recipes in this chapter. SQL databases can be complicated, but they are extremely powerful. To use PHP with a particular SQL database, PHP must be explicitly told to include support for that database when it is compiled. If PHP is built to support dynamic module loading, the database support can also be built as a dynamic module.

The SQL database examples in this chapter use PHP 5's PDO database access layer. With PDO, you use the same PHP functions no matter what database engine you're talking to. Although the syntax of the SQL may differ from database to database, the PHP code remains similar. In this regard, PDO offers data *access* abstraction, not total database abstraction. There are other libraries that attempt to solve the total database abstraction problem—they hide the implementation details of different databases such as date handling and column types behind a layer of code. Although this sort of abstraction can save you some work if you're writing software that is intended to be used with lots of different types of databases, it can cause other problems. When you write SQL focused on a particular type of database, you can take advantage of that database's features for maximum performance.

PHP 5 comes bundled with SQLite, a powerful database that doesn't require a separate server. It's a great choice when you have a moderate amount of traffic and don't want to deal with the hassles of running a database server. Recipe 10.2 discusses the ins and outs of SQLite.

Many SQL examples in this chapter use a table of information about zodiac signs. The table's structure is shown in Example 10-1. The data in the table is shown in Example 10-2.

Example 10-1. Sample table structure

```
CREATE TABLE zodiac (
    id INT UNSIGNED NOT NULL,
    sign CHAR(11),
    symbol CHAR(13),
    planet CHAR(7),
    element CHAR(5),
    start_month TINYINT,
    start_day TINYINT,
    end_month TINYINT,
    end_day TINYINT,
    PRIMARY KEY(id)
);
```

Example 10-2. Sample table data

```
INSERT INTO zodiac VALUES (1,'Aries','Ram','Mars','fire',3,21,4,19);
INSERT INTO zodiac VALUES (2,'Taurus','Bull','Venus','earth',4,20,5,20);
INSERT INTO zodiac VALUES (3,'Gemini','Twins','Mercury','air',5,21,6,21);
INSERT INTO zodiac VALUES (4,'Cancer','Crab','Moon','water',6,22,7,22);
INSERT INTO zodiac VALUES (5,'Leo','Lion','Sun','fire',7,23,8,22);
INSERT INTO zodiac VALUES (6,'Virgo','Virgin','Mercury','earth',8,23,9,22);
INSERT INTO zodiac VALUES (7,'Libra','Scales','Venus','air',9,23,10,23);
INSERT INTO zodiac VALUES (8,'Scorpio','Scorpion','Mars','water',10,24,11,21);
INSERT INTO zodiac VALUES (9,'Sagittarius','Archer','Jupiter','fire',11,22,12,↵
21);
INSERT INTO zodiac VALUES (10,'Capricorn','Goat','Saturn','earth',12,22,1,19);
INSERT INTO zodiac VALUES (11,'Aquarius','Water Carrier','Uranus','air',1,20,2,↵
18);
INSERT INTO zodiac VALUES (12,'Pisces','Fishes','Neptune','water',2,19,3,20);
```

Recipes 10.3 through 10.8 cover the basics of connecting to a database server, sending queries and getting the results back, as well as using queries that change the data in the database. Because Recipe 10.3 discusses how to connect to a database, the code in the subsequent recipes omits those lines so they can focus on the specifics of queries and result handling.

Typical PHP programs capture information from HTML form fields and store that information in the database. Some characters, such as the apostrophe and backslash, have special meaning in SQL, so you have to be careful if your form data contains those characters.

Versions of PHP prior to 5.4.0 have a feature called *magic quotes* that attempts to make this easier. When the configuration setting `magic_quotes_gpc` is on, variables coming from `get` requests, `post` requests, and cookies have single quotes, double quotes, back-slashes, and nulls escaped with a backslash. You can also turn on `magic_quotes_run time` to automatically escape quotes, backslashes, and nulls from external sources such as database queries or text files. For example, if `magic_quotes_runtime` is on and you read a file into an array with `file()`, the special characters in that array are backslash-escaped.

Unfortunately, *magic quotes* usually turns out to be more like *annoying quotes*. If you want to use submitted form data in any other context than an SQL query (for example, displaying it in a page), you need to undo the escaping so the page looks right. If you're using a version of PHP before 5.4.0, set the various magic quotes–related configuration directives mentioned to `off`. The right way to handle proper escaping of user input for database queries is discussed in Recipe 10.7, which explains PDO's *bound parameters* support. Additionally, Recipe 10.9 discusses escaping special characters in queries in more detail. General debugging techniques you can use to handle errors resulting from database queries are covered in Recipe 10.10.

The next set of recipes cover database tasks that are more involved than just simple queries. Recipe 10.11 shows how to automatically generate unique ID values you can use as record identifiers. Recipe 10.12 covers building queries at runtime from a list of fields. This makes it easier to manage INSERT and UPDATE queries with a lot of columns. Recipe 10.13 demonstrates how to display links that let you page through a result set, displaying a few records on each page. To speed up your database access, you can cache queries and their results, as explained in Recipe 10.14.

Recipe 10.15 shows techniques for managing access to a single database connection from multiple places in a large program. Then, Recipe 10.16 ties together some of the topics discussed in the chapter in a complete program that stores a threaded message board in a database.

In addition to SQL databases, PHP can work with a large number of so-called NoSQL databases—data stores that offer different models of how you organize and query for your information. There are too many NoSQL databases out there to cover them all here, so we talk about one, Redis, in Recipe 10.17.

10.1 Using DBM Databases

Problem

You have data that can be easily represented as key/value pairs, want to store it safely, and have very fast lookups based on those keys.

Solution

Use the DBA abstraction layer to access a DBM-style database, as shown in Example 10-3.

Example 10-3. Using a DBM database

```
$dbh = dba_open(__DIR__ . '/fish.db','c','db4') or die($php_errormsg);

// retrieve and change values
if (dba_exists('flounder',$dbh)) {
  $flounder_count = dba_fetch('flounder',$dbh);
  $flounder_count++;
  dba_replace('flounder',$flounder_count, $dbh);
  print "Updated the flounder count.";
} else {
  dba_insert('flounder',1, $dbh);
  print "Started the flounder count.";
}

// no more tilapia
dba_delete('tilapia',$dbh);

// what fish do we have?
for ($key = dba_firstkey($dbh); $key !== false; $key = dba_nextkey($dbh)) {
    $value = dba_fetch($key, $dbh);
    print "$key: $value\n";
}

dba_close($dbh);
```

Discussion

PHP can support many DBM backends, such as GDBM, NDBM, QDBM, DB2, DB3, DB4, DBM, and CDB. The DBA abstraction layer lets you use the same functions on any DBM backend. All these backends store key/value pairs. You can iterate through all the keys in a database, retrieve the value associated with a particular key, and find if a particular key exists. Both the keys and the values are strings.

The program in Example 10-4 maintains a list of usernames and passwords in a DBM database. The username is the first command-line argument, and the password is the second argument. If the given username already exists in the database, the password is changed to the given password; otherwise, the user and password combination are added to the database.

Example 10-4. Tracking users and passwords with a DBM database

```
$user = $argv[1];
$password = $argv[2];

$data_file = '/tmp/users.db';

$dbh = dba_open($data_file,'c','db4') or die("Can't open db $data_file");

if (dba_exists($user,$dbh)) {
    print "User $user exists. Changing password.";
} else {
    print "Adding user $user.";
}

dba_replace($user,$password,$dbh) or die("Can't write to database $data_file");

dba_close($dbh);
```

The dba_open() function returns a handle to a DBM file (or false on error). It takes three arguments. The first is the filename of the DBM file. The second argument is the mode for opening the file. A mode of r opens an existing database for read-only access, and w opens an existing database for read-write access. The c mode opens a database for read-write access and creates the database if it doesn't already exist. Last, n does the same thing as c, but if the database already exists, n empties it. The third argument to dba_open() is which DBM handler to use; this example uses db4.

To find what DBM handlers are compiled into your PHP installation, use the dba_han dlers() function. It returns an array of the supported handlers.

To find if a key has been set in a DBM database, use dba_exists(). It takes two arguments: a string key and a DBM file handle. It looks for the key in the DBM file and returns true if it finds the key (or false if it doesn't). The dba_replace() function takes three arguments: a string key, a string value, and a DBM file handle. It puts the key/value pair into the DBM file. If an entry already exists with the given key, it overwrites that entry with the new value.

To close a database, call dba_close(). A DBM file opened with dba_open() is automatically closed at the end of a request, but you need to call dba_close() explicitly to close persistent connections created with dba_popen().

You can use dba_firstkey() and dba_nextkey() to iterate through all the keys in a DBM file and dba_fetch() to retrieve the values associated with each key. The program in Example 10-5 calculates the total length of all passwords in a DBM file.

Example 10-5. Calculating password length with DBM

```
$data_file = '/tmp/users.db';
$total_length = 0;
$dbh = dba_open($data_file,'r','db4');
$dbh or die("Can't open database $data_file");

$k = dba_firstkey($dbh);
while ($k) {
    $total_length += strlen(dba_fetch($k,$dbh));
    $k = dba_nextkey($dbh);
}

print "Total length of all passwords is $total_length characters.";

dba_close($dbh);
```

The dba_firstkey() function initializes $k to the first key in the DBM file. Each time through the while loop, dba_fetch() retrieves the value associated with key $k and $total_length is incremented by the length of the value (calculated with strlen()). With dba_nextkey(), $k is set to the next key in the file.

One way to store complex data in a DBM database is with serialize(). Example 10-6 stores structured user information in a DBM database by serializing the structure before storing it and unserializing when retrieving it.

Example 10-6. Storing structured data in a DBM database

```
$dbh = dba_open('users.db','c','db4') or die($php_errormsg);

// read in and unserialize the data
$exists = dba_exists($_POST['username'], $dbh);
if ($exists) {
    $serialized_data = dba_fetch($_POST['username'], $dbh) or die($php_errormsg);
    $data = unserialize($serialized_data);
} else {
    $data = array();
}

// update values
if ($_POST['new_password']) {
    $data['password'] = $_POST['new_password'];
}
$data['last_access'] = time();

// write data back to file
if ($exists) {
    dba_replace($_POST['username'],serialize($data), $dbh);
} else {
    dba_insert($_POST['username'],serialize($data), $dbh);
}
```

```
dba_close($dbh);
```

Though Example 10-6 can store multiple users' data in the same file, you can't search for, for example, a user's last access time, without looping through each key in the file. If you need to do those kinds of searches, put your data in an SQL database.

Using a DBM database is a step up from a plain-text file but it lacks most features of an SQL database. Your data structure is limited to key/value pairs, and locking robustness varies greatly depending on the DBM handler. Still, DBM handlers can be a good choice for heavily accessed read-only data.

See Also

Recipe 5.7 discusses serializing data; documentation on the DBA functions (*http://www.php.net/dba*); for more information on the DB4 DBM handlers, see the Oracle website (*http://bit.ly/1kIIkS6*).

10.2 Using an SQLite Database

Problem

You want to use a relational database that doesn't involve a separate server process.

Solution

Use SQLite. This robust, powerful database program is easy to use and doesn't require running a separate server. An SQLite database is just a file. Example 10-7 creates an SQLite database, populates it with a table if it doesn't already exist, and then puts some data into the table.

Example 10-7. Creating an SQLite database

```
<programlisting>$db = new PDO('sqlite:/tmp/zodiac');

// Create the table and insert the data atomically
$db-&gt;beginTransaction();
// Try to find a table named 'zodiac'
$q = $db-&gt;query("SELECT name FROM sqlite_master WHERE type = 'table'" .
               " AND name = 'zodiac'");
// If the query didn't return a row, then create the table
// and insert the data
if ($q-&gt;fetch() === false) {
    $db-&gt;exec(&lt;&lt;&lt;_SQL_
CREATE TABLE zodiac (
  id INT UNSIGNED NOT NULL,
  sign CHAR(11),
  symbol CHAR(13),
```

```
    planet CHAR(7),
    element CHAR(5),
    start_month TINYINT,
    start_day TINYINT,
    end_month TINYINT,
    end_day TINYINT,
    PRIMARY KEY(id)
)
_SQL_
);

    // The individual SQL statements
    $sql=&lt;&lt;&lt;_SQL_
INSERT INTO zodiac VALUES (1,'Aries','Ram','Mars','fire',3,21,4,19);
INSERT INTO zodiac VALUES (2,'Taurus','Bull','Venus','earth',4,20,5,20);
INSERT INTO zodiac VALUES (3,'Gemini','Twins','Mercury','air',5,21,6,21);
INSERT INTO zodiac VALUES (4,'Cancer','Crab','Moon','water',6,22,7,22);
INSERT INTO zodiac VALUES (5,'Leo','Lion','Sun','fire',7,23,8,22);
INSERT INTO zodiac VALUES (6,'Virgo','Virgin','Mercury','earth',8,23,9,22);
INSERT INTO zodiac VALUES (7,'Libra','Scales','Venus','air',9,23,10,23);
INSERT INTO zodiac VALUES (8,'Scorpio','Scorpion','Mars','water',10,24,11,21);
INSERT INTO zodiac VALUES (9,'Sagittarius','Archer','Jupiter','fire',11,22,12,<?pdf-cr?>21);
INSERT INTO zodiac VALUES (10,'Capricorn','Goat','Saturn','earth',12,22,1,19);
INSERT INTO zodiac VALUES (11,'Aquarius','Water Carrier','Uranus','air',1,20,2,<?pdf-cr?>18)
INSERT INTO zodiac VALUES (12,'Pisces','Fishes','Neptune','water',2,19,3,20);
_SQL_;

    // Chop up each line of SQL and execute it
    foreach (explode("\n",trim($sql)) as $q) {
        $db-&gt;exec(trim($q));
    }
    $db-&gt;commit();
} else {
    // Nothing happened, so end the transaction
    $db-&gt;rollback();
}</programlisting>
```

Discussion

Because SQLite databases are just regular files, all the precautions and gotchas that apply to file access in PHP apply to SQLite databases. The user that your PHP process is running as must have permission to read from and write to the location where the SQLite database is. It is an extremely good idea to make this location somewhere outside your web server's document root. If the database file can be read directly by the web server, then a user who guesses its location can retrieve the entire thing, bypassing any restrictions you've built into the queries in your PHP programs.

In PHP, the sqlite extension provides regular SQLite access as well as a PDO driver for SQLite version 2. The pdo_sqlite extension provides a PDO driver for SQLite version 3. If you're starting from scratch, use the PDO driver for SQLite 3, because it's faster and has more features. If you already have an SQLite 2 database, consider using the PDO drivers to migrate to SQLite 3.

The `sqlite_master` table referenced in Example 10-7 is special system table that holds information about other tables—so it's useful in determining whether a particular table exists yet. Other databases have their own ways of providing this sort of system metadata.

See Also

Documentation on SQLite (*http://www.sqlite.org/docs.html*) and on `sqlite_master` (*http://www.sqlite.org/faq.html#q7*).

10.3 Connecting to an SQL Database

Problem

You want access to a SQL database to store or retrieve information. Without a database, dynamic websites aren't very dynamic.

Solution

Create a new `PDO` object with the appropriate connection string. Example 10-8 shows PDO object creation for a few different kinds of databases.

Example 10-8. Connecting with PDO

```
// MySQL expects parameters in the string
$mysql = new PDO('mysql:host=db.example.com', $user, $password);
// Separate multiple parameters with ;
$mysql = new PDO('mysql:host=db.example.com;port=31075', $user, $password);
$mysql = new PDO('mysql:host=db.example.com;port=31075;dbname=food', $user,
                $password);
// Connect to a local MySQL Server
$mysql = new PDO('mysql:unix_socket=/tmp/mysql.sock', $user, $password);

// PostgreSQL also expects parameters in the string
$pgsql = new PDO('pgsql:host=db.example.com', $user, $password);
// Separate multiple parameters with ' ' or ;
$pgsql = new PDO('pgsql:host=db.example.com port=31075', $user, $password);
$pgsql = new PDO('pgsql:host=db.example.com;port=31075;dbname=food', $user,
                $password);
// You can put the user and password in the DSN if you like.
$pgsql = new PDO("pgsql:host=db.example.com port=31075 dbname=food user=$user
                password=$password");

// Oracle
// If a database name is defined in tnsnames.ora, just put that in the DSN
// as the value of the dbname parameter
$oci = new PDO('oci:dbname=food', $user, $password);
```

```
// Otherwise, specify an Instant Client URI
$oci = new PDO('oci:dbname=//db.example.com:1521/food', $user, $password);

// Sybase (If PDO is using Sybase's ct-lib library)
$sybase = new PDO('sybase:host=db.example.com;dbname=food', $user, $password);
// Microsoft SQL Server (If PDO is using MS SQL Server libraries)
$mssql = new PDO('mssql:host=db.example.com;dbname=food', $user, $password);
// DBLib (for FreeTDS)
$dblib = new PDO('dblib:host=db.example.com;dbname=food', $user, $password);

// ODBC -- a predefined connection
$odbc = new PDO('odbc:food');
// ODBC -- an ad-hoc connection. Provide whatever the underlying driver needs
$odbc = new PDO('odbc:Driver={Microsoft Access Driver
                (*.mdb)};DBQ=C:\\data\\food.mdb;Uid=Chef');

// SQLite just expects a filename -- no user or password
$sqlite = new PDO('sqlite:/usr/local/zodiac.db');
$sqlite = new PDO('sqlite:c:/data/zodiac.db');
// SQLite can also handle in-memory, temporary databases
$sqlite = new PDO('sqlite::memory:');
// SQLite v2 DSNs look similar to v3
$sqlite2 = new PDO('sqlite2:/usr/local/old-zodiac.db');
```

Discussion

If all goes well, the PDO constructor returns a new object that can be used for querying the database. If there's a problem, a PDOException is thrown.

As you can see from Example 10-8, the format of the DSN is highly dependent on which kind of database you're attempting to connect to. In general, though, the first argument to the PDO constructor is a string that describes the location and name of the database you want and the second and third arguments are the username and password to connect to the database with. Note that to use a particular PDO backend, PHP must be built with support for that backend. Use the output from the PDO::getAvailableDriv ers() method to determine what PDO backends your PHP setup has.

See Also

Recipe 10.4 for querying an SQL database; Recipe 10.6 for modifying an SQL database; documentation on PDO (*http://www.php.net/PDO*).

10.4 Querying an SQL Database

Problem

You want to retrieve some data from your database.

Solution

Use PDO::query() to send the SQL query to the database, and then a foreach loop to retrieve each row of the result, as shown in Example 10-9.

Example 10-9. Sending a query to the database

```
$st = $db->query('SELECT symbol,planet FROM zodiac');
foreach ($st->fetchAll() as $row) {
    print "{$row['symbol']} goes with {$row['planet']} <br/>\n";
}
```

Discussion

The query() method returns a PDOStatement object. Its fetchAll() method provides a concise way to operate on each row returned from a query.

The fetch() method returns a row at a time, as shown in Example 10-10.

Example 10-10. Fetching individual rows

```
$rows = $db->query('SELECT symbol,planet FROM zodiac ORDER BY planet');
$firstRow = $rows->fetch();
print "The first results are that {$firstRow['symbol']} goes with ↵
{$firstRow['planet']}";
```

Each call to fetch() returns the next row in the result set. When there are no more rows available, fetch() returns false.

By default, fetch() returns an array containing each column in the result set row *twice* —once with an index corresponding to the column name and once with a numerical index. That means that the $firstRow variable in Example 10-10 has four elements: $firstRow[0] is Archer, $firstRow[1] is Jupiter, $firstRow['symbol'] is Archer, and $firstRow['planet'] is Jupiter.

To have fetch() return rows in a different format, pass a PDO::FETCH_* constant to query() as a second argument. You can also pass one of the constants as the first argument to fetch(). The allowable constants and what they make fetch() return are listed in Table 10-1.

Table 10-1. PDO::FETCH_* constants

Constant	Row format
PDO::FETCH_BOTH	Array with both numeric and string (column names) keys. The default format.
PDO::FETCH_NUM	Array with numeric keys.
PDO::FETCH_ASSOC	Array with string (column names) keys.
PDO::FETCH_OBJ	Object of class stdClass with column names as property names.

Constant	Row format
PDO::FETCH_LAZY	Object of class PDORow with column names as property names. The properties aren't populated until accessed, so this is a good choice if your result row has a lot of columns. Note that if you store the returned object and fetch another row, the stored object is updated with values from the new row.

In addition to the choices in Table 10-1, there are other ways a row can be structured. These other ways require more than just passing a constant to `query()` or `fetch()`, however.

In combination with `bindColumn()`, the `PDO::FETCH_BOUND` fetch mode lets you set up variables whose values get refreshed each time `fetch()` is called. Example 10-11 shows how this works.

Example 10-11. Binding result columns

```
$row = $db->query('SELECT symbol,planet FROM zodiac',PDO::FETCH_BOUND);
// Put the value of the 'symbol' column in $symbol
$row->bindColumn('symbol', $symbol);
// Put the value of the second column ('planet') in $planet
$row->bindColumn(2, $planet);
while ($row->fetch()) {
    print "$symbol goes with $planet. <br/>\n";
}
```

In Example 10-11, each time `fetch()` is called, `$symbol` and `$planet` are assigned new values. Note that you can use either a column name or number with `bindColumn()`. Column numbers start at 1.

When used with `query()`, the `PDO::FETCH_INTO` and `PDO::FETCH_CLASS` constants put result rows into specialized objects of particular classes. To use these modes, first create a class that extends the built-in `PDOStatement` class. Example 10-12 extends `PDOStatement` with a method that reports the average length of all the column values and then sets up a query to use it.

Example 10-12. Extending PDOStatement

```
class AvgStatement extends PDOStatement {
    public function avg() {
        $sum = 0;
        $vars = get_object_vars($this);
        // Remove PDOStatement's built-in 'queryString' variable
        unset($vars['queryString']);
        foreach ($vars as $var => $value) {
            $sum += strlen($value);
        }
        return $sum / count($vars);
    }
}
$row = new AvgStatement;
$results = $db->query('SELECT symbol,planet FROM zodiac',PDO::FETCH_INTO, $row);
```

```
// Each time fetch() is called, $row is repopulated
while ($results->fetch()) {
    print "$row->symbol belongs to $row->planet (Average: {$row->avg()}) <br/>
    \n";
}
```

In Example 10-12, the second and third arguments to query() tell PDO "each time you fetch a new row, stuff the values into properties of the $row variable." Then, inside the while() loop, the properties of $row are available, as well as the newly defined avg() method.

PDO::FETCH_INTO is useful when you want to keep data around in the same object, such as whether you're displaying an odd- or even-numbered row, throughout all the calls to fetch(). But when you want a new object for each row, use PDO::FETCH_CLASS. Pass it to query() like PDO::FETCH_INTO, but make the third argument to query() a class name, not an object instance. The class name you provide with PDO::FETCH_CLASS must extend PDOStatement.

See Also

Recipe 10.5 for other ways to retrieve data; Recipe 10.6 for modifying an SQL database; Recipe 10.7 for repeating queries efficiently; documentation on PDO (*http://www.php.net/PDO*).

10.5 Retrieving Rows Without a Loop

Problem

You want a concise way to execute a query and retrieve the data it returns.

Solution

Use fetchAll() to get all the results from a query at once, as shown in Example 10-13.

Example 10-13. Getting all results at once

```
$st = $db->query('SELECT planet, element FROM zodiac');
$results = $st->fetchAll();
foreach ($results as $i => $result) {
    print "Planet $i is {$result['planet']} <br/>\n";
}
```

Discussion

The fetchAll() method is useful when you need to do something that depends on all the rows a query returns, such as counting how many rows there are or handling rows out of order. Like `fetch()`, `fetchAll()` defaults to representing each row as an array with both numeric and string keys and accepts the various `PDO::FETCH_*` constants to change that behavior.

`fetchAll()` also accepts a few other constants that affect the results it returns. To retrieve just a single column from the results, pass `PDO::FETCH_COLUMN` and a second argument, the index of the column you want. The first column is 0, not 1.

See Also

Recipe 10.4 for querying an SQL database and more information on fetch modes; Recipe 10.6 for modifying an SQL database; Recipe 10.7 for repeating queries efficiently; documentation on PDO (*http://www.php.net/PDO*).

10.6 Modifying Data in an SQL Database

Problem

You want to add, remove, or change data in an SQL database.

Solution

Use `PDO::exec()` to send an `INSERT`, `DELETE`, or `UPDATE` command, as shown in Example 10-14.

Example 10-14. Using PDO::exec()

```
$db->exec("INSERT INTO family (id,name) VALUES (1,'Vito')");

$db->exec("DELETE FROM family WHERE name LIKE 'Fredo'");

$db->exec("UPDATE family SET is_naive = 1 WHERE name LIKE 'Kay'");
```

You can also prepare a query with `PDO::prepare()` and execute it with `PDOState ment::execute()`, as shown in Example 10-15.

Example 10-15. Preparing and executing a query

```
$st = $db->prepare('INSERT INTO family (id,name) VALUES (?,?)');
$st->execute(array(1,'Vito'));

$st = $db->prepare('DELETE FROM family WHERE name LIKE ?');
$st->execute(array('Fredo'));

$st = $db->prepare('UPDATE family SET is_naive = ? WHERE name LIKE ?');
$st->execute(array(1,'Kay'));
```

Discussion

The exec() method sends to the database whatever it's passed. For INSERT, UPDATE, and DELETE queries, it returns the number of rows affected by the query.

The prepare() and execute() methods are especially useful for queries that you want to execute multiple times. Once you've prepared a query, you can execute it with new values without repreparing it. Example 10-16 reuses the same prepared query three times.

Example 10-16. Reusing a prepared statement

```
$st = $db->prepare('DELETE FROM family WHERE name LIKE ?');
$st->execute(array('Fredo'));
$st->execute(array('Sonny'));
$st->execute(array('Luca Brasi'));
```

See Also

Recipe 10.7 for information on repeating queries; documentation on PDO::exec() (*http://bit.ly/1mfhEqO*), on PDO::prepare() (*http://bit.ly/UEU3u7*), and on PDOState ment::execute() (*http://bit.ly/1qGJovZ*).

10.7 Repeating Queries Efficiently

Problem

You want to run the same query multiple times, substituting in different values each time.

Solution

Set up the query with PDO::prepare() and then run it by calling execute() on the prepared statement that prepare() returns. The placeholders in the query passed to prepare() are replaced with data by execute(), as shown in Example 10-17.

Example 10-17. Running prepared statements

```
// Prepare
$st = $db->prepare("SELECT sign FROM zodiac WHERE element LIKE ?");
// Execute once
$st->execute(array('fire'));
while ($row = $st->fetch()) {
    print $row[0] . "<br/>\n";
}
// Execute again
$st->execute(array('water'));
while ($row = $st->fetch()) {
```

```
        print $row[0] . "<br/>\n";
    }
```

Discussion

The values passed to execute() are called *bound parameters*—each value is associated with (or "bound to") a placeholder in the query. Two great things about bound parameters are security and speed. With bound parameters, you don't have to worry about SQL injection attacks. PDO appropriately quotes and escapes each parameter so that special characters are neutralized. Also, upon prepare(), many database backends do some parsing and optimizing of the query, so each call to execute() is faster than calling exec() or query() with a fully formed query in a string you've built yourself.

In Example 10-17, the first execute() runs the query SELECT sign FROM zodiac WHERE element LIKE 'fire'. The second execute() runs SELECT sign FROM zodiac WHERE element LIKE 'water'.

Each time, execute() substitutes the value in its second argument for the ? placeholder. If there is more than one placeholder, put the arguments in the array in the order they should appear in the query. Example 10-18 shows prepare() and execute() with two placeholders.

Example 10-18. Multiple placeholders

```
$st = $db->prepare(
    "SELECT sign FROM zodiac WHERE element LIKE ? OR planet LIKE ?");

// SELECT sign FROM zodiac WHERE element LIKE 'earth' OR planet LIKE 'Mars'
$st->execute(array('earth','Mars'));
```

In addition to the ? placeholder style, PDO also supports named placeholders. If you've got a lot of placeholders in a query, this can make them easier to read. Instead of ?, put a placeholder name (which has to begin with a colon) in the query, and then use those placeholder names (without the colons) as keys in the parameter array you pass to execute(). Example 10-19 shows named placeholders in action.

Example 10-19. Using named placeholders

```
$st = $db->prepare(
    "SELECT sign FROM zodiac WHERE element LIKE :element OR planet LIKE :planet");
// SELECT sign FROM zodiac WHERE element LIKE 'earth' OR planet LIKE 'Mars'
$st->execute(array('planet' => 'Mars', 'element' => 'earth'));
$row = $st->fetch();
```

With named placeholders, your queries are easier to read and you can provide the values to execute() in any order. Note, though, that each placeholder name can only appear in a query once. If you want to provide the same value more than once in a query, use two different placeholder names and include the value twice in the array passed to execute().

Aside from ? and named placeholders, prepare() offers a third way to stuff values into queries: bindParam(). This method automatically associates what's in a variable with a particular placeholder. Example 10-20 shows how to use bindParam().

Example 10-20. Using bindParam()

```
$pairs = array('Mars' => 'water',
               'Moon' => 'water',
               'Sun' => 'fire');
$st = $db->prepare(
  "SELECT sign FROM zodiac WHERE element LIKE :element AND planet LIKE
  :planet");
$st->bindParam(':element', $element);
$st->bindparam(':planet', $planet);
foreach ($pairs as $planet => $element) {
    // No need to pass anything to execute() --
    // the values come from $element and $planet
    $st->execute();
    var_dump($st->fetch());
}
```

In Example 10-20, there's no need to pass any values to execute(). The two calls to bindParam() tell PDO "whenever you execute $st, use whatever's in the $element variable for the :element placeholder and whatever's in the $planet variable for the :planet placeholder." The values in those variables when you call bindParam() don't matter—it's the values in those variables when execute() is called that counts. Because the foreach statement puts array keys in $planet and array values in $element, the keys and values from $pairs are substituted into the query.

If you use ? placeholders with prepare(), provide a placeholder position as the first argument to bindParam() instead of a parameter name. Placeholder positions start at 1, not 0.

bindParam() takes its cue on how to deal with the provided value based on that value's PHP type. Force bindParam() to treat the value as a particular type by passing a type constant as a third argument. The type constants that bindParam() understands are listed in Table 10-2.

Table 10-2. PDO::PARAM_* constants

Constant	Type
PDO::PARAM_NULL	NULL
PDO::PARAM_BOOL	boolean
PDO::PARAM_INT	integer

Constant	Type
PDO::PARAM_STR	string
PDO::PARAM_LOB	"large object"

The PDO::PARAM_LOB type is particularly handy because it treats the parameter as a stream. It makes for an efficient way to stuff the contents of files (or anything that can be represented by a stream, such as a remote URL) into a database table. Example 10-21 uses glob() to slurp the contents of all the files in a directory into a database table.

Example 10-21. Putting file contents into a database with PDO::PARAM_LOB

```
$st = $db->prepare('INSERT INTO files (path,contents) VALUES (:path,:contents)');
$st->bindParam(':path',$path);
$st->bindParam(':contents',$fp,PDO::PARAM_LOB);
foreach (glob('/usr/local/*') as $path) {
    // Get a filehandle that PDO::PARAM_LOB can work with
    $fp = fopen($path,'r');
    $st->execute();
}
```

Using PDO::PARAM_LOB effectively depends on your underlying database. For example, with Oracle your query must create an empty LOB handle and be inside a transaction. The "Inserting an image into a database: Oracle" example (*http://www.php.net/pdo.lobs*) of the PDO manpage shows the proper syntax to do this.

See Also

Check out the documentation on PDO::prepare() (*http://bit.ly/UEU3u7*), on PDOStatement::execute() (*http://bit.ly/1qGJovZ*), on PDOStatement::bindParam() (*http://bit.ly/1pIEgpo*), and on PDO::PARAM_LOB in the Large Objects (*http://bit.ly/1v1e7BQ*) section.

10.8 Finding the Number of Rows Returned by a Query

Problem

You want to know how many rows a SELECT query returned, or you want to know how many rows an INSERT, UPDATE, or DELETE query changed.

Solution

If you're issuing an INSERT, UPDATE, or DELETE with PDO::exec(), the return value from exec() is the number of modified rows.

If you're issuing an INSERT, UPDATE, or DELETE with PDO::prepare() and PDOState ment::execute(), call PDOStatement::rowCount() to get the number of modified rows, as shown in Example 10-22.

Example 10-22. Counting rows with rowCount()

```
$st = $db->prepare('DELETE FROM family WHERE name LIKE ?');
$st->execute(array('Fredo'));
print "Deleted rows: " . $st->rowCount();
$st->execute(array('Sonny'));
print "Deleted rows: " . $st->rowCount();
$st->execute(array('Luca Brasi'));
print "Deleted rows: " . $st->rowCount();
```

If you're issuing a SELECT statement, the only foolproof way to find out how many rows are returned is to retrieve them all with fetchAll() and then count how many rows you have, as shown in Example 10-23.

Example 10-23. Counting rows from a SELECT

```
$st = $db->query('SELECT symbol,planet FROM zodiac');
$all= $st->fetchAll(PDO::FETCH_COLUMN, 1);
print "Retrieved ". count($all) . " rows";
```

Discussion

Although some database backends provide information to PDO about the number of rows retrieved by a SELECT, so that rowCount() can work in those circumstances, not all do. So relying on that behavior isn't a good idea.

However, retrieving everything in a large result set can be inefficient. As an alternative, ask the database to calculate a result set size with the COUNT(*) function. Use the same WHERE clause as you would otherwise, but ask SELECT to return COUNT(*) instead of a list of fields.

See Also

Documentation on PDOStatement::rowCount (*http://www.php.net/pdostate ment.rowcount*) and on PDO::exec() (*http://www.php.net/pdo.exec*).

10.9 Escaping Quotes

Problem

You need to make text or binary data safe for queries.

Solution

Write all your queries with placeholders so that `prepare()` and `execute()` can escape strings for you. Recipe 10.7 details the different ways to use placeholders.

If you need to apply escaping yourself, use the `PDO::quote()` method. The rare circumstance you might need to do this could be if you want to escape SQL wildcards coming from user input, as shown in Example 10-24.

Example 10-24. Manual quoting

```
$safe = $db->quote($_GET['searchTerm']);
$safe = strtr($safe,array('_' => '\_', '%' => '\%'));
$st = $db->query("SELECT * FROM zodiac WHERE planet LIKE $safe");
```

Discussion

The `PDO::quote()` method makes sure that text or binary data is appropriately quoted, but you may also need to quote the SQL wildcard characters % and _ to ensure that `SELECT` statements using the `LIKE` operator return the right results. If `$_GET['search Term']` is set to `Melm%` and Example 10-24 doesn't call `strtr()`, its query returns rows with `planet` set to `Melmac`, `Melmacko`, `Melmacedonia`, or anything else beginning with `Melm`.

Because % is the SQL wildcard meaning *match any number of characters* (like * in shell globbing) and _ is the SQL wildcard meaning *match one character* (like ? in shell globbing), those need to be backslash-escaped as well.

`strtr()` must be called after `PDO::quote()`. Otherwise, `PDO::quote()` would backslash-escape the backslashes `strtr()` adds. With `PDO::quote()` first, `Melm_` is turned into `Melm\_`, which is interpreted by the database to mean the string "M e l m followed by a literal underscore character." With `PDO::quote()` after `strtr()`, `Melm_` is turned into `Melm\\_`, which is interpreted by the database to mean the string "Melm followed by a literal backslash character, followed by the underscore wildcard." This is the same thing that would happen if we escaped the SQL wildcards and then used the resulting value as a bound parameter.

Quoting of placeholder values happens even if `magic_quotes_gpc` or `magic_quotes_runtime` is turned on. Similarly, if you call `PDO::quote()` on a value when magic quotes are active, the value gets quoted anyway. For maximum portability, remove the magic quotes–supplied backslashes before you use a query with placeholders or call `PDO::quote()`. Example 10-25 shows this check.

Example 10-25. Checking for magic quotes

```
// The behavior of magic_quotes_sybase can also affect things
if (get_magic_quotes_gpc() && (! ini_get('magic_quotes_sybase'))) {
```

```
    $fruit = stripslashes($_GET['fruit']);
} else {
    $fruit = $_GET['fruit'];
}
$st = $db->prepare('UPDATE orchard SET trees = trees - 1 WHERE fruit = ?');
$st->execute(array($fruit));
```

 If you have any control over your server, turn magic quotes off and make your life a lot easier. However, if you're trying to write maximally portable code that could run in an environment you don't control, you need to look out for this problem.

See Also

Documentation on PDO::quote() (*http://www.php.net/PDO.quote*) and on magic quotes (*http://bit.ly/1iZ6GUQ*).

10.10 Logging Debugging Information and Errors

Problem

You want access to information to help you debug database problems. For example, when a query fails, you want to see what error message the database returns.

Solution

Use PDO::errorCode() or PDOStatement::errorCode() after an operation to get an error code if the operation failed. The corresponding errorInfo() method returns more information about the error. Example 10-26 handles the error that results from trying to access a nonexistent table.

Example 10-26. Printing error information

```
$st = $db->prepare('SELECT * FROM imaginary_table');
if (! $st) {
    $error = $db->errorInfo();
    print "Problem ({$error[2]})";
}
```

Discussion

The errorCode() method returns a five-character error code. PDO uses the SQL 92 SQLSTATE error codes. By that standard, 00000 means "no error," so a call to error Code() that returns 00000 indicates success.

The errorInfo() method returns a three-element array. The first element contains the five-character SQLSTATE code (the same thing that errorCode() returns). The second element is a database backend-specific error code. The third element is a database backend-specific error message.

Make sure to call errorCode() or errorInfo() on the same object on which you called the method that you're checking for an error. In Example 10-26, the prepare() method is called on the PDO object, so errorInfo() is called on the PDO object. If you want to check whether a fetch() called on a PDOStatement object succeeded, call error Code() or errorInfo() on the PDOStatement object.

One exception to this rule is when creating a new PDO object. If that fails, PDO throws an exception. It does this because otherwise there'd be no object on which you could call errorCode() or errorInfo(). The message in the exception details why the connection failed.

To have PDO throw exceptions *every* time it encounters an error, call setAttri bute(PDO::ATTR_ERRMODE, PDO::ERRMODE_EXCEPTION) on your PDO object after it's created. This way, you can handle database problems uniformly instead of larding your code with repeated calls to errorCode() and errorInfo(). Example 10-27 performs a series of database operations wrapped inside a try/catch block.

Example 10-27. Catching database exceptions

```
try {
    $db = new PDO('sqlite:/tmp/zodiac.db');
    // Make all DB errors throw exceptions
    $db->setAttribute(PDO::ATTR_ERRMODE, PDO::ERRMODE_EXCEPTION);
    $st = $db->prepare('SELECT * FROM zodiac');
    $st->execute();
    while ($row = $st->fetch(PDO::FETCH_NUM)) {
        print implode(',',$row). "<br/>\n";
    }
} catch (Exception $e) {
    print "Database Problem: " . $e->getMessage();
}
```

Handling PDO errors as exceptions is useful inside of transactions, too. If there's a problem with a query once the transaction's started, just roll back the transaction when handling the exception.

Similar to the exception error mode is the "warning" error mode. setAttri bute(PDO::ATTR_ERRMODE, PDO::ERRMODE_WARNING) tells PDO to issue warnings when a database error is encountered. If you prefer to work with regular PHP errors instead of exceptions, this is the error mode for you. Set up a custom error handler with set_error_handler() to handle E_WARNING level events and you can deal with your database problems in the error handler.

Whatever the error mode, PDO throws an exception if the initial PDO object creation fails. When using PDO, it's an extremely good idea to set up a default exception handler with `set_exception_handler()`. Without a default exception handler, an uncaught exception causes the display of a complete stack trace if `display_errors` is on. If an exception is thrown when connecting to the database, this stack trace may contain sensitive information, including database connection credentials.

See Also

Documentation on `PDO::errorCode()` (*http://bit.ly/1nEbmDV*), on `PDO::errorIn fo()` (*http://bit.ly/1wxUT9x*), on `PDOStatement::errorCode()` (*http://bit.ly/Vo2o61*), on `PDOStatement::errorInfo()` (*http://bit.ly/1lQ81D3*), on `set_exception_han dler()` (*http://bit.ly/1ryZ3v0*), and on `set_error_handler()` (*http://bit.ly/TjyjT4*). Page 619 of the SQL 92 standard (*http://bit.ly/14R3PYK*) contains the SQLSTATE error codes that PDO knows about is available, but some database backends may raise errors other than the ones listed.

10.11 Creating Unique Identifiers

Problem

You want to assign unique IDs to users, articles, or other objects as you add them to your database.

Solution

Use PHP's `uniqid()` function to generate an identifier. To restrict the set of characters in the identifier, pass it through `md5()`, which returns a string containing only numerals and the letters `a` through `f`. Example 10-28 creates identifiers using both techniques.

Example 10-28. Creating unique identifiers

```
$st = $db->prepare('INSERT INTO users (id, name) VALUES (?,?)');
$st->execute(array(uniqid(), 'Jacob'));
$st->execute(array(md5(uniqid()), 'Ruby'));
```

You can also use a database-specific method to have the database generate the ID. For example, SQLite 3 and MySQL support AUTOINCREMENT columns that automatically assign increasing integers to a column as rows are inserted.

Discussion

`uniqid()` uses the current time (in microseconds) and a random number to generate a string that is extremely difficult to guess. `md5()` computes a hash of whatever you give it. It doesn't add any randomness to the identifier, but restricts the characters that appear in it. The results of md5() don't contain any punctuation, so you don't have to worry about escaping issues. Plus, you can't spell any naughty words with just the first six letters of the alphabet (in English, at least).

If you'd rather give your database the responsibility of generating the unique identifier, use the appropriate syntax when creating a table. Example 10-29 shows how to create a table in SQLite with a column that gets an auto-incremented integer ID each time a new row is inserted.

Example 10-29. Creating an auto-increment column with SQLite

```
// the type INTEGER PRIMARY KEY AUTOINCREMENT tells SQLite
// to assign ascending IDs
$db->exec(<<<_SQL_
  CREATE TABLE users (
    id  INTEGER PRIMARY KEY AUTOINCREMENT,
    name VARCHAR(255)
  )
_SQL_
);

// No need to insert a value for 'id' -- SQLite assigns it
$st = $db->prepare('INSERT INTO users (name) VALUES (?)');

// These rows are assigned 'id' values
foreach (array('Jacob','Ruby') as $name) {
    $st->execute(array($name));
}
```

Example 10-30 shows the same thing for MySQL.

Example 10-30. Creating an auto-increment column with MySQL

```
// the AUTO_INCREMENT tells MySQL to assign ascending IDs
// that column must be the PRIMARY KEY
$db->exec(<<<_SQL_
  CREATE TABLE users (
    id  INT NOT NULL AUTO_INCREMENT,
    name VARCHAR(255),
    PRIMARY KEY(id)
  )
_SQL_
);

// No need to insert a value for 'id' -- MySQL assigns it
$st = $db->prepare('INSERT INTO users (name) VALUES (?)');

// These rows are assigned 'id' values
foreach (array('Jacob','Ruby') as $name) {
    $st->execute(array($name));
}
```

When the database creates ID values automatically, the PDO::lastInsertId() method retrieves them. Call lastInsertId() on your PDO object to get the auto-generated ID of the last inserted row. Some database backends also let you pass a sequence name to lastInsertId() to get the last value from the sequence. Some database backends don't support PDO::lastInsertId() at all. In that case, PDO::lastInsertId() causes an error with SQLSTATE set to IM001.

See Also

Documentation on uniqid() (*http://www.php.net/uniqid*), on md5() (*http://www.php.net/md5*), on PDO::lastInsertId() (*http://www.php.net/PDO.lastInsertId*), on SQLite and AUTOINCREMENT (*http://www.sqlite.org/autoinc.html*), and on MySQL and AUTO_INCREMENT (*http://bit.ly/1kS760t*).

10.12 Building Queries Programmatically

Problem

You want to construct an INSERT or UPDATE query from an array of field names. For example, you want to insert a new user into your database. Instead of hardcoding each field of user information (such as username, email address, postal address, birthdate, etc.), you put the field names in an array and use the array to build the query. This is easier to maintain, especially if you need to conditionally INSERT or UPDATE with the same set of fields.

Solution

To construct an UPDATE query, build an array of field/value pairs and then implode() together each element of that array, as shown in Example 10-31.

Example 10-31. Building an UPDATE query

```
// A list of field names
$fields = array('symbol','planet','element');

$update_fields = array();
$update_values = array();
foreach ($fields as $field) {
    $update_fields[] = "$field = ?";
    // Assume the data is coming from a form
    $update_values[] = $_POST[$field];
}

$st = $db->prepare("UPDATE zodiac SET " .
                    implode(',', $update_fields) .
                    'WHERE sign = ?');
```

```
// Add 'sign' to the values array
$update_values[] = $_GET['sign'];

// Execute the query
$st->execute($update_values);
```

For an INSERT query, do the same thing, although the SQL syntax is a little different, as Example 10-32 demonstrates.

Example 10-32. Building an INSERT query

```
// A list of field names
$fields = array('symbol','planet','element');
$placeholders = array();
$values = array();
foreach ($fields as $field) {
    // One placeholder per field
    $placeholders[] = '?';
    // Assume the data is coming from a form
    $values[] = $_POST[$field];
}

$st = $db->prepare('INSERT INTO zodiac (' .
                    implode(',',$fields) .
                    ') VALUES (' .
                    implode(',', $placeholders) .
                    ')');
// Execute the query
$st->execute($values);
```

Discussion

Placeholders make this sort of thing a breeze. Because they take care of escaping the provided data, you can easily stuff user-submitted data into programatically generated queries.

If you use sequence-generated integers as primary keys, you can combine the two query-construction techniques into one function. That function determines whether a record exists and then generates the correct query, including a new ID, as shown in the build_query() function in Example 10-33.

Example 10-33. build_query()

```
function build_query($db,$key_field,$fields,$table) {
    $values = array();
    if (! empty($_POST[$key_field])) {
        $update_fields = array();
        foreach ($fields as $field) {
            $update_fields[] = "$field = ?";
            // Assume the data is coming from a form
```

```
                $values[] = $_POST[$field];
            }
            // Add the key field's value to the $values array
            $values[] = $_POST[$key_field];
            $st = $db->prepare("UPDATE $table SET " .
                        implode(',', $update_fields) .
                        "WHERE $key_field = ?");
        } else {
            // Start values off with a unique ID
            // If your DB is set to generate this value, use NULL instead
            $values[] = md5(uniqid());
            $placeholders = array('?');
            foreach ($fields as $field) {
                // One placeholder per field
                $placeholders[] = '?';
                // Assume the data is coming from a form
                $values[] = $_POST[$field];
            }
            $st = $db->prepare("INSERT INTO $table ($key_field," .
                            implode(',',$fields) . ') VALUES ('.
                            implode(',',$placeholders) .')'); 
        }
        $st->execute($values);
        return $st;
    }
```

Using this function, you can make a simple page to edit all the information in the zodiac table, shown in Example 10-34.

Example 10-34. A simple add/edit record page

```
// The file where build_query() is defined
include __DIR__ . '/buildquery.php';

$db = new PDO('sqlite:/tmp/zodiac.db');
$db->setAttribute(PDO::ATTR_ERRMODE, PDO::ERRMODE_EXCEPTION);

$fields = array('sign','symbol','planet','element',
                'start_month','start_day','end_month','end_day');

$cmd = isset($_REQUEST['cmd']) ? $_REQUEST['cmd'] : 'show';

switch ($cmd) {
 case 'edit':
 try {
    $st = $db->prepare('SELECT ' . implode(',',$fields) .
                        ' FROM zodiac WHERE id = ?');
    $st->execute(array($_GET['id']));
    $row = $st->fetch(PDO::FETCH_ASSOC);
 } catch (Exception $e) {
     $row = array();
 }
```

```
case 'add':
    print '<form method="post" action="' .
        htmlentities($_SERVER['PHP_SELF']) . '">';
    print '<input type="hidden" name="cmd" value="save">';
    print '<table>';
    if ('edit' == $cmd) {
        printf('<input type="hidden" name="id" value="%d">',
            $_GET['id']);
    }
    foreach ($fields as $field) {
        if ('edit' == $cmd) {
            $value = htmlentities($row[$field]);
        } else {
            $value = '';
        }
        printf('<tr><td>%s: </td><td><input type="text" name="%s" value="%s">',
            $field,$field,$value);
        printf('</td></tr>');
    }
    print '<tr><td></td><td><input type="submit" value="Save"></td></tr>';
    print '</table></form>';
    break;
case 'save':
    try {
        $st = build_query($db,'id',$fields,'zodiac');
        print 'Added info.';
    } catch (Exception $e) {
        print "Couldn't add info: " . htmlentities($e->getMessage());
    }
    print '<hr>';
case 'show':
default:
    $self = htmlentities($_SERVER['PHP_SELF']);
    print '<ul>';
    foreach ($db->query('SELECT id,sign FROM zodiac') as $row) {
        printf('<li> <a href="%s?cmd=edit&id=%s">%s</a>',
            $self,$row['id'],htmlentities($row['sign']));
    }
    print '<hr><li> <a href="'.$self.'?cmd=add">Add New</a>';
    print '</ul>';
    break;
}
```

The switch statement controls what action the program takes based on the value of
$_REQUEST['cmd']. If $_REQUEST['cmd'] is add or edit, the program displays a form
with text boxes for each field in the $fields array, as shown in Figure 10-1. If $_RE
QUEST['cmd'] is edit, values for the row with the supplied $id are loaded from the
database and displayed as defaults. If $_REQUEST['cmd'] is save, the program uses
build_query() to generate an appropriate query to either INSERT or UPDATE the data

in the database. After saving (or if no $_REQUEST['cmd'] is specified), the program displays a list of all zodiac signs, as shown in Figure 10-2.

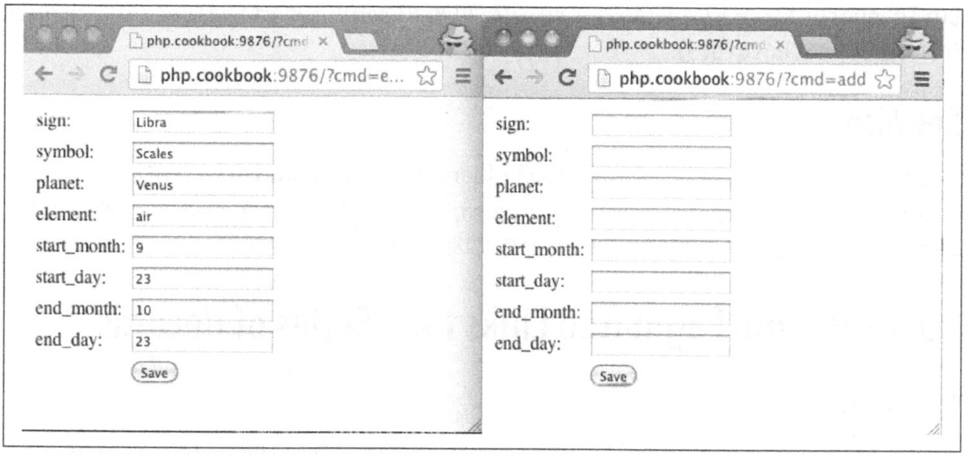

Figure 10-1. Editing and adding a record

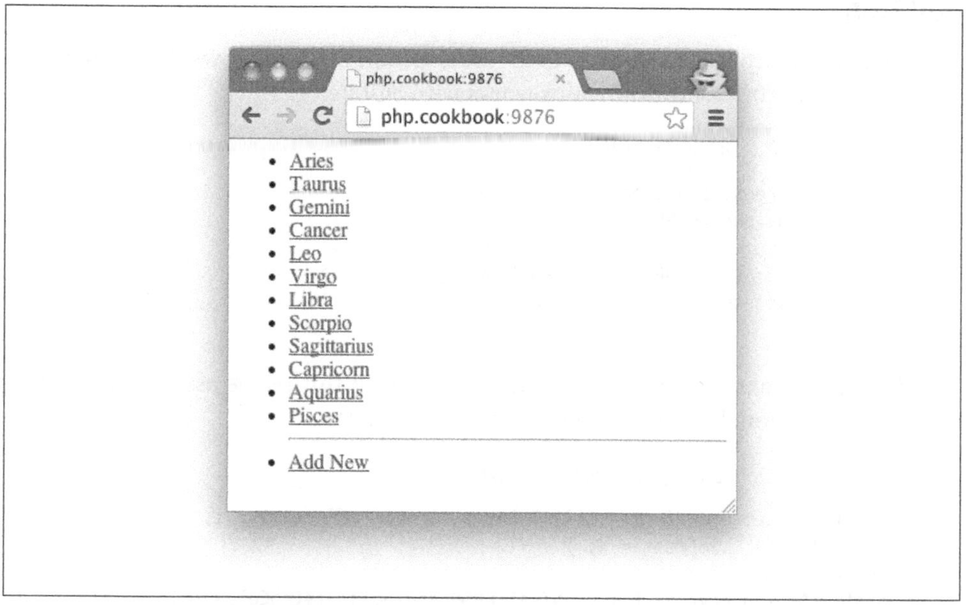

Figure 10-2. Listing records

Whether build_query() builds an INSERT or UPDATE statement is based on the presence of the request variable $_REQUEST['id'] (because id is passed in $key_field). If $_RE

QUEST['id'] is not empty, the function builds an UPDATE query to change the row with that ID. If $_REQUEST['id'] is empty (or it hasn't been set at all), the function generates a new ID and uses that new ID in an INSERT query that adds a row to the table. To have build_query() respect a database's AUTOINCREMENT setting, start $values off with null instead of md5(uniqid()).

See Also

Recipe 10.7 for information about placeholders, prepare(), and execute(); documentation on PDO::prepare() (*http://www.php.net/PDO.prepare*) and on PDOStatement::execute() (*http://www.php.net/PDOStatement.execute()*).

10.13 Making Paginated Links for a Series of Records

Problem

You want to display a large dataset a page at a time and provide links that move through the dataset.

Solution

Use database-appropriate syntax to grab just a section of all the rows that match your query. Example 10-35 shows how this works with SQLite.

Example 10-35. Paging with SQLite

```
// Select 5 rows, starting after the first 3
foreach ($db->query('SELECT * FROM zodiac ' .
                    'ORDER BY sign LIMIT 5 ' .
                    'OFFSET 3') as $row) {
    // Do something with each row
}
```

The indexed_links() and print_link() functions in this recipe assist with printing paging information. Example 10-36 shows them in action.

Example 10-36. Displaying paginated results

```
$offset = isset($_GET['offset']) ? intval($_GET['offset']) : 1;
if (! $offset) { $offset = 1; }
$per_page = 5;
$total = $db->query('SELECT COUNT(*) FROM zodiac')->fetchColumn(0);

$limitedSQL = 'SELECT * FROM zodiac ORDER BY id ' .
              "LIMIT $per_page OFFSET " . ($offset-1);
$lastRowNumber = $offset - 1;

foreach ($db->query($limitedSQL) as $row) {
```

```
        $lastRowNumber++;
        print "{$row['sign']}, {$row['symbol']} ({$row['id']}) <br/>\n";
}

indexed_links($total,$offset,$per_page);
print "<br/>";
print "(Displaying $offset - $lastRowNumber of $total)";
```

Discussion

`print_link()` is shown in Example 10-37 and `indexed_links()` is shown in Example 10-38.

Example 10-37. print_link()

```
function print_link($inactive,$text,$offset='') {
    if ($inactive) {
        print "<span class='inactive'>$text</span>";
    } else {
        print "<span class='active'>".
            "<a href='" . htmlentities($_SERVER['PHP_SELF']) .
            "?offset=$offset'>$text</a></span>";
    }
}
```

Example 10-38. indexed_links()

```
function indexed_links($total,$offset,$per_page) {
    $separator = ' | ';

    // print "<<Prev" link
    print_link($offset == 1, '<< Prev', max(1, $offset - $per_page));

    // print all groupings except last one
    for ($start = 1, $end = $per_page;
        $end < $total;
        $start += $per_page, $end += $per_page) {
            print $separator;
            print_link($offset == $start, "$start-$end", $start);
    }

    /* print the last grouping -
     * at this point, $start points to the element at the beginning
     * of the last grouping
     */

    /* the text should only contain a range if there's more than
     * one element on the last page. For example, the last grouping
     * of 11 elements with 5 per page should just say "11", not "11-11"
     */
    $end = ($total > $start) ? "-$total" : '';
```

```
    print $separator;
    print_link($offset == $start, "$start$end", $start);

    // print "Next>>" link
    print $separator;
    print_link($offset == $start, 'Next >>',$offset + $per_page);
}
```

To use these functions, retrieve the correct subset of the data using appropriate PDO functions and then print it out. Call indexed_links() to display the indexed links.

After connecting to the database, you need to make sure $offset has an appropriate value. $offset is the beginning record in the result set that should be displayed. To start at the beginning of the result set, $offset should be 1. The variable $per_page is set to how many records to display on each page, and $total is the total number of records in the entire result set. For this example, all the zodiac records are displayed, so $total is set to the count of all the rows in the entire table.

The SQL query that retrieves information in the proper order is:

```
$limitedSQL = 'SELECT * FROM zodiac ORDER BY id ' .
"LIMIT $per_page OFFSET " . ($offset-1);
```

The LIMIT and OFFSET keywords are how you tell SQLite to return just a subset of all matching rows.

The relevant rows are retrieved by $db->query($limitedSQL), and then information is displayed from each row. After the rows, indexed_links() provides navigation links. The output when $offset is not set (or is 1) is shown in Figure 10-3.

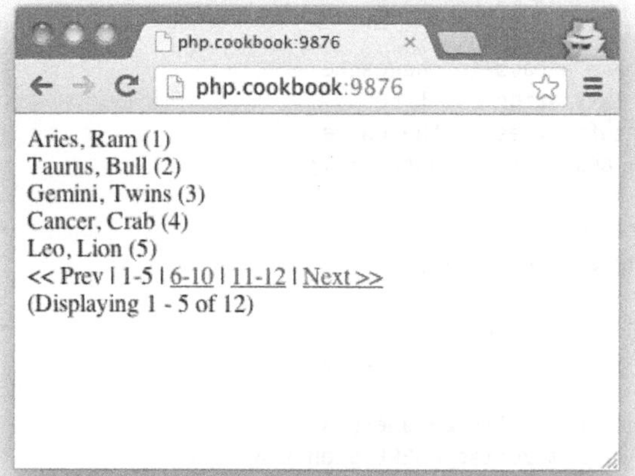

Figure 10-3. Paginated results with indexed_links()

In Figure 10-3, "6-10," "11-12," and "Next >>" are links to the same page with adjusted $offset arguments. "<< Prev" and "1-5" are grayed out, because what they would link to is what's currently displayed.

See Also

A discussion of paging in the Solar framework (*http://bit.ly/TwXYYZ*) and information on different database paging syntaxes (*http://bit.ly/1sFg4YH*).

10.14 Caching Queries and Results

Problem

You don't want to rerun potentially expensive database queries when the results haven't changed.

Solution

Use PEAR's `Cache_Lite` package. It makes it simple to cache arbitrary data. In this case, cache the results of a `SELECT` query and use the text of the query as a cache key. Example 10-39 shows how to cache query results with `Cache_Lite`.

Example 10-39. Caching query results

```
require_once 'Cache/Lite.php';
```

```
$opts = array(
    // Where to put the cached data
    'cacheDir' => '/tmp/',
    // Let us store arrays in the cache
    'automaticSerialization' => true,
    // How long stuff lives in the cache
    'lifeTime' => 600 /* ten minutes */);

// Create the cache
$cache = new Cache_Lite($opts);

// Connect to the database
$db = new PDO('sqlite:/tmp/zodiac.db');

// Define our query and its parameters
$sql = 'SELECT * FROM zodiac WHERE planet = ?';
$params = array($_GET['planet']);

// Get the unique cache key
$key = cache_key($sql, $params);

// Try to get results from the cache
$results = $cache->get($key);

if ($results === false) {
    // No results found, so do the query and put the results in the cache
    $st = $db->prepare($sql);
    $st->execute($params);
    $results = $st->fetchAll();
    $cache->save($results);
}

// Whether from the cache or not, $results has our data
foreach ($results as $result) {
    print "$result[id]: $result[planet], $result[sign] <br/>\n";
}

function cache_key($sql, $params) {
    return md5($sql .
                implode('|',array_keys($params)) .
                implode('|',$params));
}
```

Discussion

Cache_Lite is a generic, lightweight mechanism for caching arbitrary information. It uses files to store the information it's caching. The Cache_Lite constructor takes an array of options that control its behavior. The two most important ones in Example 10-39 are automaticSerialization, which makes it easier to store arrays in the cache, and `cacheDir`, which defines where the cache files go. Make sure `cacheDir` ends with a /.

The cache is just a mapping of keys to values. It's up to us to make sure that we supply a cache key that uniquely identifies the data we want to cache—in this case, the SQL query and the parameters bound to it. The `cache_key` function computes an appropriate key. After that, Example 10-39 just checks to see if the results are already in the cache. If not, it executes the query against the database and stuffs the results in the cache for next time.

Note that you can't put a `PDO` or `PDOStatement` object in the cache—you have to fetch results and then put the results in the cache.

By default, entries stay in the cache for one hour. You can adjust this by passing a different value (in seconds) as the `lifeTime` option when creating a new `Cache_Lite` object. Pass in `null` if you don't want data to automatically expire.

The cache isn't altered if you change the database with an `INSERT`, `UPDATE`, or `DELETE` query. If there are cached `SELECT` statements that refer to data no longer in the database, you need to explicitly remove everything from the cache with the `Cache_Lite::clean()` method. You can also remove an individual element from the cache by passing a cache key to `Cache_Lite::remove()`.

The `cache_key()` function in Example 10-39 is case sensitive. This means that if the results of `SELECT * FROM zodiac` are in the cache, and you run the query `SELECT * from zodiac`, the results aren't found in the cache and the query is run again. Maintaining consistent capitalization, spacing, and field ordering when constructing your SQL queries results in more efficient cache usage.

A benefit of PHP-layer solutions such as `Cache_Lite` is that they are database agnostic. However, depending on the database you're using you may be able to take advantage of database-specific query caching mechanisms. These kinds of caches, because they are more tightly integrated into the database, are able to be smarter about expiring cached data when it has changed. For example, you can read about how to enable MySQL's query cache (*http://bit.ly/1fQaVYo*).

See Also

Documentation on `Cache_Lite` (*http://bit.ly/1huOJxS*).

10.15 Accessing a Database Connection Anywhere in Your Program

Problem

You've got a program with lots of functions and classes in it, and you want to maintain a single database connection that's easily accessible from anywhere in the program.

Solution

Use a static class method that creates the connection if it doesn't exist and returns the connection (see Example 10-40).

Example 10-40. Creating a database connection in a static class method

```
class DBCxn {
    // What DSN to connect to?
    public static $dsn = 'sqlite:c:/data/zodiac.db';
    public static $user = null;
    public static $pass = null;
    public static $driverOpts = null;

    // Internal variable to hold the connection
    private static $db;
    // No cloning or instantiating allowed
    final private function __construct() { }
    final private function __clone() { }

    public static function get() {
        // Connect if not already connected
        if (is_null(self::$db)) {
            self::$db = new PDO(self::$dsn, self::$user, self::$pass,
                                self::$driverOpts);
        }
        // Return the connection
        return self::$db;
    }
}
```

Discussion

The DBCxn::get() method defined in Example 10-40 accomplishes two things: you can call it from anywhere in your program without worrying about variable scope and it prevents more than one connection from being created in a program.

To change what kind of connection DBCxn::get() provides, alter the $dsn, $user, $pass, and $driverOpts properties of the class. If you need to manage multiple different database connections during the same script execution, change $dsn and $db to an array and have `get()` accept an argument identifying which connection to use. Example 10-41 shows a version of DBCxn that provides access to three different databases.

Example 10-41. Handling connections to multiple databases

```
class DBCxn {
    // What DSNs to connect to?
    public static $dsn =
        array('zodiac' => 'sqlite:c:/data/zodiac.db',
              'users' => array('mysql:host=db.example.com','monty','7f2iuh'),
              'stats' => array('oci:statistics', 'statsuser','statspass'));


    // Internal variable to hold the connection
    private static $db = array();
    // No cloning or instantiating allowed
    final private function __construct() { }
    final private function __clone() { }

    public static function get($key) {
        if (! isset(self::$dsn[$key])) {
            throw new Exception("Unknown DSN: $key");
        }
        // Connect if not already connected
        if (! isset(self::$db[$key])) {
            if (is_array(self::$dsn[$key])) {

                $c = new ReflectionClass('PDO');
                self::$db[$key] = $c->newInstanceArgs(self::$dsn[$key]);
            } else {
                self::$db[$key] = new PDO(self::$dsn[$key]);
            }
        }
        // Return the connection
        return self::$db[$key];
    }
}
```

In Example 10-41, you must pass a key to DBCxn::get() that identifies which entry in $dsn to use. The code inside get() is a little more complicated, too, because it has to handle variable numbers of arguments to the PDO constructor. Some databases, such as SQLite, just need one argument. Others may provide two, three, or four arguments. Example 10-41 uses the ReflectionClass::newInstanceArgs() method to concisely call a constructor and provide arguments in an array.

See Also

Documentation on PDO::__construct() (*http://www.php.net/PDO.__construct*) and on ReflectionClass::newInstanceArgs() (*http://www.php.net/language.oop5.reflection*).

10.16 Program: Storing a Threaded Message Board

Storing and retrieving threaded messages requires extra care to display the threads in the correct order. Finding the children of each message and building the tree of message relationships can easily lead to a recursive web of queries. Users generally look at a list of messages and read individual messages far more often then they post messages. With a little extra processing when saving a new message to the database, the query that retrieves a list of messages to display is simpler and much more efficient.

Store messages in a table structured like this:

```
CREATE TABLE message (
    id INTEGER PRIMARY KEY AUTOINCREMENT,
    posted_on DATETIME NOT NULL,
    author CHAR(255),
    subject CHAR(255),
    body MEDIUMTEXT,
    thread_id INT UNSIGNED NOT NULL,
    parent_id INT UNSIGNED NOT NULL,
    level INT UNSIGNED NOT NULL,
    thread_pos INT UNSIGNED NOT NULL
);
```

The primary key, id, is a unique integer that identifies a particular message. The time and date that a message is posted is stored in posted_on, and author, subject, and body are (surprise!) a message's author, subject, and body. The remaining four fields keep track of the threading relationships between messages. The integer thread_id identifies each thread. All messages in a particular thread have the same thread_id. If a message is a reply to another message, parent_id is the id of the replied-to message. level is the position of the message in a thread. The first message in a thread has level 0. A reply to that level message has level 1, and a reply to that level 1 message has level 2. Multiple messages in a thread can have the same level and the same parent_id. For example, if someone starts off a thread with a message about the merits of BeOS over CP/M, the angry replies to that message from CP/M's legions of fans all have level 1 and a parent_id equal to the id of the original message.

The last field, thread_pos, is what makes the easy display of messages possible. When displayed, all messages in a thread are ordered by their thread_pos value.

Here are the rules for calculating thread_pos:

- The first message in a thread has thread_pos = 0.

- For a new message N, if there are no messages in the thread with the same parent as N, N's thread_pos is one greater than its parent's thread_pos.

- For a new message N, if there are messages in the thread with the same parent as N, N's `thread_pos` is one greater than the biggest `thread_pos` of all the messages with the same parent as N.

- After new message N's `thread_pos` is determined, all messages in the same thread with a `thread_pos` value greater than or equal to N's have their `thread_pos` value incremented by 1 (to make room for N).

The message board program, *message.php*, shown in Example 10-42 saves messages and properly calculates `thread_pos`. Sample output is shown in Figure 10-4.

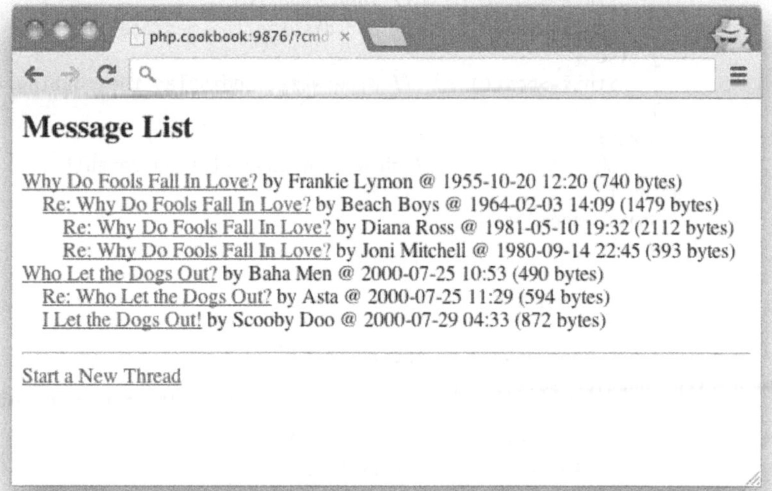

Figure 10-4. A threaded message board

Example 10-42. message.php

```php
$board = new MessageBoard();
$board->go();

class MessageBoard {
    protected $db;
    protected $form_errors = array();
    protected $inTransaction = false;

    public function __construct() {
        set_exception_handler(array($this,'logAndDie'));
        $this->db = new PDO('sqlite:/tmp/message.db');
        $this->db->setAttribute(PDO::ATTR_ERRMODE,PDO::ERRMODE_EXCEPTION);
```

```
    }

    public function go() {
        // The value of $_REQUEST['cmd'] tells us what to do
        $cmd = isset($_REQUEST['cmd']) ? $_REQUEST['cmd'] : 'show';
        switch ($cmd) {
            case 'read':            // read an individual message
              $this->read();
              break;
            case 'post':            // display the form to post a message
              $this->post();
              break;
            case 'save':            // save a posted message
              if ($this->valid()) { // if the message is valid,
                  $this->save();      // then save it
                  $this->show();      // and display the message list
              } else {
                  $this->post();     // otherwise, redisplay the posting form
              }
              break;
            case 'show':            // show a message list by default
            default:
              $this->show();
              break;
        }
    }

    // save() saves the message to the database
    protected function save() {

        $parent_id = isset($_REQUEST['parent_id']) ?
                    intval($_REQUEST['parent_id']) : 0;

        // Make sure message doesn't change while we're working with it.
        $this->db->beginTransaction();
        $this->inTransaction = true;

        // is this message a reply?
        if ($parent_id) {
            // get the thread, level, and thread_pos of the parent message
            $st = $this->db->prepare("SELECT thread_id,level,thread_pos
                            FROM message WHERE id = ?");
            $st->execute(array($parent_id));
            $parent = $st->fetch();

            // a reply's level is one greater than its parent's
            $level = $parent['level'] + 1;

            /* what's the biggest thread_pos in this thread among messages
            with the same parent? */
            $st = $this->db->prepare('SELECT MAX(thread_pos) FROM message
                    WHERE thread_id = ? AND parent_id = ?');
```

```
                $st->execute(array($parent['thread_id'], $parent_id));
                $thread_pos = $st->fetchColumn(0);

                // are there existing replies to this parent?
                if ($thread_pos) {
                    // this thread_pos goes after the biggest existing one
                    $thread_pos++;
                } else {
                    // this is the first reply, so put it right after the parent
                    $thread_pos = $parent['thread_pos'] + 1;
                }

                /* increment the thread_pos of all messages in the thread that
                come after this one */
                $st = $this->db->prepare('UPDATE message SET thread_pos = thread_pos
                                    + 1 WHERE thread_id = ? AND thread_pos >= ?');
                $st->execute(array($parent['thread_id'], $thread_pos));

                // the new message should be saved with the parent's thread_id
                $thread_id = $parent['thread_id'];
            } else {
                // the message is not a reply, so it's the start of a new thread
                $thread_id = $this->db->query('SELECT MAX(thread_id) + 1 FROM
                                        message')->fetchColumn(0);
                // If there are no rows yet, make sure we start at 1 for thread_id
                if (! $thread_id) {
                    $thread_id = 1;
                }
                $level = 0;
                $thread_pos = 0;
            }

            /* insert the message into the database. Using prepare() and execute()
            makes sure that all fields are properly quoted */
            $st = $this->db->prepare("INSERT INTO message (id,thread_id,parent_id,
                        thread_pos,posted_on,level,author,subject,body)
                        VALUES (?,?,?,?,?,?,?,?,?)");

            $st->execute(array(null,$thread_id,$parent_id,$thread_pos,
                        date('c'),$level,$_REQUEST['author'],
                        $_REQUEST['subject'],$_REQUEST['body']));

        // Commit all the operations
        $this->db->commit();
        $this->inTransaction = false;
    }

    // show() displays a list of all messages
    protected function show() {
        print '<h2>Message List</h2><p>';

        /* order the messages by their thread (thread_id) and their position
```

```
                within the thread (thread_pos) */
                $st = $this->db->query("SELECT id,author,subject,LENGTH(body)
                    AS body_length,posted_on,level FROM message
                            ORDER BY thread_id,thread_pos");
                while ($row = $st->fetch()) {
                    // indent messages with level > 0
                    print str_repeat(' ',4 * $row['level']);
                    // print out information about the message with a link to read it
                    $when = date('Y-m-d H:i', strtotime($row['posted_on']));
                    print "<a href='" . htmlentities($_SERVER['PHP_SELF']) .
                    "?cmd=read&amp;id={$row['id']}'>" .
                    htmlentities($row['subject']) . '</a> by ' .
                    htmlentities($row['author']) . ' @ ' .
                    htmlentities($when) .
                    " ({$row['body_length']} bytes) <br/>";
                }

                // provide a way to post a non-reply message
                print "<hr/><a href='" .
                    htmlentities($_SERVER['PHP_SELF']) .
                    "?cmd=post'>Start a New Thread</a>";
        }

        // read() displays an individual message
        public function read() {

            /* make sure the message id we're passed is an integer and really
            represents a message */
            if (! isset($_REQUEST['id'])) {
                throw new Exception('No message ID supplied');
            }
            $id = intval($_REQUEST['id']);
            $st = $this->db->prepare("SELECT author,subject,body,posted_on
                            FROM message WHERE id = ?");
            $st->execute(array($id));
            $msg = $st->fetch();
            if (! $msg) {
                throw new Exception('Bad message ID');
            }

            /* don't display user-entered HTML, but display newlines as
            HTML line breaks */
            $body = nl2br(htmlentities($msg['body']));

            // display the message with links to reply and return to the message list
            $self = htmlentities($_SERVER['PHP_SELF']);
            $subject = htmlentities($msg['subject']);
            $author = htmlentities($msg['author']);
            print<<<_HTML_
<h2>$subject</h2>
<h3>by $author</h3>
<p>$body</p>
```

```
<hr/>
<a href="$self?cmd=post&parent_id=$id">Reply</a>
<br/>
<a href="$self?cmd=list">List Messages</a>
_HTML_;
    }

    // post() displays the form for posting a message
    public function post() {
        $safe =  array();
        foreach (array('author','subject','body') as $field) {
            // escape characters in default field values
            if (isset($_POST[$field])) {
                $safe[$field] = htmlentities($_POST[$field]);
            } else {
                $safe[$field] = '';
            }
            // make the error messages display in red
            if (isset($this->form_errors[$field])) {
                $this->form_errors[$field] = '<span style="color: red">' .
                    $this->form_errors[$field] . '</span><br/>';
            } else {
                $this->form_errors[$field] = '';
            }
        }

        // is this message a reply
        if (isset($_REQUEST['parent_id']) &&
        $parent_id = intval($_REQUEST['parent_id'])) {

        // send the parent_id along when the form is submitted
        $parent_field =
            sprintf('<input type="hidden" name="parent_id" value="%d" />',
                    $parent_id);

        // if no subject's been passed in, use the subject of the parent
        if (! strlen($safe['subject'])) {
            $st = $this->db->prepare('SELECT subject FROM message WHERE
                        id = ?');
            $st->execute(array($parent_id));
            $parent_subject = $st->fetchColumn(0);

            /* prefix 'Re: ' to the parent subject if it exists and
               doesn't already have a 'Re:' */
            $safe['subject'] = htmlentities($parent_subject);
            if ($parent_subject && (! preg_match('/^re:/i',$parent_subject))) {
                $safe['subject'] = "Re: {$safe['subject']}";
            }
        }
    } else {
        $parent_field = '';
    }
```

```php
        // display the posting form, with errors and default values
        $self = htmlentities($_SERVER['PHP_SELF']);
        print<<<_HTML_
<form method="post" action="$self">
<table>
<tr>
 <td>Your Name:</td>
 <td>{$this->form_errors['author']}
     <input type="text" name="author" value="{$safe['author']}" />
</td>
<tr>
 <td>Subject:</td>
 <td>{$this->form_errors['subject']}
     <input type="text" name="subject" value="{$safe['subject']}" />
</td>
<tr>
 <td>Message:</td>
 <td>{$this->form_errors['body']}
     <textarea rows="4" cols="30" wrap="physical"
              name="body">{$safe['body']}</textarea>
</td>
<tr><td colspan="2"><input type="submit" value="Post Message" /></td></tr>
</table>
$parent_field
<input type="hidden" name="cmd" value="save" />
</form>
_HTML_;
    }

    // validate() makes sure something is entered in each field
    public function valid() {
        $this->form_errors = array();
        if (! (isset($_POST['author']) && strlen(trim($_POST['author'])))) {
            $this->form_errors['author'] = 'Please enter your name.';
        }
        if (! (isset($_POST['subject']) && strlen(trim($_POST['subject'])))) {
            $this->form_errors['subject'] = 'Please enter a message subject.';
        }
        if (! (isset($_POST['body']) && strlen(trim($_POST['body'])))) {
            $this->form_errors['body'] = 'Please enter a message body.';
        }

        return (count($this->form_errors) == 0);
    }

    public function logAndDie(Exception $e) {
        print 'ERROR: ' . htmlentities($e->getMessage());
        if ($this->db && $this->db->inTransaction()) {
            $this->db->rollback();
        }
```

```
        exit();
    }
}
```

To properly handle concurrent usage, `save()` needs exclusive access to the `msg` table between the time it starts calculating the `thread_pos` of the new message and when it actually inserts the new message into the database. We've used PDO's `beginTransaction()` and `commit()` methods to accomplish this. Note that `logAndDie()`, the exception handler, rolls back the transaction when appropriate if an error occurred inside the transaction. Although PDO always calls `rollback()` at the end of a script if a transaction was started, explicitly including the call inside `logAndDie()` makes clearer what's happening to someone reading the code.

The `level` field can be used when displaying messages to limit what you retrieve from the database. If discussion threads become very deep, this can help prevent your pages from growing too large. Example 10-43 shows how to display just the first message in each thread and any replies to that first message.

Example 10-43. Limiting thread depth

```
$st = $this->db->query(
    "SELECT * FROM message WHERE level <= 1 ORDER BY thread_id,thread_pos");
while ($row = $st->fetch()) {
    // display each message
}
```

If you're interested in having a discussion group on your website, you may want to use one of the existing PHP message board packages. Two popular ones are FUDForum (*http://fudforum.org/forum/*) and Vanilla Forums (*http://vanillaforums.org/*).

10.17 Using Redis

Problem

You want to use the Redis key-value store from your PHP program.

Solution

If you can install PECL extensions, install the `redis` extension and then use it as follows:

```
$redis = new Redis();
$redis->connect('127.0.0.1');
$redis->set('counter', 0);
$redis->incrBy('counter', 7);
$counter = $redis->get('counter');
print $counter;
```

If you can't, use the Predis library (*https://github.com/nrk/predis*):

```
require 'Predis/Autoloader.php';
Predis\Autoloader::register();

$redis = new Predis\Client(array('host' => '127.0.0.1'));
$redis->set('counter', 0);
$redis->incrBy('counter', 7);
$counter = $redis->get('counter');
print $counter;
```

Discussion

Although the redis extension and Predis library differ in how they are installed and how you connect to a server, they behave similarly in many respects. Each gives you an object representing a connection to a Redis server (or a pool of Redis servers) and that object has methods corresponding to the different operations you can send to the server(s).

To install the redis extension, use the pecl command:

```
pecl install redis
```

To install Predis, use pear:

```
pear channel-discover pear.nrk.io
pear install nrk/Predis
```

If you are using the Composer package manager, install Predis with a dependency string of "predis/predis".

See Also

The Redis server (*http://redis.io*) itself is available online. Check out the PECL page (*http://pecl.php.net/package/redis*) for the redis extension and its documentation (*https://github.com/nicolasff/phpredis*). Documentation for the Predis library is on GitHub (*https://github.com/nrk/predis*). Get more information about Composer at the Composer website (*http://getcomposer.org/*).

CHAPTER 11

Sessions and Data Persistence

11.0 Introduction

As web applications have matured, the need for *statefulness* has become a common requirement. Stateful web applications, meaning applications that keep track of a particular visitor's information as he travels throughout a site, are now so common that they are taken for granted.

Given the prevalence of web applications that keep track of things for their visitors—such as shopping carts, online banking, personalized home page portals, and social networking community sites—it is hard to imagine the Internet we use every day without stateful applications.

HTTP, the protocol that web servers and clients use to talk to each other, is a stateless protocol by design. However, PHP gives you a convenient set of session management functions that makes the challenge of implementing statefulness much easier. This chapter focuses on several good practices to keep in mind while developing stateful applications.

Sessions are focused on maintaining visitor-specific state between requests. Some applications also require an equivalent type of lightweight storage of nonvisitor-specific state for a period of time at the server-side level. This is known as *data persistence*.

Recipe 11.1 explains PHP's session module, which lets you easily associate persistent data with a user as he moves through your site. Recipe 11.2 and Recipe 11.3 explore session hijacking and session fixation vulnerabilities and how to avoid them.

Session data is stored in flat files in the server's */tmp* directory by default. Recipe 11.4 and Recipe 11.5 explain how to store session data in alternate locations, such as Memcached and a database, and discuss the pros and cons of these different approaches.

Recipe 11.6 demonstrates how to use shared memory for more than just session data storage, and Recipe 11.7 illustrates techniques for longer-term storage of summary information that has been gleaned from logfiles.

11.1 Using Session Tracking

Problem

You want to maintain information about a user as she moves through your site.

Solution

Use the sessions module. The `session_start()` function initializes a session, and accessing an element in the superglobal `$_SESSION` array tells PHP to keep track of the corresponding variable:

```
session_start();
if (! isset($_SESSION['visits'])) {
    $_SESSION['visits'] = 0;
}
$_SESSION['visits']++;
print 'You have visited here '.$_SESSION['visits'].' times.';
```

Discussion

The sessions module keeps track of users by issuing them cookies with randomly generated session IDs.

By default, PHP stores session data in files in the */tmp* directory on your server. Each session is stored in its own file. To change the directory in which the files are saved, set the `session.save_path` configuration directive to the new directory in *php.ini* or with `ini_set()`. You can also call `session_save_path()` with the new directory to change directories, but you need to do this before starting the session or accessing any session variables.

To start a session automatically on each request, set `session.auto_start` to 1 in *php.ini*. With `session.auto_start`, there's no need to call `session_start()`, so if you have the ability to change your *php.ini* file, this is easiest.

With the `session.use_trans_sid` configuration directive turned on, if PHP detects that a user doesn't accept the session ID cookie, it automatically adds the session ID to URLs and forms. For example, consider this code that prints a URL:

```
print '<a href="train.php">Take the A Train</a>';
```

If sessions are enabled, but a user doesn't accept cookies, what's sent to the browser is something like:

```
<a href="train.php?PHPSESSID=2eb89f3344520d11969a79aea6bd2fdd">↵
Take the A Train</a>
```

In this example, the session name is `PHPSESSID` and the session ID name is `2eb89f3344520d11969a79aea6bd2fdd`. PHP adds those to the URL so they are passed along to the next page. Forms are modified to include a hidden element that passes the session ID.

Due to a variety of security concerns relating to embedding session IDs in URLs, this behavior is disabled by default. To enable transparent session IDs in URLs, you need to turn on `session.use_trans_sid` in *php.ini* or through the use of `ini_set('ses sion.use_trans_sid', true)` in your scripts before the session is started.

Although `session.use_trans_sid` is convenient, it can cause you some security-related headaches. Because URLs have session IDs in them, distribution of such a URL lets anybody who receives the URL act as the user to whom the session ID was given. A user who copies a URL from his web browser and pastes it into an email message sent to friends unwittingly allows all those friends (and anybody else to whom the message is forwarded) to visit your site and impersonate him.

What's worse, when a user clicks a link on your site that takes him to another site, the user's browser passes along the session ID–containing URL as the referring URL to the external site. Even if the folks who run that external site don't maliciously mine these referrer URLs, referrer logs are often inadvertently exposed to search engines. Search for "PHPSESSID referer" on your favorite search engine, and you'll probably find some referrer logs with PHP session IDs embedded in them.

Separately, redirects with the `Location` header aren't automatically modified, so you have to add a session ID to them yourself using the `SID` constant:

```
$redirect_url = 'http://www.example.com/airplane.php';
if (defined('SID') && (!isset($_COOKIE[session_name()]))) {
    $redirect_url .= '?' . SID;
}

header("Location: $redirect_url");
```

The `session_name()` function returns the name of the cookie that stores the session ID, so this code appends the `SID` constant to `$redirect_url` if the constant is defined, and the session cookie isn't set.

See Also

Documentation on `session_start()` (*http://www.php.net/session-start*) and `ses sion_save_path()` (*http://www.php.net/session-save-path*). The session module has a number of configuration directives that help you do things like manage how long sessions can last and how they are cached. These options are detailed in the "Sessions" section of the online manual (*http://www.php.net/session*).

11.2 Preventing Session Hijacking

Problem

You want make sure an attacker can't access another user's session.

Solution

Allow passing of session IDs via cookies only, and generate an additional session token that is passed via URLs. Only requests that contain a valid session ID and a valid session token may access the session:

```
ini_set('session.use_only_cookies', true);
session_start();

$salt     = 'YourSpecialValueHere';
$tokenstr = strval(date('W')) . $salt;
$token    = md5($tokenstr);

if (!isset($_REQUEST['token']) || $_REQUEST['token'] != $token) {
    // prompt for login
    exit;
}

$_SESSION['token'] = $token;
output_add_rewrite_var('token', $token);
```

Discussion

This example creates an auto-shifting token by joining the current week number with a salt string of your choice. With this technique, tokens will be valid for a reasonable period of time without being fixed. The salt prevents someone from calculating their own MD5 hash of a date far in the future and using it to extend a session. Without knowing the particular salt you've chosen, someone can't easily produce a valid token.

We then check for the token in the request, and if it's not found, we prompt for a new login. If it is found, it needs to be added to generated links. `output_add_re write_var()` does this easily.

Note that this mechanism won't defeat an attacker who can sniff all of the traffic between a user and your server (for example, on an unencrypted WiFi network). Running your site over SSL is the best way to prevent that kind of attack.

See Also

Recipes 18.1 and 11.3 for more information on regenerating IDs to prevent session fixation.

11.3 Preventing Session Fixation

Problem

You want to make sure that your application is not vulnerable to session fixation attacks, in which an attacker forces a user to use a predetermined session ID.

Solution

Require the use of session cookies without session identifiers appended to URLs, and generate a new session ID frequently:

```
ini_set('session.use_only_cookies', true);
session_start();
if (!isset($_SESSION['generated'])
    || $_SESSION['generated'] < (time() - 30)) {
    session_regenerate_id();
    $_SESSION['generated'] = time();
}
```

Discussion

In this example, we start by setting PHP's session behavior to use cookies only. This ensures PHP won't pay attention to a session ID if an attacker has put one in a URL.

Once the session is started, we set a value that will keep track of the last time a session ID was generated. By requiring a new one to be generated on a regular basis—every 30 seconds in this example—the opportunity for an attacker to obtain a valid session ID is dramatically reduced.

These two approaches combine to virtually eliminate the risk of session fixation. An attacker has a hard time obtaining a valid session ID because it changes so often, and because sessions IDs can only be passed in cookies, a URL-based attack is not possible. Finally, because we enabled the session.use_only_cookies setting, no session cookies will be left lying around in browser histories or in server referrer logs.

See Also

"Session Fixation Vulnerability in Web-based Applications" (*http://bit.ly/1wtGgoN*); Recipe 18.1 for information about regenerating session IDs on privilege escalation.

11.4 Storing Sessons in Memcached

Problem

You want to store session data somewhere that's fast and can be accessed by multiple webservers.

Solution

Use the session handler built into the memcached extension to store your sessions in one or more Memcached servers. With the memcached extension installed, set the session.save_handler configuration directive to memcached and then set session.save_path to the host and port of your Memcached server. For example, if your Memcached server is running on port 11211 of host 10.5.7.12, set session.save_path to 10.5.7.12:11211. If you are using multiple Memcached servers, make session.save_path a comma-separated list of the host:port values.

Once you specify the appropriate session.save_handler and session.save_path that tells PHP to store your session info in Memcached, you don't have to do anything to your $_SESSION-using code to make it work properly. Because the session persistence backend is so easily pluggable, you can just change the configuration and it works.

If you are using consistent hashing with multiple Memcached servers to distribute your values across servers, set the configuration directive memcached.sess_consistent_hash to on. This ensures that your session data is also spread across the multiple Memcached servers.

Note that apart from the memcached PHP extension, there is also a memcache (no d on the end) PHP extension. It *also* has a built-in session handler. To use that session handler, set session.save_handler to memcache. The session.save_path configuration directive is used to indicate your Memcached servers, but the syntax is slightly different than the memcached extension. You need to prefix the hostname with the appropriate protocol (e.g., tcp://) and you can add query string–style name=value pairs to set any option that Memcache::addServer() accepts. For example, you could set session.save_path to tcp://10.5.7.12:11211?weight=3,tcp://10.5.7.13:11211?weight=5 to specify two servers—10.5.7.12 and 10.5.7.12—each running on port 11211 but weighted differently.

Both extensions can capably store sessions in Memcache. The memcached extension supports some different compression schemes for storing large pieces of data in Memcache. The memcache extension has a few less features but does not depend on any external libraries.

Note that a Memcached server itself does not persist the data it stores across restarts—it only holds it in memory while it's running. That means that session data in Memcached could disappear if one of your Memcached servers crashes or is restarted.

See Also

Documentation on how to configure the memcached extension (*http://www.php.net/memcached.configuration*) and on how to configure the memcache extension (*http://www.php.net/memcache.ini*); information about Memcached itself (*http://memcached.org*).

11.5 Storing Sessions in a Database

Problem

You want to store session data in a database instead of in files. If multiple web servers all have access to the same database, the session data is then mirrored across all the web servers.

Solution

Use a class in conjunction with the session_set_save_handler() function to define database-aware routines for session management. For example, Example 11-1 shows a class that uses PDO to store session information in a database table.

Example 11-1. Database-backed session handler

```
/** Implementing SessionHandlerInterface is mandatory as of PHP 5.4
 * and will fail in previous versions.
 */
class DBHandler implements SessionHandlerInterface {

    protected $dbh;

    public function open($save_path, $name) {
        try {
            $this->connect($save_path, $name);
            return true;
        } catch (PDOException $e) {
            return false;
        }
    }

    public function close() {
        return true;
    }

    public function destroy($session_id) {
```

```php
        $sth = $this->dbh->prepare("DELETE FROM sessions WHERE session_id = ?");
        $sth->execute(array($session_id));
        return true;
    }

    public function gc($maxlifetime) {
        $sth = $this->dbh->prepare("DELETE FROM sessions WHERE last_update < ?");
        $sth->execute(array(time() - $maxlifetime));
        return true;
    }

    public function read($session_id) {
        $sth = $this->dbh->prepare("SELECT session_data FROM sessions WHERE
                                    session_id = ?");
        $sth->execute(array($session_id));
        $rows = $sth->fetchAll(PDO::FETCH_NUM);
        if (count($rows) == 0) {
            return '';
        } else {
            return $rows[0][0];
        }
    }

    public function write($session_id, $session_data) {
        $now = time();
        $sth = $this->dbh->prepare("UPDATE sessions SET session_data = ?,
                                    last_update = ? WHERE session_id = ?");
        $sth->execute(array($session_data, $now, $session_id));
        if ($sth->rowCount() == 0) {
            $sth2 = $this->dbh->prepare('INSERT INTO sessions (session_id,
                                         session_data, last_update)
                                         VALUES (?,?,?)');
            $sth2->execute(array($session_id, $session_data, $now));
        }
    }

    public function createTable($save_path, $name, $connect = true) {
        if ($connect) {
            $this->connect($save_path, $name);
        }
        $sql=<<<_SQL_
CREATE TABLE sessions (
  session_id VARCHAR(64) NOT NULL,
  session_data MEDIUMTEXT NOT NULL,
  last_update TIMESTAMP NOT NULL,
  PRIMARY KEY (session_id)
)
_SQL_;
        $this->dbh->exec($sql);
    }

    protected function connect($save_path) {
```

```
/* Look for user and password in DSN as "query string" params */
$parts = parse_url($save_path);
if (isset($parts['query'])) {
    parse_str($parts['query'], $query);
    $user = isset($query['user']) ? $query['user'] : null;
    $password = isset($query['password']) ? $query['password'] : null;
    $dsn = $parts['scheme'] . ':';
    if (isset($parts['host'])) {
        $dsn .= '//' . $parts['host'];
    }
    $dsn .= $parts['path'];
    $this->dbh = new PDO($dsn, $user, $password);
} else {
    $this->dbh = new PDO($save_path);
}
$this->dbh->setAttribute(PDO::ATTR_ERRMODE, PDO::ERRMODE_EXCEPTION);
// A very simple way to create the sessions table if it doesn't exist.
try {
    $this->dbh->query('SELECT 1 FROM sessions LIMIT 1');
} catch (Exception $e) {
    $this->createTable($save_path, NULL, false);
}
    }
}
```

Discussion

One of the most powerful aspects of the session module is its abstraction of how sessions get saved. The `session_set_save_handler()` function tells PHP to use different functions for the various session operations such as saving a session and reading session data.

In PHP 5.4 and later, you give `session_set_save_handler()` an instance of a class that implements the `SessionHandlerInterface` interface. In earlier versions, there's no explicit interface, but the methods to define are the same: the public methods `open()`, `close()`, `destroy()`, `gc()`, `read()`, and `write()` are called from PHP's internal session handling code when necessary. To use this session handler, instantiate the class and pass it to `session_set_save_handler()`:

```
include __DIR__ . '/db.php';
ini_set('session.save_path', 'sqlite:/tmp/sessions.db');
session_set_save_handler(new DBHandler);

session_start();
if (! isset($_SESSION['visits'])) {
    $_SESSION['visits'] = 0;
}
$_SESSION['visits']++;
print 'You have visited here '.$_SESSION['visits'].' times.';
```

This code block assumes that the DBHandler class is defined in a file called *db.php* in the same directory as itself. Once session.save_path is set to the PDO DSN describing the database that holds the sessions table, session_set_save_handler(new DBHandler) is all that's necessary to wire up PHP to the handler. From then on, your session-using code is the same as if you were using PHP's default handler.

In Example 11-1, the additional public createTable() method is provided as a convenient way to create the table into which session data is stored. The connect() method calls it if it can't find a sessions table to use.

The createTable() and open() functions are also passed the session name as a separate variable. The default value for this is PHPSESSID. It is used as the cookie name by PHP when setting a cookie containing the session ID. If you need to distinguish between differently named sessions that might be assigned to the same user, modify the DBHandler class to incorporate the $name argument into the database table name or as an additional column in the sessions table.

See Also

Documentation on session_set_save_handler() (*http://bit.ly/1hCMhpv*) and on SessionHandlerInterface (*http://bit.ly/Siqj4I*).

11.6 Storing Arbitrary Data in Shared Memory

Problem

You want a chunk of data to be available to all server processes through shared memory.

Solution

If you want to share data only amongst PHP processes, use APC, as described in Recipe 5.6. If you want to share data with other processes as well, use the pc_Shm class shown in Example 11-2.

For example, to store a string in shared memory, use the pc_Shm::write() method, which accepts a key, a length, and a value:

```
$shm = new pc_Shm();
$secret_code = 'land shark';
$shm->write('mysecret', strlen($secret_code), $secret_code);
```

Discussion

The pc_Shm class is shown in Example 11-2.

Example 11-2. Storing arbitrary data in shared memory

```php
class pc_Shm {

    protected $tmp;

    public function __construct($tmp = '') {
        if (!function_exists('shmop_open')) {
            trigger_error('pc_Shm: shmop extension is required.', E_USER_ERROR);
            return;
        }

        if ($tmp != '' && is_dir($tmp) && is_writable($tmp)) {
            $this->tmp = $tmp;
        } else {
            $this->tmp = '/tmp';
        }
    }

    public function read($id, $size) {
        $shm = $this->open($id, $size);
        $data = shmop_read($shm, 0, $size);
        $this->close($shm);
        if (!$data) {
            trigger_error('pc_Shm: could not read from shared memory block',
                          E_USER_ERROR);
            return false;
        }
        return $data;
    }


    public function write($id, $size, $data) {
        $shm = $this->open($id, $size);
        $written = shmop_write($shm, $data, 0);
        $this->close($shm);
        if ($written != strlen($data)) {
            trigger_error('pc_Shm: could not write entire length of data',
                          E_USER_ERROR);
            return false;
        }
        return true;
    }


    public function delete($id, $size) {
        $shm = $this->open($id, $size);
        if (shmop_delete($shm)) {
            $keyfile = $this->getKeyFile($id);
            if (file_exists($keyfile)) {
                unlink($keyfile);
            }
        }
```

```
        return true;
    }

    protected function open($id, $size) {
        $key = $this->getKey($id);
        $shm = shmop_open($key, 'c', 0644, $size);
        if (!$shm) {
            trigger_error('pc_Shm: could not create shared memory segment',
                          E_USER_ERROR);
            return false;
        }
        return $shm;
    }

    protected function close($shm) {
        return shmop_close($shm);
    }

    protected function getKey($id) {
        $keyfile = $this->getKeyFile($id);
        if (! file_exists($keyfile)) {
            touch($keyfile);
        }
        return ftok($keyfile, 'R');
    }

    protected function getKeyFile($id) {
        return $this->tmp . DIRECTORY_SEPARATOR . 'pcshm_' . $id;
    }
}
```

Because `pc_Shm` uses standard system functions for accessing shared memory, other programs (no matter what language they're written in) can access that data as well. For example, Example 11-3 shows a short C program that can read data written by `pc_Shm`.

Example 11-3. Reading shared memory data from C

```c
#include <sys/ipc.h>
#include <sys/shm.h>

#include <stdio.h>

int main(int argc, char **argv) {
    char *id;
    size_t size;

    if (argc != 3) {
        fprintf(stderr, "Usage: %s ID SIZE\n", argv[0]);
        return -1;
    }

    id = argv[1];
```

```
    size = atoi(argv[2]);

    char *path;
    asprintf(&path, "/tmp/pcshm_%s", id);
    key_t token = ftok(path, (int) 'R');
    int shmid = shmget(token, size, 0);
    void *ptr = shmat(shmid, 0, SHM_RDONLY);
    printf("%*s\n", (int) size, (char *) ptr);
    shmdt(ptr);
    free(path);
}
```

Compiling that program and then invoking it with arguments `mysecret` and `10` (or any sufficiently long length) will print the data inserted into shared memory by the PHP code.

It's important to remember that, unlike setting a key/value pair in a regular PHP array, the `shmop` functions need to allocate a specific amount of space that the data stored there is *expected* to consume. That is why the read and write operations require a size to be passed to them.

See Also

Recipe 5.6 has more information on how to use APC to share memory among PHP processes; documentation on PHP's `shmop` functions (*http://www.php.net/shmop*).

11.7 Caching Calculated Results in Summary Tables

Problem

You need to collect statistics from log tables that are too large to efficiently query in real time.

Solution

Create a table that stores summary data from the complete log table, and query the summary table to generate reports in nearly real time.

Discussion

Let's say that you are logging search queries that website visitors use on search engines like Google and Yahoo! to find your website, and tracking those queries in MySQL. Your search term tracking log table has this structure:

```
CREATE TABLE searches
(
  searchterm    VARCHAR(255) NOT NULL,  -- search term determined from
```

```
                                          -- HTTP_REFERER parsing
    dt              DATETIME NOT NULL,    -- request date
    source          VARCHAR(15) NOT NULL  -- site where search was performed
);
```

If you are fortunate enough to be logging thousands or tens of thousands of visits from the major search engines per hour, the `searches` table could grow to an unmanageable size over a period of several months.

You may wish to generate reports that illustrate trends of search terms that have driven traffic to your website over time from each major search engine so that you can determine which search engine to purchase advertising with.

Create a summary table that reflects what your report needs to display, and then query the full dataset hourly and store the result in the summary table for speedy retrieval during report generation. Your summary table would have this structure:

```
CREATE TABLE searchsummary
(
    searchterm      VARCHAR(255) NOT NULL,  -- search term
    source          VARCHAR(15) NOT NULL,   -- site where search was performed
    sdate           DATE NOT NULL,          -- date search performed
    searches        INT UNSIGNED NOT NULL,  -- number of searches
    PRIMARY KEY (searchterm, source, sdate)
);
```

Your report generation script can then use PDO to query the `searchsummary` table, and if results are not available, collect them from the `searches` table and cache the result in `searchsummary`:

```
$st = $db->prepare('SELECT COUNT(*)
                    FROM
                        searchsummary
                    WHERE
                        sdate = ?');
$st->execute(array(date('Y-m-d', strtotime('yesterday'))));

$row = $st->fetch();

// no matches in cache
if ($row[0] == 0) {
    $st2 = $db->prepare('SELECT
                        searchterm,
                        source,
                        date(dt) AS sdate,
                        COUNT(*) as searches
                    FROM
                        searches
                    WHERE
                        date(dt) = ?');
    $st2->execute(array(date('Y-m-d', strtotime('yesterday'))));
```

```
$stInsert = $db->prepare('INSERT INTO searchsummary
                         (searchterm,source,sdate,searches)
                         VALUES (?,?,?,?)');
while ($row = $st2->fetch(PDO::FETCH_NUM)) {
    $stInsert->execute($row);
}
}
```

Using this technique, your script will only incur the overhead of querying the full log table once, and all subsequent requests will retrieve a single row of summary data per search term.

See Also

Recipe 10.6 for information about PDO::prepare() and PDOStatement::execute().

CHAPTER 12

XML

12.0 Introduction

XML is a popular data-exchange, configuration, and message-passing format. Although JSON has displaced XML for many basic situations, XML still plays an important role in a developer's life. With the help of a few extensions, PHP lets you read and write XML for every occasion.

XML provides developers with a structured way to mark up data with tags arranged in a tree-like hierarchy. One perspective on XML is to treat it as CSV on steroids. You can use XML to store records broken into a series of fields. But instead of merely separating each field with a comma, you can include a field name, a type, and attributes alongside the data.

Another view of XML is as a document representation language. For instance, this book was written using XML. The book is divided into chapters; each chapter into recipes; and each recipe into Problem, Solution, and Discussion sections. Within any individual section, we further subdivide the text into paragraphs, tables, figures, and examples. An article on a web page can similarly be divided into the page title and headline, the authors of the piece, the story itself, and any sidebars, related links, and additional content.

XML content looks similar to HTML. Both use tags bracketed by < and > for marking up text. But XML is both stricter and looser than HTML. It's stricter because all container tags must be properly closed. No opening elements are allowed without a corresponding closing tag. It's looser because you're not forced to use a set list of tags, such as <a>, <img>, and <h1>. Instead, you have the freedom to choose a set of tag names that best describe your data.

Other key differences between XML and HTML are case sensitivity, attribute quoting, and whitespace. In HTML, <B> and <b> are the same bold tag; in XML, they're two different tags. In HTML, you can often omit quotation marks around attributes; XML, however, requires them. So you must always write:

```
<element attribute="value">
```

Additionally, HTML parsers generally ignore whitespace, so a run of 20 consecutive spaces is treated the same as one space. XML parsers preserve whitespace, unless explicitly instructed otherwise. Because all elements must be closed, empty elements must end with />. For instance, in HTML, the line break is <br>, whereas in XHTML, which is HTML that validates as XML, it's written as <br />.[1]

There is another restriction on XML documents. When XML documents are parsed into a tree of elements, the outermost element is known as the root element. Just as a tree has only one trunk, an XML document must have exactly one root element. In the previous book example, this means chapters must be bundled inside a book tag. If you want to place multiple books inside a document, you need to package them inside a bookcase or another container. This limitation applies only to the document root. Again, just like trees can have multiple branches off of the trunk, it's legal to store multiple books inside a bookcase.

This chapter doesn't aim to teach you XML; for an introduction to XML, see *Learning XML* by Erik T. Ray (O'Reilly). A solid nuts-and-bolts guide to all aspects of XML is *XML in a Nutshell* by Elliotte Rusty Harold and W. Scott Means (O'Reilly).

Now that we've covered the rules, here's an example. If you are a librarian and want to convert your card catalog to XML, start with this basic set of XML tags:

```
<book>
    <title>PHP Cookbook</title>
    <author>Sklar, David and Trachtenberg, Adam</author>
    <subject>PHP</subject>
</book>
```

From there, you can add new elements or modify existing ones. For example, <author> can be divided into first and last name, or you can allow for multiple records so two authors aren't placed in one field.

PHP has a set of XML extensions that:

- Work together as a unified whole
- Are standardized on a single XML library: libxml2
- Fully comply with W3C specifications
- Efficiently process data

---

1. This is why nl2br() outputs <br /> by default; that output is XHTML compatible.

- Provide you with the right XML tool for your job

Additionally, following the PHP tenet that creating web applications should be easy, there's an XML extension that makes it simple to read and alter XML documents. The aptly named SimpleXML extension allows you to interact with the information in an XML document as though these pieces of information are arrays and objects, iterating through them with `foreach` loops and editing them in place merely by assigning new values to variables.

The first two recipes in this chapter cover parsing XML. Recipe 12.1 shows how to write XML without additional tools. To use DOM extension to write XML in a standardized fashion, see Recipe 12.2.

The complement to writing XML is parsing XML. That's the subject of the next three recipes. They're divided based upon the complexity and size of the XML document you're trying to parse. Recipe 12.3 covers how to parse basic XML documents. If you need more sophisticated XML parsing tools, move onto Recipe 12.4. When your XML documents are extremely large and memory intensive, turn to Recipe 12.5. If this is your first time using XML, and you're unsure which recipe is right for you, try them in order, because the code becomes increasingly complex as your requirements go up.

XPath is the topic of Recipe 12.6. It's a W3C standard for extracting specific information from XML documents. We like to think of it as regular expressions for XML. XPath is one of the most useful, yet unused parts of the XML family of specifications. If you process XML on a regular basis, you should be familiar with XPath.

With XSLT, you can take an XSL stylesheet and turn XML into viewable output. By separating content from presentation, you can make one stylesheet for web browsers, another for mobile phones, and a third for print, all without changing the content itself. This is the subject of Recipe 12.7.

After introducing XSLT, the two recipes that follow show how to pass information back and forth between PHP and XSLT. Recipe 12.8 tells how to send data from PHP to an XSLT stylesheet; Recipe 12.9 shows how to call out to PHP from within an XSLT stylesheet.

As long as your XML document abides by the structural rules of XML, it is known as *well-formed*. However, unlike HTML, which has a specific set of elements and attributes that must appear in set places, XML has no such restrictions.

Yet, in some cases, it's useful to make sure your XML documents abide by a specification. This allows tools, such as web browsers, RSS readers, or your own scripts, to easily process the input. When an XML document follows all the rules set out by a specification, it is known as *valid*. Recipe 12.10 covers how to validate an XML document.

One of PHP's major limitations is its handling of character sets and document encodings. PHP strings are not associated with a particular encoding, but all the XML extensions require UTF-8 input and emit UTF-8 output. Therefore, if you use a character set incompatible with UTF-8, you must manually convert your data both before sending it into an XML extension and after you receive it back. Recipe 12.11 explores the best ways to handle this process.

The chapter concludes with a number of recipes dedicated to reading and writing a number of common types of XML documents, specifically RSS and Atom. These are the two most popular data syndication formats, and are useful for exchanging many types of data, including blog posts, podcasts, and even mapping information.

PHP Cookbook also covers RESTful APIs. This topic is so important, it gets two dedicated chapters of its own. Chapter 14 describes how to consume RESTful APIs, and Chapter 15 tells how to implement RESTful APIs of your very own.

12.1 Generating XML as a String

Problem

You want to generate XML. For instance, you want to provide an XML version of your data for another program to parse.

Solution

Loop through your data and print it out surrounded by the correct XML tags:

```
header('Content-Type: text/xml');
print '<?xml version="1.0"?>' . "\n";
print "<shows>\n";

$shows = array(array('name'     => 'Modern Family',
                     'channel'  => 'ABC',
                     'start'    => '9:00 PM',
                     'duration' => '30'),

                array('name'     => 'Law & Order: SVU',
                      'channel'  => 'NBC',
                      'start'    => '9:00 PM',
                      'duration' => '60'));

foreach ($shows as $show) {
    print "  <show>\n";
    foreach($show as $tag => $data) {
        print "    <$tag>" . htmlspecialchars($data) . "</$tag>\n";
    }
    print "  </show>\n";
}

print "</shows>\n";
```

Discussion

Printing out XML manually mostly involves lots of `foreach` loops as you iterate through arrays. However, there are a few tricky details. First, you need to call `header()` to set the correct `Content-Type` header for the document. Because you're sending XML instead of HTML, it should be `text/xml`.

Next, depending on your settings for the `short_open_tag` configuration directive, trying to print the XML declaration may accidentally turn on PHP processing. Because the `<?` of `<?xml version="1.0"?>` is the short PHP open tag, to print the declaration to the browser you need to either disable the directive or print the line from within PHP. We do the latter in the Solution.

Last, entities must be escaped. For example, the & in the show `Law & Order` needs to be `&amp;`. Call `htmlspecialchars()` to escape your data.

The output from the example in the Solution is shown in Example 12-1.

Example 12-1. Tonight's TV listings

```
<?xml version="1.0"?>
<shows>
    <show>
        <name>Modern Family</name>
        <channel>ABC</channel>
        <start>9:00 PM</start>
        <duration>30</duration>
    </show>
    <show>
        <name>Law &amp; Order: SVU</name>
        <channel>NBC</channel>
        <start>9:00 PM</start>
        <duration>60</duration>
    </show>
</shows>
```

See Also

Recipe 12.2 for generating XML using DOM; documentation on `htmlspecial chars()` (*http://www.php.net/htmlspecialchars*).

12.2 Generating XML with DOM

Problem

You want to generate XML but want to do it in an organized way instead of using `print` and loops.

Solution

Use the DOM extension to create a DOMDocument object. After building up the document, call DOMDocument::save() or DOMDocument::saveXML() to generate a well-formed XML document:

```
// create a new document
$dom = new DOMDocument('1.0');

// create the root element, <book>, and append it to the document
$book = $dom->appendChild($dom->createElement('book'));

// create the title element and append it to $book
$title = $book->appendChild($dom->createElement('title'));

// set the text and the cover attribute for $title
$title->appendChild($dom->createTextNode('PHP Cookbook'));
$title->setAttribute('edition', '3');

// create and append author elements to $book
$sklar = $book->appendChild($dom->createElement('author'));
// create and append the text for each element
$sklar->appendChild($dom->createTextNode('Sklar'));

$trachtenberg = $book->appendChild($dom->createElement('author'));
$trachtenberg->appendChild($dom->createTextNode('Trachtenberg'));

// print a nicely formatted version of the DOM document as XML
$dom->formatOutput = true;
echo $dom->saveXML();
```

```
<?xml version="1.0"?>
<book>
  <title edition="3">PHP Cookbook</title>
  <author>Sklar</author>
  <author>Trachtenberg</author>
</book>
```

Discussion

The DOM methods follow a pattern. You create an object as either an element or a text node, add and set any attributes you want, and then append it to the tree in the spot it belongs.

Before creating elements, create a new document, passing the XML version as the sole argument:

```
$dom = new DOMDocument('1.0');
```

Now create new elements belonging to the document. Despite being associated with a specific document, nodes don't join the document tree until appended:

```
$book_element = $dom->createElement('book');
$book = $dom->appendChild($book_element);
```

Here a new book element is created and assigned to the object $book_element. To create the document root, append $book_element as a child of the $dom document. The result, $book, refers to the specific element and its location within the DOM object.

All nodes are created by calling a method on $dom. Once a node is created, it can be appended to any element in the tree. The element from which we call the append Child() method determines the location in the tree where the node is placed. In the previous case, $book_element is appended to $dom. The element appended to $dom is the top-level node, or the root node.

You can also append a new child element to $book. Because $book is a child of $dom, the new element is, by extension, a grandchild of $dom:

```
$title_element = $dom->createElement('title');
$title = $book->appendChild($title_element);
```

By calling $book->appendChild(), this code places the $title_element element under the $book element.

To add the text inside the <title></title> tags, create a text node using createText Node() and append it to $title:

```
$text_node = $dom->createTextNode('PHP Cookbook');
$title->appendChild($text_node);
```

Because $title is already added to the document, there's no need to reappend it to $book.

The order in which you append children to nodes isn't important. The following four lines, which first append the text node to $title_element and then to $book, are equivalent to the previous code:

```
$title_element = $dom->createElement('title');
$text_node = $dom->createTextNode('PHP Cookbook');

$title_element->appendChild($text_node);
$book->appendChild($title_element);
```

To add an attribute, call setAttribute() upon a node, passing the attribute name and value as arguments:

```
$title->setAttribute('edition', '3');
```

If you print the title element now, it looks like this:

```
<title edition="3">PHP Cookbook</title>
```

Once you're finished, you can output the document as a string or to a file:

```
// put the string representation of the XML document in $books
$books = $dom->saveXML();

// write the XML document to books.xml
$dom->save('books.xml');
```

By default, these methods generate XML output in one long line without any whitespace, including indentations and line breaks. To fix this, set the formatOutput attribute of your DOMDocument to true:

```
// print a nicely formatted version of the DOM document as XML
$dom->formatOutput = true;
```

This causes the DOM extension to generate XML like this:

```
<?xml version="1.0"?>
<book>
  <title cover="soft">PHP Cookbook</title>
</book>
```

See Also

Recipe 12.1 for writing XML without DOM; Recipe 12.4 for parsing XML with DOM; documentation on DOMDocument (*http://www.php.net/domdocument*) and the DOM functions in general (*http://www.php.net/dom*); more information about the underlying libxml2 C library (*http://xmlsoft.org/*).

12.3 Parsing Basic XML Documents

Problem

You want to parse a basic XML document that follows a known schema, and you don't need access to more esoteric XML features, such as processing instructions.

Solution

Use the SimpleXML extension. Here's how to read XML from a file:

```
$sx = simplexml_load_file(__DIR__ . '/address-book.xml');

foreach ($sx->person as $person) {
    $firstname_text_value = $person->firstname;
    $lastname_text_value = $person->lastname;

    print "$firstname_text_value $lastname_text_value\n";
}
David Sklar
Adam Trachtenberg
```

Discussion

SimpleXML has been described as "the mostest bestest thing ever." Though it's hard to live up to such grand praise, SimpleXML does do a remarkable job of making it—dare we say—simple to interact with XML. When you want to read a configuration file written in XML, parse an RSS feed, or process the result of a REST request, SimpleXML excels at these tasks. It doesn't work well for more complex XML-related jobs, such as reading a document where you don't know the format ahead of time or when you need to access processing instructions or comments.

SimpleXML turns elements into object properties. The text between the tags is assigned to the property. If more than one element with the same name lives in the same place (such as multiple <people>s), then they're placed inside a list.

Element attributes become array elements, where the array key is the attribute name and the key's value is the attribute's value.

To access a single value, reference it directly using object method notation. Let's use this XML fragment as an example:

```
<firstname>David</firstname>
```

If you have this in a SimpleXML object, $firstname, here's all you need to do to access David:

```
$firstname
```

SimpleXML assumes that when you have a node that contains only text, you're interested in the text. Therefore, print $firstname does what you expect it to: it prints David.

Iteration methods, like foreach, are the best choice for cycling through multiple elements. Code for this is shown in later examples.

Attributes are stored as array elements. For example, this prints out the id attribute for the first person element:

```
$ab = simplexml_load_file(__DIR__ . '/address-book.xml');

// the id attribute of the first person
print $ab->person['id'] . "\n";
```

which gives you:

```
1
```

Here's a more complete example based on this simple address book in XML. It's used in the code examples that follow.

```
<?xml version="1.0"?>
<address-book>
    <person id="1">
        <!--David Sklar-->
```

```
        <firstname>David</firstname>
        <lastname>Sklar</lastname>
        <city>New York</city>
        <state>NY</state>
        <email>sklar@php.net</email>
    </person>

    <person id="2">
        <!--Adam Trachtenberg-->
        <firstname>Adam</firstname>
        <lastname>Trachtenberg</lastname>
        <city>San Francisco</city>
        <state>CA</state>
        <email>amt@php.net</email>
    </person>
</address-book>
```

Use SimpleXML to pull out all the first and last names:

```
$sx = simplexml_load_file(__DIR__ . '/address-book.xml');

foreach ($sx->person as $person) {
    $firstname_text_value = $person->firstname;
    $lastname_text_value = $person->lastname;

    print "$firstname_text_value $lastname_text_value\n";
}
```

David Sklar
Adam Trachtenberg

When you use SimpleXML, you can directly iterate over elements using `foreach`. Here, the iteration occurs over `$sx->person`, which holds all the `person` nodes.

You can also directly print SimpleXML objects:

```
foreach ($sx->person as $person) {
    print "$person->firstname $person->lastname\n";
}
```

David Sklar
Adam Trachtenberg

PHP interpolates SimpleXML objects inside of quoted strings and retrieves the text stored in them.

See Also

Recipe 12.4 for parsing complex XML documents; Recipe 12.5 for parsing large XML documents; documentation on SimpleXML (*http://www.php.net/simplexml*); more information about the underlying `libxml2` C library (*http://xmlsoft.org/*).

12.4 Parsing Complex XML Documents

Problem

You have a complex XML document, such as one where you need to introspect the document to determine its schema, or you need to use more esoteric XML features, such as processing instructions or comments.

Solution

Use the DOM extension. It provides a complete interface to all aspects of the XML specification:

```
// $node is the DOM parsed node <book cover="soft">PHP Cookbook</book>
$type = $node->nodeType;

switch($type) {
case XML_ELEMENT_NODE:
    // I'm a tag. I have a tagname property.
    print $node->tagName;  // prints the tagname property: "book"
    break;
case XML_ATTRIBUTE_NODE:
    // I'm an attribute. I have a name and a value property.
    print $node->name;  // prints the name property: "cover"
    print $node->value; // prints the value property: "soft"
    break;
case XML_TEXT_NODE:
    // I'm a piece of text inside an element.
    // I have a name and a content property.
    print $node->nodeName;  // prints the name property: "#text"
    print $node->nodeValue; // prints the text content: "PHP Cookbook"
    break;
default:
    // another type
    break;
}
book
```

Discussion

The W3C's DOM provides a platform- and language-neutral method that specifies the structure and content of a document. Using DOM, you can read an XML document into a tree of nodes and then maneuver through the tree to locate information about a particular element or elements that match your criteria. This is called *tree-based parsing*.

Additionally, you can modify the structure by creating, editing, and deleting nodes. In fact, you can use the DOM functions to author a new XML document from scratch; see Recipe 12.2.

One of the major advantages of DOM is that by following the W3C's specification, many languages implement DOM functions in a similar manner. Therefore, the work of translating logic and instructions from one application to another is considerably simplified.

DOM is large and complex. For more information, read the specification (*http://www.w3.org/DOM/*) or pick up a copy of *XML in a Nutshell*.

DOM functions in PHP are object oriented. To move from one node to another, access properties such as `$node->childNodes`, which contains an array of node objects, and `$node->parentNode`, which contains the parent node object. Therefore, to process a node, check its type and call a corresponding method, as shown:

```
// $node is the DOM parsed node <book cover="soft">PHP Cookbook</book>
$type = $node->nodeType;

switch($type) {
case XML_ELEMENT_NODE:
    // I'm a tag. I have a tagname property.
    print $node->tagName;  // prints the tagname property: "book"
    break;
case XML_ATTRIBUTE_NODE:
    // I'm an attribute. I have a name and a value property.
    print $node->name;  // prints the name property: "cover"
    print $node->value; // prints the value property: "soft"
    break;
case XML_TEXT_NODE:
    // I'm a piece of text inside an element.
    // I have a name and a content property.
    print $node->nodeName;  // prints the name property: "#text"
    print $node->nodeValue; // prints the text content: "PHP Cookbook"
    break;
default:
    // another type
    break;
}
```

To automatically search through a DOM tree for specific elements, use `getElements ByTagname()`. Here's how to do so with multiple book records:

```
<books>
    <book>
        <title>PHP Cookbook</title>
        <author>Sklar</author>
        <author>Trachtenberg</author>
        <subject>PHP</subject>
    </book>
    <book>
        <title>Perl Cookbook</title>
        <author>Christiansen</author>
        <author>Torkington</author>
```

```
            <subject>Perl</subject>
        </book>
    </books>
```

And to find all authors:

```
// find and print all authors
$authors = $dom->getElementsByTagname('author');

// loop through author elements
foreach ($authors as $author) {
    // childNodes holds the author values
    $text_nodes = $author->childNodes;

    foreach ($text_nodes as $text) {
        print $text->nodeValue . "\n";
    }
}
Sklar
Trachtenberg
Christiansen
Torkington
```

The getElementsByTagname() method returns an array of element node objects. By looping through each element's children, you can get to the text node associated with that element. From there, you can pull out the node values, which in this case are the names of the book authors, such as Sklar and Trachtenberg.

See Also

Recipe 12.3 for parsing simple XML documents; Recipe 12.5 for parsing large XML documents; documentation on DOM (*http://www.php.net/dom*); more information about the underlying libxml2 C library (*http://xmlsoft.org/*).

12.5 Parsing Large XML Documents

Problem

You want to parse a large XML document. This document is so large that it's impractical to use SimpleXML or DOM because you cannot hold the entire document in memory. Instead, you must load the document in one section at a time.

Solution

Use the XMLReader extension:

```
$reader = new XMLReader();
$reader->open(__DIR__ . '/card-catalog.xml');
```

```
/* Loop through document */
while ($reader->read()) {
    /* If you're at an element named 'author' */
    if($reader->nodeType == XMLREADER::ELEMENT &&
    $reader->localName == 'author') {
        /* Move to the text node and print it out */
        $reader->read();
        print $reader->value . "\n";
    }
}
```

Discussion

There are two major types of XML parsers: ones that hold the entire document in memory at once, and ones that hold only a small portion of the document in memory at any given time.

The first kind are called tree-based parsers, because they store the document into a data structure known as a tree. The SimpleXML and DOM extensions, from Recipes 12.3 and 12.4, are tree-based parsers. Using a tree-based parser is easier for you, but requires PHP to use more RAM. With most XML documents, this isn't a problem. However, when your XML document is quite large, this can cause major performance issues.

The other kind of XML parser is a stream-based parser. Stream-based parsers don't store the entire document in memory; instead, they read in one node at a time and allow you to interact with it in real time. Once you move onto the next node, the old one is thrown away—unless you explicitly store it yourself for later use. This makes stream-based parsers faster and less memory-consuming, but you may have to write more code to process the document.

The easiest way to process XML data using a stream-based parser is using the *XMLReader* extension. This extension is based on the C# XmlTextReader API. If you're familiar with SAX (Simple API for XML), XMLReader is more intuitive, feature-rich, and faster.

Begin by creating a new instance of the XMLReader class and specifying the location of your XML data:

```
// Create a new XMLReader object
$reader = new XMLReader();

// Load from a file or URL
$reader->open('document.xml');

// Or, load from a PHP variable
$reader->XML($document);
```

Most of the time, you'll use the XMLReader::open() method to pull in data from an external source, but you can also load it from an existing PHP variable with XMLReader::XML().

Once the object is configured, you begin processing the data. At the start, you're positioned at the top of the document. You can maneuver through the document using a combination of the two navigation methods XMLReader provides: XMLReader::read() and XMLReader::next(). The first method reads in the piece of XML data that immediately follows the current position. The second method moves to the next sibling element after the current position.

For example, look at this XML:

```
<books>
    <book isbn="1565926811">
        <title>PHP Cookbook</title>
        <author>Sklar</author>
        <author>Trachtenberg</author>
        <subject>PHP</subject>
    </book>
    <book isbn="0596003137">
        <title>Perl Cookbook</title>
        <author>Christiansen</author>
        <author>Torkington</author>
        <subject>Perl</subject>
    </book>
</books>
```

When the object is positioned at the first <book> element, the read() method moves you to the next element underneath <book>. (This is technically the whitespace between <book> and <title>.) In comparison, next() moves you to the next <book> element and skips the entire *PHP Cookbook* subtree.

These methods return true when they're able to successfully move to another node, and false when they cannot. So, it's typical to use them inside a while loop, as such:

```
/* Loop through document */
while ($reader->read()) {
    /* Process XML */
}
```

This causes the object to read in the entire XML document one piece at a time. Inside the while(), examine $reader and process it accordingly.

A common aspect to check is the node type. This lets you know if you've reached an element (and then check the name of that element), a closing element, an attribute, a piece of text, some whitespace, or any other part of an XML document. Do this by referencing the nodeType attribute:

```
/* Loop through document */
while ($reader->read()) {
    /* If you're at an element named 'author' */
    if($reader->nodeType == XMLREADER::ELEMENT &&
    $reader->localName == 'author') {
        /* Process author element */
    }
}
```

This code checks if the node is an element and, if so, that its name is author. For a complete list of possible values stored in nodeType, check out Table 12-1.

Table 12-1. XMLReader node type values

Node type	Description
XMLReader::NONE	No node type
XMLReader::ELEMENT	Start element
XMLReader::ATTRIBUTE	Attribute node
XMLReader::TEXT	Text node
XMLReader::CDATA	CDATA node
XMLReader::ENTITY_REF	Entity Reference node
XMLReader::ENTITY	Entity Declaration node
XMLReader::PI	Processing Instruction node
XMLReader::COMMENT	Comment node
XMLReader::DOC	Document node
XMLReader::DOC_TYPE	Document Type node
XMLReader::DOC_FRAGMENT	Document Fragment node
XMLReader::NOTATION	Notation node
XMLReader::WHITESPACE	Whitespace node
XMLReader::SIGNIFICANT_WHITESPACE	Significant Whitespace node
XMLReader::END_ELEMENT	End Element
XMLReader::END_ENTITY	End Entity
XMLReader::XML_DECLARATION	XML Declaration node

From there, you can decide how to handle that element and the data it contains. For example, we can print out all the author names in the card catalog:

```
$reader = new XMLReader();
$reader->open(__DIR__ . '/card-catalog.xml');

/* Loop through document */
while ($reader->read()) {
    /* If you're at an element named 'author' */
    if($reader->nodeType == XMLREADER::ELEMENT &&
    $reader->localName == 'author') {
```

```
        /* Move to the text node and print it out */
        $reader->read();
        print $reader->value . "\n";
    }
}

Sklar
Trachtenberg
Christiansen
Torkington
```

Once you've reached the `<author>` element, call `$reader->read()` to advance to the text *inside* it. From there, you can find the author names inside of `$reader->value`.

The `XMLReader::value` attribute provides you access with a node's value. This only applies to nodes where this is a meaningful concept, such as text nodes or CDATA nodes. In all other cases, such as element nodes, this attribute is set to the empty string.

Table 12-2 contains a complete listing of XMLReader object properties, including `value`.

Table 12-2. XMLReader node type values

Name	Type	Description
attributeCount	int	Number of node attributes
baseURI	string	Base URI of the node
depth	int	Tree depth of the node, starting at 0
hasAttributes	bool	If the node has attributes
hasValue	bool	If the node has a text value
isDefault	bool	If the attribute value is defaulted from DTD
isEmptyElement	bool	If the node is an empty element tag
localName	string	Local name of the node
name	string	Qualified name of the node
namespaceURI	string	URI of the namespace associated with the node
nodeType	int	Node type of the node
prefix	string	Namespace prefix associated with the node
value	string	Text value of the node
xmlLang	string	xml:lang scope of the node

There's one remaining major piece of XMLReader functionality: attributes. XMLReader has a special set of methods to access attribute data when it's on top of an element node, including the following: `moveToAttribute()`, `moveToFirstAttribute()`, and `moveToNextAttribute()`.

The `moveToAttribute()` method lets you specify an attribute name. For example, here's code using the card catalog XML to print out all the ISBN numbers:

```
$reader = new XMLReader();
$reader->XML($catalog);

/* Loop through document */
while ($reader->read()) {
    /* If you're at an element named 'book' */
    if ($reader->nodeType == XMLREADER::ELEMENT &&
    $reader->localName == 'book') {
        $reader->moveToAttribute('isbn');
        print $reader->value . "\n";
    }
}
```

Once you've found the <book> element, call moveToAttribute('isbn') to advance to the isbn attribute, so you can read its value and print it out:

1565926811
0596003137

In the examples in this recipe, we print out information on all books. However, it's easy to modify them to retrieve data only for one specific book. For example, this code combines pieces of the examples to print out all the data for *Perl Cookbook* in an efficient fashion:

```
$reader = new XMLReader();
$reader->XML($catalog);

// Perl Cookbook ISBN is 0596003137
// Use array to make it easy to add additional ISBNs
$isbns = array('0596003137' => true);

/* Loop through document to find first <book> */
while ($reader->read()) {
    /* If you're at an element named 'book' */
    if ($reader->nodeType == XMLREADER::ELEMENT &&
        $reader->localName == 'book') {
        break;
    }
}

/* Loop through <book>s to find right ISBNs */
do {
    if ($reader->moveToAttribute('isbn') &&
        isset($isbns[$reader->value])) {
        while ($reader->read()) {
            switch ($reader->nodeType) {
            case XMLREADER::ELEMENT:
                print $reader->localName . ": ";
                break;
            case XMLREADER::TEXT:
                print $reader->value . "\n";
                break;
```

```
                case XMLREADER::END_ELEMENT;
                    if ($reader->localName == 'book') {
                        break 2;
                    }
                }
            }
        }
    }
} while ($reader->next());

title: Perl Cookbook
author: Christiansen
author: Torkington
subject: Perl
```

The first while() iterates sequentially until it finds the first <book> element.

Having lined yourself up correctly, you then break out of the loop and start checking ISBN numbers. That's handled inside a do... while() loop that uses $reader->next() to move down the <book> list. You cannot use a regular while() here or you'll skip over the first <book>. Also, this is a perfect example of when to use $reader->next() instead of $reader->read().

If the ISBN matches a value in $isbns, then you want to process the data inside the current <book>. This is handled using yet another while() and a switch().

There are three different switch() cases: an opening element, element text, and a closing element. If you're opening an element, you print out the element's name and a colon. If you're visiting text, you print out the textual data. And if you're closing an element, you check to see whether you're closing the <book>. If so, then you've reached the end of the data for that particular book, and you need to return to the do... while() loop. This is handled using a break 2;—while jumps back two levels, instead of the usual one level.

See Also

Recipe 12.3 for parsing simple XML documents; Recipe 12.4 for parsing complex XML documents; documentation on XMLReader (*http://www.php.net/xmlreader*); more information about the underlying libxml2 C library's XMLReader functions (*http://xmlsoft.org/xmlreader.html*).

12.6 Extracting Information Using XPath

Problem

You want to make sophisticated queries of your XML data without parsing the document node by node.

Solution

Use XPath.

XPath is available in SimpleXML:

```
$s = simplexml_load_file(__DIR__ . '/address-book.xml');
$emails = $s->xpath('/address-book/person/email');

foreach ($emails as $email) {
    // do something with $email
}
```

And in DOM:

```
$dom = new DOMDocument;
$dom->load(__DIR__ . '/address-book.xml');
$xpath = new DOMXPath($dom);
$emails = $xpath->query('/address-book/person/email');

foreach ($emails as $email) {
    // do something with $email
}
```

Discussion

Except for the simplest documents, it's rarely easy to access the data you want one element at a time. As your XML files become increasingly complex and your parsing desires grow, using XPath is easier than filtering the data inside a `foreach`.

PHP has an XPath class that takes a DOM object as its constructor. You can then search the object and receive DOM nodes in reply. SimpleXML also supports XPath, and it's easier to use because it's integrated into the SimpleXML object.

DOM supports XPath queries, but you do not perform the query directly on the DOM object itself. Instead, you create a `DOMXPath` object, as shown:

```
$dom = new DOMDocument;
$dom->load(__DIR__ . '/address-book.xml');
$xpath = new DOMXPath($dom);
$emails = $xpath->query('/address-book/person/email');
```

Instantiate `DOMXPath` by passing in a `DOMDocument` to the constructor. To execute the XPath query, call `query()` with the query text as your argument. This returns an iterable DOM node list of matching nodes:

```
$dom = new DOMDocument;
$dom->load(__DIR__ . '/address-book.xml');
$xpath = new DOMXPath($dom);
$emails = $xpath->query('/address-book/person/email');

foreach ($emails as $e) {
```

```
        $email = $e->firstChild->nodeValue;
        // do something with $email
    }
```

After creating a new `DOMXPath` object, query this object using `DOMXPath::query()`, passing the XPath query as the first parameter (in this example, it's `/people/person/email`). This function returns a node list of matching DOM nodes.

By default, `DOMXPath::query()` operates on the entire XML document. Search a subsection of the tree by passing in the subtree as a final parameter to `query()`. For instance, to gather all the first and last names of people in the address book, retrieve all the `person` nodes and query each node individually:

```
    $dom = new DOMDocument;
    $dom->load(__DIR__ . '/address-book.xml');
    $xpath = new DOMXPath($dom);
    $people = $xpath->query('/address-book/person');

    foreach ($people as $p) {
        $fn = $xpath->query('firstname', $p);
        $firstname = $fn->item(0)->firstChild->nodeValue;

        $ln = $xpath->query('lastname', $p);
        $lastname = $ln->item(0)->firstChild->nodeValue;

        print "$firstname $lastname\n";
    }
```

Inside the foreach, call `DOMXPath::query()` to retrieve the firstname and lastname nodes. Now, in addition to the XPath query, also pass $p to the method. This makes the search local to the node.

In contrast to DOM, all SimpleXML objects have an integrated `xpath()` method. Calling this method queries the current object using XPath and returns a SimpleXML object containing the matching nodes, so you don't need to instantiate another object to use XPath. The method's one argument is your XPath query.

Here's how to find all the matching email addresses in the sample address book:

```
    $s = simplexml_load_file(__DIR__ . '/address-book.xml');
    $emails = $s->xpath('/address-book/person/email');

    foreach ($emails as $email) {
        // do something with $email
    }
```

This is shorter because there's no need to dereference the `firstChild` or to take the `nodeValue`.

SimpleXML handles the more complicated example, too. Because `xpath()` returns SimpleXML objects, you can query them directly:

```
$s = simplexml_load_file(__DIR__ . '/address-book.xml');
$people = $s->xpath('/address-book/person');

foreach($people as $p) {
    list($firstname) = $p->xpath('firstname');
    list($lastname) = $p->xpath('lastname');

    print "$firstname $lastname\n";
}
```
David Sklar
Adam Trachtenberg

Because the inner XPath queries return only one element, use `list` to grab it from the array.

See Also

Documentation on DOM XPath (*http://www.php.net/domxpath.construct*); the offical XPath specification (*http://www.w3.org/TR/xpath*); the XPath chapter (*http://oreil.ly/1m03r5y*) from *XML in a Nutshell*.

12.7 Transforming XML with XSLT

Problem

You have an XML document and an XSL stylesheet. You want to transform the document using XSLT and capture the results. This lets you apply stylesheets to your data and create different versions of your content for different media.

Solution

Use PHP's XSLT extension:

```
// Load XSL template
$xsl = new DOMDocument;
$xsl->load(__DIR__ . '/stylesheet.xsl');

// Create new XSLTProcessor
$xslt = new XSLTProcessor();
// Load stylesheet
$xslt->importStylesheet($xsl);

// Load XML input file
$xml = new DOMDocument;
$xsl->load(__DIR__ . '/address-book.xml');

// Transform to string
$results = $xslt->transformToXML($xml);
```

```
// Transform to a file
$results = $xslt->transformToURI($xml, 'results.txt');

// Transform to DOM object
$results = $xslt->transformToDoc($xml);
```

The transformed text is stored in $results.

Discussion

XML documents describe the content of data, but they don't contain any information about how that data should be displayed. However, when XML content is coupled with a stylesheet described using XSL (eXtensible Stylesheet Language), the content is displayed according to specific visual rules.

The glue between XML and XSL is XSLT (eXtensible Stylesheet Language Transformations). These transformations apply the series of rules enumerated in the stylesheet to your XML data. So just as PHP parses your code and combines it with user input to create a dynamic page, an XSLT program uses XSL and XML to output a new page that contains more XML, HTML, or any other format you can describe.

There are a few XSLT programs available, each with different features and limitations. PHP supports only the libxslt processor.

Using XSLT in PHP involves two main steps: preparing the XSLT object and then triggering the actual transformation for each XML file.

To begin, load in the stylesheet using DOM. Then, instantiate a new XSLTProcessor object, and import the XSLT document by passing in your newly created DOM object to the importStylesheet() method, as shown:

```
// Load XSL template
$xsl = new DOMDocument;
$xsl->load(__DIR__ . '/stylesheet.xsl');

// Create new XSLTProcessor
$xslt = new XSLTProcessor();
// Load stylesheet
$xslt->importStylesheet($xsl);
```

Now the transformer is up and running. You can transform any DOM object in one of three ways—into a string, into a file, or back into another DOM object, as shown:

```
// Load XML input file
$xml = new DOMDocument;
$xsl->load(__DIR__ . '/stylesheet.xsl');

// Transform to string
$results = $xslt->transformToXML($xml);
```

```
// Transform to a file
$results = $xslt->transformToURI($xml, 'results.txt');

// Transform to DOM object
$results = $xslt->transformToDoc($xml);
```

When you call `transformToXML()` or `transformToDoc()`, the extension returns the resulting string or object. In contrast, `transformToURI()` returns the number of bytes written to the file, not the actual document.

These methods return `false` when they fail, so to accurately check for failure, write:

```
if (false === ($results = $xslt->transformToXML($xml))) {
    // an error occurred
}
```

Using === prevents a return value of 0 from being confused with an actual error.

See Also

Documentation on XSL functions (*http://www.php.net/xsl*); *XSLT* by Doug Tidwell (O'Reilly).

12.8 Setting XSLT Parameters from PHP

Problem

You want to set parameters in your XSLT stylesheet from PHP.

Solution

Use the `XSLTProcessor::setParameter()` method:

```
// This could also come from $_GET['city'];
$city = 'San Francisco';

$dom  = new DOMDocument;
$dom->load(__DIR__ . '/address-book.xml');
$xsl  = new DOMDocument;
$xsl->load(__DIR__ . '/stylesheet.xsl');

$xslt = new XSLTProcessor();
$xslt->importStylesheet($xsl);
$xslt->setParameter(NULL, 'city', $city);
print $xslt->transformToXML($dom);
```

This code sets the XSLT `city` parameter to the value stored in the PHP variable `$city`.

Discussion

You can pass data from PHP into your XSLT stylesheet with the `setParameter()` method. This allows you to do things such as filter data in your stylesheet based on user input.

For example, this program allows you to find people based on their city:

```php
// This could also come from $_GET['city'];
$city = 'San Francisco';

$dom  = new DOMDocument;
$dom->load(__DIR__ . '/address-book.xml');
$xsl  = new DOMDocument;
$xsl->load(__DIR__ . '/stylesheet.xsl');

$xslt = new XSLTProcessor();
$xslt->importStylesheet($xsl);
$xslt->setParameter(NULL, 'city', $city);
print $xslt->transformToXML($dom);
```

The program uses the following stylesheet:

```xml
<?xml version="1.0" ?>
<xsl:stylesheet version="1.0"
  xmlns:xsl="http://www.w3.org/1999/XSL/Transform">

<xsl:template match="@*|node()">
  <xsl:copy>
    <xsl:apply-templates select="@*|node()"/>
  </xsl:copy>
</xsl:template>

<xsl:template match="/address-book/person">
  <xsl:if test="city=$city">
    <xsl:copy>
      <xsl:apply-templates select="@*|node()"/>
    </xsl:copy>
  </xsl:if>
</xsl:template>
</xsl:stylesheet>
```

The program and stylesheet combine to produce the following results:

```xml
<?xml version="1.0"?>
<address-book>


    <person id="2">
        <!--Adam Trachtenberg-->
        <firstname>Adam</firstname>
        <lastname>Trachtenberg</lastname>
        <city>San Francisco</city>
        <state>CA</state>
        <email>amt@php.net</email>
```

```
        </person>
    </address-book>
```

The PHP script does a standard XSLT transformation, except it calls `$xslt->setParameter(NULL, city, $city)`. The first argument is the parameter's namespace, the second is the parameter's name, and the third is the parameter's value.

Here, the value stored in the PHP variable `$city`—in this case, `San Francisco`—is assigned to the XSLT parameter `city`, which does not live under a namespace. This is equal to placing the following in an XSLT file:

```
<xsl:param name="city">San Francisco</xsl:param>
```

You usually access a parameter inside a stylesheet like you do a PHP variable, by placing a dollar sign ($) in front of its name. The stylesheet example creates a template that matches `/address-book/person` nodes.

Inside the template, you test whether `city=$city`; in other words, is the `city` child of the current node equal to the value of the `city` parameter? If there's a match, the children are copied along; otherwise, the records are eliminated.

In this case, `city` is set to `San Francisco`, so David's record is removed and Adam's remains.

See Also

Documentation on `XSLTProcessor::setParameter()` (*http://www.php.net/xsltproces sor.setparameter*); *XSLT* by Doug Tidwell (O'Reilly).

12.9 Calling PHP Functions from XSLT Stylesheets

Problem

You want to call PHP functions from within an XSLT stylesheet.

Solution

Invoke the `XSLTProcessor::registerPHPFunctions()` method to enable this functionality:

```
$xslt = new XSLTProcessor();
$xslt->registerPHPFunctions();
```

And use the `function()` or `functionString()` function within your stylesheet:

```
<?xml version="1.0" ?>
<xsl:stylesheet version="1.0"
    xmlns:xsl="http://www.w3.org/1999/XSL/Transform"
    xmlns:php="http://php.net/xsl"
```

```
    xsl:extension-element-prefixes="php">

<xsl:template match="/">
    <xsl:value-of select="php:function('strftime', '%c')" />
</xsl:template>

</xsl:stylesheet>
```

Discussion

XSLT parameters are great when you need to communicate from PHP to XSLT. However, they're not very useful when you require the reverse. You can't use parameters to extract information from the stylesheet during the transformation. Ideally, you could call PHP functions from a stylesheet and pass information back to PHP.

Fortunately, there's a method that implements this functionality: `registerPHPFunctions()`. Here's how it's enabled:

```
$xslt = new XSLTProcessor();
$xslt->registerPHPFunctions();
```

This allows you to call any PHP function from your stylesheets. It's not available by default because it presents a security risk if you're processing stylesheets controlled by other people.

Both built-in and user-defined functions work. Inside your stylesheet, you must define a namespace and call the `function()` or `functionString()` methods, as shown:

```
<?xml version="1.0" ?>
<xsl:stylesheet version="1.0"
    xmlns:xsl="http://www.w3.org/1999/XSL/Transform"
    xmlns:php="http://php.net/xsl"
    xsl:extension-element-prefixes="php">

<xsl:template match="/">
    <xsl:value-of select="php:function('strftime', '%c')" />
</xsl:template>

</xsl:stylesheet>
```

At the top of the stylesheet, define the namespace for PHP: `http://php.net/xsl`. This example sets the namespace prefix to `php`. Also, set the `extension-element-prefixes` value to `php` so XSLT knows these are functions.

To call a PHP function, reference `php:function()`. The first parameter is the function name; additional parameters are the function arguments. In this case, the function name is `strftime` and the one argument is `%c`. This causes `strftime` to return the current date and time.

This example uses the stylesheet, stored as *strftime.xsl*, to process a single-element XML document:

```
$dom  = new DOMDocument;
$dom->loadXML('<blank/>');
$xsl  = new DOMDocument;
$xsl->load(__DIR__ . '/strftime.xsl');

$xslt = new XSLTProcessor();
$xslt->importStylesheet($xsl);
$xslt->registerPHPFunctions();
print $xslt->transformToXML($dom);
```

Mon Jul 22 06:01:10 2014

This works like standard XSLT processing, but there's an additional call to `registerPHP Functions()` to activate PHP function support.

You can also return DOM objects. Example 12-2 takes the XML address book and mangles all the email addresses to turn the hostname portion into three dots. Everything else in the document is left untouched.

Example 12-2. Spam protecting email addresses

```
function mangle_email($nodes) {
    return preg_replace('/([^@\s]+)@([-a-z0-9]+\.)+[a-z]{2,}/is',
                        '$1@...',
                        $nodes[0]->nodeValue);
}

$dom  = new DOMDocument;
$dom->load(__DIR__ . '/address-book.xml');
$xsl  = new DOMDocument;
$xsl->load(__DIR__ . '/mangle-email.xsl');

$xslt = new XSLTProcessor();
$xslt->importStylesheet($xsl);
$xslt->registerPhpFunctions();
print $xslt->transformToXML($dom);
```

Inside your stylesheet, create a special template for `/address-book/person/email` elements. As an example:

```
<?xml version="1.0" ?>
<xsl:stylesheet version="1.0"
  xmlns:xsl="http://www.w3.org/1999/XSL/Transform"
  xmlns:php="http://php.net/xsl"
  xsl:extension-element-prefixes="php">

<xsl:template match="@*|node()">
  <xsl:copy>
    <xsl:apply-templates select="@*|node()"/>
  </xsl:copy>
```

```
    </xsl:template>

    <xsl:template match="/address-book/person/email">
      <xsl:copy>
        <xsl:value-of select="php:function('mangle_email', node())" />
      </xsl:copy>
    </xsl:template>
    </xsl:stylesheet>
```

The first template ensures that the elements aren't modified, and the second passes the current node to PHP for mangling. In the second template, the mangle_email() function is passed the current node, represented in XPath as node(), instead of a string. Be sure not to place the node() inside quotation marks, or you'll pass the literal text node().

Nodes become DOM objects inside PHP and always arrive in an array. In this case, mangle_email() knows there's always only one object and it's a DOMText object, so the email address is located in $nodes[0]->nodeValue.

When you know that you're only interested in the text portion of a node, use the func tionString() function. This function converts nodes to PHP strings, which allows you to omit the array access and nodeValue dereference:

```
function mangle_email($email) {
    return preg_replace('/([^@\s]+)@([-a-z0-9]+\.)+[a-z]{2,}/is',
                        '$1@...',
                        $email);
}

// all other code is the same as before
```

The new stylesheet template for /address-book/person/email is:

```
<xsl:template match="/address-book/person/email">
  <xsl:copy>
    <xsl:value-of
        select="php:functionString('mangle_email', node())" />
  </xsl:copy>
</xsl:template>
```

The mangle_email() function now processes $email instead of $nodes[0]->nodeValue because the template now calls the functionString() function.

The function() and functionString() methods are incredibly useful, but using them undermines the premise of XSL as a language-neutral transformation engine. When you call PHP from XSLT, you cannot easily reuse your stylesheets in projects that use Java, Perl, and other languages, because they cannot call PHP. Therefore, you should consider the trade-off between convenience and portability before using this feature.

See Also

Documentation on XSLTProcessor::registerPHPFunctions() (*http://bit.ly/ 1g63neD*); *XSLT* by Doug Tidwell (O'Reilly).

12.10 Validating XML Documents

Problem

You want to make sure your XML document abides by a schema, such as XML Schema, Relax NG (*http://relaxng.org*), and DTDs.

Solution

Use the DOM extension.

To validate a DOM object against a schema stored in a file, call DOMDocument::schema Validate() or DOMDocument::relaxNGValidate():

```
$file = __DIR__ . '/address-book.xml';
$schema = __DIR__ . '/address-book.xsd';
$ab = new DOMDocument;
$ab->load($file);

if ($ab->schemaValidate($schema)) {
    print "$file is valid.\n";
} else {
    print "$file is invalid.\n";
}
```

If your XML document specifies a DTD at the top, call DOMDocument::validate() to validate it against the DTD.

To validate a DOM object against a schema stored in a variable, call DOMDocument::sche maValidateSource() or DOMDocument::relaxNGValidateSource():

```
$file = __DIR__ . '/address-book.xml';
$ab = new DOMDocument;
$ab->load($file);

$schema = file_get_contents(__DIR__ . '/address-book.xsd');

if ($ab->schemaValidateSource($schema)) {
    print "XML is valid.\n";
} else {
    print "XML is invalid.\n";
}
```

Discussion

Schemas are a way of defining a specification for your XML documents. Though the goal is the same, there are multiple ways to encode a schema, each with a different syntax.

Some popular formats are DTDs (Document Type Definitions), XML Schema, and Relax NG. DTDs have been around longer, but they are not written in XML and have other issues, so they can be difficult to work with. XML Schema and Relax NG are more recent schemas and attempt to solve some of the issues surrounding DTDs.

PHP uses the libxml2 library to provide its validation support. Therefore, it lets you validate files against all three types. It is most flexible when you're using XML Schema and Relax NG, but its XML Schema support is incomplete. You shouldn't run into issues in most XML Schema documents; however, you may find that libxml2 cannot handle some complex schemas or schemas that use more esoteric features.

Within PHP, the DOM extension supports DTD, XML Schema, and Relax NG validation, whereas SimpleXML provides only an XML Schema validator.

Validating any file using DOM is a similar process, regardless of the underlying schema format. To validate, call a validation method on a DOM object. For example:

```
$file = __DIR__ . '/address-book.xml';
$schema = __DIR__ . '/address-book.xsd';
$ab = new DOMDocument;
$ab->load($file);

if ($ab->schemaValidate($schema)) {
    print "$file is valid.\n";
} else {
    print "$file is invalid.\n";
}
```

It returns true if the file passes. If there's an error, it returns false and prints a message to the error log. There is no method for *capturing* the error message.

If the schema is stored in a string, use DOMDocument::schemaValidateSource() instead of schemaValidate().

Table 12-3 lists all the validation methods.

Table 12-3. DOM schema validation methods

Method name	Schema type	Data location
schemaValidate	XML Schema	File
schemaValidateSource	XML Schema	String
relaxNGValidate	Relax NG	File
relaxNGValidateSource	Relax NG	String
validate	DTD	N/A

All of the validation methods behave in a similar manner, so you only need to switch the method name in the previous example to switch to a different validation scheme.

Both XML Schema and Relax NG support validation against files and strings. You can validate a DOM object only against the DTD defined at the top of the XML document.

See Also

The XML Schema specification (*http://www.w3.org/XML/Schema*) and the Relax NG specification (*http://www.relaxng.org/*).

12.11 Handling Content Encoding

Problem

PHP XML extensions use UTF-8, but your data is in a different content encoding.

Solution

Use the `iconv` library to convert data before passing it into an XML extension:

```
$utf_8 = iconv('ISO-8859-1', 'UTF-8', $iso_8859_1);
```

Then convert the data back when you are finished:

```
$iso_8859_1 = iconv('UTF-8', 'ISO-8859-1', $utf_8);
```

Discussion

Character encoding is a major PHP weakness, so you can run into problems if you're trying to use XML extensions with arbitrary encoded data.

For simplicity, the XML extensions all exclusively use the UTF-8 character encoding. That means they all expect data in UTF-8 and output all data in UTF-8. If your data is ASCII, then you don't need to worry; UTF-8 is a superset of ASCII. However, if you're using other encodings, you will run into trouble sooner or later.

To work around this issue, use the `iconv` extension to manually encode data back and forth between your character sets and UTF-8. For example, to convert from ISO-8859-1 to UTF-8:

```
$utf_8 = iconv('ISO-8859-1', 'UTF-8', $iso_8859_1);
```

The `iconv` function supports two special modifiers for the destination encoding: `//TRANSLIT` and `//IGNORE`. The first option tells `iconv` that whenever it cannot exactly duplicate a character in the destination encoding, it should try to approximate it using a series of other characters. The other option makes `iconv` silently ignore any unconvertible characters.

For example, the string `$geb` holds the text Gödel, Escher, Bach. A straight conversion to ASCII produces an error:

```
echo iconv('UTF-8', 'ASCII', $geb);

PHP Notice:  iconv(): Detected an illegal character in input string...
```

Enabling the `//IGNORE` feature allows the conversion to occur:

```
echo iconv('UTF-8', 'ASCII//IGNORE', $geb);
```

However, the output isn't nice, because the ö is missing:

```
Gdel, Escher, Bach
```

The best solution is to use `//TRANSLIT`:

```
echo iconv('UTF-8', 'ASCII//TRANSLIT', $geb);
```

This produces a better-looking string:

```
G"odel, Escher, Bach
```

However, be careful when you use `//TRANSLIT`, because it can increase the number of characters. For example, the single character ö becomes two characters: " and o.

See Also

More information about working with UTF-8 text is in Recipe 19.12; documentation on iconv (*http://www.php.net/iconv*); the GNU libiconv homepage (*http://www.gnu.org/software/libiconv/*).

12.12 Reading RSS and Atom Feeds

Problem

You want to retrieve RSS and Atom feeds and look at the items. This allows you to incorporate newsfeeds from multiple websites into your application.

Solution

Use the MagpieRSS parser (*http://magpierss.sourceforge.net/*). Here's an example that reads the RSS feed for the *php.announce* mailing list:

```
require __DIR__ . '/magpie/rss_fetch.inc';

$feed = 'http://news.php.net/group.php?group=php.announce&format=rss';

$rss = fetch_rss( $feed );

print "<ul>\n";
```

```
foreach ($rss->items as $item) {
    print '<li><a href="' . $item['link'] . '">' . $item['title'] .
        "</a></li>\n";
}
print "</ul>\n";
```

Discussion

RSS is an easy-to-use headline or article syndication format written in XML. Many news websites, such as the *New York Times* and the *Washington Post*, provide RSS feeds that update whenever new stories are published. Weblogs have also embraced RSS and having an RSS feed for your blog is a standard feature. The PHP website also publishes RSS feeds for most PHP mailing lists.

Atom is a similar XML syndication format. It extends many of the concepts in RSS, including a way to read and write Atom data. It also attempts to provide a more well-defined syntax for syndication than RSS, because the RSS specification doesn't always clearly enumerate exactly what is or isn't permissible in a feed.

Using MagpieRSS, retrieving and parsing RSS and Atom feeds are simple:

```
$feed = 'http://news.php.net/group.php?group=php.announce&format=rss';

$rss = fetch_rss($feed);
```

This example reads in the RSS feed for the *php.announce* mailing list. The feed is then parsed by fetch_rss() and stored internally within $rss.

Although this feed is RSS 0.93, there's no need to specify this to MagpieRSS. Its fetch_rss() function detects the syndication format, including Atom, and formats the document accordingly.

Each RSS item is then retrieved as an associative array using the items property:

```
print "<ul>\n";

foreach ($rss->items as $item) {
    print '<li><a href="' . $item['link'] . '">' . $item['title'] .
        "</a></li>\n";
}

print "</ul>\n";
```

This foreach loop creates an unordered list of items with the item title linking back to the URL associated with the complete article, as shown in Figure 12-1. Besides the required title and link fields, an item can have an optional description field that contains a brief write-up about the item.

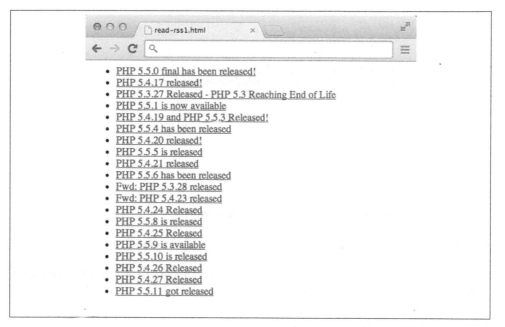

Figure 12-1. php.announce RSS feed

Each channel also has an entry with information about the feed, as shown in Figure 12-2. To retrieve this data, access the channel attribute:

```
$feed = 'http://news.php.net/group.php?group-php.announce&format=rss';
$rss = fetch_rss($feed);


print "<ul>\n";

foreach ($rss->channel as $key => $value) {
    print "<li>$key: $value</li>\n";
}

print "</ul>\n";
```

- title: news.php.net: php.announce
- link: http://news.php.net/group.php?group=php.announce
- tagline:

Figure 12-2. php.announce RSS channel information

See Also

The MagpieRSS homepage (*http://magpierss.sourceforge.net/*); more information on RSS at Wikipedia (*http://en.wikipedia.org/wiki/RSS_(protocol)*).

12.13 Writing RSS Feeds

Problem

You want to generate RSS feeds from your data. This will allow you to syndicate your content.

Solution

Use this class:

```
class rss2 extends DOMDocument {
    private $channel;

    public function __construct($title, $link, $description) {
        parent::__construct();
        $this->formatOutput = true;

        $root = $this->appendChild($this->createElement('rss'));
        $root->setAttribute('version', '2.0');

        $channel= $root->appendChild($this->createElement('channel'));

        $channel->appendChild($this->createElement('title', $title));
        $channel->appendChild($this->createElement('link', $link));
        $channel->appendChild($this->createElement('description',
                                                   $description));
```

```
            $this->channel = $channel;
        }

        public function addItem($title, $link, $description) {
            $item = $this->createElement('item');
            $item->appendChild($this->createElement('title', $title));
            $item->appendChild($this->createElement('link', $link));
            $item->appendChild($this->createElement('description', $description));

            $this->channel->appendChild($item);
        }
    }

    $rss = new rss2('Channel Title', 'http://www.example.org',
                    'Channel Description');

    $rss->addItem('Item 1', 'http://www.example.org/item1',
                    'Item 1 Description');
    $rss->addItem('Item 2', 'http://www.example.org/item2',
                    'Item 2 Description');

    print $rss->saveXML();
```

Discussion

RSS is XML, so you can leverage all the XML-generation features of the DOM extension. The code in the Solution extends the DOMDocument class to build up a DOM tree by creating elements and appending them in the appropriate structure.

The class constructor sets up the <rss> and <channel> elements. It takes three arguments—the channel title, link, and description:

```
    public function __construct($title, $link, $description) {
            parent::__construct();
            $this->formatOutput = true;

            $root = $this->appendChild($this->createElement('rss'));
            $root->setAttribute('version', '2.0');

            $channel= $root->appendChild($this->createElement('channel'));

            $channel->appendChild($this->createElement('title', $title));
            $channel->appendChild($this->createElement('link', $link));
            $channel->appendChild($this->createElement('description',
                                                        $description));

            $this->channel = $channel;
        }
```

Inside the method, you call the parent::__construct() method to invoke the actual DOMDocument::__construct(). Now you can begin building up the document.

First, set the `formatOutput` attribute to `true`. This adds indentation and carriage returns to the output, so it's easy to read.

From there, create the document's root element, `rss`, and set its `version` attribute to 2.0, because this is an RSS 2.0 feed.

All the actual data lives inside a `channel` element underneath the `rss` node, so the next step is to make that element and also to set its `title`, `link`, and `description` child elements.

That data comes from the arguments passed to the constructor. It's set using a handy feature of the `createElement()` method, which lets you specify both an element's name and a text node with data in one call. This is a PHP extension to the DOM specification.

Last, the `channel` element is saved for easy access later on.

With the main content defined, use the `addItem()` method to add item entries:

```
public function addItem($title, $link, $description) {
    $item = $this->createElement('item');
    $item->appendChild($this->createElement('title', $title));
    $item->appendChild($this->createElement('link', $link));
    $item->appendChild($this->createElement('description', $description));
    $this->channel->appendChild($item);
}
```

Because `item` elements contain the same data as the `channel`, this code is almost identical to what appears in the constructor.

Although a title, link, and description are required elements of the channel, they are actually optional in the item. The only requirement of an item is that it contains *either* a title or a description. That's it.

For simplicity, this code requires all three elements. Likewise, it doesn't provide a way to add in additional channel or item elements, such as the date the item was published or a GUID that uniquely identifies the item.

But 43 lines later, the basic RSS 2.0 class is finished. Use it like this:

```
$rss = new rss2('Channel Title', 'http://www.example.org',
                'Channel Description');

$rss->addItem('Item 1', 'http://www.example.org/item1',
              'Item 1 Description');
$rss->addItem('Item 2', 'http://www.example.org/item2',
              'Item 2 Description');

print $rss->saveXML();

<?xml version="1.0"?>
<rss version="2.0">
  <channel>
```

```
    <title>Channel Title</title>
    <link>http://www.example.org</link>
    <description>Channel Description</description>
    <item>
      <title>Item 1</title>
      <link>http://www.example.org/item1</link>
      <description>Item 1 Description</description>
    </item>
    <item>
      <title>Item 2</title>
      <link>http://www.example.org/item2</link>
      <description>Item 2 Description</description>
    </item>
  </channel>
</rss>
```

Create a new instance of the rss2 class and pass along the channel data. Then call its addItem() method to add individual items to the channel. Once you're finished, you can convert the class to XML by using the parent DOMDocument::saveXML() method.

12.14 Writing Atom Feeds

Problem

You want to generate Atom feeds from your data. This will allow you to syndicate your content.

Solution

Use this class:

```
class atom1 extends DOMDocument {
    private $ns;

    public function __construct($title, $href, $name, $id) {
        parent::__construct();
        $this->formatOutput = true;

        $this->ns = 'http://www.w3.org/2005/Atom';

        $root = $this->appendChild($this->createElementNS($this->ns, 'feed'));

        $root->appendChild($this->createElementNS($this->ns, 'title', $title));
        $link = $root->appendChild($this->createElementNS($this->ns, 'link'));
        $link->setAttribute('href', $href);
        $root->appendChild($this->createElementNS($this->ns, 'updated',
            date(DATE_ATOM)));
        $author = $root->appendChild($this->createElementNS($this->ns,
                                                            'author'));
        $author->appendChild($this->createElementNS($this->ns, 'name', $name));
```

```
        $root->appendChild($this->createElementNS($this->ns, 'id', $id));
    }

    public function addEntry($title, $link, $summary) {
        $entry = $this->createElementNS($this->ns, 'entry');
        $entry->appendChild($this->createElementNS($this->ns, 'title', $title));
        $entry->appendChild($this->createElementNS($this->ns, 'link', $link));

        $id = uniqid('http://example.org/atom/entry/ids/');
        $entry->appendChild($this->createElementNS($this->ns, 'id', $id));

        $entry->appendChild($this->createElementNS($this->ns, 'updated',
            date(DATE_ATOM)));
        $entry->appendChild($this->createElementNS($this->ns, 'summary',
            $summary));

        $this->documentElement->appendChild($entry);
    }
}

$atom = new atom1('Channel Title', 'http://www.example.org',
            'John Quincy Atom', 'http://example.org/atom/feed/ids/1');

$atom->addEntry('Item 1', 'http://www.example.org/item1',
            'Item 1 Description', 'http://example.org/atom/entry/ids/1');

$atom->addEntry('Item 2', 'http://www.example.org/item2',
            'Item 2 Description', 'http://example.org/atom/entry/ids/2');

print $atom->saveXML();
```

Discussion

The atom1 class is structured similar to the rss2 class from Recipe 12.13. Read its Discussion for a more detailed explanation of the overall code structure and DOM extension behavior. This recipe covers the differences between RSS and Atom and how the class is updated to handle them.

The Atom specification is more complex than RSS. It requires you to place elements inside a namespace and also forces the generation of unique identifiers for a feed and individual items, along with the last updated times for those entries.

Also, though its general structure is similar to RSS, it uses different terminology. The root element is now a feed and an item is now an entry. You don't need a feed description, but you do need an author. And inside the entries, the description is a summary.

Last, there is no concept of a channel. Both feed data and entries are located directly under the document element.

Here's the updated constructor:

```
public function __construct($title, $href, $name, $id) {
        parent::__construct();
        $this->formatOutput = true;

        $this->ns = 'http://www.w3.org/2005/Atom';

        $root = $this->appendChild($this->createElementNS($this->ns, 'feed'));

        $root->appendChild(
            $this->createElementNS($this->ns, 'title', $title));
        $link = $root->appendChild(
            $this->createElementNS($this->ns, 'link'));
        $link->setAttribute('href', $href);
        $root->appendChild($this->createElementNS(
            $this->ns, 'updated', date(DATE_ATOM)));
        $author = $root->appendChild(
            $this->createElementNS($this->ns, 'author'));
        $author->appendChild(
            $this->createElementNS($this->ns, 'name', $name));
        $root->appendChild(
            $this->createElementNS($this->ns, 'id', $id'));
    }
```

All Atom elements live under the http://www.w3.org/2005/Atom XML namespace. Therefore, all atom1 methods use DOMDocument::createElementNS(), which is the *namespace* version of DOMDocument::createElement(). The Atom namespace is stored in atom1::ns, so it's easy to access.

The constructor now takes four arguments: title, link, author name, and feed ID. The title and id are defined similar to RSS channel elements. However, the link is actually set as the href attribute of the link element, and the name is a child of the author element.

Additionally, there is an updated element, which is set to the last update time. In this case, it's set to the current time and formatted using PHP's built-in DATE_ATOM constant formatting specification.

The addItem() method is renamed to addEntry() to be consistent with the Atom specification:

```
public function addEntry($title, $link, $summary, $id) {
        $entry = $this->createElementNS($this->ns, 'entry');
        $entry->appendChild(
            $this->createElementNS($this->ns, 'title', $title));
        $entry->appendChild(
            $this->createElementNS($this->ns, 'link', $link));
        $entry->appendChild(
            $this->createElementNS($this->ns, 'id', $id));
        $entry->appendChild(
```

```
        $this->createElementNS($this->ns, 'updated', date(DATE_ATOM)));
    $entry->appendChild(
        $this->createElementNS($this->ns, 'summary', $summary));

    $this->documentElement->appendChild($entry);
}
```

It behaves very similar to its counterpart, with the few additions of new elements, such as id and updated.

Everything comes together like this:

```
$atom = new atom1('Channel Title', 'http://www.example.org',
            'John Quincy Atom', 'http://example.org/atom/feed/ids/1');

$atom->addEntry('Item 1', 'http://www.example.org/item1',
            'Item 1 Description', 'http://example.org/atom/entry/ids/1');

$atom->addEntry('Item 2', 'http://www.example.org/item2',
            'Item 2 Description', 'http://example.org/atom/entry/ids/2');

print $atom->saveXML();

<?xml version="1.0"?>
<feed xmlns="http://www.w3.org/2005/Atom">
  <title>Channel Title</title>
  <link href="http://www.example.org"/>
  <updated>2006-10-23T22:33:59-07:00</updated>
  <author>
    <name>John Quincy Atom</name>
  </author>
  <id>http://example.org/atom/feed/ids/1</id>
  <entry>
    <title>Item 1</title>
    <link>http://www.example.org/item1</link>
    <id>http://example.org/atom/entry/ids/1</id>
    <updated>2014-10-23T20:23:32-07:00</updated>
    <summary>Item 1 Description</summary>
  </entry>
  <entry>
    <title>Item 2</title>
    <link>http://www.example.org/item2</link>
    <id>http://example.org/atom/entry/ids/2</id>
    <updated>2014-10-23T21:53:44-07:00</updated>
    <summary>Item 2 Description</summary>
  </entry>
</feed>
```

Like the rss2 class, atom1 implements only a small subset of the full specification. It's enough to generate a valid feed, but if you need to do more, you will need to extend the class.

See Also

The Atom homepage (*http://www.atomenabled.org/*); the Atom Wiki (*http://www.inter twingly.net/wiki/pie/*); more information on Atom (*http://en.wikipedia.org/wiki/ Atom_(standard)*).

CHAPTER 13

Web Automation

13.0 Introduction

Most of the time, PHP is part of a web server, sending content to browsers. Even when you run it from the command line, it usually performs a task and then prints some output. PHP can also be useful, however, playing the role of a web client, retrieving URLs and then operating on the content. Whereas Chapter 14 discusses retrieving URLs from within PHP, this chapter explores how to process the received content.

Recipes 13.1 through 13.6 help you manipulate those page contents. Recipe 13.1 demonstrates how to mark up certain words in a page with blocks of color. This technique is useful for highlighting search terms, for example. Cleaning up HTML so it's easier to parse and is standards compliant, is the topic of Recipe 13.2. Recipe 13.3 provides a function to find all the links in a page. This is an essential building block for a web spider or a link checker. Converting between plain text and HTML is covered in Recipes 13.4 and 13.5. Recipe 13.6 shows how to remove all HTML and PHP tags from a web page.

Recipes 13.7 and 13.8 discuss how PHP and JavaScript can work together. Recipe 13.7 explores using PHP to respond to requests made by JavaScript, in which you have to be concerned about caching and using alternate content types. Recipe 13.8 provides a full-fledged example of PHP–JavaScript integration using the popular and powerful jQuery toolkit.

Two sample programs use the link extractor from Recipe 13.3. The program in Recipe 13.9 scans the links in a page and reports which are still valid, which have been moved, and which no longer work. The program in Recipe 13.10 reports on the freshness of links. It tells you when a linked-to page was last modified and if it's been moved.

13.1 Marking Up a Web Page

Problem

You want to display a web page—for example, a search result—with certain words highlighted.

Solution

Build an array replacement for each word you want to highlight. Then, chop up the page into "HTML elements" and "text between HTML elements" and apply the replacements to just the text between HTML elements. Example 13-1 applies highlighting in the HTML in $body to the words found in $words.

Example 13-1. Marking up a web page

```
$body = '
<p>I like pickles and herring.</p>

<a href="pickle.php"><img src="pickle.jpg"/>A pickle picture</a>

I have a herringbone-patterned toaster cozy.

<herring>Herring is not a real HTML element!</herring>
';

$words = array('pickle','herring');
$replacements = array();
foreach ($words as $i => $word) {
    $replacements[] = "<span class='word-$i'>$word</span>";
}

// Split up the page into chunks delimited by a
// reasonable approximation of what an HTML element
// looks like.
$parts = preg_split("{(<(?:\"[^\"]*\"|'[^']*'|[^'\"]*>)*)}",
                    $body,
                    -1,  // Unlimited number of chunks
                    PREG_SPLIT_DELIM_CAPTURE);
foreach ($parts as $i => $part) {
    // Skip if this part is an HTML element
    if (isset($part[0]) && ($part[0] == '<')) { continue; }
    // Wrap the words with <span/>s
    $parts[$i] = str_replace($words, $replacements, $part);
}

// Reconstruct the body
$body = implode('',$parts);

print $body;
```

Discussion

Example 13-1 prints:

```
<p>I like <span class='word-0'>pickle</span>s and <span class='word-1'>↵
herring</span>.</p>

<a href="pickle.php"><img src="pickle.jpg"/>A <span class='word-0'>pickle</span>↵
 picture</a>

I have a <span class='word-1'>herring</span>bone-patterned toaster cozy.

<herring>Herring is not a real HTML element!</herring>
```

Each of the words in $words (pickle and herring) has been wrapped with a <span/>
that has a specific class attribute. Use a CSS stylesheet to attach particular display
attributes to these classes, such as a bright yellow background or a border.

The regular expression in Example 13-1 chops up $body into a series of chunks delimited
by HTML elements. This lets us just replace the text between HTML elements and leaves
HTML elements or attributes alone whose values might contain a search term. The
regular expression does a pretty good job of matching HTML elements, but if you have
some particularly crazy, malformed markup with mismatched or unescaped quotes, it
might get confused.

Because str_replace() is case sensitive, only strings that exactly match words in
$words are replaced. The last Herring in Example 13-1 doesn't get highlighted because
it begins with a capital letter. To do case-insensitive matching, we need to switch from
str_replace() to regular expressions. (We can't use str_ireplace() because the replacement has to preserve the case of what matched.) Example 13-2 shows the altered
code that uses regular expressions to do the replacement.

Example 13-2. Marking up a web page with regular expressions

```
$body = '
<p>I like pickles and herring.</p>

<a href="pickle.php"><img src="pickle.jpg"/>A pickle picture</a>

I have a herringbone-patterned toaster cozy.

<herring>Herring is not a real HTML element!</herring>
';

$words = array('pickle','herring');
$patterns = array();
$replacements = array();
foreach ($words as $i => $word) {
    $patterns[] = '/' . preg_quote($word) .'/i';
    $replacements[] = "<span class='word-$i'>\\0</span>";
```

```
    }

    // Split up the page into chunks delimited by a
    // reasonable approximation of what an HTML element
    // looks like.
    $parts = preg_split("{(<(?:\"[^\"]*\"|'[^']*'|[^'\"]>)*>)}",
                        $body,
                        -1, // Unlimited number of chunks
                        PREG_SPLIT_DELIM_CAPTURE);
    foreach ($parts as $i => $part) {
        // Skip if this part is an HTML element
        if (isset($part[0]) && ($part[0] == '<')) { continue; }
        // Wrap the words with <span/>s
        $parts[$i] = preg_replace($patterns, $replacements, $part);
    }

    // Reconstruct the body
    $body = implode('',$parts);

    print $body;
```

The two differences in Example 13-2 are that it builds a $patterns array in the loop at the top and it uses preg_replace() (with the $patterns array) instead of str_re place(). The i at the end of each element in $patterns makes the match case insensitive. The \\0 in the replacement preserves the case in the replacement with the case of what it matched.

Switching to regular expressions also makes it easy to prevent substring matching. In both Example 13-1 and Example 13-2, the herring in herringbone gets highlighted. To prevent this, change $patterns[] = '/' . preg_quote($word) .'/i'; in Example 13-2 to $patterns[] = '/\b' . preg_quote($word) .'\b/i';. The additional \b items in the pattern tell preg_replace() only to match a word if it stands on its own.

See Also

Documentation on str_replace() (*http://bit.ly/V8RFMO*), on str_ireplace() (*http://bit.ly/1nzhGMS*), on preg_replace() (*http://bit.ly/1nZKuzU*), and on preg_split() (*http://bit.ly/1q4jzG8*). If you're feeling squeamish about using regular expressions to parse HTML, see the end of the Discussion of Recipe 13.2.

13.2 Cleaning Up Broken or Nonstandard HTML

Problem

You've got some HTML with malformed syntax that you'd like to clean up. This makes it easier to parse and ensures that the pages you produce are standards compliant.

Solution

Use PHP's Tidy extension. It relies on the popular, powerful, HTML Tidy library to turn frightening piles of tag soup into well-formed, standards-compliant HTML or XHTML. Example 13-3 shows how to repair a file.

Example 13-3. Repairing an HTML file with Tidy

```
$fixed = tidy_repair_file('bad.html');
file_put_contents('good.html', $fixed);
```

Discussion

The HTML Tidy library has a large number of rules and features built up over time that creatively handle a wide variety of HTML abominations. Fortunately, you don't have to care about what all those rules are to reap the benefits of Tidy. Just pass a filename to `tidy_repair_file()` and you get back a cleaned-up version. For example, if *bad.html* contains:

```
<img src="monkey.jpg">

<b>I <em>love</b> monkeys</em>.
```

then Example 13-3 writes the following out to *good.html*:

```
<!DOCTYPE html PUBLIC "-//W3C//DTD HTML 3.2//EN">
<html>
<head>
<title></title>
</head>
<body>
<img src="monkey.jpg"> <b>I <em>love</em> monkeys</b>.
</body>
</html>
```

Tidy has a large number of configuration options (*http://bit.ly/TrxOqt*) that affect the output it produces. Pass configuration to `tidy_repair_file()` by providing a second argument that is an array of configuration options and values. Example 13-4 uses the `output-xhtml` option, which tells Tidy to produce valid XHTML.

Example 13-4. Production of XHTML with Tidy

```
$config = array('output-xhtml' => true);
$fixed = tidy_repair_file('bad.html', $config);
file_put_contents('good.xhtml', $fixed);
```

Example 13-4 writes the following to *good.xhtml*:

```
<!DOCTYPE html PUBLIC "-//W3C//DTD XHTML 1.0 Transitional//EN"
    "http://www.w3.org/TR/xhtml1/DTD/xhtml1-transitional.dtd">
<html xmlns="http://www.w3.org/1999/xhtml">
<head>
<title></title>
</head>
<body>
<img src="monkey.jpg" /> <b>I <em>love</em> monkeys</b>.
</body>
</html>
```

If your source HTML is in a string instead of a file, use `tidy_repair_string()`. It expects a first argument that contains HTML, not a filename.

The cleaned-up XHTML produced by Tidy also provides a way to mark up HTML (as in Recipe 13.1) without using regular expressions. After the HTML has been converted to a well-formed XHTML document, it can be systematically processed and converted by PHP's DOM functions. Example 13-5 shows this in action.

Example 13-5. Marking up a web page with Tidy and DOM

```
$body = '
<p>I like pickles and herring.</p>

<a href="pickle.php"><img src="pickle.jpg"/>A pickle picture</a>

I have a herringbone-patterned toaster cozy.

<herring>Herring is not a real HTML element!</herring>
';

$words = array('pickle','herring');
$patterns = array();
$replacements = array();
foreach ($words as $i => $word) {
    $patterns[] = '/' . preg_quote($word) . '/i';
    $replacements[] = "<span class='word-$i'>$word</span>";
}

/* Tell Tidy to produce XHTML */
$xhtml = tidy_repair_string($body, array('output-xhtml' => true));

/* Load the XHTML as an XML document */
$doc = new DOMDocument;
$doc->loadXml($xhtml);
```

```
/* When turning our input HTML into a proper XHTML document,
 * Tidy puts the input HTML inside the <body/> element of the
 * XHTML document */
$body = $doc->getElementsByTagName('body')->item(0);

/* Visit all text nodes and mark up words if necessary */
$xpath = new DOMXpath($doc);
foreach ($xpath->query("descendant-or-self::text()", $body) as $textNode) {
    $replaced = preg_replace($patterns, $replacements, $textNode->wholeText);
    if ($replaced !== $textNode->wholeText) {
        $fragment = $textNode->ownerDocument->createDocumentFragment();
        /* This makes sure that the <span/> sub-nodes are created properly */
        $fragment->appendXml($replaced);
        $textNode->parentNode->replaceChild($fragment, $textNode);
    }
}

/* Build the XHTML consisting of the content of everything under <body/> */
$markedup = '';
foreach ($body->childNodes as $node) {
    $markedup .= $doc->saveXml($node);
}
print $markedup;
```

In Example 13-5, the `preg_replace()` command to add the markup is run on all text nodes of the DOM tree that results from loading a Tidy-repaired version of the input HTML into a `DOMDocument` object. The great thing about this is that we can be certain that the replacements are only being run on text. Any broken HTML that would have confused the regular expression used for finding HTML tags in Recipe 13.1 is repaired by Tidy before the `DOMDocument` is created.

The downside of this approach is that, depending on how broken your input HTML is, the results of Tidy's conversion may not be what you expect. Here is the output of Example 13-5:

```
<p>I like <span class="word-0">pickle</span>s and <span class="word-1">herring
</span>.</p>
<a href="pickle.php"><img src="pickle.jpg" />A <span class="word-0">pickle
</span> picture</a> I
have a <span class="word-1">herring</span>bone-patterned toaster cozy.
<span class="word-1">herring</span> is not a real HTML element!
```

Note that the final part of it is `<span class="word-1">herring</span> is not a real HTML element!`. Because `<herring/>` is not a valid XHTML element, Tidy has stripped the `<herring>` and `</herring>` out, leaving the enclosed text. This is a reasonable thing to do in order to produce a valid XHTML document, but could be confusing if you're not expecting it.

See Also

Documentation on `tidy_repair_file()` (*http://bit.ly/1v1eQmE*), on `tidy_re pair_string()` (*http://bit.ly/1lmAIb6*), and on Tidy configuration options (*http://bit.ly/TrxOqt*). The XHTML 1.0 specification (*http://bit.ly/1rtPfCv*); more information about PHP's DOM functions is in Recipe 12.4.

13.3 Extracting Links from an HTML File

Problem

You need to extract the URLs that are specified inside an HTML document.

Solution

Use Tidy to convert the document to XHTML, then use an XPath query to find all the links, as shown in Example 13-6.

Example 13-6. Extracting links with Tidy and XPath

```
$html=<<<_HTML_
<p>Some things I enjoy eating are:</p>
<ul>
<li><a href="http://en.wikipedia.org/wiki/Pickle">Pickles</a></li>
<li><a href="http://www.eatingintranslation.com/2011/03/great_ny_noodle.html">
                Salt-Baked Scallops</a></li>
<li><a href="http://www.thestoryofchocolate.com/">Chocolate</a></li>
</ul>
_HTML_;

$doc = new DOMDocument();
$opts = array('output-xhtml' => true,
              // Prevent DOMDocument from being confused about entities
              'numeric-entities' => true);
$doc->loadXML(tidy_repair_string($html,$opts));
$xpath = new DOMXPath($doc);
// Tell $xpath about the XHTML namespace
$xpath->registerNamespace('xhtml','http://www.w3.org/1999/xhtml');
foreach ($xpath->query('//xhtml:a/@href') as $node) {
    $link = $node->nodeValue;
    print $link . "\n";
}
```

If Tidy isn't available, use the `pc_link_extractor()` function shown in Example 13-7.

Example 13-7. Extracting links without Tidy

```
$html=<<<_HTML_
<p>Some things I enjoy eating are:</p>
<ul>
```

```
<li><a href="http://en.wikipedia.org/wiki/Pickle">Pickles</a></li>
<li><a href="http://www.eatingintranslation.com/2011/03/great_ny_noodle.html">
                Salt-Baked Scallops</a></li>
<li><a href="http://www.thestoryofchocolate.com/">Chocolate</a></li>
</ul>
_HTML_;

$links = pc_link_extractor($html);
foreach ($links as $link) {
    print $link[0] . "\n";
}

function pc_link_extractor($html) {
    $links = array();
    preg_match_all('/<a\s+.*?href=[\"\']?([^\"\' >]*)[\"\']?[^>]*>(.*?)<\/a>/i',
                   $html,$matches,PREG_SET_ORDER);
    foreach($matches as $match) {
        $links[] = array($match[1],$match[2]);
    }
    return $links;
}
```

Discussion

The XHTML document that Tidy generates when the output-xhtml option is turned
on may contain entities other then the four that are defined by the base XML specification (<, >, &, "). Turning on the numeric-entities option prevents
those other entities from appearing in the generated XHTML document. Their presence
would cause DOMDocument to complain about undefined entities. An alternative is to
leave out the numeric-entities option but set $doc->resolveExternals to true. This
tells DOMDocument to fetch any Document Type Definition (DTD) referenced in the file
it's loading and use that to resolve the entities. Tidy generates XML with an appropriate
DTD in it. The downside of this approach is that the DTD URL points to a resource on
an external web server, so your program would have to download that resource each
time it runs.

XHTML is an XML application—a defined XML vocabulary for expressing HTML. As
such, all of its elements (the familiar <a/>, <h1/>, and so on) live in a namespace (*http://
www.w3.org/1999/xhtml*). For XPath queries to work properly, the namespace has to be
attached to a prefix (that's what the registerNamespace() method does) and then used
in the XPath query.

The pc_link_extractor() function is a useful alternative if Tidy isn't available. Its regular expression won't work on all links, such as those that are constructed with some
hexadecimal escapes, but it should function on the majority of reasonably well-formed
HTML. The function returns an array. Each element of that array is itself a two-element

array. The first element is the target of the link, and the second element is the link anchor —text that is linked.

The XPath expression in Example 13-6 only grabs links, not anchors. Example 13-8 shows an alternative that produces both links and anchors.

Example 13-8. Extracting links and anchors with Tidy and XPath

```
$html=<<<_HTML_
<p>Some things I enjoy eating are:</p>
<ul>
<li><a href="http://en.wikipedia.org/wiki/Pickle">Pickles</a></li>
<li><a href="http://www.eatingintranslation.com/2011/03/great_ny_noodle.html">
                Salt-Baked Scallops</a></li>
<li><a href="http://www.thestoryofchocolate.com/">Chocolate</a></li>
</ul>
_HTML_;

$doc = new DOMDocument();
$opts = array('output-xhtml'=>true,
              'wrap' => 0,
              // Prevent DOMDocument from being confused about entities
              'numeric-entities' => true);
$doc->loadXML(tidy_repair_string($html,$opts));
$xpath = new DOMXPath($doc);
// Tell $xpath about the XHTML namespace
$xpath->registerNamespace('xhtml','http://www.w3.org/1999/xhtml');
foreach ($xpath->query('//xhtml:a') as $node) {
    $anchor = trim($node->textContent);
    $link = $node->getAttribute('href');
    print "$anchor -> $link\n";
}
```

In Example 13-8, the XPath query finds all the <a/> element nodes. The textContent property of the node holds the anchor text and the link is in the href attribute. The additional 'wrap' => 0 Tidy option tells Tidy not to do any line-wrapping on the generated XHTML. This keeps all the link anchors on one line when extracting them.

See Also

Documentation on DOMDocument (*http://www.php.net/DOM*), on DOMXPath::query() (*http://bit.ly/T59o5A*), on DOMXPath::registerNamespace() (*http://bit.ly/UEVzwn*), on tidy_repair_file() (*http://bit.ly/1v1eQmE*), and on preg_match_all() (*http://www.php.net/preg_match_all*); Recipe 13.2 has more information about Tidy; XPath (*http://www.w3.org/TR/xpath*); XHTML (*http://www.w3.org/TR/xhtml1/*).

13.4 Converting Plain Text to HTML

Problem

You want to turn plain text into reasonably formatted HTML.

Solution

First, encode entities with `htmlentities()`. Then, transform the text into various HTML structures. The `pc_text2html()` function shown in Example 13-9 has basic transformations for links and paragraph breaks.

Example 13-9. pc_text2html()

```
function pc_text2html($s) {
  $s = htmlentities($s);
  $grafs = split("\n\n",$s);
  for ($i = 0, $j = count($grafs); $i < $j; $i++) {
    // Link to what seem to be http or ftp URLs
    $grafs[$i] = preg_replace('/((ht|f)tp:\/\/[^\s&]+)/',
                              '<a href="$1">$1</a>',$grafs[$i]);

    // Link to email addresses
    $grafs[$i] = preg_replace('/[^@\s]+@([-a-z0-9]+\.)+[a-z]{2,}/i',
        '<a href="mailto:$1">$1</a>',$grafs[$i]);

    // Begin with a new paragraph
    $grafs[$i] = '<p>'.$grafs[$i].'</p>';
  }
  return implode("\n\n",$grafs);
}
```

Discussion

The more you know about what the plain text looks like, the better your HTML conversion can be. For example, if emphasis is indicated with asterisks (*) or slashes (/) around words, you can add rules that take care of that, as shown in Example 13-10.

Example 13-10. More text-to-HTML rules

```
$grafs[$i] = preg_replace('/(\A|\s)\*([^*]+)\*(\s|\z)/',
                          '$1<b>$2</b>$3',$grafs[$i]);
$grafs[$i] = preg_replace('{(\A|\s)/([^/]+)/(\s|\z)}',
                          '$1<i>$2</i>$3',$grafs[$i]);
```

See Also

Documentation on `preg_replace()` (*http://www.php.net/preg_replace*).

13.5 Converting HTML to Plain Text

Problem

You need to convert HTML to readable, formatted plain text.

Solution

Use the `html2text` class (*http://www.chuggnutt.com/html2text*). Example 13-11 shows it in action.

Example 13-11. Converting HTML to plain text

```
require_once 'class.html2text.inc';
/* Give file_get_contents() the path or URL of the HTML you want to process */
$html = file_get_contents(__DIR__ . '/article.html');
$converter = new html2text($html);
$plain_text = $converter->get_text();
```

Discussion

The `html2text` class has a large number of formatting rules built in so your generated plain text has some visual layout for headings, paragraphs, and so on. It also includes a list of all the links in the HTML at the bottom of the text it generates.

 The `html2text` class version 1.0 uses the `/e` modifier with `preg_re place()` in a few places. This is deprecated in PHP 5.5 and so will generate some deprecation warnings if your error level is configured to include them. To remove those warnings, change the patterns that end on `/ie` to end in just `/i` in lines 153, 156, 157, 164, and 170.

See Also

More information on `html2text` (*http://www.chuggnutt.com/html2text.php*) and links to download it.

13.6 Removing HTML and PHP Tags

Problem

You want to remove HTML and PHP tags from a string or file. For example, you want to make sure there is no HTML in a string before printing it or PHP in a string before passing it to `eval()`.

Solution

Use `strip_tags()` or `filter_var()` to remove HTML and PHP tags from a string, as shown in Example 13-12.

Example 13-12. Removing HTML and PHP tags

```
$html = '<a href="http://www.oreilly.com">I <b>love computer books.</b></a>';
$html .= '<?php echo "Hello!" ?>';
print strip_tags($html);
print "\n";
print filter_var($html, FILTER_SANITIZE_STRING);
```

Example 13-12 prints:

```
I love computer books.
I love computer books.
```

To strip tags from a stream as you read it, use the `string.strip_tags` stream filter, as shown in Example 13-13.

Example 13-13. Removing HTML and PHP tags from a stream

```
$stream = fopen(__DIR__ . '/elephant.html','r');
stream_filter_append($stream, 'string.strip_tags');
print stream_get_contents($stream);
```

Discussion

Both `strip_tags()` and the `string.strip_tags` filter can be told not to remove certain tags. Provide a string containing allowable tags to `strip_tags()` as a second argument. The tag specification is case insensitive, and for pairs of tags, you only have to specify the opening tag. For example, to remove all but `<b></b>` and `<i></i>` tags from `$html`, call `strip_tags($html,'<b><i>')`.

With the `string.strip_tags` filter, pass a similar string as a fourth argument to `stream_filter_append()`. The third argument to `stream_filter_append()` controls whether the filter is applied on reading (STREAM_FILTER_READ), writing (STREAM_FIL TER_WRITE), or both (STREAM_FILTER_ALL). Example 13-14 does what Example 13-13 does, but allows `<b></b><i></i>` tags.

Example 13-14. Removing some HTML and PHP tags from a stream

```
$stream = fopen(__DIR__ . '/elephant.html','r');
stream_filter_append($stream, 'string.strip_tags',STREAM_FILTER_READ,'b,i');
print stream_get_contents($stream);
```

`stream_filter_append()` also accepts an array of tag names instead of a string: ar ray('b','i') instead of '<b><i>'.

Whether with strip_tags() or the stream filter, attributes are not removed from allowed tags. This means that an attribute that changes display (such as style) or executes JavaScript (any event handler) is preserved. If you are displaying "stripped" text of arbitrary origin in a web browser to a user without escaping it first, this could result in cross-site scripting attacks.

A more robust approach that avoids the problems that could result from strip_tags() reacting poorly to a broken tag or not removing a dangerous attribute is to allow only a whitelist of known-good tags and attributes in your stripped HTML. With this approach, you don't remove bad things (which leaves you open to the possibility that your list of bad things is incomplete) but instead only keep good things. The TagStripper class in Example 13-15 operates this way.

Example 13-15. "Stripping" tags with a whitelist

```
class TagStripper {

    protected $allowed =
        array(
            /* Allow <a/> and only an "href" attribute */
            'a'=> array('href' => true),
            /* Allow <p/> with no attributes */
            'p' => array());

    public function strip($html) {
        /* Tell Tidy to produce XHTML */
        $xhtml = tidy_repair_string($html, array('output-xhtml' => true));

        /* Load the dirty HTML into a DOMDocument */
        $dirty = new DOMDocument;
        $dirty->loadXml($xhtml);
        $dirtyBody = $dirty->getElementsByTagName('body')->item(0);

        /* Make a blank DOMDocument for the clean HTML */
        $clean = new DOMDocument();
        $cleanBody = $clean->appendChild($clean->createElement('body'));

        /* Copy the allowed nodes from dirty to clean */
        $this->copyNodes($dirtyBody, $cleanBody);

        /* Return the contents of the clean body */
        $stripped = '';
        foreach ($cleanBody->childNodes as $node) {
            $stripped .= $clean->saveXml($node);
        }
        return trim($stripped);
    }
```

```
        protected function copyNodes(DOMNode $dirty, DOMNode $clean) {
            foreach ($dirty->attributes as $name => $valueNode) {
                /* Copy over allowed attributes */
                if (isset($this->allowed[$dirty->nodeName][$name])) {
                    $attr = $clean->ownerDocument->createAttribute($name);
                    $attr->value = $valueNode->value;
                    $clean->appendChild($attr);
                }
            }
            foreach ($dirty->childNodes as $child) {
                /* Copy allowed elements */
                if (($child->nodeType == XML_ELEMENT_NODE) &&
                    (isset($this->allowed[$child->nodeName]))) {
                        $node = $clean->ownerDocument->createElement(
                        $child->nodeName);
                        $clean->appendChild($node);
                        /* Examine children of this allowed element */
                        $this->copyNodes($child, $node);
                }
                /* Copy text */
                else if ($child->nodeType == XML_TEXT_NODE) {
                    $text = $clean->ownerDocument->createTextNode(
                    $child->textContent);
                    $clean->appendChild($text);
                }
            }
        }
    }
}
```

Given some input HTML, its `strip()` method of the class in Example 13-15 regularizes it into XHTML with Tidy, then walks down its DOM tree of elements, copying only allowed attributes and elements into a new DOM structure. Then, it returns the contents of that new DOM structure.

Here's `TagStripper` in action:

```
$html=<<<_HTML_
<a href=foo onmouseover="bad()" >this is some</b>
stuff
    <p>This should be OK, as <a href="beep">well</a> as this. </p>
<script>alert('whoops')<p>This gets removed.</p></script>

<p>But this <script>bad</script> stuff has the script removed.</p>
_HTML_;


$ts = new TagStripper();
print $ts->strip($html);
```

This prints:

```
<a href="foo">this is some stuff</a>
<p>This should be OK, as <a href="beep">well</a> as this.</p>

<p>But this  stuff has the script removed.</p>
```

The initial set of allowed elements and attributes, as defined by the `$allowed` property of the `TagStripper` class in Example 13-15, is intentionally sparse. Add new elements and attributes carefully as you need them.

See Also

Documentation on `strip_tags()` (*http://www.php.net/strip-tags*), on `stream_fil` `ter_append()` (*http://www.php.net/stream_filter_append*), and on stream filters (*http://www.php.net/filters*). Recipe 18.4 has more details on cross-site scripting.

13.7 Responding to an Ajax Request

Problem

You're using JavaScript to make in-page requests with `XMLHTTPRequest` and need to send data in reply to one of those requests.

Solution

Set an appropriate `Content-Type` header and then emit properly formatted data. Example 13-16 sends a small XML document as a response.

Example 13-16. Sending an XML response

```
<?php header('Content-Type: text/xml'); ?>
<menu>
 <dish type="appetizer">Chicken Soup</dish>
 <dish type="main course">Fried Monkey Brains</dish>
</menu>
```

Example 13-17 uses the `json_encode()` function to send a JSON response.

Example 13-17. Sending a JSON response

```
$menu = array();
$menu[] = array('type' => 'appetizer',
                'dish' => 'Chicken Soup');
$menu[] = array('type' => 'main course',
                'dish' => 'Fried Monkey Brains');
header('Content-Type: application/json');
print json_encode($menu);
```

Discussion

From a purely PHP perspective, sending a response to an XMLHTTPRequest-based request is no different than any other response. You send any necessary headers and then spit out some text. What's different, however, is what those headers are and, usually, what the text looks like.

JSON is a particularly useful format for these sorts of responses, because it's super easy to deal with the JSON-formatted data from within JavaScript. The output from Example 13-17 looks like this:

```
[{"type":"appetizer","dish":"Chicken Soup"},
 {"type":"main course","dish":"Fried Monkey Brains"}]
```

This encodes a two-element JavaScript array of hashes. The json_encode() function is an easy way to turn PHP data structures (scalars, arrays, and objects) into JSON strings and vice versa. This function and the complementary json_decode() function turn PHP data structures to JSON strings and back again.

With these types of responses, it's also important to pay attention to caching. Different browsers have a creative variety of caching strategies when it comes to requests made from within JavaScript. If your responses are sending dynamic data (which they usually are), you probably don't want them to be cached. The two tools in your anti-caching toolbox are headers and URL poisoning. Example 13-18 shows the full complement of anti-caching headers you can issue from PHP to prevent a browser from caching a response.

Example 13-18. Anti-caching headers

```
header("Expires: 0");
header("Last-Modified: " . gmdate("D, d M Y H:i:s") . " GMT");
header("Cache-Control: no-store, no-cache, must-revalidate");
// Add some IE-specific options
header("Cache-Control: post-check=0, pre-check=0", false);
// For HTTP/1.0
header("Pragma: no-cache");
```

The other anti-caching tool, URL poisoning, requires cooperation from the JavaScript that is making the request. It adds a name/value pair to the query string of each request it makes using an arbitrary value. This makes the request URL different each time the request is made, preventing any misbehaving caches from getting in the way. The JavaScript Math.random() function is useful for generating these values.

See Also

Documentation on header() (*http://www.php.net/header*). Read more about XMLHTTPRequest (*http://en.wikipedia.org/wiki/XMLHttpRequest*), JSON (*http://www.json.org*), and the json extension (*http://www.php.net/json*). Michael Radwin's

HTTP Caching and Cache-Busting for Content Publishers (*http://public.yahoo.com/ ~radwin/talks/http-caching-apachecon2005.htm*) is a good introduction to HTTP caching. Section 13 of RFC 2616 (*http://www.w3.org/Protocols/rfc2616/rfc2616-sec13.html#sec13*) has the gory details on HTTP caching.

13.8 Integrating with JavaScript

Problem

You want part of your page to update with server-side data without reloading the whole page. For example, you want to populate a list with search results.

Solution

Use a JavaScript toolkit such as jQuery to wire up the client side of things so that a particular user action (such as clicking a button) fires off a request to the server. Write appropriate PHP code to generate a response containing the right data. Then, use your JavaScript toolkit to put the results in the page correctly.

Example 13-19 shows a simple HTML document that loads jQuery and the code in Example 13-20. Example 13-20 is the JavaScript glue that sends a request off to the server when the Search button is clicked and makes sure the results end up on the page in the right place when they come back. Example 13-21 is the PHP code that does the searching and sends back a JSON-formatted response.

Example 13-19. Basic HTML for JavaScript integration

```html
<!-- Load jQuery -->
<script type="text/javascript"
        src="//code.jquery.com/jquery-1.9.1.min.js"></script>
<!-- Load our JavaScript -->
<script type="text/javascript" src="search.js"></script>

<!-- Some input elements -->
<input type="text" id="q" />
<input type="button" id="go" value="Search"/>
<hr/>
<!-- Where the output goes -->
<div id="output"></div>
```

Example 13-20. JavaScript integration glue

```javascript
// When the page loads, run this code
$(document).ready(function() {
    // Call the search() function when the 'go' button is clicked
    $("#go").click(search);
});
```

```
function search() {
    // What's in the text box?
    var q = $("#q").val();
    // Send request to the server
    // The first argument should be to wherever you save the search page
    // The second argument sends a query string parameter
    // The third argument is the function to run with the results
    $.get('/search.php', { 'q': q }, showResults);
}

// Handle the results
function showResults(data) {
    var html = '';
    // If we got some results...
    if (data.length > 0) {
        html = '<ul>';
        // Build a list of them
        for (var i in data) {
            var escaped = $('<div/>').text(data[i]).html();
            html += '<li>' + escaped + '</li>';
        }
        html += '</ul>';
    } else {
        html = 'No results.';
    }
    // Put the result HTML in the page
    $("#output").html(html);
}
```

Example 13-21. PHP to generate a response for JavaScript

```
$results = array();
$q = isset($_GET['q']) ? $_GET['q'] : '';

// Connect to the database from Chapter 10
$db = new PDO('sqlite:/tmp/zodiac.db');

// Do the query
$st = $db->prepare('SELECT symbol FROM zodiac WHERE planet LIKE ? ');
$st->execute(array($q.'%'));

// Build an array of results
while ($row = $st->fetch()) {
    $results[] = $row['symbol'];
}

if (count($results) == 0) {
    $results[] = "No results";
}

// Splorp out all the anti-caching stuff
header("Expires: 0");
header("Last-Modified: " . gmdate("D, d M Y H:i:s") . " GMT");
```

```
header("Cache-Control: no-store, no-cache, must-revalidate");
// Add some IE-specific options
header("Cache-Control: post-check=0, pre-check=0", false);
// For HTTP/1.0
header("Pragma: no-cache");

// The response is JSON
header('Content-Type: application/json');

// Output the JSON data
print json_encode($results);
```

Discussion

The HTML in Example 13-19 is pretty minimal by design. All that's there are a few elements and calls to load external scripts. Separating JavaScript from HTML is good development practice—similar to segregating your presentation logic and your business logic on the server side. The first `<script/>` tag in Example 13-19 loads jQuery from a CDN. This is convenient so you don't have to install it on your own server. Using `//` at the beginning of the URL is a handy trick to ensure it works well on both `http` and `https` pages.

The second should point to wherever you've put the code in Example 13-20. That handful of JavaScript functions provides the bridge between the HTML elements in Example 13-19 and the server-side code in Example 13-21. The first call to `$(docu ment).ready` tells the web browser, "When the page is finished loading, run the Java-Script code that tells the web browser, 'When the go button is clicked, run the `search()` function.'"

A lot of JavaScript programming is *event based*—along the lines of setting up rules like "when such-and-such happens, run this function." A web page studded with JavaScript does not have a strictly procedural flow from start to finish. Instead, it presents the user with lots of possibilities—clicking buttons, typing stuff in text boxes, clicking links, and so on. Your JavaScript code usually sets up various *event handlers*—functions that run in response to clicking, typing, and other events.

In Example 13-20, the `search()` function uses jQuery's `$.get` function to send a request back to the server, passing whatever's in the text box as the q query string parameter. The other argument to `$.get` indicates that when the request arrives, it should be passed to the `showResults()` function.

The `showResults()` function, in turn, takes those results and builds an HTML list out of them. Once the list has been built up, it sets the content of the `output <div/>` to contain that HTML.

Example 13-21 is the familiar part of this triumvirate. It's very similar to any "search the database for some stuff based on user input" PHP script, except for how it returns results.

Instead of printing HTML, it uses the techniques described in Recipe 13.7 to send back an uncacheable JSON response.

Writing applications that rely on JavaScript-based client-side activity requires a different programming paradigm than your typical PHP application. Instead of thinking about how to generate entire dynamic pages, you have to think about how to generate bits of dynamic data that client-side logic can display or manipulate in convenient ways. A toolkit such as jQuery gives you a robust platform on which to build such applications. It abstracts away many of the messy practicalities of JavaScript programming—cross-browser incompatibilities, the guts of asynchronous I/O, and other housekeeping.

See Also

Recipe 13.7 details sending JSON responses; more information on jQuery (*http:// jquery.com/*).

13.9 Program: Finding Stale Links

The *stale-links.php* program in Example 13-22 produces a list of links in a page and their status. It tells you if the links are okay, if they've been moved somewhere else, or if they're bad. Run the program by passing it a URL to scan for links:

```
http://oreilly.com: OK
https://members.oreilly.com: MOVED: https://members.oreilly.com/account/login
http://shop.oreilly.com/basket.do: OK
http://shop.oreilly.com: OK
http://radar.oreilly.com: OK
http://animals.oreilly.com: OK
http://programming.oreilly.com: OK
...
```

The *stale-links.php* program uses the cURL extension to retrieve web pages (see Example 13-22). First, it retrieves the URL specified on the command line. Once a page has been retrieved, the program uses the XPath technique from Recipe 13.3 to get a list of links in the page. Then, after prepending a base URL to each link if necessary, the link is retrieved. Because we need just the headers of these responses, we use the HEAD method instead of GET by setting the CURLOPT_NOBODY option. Setting CURLOPT_HEADER tells curl_exec() to include the response headers in the string it returns. Based on the response code, the status of the link is printed, along with its new location if it's been moved.

Example 13-22. stale-links.php

```
if (! isset($_SERVER['argv'][1])) {
    die("No URL provided.\n");
}

$url = $_SERVER['argv'][1];
```

```php
// Load the page
list($page,$pageInfo) = load_with_curl($url);

if (! strlen($page)) {
    die("No page retrieved from $url");
}

// Convert to XML for easy parsing
$opts = array('output-xhtml' => true,
              'numeric-entities' => true);
$xml = tidy_repair_string($page, $opts);
$doc = new DOMDocument();
$doc->loadXML($xml);
$xpath = new DOMXPath($doc);
$xpath->registerNamespace('xhtml','http://www.w3.org/1999/xhtml');

// Compute the Base URL for relative links
$baseURL = '';
// Check if there is a <base href=""/> in the page
$nodeList = $xpath->query('//xhtml:base/@href');
if ($nodeList->length == 1) {
    $baseURL = $nodeList->item(0)->nodeValue;
}
// No <base href=""/>, so build the Base URL from $url
else {
    $URLParts = parse_url($pageInfo['url']);
    if (! (isset($URLParts['path']) && strlen($URLParts['path']))) {
        $basePath = '';
    } else {
        $basePath = preg_replace('#/[^/]*$#','',$URLParts['path']);
    }
    if (isset($URLParts['username']) || isset($URLParts['password'])) {
        $auth = isset($URLParts['username']) ? $URLParts['username'] : '';
        $auth .= ':';
        $auth .= isset($URLParts['password']) ? $URLParts['password'] : '';
        $auth .= '@';
    } else {
        $auth = '';
    }
    $baseURL = $URLParts['scheme'] . '://' .
               $auth . $URLParts['host'] .
               $basePath;
}

// Keep track of the links we visit so we don't visit each more than once
$seenLinks = array();

// Grab all links
$links = $xpath->query('//xhtml:a/@href');

foreach ($links as $node) {
```

```php
    $link = $node->nodeValue;
    // Resolve relative links
    if (! preg_match('#^(http|https|mailto):#', $link)) {
        if (((strlen($link) == 0)) || ($link[0] != '/')) {
            $link = '/' . $link;
        }
        $link = $baseURL . $link;
    }
    // Skip this link if we've seen it already
    if (isset($seenLinks[$link])) {
        continue;
    }
    // Mark this link as seen
    $seenLinks[$link] = true;
    // Print the link we're visiting
    print $link.': ';
    flush();

    list($linkHeaders, $linkInfo) = load_with_curl($link, 'HEAD');
    // Decide what to do based on the response code
    // 2xx response codes mean the page is OK
    if (($linkInfo['http_code'] >= 200) && ($linkInfo['http_code'] < 300)) {
        $status = 'OK';
    }
    // 3xx response codes mean redirection
    else if (($linkInfo['http_code'] >= 300) && ($linkInfo['http_code'] < 400)) {
        $status = 'MOVED';
        if (preg_match('/^Location: (.*)$/m',$linkHeaders,$match)) {
            $status .= ': ' . ltrim($match[1]);
        }
    }
    // Other response codes mean errors
    else {
        $status = "ERROR: {$linkInfo['http_code']}";
    }
    // Print what we know about the link
    print "$status\n";
}

function load_with_curl($url, $method = 'GET') {
    $c = curl_init($url);
    curl_setopt($c, CURLOPT_RETURNTRANSFER, true);
    if ($method == 'GET') {
        curl_setopt($c,CURLOPT_FOLLOWLOCATION, true);
    }
    else if ($method == 'HEAD') {
        curl_setopt($c, CURLOPT_NOBODY, true);
        curl_setopt($c, CURLOPT_HEADER, true);
    }
    $response = curl_exec($c);
    return array($response, curl_getinfo($c));
}
```

13.10 Program: Finding Fresh Links

Example 13-23 is a modification of the program in Example 13-22 that produces a list of links and their last-modified time. If the server on which a URL lives doesn't provide a last-modified time, the program reports the URL's last-modified time as the time the URL was requested. If the program can't retrieve the URL successfully, it prints out the status code it got when it tried to retrieve the URL. Run the program by passing it a URL to scan for links:

```
http://oreilly.com: OK; Last Modified: Fri, 24 May 2013 18:09:11 GMT
https://members.oreilly.com: MOVED: https://members.oreilly.com/account/login
http://shop.oreilly.com/basket.do: OK
http://shop.oreilly.com: OK
http://radar.oreilly.com: OK; Last Modified: Fri, 24 May 2013 20:40:56 GMT
http://animals.oreilly.com: OK; Last Modified: Fri, 24 May 2013 20:40:18 GMT
http://programming.oreilly.com: OK; Last Modified: Fri, 24 May 2013 20:42:44 GMT
...
```

This output is from a run of the program at about 8:43 P.M. GMT on May 24, 2013. The links that aren't accompanied by a last-modified time means the server didn't provide one, so those pages are probably dynamic.

The program to find fresh links is conceptually almost identical to the program to find stale links. It uses the same techniques to pull links out of a page and the same code to retrieve URLs.

Once a page has been retrieved, each linked URL is retrieved with the head method. Instead of just printing out a new location for moved links, however, it prints out a formatted version of the Last-Modified header if it's available.

Example 13-23. fresh-links.php

```php
error_reporting(E_ALL);

if (! isset($_SERVER['argv'][1])) {
    die("No URL provided.\n");
}

$url = $_SERVER['argv'][1];

// Load the page
list($page, $pageInfo) = load_with_curl($url);

if (! strlen($page)) {
    die("No page retrieved from $url");
}

// Convert to XML for easy parsing
$opts = array('output-xhtml' => true,
              'numeric-entities' => true);
```

```php
$xml = tidy_repair_string($page, $opts);
$doc = new DOMDocument();
$doc->loadXML($xml);
$xpath = new DOMXPath($doc);
$xpath->registerNamespace('xhtml','http://www.w3.org/1999/xhtml');

// Compute the Base URL for relative links.
$baseURL = '';
// Check if there is a <base href=""/> in the page
$nodeList = $xpath->query('//xhtml:base/@href');
if ($nodeList->length == 1) {
    $baseURL = $nodeList->item(0)->nodeValue;
}
// No <base href=""/>, so build the Base URL from $url
else {
    $URLParts = parse_url($pageInfo['url']);
    if (! (isset($URLParts['path']) && strlen($URLParts['path']))) {
        $basePath = '';
    } else {
        $basePath = preg_replace('#/[^/]*$#','',$URLParts['path']);
    }
    if (isset($URLParts['username']) || isset($URLParts['password'])) {
        $auth = isset($URLParts['username']) ? $URLParts['username'] : '';
        $auth .= ':';
        $auth .= isset($URLParts['password']) ? $URLParts['password'] : '';
        $auth .= '@';
    } else {
        $auth = '';
    }
    $baseURL = $URLParts['scheme'] . '://' .
               $auth . $URLParts['host'] .
               $basePath;
}

// Keep track of the links we visit so we don't visit each more than once
$seenLinks = array();

// Grab all links
$links = $xpath->query('//xhtml:a/@href');

foreach ($links as $node) {
    $link = $node->nodeValue;
    // Resolve relative links
    if (! preg_match('#^(http|https|mailto):#', $link)) {
        if (((strlen($link) == 0)) || ($link[0] != '/')) {
            $link = '/' . $link;
        }
        $link = $baseURL . $link;
    }
    // Skip this link if we've seen it already
    if (isset($seenLinks[$link])) {
        continue;
```

```php
    }
    // Mark this link as seen
    $seenLinks[$link] = true;
    // Print the link we're visiting
    print $link.': ';
    flush();

    list ($linkHeaders, $linkInfo) = load_with_curl($link, 'HEAD');
    // Decide what to do based on the response code
    // 2xx response codes mean the page is OK

    if (($linkInfo['http_code'] >= 200) && ($linkInfo['http_code'] < 300)) {
        $status = 'OK';
    }
    // 3xx response codes mean redirection
    else if (($linkInfo['http_code'] >= 300) && ($linkInfo['http_code'] < 400)) {
        $status = 'MOVED';
        if (preg_match('/^Location: (.*)$/m',$linkHeaders,$match)) {
                $status .= ': ' . trim($match[1]);
        }
    }
    // Other response codes mean errors
    else {
        $status = "ERROR: {$linkInfo['http_code']}";
    }
    if (preg_match('/^Last-Modified: (.*)$/mi', $linkHeaders, $match)) {
        $status .= "; Last Modified: " . trim($match[1]);
    }
    // Print what we know about the link
    print "$status\n";
}


function load_with_curl($url, $method = 'GET') {
    $c = curl_init($url);
    curl_setopt($c, CURLOPT_RETURNTRANSFER, true);
    if ($method == 'GET') {
        curl_setopt($c,CURLOPT_FOLLOWLOCATION, true);
    }
    else if ($method == 'HEAD') {
        curl_setopt($c, CURLOPT_NOBODY, true);
        curl_setopt($c, CURLOPT_HEADER, true);
    }
    $response = curl_exec($c);
    return array($response, curl_getinfo($c));
}
```

CHAPTER 14

Consuming RESTful APIs

14.0 Introduction

When you want to find out the weather forecast for New York City, the latest tweets from @rasmus, or update a stored file, you can write a short REST script to process that data in a format you can easily manipulate.

REST is a straightforward style of web APIs in which you make requests to a URL using HTTP methods, such as GET and POST. The URL and body, often in JSON or XML, describes the resource you want to manipulate and the method tells the server what action it should take.

GET tells the server you want to retrieve existing data, whereas POST means you want to add a new resource. Use PUT to replace a resource or create a specifically named resource. And DELETE, of course, deletes the resource.

The brilliance of REST is in use of existing standards. Because most developers are familiar with HTTP and JSON, the learning curve for REST is short and shallow.

The one downside to REST is there's no standard schema for data that's passed in or returned. Every site is free to use what it feels is the best. Though this is not a problem for small services, if not designed properly, this can cause complexity when a service grows.

Still, REST is a very popular format and its simplicity is a key factor in its success. Recipe 14.1 covers making REST requests.

Recipes in this chapter cover how to generate an HTTP request for your desired REST call. Because the data returned is (almost always) in a standard file format, there's no need to show how to parse the results. Given the nature of REST documents, and that you're usually familiar with the schema of the response, the JSON and SimpleXML extensions are often the best choice. They're covered in Recipes 5.7 and 12.3.

There are many ways to retrieve a remote URL in PHP. Choosing one method over another depends on your needs for simplicity, control, and portability. The three methods discussed in this chapter are standard file functions, the cURL extension, and the HTTP_Request2 class from PEAR. These three methods can generally do everything you need and at least one of them should be available to you whatever your server configuration or ability to install custom extensions. Other ways to retrieve remote URLs include the pecl_http extension (*http://pecl.php.net/package/pecl_http*), which, though still in development, offers some promising features, and using the fsockopen() function to open a socket over which you send an HTTP request that you construct piece by piece.

Using a standard file function such as file_get_contents() is simple and convenient. It automatically follows redirects, so if you use this function to retrieve the directory at *http://www.example.com/people* and the server redirects you to *http://www.example.com/people/*, you'll get the contents of the directory index page, not a message telling you that the URL has moved. Standard file functions also work with both HTTP and FTP. The downside to this method is that it requires the allow_url_fopen configuration directive to be turned on.

The cURL extension is a powerful jack-of-all-request-trades. It relies on the popular libcurl (*http://curl.haxx.se/*) to provide a fast, configurable mechanism for handling a wide variety of network requests. If this extension is available on your server, we recommend you use it.

If allow_url_fopen is turned off and cURL is not available, the PEAR HTTP_Re. quest2 module saves the day. Like all PEAR modules, it's plain PHP, so if you can save a PHP file on your server, you can use it. HTTP_Request2 supports just about anything you'd like to do when requesting a remote URL, including modifying request headers and body, using an arbitrary method, and retrieving response headers.

Recipe 14.1 through Recipe 14.7 explain how to make various kinds of HTTP requests, tweaking headers, method, body, and timing. Recipe 14.8 helps you go behind the scenes of an HTTP request to examine the headers in a request and response. If a request you're making from a program isn't giving you the results you're looking for, examining the headers often provides clues as to what's wrong.

14.1 Fetching a URL with the GET Method

Problem

You want to retrieve the contents of a URL. For example, you want to include part of one site in another site's content.

Solution

Provide the URL to `file_get_contents()`:

```
$page = file_get_contents('http://www.example.com/robots.txt');
```

Or you can use the cURL extension:

```
$c = curl_init('http://www.example.com/robots.txt');
curl_setopt($c, CURLOPT_RETURNTRANSFER, true);
$page = curl_exec($c);
curl_close($c);
```

You can also use the `HTTP_Request2` class from PEAR:

```
require_once 'HTTP/Request2.php';
$r = new HTTP_Request2('http://www.example.com/robots.txt');
$page = $r->send()->getBody();
```

Discussion

`file_get_contents()`, like all PHP file-handling functions, uses PHP's *streams* feature. This means that it can handle local files as well as a variety of network resources, including HTTP URLs. There's a catch, though—the `allow_url_fopen` configuration setting must be turned on (which it usually is).

This makes for extremely easy retrieval of remote documents. You can use the same technique to grab a remote XML document:

```
$url = 'http://rss.news.yahoo.com/rss/oddlyenough';
$rss = simplexml_load_file($url);
print '<ul>';
foreach ($rss->channel->item as $item) {
    print '<li><a href="' .
          htmlentities($item->link) .
          '">' .
          htmlentities($item->title) .
          '</a></li>';
}
print '</ul>';
```

To retrieve a page that includes query string variables, use `http_build_query()` to create the query string. It accepts an array of key/value pairs and returns a single string with everything properly escaped. You're still responsible for the ? in the URL that sets off the query string. For example:

```
$vars = array('page' => 4, 'search' => 'this & that');
$qs = http_build_query($vars);
$url = 'http://www.example.com/search.php?' . $qs;
$page = file_get_contents($url);
```

To retrieve a protected page, put the username and password in the URL. Here the username is david, and the password is hax0r:

```
$url = 'http://david:hax0r@www.example.com/secrets.php';
$page = file_get_contents($url);
```

Or with cURL:

```
$c = curl_init('http://www.example.com/secrets.php');
curl_setopt($c, CURLOPT_RETURNTRANSFER, true);
curl_setopt($c, CURLOPT_USERPWD, 'david:hax0r');
$page = curl_exec($c);
curl_close($c);
```

Likewise with HTTP_Request2:

```
require 'HTTP/Request2.php';

$r = new HTTP_Request2('http://www.example.com/secrets.php');
$r->setAuth('david', 'hax0r', HTTP_Request2::AUTH_DIGEST);
$page = $r->send()->getBody();
```

PHP's http stream wrapper automatically follows redirects. The file_get_con tents() and fopen() functions support a *stream context* argument that allows for specifying options about how the stream is retrieved. One of those options is max_re directs, the maximum number of redirects to follow.

This example sets max_redirects to 1, which turns off redirect following:

```
$url = 'http://www.example.com/redirector.php';
// Define the options
$options = array('max_redirects' => 1 );
// Create a context with options for the http stream
$context = stream_context_create(array('http' => $options));
// Pass the options to file_get_contents. The second
// argument is whether to use the include path, which
// we don't want here.
print file_get_contents($url, false, $context);
```

The max_redirects stream wrapper option really indicates not how many redirects should be followed, but the maximum number of requests that should be made when following the redirect chain. That is, a value of 1 tells PHP to make at most one request —follow no redirects. A value of 2 tells PHP to make at most two requests—follow no more than one redirect. (A value of 0, however, behaves like a value of 1—PHP makes just one request.)

If the redirect chain would have PHP make more requests than are allowed by max_re directs, PHP issues a warning.

cURL only follows redirects when the CURLOPT_FOLLOWLOCATION option is set:

```
$c = curl_init('http://www.example.com/redirector.php');
curl_setopt($c, CURLOPT_RETURNTRANSFER, true);
curl_setopt($c, CURLOPT_FOLLOWLOCATION, true);
$page = curl_exec($c);
curl_close($c);
```

To set a maximum number of redirects that cURL should follow, set CURLOPT_FOLLOWLOCATION to true and then set the CURLOPT_MAXREDIRS option to that maximum number.

HTTP_Request2 follows if the follow_redirects parameter is set to true, as shown here:

```
require 'HTTP/Request2.php';

$r = new HTTP_Request2('http://www.example.com/redirector.php');
$r->setConfig(array(
    'follow_redirects' => true,
    'max_redirects'    => 1
));

$page = $r->send()->getBody();
print $page;
```

cURL can do a few different things with the page it retrieves. As you've seen in previous examples, if CURLOPT_RETURNTRANSFER is set, curl_exec() returns the body of the page requested. If CURLOPT_RETURNTRANSFER is not set, curl_exec() prints the response body.

To write the retrieved page to a file, open a file handle for writing with fopen() and set the CURLOPT_FILE option to that file handle. This example uses cURL to copy a remote web page to a local file:

```
$fh = fopen('local-copy-of-files.html','w') or die($php_errormsg);
$c = curl_init('http://www.example.com/files.html');
curl_setopt($c, CURLOPT_FILE, $fh);
curl_exec($c);
curl_close($c);
```

To pass the cURL resource and the contents of the retrieved page to a function, set the CURLOPT_WRITEFUNCTION option to a callback for that function (either a function name or an array whose first element is an object instance or a string containing a class name and whose second element is a method name). The "write function" must return the number of bytes it was passed. Note that with large responses, the write function might get called more than once because cURL processes the response in chunks. This example uses a cURL write function to save page contents in a database:

```
class PageSaver {
    protected $db;
    protected $page ='';
```

```php
    public function __construct() {
        $this->db = new PDO('sqlite:./pages.db');
    }

    public function write($curl, $data) {
        $this->page .= $data;
        return strlen($data);
    }

    public function save($curl) {
        $info = curl_getinfo($curl);
        $st = $this->db->prepare('INSERT INTO pages '.
                          '(url,page) VALUES (?,?)');
        $st->execute(array($info['url'], $this->page));
    }
}

// Create the saver instance
$pageSaver = new PageSaver();
// Create the cURL resources
$c = curl_init('http://www.example.com/');
// Set the write function
curl_setopt($c, CURLOPT_WRITEFUNCTION, array($pageSaver,'write'));
// Execute the request
curl_exec($c);
// Save the accumulated data
$pageSaver->save($c);
```

See Also

Recipe 14.2 for fetching a URL with the POST method; documentation on
file_get_contents() (*http://bit.ly/1qu3G9P*), simplexml_load_file() (*http://bit.ly/ 1wrTD7Y*), stream_context_create() (*http://bit.ly/1wrTMrS*), curl_init() (*http:// www.php.net/curl-init*), curl_setopt() (*http://www.php.net/curl-setopt*), curl_ex ec() (*http://www.php.net/curl-exec*), curl_getinfo() (*http://www.php.net/curl_getin fo*), and curl_close() (*http://www.php.net/curl-close*); the PEAR HTTP_Request2 class (*http://bit.ly/1l6Ab8p*).

14.2 Fetching a URL with the POST Method and Form Data

Problem

You want to submit a document using the POST method, passing data formatted as an HTML form.

Solution

Set the method and content stream context options when using the http stream:

```
$url = 'http://www.example.com/submit.php';
// The submitted form data, encoded as query-string-style
// name-value pairs
$body = 'monkey=uncle&amp;rhino=aunt';
$options = array('method' => 'POST',
                 'content' => $body,
                 'header' => 'Content-type: application/x-www-form-urlencoded');
// Create the stream context
$context = stream_context_create(array('http' => $options));
// Pass the context to file_get_contents()
print file_get_contents($url, false, $context);
```

With cURL, set the CURLOPT_POST and CURLOPT_POSTFIELDS options:

```
$url = 'http://www.example.com/submit.php';
// The submitted form data, encoded as query-string-style
// name-value pairs
$body = 'monkey=uncle&rhino=aunt';
$c = curl_init($url);
curl_setopt($c, CURLOPT_POST, true);
curl_setopt($c, CURLOPT_POSTFIELDS, $body);
curl_setopt($c, CURLOPT_RETURNTRANSFER, true);
$page = curl_exec($c);
curl_close($c);
```

Using HTTP_Request2, pass HTTP_Request2::METHOD_POST to setMethod() and chain calls to addPostParameter() for each name/value pair in the data to submit:

```
require 'HTTP/Request2.php';

$url = 'http://www.example.com/submit.php';
$r = new HTTP_Request2($url);

$r->setMethod(HTTP_Request2::METHOD_POST)
    ->addPostParameter('monkey', 'uncle')
    ->addPostParameter('rhino','aunt');

$page = $r->send()->getBody();
```

Discussion

Sending a POST method request requires different handling of any form arguments. In a GET request, these arguments are in the query string, but in a POST request, they go in the request body. Additionally, the request needs a Content-Length header that tells the server the size of the content to expect in the request body.

Although they each have different mechanisms by which you specify the request method and the body content, each of the examples in the Solution automatically add the proper Content-Length header for you.

If you use a stream context to send a POST request, make sure to set the method option to post. Case matters.

See Also

Recipe 14.1 for fetching a URL with the GET method; also see the documentation on curl_setopt() (*http://www.php.net/curl-setopt*) and on stream options (*http://www.php.net/wrappers.http*); the PEAR HTTP_Request2 class (*http://bit.ly/1l6Ab8p*); RFC 2616 (*http://bit.ly/rfc-http*).

14.3 Fetching a URL with an Arbitrary Method and POST Body

Problem

You want to request a URL using any method, such as POST, PUT, or DELETE. Your POST or PUT request may contain formatted data, such as JSON or XML.

Solution

Set the method, header, and content stream context options when using the http stream:

```
$url = 'http://www.example.com/meals/123';
$header = "Content-Type: application/json";
// The request body, in JSON
$body = '[{
    "type": "appetizer",
    "dish": "Chicken Soup"
}, {
    "type": "main course",
    "dish": "Fried Monkey Brains"
}]';

$options = array('method' => 'put',
    'header' => $header,
    'content' => $body);
// Create the stream context
$context = stream_context_create(array('http' => $options));
// Pass the context to file_get_contents()
print file_get_contents($url, false, $context);
```

With cURL, set the CURLOPT_CUSTOMREQUEST option to the method name. To include a request body, set CURLOPT_HTTPHEADER to the Content-Type and CURLOPT_POST FIELDS to the body:

```
$url = 'http://www.example.com/meals/123';
// The request body, in JSON
$body = '[{
    "type": "appetizer",
    "dish": "Chicken Soup"
}, {
    "type": "main course",
    "dish": "Fried Monkey Brains"
}]';
$c = curl_init($url);
curl_setopt($c, CURLOPT_CUSTOMREQUEST, 'PUT');
curl_setopt($c, CURLOPT_HTTPHEADER, array('Content-Type: application/json'));
curl_setopt($c, CURLOPT_POSTFIELDS, $body);
curl_setopt($c, CURLOPT_RETURNTRANSFER, true);
$page = curl_exec($c);
curl_close($c);
```

In HTTP_Request2, call setMethod() with a method constant, setHeader() with the Content-Type, and setBody() with the contents of the request body:

```
require 'HTTP/Request2.php';
$url = 'http://www.example.com/meals/123';
// The request body, in JSON
$body = '[{
    "type": "appetizer",
    "dish": "Chicken Soup"
}, {
    "type": "main course",
    "dish": "Fried Monkey Brains"
}]';
$r = new HTTP_Request2($url);
$r->setMethod(HTTP_Request2::METHOD_PUT);
$r->setHeader('Content-Type', 'application/json');
$r->setBody($body);

$page = $r->send()->getBody();
```

Discussion

In many REST-style APIs, you need to use more than just GET and POST to modify resources, you also need to use PUT and DELETE.

The examples in the Solution make HTTP PUT requests to set a dinner menu, with data formatted in JSON. If your data is in another format, such as XML, change the Content-Type accordingly. If there is no body, such as in a HTTP DELETE request, only set the method.

The PUT method is often used for creating or modifying the contents of a specific resource. cURL has three special options to help with this: CURLOPT_PUT, CURLOPT_IN FILE, and CURLOPT_INFILESIZE. To upload a file with PUT and cURL, set CUR

LOPT_PUT to true, CURLOPT_INFILE to a filehandle opened to the file that should be uploaded, and CURLOPT_INFILESIZE to the size of that file. This is shown in Example 14-1.

Example 14-1. Uploading a file with cURL and PUT

```
$url = 'http://www.example.com/upload.php';
$filename = '/usr/local/data/pictures/piggy.jpg';
$fp = fopen($filename,'r');
$c = curl_init($url);
curl_setopt($c, CURLOPT_PUT, true);
curl_setopt($c, CURLOPT_INFILE, $fp);
curl_setopt($c, CURLOPT_INFILESIZE, filesize($filename));
curl_setopt($c, CURLOPT_RETURNTRANSFER, true);
$page = curl_exec($c);
print $page;
curl_close($c);
```

See Also

Documentation on curl_setopt() (*http://www.php.net/curl-setopt*) and on stream options (*http://www.php.net/wrappers.http*); the PEAR HTTP_Request2 class (*http://pear.php.net/package/HTTP_Request2*); Section 5.1.1 (*http://www.w3.org/Protocols/rfc2616/rfc2616-sec5.html#sec5.1.1*) of RFC 2616, which discusses request methods; a list of popular Content-Types (*http://en.wikipedia.org/wiki/Internet_media_type*).

14.4 Fetching a URL with Cookies

Problem

You want to retrieve a page that requires a cookie to be sent with the request for the page.

Solution

Use the CURLOPT_COOKIE option with cURL:

```
$c = curl_init('http://www.example.com/needs-cookies.php');
curl_setopt($c, CURLOPT_COOKIE, 'user=ellen; activity=swimming');
curl_setopt($c, CURLOPT_RETURNTRANSFER, true);
$page = curl_exec($c);
curl_close($c);
```

With HTTP_Request2, use the addCookie() method:

```
require 'HTTP/Request2.php';
$r = new HTTP_Request2('http://www.example.com/needs-cookies.php');
$r->addCookie('user', 'ellen');
$r->addCookie('activity', 'swimming');
```

```
$page = $r->send()->getBody();
echo $page;
```

Discussion

Cookies are sent to the server in the `Cookie` request header. Although in practice just another HTTP header, due to their importance, both the cURL extension and the `HTTP_Request2` package have specific functions to set cookies.

The examples in the Solution send two cookies: one named `user` with value `ellen` and one named `activity` with value `swimming`.

To request a page that sets cookies and then make subsequent requests that include those newly set cookies, use cURL's "cookie jar" feature. On the first request, set `CURLOPT_COOK IEJAR` to the name of a file in which to store the cookies. On subsequent requests, set `CURLOPT_COOKIEFILE` to the same filename, and cURL reads the cookies from the file and sends them along with the request. This is especially useful for a sequence of requests in which the first request logs in to a site that sets session or authentication cookies, and then the rest of the requests need to include those cookies to be valid.

Here's such a sequence of requests:

```
// A temporary file to hold the cookies
$cookie_jar = tempnam('/tmp','cookie');

// log in
$c = curl_init('https://bank.example.com/login.php?user=donald&password=big$');
curl_setopt($c, CURLOPT_RETURNTRANSFER, true);
curl_setopt($c, CURLOPT_COOKIEJAR, $cookie_jar);
$page = curl_exec($c);
curl_close($c);

// retrieve account balance
$c = curl_init('http://bank.example.com/balance.php?account=checking');
curl_setopt($c, CURLOPT_RETURNTRANSFER, true);
curl_setopt($c, CURLOPT_COOKIEFILE, $cookie_jar);
$page = curl_exec($c);
curl_close($c);

// make a deposit
$c = curl_init('http://bank.example.com/deposit.php');
curl_setopt($c, CURLOPT_POST, true);
curl_setopt($c, CURLOPT_POSTFIELDS, 'account=checking&amount=122.44');
curl_setopt($c, CURLOPT_RETURNTRANSFER, true);
curl_setopt($c, CURLOPT_COOKIEFILE, $cookie_jar);
$page = curl_exec($c);
curl_close($c);

// remove the cookie jar
unlink($cookie_jar) or die("Can't unlink $cookie_jar");
```

Be careful where you store the cookie jar. It needs to be in a place your web server has write access to, but if other users can read the file, they may be able to poach the authentication credentials stored in the cookies.

HTTP_Request2 offers a similar cookie-tracking feature. You need to invoke the setCookieJar() method to enable it. Then, if you make multiple requests with the same HTTP_Request2 object, cookies are automatically preserved from one request to the next. For example:

```
require 'HTTP/Request2.php';

$r = new HTTP_Request2;
$r->setCookieJar(true);

// log in
$r->setUrl('https://bank.example.com/login.php?user=donald&password=b1gmoney$');
$page = $r->send()->getBody();

// retrieve account balance
$r->setUrl('http://bank.example.com/balance.php?account=checking');
$page = $r->send()->getBody();

// make a deposit
$r->setUrl('http://bank.example.com/deposit.php');
$r->setMethod(HTTP_Request2::METHOD_POST)
    ->addPostParameter('account', 'checking')
    ->addPostParameter('amount','122.44');

$page = $r->send()->getBody();
```

See Also

Documentation on curl_setopt() (*http://bit.ly/1pxCXYF*); the PEAR HTTP_Request2 class (*http://bit.ly/1l6Ab8p*); RFC 6265 (*http://bit.ly/1jKYjOa*) and "HTTP Cookies: Standards, Privacy, and Politics" (*http://bit.ly/1lMEBWy*) by David M. Kristol.

14.5 Fetching a URL with Arbitrary Headers

Problem

You want to retrieve a URL that requires specific headers to be sent with the request for the page.

Solution

Set the `header` stream context option when using the `http` stream. The header value must be a single string. Separate multiple headers with a carriage return and newline (\r\n inside a double-quoted string). For example:

```
$url = 'http://www.example.com/special-header.php';
$header = "X-Factor: 12\r\nMy-Header: Bob";
$options = array('header' => $header);
// Create the stream context
$context = stream_context_create(array('http' => $options));
// Pass the context to file_get_contents()
print file_get_contents($url, false, $context);
```

With cURL, set the `CURLOPT_HTTPHEADER` option to an array of headers to send:

```
$c = curl_init('http://www.example.com/special-header.php');
curl_setopt($c, CURLOPT_RETURNTRANSFER, true);
curl_setopt($c, CURLOPT_HTTPHEADER, array('X-Factor: 12', 'My-Header: Bob'));
$page = curl_exec($c);
curl_close($c);
```

With HTTP_Request2, use the `setHeader()` method, as shown:

```
require 'HTTP/Request2.php';

$r = new HTTP_Request2('http://www.example.com/special-header.php');
$r->setHeader(array('X-Factor' => 12, 'My-Header','Bob'));
$page = $r->send()->getBody();
print $page;
```

Discussion

cURL has special options for setting the `Referer` and `User-Agent` request headers—`CURLOPT_REFERER` and `CURLOPT_USERAGENT`. Here's how you use each of these options:

```
$c = curl_init('http://www.example.com/submit.php');
curl_setopt($c, CURLOPT_RETURNTRANSFER, true);
curl_setopt($c, CURLOPT_REFERER, 'http://www.example.com/form.php');
curl_setopt($c, CURLOPT_USERAGENT, 'cURL via PHP');
$page = curl_exec($c);
curl_close($c);
```

See Also

Documentation on the `http` stream wrapper (*http://www.php.net/wrappers.http*), on `curl_setopt()` (*http://www.php.net/curl-setopt*), and on the PEAR HTTP_Request2 class (*http://pear.php.net/package/HTTP_Request2*). The mailing list message (*http://lists.w3.org/Archives/Public/ietf-http-wg-old/1996MayAug/0734.html*) explains the ambitious and revolutionary goals behind spelling "Referer" with one "r."

14.6 Fetching a URL with a Timeout

Problem

You want to fetch a remote URL, but don't want to wait around too long if the remote server is busy or slow.

Solution

With the `http` stream, set the `default_socket_timeout` configuration option:

```
// 15 second timeout
ini_set('default_socket_timeout', 15);
$page = file_get_contents('http://slow.example.com/');
```

This waits up to 15 seconds to establish the connection with the remote server. Changing `default_socket_timeout` affects all new sockets or remote connections created in a particular script execution.

With cURL, set the `CURLOPT_CONNECTTIMEOUT` option:

```
$c = curl_init('http://slow.example.com/');
curl_setopt($c, CURLOPT_RETURNTRANSFER, true);
curl_setopt($c, CURLOPT_CONNECTTIMEOUT, 15);
$page = curl_exec($c);
curl_close($c);
```

With `HTTP_Request2`, set the `timeout` element in a parameter array passed to the `HTTP_Request2` constructor:

```
require_once 'HTTP/Request2.php';

$r = new HTTP_Request2('http://slow.example.com/');
$r->setConfig(array(
    'connect_timeout' => 15
));

$page = $r->send()->getBody();
```

Discussion

Remote servers are fickle beasts. Even the most most robust, enterprise-class, mission-critical service can experience an outage. Alternatively, a remote service you depend on can be up and running, but be unable to handle your requests because of network problems between your server and the remote server. Limiting the amount of time that PHP waits to connect to a remote server is a good idea if using data from remote sources is part of your page construction process.

All of the techniques outlined in the Solution limit the amount of time PHP waits to connect to a remote server. Once the connection is made, though, all bets are off in terms of response time. If you're truly concerned about speedy responses, additionally set a limit on how long PHP waits to receive data from the already connected socket. For a stream connection, use the `stream_set_timeout()` function. This function needs to be passed a stream resource, so you have to open a stream with `fopen()`—no `file_get_contents()` here. This example limits the read timeout to 20 seconds:

```
$url = 'http://slow.example.com';
$stream = fopen($url, 'r');
stream_set_timeout($stream, 20);
$response_body = stream_get_contents($stream);
```

With cURL, set the `CURLOPT_TIMEOUT` to the maximum amount of time `curl_exec()` should operate. This includes both the connection timeout and the time to read the entire response body:

```
curl_setopt($c, CURLOPT_TIMEOUT, 35);
```

With `HTTP_Request2`, add a `timeout` value to the configuration array. This value is the number of seconds. Here it's 20 seconds:

```
require_once 'HTTP/Request2.php';

$r = new HTTP_Request2('http://slow.example.com/');
$r->setConfig(array(
    'timeout' => 20
));

$page = $r->send()->getBody();
```

Although setting connection and read timeouts can improve performance, it can also lead to garbled responses. Your script could read just a partial response before a timeout expires. If you've set timeouts, be sure to validate the entire response that you've received. Alternatively, in situations where fast page generation is crucial, retrieve external data in a separate process and write it to a local cache. This way, your pages can use the cache without fear of timeouts or partial responses.

See Also

Documentation on `curl_setopt()` (*http://www.php.net/curl-setopt*), on `stream_set_timeout()` (*http://www.php.net/stream_set_timeout*), on `default_sock et_timeout` (*http://www.php.net/filesystem*), and on the PEAR `HTTP_Request2` class (*http://pear.php.net/package/HTTP_Request2*).

14.7 Fetching an HTTPS URL

Problem

You want to retrieve a secure URL.

Solution

Use any of the techniques described in Recipe 14.1 or Recipe 14.2, providing a URL that begins with `https`.

Discussion

As long as PHP has been built with the OpenSSL library, all of the functions that can retrieve regular URLs can retrieve secure URLs. Look for the "openssl" section in the output of `phpinfo()` to see if your PHP setup has SSL support.

See Also

Recipes 14.1 and 14.2 for retrieving URLs; the OpenSSL Project (*http://www.openssl.org/*).

14.8 Debugging the Raw HTTP Exchange

Problem

You want to analyze the HTTP request a browser makes to your server and the corresponding HTTP response. For example, your server doesn't supply the expected response to a particular request so you want to see exactly what the components of the request are.

Solution

For simple requests, connect to the web server with Telnet and type in the request headers. A sample exchange looks like:

```
POST /submit.php HTTP/1.1
User-Agent: PEAR HTTP_Request2 class ( http://pear.php.net/ )
Content-Type: application/x-www-form-urlencoded
Connection: close
Host: www.example.com
Content-Length: 12

monkey=uncle
```

Discussion

When you type in request headers, the web server doesn't know that it's just you typing and not a web browser submitting a request. However, some web servers have timeouts on how long they'll wait for a request, so it can be useful to pretype the request and then just paste it into Telnet. The first line of the request contains the request method (POST), a space and the path of the file you want (/submit.php), and then a space and the protocol you're using (HTTP/1.1). A subsequent line, the Host header, tells the server which virtual host to use if many are sharing the same IP address. A blank line tells the server that the request is over; it then spits back its response: first headers, then a blank line, and then the body of the response. The Netcat program (*http://netcat.source forge.net/*) is also useful for this sort of task.

Pasting text into Telnet can get tedious, and it's even harder to make requests with the POST method that way. If you make a request with HTTP_Request2, you can retrieve the response headers and the response body with the getResponseHeader() and getResponseBody() methods, as shown:

```
require 'HTTP/Request2.php';
$r = new HTTP_Request2('http://www.example.com/submit.php');
$r = new HTTP_Request2('http://localhost/submit.php');
$r->setMethod(HTTP_Request2::METHOD_POST)
    ->addPostParameter('monkey', 'uncle');
$response = $r->send();


$response_headers = $response->getHeader();
$response_body    = $response->getBody();
```

To retrieve a specific response header, pass the header name to getResponseHeader(). The header name must be all lowercase. Without an argument, getResponseHead er() returns an array containing all the response headers. HTTP_Request2 saves the outgoing request. Access it by calling the getLastEvent() method, as shown:

```
require 'HTTP/Request2.php';

$r = new HTTP_Request2('http://www.example.com/submit.php');
$r = new HTTP_Request2('http://localhost/submit.php');
$r->setMethod(HTTP_Request2::METHOD_POST)
    ->addPostParameter('monkey', 'uncle');
$response = $r->send();

print_r($r->getLastEvent());
```

That request is something like:

```
POST /submit.php HTTP/1.1
User-Agent: PEAR HTTP_Request2 class ( http://pear.php.net/ )
Content-Type: application/x-www-form-urlencoded
Connection: close
```

```
Host: www.example.com
Content-Length: 12

monkey=uncle
```

Accessing response headers with the http stream is possible, but you have to use a function such as fopen() that gives you a stream resource. One piece of the metadata you get when passing that stream resource to stream_get_meta_data() after the request has been made is the set of response headers. This example demonstrates how to access response headers with a stream resource:

```
$url = 'http://www.example.com/submit.php';
$stream = fopen($url, 'r');
$metadata = stream_get_meta_data($stream);
// The headers are stored in the 'wrapper_data'
foreach ($metadata['wrapper_data'] as $header) {
    print $header . "\n";
}
// The body can be retrieved with
// stream_get_contents()
$response_body = stream_get_contents($stream);
```

stream_get_meta_data() returns an array of information about the stream. The wrap per_data element of that array contains wrapper-specific data. For the http wrapper, that means the response headers, one per subarray element. It prints something like:

```
HTTP/1.1 200 OK
Date: Sun, 07 May 2014 18:24:37 GMT
Server: Apache/2.2.2 (Unix)
Last-Modified: Sun, 07 May 2014 01:58:12 GMT
ETag: "1348011-7-16167502"
Accept-Ranges: bytes
Content-Length: 7
Connection: close
Content-Type: text/plain
```

The fopen() function accepts an optional stream context. Pass it as the fourth argument to fopen() if you want to use one. (The second argument is the mode and the third argument is the optional flag indicating whether to use include_path in looking for a file.)

With cURL, include response headers in the output from curl_exec() by setting the CURLOPT_HEADER option, as shown:

```
$c = curl_init('http://www.example.com/submit.php');
curl_setopt($c, CURLOPT_HEADER, true);
curl_setopt($c, CURLOPT_POST, true);
curl_setopt($c, CURLOPT_POSTFIELDS, 'monkey=uncle&amp;rhino=aunt');
curl_setopt($c, CURLOPT_RETURNTRANSFER, true);
```

```
$response_headers_and_page = curl_exec($c);
curl_close($c);
```

To write the response headers directly to a file, open a filehandle with `fopen()` and set `CURLOPT_WRITEHEADER` to that filehandle, as shown:

```
$fh = fopen('/tmp/curl-response-headers.txt','w') or die($php_errormsg);
$c = curl_init('http://www.example.com/submit.php');
curl_setopt($c, CURLOPT_POST, true);
curl_setopt($c, CURLOPT_POSTFIELDS, 'monkey=uncle&amp;rhino=aunt');
curl_setopt($c, CURLOPT_RETURNTRANSFER, true);
curl_setopt($c, CURLOPT_WRITEHEADER, $fh);
$page = curl_exec($c);
curl_close($c);
fclose($fh) or die($php_errormsg);
```

cURL's `CURLOPT_VERBOSE` option causes `curl_exec()` and `curl_close()` to print out debugging information to standard error, including the contents of the request, as shown:

```
$c = curl_init('http://www.example.com/submit.php');
curl_setopt($c, CURLOPT_VERBOSE, true);
curl_setopt($c, CURLOPT_POST, true);
curl_setopt($c, CURLOPT_POSTFIELDS, 'monkey=uncle&amp;rhino=aunt');
curl_setopt($c, CURLOPT_RETURNTRANSFER, true);
$page = curl_exec($c);
curl_close($c);
```

It prints something like:

```
* Connected to www.example.com (10.1.1.1)
> POST /submit.php HTTP/1.1
Host: www.example.com
Pragma: no-cache
Accept: image/gif, image/x-xbitmap, image/jpeg, image/pjpeg, */*
Content-Length: 23
Content-Type: application/x-www-form-urlencoded

monkey=uncle&rhino=aunt* Connection #0 left intact
* Closing connection #0
```

Because cURL prints the debugging information to standard error and not standard output, it can't be captured with output buffering. You can, however, open a filehandle for writing and set `CURLOUT_STDERR` to that filehandle to divert the debugging information to a file:

```
$fh = fopen('/tmp/curl.out','w') or die($php_errormsg);
$c = curl_init('http://www.example.com/submit.php');
curl_setopt($c, CURLOPT_VERBOSE, true);
curl_setopt($c, CURLOPT_POST, true);
curl_setopt($c, CURLOPT_POSTFIELDS, 'monkey=uncle&amp;rhino=aunt');
curl_setopt($c, CURLOPT_RETURNTRANSFER, true);
curl_setopt($c, CURLOPT_STDERR, $fh);
```

```
$page = curl_exec($c);
curl_close($c);
fclose($fh) or die($php_errormsg);
```

Another way to access response headers with cURL is to write a *header function*. This
is similar to a cURL *write function* except it is called to handle response headers instead
of the response body. This example defines a `HeaderSaver` class whose `header()` method
can be used as a header function to accumulate response headers:

```
class HeaderSaver {
    public $headers = array();
    public $code = null;

    public function header($curl, $data){
        if (is_null($this->code) &&
            preg_match('@^HTTP/\d\.\d (\d+) @',$data,$matches)) {
            $this->code = $matches[1];
        } else {
            // Remove the trailing newline
            $trimmed = rtrim($data);
            if (strlen($trimmed)) {
                // If this line begins with a space or tab, it's a
                // continuation of the previous header
                if (($trimmed[0] == ' ') || ($trimmed[0] == "\t")) {
                    // Collapse the leading whitespace into one space
                    $trimmed = preg_replace('@^[ \t]+@',' ', $trimmed);
                    $this->headers[count($this->headers)-1] .= $trimmed;
                }
                // Otherwise, it's a new header
                else {
                    $this->headers[] = $trimmed;
                }
            }
        }
        return strlen($data);
    }

}

$h = new HeaderSaver();
$c = curl_init('http://www.example.com/plankton.php');
// Register the header function
curl_setopt($c, CURLOPT_HEADERFUNCTION, array($h,'header'));
curl_setopt($c, CURLOPT_RETURNTRANSFER, true);
$page = curl_exec($c);
// Now $h is populated with data
print 'The response code was: ' . $h->code . "\n";
print "The response headers were: \n";
foreach ($h->headers as $header) {
    print "  $header\n";
}
```

The HTTP 1.1 standard specifies that headers can span multiple lines by putting at least one space or tab character at the beginning of the additional lines of the header. The header arrays returned by `stream_get_meta_data()` and `HTTP_Request2::getRespon seHeader()` do not properly handle multiline headers, though. The additional lines in a header are treated as separate headers. This code, however, correctly combines the additional lines in multiline headers.

See Also

Documentation on `curl_setopt()` (*http://www.php.net/curl-setopt*), on `stream_get_meta_data()` (*http://bit.ly/1iwl8us*), on `fopen()` (*http://www.php.net/ fopen*), and on the PEAR `HTTP_Request2` class (*http://bit.ly/1l6Ab8p*); the syntax of an HTTP request is defined in RFC 2616 (*http://bit.ly/rfc-http*). The rules about multiline message headers are in Section 4.2 (*http://bit.ly/1qwvPgk*). The `netcat` program is available from the GNU Netcat project (*http://netcat.sourceforge.net/*).

14.9 Making an OAuth 1.0 Request

Problem

You want to make an OAuth 1.0 signed request.

Solution

Use the PECL `oauth` extension.

Discussion

OAuth 1.0 enables API providers to let their users securely give third-party developers access to their accounts by not providing their usernames and passwords.

Instead, you use two sets of public and private tokens to sign your requests. One set of tokens is for your application; that's used for every request. The other set is user specific; they differ from user to user.

You pass along the two public tokens to identify your application and the user. You also use the two private tokens, also called secrets, to sign the request. The signature is constructed using the HTTP method and URL of the request, along with a few other pieces of metadata, such as a timestamp.

When the request is received, the API provider validates the signature and other pieces of the request to ensure its legitimacy. Because only you and the provider have these secret keys, the API provider knows that if the signatures match the request must have come from the you. If they disagree, then it's a fake and should be rejected.

Using the PECL oauth extension, you don't need to worry about the specifics of the algorithm itself. What you need to know instead is the general authorization flow, nicknamed the OAuth Dance:

1. You get an initial set of user tokens. These are also called request tokens or temporary tokens, because they're only used during the authorization process and not to make actual API calls.

2. You redirect the user to the API provider.

3. The user signs into that site, which authenticates the user and asks him to authorize your application to make API calls on his behalf.

4. After the user authorizes your application, the API provider redirects the user back to your application, passing along two pieces of data: the same temporary public key you provided to match up each reply with its corresponding user and a PIN to prevent against session fixation attacks.

5. You exchange the PIN for permanent OAuth tokens for the user.

6. You make API calls on behalf of the user.

The "Hello World" example from the Solution uses LinkedIn's REST APIs to greet the user with his first name.

For other API providers, the OAuth flow is the same, but you will need to alter URLs at the top of the example and the API call itself.

See Also

Documentation on the oauth extension (*http://www.php.net/oauth*); the OAuth 1.0 specification (*http://bit.ly/oauth-1*) is defined in RFC 5849; the LinkedIn Developer Network (*http://linkd.in/1rtUMcg*).

14.10 Making an OAuth 2.0 Request

Problem

You want to make an OAuth 2.0 signed request.

Solution

Use the stream functions.

Discussion

OAuth 2.0 enables API providers to let their users securely give third-party developers access to their accounts by not providing their usernames and passwords.

Instead, you use a token that identifies both your application and the member. This is also called a "bearer" token, because the API will accept that token as an ID from anyone who presents it. To mitigate against theft of the token, OAuth 2.0 requests are made over SSL.

Because OAuth 2.0 forgoes the signatures of OAuth 1.0, there's no need for a special extension. Instead, you can use the same HTTP functions you normally use.

The OAuth 2.0 flow goes as follows:

1. You redirect the user to the API provider, passing along a self-generated secret value, known as the state, and the URL where the user should be redirected after sign in.

2. The user signs into that site, which authenticates him and asks him to authorize your application to make API calls on his behalf.

3. After the user authorizes your application, the API provider redirects the user back to your application, passing along two pieces of data: the same state you provided to match up each reply with its corresponding user and a code.

4. You exchange the code for a permanent OAuth token for the user, passing along your application ID and secret to identify yourself.

5. You make API calls on behalf of the user.

This "Hello World" example uses LinkedIn's REST APIs to greet the user with his first name:

```
// Change these
define('API_KEY',      'YOUR_API_KEY_HERE');
define('API_SECRET',   'YOUR_API_SECRET_HERE');
define('REDIRECT_URI', 'http://' . $_SERVER['SERVER_NAME'] .
                                    $_SERVER['SCRIPT_NAME']);
define('SCOPE',        'r_fullprofile r_emailaddress rw_nus');

// You'll probably use a database
session_name('linkedin');
session_start();

// OAuth 2 Control Flow
if (isset($_GET['error'])) {
    // LinkedIn returned an error
    print $_GET['error'] . ': ' . $_GET['error_description'];
    exit;
} elseif (isset($_GET['code'])) {
    // User authorized your application
```

```php
    if ($_SESSION['state'] == $_GET['state']) {
        // Get token so you can make API calls
        getAccessToken();
    } else {
        // CSRF attack? Or did you mix up your states?
        exit;
    }
} else {
    if ((empty($_SESSION['expires_at'])) || (time() > $_SESSION['expires_at'])) {
        // Token has expired, clear the state
        $_SESSION = array();
    }
    if (empty($_SESSION['access_token'])) {
        // Start authorization process
        getAuthorizationCode();
    }
}

// Congratulations! You have a valid token. Now fetch a profile
$user = fetch('GET', '/v1/people/~:(firstName)');
print "Hello $user->firstName.\n";
exit;

function getAuthorizationCode() {
    $params = array('response_type' => 'code',
                    'client_id' => API_KEY,
                    'scope' => SCOPE,
                    'state' => uniqid('', true), // unique long string
                    'redirect_uri' => REDIRECT_URI,
            );

    // Authentication request
    $url = 'https://www.linkedin.com/uas/oauth2/authorization?' .
            http_build_query($params);

    // Needed to identify request when it returns to us
    $_SESSION['state'] = $params['state'];

    // Redirect user to authenticate
    header("Location: $url");
    exit;
}

function getAccessToken() {
    $params = array('grant_type' => 'authorization_code',
                    'client_id' => API_KEY,
                    'client_secret' => API_SECRET,
                    'code' => $_GET['code'],
                    'redirect_uri' => REDIRECT_URI,
            );

    // Access Token request
```

```php
    $url = 'https://www.linkedin.com/uas/oauth2/accessToken?' .
            http_build_query($params);

    // Tell streams to make a POST request
    $context = stream_context_create(
                    array('http' =>
                        array('method' => 'POST',
                        )
                    )
                );

    // Retrieve access token information
    $response = file_get_contents($url, false, $context);

    // Native PHP object, please
    $token = json_decode($response);

    // Store access token and expiration time
    $_SESSION['access_token'] = $token->access_token; // guard this!
    $_SESSION['expires_in']   = $token->expires_in; // relative time (in seconds)
    $_SESSION['expires_at']   = time() + $_SESSION['expires_in']; //absolute time

    return true;
}

function fetch($method, $resource, $body = '') {
    $params = array('oauth2_access_token' => $_SESSION['access_token'],
                'format' => 'json',
            );

    // Need to use HTTPS
    $url = 'https://api.linkedin.com' . $resource . '?' .
            http_build_query($params);
    // Tell streams to make a (GET, POST, PUT, or DELETE) request
    $context = stream_context_create(
                    array('http' =>
                        array('method' => $method,
                        )
                    )
                );


    // Hocus Pocus
    $response = file_get_contents($url, false, $context);

    // Native PHP object, please
    return json_decode($response);
}
```

For other API providers, the OAuth flow is the same, but you will need to alter the keys
and URLs in this example and the API call itself.

See Also

Documentation on the oauth extension (*http://www.php.net/oauth*); the OAuth 2.0 specification is defined in RFC 6749 (*http://tools.ietf.org/html/rfc6749*); the LinkedIn Developer Network (*https://developer.linkedin.com*).

CHAPTER 15

Serving RESTful APIs

15.0 Introduction

Exposing APIs using REST allows practically everyone to programmatically access your application. It doesn't matter what language they're using. Because REST embraces the basic protocol of the Web as its syntax, no special libraries are necessary. If a developer is capable of making HTTP requests, he can call your RESTful APIs.

REST does not prescribe a specific syntax for requests, the schema of the data passed back and forth, or even how to serialize data. Instead, it's an architectural style that provides a set of patterns and general rules. Each site is then free to implement its APIs according to its needs, as long as it can follow the guidelines.

A resource is the fundamental unit of REST. Resources can be people, objects, or anything you wish to act upon. Resources are identified by location, using URLs. (Or by name, using a URN.)[1] Resources have representations, which are various ways to describe the resource. Usually the representations use standard data formats, such as JSON, XML, HTML, PDF, PNG, etc.

It's a standard pattern to format URLs using */version/resource/key*. For example, Rasmus Lerdorf could be located at *http://api.example.com/v1/people/rasmus*. This maps to a person identified as "rasmus" using version 1.0 of the API.

This resource can be represented in JSON as:

```
{
    "firstName": "Rasmus"
```

---

1. URL stands for uniform resource locator, and URN stands for uniform resource name. A resource can have both a name and locations. For example, the HTTP 1.1 specification has a URN of urn:ietf:rfc:2616 and a URL of *https://www.ietf.org/rfc/rfc2616.txt*. Collectively, URNs and URLs are called URIs, for uniform resource identifiers.

```
    "lastName": "Lerdorf"
}
```

In REST, the HTTP methods, such as GET and POST, describes the requested action. So, to process a RESTful request you need to know both the URL and the HTTP method. Recipe 15.1 demonstrates how to route a request to a URL based on the client's HTTP method, and Recipe 15.2 shows to do so with "clean" URLs.

Each method has a well-defined set of behaviors. For example, GET tells the server you want to retrieve an existing resource, whereas POST means you want to add a new resource. You use PUT to modify a resource or create a specifically named resource. And DELETE, of course, deletes the resource.

Beyond this, REST imposes a few other constraints upon your API design. Specifically, some methods must be safe and others must be idempotent.

Safe methods, such as GET, don't modify resources (which is why they're safe). Other methods, such as POST and DELETE, are not safe. They are allowed to have the side effect of updating the system, by creating, modifying, or deleting a resource (which is probably what you want, but it isn't safe).

Nonsafe methods are further subdivided into two based on idempotency. When a method is idempotent, calling it multiple times is equivalent to calling it once. For instance, once you've called DELETE on a resource, trying to DELETE it again may return an error, but won't cause anything else to be deleted. In contrast, making a POST request twice can cause two new resources to be created. Table 15-1 provides an outline of this behavior.

Table 15-1. HTTP method behavior

HTTP method	Description	Safe	Idempotent
GET	Read a resource	Yes	Yes
POST	Create a resource	No	No
PUT	Update a resource	No	Yes
DELETE	Delete a resource	No	Yes

Detailed specifics of how each method behaves and how to process requests for reading, creating, updating, and deleting a resource are covered in Recipes 15.3, 15.4, 15.5, and 15.6.

REST uses HTTP status codes to indicate whether the request has succeeded or failed. The 200s indicate success; 300s indicate further action is needed for the server to respond; 400s are client errors; and 500s are server errors. For example, a GET request that's successful returns 200; a request to a resource that's at a new URL returns 301, trying to read a nonexistent resource returns 404, and a request to a server undergoing maintenance returns 503.

Common status codes and when it's appropriate to use them are described in the context of recipes as appropriate. General best practices for returning errors is covered in Recipe 15.7.

It's perfectly okay for a resource to have multiple representations. An XML version of *http://api.example.com/v1/people/rasmus* could be:

```
<person>
    <firstName>Rasmus</firstName>
    <lastName>Lerdorf</lastName>
</person>
```

Another example is a text document that has both an HTML and a PDF version, or an image that comes in both JPEG and PNG formats. How to expose the same resource in more than one way is covered in Recipe 15.8.

The recipes in this chapter look to provide the foundation for designing and implementing RESTful APIs in PHP. However, the entirety of that task is far beyond the scope of a single chapter. REST has many aspects, including caching and hypermedia as the engine of application state (HATEOAS) that aren't touched upon. To learn more, you can go to the source: the original document describing REST is Roy Fielding's thesis (*https://www.ics.uci.edu/~fielding/pubs/dissertation/top.htm*). Not unexpectedly, this is somewhat academic in nature.

A more practical book that still looks to translate the tenets of REST into specifics is *RESTful Web APIs* by Leonard Richardson, Mike Amundsen, and Sam Ruby (O'Reilly). *REST in Practice* by Jim Webber, Savas Parastatidis, and Ian Robinson (O'Reilly) is a pragmatic hands-on guide to RESTful design. Finally, a very in-depth Cookbook style guide to REST is *RESTful Web Services Cookbook* by Subbu Allamaraju (O'Reilly). Chapter 8 covers how to implement additional RESTful concepts, although without necessarily using RESTful terminology. For example, authentication is covered in Recipe 8.6, and reading and writing HTTP headers is discussed in Recipes 8.8 and 8.9.

Though an understanding of the fundamentals of RESTful design is necessary to create a RESTful API of your own, you don't need to implement all the scaffolding code from scratch. Unfortunately, there's no one-size-fits-all official PHP RESTful framework. (Some may quip that's PHP itself.) However, there are a number of PHP frameworks to simplify the overhead of exposing resources. Some are full MVC frameworks with ORM abstractions to enable the creation of fullstack applications that also expose RESTful APIs; others are micro-frameworks that provide the thinnest facade on top of your existing code. This is an area of active development, so you're bound to find a package that's perfect for your situation.

15.1 Exposing and Routing to a Resource

Problem

You want to provide access to a resource and handle requests according to the HTTP method.

Solution

Use the $_SERVER['REQUEST_METHOD'] variable to route the request:

```php
$request = explode('/', $_SERVER['PATH_INFO']);

$method = strtolower($_SERVER['REQUEST_METHOD']);
switch($method) {
    case 'get':
        // handle a GET request
        break;
    case 'post':
        // handle a POST request
        break;
    case 'put':
        // handle a PUT request
        break;
    case 'delete':
        // handle a DELETE request
        break;
    default:
        // unimplemented method
        http_response_code(405);
}
```

Discussion

When processing a request for a RESTful resource, you need to both know the requested resource and the action the client wants to take.

However, it's rare to have a one-to-one mapping between resources and the PHP script that processes them. For example, a resource for books could use a book's ISBN as the key. So, *PHP Cookbook* is at */v1/books.php/9781449363758*, *Learning PHP 5* is at */v1/books.php/9780596005603*, and so on.

But it's not a good idea to have individual files at each of those locations. Instead, use a single *books.php* file, which uses the ISBN as a parameter. In many scripts, you'd pass the ISBN as a query parameter, such as */v1/books.php?isbn=9781449363758*, and read this in your PHP code at $_GET['isbn'].

However, with REST, you use slashes to identify each resource. And you cannot use the standard PHP superglobals with a URL such as */v1/books.php/9781449363758*. Instead, parse the path into its components by breaking the $_SERVER['PATH_INFO'] apart on "/":

```
$request = explode('/', $_SERVER['PATH_INFO']);
```

This breaks a request for */v1/books.php/9781449363758* into:

```
Array
(
    [0] =>
    [1] => 9781449363758
)
```

Next, route the request based on the HTTP method, so you can handle GETs, PUTs, POSTs, and DELETEs in different functions. For this, use $_SERVER['REQUEST_METHOD']:

```
$method = strtolower($_SERVER['REQUEST_METHOD']);
switch($method) {
    case 'get':
        // handle a GET request
        get_book($request);
        break;
    case 'post':
        // handle a POST request
        post_book($request);
        break;
    case 'put':
        // handle a PUT request
        put_book($request);
        break;
    case 'delete':
        // handle a DELETE request
        delete_book($request);
        break;
    default:
        // unimplemented method
        http_response_code(405);
}
```

Because you may not choose to implement all methods for a resource, a switch statement makes it easy to insert the methods you want, while also having a default behavior of returning HTTP status code 405 to signal "Method Not Allowed".

You may find it convenient to map the RESTful resources you expose to PHP classes. Furthermore, those classes can have methods of get(), post(), and so forth. For example:

```
class books {
    static public function get($request) {
        // handle a GET request
    }
```

```
    static public function post($request) {
        // handle a POST request
    }

    // other methods, too
}

class albums {
    static public function get($request) {
        // handle a GET request
    }
}
```

Then you can modify the router to be a single *index.php* to process all resources, instead of separate files for each resource:

```
// break apart URL and extract the root resource
$request = explode('/', $_SERVER['PATH_INFO']);
$resource = array_shift($request);

// only process valid resources
$resources = array('books' => true, 'music' => true);
if (! array_key_exists($resource, $resources)) {
    http_response_code(404);
    exit;
}

// route the request to the appropriate function based on method
$method = strtolower($_SERVER["REQUEST_METHOD"]);
switch($method) {
    case 'get':
    case 'post':
    case 'put':
    case 'delete':
    // any other methods you want to support, such as HEAD
        if (method_exists($resource, $method)) {
            call_user_func(array($resource, $method), $request);
            break;
        }
        // fall through
    default:
        http_response_code(405);
}
```

First, you break apart the URL on /. Then you pop off the first element to extract the resource, such as books or albums.

Then you make sure that resource is a legitimate one to call. For instance, asking for */v1/movies/fletch* generates a 404 error, because that resource doesn't exist.

Finally, you check if the class with the same name as the resource has a class method that matches the HTTP method. If so, you use call_user_func() to invoke the method.

If not, you return a response code of 405 (Method Not Allowed). You also only handle the get(), post(), put(), and delete() methods, so people cannot invoke other class methods.

See Also

Recipe 15.2 for exposing clean-looking URLs; documentation on the $_SERVER super-global (*http://www.php.net/_server*) and http_response_code() (*http://www.php.net/ http_response_code*).

15.2 Exposing Clean Resource Paths

Problem

You want your URLs to look clean and not include file extensions.

Solution

Use Apache's mod_rewrite to map the path to your PHP script:

```
RewriteEngine on
RewriteBase /v1/
RewriteCond %{REQUEST_FILENAME} !-f
RewriteCond %{REQUEST_FILENAME} !-d
RewriteRule ^(.*)$ index.php?PATH_INFO=$1 [L,QSA]
```

Then use $_GET['PATH_INFO'] in place of $_SERVER['PATH_INFO']:

```
$request = explode('/', $_GET['PATH_INFO']);
```

Discussion

Use mod_rewrite to expose elegant URLs, such as */v1/books/9781449363758*, even when there isn't a file at that specific path. Without this, you end up with the more clumsy URL of */v1/books.php/9781449363758*. If you're running another web server, such as nginx, use its own syntax for handling this type of URL mapping.

The code in the Solution tells Apache that when it doesn't find a file or directory at the requested path, it should route it to *index.php* instead. Additionally, so you can still read in the original URL to properly process the request, extract the path and pass it in as the PATH_INFO query parameter.

Inside your script, parse the path into its components by breaking it apart on "/":

```
$request = explode('/', $_GET['PATH_INFO']);
```

This breaks a request for */v1/books/9781449363758* into:

```
Array
(
    [0] => books
    [1] => 9781449363758
)
```

Now you can take action based on the resource and path, as described in Recipe 15.1.

See Also

Recipe 15.1 for routing requests for a resource based on HTTP method; documentation on the Apache `mod_rewrite` module (*http://httpd.apache.org/docs/current/mod/mod_rewrite.html*).

15.3 Exposing a Resource for Reading

Problem

You want to let people read a resource.

Solution

Read requests using GET. Return structured results, using formats such as JSON, XML, or HTML. Don't modify any resources.

For a GET request to the resource at *http://api.example.com/v1/jobs/123*:

```
GET /v1/jobs/123 HTTP/1.1
Host: api.example.com
```

Use this PHP code:

```php
// Assume this was pulled from a database or other data store
$job[123] = [
    'id' => 123,
    'position' => [
        'title' => 'PHP Developer',
        ],
    ];

$json = json_encode($job[123]);

// Resource exists 200: OK
http_response_code(200);

// And it's being sent back as JSON
header('Content-Type: application/json');
```

```
    print $json;
```

To generate this HTTP response:

```
HTTP/1.1 200 OK
Content-Type: application/json
Content-Length: 61

{
    "id": 123,
    "position": {
        "title": "PHP Developer"
    }
}
```

Discussion

The most common type of REST request is reading data. Reads in REST correspond with HTTP GET requests. This is the same HTTP method used by your web browser to read an HTML page, so when you write PHP scripts you're almost always handling GET requests.

This makes serving up a REST resource for reading straightforward:

1. Check that the HTTP method is GET.
2. Parse the URL to determine the specific resource and, optionally, key.
3. Retrieve the necessary information, probably from a database.
4. Format the data into the proper structure
5. Send the data back, along with the necessary HTTP headers.

The first steps are covered in Recipe 15.1 and the third is specific to your application. Once you've fetched the data, the next step is formatting it for output. It's common to use JSON or XML (or both), but any structured format is perfectly fine. That could be HTML or YAML or even CSV.

This example takes a record and converts it to JSON:

```
// Assume this was pulled from a database or other data store
$job[123] = [
    'id' => 123,
    'position' => [
        'title' => 'PHP Developer',
        ],
    ];

$json = json_encode($job[123]);
```

After you have the response body, the other step is sending the appropriate HTTP headers. Because this record was found, return a status code of 200 (OK) and because you're using JSON, set the Content-Type header:

```
// Resource exists 200: OK
http_response_code(200);

// And it's being sent back as JSON
header('Content-Type: text/json');
```

Last, send the data itself:

```
print $json;
```

If there is no Job 123 in the system, tell the caller this wasn't found using status code 404:

```
// Resource exists 404: Not Found
http_response_code(404);
```

GET requests also have the requirement of not modifying the system. In other words, reading a resource shouldn't cause that resource—or any other part of your data—to change. The technical phrase for this is "safe."

See Also

Recipe 14.1 for fetching a URL with the GET method; Recipes 15.4, 15.5, and 15.6 for serving resources using other methods.

15.4 Creating a Resource

Problem

You want to let people add a new resource to the system.

Solution

Accept requests using POST. Read the POST body. Return success and the location of the new resource.

For a POST request to *http://api.example.com/v1/jobs*:

```
POST /v1/jobs HTTP/1.1
Host: api.example.com
Content-Type: application/json
Content-Length: 49

{
    "position": {
        "title": "PHP Developer"
```

```
        }
    }
```

Use this PHP code:

```php
if ($_SERVER["REQUEST_METHOD"] == 'POST') {
    $body = file_get_contents('php://input');
    switch(strtolower($_SERVER['HTTP_CONTENT_TYPE'])) {
        case "application/json":
            $job = json_decode($body);
            break;
        case "text/xml":
            // parsing here
            break;
    }

    // Validate input

    // Create new Resource
    $id = create($job); // Returns id of 456
    $json = json_encode(array('id' => $id));

    http_response_code(201); // Created
    $site = 'https://api.example.com';
    header("Location: $site/" . $_SERVER['REQUEST_URI'] . "/$id");
    header('Content-Type: application/json');
    print $json;
}
```

To generate this output:

```
HTTP/1.1 201 Created
Location: https://api.example.com/jobs/456
Content-Type: application/json
Content-Length: 15

{
    "id": 456
}
```

If the client is allowed to specify (and knows) the ID, use PUT instead:

```
PUT /v1/jobs/456 HTTP/1.1
Host: api.example.com
Content-Type: application/json
Content-Length: 49

{
    "position": {
        "title": "PHP Developer"
    }
}
```

Use this PHP code:

```php
if ($_SERVER["REQUEST_METHOD"] == 'PUT') {

    $body = file_get_contents('php://input');
    switch(strtolower($_SERVER['HTTP_CONTENT_TYPE'])) {
        case "application/json":
            $job = json_decode($body);
            break;
        case "text/xml":
            // parsing here
            break;
    }

    // Validate input

    // Create new Resource

    $request = explode('/', substr($_SERVER['PATH_INFO'], 1));
    $resource = array_shift($request);
    $id = create($job, $request[0]); // Uses id from request
    $json = json_encode(array('id' => $id));

    http_response_code(201); // Created
    $site = 'https://api.example.com';
    header("Location: $site/" . $_SERVER['REQUEST_URI'] );
    print $json;
}
```

Discussion

The standard way to add new records is by HTTP POSTing to a parent (or collection) resource. For example, to add a new job to the system, POST the data to *v1/jobs* (in contrast to a specific resource such as *v1/jobs/123*).

It's the job of the server to parse the data, validate it, and assign an ID for the newly re-created record. For example:

```php
if ($_SERVER["REQUEST_METHOD"] == 'POST') {

    $body = file_get_contents('php://input');
    switch(strtolower($_SERVER['HTTP_CONTENT_TYPE'])) {
        case "application/json":
            $job = json_decode($body);
            break;
        case "text/xml":
            $job = simplexml_load_string($body);
            break;
    }

    // Validate input

    // Create new Resource
```

```
        $id = create($job); // Returns id
    }
```

PHP automatically parses standard HTML form data into `$_POST`. However, for most REST APIs, the POST body is in JSON (or XML or another format).

This requires you to read and parse the data yourself. The raw POST body is available using the special stream *php://input*; slurp it into a variable using `file_get_contents()`.

Next, check the `Content-Type` HTTP header to learn what data format was sent. You do this via the `$_SERVER['HTTP_CONTENT_TYPE']` superglobal variable. You may only support one format, such as JSON, but you should still confirm that the client is using that format.

Based on the `Content-Type`, use the appropriate function, such as `json_decode()` or `simplexml_load_string()`, to deserialize the data to PHP.

Now you can perform the necessary business logic to validate the input, add the resource, and generate a unique ID for that record.

If everything goes OK, signal success and return the location of the new resource:

```
http_response_code(201); // Created
$site = 'https://api.example.com';
header("Location: $site/" . $_SERVER['REQUEST_URI'] . "/$id");
print $json;
```

A status code of 201 signifies a resource has been created, which is preferable over the more generic 200 (OK). Additionally, it's a best practice to return the location, either via the `Location` HTTP header or in the body. The first is more RESTful, but some clients find it easier to parse the results in a body than from a header. The `Location` HTTP must be an absolute URL.

If there's a problem with how the request was sent, return a status code in the 4xx range. Whenever possible, you should return a message explaining how the client can fix her request.

For example, if a required field is missing or the document is otherwise well-formed but has an incorrect schema, return 422 (Unprocessable Entity):

```
http_response_code(422); // Unprocessable Entity

$error_body = [
    "error" => "12",
    "message" => "Missing required field: job title"
];

print json_encode($error_body);
```

If you cannot find a specific error code for the problem, then a response code of 400 (Bad Request) is always OK.

If your system cannot definitively say whether a request is or isn't OK, return 202 (Accepted). This is the appropriate way to passive-agressively signal your noncommittal behavior. This is most frequently used when you process requests via an asynchronous queue, so the REST server is primarily handing off the request to another system, but that system doesn't immediately return a response.

When the client knows the ID associated with the new record (instead of having you assign one), have them PUT directly to the location (instead of to the parent resource). For example:

```
PUT /v1/jobs/123 HTTP/1.1
Host: api.example.com
Content-Type: application/json
Content-Length: 49

{
    "position": {
        "title": "PHP Developer"
    }
}
if ($_SERVER["REQUEST_METHOD"] == 'PUT') {

    $body = file_get_contents('php://input');
    switch(strtolower($_SERVER['HTTP_CONTENT_TYPE'])) {
        case "application/json":
            $job = json_decode($body);
            break;
        case "text/xml":
            // parsing here
            break;
    }

    // Validate input

    // Create new Resource
    $request = explode('/', substr($_SERVER['PATH_INFO'], 1));
    $resource = array_shift($request);
    $id = create($job, $request[0]); // Uses id from request
    $json = json_encode(array('id' => $id));

    http_response_code(201); // Created
    $site = 'https://api.example.com';
    header("Location: $site/" . $_SERVER['REQUEST_URI'] . "/$id");
    print $json;
}
```

Regardless whether the request is a PUT or a POST, the same set of responses are appropriate. A PUT to an already existing resource (for instance, if *v1/job/123* was already defined) will overwrite what's there. In that case, return a 200 OK response code instead of 201 Created (unless you're using some form of versioning to protect against this). If you do have a versioning conflict, return a 409 Conflict response code.

POST requests are not safe, so they are allowed to have side effects. Additionally, they are not idempotent, so making the same request multiple times causes multiple resources to be re-created. This is in contrast to PUT requests, which are not safe, but are idempotent. Making the same PUT request more than once is equivalent to making it one time.

See Also

Recipe 14.2 for fetching a URL with the POST method: Recipes 15.3, 15.5, and 15.6 for serving resources using other methods; documentation on *php://input* (*http://www.php.net/wrappers.php*).

15.5 Editing a Resource

Problem

You want to let people update a resource.

Solution

Accept requests using PUT. Read the POST body. Return success.

For a PUT request to *http://api.example.com/v1/jobs/123*:

```
PUT /v1/jobs/123 HTTP/1.1
Host: api.example.com
Content-Type: application/json
Content-Length: 49

{
    "position": {
        "title": "PHP Developer"
    }
}
```

Use this PHP code:

```php
if ($_SERVER["REQUEST_METHOD"] == 'PUT') {
    $body = file_get_contents('php://input');
    switch(strtolower($_SERVER['HTTP_CONTENT_TYPE'])) {
        case "application/json":
            $job = json_decode($body);
            break;
        case "text/xml":
            // parsing here
            break;
```

```
    }

    // Validate input

    // Modify the Resource

    $request = explode('/', substr($_SERVER['PATH_INFO'], 1));
    $resource = array_shift($request);
    $id = update($job, $request[0]); // Uses id from request

    http_response_code(204); // No Content
}
```

To generate this output:

```
HTTP/1.1 204 No Content
```

Discussion

To update a resource, accept PUT requests. The resource provided in the POST body replaces the current resource. See Recipe 15.4 for an explanation of the logic to parse this request.

If the request is successful, return 204 (No Content). You don't return 201 because the resource already exists. You can return 200, but 204 is preferable when you don't return an HTTP body. This allows the client to definitely know nothing was lost.

PUT requests are not safe, but they are idempotent because the resource being PUT entirely replaces the current entity. Unfortunately, this means that even updating a one-character typo requires you to transmit the entire resource.

Some sites allow partial updates using PUT. For example, this request keeps the resource as is, except for updating the postal code:

```
PUT /v1/jobs/123 HTTP/1.1
Host: api.example.com
Content-Type: application/json
Content-Length: 43

{
    "location" {
        "postalCode": 94043
    }
}
```

This makes it hard to disambiguate between when you want to delete a field versus intentionally not providing it. The PATCH method is a proposed standard for partial updates, so you can differentiate your behavior based on a PUT or a PATCH.

See Also

Recipe 14.3 for fetching a URL with any method; Recipes 15.3, 15.4, and 15.6 for serving resources using other methods; RFC 5789 for the HTTP PATCH method (*http://bit.ly/rfc-5789*).

15.6 Deleting a Resource

Problem

You want to let people delete a resource.

Solution

Accept requests using DELETE. Return success.

For a DELETE request to *http://api.example.com/v1/jobs/123*:

```
DELETE /v1/jobs/123 HTTP/1.1
Host: api.example.com
```

Use this PHP code:

```
if ($_SERVER["REQUEST_METHOD"] == 'DELETE') {
    // Delete the Resource

    $request = explode('/', substr($_SERVER['PATH_INFO'], 1));
    $resource = array_shift($request);
    $success = delete($request[0]); // Uses id from request

    http_response_code(204); // No Content
}
```

To generate this output:

```
HTTP/1.1 204 No Content
```

Discussion

To delete a resource, accept the DELETE method. If the request is successful, return 204 (No Content). You can return 200, but 204 is preferable when you don't return an HTTP body. This allows the client to definitely know nothing was lost.

If the resource doesn't exist (either because it never existed or someone deleted it first), return 404 (Not Found). If the resource is never coming back (versus it never existed or is temporarily deleted, but could be re-created), return 410 (Gone). This is often used when the entire parent resource has been deprecated, such as if you stopped supporting the ability to handle jobs.

DELETE requests are not safe, but they are idempotent because deleting the same resource multiple times is the same as deleting it once. It's gone.

See Also

Recipe 14.3 for fetching a URL with any method; Recipes 15.3, 15.4, and 15.5 for serving resources using other methods.

15.7 Indicating Errors and Failures

Problem

You want to indicate that a failure occurred.

Solution

Return a 4xx status code for client failures. Provide a message with more information.

```
http_response_code(401); // Unauthorized

$error_body = [
    "error" => "Unauthorized",
    "code" => 1,
    "message" => "Only authenticated users can read " . $_SERVER['REQUEST_URI'],
    "url" => "http://developer.example.com/error/1"
];

print json_encode($error_body);
```

Return a 5xx status code for server failures. Provide a message with more information:

```
http_response_code(503); // Site down

$error_body = [
    "error" => "Down for maintenance",
    "code" => 2,
    "message" => "Check back in two hours.",
    "url" => "http://developer.example.com/error/2"
];
print json_encode($error_body);
```

Discussion

Helpful and informative error messages are a blessing to consumers of your APIs. A good error message is specific, and explains what's wrong and how (if possible) to fix the problem.

For RESTful servers, this divides into two pieces: the HTTP status code and the error message returned in the response body. HTTP status codes are divided into two large buckets.

The 4xx family of codes indicate client-side failures, such as invalid authentication credentials (401), being forbidden to access the resource (403), or the resource is no longer available (410).

Receiving a 4xx error is not blaming the client, because sometimes it's impossible for it to know in advance that it's request is going to be bad (because the user has revoked the authorization token or the server has deprecated an API without notice). Instead, these are problems that can be fixed by the client, by providing the right information (such as valid authentication credentials), modifying the request (only asking for resources it's allowed to request), or stopping the request entirely (if it's gone, it's gone).

The 5xx family of codes are server-side errors. (It's not you, it's me.) For example, the service is down (503) or an unexpected error due to a bug in the code (500).

These are problems entirely outside of the client's control and can only be fixed by the API provider. They cannot be fixed by modifying the request. Instead, they need to wait until the server has fixed the bug, finished maintenance, or regained the ability to handle traffic.

Table 15-2 contains a list of common HTTP status codes used in errors.

Table 15-2. HTTP status codes used in errors

Status code	Meaning	Description
400	Bad Request	Bad syntax or other generic error
401	Unauthorized	Must provide valid authentication
403	Forbidden	Not allowed to access the resource for reasons other than invalid authentication
404	Not Found	Resource doesn't exist (but may in the future)
405	Method Not Allowed	Cannot call that method on this resource
410	Gone	The resource no longer exists and never will again
429	Too Many Requests	Past your quota or rate limit
500	Internal Server Error	Generic server error
503	Service Unavailable	Server is overloaded or down for maintenance

However, a code by itself is rarely sufficient to fully explain the error. For this, you should provide an error message in the response, ideally in the same format as the request itself (such as JSON or XML).

The minimal error message is a string of text that describes the problem. However, though this explains the error, it's hard to write code to parse from a string. Therefore, it's best to also include a numeric error code and a short string. For extra credit, include a URL to an HTML page that describes the issue in more detail or allows people to ask questions about how to resolve the problem.

For example:

```
$http_error_code = 401;
$error_body = [
    "error" => "Unauthorized",
    "code" => 1,
    "message" => "Only authenticated users can read " . $_SERVER['REQUEST_URI'],
    "url" => "http://developer.example.com/error/1"
];

http_response_code($http_error_code); // Unauthorized
print json_encode($error_body);
```

See Also

RFC 2616 Sections 10.4 and 10.5 (*http://tools.ietf.org/html/rfc2616*).

15.8 Supporting Multiple Formats

Problem

You want to support multiple formats, such as JSON and XML.

Solution

Use file extensions:

```
http://api.example.com/people/rasmus.json
http://api.example.com/people/rasmus.xml

// Break apart URL
$request = explode('/', $_SERVER['PATH_INFO']);

// Extract the root resource and type
$resource = array_shift($request);
$file = array_pop($request);
$dot = strrpos($file, ".");
if ($dot === false) { // note: three equal signs
    $request[] = $file;
    $type = 'json'; // default value
} else {
    $request[] = substr($file, 0, $dot);
    $type = substr($file, $dot + 1);
}
```

Or support the Accept HTTP header, to allow requests to *http://api.example.com/ people/rasmus*:

```
GET /people/rasmus HTTP/1.1
Host: api.example.com
Accept: application/json,text/html

require_once 'HTTP2.php';
$http = new HTTP2;
$supportedTypes = array(
    'application/json',
    'text/xml',
);

$type = $http->negotiateMimeType($supportedTypes, false);
if ($type === false) {
    http_response_code(406); // Not Acceptable
    $error_body = 'Choose one of: ' . join(',', $supportedTypes);
    print json_encode($error_body);
} else {
    // format response based on $type
}
```

If all else fails, read a query parameter:

```
http://api.example.com/people/rasmus?format=json
http://api.example.com/people/rasmus?format=xml

$type = $_GET['format'];
```

Discussion

When your RESTful API supports multiple formats, such as JSON and XML, there are a few ways to allow developers to signal which format they want to use.

One option is to use file extensions, such as *http://api.example.com/people/ rasmus.json* and *http://api.example.com/people/rasmus.xml*. Because these aren't real files, this requires some parsing of $_SERVER['PATH_INFO']:

```
// Break apart URL
$request = explode('/', $_SERVER['PATH_INFO']);

// Extract the root resource and type
$resource = array_shift($request);
$file = array_pop($request);
$dot = strrpos($file, '.');
if ($dot === false) { // note: three equal signs
    $request[] = $file;
    $type = 'json'; // default value
} else {
    $request[] = substr($file, 0, $dot);
    $type = substr($file, $dot + 1);
}

// $type is json, xml, etc.
```

You pull off the file segment of the URL and search for the trailing ".". If it's not there, fall back to a default value. If it is, then extract the resource name and type using `substr()`.

The downside to using file extensions is that clients can only request one specific representation type. If they ask for a JSON version and you don't support that, then there's no way for them to signal an acceptable alternative format in the same request.

Multiple representations for a resource can live at a single location, such as *http:// api.example.com/people/rasmus*. In this case, clients can specify a list of formats in their preferred order. Then you can negotiate with the client to return the resource in the best mutually agreeable format.

In this case, the client passes a request like so, using the `Accept` HTTP header to signal its preferences:

```
GET /people/rasmus HTTP/1.1
Host: api.example.com
Accept: application/json,text/html
```

Unfortunately, proper parsing of the `Accept` header isn't easy. So, use a library, such as PEAR's HTTP2:

```
require_once 'HTTP2.php';
$http = new HTTP2;
$supportedTypes = array(
    'application/json',
    'text/xml',
);

$type = $http->negotiateMimeType($supportedTypes, false);
if ($type === false) {
    http_response_code(406); // Not Acceptable
    $error_body = 'Choose one of: ' . join(',', $supportedTypes);
    print json_encode($error_body);
} else {
    // format response based on $type
}
```

This lets you specify that you support JSON and XML and uses the `$http->negotiateMimeType()` function to return the client's most preferred format from the list you support.

As a last result, you can accept the format as a query parameter:

```
$type = $_GET['format'];
```

Though simple and easy to implement, this is not considered a proper RESTful design.

See Also

PEAR's `HTTP2` class (*http://bit.ly/TwYR3Q*); the `Accept` HTTP header (*http://bit.ly/1pBAYT2*).

CHAPTER 16

Internet Services

16.0 Introduction

Before there was HTTP, there was FTP, IMAP, POP3, and a whole alphabet soup of other protocols. Many people quickly embraced web browsers because the browser provided an integrated program that let them check their email, transfer files, and view documents without worrying about the details surrounding the underlying means of communication. PHP provides functions, both natively and through PEAR, to use these other protocols. With them, you can use PHP to create web frontend applications that perform all sorts of network-enabled tasks, such as looking up domain names or sending web-based email. Although PHP simplifies these jobs, it is important to understand the strengths and limitations of each protocol.

Recipe 16.1 to Recipe 16.3 cover the most popular feature of all: email. Recipe 16.1 shows how to send basic email messages. Recipe 16.2 describes MIME-encoded email, which enables you to send plain text and HTML-formatted messages. The IMAP and POP3 protocols, which are used to read mailboxes, are discussed in Recipe 16.3.

Recipe 16.4 covers how to exchange files using FTP (file transfer protocol), which is a method for sending and receiving files across the Internet. FTP servers can require users to log in with a password or allow anonymous usage.

Searching LDAP servers is the topic of Recipe 16.5, and Recipe 16.6 discusses how to authenticate users against an LDAP server. LDAP servers are used as address books and as centralized stores for user information. They're optimized for information retrieval and can be configured to replicate their data to ensure high reliability and quick response times.

The chapter concludes with recipes on networking. Recipe 16.7 covers DNS lookups, both from domain name to IP and vice versa. Recipe 16.8 tells how to check if a host is up and accessible with PEAR's ping module. Learn how to get information about domains in Recipe 16.9.

Other parts of the book deal with some network protocols as well. HTTP is covered in detail in Chapter 13. Those recipes discuss how to fetch URLs in a variety of different ways. Protocols that combine HTTP and JSON are covered in Chapter 14 and Chapter 15. Those two chapters discuss consuming and serving RESTful APIs.

16.1 Sending Mail

Problem

You want to send an email message. This can be in direct response to a user's action, such as signing up for your site, or a recurring event at a set time, such as a weekly newsletter.

Solution

Use Zetacomponent's `ezcMailComposer` class:

```
$message = new ezcMailComposer();
$message->from = new ezcMailAddress('webmaster@example.com');
$message->addTo(new ezcMailAddress('adam@example.com', 'Adam'));
$message->subject = 'New Version of PHP Released!';
$body = 'Go to http://www.php.net and download it today!';
$message->plainText = $body;
$message->build();

$sender = new ezcMailMtaTransport();
$sender->send($message);
```

If you can't use Zetacomponent's `ezcMailComposer` class, use PHP's built-in `mail()` function:

```
$to = 'adam@example.com';
$subject = 'New Version of PHP Released!';
$body = 'Go to http://www.php.net and download it today!';

mail($to, $subject, $body);
```

Discussion

The Zetacomponent `ezcMailComposer` class gives you a way to construct email messages. How the component sends the message depends on which `ezcMailTransport` implementation you use. In the preceding example, `ezcMailMtaTransport()` uses the PHP `mail()` function internally, so it benefits from your PHP configuration. The `ezc MailSmtpTransport` can be used to talk to an SMTP server directly, as follows:

```
$message = new ezcMailComposer();
$message->from = new ezcMailAddress('webmaster@example.com');
$message->addTo(new ezcMailAddress('adam@example.com', 'Adam'));
$message->subject = 'New Version of PHP Released!';
$body = 'Go to http://www.php.net and download it today!';
$message->plainText = $body;
$message->build();

$host = 'smtpauth.example.com';
$username = 'philb';
$password = 'jf430k24';
$port = 587;

$smtpOptions = new ezcMailSmtpTransportOptions();
$smtpOptions->preferredAuthMethod = ezcMailSmtpTransport::AUTH_LOGIN;

$sender = new ezcMailSmtpTransport($host, $username, $password, $port,
                                   $smtpOptions);

$sender->send($message);
```

If you can't use the Zetacomponent `ezcMailComposer` class, you can use the built-in `mail()` function. The program `mail()` uses to send mail is specified in the `send mail_path` configuration variable in your *php.ini* file. If you're running Windows, set the SMTP variable to the hostname of your SMTP server. Your `From` address comes from the `sendmail_from` variable.

The first parameter to `mail()` is the recipient's email address, the second is the message subject, and the last is the message body. You can also add extra headers with an optional fourth parameter. For example, here's how to add `Reply-To` and `Organization` headers:

```
$to = 'adam@example.com';
$subject = 'New Version of PHP Released!';
$body = 'Go to http://www.php.net and download it today!';
$header = "Reply-To: webmaster@example.com\r\n"
         ."Organization: The PHP Group";

mail($to, $subject, $body, $header);
```

Separate each header with \r\n, but don't add \r\n following the last header.

Regardless of which method you choose, it's a good idea to write a wrapper function to assist you in sending mail. Forcing all your mail through this function makes it easy to add logging and other checks to every message sent:

```
function mail_wrapper($to, $subject, $body, $headers) {
    mail($to, $subject, $body, $headers);
    error_log("[MAIL][TO: $to]");
}
```

Here a message is written to the error log, recording the recipient of each message that's sent. This provides a timestamp that allows you to more easily track complaints that someone is trying to use the site to send spam. Another option is to create a list of *do not send* email addresses, which prevent those people from ever receiving another message from your site. You can also validate all recipient email addresses, which reduces the number of bounced messages.

See Also

Recipe 9.4 for validating email addresses; Recipe 16.2 for sending MIME email; Recipe 16.3 for more on retrieving mail; documentation on `mail()` (*http://www.php.net/mail*); the PEAR `Mail` class (*http://pear.php.net/package-info.php?package=Mail*); the `ezcMailComposer` class (*http://ezcomponents.org/docs/api/trunk/Mail/ezcMailComposer.html*); RFC 822 (*http://www.faqs.org/rfcs/rfc822.html*); *sendmail* by Bryan Costales with Eric Allman and *sendmail Desktop Reference* by Bryan Costales and Eric Allman (O'Reilly).

16.2 Sending MIME Mail

Problem

You want to send MIME email. For example, you want to send multipart messages with both plain text and HTML portions and have MIME-aware mail readers automatically display the correct portion.

Solution

Use Zetacomponent's `ezcMailComposer` class, specifying both a `plainText` and an `htmlText` property as follows:

```
$message = new ezcMailComposer();
$message->from = new ezcMailAddress('webmaster@example.com');
$message->addTo(new ezcMailAddress('adam@example.com', 'Adam'));
$message->subject = 'New Version of PHP Released!';
$body = 'Go to http://www.php.net and download it today!';
$message->plainText = $body;
$html = '<html><body><b>Hooray!</b> New PHP Version!</body></html>';
$message->htmlText = $html;
$message->build();

$sender = new ezcMailMtaTransport();
$sender->send($message);
```

Discussion

With the `htmlText` property specified, `ezcMailComposer` does all the hard work for you of constructing the appropriate headers and body delimiters so that mail readers interpret the e-mail message properly.

Including inline images is easy with `ezcMailComposer`. Just reference the appropriate local path in the `src` attribute of an `<img/>` tag:

```
$message = new ezcMailComposer();
$message->from = new ezcMailAddress('webmaster@example.com');
$message->addTo(new ezcMailAddress('adam@example.com', 'Adam'));
$message->subject = 'New Version of PHP Released!';
$body = 'Go to http://www.php.net and download it today!';
$message->plainText = $body;
$html = '<html>Me: <img src="file:///home/me/picture.png"/></html>';
$message->htmlText = $html;
$message->build();

$sender = new ezcMailMtaTransport();
$sender->send($message);
```

When you call `$message->build()`, `ezcMailComposer` looks for the file specified in the `<img/>` tag, includes its contents as an attachment to the message, and updates the HTML appropriately to reference the attachment.

To add an attachment to the message, such as a graphic or an archive, call `addFileAttachment()` or `addStringAttachment()`:

```
$message = new ezcMailComposer();
$message->from = new ezcMailAddress('webmaster@example.com');
$message->addTo(new ezcMailAddress('adam@example.com', 'Adam'));
$message->subject = 'New Version of PHP Released!';
$body = 'Go to http://www.php.net and download it today!';
$message->plainText = $body;
$message->addFileAttachment('/home/me/details.png','image','png');
$message->addStringAttachment('extra.txt','Some text', 'text/plain');

$message->build();

$sender = new ezcMailMtaTransport();
$sender->send($message);
```

See Also

Recipe 16.1 for sending regular email; Recipe 16.3 for more on retrieving mail; the Zetacomponent `ezcMailComposer` documentation (*http://ezcomponents.org/docs/api/ latest/Mail/ezcMailComposer.html*).

16.3 Reading Mail with IMAP or POP3

Problem

You want to read mail using IMAP or POP3, which allows you to create a web-based email client.

Solution

Use PHP's IMAP extension, which speaks both IMAP and POP3:

```
// open IMAP connection
$mail = imap_open('{mail.server.com:143}',        'username', 'password');
// or, open POP3 connection
$mail = imap_open('{mail.server.com:110/pop3}', 'username', 'password');

// grab a list of all the mail headers
$headers = imap_headers($mail);

// grab a header object for the last message in the mailbox
$last = imap_num_msg($mail);
$header = imap_header($mail, $last);

// grab the body for the same message
$body = imap_body($mail, $last);

// close the connection
imap_close($mail);
```

Discussion

The underlying library PHP uses to support IMAP and POP3 offers a seemingly unending number of features that allow you to essentially write an entire mail client. With all those features, however, comes complexity. In fact, there are currently 73 different functions in PHP beginning with the word imap, and that doesn't take into account that some also speak POP3 and NNTP.

However, the basics of talking with a mail server are straightforward. Like many features in PHP, you begin by opening the connection and grabbing a handle:

```
$mail = imap_open('{mail.server.com:143}', 'username', 'password');
```

This opens an IMAP connection to the server named *mail.server.com* on port 143. It also passes along a username and password as the second and third arguments.

To open a POP3 connection instead, append /pop3 to the end of the server and port. Because POP3 usually runs on port 110, add :110 after the server name:

```
$mail = imap_open('{mail.server.com:110/pop3}', 'username', 'password');
```

To encrypt your connection with SSL, add /ssl on to the end, just as you did with pop3. You also need to make sure your PHP installation is built with the --with-imap-ssl configuration option in addition to --with-imap. Also, you need to build the system IMAP library itself with SSL support. If you're using a self-signed certificate and wish to prevent an attempted validation, also add /novalidate-cert. Finally, most SSL connections talk on either port 993 or 995. All these options can come in any order, so the following is perfectly legal:

```
$mail = imap_open('{mail.server.com:993/novalidate-cert/pop3/ssl}',
                  'username', 'password');
```

Surrounding a variable with curly braces inside of a double-quoted string, such as {$var}, is a way to tell PHP exactly which variable to interpolate. Therefore, to use interpolated variables in this first parameter to imap_open(), escape the opening {:

```
$server = 'mail.server.com';
$port = 993;

$mail = imap_open("\{$server:$port}", 'username', 'password');
```

After you've opened a connection, you can ask the mail server a variety of questions. To get a listing of all the messages in your inbox, use imap_headers():

```
$headers = imap_headers($mail);
```

This returns an array in which each element is a formatted string corresponding to a message:

```
A   189) 5-Aug-2007 Beth Hondl            an invitation (1992 chars)
```

Alternatively, to retrieve a specific message, use imap_header() and imap_body() to pull the header object and body string:

```
$header = imap_header($message_number);
$body   = imap_body($message_number);
```

The imap_header() function returns an object with many fields. Useful ones include subject, fromaddress, and udate. All the fields are listed in Table 16-1.

Table 16-1. imap_header() fields from a server

Name	Description	Type	Example
date or Date	RFC 822–formatted date: date('r')	String	Fri, 16 Aug 2002 01:52:24 -0400
subject or Subject	Message subject	String	Re: PHP Cookbook Revisions
message_id	A unique ID identifying the message	String	<20030410020818.33915.php@news.example.com>
toaddress	The address the message was sent to	String	php-general@lists.php.net

Name	Description	Type	Example
to	Parsed version of toaddress field	Object	mailbox: 'php-general', host: 'lists-php.net'
fromaddress	The address that sent the message	String	Ralph Josephs <ralph@example.net>
from	Parsed version of fromad dress field	Object	personal: 'Ralph Josephs', mailbox: 'ralph', host: 'example.net'
reply_toad dress	The address you should reply to, if you're trying to contact the author	String	rjosephs@example.net
reply_to	Parsed version of reply_toad dress field	Object	Mailbox: 'rjosephs', host: 'example.net'
senderad dress	The person who sent the message; almost always identical to the from field, but if the from field doesn't uniquely identify who sent the message, this field does	String	Ralph Josephs <ralph@example.net>
sender	Parsed version of senderad dress field	Object	Personal: *Ralph Josephs*, mailbox: *ralph*, host: 'example.net'
Recent	If the message is recent, or new since the last time the user checked for mail	String	Y or N
Unseen	If the message is unseen	String	Y or " "
Flagged	If the message is marked	String	Y or " "
Answered	If a reply has been sent to this message	String	Y or " "
Deleted	If the message is deleted	String	Y or " "
Draft	If the message is a draft	String	Y or " "
Size	Size of the message in bytes	String	1345
udate	Unix timestamp of message date	Int	1013480645
Mesgno	The number of the message in the group	String	34943

The body element is just a string, but if the message is a multipart message, such as one that contains both an HTML and a plain-text version, $body holds both parts and the MIME lines describing them:

```
------=_Part_1046_3914492.1008372096119
Content-Type: text/plain; charset=us-ascii
Content-Transfer-Encoding: 7bit


Plain-Text Message

------=_Part_1046_3914492.1008372096119
Content-Type: text/html
Content-Transfer-Encoding: 7bit
```

```
<html>HTML Message</html>
------=_Part_1046_3914492.1008372096119--
```

To avoid this, use `imap_fetchstructure()` in combination with `imap_fetchbody()` to discover how the body is formatted and to extract just the parts you want:

```
// pull the plain text for message $n
$st = imap_fetchstructure($mail, $n);
if (!empty($st->parts)) {
    for ($i = 0, $j = count($st->parts); $i < $j; $i++) {
        $part = $st->parts[$i];
        if ($part->subtype == 'PLAIN') {
            $body = imap_fetchbody($mail, $n, $i+1);
        }
    }
} else {
    $body = imap_body($mail, $n);
}
```

If a message has multiple parts, `$st->parts` holds an array of objects describing them. The `part` property holds an integer describing the main body MIME type. Table 16-2 lists which numbers go with which MIME types. The `subtype` property holds the MIME subtype and tells if the part is `plain`, `html`, `png`, or another type, such as `octet-stream`.

Table 16-2. IMAP MIME type values

Number	MIME type	PHP constant	Description	Examples
0	text	TYPETEXT	Unformatted text	Plain text, HTML, XML
1	multipart	TYPEMULTIPART	Multipart message	Mixed, form data, signed
2	message	TYPEMESSAGE	Encapsulated message	News, HTTP
3	application	TYPEAPPLICATION	Application data	Octet stream, PDF, Zip
4	audio	TYPEAUDIO	Music file	MP3
5	image	TYPEIMAGE	Graphic image	GIF, JPEG, PNG
6	video	TYPEVIDEO	Video clip	MPEG, Quicktime
7	other	TYPEOTHER	Everything else	VRML models

See Also

Check out recipes 16.1 and 16.2 for more on sending mail; documentation on `imap_open()` (*http://bit.ly/1jcG0S7*), `imap_header()` (*http://bit.ly/T5fKSw*), `imap_body()` (*http://bit.ly/T5fLWz*), and IMAP in general (*http://www.php.net/imap*).

16.4 Getting and Putting Files with FTP

Problem

You want to transfer files using FTP.

Solution

Use PHP's built-in FTP functions:

```
$c = ftp_connect('ftp.example.com')      or die("Can't connect");
ftp_login($c, $username, $password)      or die("Can't login");
ftp_put($c, $remote, $local, FTP_ASCII) or die("Can't transfer");
ftp_close($c)                            or die("Can't close");
```

You can also use the cURL extension:

```
$c = curl_init("ftp://$username:$password@ftp.example.com/$remote");
// $local is the location to store file on local machine
$fh = fopen($local, 'w') or die($php_errormsg);
curl_setopt($c, CURLOPT_FILE, $fh);
curl_exec($c);
curl_close($c);
```

Discussion

FTP is a method of exchanging files between one computer and another. Unlike with HTTP servers, it's easy to set up an FTP server to both send and receive files.

Using the built-in FTP functions doesn't require additional libraries, but you must specifically enable them with --enable-ftp. Because these functions are specialized to FTP, they're simple to use when transferring files.

All FTP transactions begin with establishing a connection from your computer, the local client, to another computer, the remote server:

```
$c = ftp_connect('ftp.example.com')      or die("Can't connect");
```

Once connected, you need to send your username and password; the remote server can then authenticate you and allow you to enter:

```
ftp_login($c, $username, $password)      or die("Can't login");
```

Some FTP servers support a feature known as anonymous FTP. Under anonymous FTP, users can log in without an account on the remote system. When you use anonymous FTP, your username is anonymous, and your password is your email address.

Here's how to transfer files with ftp_put() and ftp_get():

```
ftp_put($c, $remote, $local,  FTP_ASCII) or die("Can't transfer");
ftp_get($c, $local,  $remote, FTP_ASCII) or die("Can't transfer");
```

The ftp_put() function takes a file on your computer and copies it to the remote server; ftp_get() copies a file on the remote server to your computer. In the previous code, $remote is the pathname to the remote file, and $local points at the file on your computer.

There are two final parameters passed to these functions. The FTP_ASCII parameter, used here, transfers the file as if it were ASCII text. Under this option, line-feed endings are automatically converted as you move from one operating system to another. The other option is FTP_BINARY, which is used for nonplain-text files, so no line-feed conversions take place.

Use ftp_fget() and ftp_fput() to download or upload a file to an existing open file pointer (opened using fopen()) instead of to a location on the filesystem. For example, here's how to retrieve a file and write it to the existing file pointer, $fp:

```
$fp = fopen($file, 'w');
ftp_fget($c, $fp, $remote, FTP_ASCII)   or die("Can't transfer");
```

Finally, to disconnect from the remote host, call ftp_close() to log out:

```
ftp_close($c)                           or die("Can't close");
```

To adjust the amount of seconds the connection takes to time out, use ftp_set_option():

```
// Up the time out value to two minutes:
set_time_limit(120);
$c = ftp_connect('ftp.example.com');
ftp_set_option($c, FTP_TIMEOUT_SEC, 120);
```

The default value is 90 seconds; however, the default max_execution_time of a PHP script is 30 seconds. So if your connection times out too early, be sure to check both values.

To use the cURL extension, you must download cURL (*http://curl.haxx.se/*) and set the --with-curl configuration option when building PHP. To use cURL, start by creating a cURL handle with curl_init(), and then specify what you want to do using curl_setopt(). The curl_setopt() function takes three parameters: a cURL resource, the name of a cURL constant to modify, and a value to assign to the second parameter. In the Solution, the CURLOPT_FILE constant is used:

```
$c = curl_init("ftp://$username:$password@ftp.example.com/$remote");
// $local is the location to store file on local client
$fh = fopen($local, 'w') or die($php_errormsg);
curl_setopt($c, CURLOPT_FILE, $fh);
curl_exec($c);
curl_close($c);
```

You pass the URL to use to curl_init(). Because the URL begins with ftp://, cURL knows to use the FTP protocol. Instead of a separate call to log on to the remote server, you embed the username and password directly into the URL. Next, you set the location to store the file on your server. Now you open a file named `$local` for writing and pass the filehandle to `curl_setopt()` as the value for `CURLOPT_FILE`. When cURL transfers the file, it automatically writes to the filehandle. Once everything is configured, you call `curl_exec()` to initiate the transaction and then `curl_close()` to close the connection.

See Also

Documentation on the FTP extension (*http://www.php.net/ftp*) and cURL (*http://www.php.net/curl*); RFC 959 (*http://www.faqs.org/rfcs/rfc969.html*).

16.5 Looking Up Addresses with LDAP

Problem

You want to query an LDAP server for address information.

Solution

Use PHP's LDAP extension:

```
$ds = ldap_connect('ldap.example.com')              or die($php_errormsg);
ldap_bind($ds)                                      or die($php_errormsg);
$sr = ldap_search($ds, 'o=Example Inc., c=US', 'sn=*') or die($php_errormsg);
$e  = ldap_get_entries($ds, $sr)                    or die($php_errormsg);

for ($i=0; $i < $e['count']; $i++) {
    echo $info[$i]['cn'][0] . ' (' . $info[$i]['mail'][0] . ')<br>';
}

ldap_close($ds)                                     or die($php_errormsg);
```

Discussion

An LDAP (Lightweight Directory Access Protocol) server stores directory information, such as names and addresses, and allows you to query it for results. In many ways, it's like a database, except that it's optimized for storing information about people.

In addition, instead of the flat structure provided by a database, an LDAP server allows you to organize people in a hierarchical fashion. For example, employees may be divided into marketing, technical, and operations divisions, or they can be split regionally into North America, Europe, and Asia. This makes it easy to find all employees of a particular subset of a company.

When using LDAP, the address repository is called as a data source. Each entry in the repository has a globally unique identifier, known as a distinguished name. The distinguished name includes both a person's name and the company information. For instance, John Q. Smith, who works at Example Inc., a U.S. company, has a distinguished name of cn=John Q. Smith, o=Example Inc., c=US. In LDAP, cn stands for common name, o for organization, and c for country.

You must enable PHP's LDAP support with --with-ldap. You can download an LDAP server (*http://www.openldap.org*). This recipe assumes basic knowledge about LDAP.

Communicating with an LDAP server requires four steps: connecting, authenticating, searching records, and logging off. Besides searching, you can also add, alter, and delete records.

The opening transactions require you to connect to a specific LDAP server and then authenticate yourself in a process known as binding:

```
$ds = ldap_connect('ldap.example.com')           or die($php_errormsg);
ldap_bind($ds)                                    or die($php_errormsg);
```

Passing only the connection handle, $ds, to ldap_bind() does an anonymous bind. To bind with a specific username and password, pass them as the second and third parameters, like so:

```
ldap_bind($ds, $username, $password)              or die($php_errormsg);
```

When you are logged in, you can request information. Because the information is arranged in a hierarchy, you need to indicate the base distinguished name as the second parameter. Finally, you pass in the search criteria. For example, here's how to find all people with a surname of Jones at company Example Inc. located in the country US:

```
$sr = ldap_search($ds, 'o=Example Inc.', c=US', 'sn=Jones') or die($php_errormsg);
$e  = ldap_get_entries($ds, $sr)                  or die($php_errormsg);
```

After ldap_search() returns results, use ldap_get_entries() to retrieve the specific data records. Then iterate through the array of entries, $e:

```
for ($i=0; $i < $e['count']; $i++) {
    echo $e[$i]['cn'][0] . ' (' . $e[$i]['mail'][0] . ')<br>';
}
```

Instead of doing count($e), use the precomputed record size located in $e['count']. Inside the loop, print the first common name and email address for each record. For example:

```
David Sklar (sklar@example.com)
Adam Trachtenberg (adam@example.com)
```

The ldap_search() function searches the entire tree equal to and below the distinguished name base. To restrict the results to a specific level, use ldap_list(). Because the search takes place over a smaller set of records, ldap_list() can be significantly faster than ldap_search().

See Also

Recipe 16.6 for authenticating users with LDAP; documentation on LDAP (*http://www.php.net/ldap*); RFC 2251 (*http://www.faqs.org/rfcs/rfc2251.html*).

16.6 Using LDAP for User Authentication

Problem

You want to restrict parts of your site to authenticated users. Instead of verifying people against a database or using HTTP Basic Authorization, you want to use an LDAP server. Holding all user information in an LDAP server makes centralized user administration easier.

Solution

Use PEAR's Auth class, which supports LDAP authentication:

```
$options = array('host'      => 'ldap.example.com',
                 'port'      => '389',
                 'base'      => 'o=Example Inc., c=US',
                 'userattr' => 'uid');

$auth = new Auth('LDAP', $options);

// begin validation
// print login screen for anonymous users
$auth->start();

if ($auth->getAuth()) {
    // content for validated users
} else {
    // content for anonymous users
}

// log users out
$auth->logout();
```

Discussion

LDAP servers are designed for address storage, lookup, and retrieval, and so are better to use than standard databases like MySQL or Oracle. LDAP servers are very fast, you can easily implement access control by granting different permissions to different groups of users, and many different programs can query the server. For example, most email clients can use an LDAP server as an address book, so if you address a message to "John Smith," the server replies with John's email address, *jsmith@example.com.*

PEAR's Auth class allows you to validate users against files, databases, and LDAP servers. The first parameter is the type of authentication to use, and the second is an array of information on how to validate users. For example:

```
$options = array('host'     => 'ldap.example.com',
                 'port'     => '389',
                 'base'     => 'o=Example Inc., c=US',
                 'userattr' => 'uid');

$auth = new Auth('LDAP', $options);
```

This creates a new Auth object that validates against an LDAP server located at *ldap.example.com* and communicates over port 389. The base directory name is o=Example Inc., c=US, and usernames are checked against the uid attribute. The uid field stands for user identifier. This is normally a username for a website or a login name for a general account. If your server doesn't store uid attributes for each user, you can substitute the cn attribute. The common name field holds a user's full name, such as "John Q. Smith."

The Auth::auth() method also takes an optional third parameter—the name of a function that displays the sign-in form. This form can be formatted however you wish; the only requirement is that the form input fields must be called username and password. Also, the form must submit the data using POST:

```
$options = array('host'     => 'ldap.example.com',
                 'port'     => '389',
                 'base'     => 'o=Example Inc., c=US',
                 'userattr' => 'uid');

function pc_auth_ldap_signin() {
    $action = htmlentities($_SERVER['PHP_SELF']);
    print<<<_HTML_
<form method="post" action="$action">
Name: <input name="username" type="text"><br />
Password: <input name="password" type="password"><br />
<input type="submit" value="Sign In">
</form>
_HTML_;
}

$auth = new Auth('LDAP', $options, 'pc_auth_ldap_signin');
```

Once the Auth object is instantiated, authenticate a user by calling Auth::start():

```
$auth->start();
```

If the user is already signed in, nothing happens. If the user is anonymous, the sign-in form is printed. To validate a user, Auth::start() connects to the LDAP server, does an anonymous bind, and searches for an address in which the user attribute specified in the constructor matches the username passed in by the form:

```
$options['userattr'] = $_POST['username'];
```

If Auth::start() finds exactly one person that fits this criterion, it retrieves the designated name for the user, and attempts to do an authenticated bind, using the designated name and password from the form as the login credentials. The LDAP server then compares the password to the userPassword attribute associated with the designated name. If it matches, the user is authenticated.

You can call Auth::getAuth() to return a boolean value describing a user's status:

```
if ($auth->getAuth()) {
    print 'Welcome member! Nice to see you again.';
} else {
    print 'Welcome guest. First time visiting?';
}
```

The Auth class uses the built-in session module to track users, so once validated, a person remains authenticated until the session expires, or you explicitly log him out with:

```
$auth->logout();
```

See Also

Recipe 16.5 for searching LDAP servers; PEAR's Auth class (*http://pear.php.net/package-info.php?package=Auth*).

16.7 Performing DNS Lookups

Problem

You want to look up a domain name or an IP address.

Solution

Use gethostbyname() and gethostbyaddr():

```
$ip   = gethostbyname('www.example.com'); // 93.184.216.119
$host = gethostbyaddr('93.184.216.119'); // www.example.com
```

Discussion

You can generally trust the address returned by gethostbyname(), but you can't trust the name returned by gethostbyaddr(). A DNS server with authority for a particular IP address can return any hostname at all. Usually, administrators set up DNS servers to reply with a correct hostname, but a malicious user may configure her DNS server to reply with incorrect hostnames. One way to combat this trickery is to call gethostbyname() on the hostname returned from gethostbyaddr() and make sure the name resolves to the original IP address.

If either function can't successfully look up the IP address or the domain name, it doesn't return `false`, but instead returns the argument passed to it. To check for failure, do this:

```
$host = 'this is not a good host name!';
if ($host == ($ip = gethostbyname($host))) {
    // failure
}
```

This assigns the return value of `gethostbyname()` to `$ip` and also checks that `$ip` is not equal to the original `$host`.

Sometimes a single hostname can map to multiple IP addresses. To find all hosts, use `gethostbynamel()`:

```
$hosts = gethostbynamel('www.yahoo.com');
print_r($hosts);
```

This prints something like the following (the specific IP addresses may vary based on your location):

```
Array
(
    [0] => 98.139.183.24
    [1] => 98.139.180.149
)
```

In contrast to `gethostbyname()` and `gethostbyaddr()`, `gethostbynamel()` returns an array, not a string.

You can also do more complicated DNS-related tasks. For instance, you can get the MX records using `getmxrr()`:

```
getmxrr('yahoo.com', $hosts, $weight);
for ($i = 0; $i < count($hosts); $i++) {
    echo "$weight[$i] $hosts[$i]\n";
}
```

This prints:

Whereas `gethostbyname()` retrieves IPv4 A records, and `getmxrr()` retrieves MX records, the `dns_get_record()` function retrieves whichever type of DNS record you specify. This is useful, for example, to retrieve IPv6 AAAA records, as follows:

```
$addrs = dns_get_record('www.yahoo.com', DNS_AAAA);
print_r($addrs);
```

This prints something like the following (again, the specifics will vary based on your location):

```
Array
(
    [0] => Array
        (
```

```
            [host] => ds-any-fp3-real.wa1.b.yahoo.com
            [type] => AAAA
            [ipv6] => 2001:4998:f00b:1fe::3001
            [class] => IN
            [ttl] => 34
        )

    [1] => Array
        (
            [host] => ds-any-fp3-real.wa1.b.yahoo.com
            [type] => AAAA
            [ipv6] => 2001:4998:f00d:1fe::3001
            [class] => IN
            [ttl] => 34
        )

    [2] => Array
        (
            [host] => ds-any-fp3-real.wa1.b.yahoo.com
            [type] => AAAA
            [ipv6] => 2001:4998:f00d:1fe::3000
            [class] => IN
            [ttl] => 34
        )

    [3] => Array
        (
            [host] => ds-any-fp3-real.wa1.b.yahoo.com
            [type] => AAAA
            [ipv6] => 2001:4998:f00b:1fe::3000
            [class] => IN
            [ttl] => 34
        )

)
```

Each element of the returned array is a subarray containing information about the record type, hostname, IPv6 address, record class, and the TTL—how long the record is cacheable for.

Read the manual page for `dns_get_record()` to learn how to indicate which type of DNS record you are interested in.

To perform zone transfers, dynamic DNS updates, and more, see PEAR's `Net_DNS2` package.

See Also

Documentation on `gethostbyname()` (*http://bit.ly/1sFgMoV*), `gethostbyaddr()` (*http://bit.ly/UJZE2g*), `gethostbynamel()` (*http://bit.ly/1jOEeGS*), `getmxrr()` (*http://*

---

bit.ly/UJZI1S), and `dns_get_record()` (*http://bit.ly/1lpOJF3*); PEAR's `Net_DNS2` package (*http://bit.ly/TjyZI8*); *DNS and BIND* by Paul Albitz and Cricket Liu (O'Reilly).

16.8 Checking If a Host Is Alive

Problem

You want to ping a host to see if it is still up and accessible from your location.

Solution

Use PEAR's `Net_Ping` package:

```
require 'Net/Ping.php';

$ping = Net_Ping::factory();
if ($ping->checkHost('www.oreilly.com')) {
    print 'Reachable';
} else {
    print 'Unreachable';
}

$data = $ping->ping('www.oreilly.com');
```

Discussion

The *ping* program tries to send a message from your machine to another. If everything goes well, you get a series of statistics chronicling the transaction. An error means that *ping* can't reach the host for some reason.

On error, `Net_Ping::checkhost()` returns `false`, and `Net_Ping::ping()` returns the constant `PING_HOST_NOT_FOUND`. If there's a problem running the *ping* program (because `Net_Ping` is really just a wrapper for the program), `PING_FAILED` is returned.

If everything is okay, you receive a `Net_Ping_Result` object. This object has assorted methods allowing you to retrieve the information about the ping operation. For example:

```
require 'Net/Ping.php';
$ping = Net_Ping::factory();

$result = $ping->ping('www.oreilly.com');
print<<<_INFO_
Ping of www.oreilly.com ({$result->getTargetIp()})
with {$result->getTransmitted()} requests had
a minimum time of {$result->getMin()} ms and
a maximum time of {$result->getMax()} ms.
_INFO_
;
```

This prints something like:

```
Ping of www.oreilly.com (23.67.61.152)
with 3 requests had
a minimum time of 35.4 ms and
a maximum time of 40.586 ms.
```

The `Net_Ping::setArgs()` method lets you change a few things about how the `ping` program is run. For example, you can call `$ping->setArgs(array('count' => 7))` to tell `Net_Ping` to send seven ping packets instead of the default (usually three or four).

See Also

PEAR's `Net_Ping` package (*http://pear.php.net/package-info.php?package=Net_Ping*).

16.9 Getting Information About a Domain Name

Problem

You want to look up contact information or other details about a domain name.

Solution

Use PEAR's `Net_Whois` class:

```
require 'Net/Whois.php';
$server = 'whois.godaddy.com';
$query = 'oreilly.com';

$whois = new Net_Whois();
$data = $whois->query($query, $server);
```

Discussion

The `Net_Whois::query()` method returns a large text string whose contents reinforce how hard it can be to parse different Whois results. For example, the code in the Solution puts 55 lines of information in `$data`, beginning with:

```
Domain Name: OREILLY.COM
Registrar URL: http://www.godaddy.com
Updated Date: 2013-04-22 17:52:42
Creation Date: 1997-05-26 23:00:00
Registrar Expiration Date: 2014-05-25 23:00:00
Registrar: GoDaddy.com, LLC
Registrant Name: O'Reilly Media, Inc.
Registrant Organization: O'Reilly Media, Inc.
Registrant Street: 1005 Gravenstein Highway North
Registrant City: Sebastopol
Registrant State/Province: California
```

```
Registrant Postal Code: 95472
Registrant Country: United States
Admin Name: Admin Contact
Admin Organization: O'Reilly Media, Inc.
Admin Street: 1005 Gravenstein Highway North
Admin City: Sebastopol
Admin State/Province: California
Admin Postal Code: 95472
Admin Country: United States
Admin Phone: +1.7078277000
Admin Fax: +1.7078290104
Admin Email: nic-ac@oreilly.com
Tech Name: Tech Contact
Tech Organization: O'Reilly Media, Inc.
Tech Street: 1005 Gravenstein Highway North
Tech City: Sebastopol
Tech State/Province: California
Tech Postal Code: 95472
Tech Country: United States
Tech Phone: +1.7078277000
Tech Fax: +1.7078290104
Tech Email: nic-tc@oreilly.com
Name Server: NSAUTHA.OREILLY.COM
Name Server: NSAUTHB.OREILLY.COM


The data contained in GoDaddy.com, LLC's WhoIs database,
while believed by the company to be reliable, is provided "as is"
with no guarantee or warranties regarding its accuracy.  This
information is provided for the sole purpose of assisting you
in obtaining information about domain name registration records.
Any use of this data for any other purpose is expressly forbidden without the
prior written permission of GoDaddy.com, LLC.  By submitting an inquiry,
you agree to these terms of usage and limitations of warranty.  In particular,
you agree not to use this data to allow, enable, or otherwise make possible,
dissemination or collection of this data, in part or in its entirety, for any
purpose, such as the transmission of unsolicited advertising and
and solicitations of any kind, including spam.  You further agree
not to use this data to enable high volume, automated or robotic electronic
processes designed to collect or compile this data for any purpose,
including mining this data for your own personal or commercial purposes.


Please note: the registrant of the domain name is specified
in the "registrant" section.  In most cases, GoDaddy.com, LLC
is not the registrant of domain names listed in this database.
```

Different domains use different Whois servers. And different Whois servers return differently formatted results. To find the correct Whois server for a domain, start by querying against whois.iana.org. That server's output will contain a line beginning with whois: which indicates the right server to use for the top-level domain of the particular domain you're interested in. And then you can query *that* server for the specific details of the domain:

```
require 'Net/Whois.php';
$query  = 'oreilly.com';

$iana_server = 'whois.iana.org';

$whois = new Net_Whois();
$iana_data = $whois->query($query, $iana_server);
preg_match('/^whois:\s+(.+)$/m', $iana_data, $matches);
$tld_whois_server = $matches[1];

$tld_data = $whois->query($query, $tld_whois_server);

print $tld_data;
```

And then depending on the details of the domain, you may have to query an additional
server. For example, the second query in the preceding code returns that whois.godad
dy.com is the authoritative Whois server for oreilly.com.

See Also

PEAR's Net_Whois class (*http://bit.ly/1mqwdN6*).

CHAPTER 17

Graphics

17.0 Introduction

With the assistance of the GD library, you can use PHP to create applications that use dynamic images to display stock quotes, reveal poll results, monitor system performance, and even create games. However, it's not like using Photoshop or GIMP; you can't draw a line by moving your mouse. Instead, you need to precisely specify a shape's type, size, and position.

GD has an existing API, and PHP tries to follows its syntax and function-naming conventions. So if you're familiar with GD from other languages, such as C or Perl, you can easily use GD with PHP. If GD is new to you, it may take a few minutes to figure it out, but soon you'll be drawing like Picasso.

The feature set of GD varies greatly depending on which version of GD you're running and which features were enabled during configuration. GD can support GIFs, JPEGs, PNGs, and WBMPs. GD reads in PNGs and JPEGs with almost no loss in quality. Also, GD supports PNG alpha channels, which allow you to specify a transparency level for each pixel.

Besides supporting multiple file formats, GD lets you draw pixels, lines, rectangles, polygons, arcs, ellipses, and circles in any color you want. Recipe 17.1 covers straight shapes, and Recipe 17.2 covers the curved ones. To fill shapes with a pattern instead of a solid color, see Recipe 17.3.

You can also draw text using a variety of font types, including built-in and TrueType fonts. Recipe 17.4 shows the ins and outs of the three main text-drawing functions, and Recipe 17.5 shows how to center text within a canvas. These two recipes form the basis for Recipe 17.6, which combines an image template with real-time data to create dynamic images. GD also lets you make transparent GIFs and PNGs. Setting a color as transparent and using transparencies in patterns are discussed in Recipe 17.7.

Beyond creating new images, you can work with existing images. For example, add a watermark to identify yourself by overlaying text or an image on top of the picture. This is the subject of Recipe 17.8. Generating thumbnail images is covered in Recipe 17.9, which shows how to create scaled-down versions of larger images. To extract image metadata from digital photos and other images that store information using the EXIF standard, read Recipe 17.10.

Recipe 17.11 moves away from GD and shows how to securely serve images by restricting user access. Last, there's an example application taking poll results and producing a dynamic bar graph showing what percentage of users voted for each answer.

GD is bundled with PHP. The GD section of the online PHP Manual (*http://www.php.net/image*) also lists the location of the additional libraries necessary to provide support for additional graphics formats, such as JPEG and PNG, and fonts, such as TrueType.

There are two easy ways to see which version, if any, of GD is installed on your server and how it's configured. One way is to call `phpinfo()`. You should see `--with-gd` at the top under *Configure Command*; further down the page there is also a section titled *gd* that has more information about which version of GD is installed and what features are enabled. The other option is to check the return value of `function_exists('image create')`. If it returns `true`, GD is installed. The `imagetypes()` function returns a bit field indicating which graphics formats are available. See PHP's website (*http://www.php.net/imagetypes*) for more on how to use this function. If you want to use a feature that isn't enabled, you need to rebuild PHP yourself or get your ISP to do so.

The basic image-generation process has three steps: creating the image, adding graphics and text to the canvas, and displaying or saving the image. For example:

```
$image = ImageCreateTrueColor(200, 50); // defaults to black

// color the background grey
$grey = 0xCCCCCC;
ImageFilledRectangle($image, 0, 0, 200 - 1, 50 - 1, $grey);

// draw a white rectangle on top
$white = 0xFFFFFF;
ImageFilledRectangle($image, 50, 10, 150, 40, $white);

// send it as PNG
header('Content-type: image/png');
ImagePNG($image);
ImageDestroy($image);
```

The output of this code, which prints a white rectangle on a grey background, is shown in Figure 17-1.

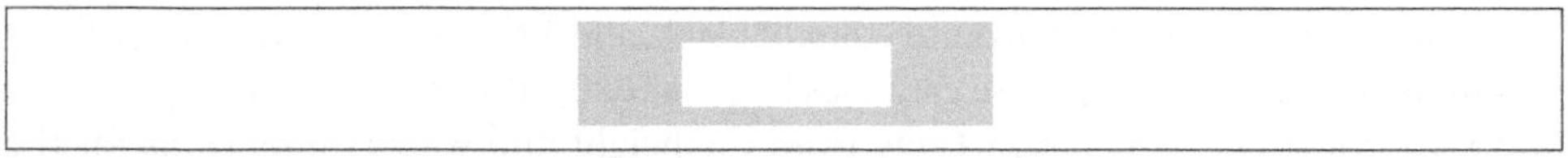

Figure 17-1. A white rectangle on a grey background

To begin, you create an image canvas. The `ImageCreateTrueColor()` function doesn't return an actual image. Instead, it provides you with a handle to an image; it's not an actual graphic until you specifically tell PHP to write the image out. Using `ImageCreateTrueColor()`, you can juggle multiple images at the same time.

The parameters passed to `ImageCreateTrueColor()` are the width and height of the graphic in pixels. In this case, it's 200 pixels across and 50 pixels high. The default background color for new canvases is black.

In addition to creating a new image, you can also edit existing images. To open a graphic, call `ImageCreateFromPNG()` or a similarly named function (such as `ImageCreateFromGIF()`, `ImageCreateFromJPEG()`, `ImageCreateFromWBMP()`, …) to open a different file format. The filename is the only argument, and files can live locally or on remote servers:

```
// open a PNG from the local machine
$graph = ImageCreateFromPNG('/path/to/graph.png');

// open a JPEG from a remote server
$icon  = ImageCreateFromJPEG('http://www.example.com/images/icon.jpeg');
```

Call `ImageFilledRectangle()` to place a box onto the canvas. `ImageFilledRectangle()` takes many parameters: the image to draw on, the *x* and *y* coordinates of the upper-left corner of the rectangle, the *x* and *y* coordinates of the lower-right corner of the rectangle, and finally, the color to use to draw the shape.

The color is a number representing its RGB values, similar to how you do it with HTML and CSS. For example, the HTML hex code for white is #FFFFFF. In PHP, you write this in hex as 0xFFFFFF (or you can use the decimal value, which is 16777215).

Another option is to use the `ImageAllocate()` function, which takes a canvas, and the red, green, and blue values:

```
$color = ImageAllocate($image, $r, $g, $b);

// For example, white
$white = ImageAllocate($image, 0xFF, 0xFF, 0xFF); // hex
$white = ImageAllocate($image,  255,  255,  255); // decimal

// Or...
$grey = ImageColorAllocate($image, 204, 204, 204);
$orange = ImageColorAllocate($image, 0xE9, 0x52, 0x22);
```

To paint over the default background color of black, allocate a color and then put a filled rectangle on the canvas. Because canvases begin at (0,0), use those for the first set of *x* and *y* coordinates. Then subtract one from the height and width dimensions for the second set of *x* and *y* coordinates:

```
// color the background grey
$grey = 0xCCCCCC;
ImageFilledRectangle($image, 0, 0, 200 - 1, 50 - 1, $grey);
```

Then you can begin drawing other items. For example, to draw a rectangle on $image, starting at (50,10) and going to (150,40), in the color white:

```
// draw a white rectangle on top
$white = 0xFFFFFF;
ImageFilledRectangle($image, 50, 10, 150, 40, $white);
```

Unlike what you might expect, (0,0) is in the upper-left corner. Therefore, as you move down the canvas, the coordinates become larger. For example, in a 50-pixel-high canvas, the vertical coordinate of a spot 10 pixels from the top of canvas is 10. It's neither 40 nor −10.

Now that the image is all ready to go, you can serve it up. First, send a Content-Type header to let the browser know what type of image you're sending. In this case, display a PNG. Next, have PHP write the PNG image out using ImagePNG():

```
header('Content-type: image/png');
ImagePNG($image);
```

To write the image to disk instead of sending it to the browser, provide a second argument to ImagePNG() with where to save the file:

```
ImagePNG($image, '/path/to/your/new/image.png');
```

Because the file isn't going to the browser, there's no need to call header(). Make sure to specify a path and an image name, and be sure PHP has permission to write to that location.

PHP cleans up the image when the script ends, but to manually deallocate the memory used by the image, call ImageDestroy($image) and PHP immediately gets rid of it:

```
ImageDestroy($image);
```

17.1 Drawing Lines, Rectangles, and Polygons

Problem

You want to draw a line, rectangle, or polygon. You also want to be able to control if the rectangle or polygon is open or filled in. For example, you want to be able to draw bar charts or create graphs of stock quotes.

Solution

To draw a line, use `ImageLine()`:

```
$width = 200;
$height = 50;
$image = ImageCreateTrueColor($width, $height);

$background_color = 0xFFFFFF; // white
ImageFilledRectangle($image, 0, 0, $width - 1, $height - 1, $background_color);

$x1 = $y1 = 0 ; // 0
$x2 = $y2 = $height - 1; // 49
$color = 0xCCCCCC; // gray

ImageLine($image, $x1, $y1, $x2, $y2, $color);

header('Content-type: image/png');
ImagePNG($image);
ImageDestroy($image);
```

To draw an open rectangle, use `ImageRectangle()`:

```
ImageRectangle($image, $x1, $y1, $x2, $y2, $color);
```

To draw a solid rectangle, use `ImageFilledRectangle()`:

```
ImageFilledRectangle($image, $x1, $y1, $x2, $y2, $color);
```

To draw an open polygon, use `ImagePolygon()`:

```
$points = array($x1, $y1, $x2, $y2, $x3, $y3);
ImagePolygon($image, $points, count($points)/2, $color);
```

To draw a filled polygon, use `ImageFilledPolygon()`:

```
$points = array($x1, $y1, $x2, $y2, $x3, $y3);
ImageFilledPolygon($image, $points, count($points)/2, $color);
```

Discussion

The prototypes for all five functions in the Solution are similar. The first parameter is the canvas to draw on. The next set of parameters are the x and y coordinates to specify where GD should draw the shape. In `ImageLine()`, the four coordinates are the endpoints of the line, and in `ImageRectangle()`, they're the opposite corners of the rectangle. For example, `ImageLine($image, 0, 0, 100, 100, $color)` produces a diagonal line. Passing the same parameters to `ImageRectangle()` produces a rectangle with corners at (0,0), (100,0), (0,100), and (100,100). Both shapes are shown in Figure 17-2.

Figure 17-2. A diagonal line and a square

The ImagePolygon() function is slightly different because it can accept a variable number of vertices. Therefore, the second parameter is an array of *x* and *y* coordinates. The function starts at the first set of points and draws lines from vertex to vertex before finally completing the figure by connecting back to the original point. You must have a minimum of three vertices in your polygon (for a total of six elements in the array). The third parameter is the number of vertices in the shape; since that's always half of the number of elements in the array of points, a flexible value for this is count($points) / 2 because it allows you to update the array of vertices without breaking the call to ImageLine().

For example, to draw a right triangle, this generates the image in Figure 17-3:

```
$size = 50;
$image = ImageCreateTrueColor($size, $size);

$background_color = 0xFFFFFF // white
ImageFilledRectangle($image, 0, 0, $size - 1, $size - 1, $background_color);

// three points for right triangle
$x1 = $y1 = 0 ;          // ( 0, 0)
$x2 = $y2 = $size - 1;   // (49,49)
$x3 = 0; $y3 = $size - 1; // ( 0,49)

$gray = 0xCCCCCC; // gray

$points = array($x1, $y1, $x2, $y2, $x3, $y3);
ImagePolygon($image, $points, count($points)/2, $gray);

header('Content-type: image/png');
ImagePNG($image);
ImageDestroy($image);
```

Figure 17-3. A right triangle

Last, all the functions take a final parameter that specifies the drawing color. This is usually a color value (e.g., 0xCCCCCC), but can also be the constants IMG_COL OR_STYLED or IMG_COLOR_STYLEDBRUSHED, if you want to draw nonsolid lines, as discussed in Recipe 17.3.

These functions all draw open shapes. To get GD to fill the region with the drawing color, use ImageFilledRectangle() and ImageFilledPolygon() with the identical set of arguments as their unfilled cousins.

See Also

Recipe 17.2 for more on drawing other types of shapes; Recipe 17.3 for more on drawing with styles and brushes; documentation on ImageLine() (*http://www.php.net/image line*), ImageRectangle() (*http://www.php.net/imagerectangle*), and ImagePolygon() (*http://www.php.net/imagepolygon*).

17.2 Drawing Arcs, Ellipses, and Circles

Problem

You want to draw open or filled curves. For example, you want to draw a pie chart showing the results of a user poll.

Solution

To draw an arc, use ImageArc():

```
ImageArc($image, $x, $y, $width, $height, $start, $end, $color);
```

To draw an ellipse, use ImageEllipse():

```
ImageEllipse($image, $x, $y, $width, $height, $color);
```

To draw a circle, use ImageEllipse(), and use the same value for both $width and $height:

```
ImageEllipse($image, $x, $y, $diameter, $diameter, $color);
```

Discussion

Because the ImageArc() function is highly flexible, you can create many types of curves. Like many GD functions, the first parameter is the canvas. The next two parameters are the *x* and *y* coordinates for the center position of the arc. After that comes the arc width and height.

The sixth and seventh parameters are the starting and ending angles, in degrees. A value of 0 is at three o'clock. The arc then moves clockwise, so 90 is at six o'clock, 180 is at nine o'clock, and 270 is at the top of the hour. (Be careful—this behavior is not consistent among all GD functions. For example, when you rotate text, you turn in a counter-clockwise direction.) Because the arc's center is located at ($x,$y), if you draw a sem-

icircle from 0 to 180, it doesn't start at ($x,$y); instead, it begins at ($x+
($diameter/2),$y).

As usual, the last parameter is the arc color.

The ImageEllipse() function is similar ImageArc(), except that the starting and ending
angles are omitted because they're hardcoded to 0 and 360. Because a circle is an ellipse
with the same width and height, to draw a circle, set both numbers to the diameter of
the circle.

For example, this draws an open black circle with a diameter of 100 pixels centered on
the canvas, as shown in the left half of Figure 17-4:

```
$size = 100;
$image = ImageCreateTrueColor($size, $size);

$background_color = 0xFFFFFF; // white
ImageFilledRectangle($image, 0, 0, $size - 1, $size - 1, $background_color);

$black = 0x000000;
ImageEllipse($image, $size / 2, $size / 2, $size - 1, $size - 1, $black);
```

To produce a solid ellipse or circle, call ImageFilledEllipse():

```
ImageFilledEllipse($image, $size / 2, $size / 2, $size - 1, $size - 1, $black);
```

The output is shown in the right half of Figure 17-4.

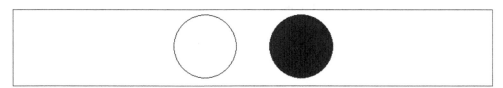

Figure 17-4. An open black circle and a filled black circle

There is also an ImageFilledArc() function. It takes an additional final parameter that
describes the fill style. Use IMG_ARC_CHORD to connect the start and end points of the arc
with a straight line or IMG_ARC_PIE to only draw the arc itself. To avoid filling the arc,
use IMG_ARC_NOFILL. These can be bitwise ored together in a variety of combinations
to create pie wedges and other interesting shapes. For example:

```
$styles = [IMG_ARC_PIE,
           IMG_ARC_CHORD,
           IMG_ARC_PIE | IMG_ARC_NOFILL,
           IMG_ARC_PIE | IMG_ARC_NOFILL | IMG_ARC_EDGED];

$size = 100;
$image = ImageCreateTrueColor($size * count($styles), $size);
```

```
$background_color = 0xFFFFFF; // white
ImageFilledRectangle($image, 0, 0,
    $size * count($styles) - 1, $size * count($styles) - 1, $background_color);

$black = 0x000000; // aka 0

for ($i = 0; $i < count($styles); $i++) {
    ImageFilledArc($image, $size / 2 + $i * $size, $size / 2,
        $size - 1, $size - 1, 0, 135, $black, $styles[$i]);
}

header('Content-type: image/png');
ImagePNG($image);
ImageDestroy($image);
```

This generates the shapes in Figure 17-5.

Figure 17-5. An assortment of pie wedges

See Also

Recipe 17.2 for more on drawing other types of shapes; documentation on Image
Arc() (*http://www.php.net/imagearc*), ImageFilledArc() (*http://www.php.net/image
filledarc*), ImageEllipse() (*http://www.php.net/imageellipse*), and ImageFilledEl
lipse() (*http://www.php.net/imagefilledellipse*).

17.3 Drawing with Patterned Lines

Problem

You want to draw shapes using line styles other than the default, a solid line.

Solution

To draw shapes with a patterned line, use ImageSetStyle() and pass in
IMG_COLOR_STYLED as the image color:

```
// make a two-pixel thick black and white dashed line
$black = 0x000000;
$white = 0xFFFFFF;

$style = array($black, $black, $white, $white);
```

```
ImageSetStyle($image, $style);

ImageLine($image, 0, 0, 50, 50, IMG_COLOR_STYLED);
ImageFilledRectangle($image, 50, 50, 100, 100, IMG_COLOR_STYLED);
```

Discussion

The line pattern is defined by an array of colors. Each element in the array is another pixel in the brush. It's often useful to repeat the same color in successive elements because this increases the size of the stripes in the pattern.

For instance, here is code for a square drawn with alternating white and black pixels, as shown on the left side of Figure 17-6:

```
// make a two-pixel thick black and white dashed line
$style = array($white, $black);
ImageSetStyle($image, $style);
ImageFilledRectangle($image, 0, 0, 49, 49, IMG_COLOR_STYLED);
```

This is the same square, but drawn with a style of five white pixels followed by five black ones, as shown on the right side of Figure 17-6:

```
// make a five-pixel thick black and white dashed line
$style = array($white, $white, $white, $white, $white,
               $black, $black, $black, $black, $black);
ImageSetStyle($image, $style);
ImageFilledRectangle($image, 0, 0, 49, 49, IMG_COLOR_STYLED);
```

Figure 17-6. Two squares with alternating white and black pixels

The patterns look completely different, even though both styles are just white and black pixels.

See Also

Recipes 17.1 and 17.2 for more on drawing shapes; documentation on `ImageSetStyle()` (*http://www.php.net/imagesetstyle*).

17.4 Drawing Text

Problem

You want to draw text as a graphic. This allows you to make dynamic buttons or hit counters.

Solution

For built-in GD fonts, use `ImageString()`:

```
ImageString($image, 1, $x, $y, 'I love PHP Cookbook', $text_color);
```

For TrueType fonts, use `ImageFTText()`:

```
ImageFTText($image, $size, 0, $x, $y, $text_color, '/path/to/font.ttf',
            'I love PHP Cookbook');
```

Discussion

Call `ImageString()` to place text onto the canvas. Like other GD drawing functions, `ImageString()` needs many inputs: the image to draw on, the font number, the x and y coordinates of the upper-right position of the first characters, the text string to display, and finally, the color to use to draw the string.

With `ImageString()`, there are five possible font choices, from 1 to 5. Font number 1 is the smallest, and font 5 is the largest, as shown in Figure 17-7. Anything above or below that range generates a size equivalent to the closest legal number.

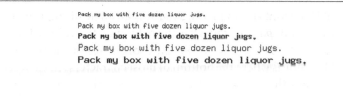

Figure 17-7. Built-in GD font sizes

To draw text vertically instead of horizontally, use the function `ImageStringUp()` instead. Figure 17-8 shows the output:

```
ImageStringUp($image, 1, $x, $y, 'I love PHP Cookbook', $text_color);
```

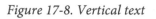

Figure 17-8. Vertical text

To use TrueType fonts, you must also install the FreeType library and configure PHP during installation to use FreeType (*http://www.freetype.org*). To enable FreeType 2.x, use `--with-freetype-dir=DIR`.

Like `ImageString()`, `ImageFTText()` prints a string to a canvas, but it takes slightly different options and needs them in a different order:

```
$image = ImageCreateTrueColor(200, 50);
ImageFilledRectangle($image, 0, 0, 199, 49, 0xFFFFFF); // white

$size = 20;
$angle = 0;
$x = 20;
$y = 35;
$text_color = 0x000000; // black
$text = 'Hello PHP!';
$fontpath = __DIR__ . '/stocky/stocky.ttf';

ImageFTText($image, $size, $angle, $x, $y, $text_color, $fontpath,
            $text);

header('Content-type: image/png');
ImagePNG($image);
```

The `$size` argument is the font size in pixels; `$angle` is an angle of rotation, in degrees going counterclockwise; and */path/to/font.ttf* is the pathname to the TrueType font file. Unlike `ImageString()`, (`$x,$y`) are the lower-left coordinates of the baseline for the first character. (The baseline is where the bottom of most characters sit. Characters such as "g" and "j" extend below the baseline; "a" and "z" sit on the baseline.)

Put them together, and you get Figure 17-9.

Figure 17-9. TrueType text

.See Also

Recipe 17.5 for drawing centered text; documentation on `ImageString()` (*http://www.php.net/imagestring*), `ImageStringUp()` (*http://www.php.net/imagestringup*), `ImageFTText()` (*http://www.php.net/imagefttext*).

17.5 Drawing Centered Text

Problem

You want to draw text in the center of an image.

Solution

Find the size of the image and the bounding box of the text. Using those coordinates, compute the correct spot to draw the text.

For TrueType fonts, use the `ImageFTCenter()` function:

```
function ImageFTCenter($image, $size, $angle, $font, $text, $extrainfo =
                       array()) {

    // find the size of the image
    $xi = ImageSX($image);
    $yi = ImageSY($image);

    // find the size of the text
    $box = ImageFTBBox($size, $angle, $font, $text, $extrainfo);

    $xr = abs(max($box[2], $box[4]));
    $yr = abs(max($box[5], $box[7]));

    // compute centering
    $x = intval(($xi - $xr) / 2);
    $y = intval(($yi + $yr) / 2);

    return array($x, $y);
}
```

For example:

```
list($x, $y) = ImageFTCenter($image, $size, $angle, $font, $text);
ImageFTText($image, $size, $angle, $x, $y, $fore, $font, $text);
```

For built-in GD fonts, use the `ImageStringCenter()` function:

```
function ImageStringCenter($image, $text, $font) {

    // font sizes
    $width  = array(1 => 5, 6, 7, 8, 9);
    $height = array(1 => 6, 8, 13, 15, 15);

    // find the size of the image
    $xi = ImageSX($image);
    $yi = ImageSY($image);

    // find the size of the text
    $xr = $width[$font] * strlen($text);
```

```
    $yr = $height[$font];

    // compute centering
    $x = intval(($xi - $xr) / 2);
    $y = intval(($yi - $yr) / 2);

    return array($x, $y);
}
```

For example:

```
list($x, $y) = ImageStringCenter($image, $text, $font);
ImageString($image, $font, $x, $y, $text, $fore);
```

Discussion

The two solution functions return the *x* and *y* coordinates for drawing. Depending on font type, size, and settings, the method used to compute these coordinates differs.

For TrueType fonts, pass `ImageFTCenter()` an image allocated from `ImageCreateTrueColor()` (or one of its friends) and a number of parameters to specify how to draw the text. Four parameters are required: the font size, the angle, text to be drawn, and the font. The final one is optional: the array of extra information that can be passed to `ImageFTBBox()`.

Inside the function, use `ImageSX()` and `ImageSY()` to find the size of the canvas; they return the width and height of the graphic. Then call `ImageFTBBox()`. It returns eight numbers: the (x,y) coordinates of the four corners of the text starting in the lower left and moving around counterclockwise. So the second two coordinates are for the lower-right spot, and so on. Because the coordinates are relative to the baseline of the text, it's typical for these not to be 0. For instance, a lowercase "g" hangs below the bottom of the rest of the letters; so in that case, the lower-left *y* value is negative.

Armed with these values, you can now calculate the correct centering values. Because coordinates of the canvas have (0,0) in the upper-left corner, but `ImageFTText()` wants the lower-left corner, the formula for finding $x and $y isn't the same. For $x, take the difference between the size of the canvas and the text. This gives the amount of whitespace that surrounds the text. Then divide that number by two to find the number of pixels you should leave to the left of the text. For $y, do the same, but add $yi and $yr. By adding these numbers, you can find the coordinate of the far side of the box, which is what is needed here because of the inverted way the *y* coordinate is entered in GD.

Intentionally ignore the lower-left coordinates in making these calculations. Because the bulk of the text sits above the baseline, adding the descending pixels into the centering algorithm actually worsens the code; it appears off-center to the eye.

To center text, put it together like this:

```
list($x, $y) = ImageFTCenter($image, $size, $angle, $font, $text);
ImageFTText($image, $size, $angle, $x, $y, $color, $font, $text);
```

Unfortunately, this example doesn't work for GD's built-in fonts or for TrueType fonts. There's no function to return the size of a string using the built-in fonts. With a few modifications, however, you can accommodate these differences.

Because the built-in fonts are fixed width, you can easily measure the size of a character to create a function that returns the size of the text based on its length. Table 17-1 isn't 100 percent accurate, but it should return results within one or two pixels, which should be good enough for most cases.

Table 17-1. GD built-in font character sizes

Font number	Width	Height
1	5	6
2	6	8
3	7	13
4	8	15
5	9	15

Inside `ImageStringCenter()`, calculate the length of the string as an integral multiple based on its length; the height is just one character high. Note that `ImageString()` takes its *y* coordinate as the uppermost part of the text, so you should switch the sign back to a minus when you compute $y.

Here is an example using all five fonts that centers text horizontally:

```
$w = 400; $h = 75;
$image = ImageCreateTrueColor($w, $h);
ImageFilledRectangle($image, 0, 0, $w-1, $h-1, 0xFFFFFF);

$color = 0x000000; // black
$text = 'Pack my box with five dozen liquor jugs.';

for ($font = 1, $y = 5; $font <= 5; $font++, $y += 20) {
    list($x) = ImageStringCenter($image, $text, $font);
    ImageString($image, $font, $x, $y, $text, $color);
}
```

The output is shown in Figure 17-10.

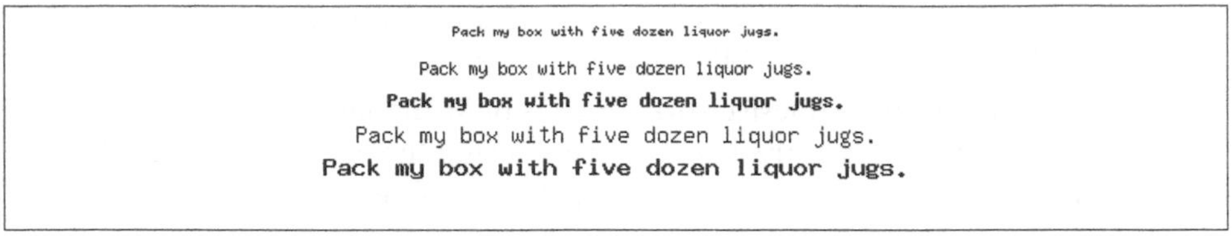

Pack my box with five dozen liquor jugs.
Pack my box with five dozen liquor jugs.
Pack my box with five dozen liquor jugs.
Pack my box with five dozen liquor jugs.
Pack my box with five dozen liquor jugs.

Figure 17-10. Centered GD built-in fonts

See Also

Recipe 17.4 for more on drawing text; Recipe 17.5 for more on centering text; documentation on ImageSX() (*http://www.php.net/imagesx*), ImageSY() (*http://www.php.net/imagesy*), and ImageFTBBox() (*http://www.php.net/imageftbbox*).

17.6 Building Dynamic Images

Problem

You want to create an image based on an existing image template and dynamic data (typically text). For instance, you want to create a hit counter.

Solution

Load the template image, find the correct position to properly center your text, add the text to the canvas, and send the image to the browser:

```
include 'imageftcenter.php';

// Configuration settings
$image    = ImageCreateFromPNG('/path/to/button.png'); // Template image
$size     = 24;
$angle    = 0;
$color    = 0x000000;
$fontfile = '/path/to/font.ttf'; // Edit accordingly
$text     = $_GET['text']; // Or any other source

// Print-centered text
list($x, $y) = ImageFTCenter($image, $size, $angle, $fontfile, $text);
ImageFTText($image, $size, $angle, $x, $y, $color, $fontfile, $text);

// Preserve Transparency
ImageColorTransparent($image,
    ImageColorAllocateAlpha($image, 0, 0, 0, 127));
ImageAlphaBlending($image, false);
ImageSaveAlpha($image, true);

// Send image
header('Content-type: image/png');
```

```
ImagePNG($image);

// Clean up
ImagePSFreeFont($font);
ImageDestroy($image);
```

Discussion

Building dynamic images with GD is easy; all you need to do is combine a few recipes. At the top of the code in the Solution, you load in an image from a stock template button; it acts as the background on which you overlay the text. You define the text to come directly from the query string. Alternatively, you can pull the string from a database (in the case of access counters) or a remote server (stock quotes or weather report icons).

After that, continue with the other settings: loading a font and specifying its size, color, and background color. Before printing the text, however, you need to compute its position; ImageFTCenter() from Recipe 17.5 nicely solves this task. Last, serve the image, and deallocate the image from memory.

For example, the following code generates a page of HTML and image tags using dynamic buttons, as shown in Figure 17-11:

```php
<?php
if (isset($_GET['button'])) {

    // Configuration settings
    $image    = ImageCreateFromPNG(__DIR__ . '/button.png');
    $text     = $_GET['button']; // dynamically generated text
    $font     = '/Library/Fonts/Hei.ttf';
    $size     = 24;
    $color    = 0x000000;
    $angle    = 0;

    // Print-centered text
    list($x, $y) = ImageFTCenter($image, $size, $angle, $font, $text);
    ImageFTText($image, $size, $angle, $x, $y, $color, $font, $text);

    // Preserve Transparency
    ImageColorTransparent($image,
        ImageColorAllocateAlpha($image, 0, 0, 0, 127));
    ImageAlphaBlending($image, false);
    ImageSaveAlpha($image, true);

    // Send image
    header('Content-type: image/png');
    ImagePNG($image);

    // Clean up
    ImagePSFreeFont($font);
    ImageDestroy($image);
```

```
} else {
    $url = htmlentities($_SERVER['PHP_SELF']);
?>
<html>
<head>
    <title>Sample Button Page</title>
</head>
<body>
    <img src="<?php echo $url; ?>?button=Previous"
        alt="Previous" width="132" height="46">
    <img src="<?php echo $url; ?>?button=Next"
        alt="Next"     width="132" height="46">
</body>
</html>
<?php
}
?>
```

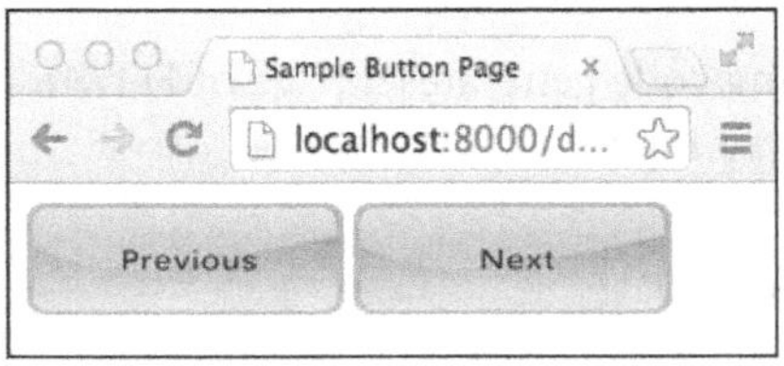

Figure 17-11. Sample button page

In this script, if a value is passed in for $_GET['button'], you generate a button and send out the PNG. If $_GET['button'] isn't set, you print a basic HTML page with two embedded calls back to the script with requests for button images—one for a Previous button and one for a Next button. A more general solution is to create a separate *button.php* page that returns only graphics and set the image source to point at that page.

See Also

Recipe 17.4 for more on drawing text; Recipe 17.5 for more on centering text; Chapter 9, "Graphics," in *Programming PHP*, Third Edition, by Rasmus Lerdorf, Kevin Tatroe, and Peter MacIntyre (O'Reilly).

17.7 Getting and Setting a Transparent Color

Problem

You want to set one color in an image as transparent. When the image is overlayed on a background, the background shows through the transparent section of the image.

Solution

Use ImageColorTransparent():

```
$color = 0xFFFFFF;
ImageColorTransparent($image, $color);
```

Discussion

Both GIFs and PNGs support transparencies; JPEGs, however, do not. To refer to the transparent color within GD, use the constant IMG_COLOR_TRANSPARENT. For example, here's how to make a dashed line that alternates between black and transparent:

```
// make a two-pixel thick black and white dashed line
$style = array($black, $black, IMG_COLOR_TRANSPARENT, IMG_COLOR_TRANSPARENT);
ImageSetStyle($image, $style);
```

To find the current transparency setting, take the return value of ImageColorTranspar ent() and pass it to ImageColorsForIndex():

```
$transparent = ImageColorsForIndex($image, ImageColorTransparent($image));
print_r($transparent);
```

This prints:

```
Array
(
    [red] => 255
    [green] => 255
    [blue] => 255
)
```

The ImageColorsForIndex() function returns an array with the red, green, and blue values. In this case, the transparent color is white.

See Also

Documentation on ImageColorTransparent() (*http://www.php.net/imagecolortrans parent*) and on ImageColorsForIndex() (*http://www.php.net/imagecolorsforindex*).

17.8 Overlaying Watermarks

Problem

You want to overlay a watermark stamp on top of images.

Solution

If your watermark stamp has a transparent background, use `ImageCopy()` to use alpha channels:

```
$image = ImageCreateFromPNG('/path/to/image.png');
$stamp = ImageCreateFromPNG('/path/to/stamp.png');

$margin = ['right' => 10, 'bottom' => 10]; // offset from the edge

ImageCopy($image, $stamp,
    imagesx($image) - imagesx($stamp) - $margin['right'],
    imagesy($image) - imagesy($stamp) - $margin['bottom'],
    0, 0, imagesx($stamp), imagesy($stamp));
```

Otherwise, use `ImageCopyMerge()` with an opacity;

```
$image = ImageCreateFromPNG('/path/to/image.png');
$stamp = ImageCreateFromPNG('/path/to/stamp.png');

$margin = ['right' => 10, 'bottom' => 10]; // offset from the edge
$opacity = 50; // between 0 and 100%

ImageCopyMerge($image, $stamp,
    imagesx($image) - imagesx($stamp) - $margin['right'],
    imagesy($image) - imagesy($stamp) - $margin['bottom'],
    0, 0, imagesx($stamp), imagesy($stamp),
    $opacity);
```

Discussion

When you overlay a watermark stamp on top of an image, you want the stamp to be clearly visible, but you would also like to allow the original image to show through. Also, to improve attractiveness, it's nice to offset the watermark from the edge. In this example, there's a 10-pixel border.

The `ImageCopy()` and `ImageCopyMerge()` functions let you take one image and place it on top of another. In this case, you copy the stamp on top of the base image.

The first two arguments are destination (your image) and the source (your stamp). Next are the *x* and *y* coordinates for where you'd like the stamp to be. In this case, you want to put the entire stamp in the lower-right corner, so the *x* coordinate is the width of the destination image minus the width of the stamp and the right offset; likewise for the *y* coordinate, but using heights instead of widths. To avoid hardcoding the image sizes into the script, use the ImageSX() and ImageSY() functions, because they dynamically compute those sizes.

When you know where the stamp is to be placed, you pass four coordinates for the size of the stamp. Here you pass 0, 0, ImageSX($stamp), and ImageSY($stamp) to copy the entire stamp. However, you could choose to copy just a portion of the image.

Finally, for ImageCopyMerge(), there's an argument for the opacity. This sets the translucence of the copied image. Values range from 0 to 100. The smaller the number, the lighter the stamp's appearance.

Putting this together in action generates Figure 17-12:

```
$image = ImageCreateFromJPEG(__DIR__ . '/iguana.jpg');

// Stamp
$w = 400; $h = 75;
$stamp = ImageCreateTrueColor($w, $h);
ImageFilledRectangle($stamp, 0, 0, $w-1, $h-1, 0xFFFFFF);

// Attribution text
$color = 0x000000; // black
ImageString($stamp, 4, 10, 10,
    'Galapagos Land Iguana by Nicolas de Camaret', $color);
ImageString($stamp, 4, 10, 28,
    'http://flic.kr/ndecam/6215259398', $color);
ImageString($stamp, 2, 10, 46,
    'Licence at http://creativecommons.org/licenses/by/2.0.', $color);

// Add watermark
$margin = ['right' => 10, 'bottom' => 10]; // offset from the edge
$opacity = 50; // between 0 and 100%
ImageCopyMerge($image, $stamp,
    imagesx($image) - imagesx($stamp) - $margin['right'],
    imagesy($image) - imagesy($stamp) - $margin['bottom'],
    0, 0, imagesx($stamp), imagesy($stamp),
    $opacity);

// Send
header('Content-type: image/png');
ImagePNG($image);
ImageDestroy($image);
ImageDestroy($stamp);
```

Figure 17-12. Iguana with a watermark

See Also

Documentation on `ImageCopy()` (*http://bit.ly/UJZTuh*), on `ImageCopyMerge()` (*http://bit.ly/1iGuJOW*), `ImageSX()` (*http://bit.ly/1pjO9fH*), and `ImageSY()` (*http://bit.ly/1v6fejI*).

17.9 Creating Thumbnail Images

Problem

You want to create scaled-down thumbnail images.

Solution

Use the `ImageCopyResampled()` function, scaling the image as needed.

To shrink proportionally:

```
$filename = __DIR__ . '/php.png';
$scale = 0.5; // Scale

// Images
$image = ImageCreateFromPNG($filename);
```

```
$thumbnail = ImageCreateTrueColor(
    ImageSX($image) * $scale,
    ImageSY($image) * $scale);

// Preserve Transparency
ImageColorTransparent($thumbnail,
    ImageColorAllocateAlpha($thumbnail, 0, 0, 0, 127));
ImageAlphaBlending($thumbnail, false);
ImageSaveAlpha($thumbnail, true);

// Scale & Copy
ImageCopyResampled($thumbnail, $image, 0, 0, 0, 0,
    ImageSX($thumbnail), ImageSY($thumbnail),
    ImageSX($image), ImageSY($image));

// Send
header('Content-type: image/png');
ImagePNG($thumbnail);
ImageDestroy($image);
ImageDestroy($thumbnail);
```

To shrink to a fixed-size rectangle:

```
// Rectangle Version

$filename = __DIR__ . '/php.png';
// Thumbnail Dimentions
$w = 50; $h = 20;

// Images
$original = ImageCreateFromPNG($filename);
$thumbnail = ImageCreateTrueColor($w, $h);

// Preserve Transparency
ImageColorTransparent($thumbnail,
    ImageColorAllocateAlpha($thumbnail, 0, 0, 0, 127));
ImageAlphaBlending($thumbnail, false);
ImageSaveAlpha($thumbnail, true);

// Scale & Copy
$x = ImageSX($original);
$y = ImageSY($original);
$scale = min($x / $w, $y / $h);

ImageCopyResampled($thumbnail, $original,
    0, 0, ($x - ($w * $scale)) / 2, ($y - ($h * $scale)) / 2,
    $w, $h, $w * $scale, $h * $scale);

// Send
header('Content-type: image/png');
ImagePNG($thumbnail);
ImageDestroy($original);
ImageDestroy($thumbnail);
```

Discussion

Thumbnail images allow you to quickly display a large number of photos in a small amount of space. The hardest part is knowing the best algorithm to scale or crop (or both) when your original pictures may be a wide variety of sizes and ratios.

The entire image is preserved when you shrink proportionally; however, this works best when all your pictures are about the same size and shape. Otherwise, you risk an unwieldy layout and pictures that are oddly shaped.

Another option is shrinking to a fixed size. This simplifies laying out the thumbnails, but when your ratio doesn't match the source ratio, you end up with very small pictures. This recipe compensates by cropping out the largest proportional rectangle from the image's center.

For example, Figure 17-13 is a scaled and cropped version of the Iguana image from Figure 17-12.

Figure 17-13. Iguana scaled and cropped

The two algorithms are similar: first, you load in the original and create the thumbnail canvas; then you adjust the thumbnail to preserve the transparencies; next you calculate the parameters to pass to the `ImageCopyResampled()` function, which does the work of scaling the original image to the new size and copying it to the thumbnail canvas; finally, you save the thumbnail as a PNG.

When scaling to a proportional size, the thumbnail canvas is a factor of the original dimensions. The `ImageSX()` and `ImageSY()` functions allow you to dynamically extract that data:

```
$thumbnail = ImageCreateTrueColor(
    ImageSX($image) * $scale,
    ImageSY($image) * $scale);
```

Then, when it's time to scale the image, you again use those two functions to specify the size of the images:

```
// Scale & Copy
ImageCopyResampled($thumbnail, $image, 0, 0, 0, 0,
    ImageSX($thumbnail), ImageSY($thumbnail),
    ImageSX($image), ImageSY($image));
```

The `ImageCopyResampled()` function takes 10 (yes, 10) arguments: the first two are the new and existing images. The next two are the *x* and *y* coordinates of where to put the new copied image; in this case, because you are overwriting the entire thumbnail, it's always 0 and 0. The fifth and sixth arguments are the similar coordinates for the original image. Again, these are 0 and 0 because you're scaling down the entire picture.

The final four arguments are another two pairs of coordinates. The first set are the width and height of the destination rectangle. The second are the same for the origin rectangle. Here, it's the full canvas for both.

When scaling to a constant size, the thumbnail canvas is simple. It's the width and height you choose:

```
$thumbnail = ImageCreateTrueColor($w, $h);
```

However, the code to scale and copy the image is more complicated:

```
// Scale & Copy
$x = ImageSX($original);
$y = ImageSY($original);
$scale = min($x / $w, $y / $h);

ImageCopyResampled($thumbnail, $original,
    0, 0, ($x - ($w * $scale)) / 2, ($y - ($h * $scale)) / 2,
    $w, $h, $w * $scale, $h * $scale);
```

First, you compute the smallest possible proportional rectangle that can fit inside the original image. You do that by finding the smaller of the two ratios of the original and thumbnail width and length. Now you know the size of the original rectangle you're cropping out: `$w * $scale` and `$h * $scale`.

You could crop this from (0,0); however, the middle of the image is more likely to be representative of the whole. Therefore, find the offset within the original by subtracting out half of the scaled rectangle from the middle of the image: `$x - ($w * $scale)) / 2` and `($y - ($h * $scale)) / 2`.

With this information, `ImageCopyResampled()` can do its job, scaling and smoothing the image down to a pretty looking, but smaller, picture.

See Also

Documentation on `ImageCopyResampled()` (*http://bit.ly/T5gfw7*), `ImageSX()` (*http://www.php.net/imagesx*), and `ImageSY()` (*http://www.php.net/imagesy*).

17.10 Reading EXIF Data

Problem

You want to extract metainformation from an image file. This lets you find out when the photo was taken, the image size, and the MIME type.

Solution

Use the `exif_read_data()` function:

```
$exif = exif_read_data('beth-and-seth.jpeg');

print_r($exif);

Array
(
    [FileName] => beth-and-seth.jpg
    [FileDateTime] => 1096055414
    [FileSize] => 182080
    [FileType] => 2
    [MimeType] => image/jpeg
    [SectionsFound] => APP12
    [COMPUTED] => Array
        (
            [html] => width="642" height="855"
            [Height] => 855
            [Width] => 642
            [IsColor] => 1
        )

    [Company] => Ducky
    [Info] =>
)
```

Discussion

The Exchangeable Image File Format (EXIF) is a standard for embedding metadata inside of pictures. Most digital cameras use EXIF, so it's an popular way of providing rich data in photo galleries.

PHP has a number of EXIF functions. They don't require external libraries, but must be enabled by passing the `--enable-exif` configuration flag.

The easiest way to extract data is through the `exif_read_data()` method. It returns an array of metadata, including the creation date of the photo, the MIME type (which you can use to help serve up the image), and the image dimensions:

```
$exif = exif_read_data('beth-and-seth.jpeg');
```

Use the `html` value to directly embed height and width attributes within an `<img>` source tag.

You can also use the EXIF functions to retrieve a thumbnail image associated with the picture. To access this, call `exif_thumbnail()`:

```
$thumb = exif_thumbnail('beth-and-seth.jpeg', $width, $height, $type);
```

The `exif_thumbnail()` function takes four parameters. The first is the filename. The last three are variables passed by reference where the width, height, and image type will be stored. The function returns the thumbnail image as a binary string, or `false` on failure.

To serve up the image directly, use the `image_type_to_mime_type()` to get the correct MIME type. Pass that along as an HTTP header and then display the image:

```
$thumb = exif_thumbnail('beth-and-seth.jpeg', $width, $height, $type);

if ($thumb !== false) {
    $mime = image_type_to_mime_type($type);
    header("Content-type: $mime");
    print $thumb;
} else {
    print "Sorry. No thumbnail.";
}
```

Alternatively, you can create an `<img>` link:

```
$file = 'beth-and-seth.jpeg';
$thumb = exif_thumbnail($file, $width, $height, $type);

if ($thumb !== false) {
    $img = "<img src=\"$file\" alt=\"Beth and Seth\"
                width=\"$width\" height=\"$height\">";
    print $img;
}
```

See Also

Documentation on `exif_read_data()` (*http://www.php.net/exif-read-data*) and on `exif_thumbnail()` (*http://www.php.net/exif-thumbnail*).

17.11 Serving Images Securely

Problem

You want to control who can view a set of images.

Solution

Don't keep the images in your document root, but store them elsewhere. To deliver a file, manually open it and send it to the browser:

```
header('Content-Type: image/png');
readfile('/path/to/graphic.png');
```

Discussion

The first line in the Solution sends the `Content-Type` header to the browser, so the browser knows what type of object is coming and displays it accordingly. The second opens a file off a disk (or from a remote URL) for reading, reads it in, dumps it directly to the browser, and closes the file.

The typical way to serve up an image is to use an `<img>` tag and set the `src` attribute to point to a file on your website. If you want to protect those images, you probably should use some form of password authentication. Two methods are HTTP Basic and Digest Authentication, which are covered in Recipe 8.6.

The typical way, however, may not always be the best. First, what happens if you want to restrict the files people can view, but you don't want to make things complex by using usernames and passwords? One option is to link only to the files; if users can't click the link, they can't view the file. They might, however, bookmark old files, or they may also try and guess other filenames based on your naming scheme and manually enter the URL into the browser.

If your content is embargoed, you don't want people to be able to guess your naming scheme and view images. When information is embargoed, a select group of people, usually reporters, are given a preview release, so they can write stories about the topic or be ready to distribute it the moment the embargo is lifted. You can fix this by making sure only legal content is under the document root, but this requires a lot of file shuffling back and forth from directory to directory. Instead, you can keep all the files in one constant place, and deliver only files that pass a check inside your code.

For example, let's say you have a contract with a publishing corporation to redistribute one of its comics on your website. However, it doesn't want you to create a virtual archive, so you agree to let your users view only the last two weeks' worth of strips. For everything else, they'll need to go to the official site. Also, you may get comics in advance of their publication date, but you don't want to let people get a free preview; you want them to keep coming back to your site on a daily basis.

Here's the solution. Files arrive named by date, so it's easy to identify which files belong to which day. Now, to lock out strips outside the rolling 14-day window, use code like this:

```
// display a comic if it's less than 14 days old and not in the future

// calculate the current date
list($now_m,$now_d,$now_y) = explode(',',date('m,d,Y'));
$now = mktime(0,0,0,$now_m,$now_d,$now_y);

// two-hour boundary on either side to account for dst
$min_ok = $now - 14*86400 - 7200; // 14 days ago
$max_ok = $now + 7200;            // today

$mo = (int) $_GET['mo'];
$dy = (int) $_GET['dy'];
$yr = (int) $_GET['yr'];

// find the time stamp of the requested comic
$asked_for = mktime(0,0,0,$mo,$dy,$yr);

// compare the dates
if (($min_ok > $asked_for) || ($max_ok < $asked_for)) {
    echo 'You are not allowed to view the comic for that day.';
} else {
    header('Content-type: image/png');
    readfile("/www/comics/{$mo}{$dy}{$yr}.png");
}
```

See Also

Recipe 24.5 for more on reading files.

17.12 Program: Generating Bar Charts from Poll Results

When displaying the results of a poll, it can be more effective to generate a colorful bar chart instead of just printing the results as text. The function shown in Example 17-1 uses GD to create an image that displays the cumulative responses to a poll question.

Example 17-1. Graphical bar charts

```
function bar_chart($question, $answers) {

    // define colors to draw the bars
    $colors = array(0xFF6600, 0x009900, 0x3333CC,
        0xFF0033, 0xFFFF00, 0x66FFFF, 0x9900CC);

    $total = array_sum($answers['votes']);

    // define spacing values and other magic numbers
    $padding = 5;
    $line_width = 20;
    $scale = $line_width * 7.5;
    $bar_height = 10;
```

```php
$x = $y = $padding;

// allocate a large palette for drawing, since you don't know
// the image length ahead of time
$image = ImageCreateTrueColor(150, 500);
ImageFilledRectangle($image, 0, 0, 149, 499, 0xE0E0E0);
$black = 0x000000;

// print the question
$wrapped = explode("\n", wordwrap($question, $line_width));
foreach ($wrapped as $line) {
    ImageString($image, 3, $x, $y , $line, $black);
    $y += 12;
}

$y += $padding;

// print the answers
for ($i = 0; $i < count($answers['answer']); $i++) {

    // format percentage
    $percent = sprintf('%1.1f', 100*$answers['votes'][$i]/$total);
    $bar = sprintf('%d', $scale*$answers['votes'][$i]/$total);

    // grab color
    $c = $i % count($colors); // handle cases with more bars than colors
    $text_color = $colors[$c];

    // draw bar and percentage numbers
    ImageFilledRectangle($image, $x, $y, $x + $bar,
                         $y + $bar_height, $text_color);
    ImageString($image, 3, $x + $bar + $padding, $y,
                "$percent%", $black);

     $y += 12;

    // print answer
    $wrapped = explode("\n", wordwrap($answers['answer'][$i], $line_width));
    foreach ($wrapped as $line) {
        ImageString($image, 2, $x, $y, $line, $black);
        $y += 12;
    }

     $y += 7;
 }

// crop image by copying it
$chart = ImageCreateTrueColor(150, $y);
ImageCopy($chart, $image, 0, 0, 0, 0, 150, $y);

// PHP 5.5+ supports
// $chart = ImageCrop($image, array('x' => 0, 'y' => 0,
```

```
//                                      'width' => 150, 'height' => $y));

    // deliver image
    header ('Content-type: image/png');
    ImagePNG($chart);

    // clean up
    ImageDestroy($image);
    ImageDestroy($chart);
}
```

To call this program, create an array holding two parallel arrays: $answers['answ er'] and $answer['votes']. Element $i of each array holds the answer text and the total number of votes for answer $i. Figure 17-14 shows this sample output:

```
// Act II. Scene II.
$question = 'What a piece of work is man?';

$answers['answer'][] = 'Noble in reason';
$answers['votes'][]  = 29;

$answers['answer'][] = 'Infinite in faculty';
$answers['votes'][]  = 22;

$answers['answer'][] = 'In form, in moving, how express and admirable';
$answers['votes'][]  = 59;

$answers['answer'][] = 'In action how like an angel';
$answers['votes'][]  = 45;

bar_chart($question, $answers);
```

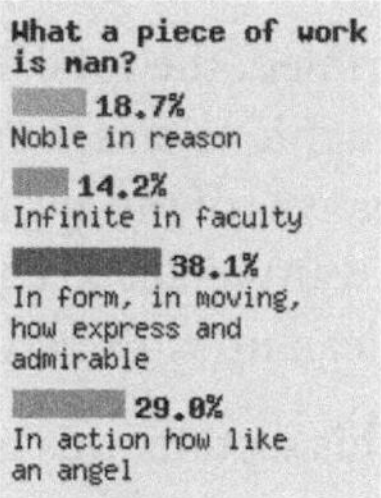

Figure 17-14. Graphic bar chart of poll results

Here the answers are manually assigned, but for a real poll, this data could be pulled from a database instead.

This program is a good start, but because it uses the built-in GD fonts, there are a lot of magic numbers embedded in the program corresponding to the font height and width.

Also, the amount of space between each answer is hardcoded. If you modify this to handle more advanced fonts, such as TrueType, you'll need to update the algorithms that control those numbers.

At the top of the function, a bunch of RGB combinations are defined; they are used as the colors to draw the bars. A variety of constants are broken out, such as `$line_width`, which is the maximum number of characters per line. The `$bar_height` variable determines how high the bars should be, and `$scale` scales the length of the bar as a function of the longest possible line. `$padding` is used to push the results five pixels away from the edge of the canvas.

You then make a very large canvas to draw the chart; later, you will crop the canvas down to size, but it can be difficult to know ahead of time how large your total size will be. The default background color of the bar chart is #E0E0E0, a light grey.

To restrict the width of the chart to a reasonable size, use `wordwrap()` to break your `$question` down to size and `explode()` it on \n. This gives an array of correctly sized lines, which you loop on to print out one line at a time.

After printing the question, move on to the answers. First, format the results numbers with `sprintf()`. To format the total percentage of votes for an answer as a floating-point number with one decimal point, use `%1.1f`. To find the length of the bar corresponding to that number, you compute a similar number, but instead of multiplying it by 100, multiply by a magic number, `$scale`, and return an integer.

The text color is pulled from the `$colors` array of RGB triplets. Then, call `ImageFilledRectangle()` to draw the bar and `ImageString()` to draw the percentage text to the right of the bar. After adding some padding, print the answer using the same algorithm used to print the question.

When all the answers have been printed, the total size of the bar chart is stored in `$y`. Now you can correctly crop the graphic to size, but there's no `ImageCrop()` function. To work around this, make a new canvas of the appropriate size and `ImageCopy()` over the part of the original canvas you want to keep. Then, serve the correctly sized image as a PNG using `ImagePNG()`, and clean up with two calls to `ImageDestroy()`.

As mentioned at the beginning of this section, this is just a quick-and-dirty function to print bar charts. It works and solves some problems, such a wrapped lines, but isn't 100 percent perfect. For instance, it's not very customizable. Many settings are baked directly into the code. Still, it shows how to put together a variety of GD functions to create a useful graphical application.

CHAPTER 18

Security and Encryption

18.0 Introduction

Web application security is an important topic that attracts attention from both the developers who create web applications and the attackers who try to exploit them. As a PHP developer, your applications are sure to be the target of many attacks, and you need to be prepared.

A large number of web application vulnerabilities are due to a misplaced trust in data provided by third parties. Such data is known as *input*, and it should be considered tainted until proven otherwise. If you display tainted data to your users, you create cross-site scripting (XSS) vulnerabilities. Recipe 18.4 explains how to avoid these by escaping your output. If you use tainted data in your SQL queries, you can create SQL injection vulnerabilities. Recipe 18.5 shows you how to eliminate these.

When using data provided by third parties, including the data provided by your users, it is important to first verify that it is valid. This process is known as *filtering*, and Recipe 18.3 shows you how to guarantee that all input is filtered.

Not all security problems can be solved by filtering input and escaping output. Session fixation, an attack discussed in Recipe 18.1, causes a victim to use a session identifier chosen by an attacker. Cross-site request forgeries, a type of attack discussed in Recipe 18.2, cause a victim to send a request of an attacker's choosing.

Closely related to security is encryption, a powerful tool that can help boost your application's security. Just like any other tool, however, it must be used properly.

Encryption scrambles data. Some data scrambling can't be unscrambled without unreasonable amounts of processing. This is called *one-way encryption* or *hashing*. Other encryption methods work in two directions: data is encrypted, and then it's decrypted.

PHP supplies tools to encrypt and secure your data. Some tools, such as the `pass word_hash()` function, are part of PHP's base set of functions, and some are extensions that need to be explicitly included when PHP is compiled (e.g., *mcrypt*, *mhash*, and *cURL*).

Recipe 18.7 discusses using `password_hash()`, which lets you securely hash a password for storage.

mcrypt is a more full-featured encryption library that offers different algorithms and encryption modes. Because it supports different kinds of encryption, *mcrypt* is especially helpful when you need to exchange encrypted data with other systems or with programs not written in PHP. *mcrypt* is discussed in detail in Recipe 18.10.

PHP gives you the tools to protect your data with robust encryption, but encryption is just part of the large and often complex security picture. Your encrypted data can be unlocked with a key, so protecting that key is very important. If your encryption keys are accessible to unauthorized users (because they're stored in a file accessible via your web server or because they're stored in a file accessible by other users in a shared hosting environment, for example), your data is at risk, no matter how secure your chosen encryption algorithm is.

Sensitive data needs to be protected not only on the server, but also when it's traveling over the network between the server and your users. Data sent over regular HTTP is visible to anyone with access to the network at any point between your server and a user. Recipe 18.13 discusses how to use SSL to prevent network snoopers from observing data as it passes by. For a complete discussion on securing PHP applications, read *PHP Security* by Chris Shiflett (O'Reilly).

18.1 Preventing Session Fixation

Problem

You need to ensure that a user's session identifier cannot be provided by a third party, such as an attacker who seeks to hijack the user's session.

Solution

Regenerate the session identifier with `session_regenerate_id()` whenever there is a change in the user's privilege, such as after a successful login:

```
session_regenerate_id();
$_SESSION['logged_in'] = true;
```

Discussion

Sessions allow you to create variables that persist between requests. For sessions to work, each of the users' requests must include a session identifier that uniquely identifies a session.

By default, PHP accepts a session identifier sent in a cookie, but if `session.use_on ly_cookies` is set to 1, it will accept a session identifier in the URL. An attacker can trick a victim into following a link to your application that includes an embedded session identifier:

```
<a href="http://example.org/login.php?PHPSESSID=1234">Click Here!</a>
```

A user who follows this link will resume the session identified as 1234. Therefore, the attacker now knows the user's session identifier and can attempt to hijack the user's session by presenting the same session identifier.

If the user never logs in or performs any action that differentiates the user from among the other users of your application, the attacker gains nothing by hijacking the session. Therefore, by ensuring that the session identifier is regenerated whenever there is a change in privilege level, you effectively eliminate session fixation attacks. PHP takes care of updating the session data store and propagating the new session identifier, so you must only call this one function as appropriate.

As of PHP 5.5.2, a new configuration setting, `session.use_strict_mode` helps prevent session hijacking. When this is enabled, PHP accepts only already initialized session IDs. If a browser sends a new session ID, PHP rejects it and generates a new one.

See Also

Recipe 11.2 for more information about session options that can help to prevent hijacking and fixation. Recipe 11.3 shows a time-based session ID regeneration scheme.

18.2 Protecting Against Form Spoofing

Problem

You want to be sure that a form submission is valid and intentional.

Solution

Add a hidden form field with a one-time token, and store this token in the user's session:

```
<?php

session_start();
```

```
$_SESSION['token'] = md5(uniqid(mt_rand(), true));

?>

<form action="buy.php" method="POST">
<input type="hidden" name="token" value="<?php echo $_SESSION['token']; ?>" />
<p>Stock Symbol: <input type="text" name="symbol" /></p>
<p>Quantity: <input type="text" name="quantity" /></p>
<p><input type="submit" value="Buy Stocks" /></p>
</form>
```

When you receive a request that represents a form submission, check the tokens to be sure they match:

```
session_start();

if ((! isset($_SESSION['token'])) ||
    ($_POST['token'] != $_SESSION['token'])) {

    /* Prompt user for password. */
} else {
    /* Continue. */
}
```

Discussion

This technique protects against a group of attacks known as *cross-site request forgeries (CSRF)*. These attacks all cause a victim to send requests to a target site without the victim's knowledge. Typically, the victim has an established level of privilege with the target site, so these attacks allow an attacker to perform actions that the attacker cannot otherwise perform. For example, imagine Alice is logged in via cookies to a social networking website, then visits another website. That second website could display a form to Alice that looks harmless, but really submits itself to a URL on that social networking website. Because Alice's browser would send login cookies along with the form submission, the social networking website wouldn't be able to distinguish this malicious form submission from a good one without CSRF protection.

Adding a token to your forms in this way does not prevent a user from forging his own request from himself, but this is not something you can prevent, nor is it something to be concerned with. If you filter input as discussed in Recipe 18.3, you force requests to abide by your rules. The technique shown in this recipe helps to make sure the request is intentional.

18.3 Ensuring Input Is Filtered

Problem

You want to filter all input prior to use.

Solution

Initialize an empty array in which to store filtered data. After you've proven that something is valid, store it in this array:

```
$filters = array('name' => array('filter' => FILTER_VALIDATE_REGEXP,
                                 'options' => array('regexp' => '/^[a-z]+$/i')),
                 'age' => array('filter' => FILTER_VALIDATE_INT,
                                'options' => array('min_range' => 13)));

$clean = filter_input_array(INPUT_POST, $filters);
```

Discussion

By using a strict naming convention, you can more easily keep up with what input has
been filtered. Always initializing $clean to an empty array ensures that data cannot be
injected into the array; you must explicitly add it. In the preceding code, the call to
filter_input_array() initializes $clean to contain only the filtered information.

Once you adopt a technique such as the use of $clean, it is important that you only use
data from this array in your business logic.

See Also

Recipe 9.2 through Recipe 9.9 discuss form input validation for different types of data
in detail.

18.4 Avoiding Cross-Site Scripting

Problem

You need to safely avoid cross-site scripting (XSS) attacks in your PHP applications.

Solution

Escape all HTML output with htmlentities(), being sure to indicate the correct character encoding:

```
/* Note the character encoding. */
header('Content-Type: text/html; charset=UTF-8');

/* Initialize an array for escaped data. */
$html = array();

/* Escape the filtered data. */
$html['username'] = htmlentities($clean['username'], ENT_QUOTES, 'UTF-8');

echo "<p>Welcome back, {$html['username']}.</p>";
```

Discussion

The `htmlentities()` function replaces each character with its HTML entity, if it has one. For example, > is replaced with `&gt;`. Although the immediate effect is that the data is modified, the purpose of the escaping is to preserve the data in a different context. Whenever a browser renders `&gt;` as HTML, it appears on the screen as >.

XSS attacks try to take advantage of a situation where data provided by a third party is included in the HTML without being escaped properly. A clever attacker can provide code that can be very dangerous to your users when interpreted by their browsers. By using `htmlentities()`, you can be sure that such third-party data is displayed properly and not interpreted.

See Also

Recipe 9.10 discusses cross-site scripting prevention in the context of submitted form data.

18.5 Eliminating SQL Injection

Problem

You need to eliminate SQL injection vulnerabilities in your PHP applications.

Solution

Use a database library such as PDO that performs the proper escaping for your database:

```
$statement = $db->prepare("INSERT
                           INTO   users (username, password)
                           VALUES (:username, :password)");

$statement->bindParam(':username', $clean['username']);
$statement->bindParam(':password', $clean['password']);

$statement->execute();
```

Discussion

Using bound parameters ensures your data never enters a context where it is considered to be anything except raw data, so no value can possibly modify the format of the SQL query.

See Also

Chapter 10 for more information about PDO, particularly Recipe 10.6 and Recipe 10.7; documentation on PDO (*http://www.php.net/pdo*).

18.6 Keeping Passwords Out of Your Site Files

Problem

You need to use a password to connect to a database, for example. You don't want to put the password in the PHP files you use on your site in case those files are exposed.

Solution

Store the password in an environment variable in a file that the web server loads when starting up. Then, just reference the environment variable in your code:

```
$db = new PDO($dsn, $_SERVER['DB_USER'], $_SERVER['DB_PASSWORD']);
```

Discussion

Although this technique removes passwords from the source code of your pages, it makes them available in other places that need to be protected. Most importantly, make sure that there are no publicly viewable pages that call phpinfo(). Because phpinfo() displays all of the environment variables, it exposes any passwords you store there. Also, make sure not to expose the contents of $_SERVER in other ways, such as with the print_r() function.

Next, especially if you are using a shared host, make sure the environment variables are set in such a way that they are only available to your virtual host, not to all users. With Apache, you can do this by setting the variables in a separate file from the main configuration file:

```
SetEnv   DB_USER     "susannah"
SetEnv   DB_PASSWORD "y23a!t@ce8"
```

Inside the <VirtualHost> directive for the site in the main configuration file (*httpd.conf*), include this separate file as follows:

```
Include "/usr/local/apache/database-passwords"
```

Make sure that this separate file containing the password (e.g., */usr/local/apache/database-passwords*) is not readable by any user other than the one that controls the appropriate virtual host. When Apache starts up and is reading in configuration files, it's usually running as root, so it is able to read the included file. A child process that handles requests typically runs as an unprivileged user, so rogue scripts cannot read the protected file.

See Also

Documentation on Apache's Include directive (*http://httpd.apache.org/docs/current/mod/core.html#include*).

18.7 Storing Passwords

Problem

You need to keep track of users' passwords, so they can log in to your website.

Solution

When a user signs up or registers, hash the chosen password with bcrypt and store the hashed password in your database of users.

With PHP 5.5 and later, use the built-in `password_hash()` function:

```
/* Initialize an array for filtered data. */
$clean = array();

/* Hash the password. */
$hashed_password = password_hash($_POST['password'], PASSWORD_DEFAULT);

/* Allow alphanumeric usernames. */
if (ctype_alnum($_POST['username'])) {
    $clean['username'] = $_POST['username'];
} else {
    /* Error */
}

/* Store user in the database. */
$st = $db->prepare('INSERT
            INTO   users (username, password)
            VALUES (?, ?)');
$st->execute(array($clean['username'], $hashed_password));
```

Then, when that user attempts to log in to your website, use the `password_verify()` function to see if the supplied password matches the stored, hashed value:

```
/* Initialize an array for filtered data. */
$clean = array();

/* Allow alphanumeric usernames. */
if (ctype_alnum($_POST['username'])) {
    $clean['username'] = $_POST['username'];
} else {
    /* Error */
}
```

```
$stmt = $db->prepare('SELECT password
                      FROM    users
                      WHERE   username = ?');
$stmt->execute(array($clean['username']));
$hashed_password = $stmt->fetchColumn();

if (password_verify($_POST['password'], $hashed_password)) {
    /* Login succeeds. */
    print "Login OK!";
} else {
    /* Login fails. */
}
```

If you are not using PHP 5.5 but are using PHP 5.3.7 or later, install the `password_com pat` library (*https://github.com/ircmaxell/password_compat*) for implementations of `password_hash()` and `password_verify()`.

If you are using an older version of PHP, the following Discussion outlines your options for secure password storage.

Discussion

Storing hashed passwords prevents users' accounts from becoming compromised if an unauthorized person gets a peek at your username and password database (although such unauthorized peeks may foreshadow other security problems).

The `password_hash()` and `password_verify()` functions do two things to make it hard for a bad guy to exploit access to the hashed passwords. First, they incorporate a "salt" string into the value that gets hashed. This means that even if two of your users choose the same plain-text password, the hashed value of that password will be different for each user. If the bad guy figures out one of the user's passwords, he won't easily be able to figure out the other.

The second notable feature of these functions is they use an algorithm (currently bcrypt) whose cost can be adjusted. This means that as the computers of bad guys grow more powerful over time, you can easily make it more expensive (computationally) to turn a hashed password into a plain-text password.

Because it's hard to turn hashed passwords into plain-text passwords, your stored passwords are somewhat more secure. This also means that you can't get at the plain text of users' passwords, even if you need to. For example, if a user forgets his password, you won't be able to tell him what it is. The best you can do is reset the password to a new value and then tell the user the new password. A method for dealing with lost passwords is covered in Recipe 18.8.

If you're using a version of PHP prior to 5.3.7, you can generate reasonably secure password hashes by using the built-in `crypt()` function:

```
/* Initialize an array for filtered data. */
$clean = array();

/* Generate an appropriate salt. '$2a$' tells crypt() to
 * use the Blowfish algorithm, and the 08 tells it to do
 * 256 (2^8) rounds of hashing */
$salt = '$2a$08$';
/* Blowfish hashes are 22 bytes long, each byte is
 * from 0-9, A-Z, a-z */
for ($i = 0; $i < 22; $i++) {
    $r = mt_rand(0, 61);
    if ($r < 10) {
        $c = ord('0') + $r;
    }
    else if ($r < 36) {
        $c = ord('A') + $r - 10;
    }
    else {
        $c = ord('a') + $r - 36;
    }
    $salt .= chr($c);
}

$hashed_password = crypt($_POST['password'], $salt);

/* Allow alphanumeric usernames. */
if (ctype_alnum($_POST['username'])) {
    $clean['username'] = $_POST['username'];
} else {
    /* Error */
}

/* Store user in the database. */
$st = $db->prepare('INSERT
            INTO   users (username, password)
            VALUES (?, ?)');
$st->execute(array($clean['username'], $hashed_password));
```

And then verify those passwords by retrieving the stored salt and providing it to `crypt()` with a user-entered password:

```
/* Initialize an array for filtered data. */
$clean = array();

/* Allow alphanumeric usernames. */
if (ctype_alnum($_POST['username'])) {
    $clean['username'] = $_POST['username'];
} else {
    /* Error */
}

$stmt = $db->prepare('SELECT password
                      FROM   users
```

```
                            WHERE  username = ?');
$stmt->execute(array($clean['username']));
$hashed_password = $stmt->fetchColumn();

$salt = substr($hashed_password, 0, strlen('$2a$08$') + 22);

if (crypt($_POST['password'], $salt) === $hashed_password) {
    /* Login succeeds. */
    print "Login OK!";
} else {
    /* Login fails. */
}
```

When using `crypt()`, you need to grab the appropriate salt (and the $2a$08$ prefix that tells `crypt()` to use Blowfish) out of the stored value in order to provide it to `crypt()` with whatever attempted password the user entered. This ensures that the re-hashed value will match if the passwords match.

If you are using a version of PHP prior to 5.3.0 *and* your system's library that `crypt()` relies on does not include support for Blowfish, the preceding code will not work, because `crypt()` will not be able to use the Blowfish algorithm. Test for this by checking the value of the `CRYPT_BLOWFISH` constant. If that is 0, then you do not have Blowfish support.

In that case, you can either upgrade to PHP 5.3 (which bundles its own Blowfish implementation) or use a different password hashing function, such as the `sha1()` function. If you want to maximize your password security, upgrading your version of PHP is the better choice. The SHA1 algorithm is much faster to compute than Blowfish, so it is easier for attackers to find plain-text passwords that match a given hashed value.

See Also

Recipe 18.11 for information on storing encrypted data; the `password_compat` library (*https://github.com/ircmaxell/password_compat*); documentation on `password_hash()` (*http://php.net/password_hash*), on `password_verify()` (*http://php.net/password_verify*), on `crypt()` (*http://php.net/crypt*), and on `sha1()` (*http://php.net/sha1*).

18.8 Dealing with Lost Passwords

Problem

You want to issue a password to a user who has lost her password.

Solution

Generate a new password and send it to the user's email address (which you should have on file):

```
/* Generate new password. */
$new_password = '';

for ($i = 0; $i < 8; $i++) {
    $new_password .= chr(mt_rand(33, 126));
}

/* Hash new password. */
$hashed_password = password_hash($new_password, PASSWORD_DEFAULT);

/* Save new hashed password to the database. */
$st = $db->prepare('UPDATE users
        SET     password = ?
        WHERE   username = ?');

$st->execute(array($hashed_password, $clean['username']));

/* Email new plain text password to user. */
mail($clean['email'], 'New Password', "Your new password is: $new_password");
```

Note that this code uses the PHP 5.5–only `password_hash()` function. If you're using an older version of PHP, follow the recommendations in "Discussion" on page 553.

Discussion

If a user forgets her password, and you store hashed passwords as recommended in Recipe 18.7, you can't provide the forgotten password. The one-way nature of hashing prevents you from retrieving the plain-text password.

Instead, generate a new password and send that to her email address. If you send the new password to an address you don't already have on file for that user, you don't have a way to verify that the new address really belongs to the user. It may be an attacker attempting to impersonate the real user.

Because the email containing the new password isn't hashed, the code in the Solution doesn't include the username in the email message to reduce the chances that an attacker that eavesdrops on the email message can steal the password. To avoid disclosing a new password by email at all, let a user authenticate herself without a password by answering one or more personal questions (the answers to which you have on file). These questions can be "What was the name of your first pet?" or "What's your mother's maiden name?" —anything a malicious attacker is unlikely to know. If the user provides the correct answers to your questions, you can let her choose a new password.

One way to compromise between security and readability is to generate a password for a user out of actual words interrupted by some numbers:

```
$words = array('mother', 'basset', 'detain', 'sudden', 'fellow', 'logged',
               'remove', 'snails', 'direct', 'serves', 'daring', 'chirps',
               'reward', 'snakes', 'uphold', 'wiring', 'nurses', 'regent',
               'ornate', 'dogmas', 'mended', 'hinges', 'verbal', 'grimes',
               'ritual', 'drying', 'chests', 'newark', 'winged', 'hobbit');

$word_count = count($words);

$password = sprintf('%s%02d%s',
                    $words[mt_rand(0,$word_count - 1)],
                    mt_rand(0,99),
                    $words[mt_rand(0,$word_count - 1)]);

echo $password;
```

This code produces passwords that are two six-letter words with two numbers between them, like `mother43hobbit` or `verbal68nurses`. The passwords are long, but remembering them is made easier by the words in them.

Sending a new password to a user's email address implicitly assumes that the person reading the email at that address is authorized to log in. Based on that assumption you could also just email the user a one-time-use URL. When she visits that URL, show her a page that lets her reset her password. If the URL is sufficiently hard to guess, then you can be confident that only the email recipient will access it.

See Also

Recipe 18.7 for information about storing hashed passwords; sitepoint (*http://bit.ly/ 1itkpu0*) describes how to make one-time-use URLs that you could use with a password reset capability.

18.9 Verifying Data with Hashes

Problem

You want to make sure users don't alter data you've sent them in a cookie or form element.

Solution

Along with the data, send a "message digest" hash of the data that uses a salt. When you receive the data back, compute the hash of the received value with the same salt. If they don't match, the user has altered the data.

Here's how to generate a hash in a hidden form field:

```php
<?php

/* Define a salt. */
define('SALT', 'flyingturtle');

$id = 1337;
$idcheck = hash_hmac('sha1', $id, SALT);

?>
<input type="hidden" name="id" value="<?php echo $id; ?>" />
<input type="hidden" name="idcheck" value="<?php echo $idcheck; ?>" />
```

Here's how to verify the hidden form field data when it's submitted:

```php
/* Initialize an array for filtered data. */
$clean = array();

/* Define a salt. */
define('SALT', 'flyingturtle');

if (hash_hmac('sha1', $_POST['id'], SALT) === $_POST['idcheck']) {
    $clean['id'] = $_POST['id'];
} else {
    /* Error */
}
```

Discussion

When processing the submitted form data, compute the hash of the submitted value of $_POST['id'] with the same salt. If it matches $_POST['idcheck'], the value of $_POST['id'] has not been altered by the user. If the values don't match, you know that the value of $_POST['id'] you received is not the same as the one you sent.

To use the same hashing technique with a cookie, add it to the cookie value with implode():

```php
/* Define a salt. */
define('SALT', 'flyingturtle');

$name = 'Ellen';

$namecheck = hash_hmac('sha1', $name, SALT);

setcookie('name', implode('|',array($name, $namecheck)));
```

Parse the hash from the cookie value with explode():

```php
/* Define a salt. */
define('SALT', 'flyingturtle');
```

```
list($cookie_value, $cookie_check) = explode('|', $_COOKIE['name'], 2);

if (hash_hmac('sha1', $cookie_value, SALT) === $cookie_check) {
    $clean['name'] = $cookie_value;
} else {
    /* Error */
}
```

Using a data verification hash in a form or cookie obviously depends on the salt used in hash computation. If a malicious user discovers your salt, the hash offers no protection. Besides guarding the salt zealously, changing it frequently is a good idea. For an additional layer of protection, use different salts, choosing the specific salt to use in the hash based on some property of the $id value (10 different words selected by $id%10, for example). That way, the damage is slightly mitigated if one of the words is compromised.

See Also

hash_hmac( ) documentation (*http://www.php.net/hash_hmac*).

18.10 Encrypting and Decrypting Data

Problem

You want to encrypt and decrypt data using one of a variety of popular algorithms.

Solution

Use PHP's *mcrypt* extension:

```
$algorithm = MCRYPT_BLOWFISH;
$key = 'That golden key that opens the palace of eternity.';
$data = 'The chicken escapes at dawn. Send help with Mr. Blue.';
$mode = MCRYPT_MODE_CBC;

$iv = mcrypt_create_iv(mcrypt_get_iv_size($algorithm, $mode),
                       MCRYPT_DEV_URANDOM);

$encrypted_data = mcrypt_encrypt($algorithm, $key, $data, $mode, $iv);
$plain_text = base64_encode($encrypted_data);
echo $plain_text . "\n";

$encrypted_data = base64_decode($plain_text);
$decoded = mcrypt_decrypt($algorithm, $key, $encrypted_data, $mode, $iv);
// trim() will remove any trailing NULL bytes that mcrypt_decrypt() may
// have added to pad the output to be a whole number of 8-byte blocks
echo trim($decoded) . "\n";
```

This prints:

Cd4Uzc1c5lDxxWc7rXv+mbsElwj2ENrYg5HAPiaOpe7Wr8UAG5aXD9CoG6NdKoOWLSumg9ffSnE=
The chicken escapes at dawn. Send help with Mr. Blue.

Discussion

The *mcrypt* extension is an interface with *mcrypt*, a library that implements many different encryption algorithms. The data is encrypted and decrypted by mcrypt_en crypt() and mcrypt_decrypt(), respectively. They each take five arguments. The first is the algorithm to use. To find which algorithms *mcrypt* supports on your system, call mcrypt_list_algorithms(). The second argument is the encryption key; the third argument is the data to encrypt or decrypt. The fourth argument is the mode for the encryption or decryption (a list of supported modes is returned by mcrypt_list_modes()). The fifth argument is an initialization vector (IV), used by some modes as part of the encryption or decryption process.

Except for the data to encrypt or decrypt, all the other arguments must be the same when encrypting and decrypting. If you're using a mode that requires an initialization vector, it's OK to pass the initialization vector in the clear with the encrypted text.

The different modes are appropriate in different circumstances. Cipher Block Chaining (CBC) mode encrypts the data in blocks, and uses the encrypted value of each block (as well as the key) to compute the encrypted value of the next block. The initialization vector affects the encrypted value of the first block. Cipher Feedback (CFB) and Output Feedback (OFB) also use an initialization vector, but they encrypt data in units smaller than the block size. Note that OFB mode has security problems if you encrypt data in smaller units than its block size. Electronic Code Book (ECB) mode encrypts data in discrete blocks that don't depend on each other. ECB mode doesn't use an initialization vector. It is also less secure than other modes for repeated use, because the same plain text with a given key always produces the same cipher text. Constants to set each mode are listed in Table 18-1.

Table 18-1. mcrypt mode constants

Mode constant	Description
MCRYPT_MODE_ECB	Electronic Code Book mode
MCRYPT_MODE_CBC	Cipher Block Chaining mode
MCRYPT_MODE_CFB	Cipher Feedback mode
MCRYPT_MODE_OFB	Output Feedback mode with 8 bits of feedback
MCRYPT_MODE_NOFB	Output Feedback mode with n bits of feedback, where n is the block size of the algorithm used
MCRYPT_MODE_STREAM	Stream Cipher mode, for algorithms such as RC4 and WAKE

Different algorithms have different block sizes. You can retrieve the block size for a particular algorithm with mcrypt_get_block_size(). Similarly, the initialization vector size is determined by the algorithm and the mode. mcrypt_create_iv() and `mcrypt_get_iv_size()` make it easy to create an appropriate random initialization vector:

```
$iv = mcrypt_create_iv(mcrypt_get_iv_size($algorithm, $mode),
                       MCRYPT_DEV_URANDOM);
```

The first argument to `mcrypt_create_iv()` is the size of the vector, and the second is a source of randomness. You have three choices for the source of randomness: `MCRYPT_DEV_RANDOM` reads from the pseudodevice */dev/random*, `MCRYPT_DEV_URANDOM` reads from the pseudodevice */dev/urandom*, and `MCRYPT_RAND` uses an internal random number generator. Not all operating systems support random-generating pseudodevices. Make sure to call `srand()` before using `MCRYPT_RAND` in order to get a nonrepeating random number stream.

See Also

The *mcrypt* extension documentation (*http://www.php.net/mcrypt*); the *mcrypt* library (*http://mcrypt.sourceforge.net*). Choosing an appropriate algorithm and using it securely requires care and planning: for more information about *mcrypt* and the cipher algorithms it uses, see the *mcrypt* extension documentation (*http://mcrypt.source forge.net*), the *mcrypt* home page (*http://mcrypt.sourceforge.net*), and the Wikipedia page about */dev/urandom* and */dev/urandom* (*http://bit.ly/1sFhen9*); good books about cryptography include *Applied Cryptography* by Bruce Schneier (Wiley) and *Cryptography: Theory and Practice* by Douglas R. Stinson (Chapman & Hall).

18.11 Storing Encrypted Data in a File or Database

Problem

You want to store encrypted data that needs to be retrieved and decrypted later by your web server.

Solution

Store the additional information required to decrypt the data (such as algorithm, cipher mode, and initialization vector) along with the encrypted information, but not the key:

```
/* Encrypt the data. */
$algorithm  = MCRYPT_BLOWFISH;
$mode = MCRYPT_MODE_CBC;
$iv = mcrypt_create_iv(mcrypt_get_iv_size($algorithm, $mode),
                       MCRYPT_DEV_URANDOM);
$ciphertext = mcrypt_encrypt($algorithm, $_POST['key'], $_POST['data'],
                             $mode, $iv);

/* Store the encrypted data. */
```

```
$st = $db->prepare('INSERT
            INTO    noc_list (algorithm, mode, iv, data)
            VALUES (?, ?, ?, ?)');
$st->execute(array($algorithm, $mode, $iv, $ciphertext));
```

To decrypt the data, retrieve a key from the user and use it with the saved data:

```
$row = $db->query('SELECT *
                    FROM    noc_list
                    WHERE   id = 27')->fetch();
$plaintext = mcrypt_decrypt($row['algorithm'],
                            $_POST['key'],
                            $row['data'],
                            $row['mode'],
                            $row['iv']);
```

Discussion

The *save-crypt.php* script shown in Example 18-1 stores encrypted data to a file.

Example 18-1. save-crypt.php

```
function show_form() {
    $html = array();
    $html['action'] = htmlentities($_SERVER['PHP_SELF'], ENT_QUOTES, 'UTF-8');

    print<<<FORM
<form method="POST" action="{$html['action']}">
<textarea name="data"
        rows="10" cols="40">Enter data to be encrypted here.</textarea>
<br />
Encryption Key: <input type="text" name="key" />
<br />
<input name="submit" type="submit" value="Save" />
</form>
FORM;
}

function save_form() {
    $algorithm  = MCRYPT_BLOWFISH;
    $mode = MCRYPT_MODE_CBC;

    /* Encrypt data. */
    $iv = mcrypt_create_iv(mcrypt_get_iv_size($algorithm, $mode),
                            MCRYPT_DEV_URANDOM);
    $ciphertext = mcrypt_encrypt($algorithm,
                                $_POST['key'],
                                $_POST['data'],
                                $mode,
                                $iv);

    /* Save encrypted data. */
    $filename = tempnam('/tmp','enc') or exit($php_errormsg);
```

```
    $file = fopen($filename, 'w') or exit($php_errormsg);
    if (FALSE === fwrite($file, $iv.$ciphertext)) {
        fclose($file);
        exit($php_errormsg);
    }

    fclose($file) or exit($php_errormsg);

    return $filename;
}

if (isset($_POST['submit'])) {
    $file = save_form();
    echo "Encrypted data saved to file: $file";
} else {
    show_form();
}
```

Example 18-2 shows the corresponding program, *get-crypt.php*, that accepts a filename and key and produces the decrypted data.

Example 18-2. get-crypt.php

```
function show_form() {
    $html = array();
    $html['action'] = htmlentities($_SERVER['PHP_SELF'], ENT_QUOTES, 'UTF-8');

    print<<<FORM
<form method="POST" action="{$html['action']]"
Encrypted File: <input type="text" name="file" />
<br />
Encryption Key: <input type="text" name="key" />
<br />
<input name="submit" type="submit" value="Display" />
</form>
FORM;
}

function display() {
    $algorithm = MCRYPT_BLOWFISH;
    $mode = MCRYPT_MODE_CBC;

    $file = fopen($_POST['file'], 'r') or exit($php_errormsg);
    $iv = fread($file, mcrypt_get_iv_size($algorithm, $mode));
    $ciphertext = fread($file, filesize($_POST['file']));
    fclose($file);

    $plaintext = mcrypt_decrypt($algorithm, $_POST['key'], $ciphertext,
                                $mode, $iv);
    echo "<pre>$plaintext</pre>";
}
```

```
if (isset($_POST['submit'])) {
    display();
} else {
    show_form();
}
```

These two programs have their encryption algorithm and mode hardcoded in them, so there's no need to store this information in the file. The file consists of the initialization vector immediately followed by the encrypted data. There's no need for a delimiter after the initialization vector (IV), because `mcrypt_get_iv_size()` returns exactly how many bytes the decryption program needs to read to get the whole IV. Everything after that in the file is encrypted data.

Encrypting files using the method in this recipe offers protection if an attacker gains access to the server on which the files are stored. Without the appropriate key or tremendous amounts of computing power, the attacker won't be able to read the files. However, the security that these encrypted files provide is undercut if the data to be encrypted and the encryption keys travel between your server and your users' web browsers in the clear. Someone who can intercept or monitor network traffic can see data before it even gets encrypted. To prevent this kind of eavesdropping, use SSL.

An additional risk when your web server encrypts data as in this recipe comes from how the data is visible before it's encrypted and written to a file. Someone with root or administrator access to the server can look in the memory the web server process is using and snoop on the unencrypted data and the key. If the operating system swaps the memory image of the web server process to disk, the unencrypted data might also be accessible in this swap file. This kind of attack can be difficult to pull off but can be devastating. Once the encrypted data is in a file, it's unreadable even to an attacker with root access to the web server, but if the attacker can peek at the unencrypted data before it's in that file, the encryption offers little protection.

See Also

Recipe 18.13 discusses SSL and protecting data as it moves over the network; documentation on `mcrypt_encrypt()` (*http://bit.ly/1pjOEGo*), `mcrypt_decrypt()` (*http://bit.ly/UK0fku*), `mcrypt_create_iv()` (*http://bit.ly/1nEd5Jl*), and `mcrypt_get_iv_size()` (*http://bit.ly/1qJmYu6*).

18.12 Sharing Encrypted Data with Another Website

Problem

You want to exchange data securely with another website.

Solution

If the other website is pulling the data from your site, put the data up on a password-protected page. You can also make the data available in encrypted form, with or without a password. If you need to push the data to another website, submit the potentially encrypted data via post to a password-protected URL.

Discussion

The following page requires a username and password and then encrypts and displays the contents of a file containing yesterday's account activity:

```
$user = 'bank';
$password = 'fas8uj3';

if ($_SERVER['PHP_AUTH_USER'] != $user ||
    $_SERVER['PHP_AUTH_PW'] != $password) {
    header('WWW-Authenticate: Basic realm="Secure Transfer"');
    header('HTTP/1.0 401 Unauthorized');
    echo "You must supply a valid username and password for access.";
    exit;
}

header('Content-type: text/plain; charset=UTF-8');
$filename = strftime('/usr/local/account-activity.%Y-%m-%d', time() - 86400);
$data = implode('', file($filename));

$algorithm = MCRYPT_BLOWFISH;
$mode = MCRYPT_MODE_CBC;
$key  = "There are many ways to butter your toast.";

/* Encrypt data. */
$iv = mcrypt_create_iv(mcrypt_get_iv_size($algorithm, $mode),
                                        MCRYPT_DEV_URANDOM);
$ciphertext = mcrypt_encrypt($algorithm, $key, $data, $mode, $iv);

echo base64_encode($iv.$ciphertext);
```

Here's the corresponding code to retrieve the encrypted page and decrypt the information:

```
$user = 'bank';
$password = 'fas8uj3';
$algorithm = MCRYPT_BLOWFISH;
$mode = MCRYPT_MODE_CBC;
$key  = "There are many ways to butter your toast.";

$url = 'https://bank.example.com/accounts.php';

$c = curl_init($url);
curl_setopt($c, CURLOPT_USERPWD, "$user:$password");
```

```
curl_setopt($c, CURLOPT_RETURNTRANSFER, TRUE);
$data = curl_exec($c);
if (FALSE === $data) {
    exit("Transfer failed: " . curl_error($c));
}

$binary_data = base64_decode($data);
$iv_size = mcrypt_get_iv_size($algorithm, $mode);
$iv = substr($binary_data, 0, $iv_size);
$ciphertext = substr($binary_data, $iv_size, strlen($binary_data));

echo mcrypt_decrypt($algorithm, $key, $ciphertext, $mode, $iv);
```

The retrieval program does all the steps of the encryption program, but in reverse. It retrieves the Base64-encoded encrypted data, supplying a username and password. Then, it decodes the data with Base64 and separates out the initialization vector. Last, it decrypts the data and prints it out.

In the previous examples, the username and password are still sent over the network in clear text, unless the connections happen over SSL. However, if you're using SSL, it's probably not necessary to encrypt the contents of the file. We included both password-prompting and file encryption in these examples to show how it can be done.

There's one circumstance, however, in which both password protection and file encryption is helpful: if the file isn't automatically decrypted when it's retrieved. An automated program can retrieve the encrypted file and put it, still encrypted, in a place that can be accessed later. The decryption key thus doesn't need to be stored in the retrieval program.

See Also

Recipe 18.13 discusses SSL and protecting data as it moves over the network; documentation on mcrypt_encrypt() (*http://php.net/mcrypt-encrypt*) and mcrypt_decrypt() (*http://php.net/mcrypt-decrypt*).

18.13 Detecting SSL

Problem

You want to know if a request arrived over SSL.

Solution

Test the value of $_SERVER['HTTPS']:

```
if ('on' == $_SERVER['HTTPS']) {
  echo 'The secret ingredient in Coca-Cola is Soylent Green.';
} else {
```

```
    echo 'Coca-Cola contains many delicious natural and artificial flavors.';
}
```

Discussion

SSL operates on a lower level than HTTP. The web server and a browser negotiate an appropriately secure connection, based on their capabilities, and the HTTP messages can pass over that secure connection. To an attacker intercepting the traffic, it's just a stream of nonsense bytes that can't be read.

Different web servers have different requirements to use SSL, so check your server's documentation for specific details. No changes have to be made to PHP to work over SSL.

In addition to altering code based on $_SERVER['HTTPS'], you can also set cookies to be exchanged only over SSL connections. If the last argument to setcookie() is true, the browser sends the cookie back to the server only over a secure connection:

```
/* Set an SSL-only cookie named "sslonly" with value "yes" that expires at the
   end of the current browser session. */
if ('on' === $_SERVER['HTTPS']) {
    setcookie('sslonly', 'yes', 0, '/', 'example.org', true);
}
```

Although the browser sends these cookies back to the server only over an SSL connection, the server sends them to the browser (when you call setcookie() in your page) whether or not the request for the page that sets the cookie is over SSL. If you're putting sensitive data in the cookie, make sure that you set the cookie only in an SSL request as well. Also, keep in mind that the cookie data is unencrypted on the user's computer.

See Also

Documentation on setcookie() (*http://php.net/setcookie*).

18.14 Encrypting Email with GPG

Problem

You want to send encrypted email messages. For example, you take orders on your website and need to send an email to your factory with order details for processing. By encrypting the email message, you prevent sensitive data such as credit card numbers from passing over the network in the clear.

Solution

Use the functions provided by the gnupg extension to encrypt the body of the email message with GNU Privacy Guard (GPG) before sending it:

```
$plaintext_body = 'Some sensitive order data';
$recipient = 'ordertaker@example.com';

$g = gnupg_init();
gnupg_seterrormode($g, GNUPG_ERROR_WARNING);
// Fingerprint of the recipient's key
$a = gnupg_addencryptkey($g, "5495F0CA9C8F30A9274C2259D7EBE8584CEF302B");
// Fingerprint of the sender's key
$b = gnupg_addsignkey($g, "520D5FC5C85EF4F4F9D94E1C1AF1F7C5916FC221",
                  "passphrase");

$encrypted_body = gnupg_encryptsign($g, $plaintext_body);

mail($recipient, 'Web Site Order', $encrypted_body);
```

The email message can be decrypted by GPG, Pretty Good Privacy (PGP), or an email client plug-in that supports either program.

Discussion

The code in the Solution uses PHP's gnupg extension, which, in turn, relies on the GPGME library, in order to perform OpenPGP-standard operations to encrypt and sign a message.

The resource returned by gnupg_init() is used in the rest of the function calls as a container for the specific settings related to the encryption we're doing. Next, gnupg_se terrormode($g, GNUPG_ERROR_WARNING) ensures that we'll get some PHP warnings generated if there are problems with any GnuPG operations.

This example encrypts and signs a message. The encryption ensures that only the desired recipient can decrypt and read the message. The signature lets the recipient be sure that this sender sent the message.

The key fingerprint passed to gnupg_addencryptkey() specifies which key should be used to encrypt the message. Only someone with access to the private key associated with this fingerprint will be able to decrypt the message.

The key fingerprint passed to gnupg_addsignkey() specifies which key should be used to sign the message. The third argument to gnupg_addsignkey() is the passphrase associated with this private key.

The functions in the gnupg extension look for keys in the same place that the command-line gpg executable does: a directory named *.gnupg* under your home directory (or under the home directory of the user that PHP is running as). To tell PHP to look in a different place for keys, set the GNUPGHOME environment variable to the desired directory.

After the keys have been set on the gnupg resource, the call to gnupg_encryptsign() produces the encrypted, signed message. By default, this value is "armored" as plain ASCII.

If you need to identify the correct fingerprint to pass to gnupg_addencryptkey() or gnupg_addsignkey(), use gnupg_keyinfo(), as shown here:

```
$email = 'friend@example.com';

$g = gnupg_init();
$keys = gnupg_keyinfo($g, $email);
if (count($keys) == 1) {
    $fingerprint = $keys[0]['subkeys'][0]['fingerprint'];
    print "Fingerprint for $email is $fingerprint";
}
else {
    print "Expected 1, found " . count($keys) .
        " keys for $email";
}
```

Given a gnupg resource and a search string, gnupg_keyinfo() returns an array containing information about each key in the keyring whose UID (or part of a UID) matches the search string. Each element in that returned array is itself an array composed of many elements and subarrays describing lots of per-key information. The finger print key of the first element of the subkeys array gives us the appropriate value to pass to other gnupg functions.

See Also

The GNU Privacy Guard homepage (*http://gnupg.org/*) and information about the GPGME library (*http://bit.ly/TjA1nx*). The PECL page (*http://pecl.php.net/package/ gnupg*) for the gnupg extension and its documentation (*http://www.php.net/gnupg*).

CHAPTER 19

Internationalization and Localization

19.0 Introduction

Though everyone who programs in PHP has to learn some English eventually to get a handle on its function names and language constructs, PHP can create applications that speak just about any language. Some applications need to be used by speakers of many different languages. Taking an application written for French speakers and making it useful for German speakers is made easier by PHP's support for internationalization and localization.

The recipies in this chapter rely on the capabilities of PHP's intl extension for internationalization and localization tasks. Underlying this extension is the powerful ICU library. ICU (*http://site.icu-project.org/*) is widely used and has both C/C++ and Java implementations. This means that the concepts around working with in PHP translate well if you are doing globalization work in other (programming) languages.

The intl extension is bundled with PHP versions 5.3.0 and later. To use it with PHP 5.2.0 or later, install it from PECL (*http://pecl.php.net/intl*).

Internationalization (often abbreviated I18N) is the process of taking an application designed for just one locale and restructuring it so that it can be used in many different locales.[1] *Localization* (often abbreviated L10N) is the process of adding support for a new locale to an internationalized application.[2]

A *locale* is a group of settings that describe text formatting and language customs in a particular area of the world. Locales describe behavior for:

---

1. The word "internationalization" has 18 letters between the first "i" and the last "n."

2. The word "localization" has 10 letters between the first "l" and the "n."

Collation

How text is sorted: which letters go before and after others in alphabetical order.

Numbers

How numeric information (including currency amounts) is displayed, including how to group digits, what characters to use as the thousands separator and decimal point, and how to indicate negative amounts.

Times and Dates

How time and date information is formatted and displayed, such as names of months and days and whether to use 24- or 12-hour time.

Messages

Text messages used by applications that need to display information in multiple languages.

A locale ID has a few components, each separated by underscores. The first is the *language code*, an abbreviation that indicates a language. This is, for example, "en" for English or "pt" for Portuguese. The language codes are the two-letter codes specified in the ISO 639-1 standard (*http://1.usa.gov/14iSOkR*).

Next comes an optional *script code*, which indicates what set of characters should be used to represent text in this locale. For example, `Arab` indicates Arabic and `Cyrl` indicates Cyrillic. These script codes are enumerated as part of ISO 15924 (*http://bit.ly/1lXTnJM*).

After that comes an optional *country code*, to distinguish between different countries that speak different versions of the same language. For example, "en_US" for US English and "en_UK" for British English, or "pt_BR" for Brazilian Portuguese and "pt_PT" for Portuguese Portuguese. The country codes are the two-letter codes specified in the ISO 3166 standard (*http://bit.ly/1jzRlyB*).

To further allow for specifying differences among the same language and country, the next component of a locale ID can be an optional *variant code*. These variant codes, documented in the IANA language subtag registry (*http://bit.ly/1opFUKn*), indicate variations such as using the Biscayan dialect of Basque (variant `biscayan`), or that the Høgnorsk orthography of Norwegian should be used (variant `hognorsk`). Your basic day-to-day use of locales will probably not involve variants.

After the exotic variant can be an optional list of keywords, prefixed by a `@`. These keywords are semicolon-separated `name=value` pairs that offer a further way to provide customized information about the locale. For example, the locale `fr_CA@currency=USD` indicates a French-language locale in Canada, but using US dollars for currency. Useful for merchants on the Quebec-Vermont border, perhaps.

To help you deal with locales, Recipe 19.1 demonstrates how to set the locale as asked for by a user's web browser.

Different techniques are necessary for correct localization of plain text, numbers, dates and times, and currency. Localization can also be applied to external entities your program uses, such as images and included files. Localizing these kinds of content is covered in Recipe 19.2 through Recipe 19.7.

Locale-aware sorting is discussed in Recipe 19.8 and dealing with large amounts of localization data is discussed in Recipe 19.9.

Recipe 19.10 through Recipe 19.12 discuss how to make sure your programs work well with a variety of character encodings so they can handle strings such as à l'Opéra-Théâtre, поленика, and 優之良品. One way to do this is to have all text your programs process be encoded as UTF-8. This encoding scheme can handle the Western characters in the familiar ISO-8859-1 encoding as well as characters for other writing systems around the world. These recipes focus on using UTF-8 to provide a seamless, language-independent experience for your users.

19.1 Determining the User's Locale

Problem

You want to use the correct locale as specified by a user's web browser.

Solution

Pass the incoming `Accept-Language` HTTP header value to the `Locale::accept FromHttp()` function to get the proper locale identifier:

```
if (isset($_SERVER['HTTP_ACCEPT_LANGUAGE'])) {
    $localeToUse = Locale::acceptFromHttp($_SERVER['HTTP_ACCEPT_LANGUAGE']);
}
else {
    $localeToUse = Locale::getDefault();
}
```

Discussion

Section 14.4 of RFC 2616, which specifies how HTTP works, provides rules for how web browsers can send an `Accept-Language` header with a request to indicate what languages are preferred as a response to the request. A web browser may send more than one possible language with values indicating the relative preference for those languages. The `Locale::acceptFromHttp()` function sorts through those values and returns an ICU locale ID corresponding to the desired language.

If no preferred language is specified, you can use the locale returned by the `Locale::get Default()` function, whose value comes from the `intl.default_locale` configuration directive (if not overridden by a call to `Locale::setDefault()`).

See Also

Documentation for `Locale::acceptFromHttp()` (*http://www.php.net/Locale.accept FromHttp*), `Locale::getDefault()` (*http://www.php.net/Locale.getDefault*), and `Lo cale::setDefault()` (*http://www.php.net/Locale.setDefault*). See more information about RFC 2616 (*http://www.w3.org/Protocols/rfc2616/rfc2616.html*).

19.2 Localizing Text Messages

Problem

You want to display text messages in a locale-appropriate language.

Solution

Maintain a message catalog of words and phrases and retrieve the appropriate string from the message catalog before passing it to a `MessageFormatter` object to format it for printing:

```
$messages = array();
$messages['en_US'] =
    array('FAVORITE_FOODS' => 'My favorite food is {0}.',
          'FRIES' => 'french fries',
          'CANDY' => 'candy',
          'CHIPS' => 'potato chips',
          'EGGPLANT' => 'eggplant');
$messages['en_GB'] =
    array('FAVORITE_FOODS' => 'My favourite food is {0}.',
          'FRIES' => 'chips',
          'CANDY' => 'sweets',
          'CHIPS' => 'crisps',
          'EGGPLANT' => 'aubergine');


foreach (array('en_US', 'en_GB') as $locale) {
    $candy = new MessageFormatter($locale, $messages[$locale]['CANDY']);
    $favs = new MessageFormatter($locale, $messages[$locale]['FAVORITE_FOODS']);
    print $favs->format(array($candy->format(array()))) . "\n";
}
```

This prints:

```
My favorite food is candy.
My favourite food is sweets.
```

Discussion

The first argument to the `MessageFormatter` constructor is the locale for which the message should be formatted. The second argument is the message pattern. The power of `MessageFormatter` comes from the special bits in the pattern delimited by curly braces. This is where the arguments supplied to the `format()` method get inserted into the pattern. In the code in the Solution, the `{0}` in the pattern is replaced by the first element in the array passed to `format()`. A `{1}` in a pattern would be replaced by the second element of the array, and so on.

The easiest way to specify pattern arguments is with numbers—`{0}` is the first argument, `{1}` the second, and so on. Then the value of the first element in the array passed to `format()` replaces the `{0}`, the second replaces the `{1}`, and so forth down the line. In the example above, there is one replacement in the `FAVORITE_FOODS` pattern and no replacements in the `CANDY` pattern, so the array passed to `$favs->format()` has one element, and the array passed to `$candy->format()` is empty.

Admittedly, a plain old formatting pattern argument such as `{0}` is not very exciting. Using all the machinery of ICU for simple string replacement is underwhelming. More complicated pattern arguments show how `MessageFormatter` shines. For example, consider a message where the text needs to be different based on how many objects are involved. For example, "You have one item in your shopping cart" versus "You have two items in your shopping cart." Here's how to express that with `MessageFormatter`:

```
$messages = array();
$messages['en_US'] =
    array('CART' => "You have {0,spellout} " .
                    "{0, plural, " .
                    " =1     {item} " .
                    " other {items} } " .
                    "in your shopping cart.");
$messages['fr_FR'] =
    array('CART' => "Vous {0, plural, " .
                    " =0 {n'avez pas d'articles} ".
                    " =1 {avez un article} ".
                    " other {avez {0,spellout} articles}} ".
                    "dans votre panier.");

$fmts = array();
foreach (array_keys($messages) as $locale) {
    $fmts[$locale] = new MessageFormatter($locale, $messages[$locale]['CART']);
}

for ($i = 0; $i < 10; $i++) {
    foreach ($fmts as $locale => $obj) {
        print $obj->format(array($i)) . "\n";
    }
}
```

This prints:

```
You have zero items in your shopping cart.
Vous n'avez pas d'articles dans votre panier.
You have one item in your shopping cart.
Vous avez un article dans votre panier.
You have two items in your shopping cart.
Vous avez deux articles dans votre panier.
You have three items in your shopping cart.
Vous avez trois articles dans votre panier.
You have four items in your shopping cart.
Vous avez quatre articles dans votre panier.
You have five items in your shopping cart.
Vous avez cinq articles dans votre panier.
You have six items in your shopping cart.
Vous avez six articles dans votre panier.
You have seven items in your shopping cart.
Vous avez sept articles dans votre panier.
You have eight items in your shopping cart.
Vous avez huit articles dans votre panier.
You have nine items in your shopping cart.
Vous avez neuf articles dans votre panier.
```

The pattern arguments in this example are more extensive than a simple {0}. The {0,spellout} argument says "use argument 0, but treat it as type spellout". This is a built-in ICU type which turns numerals into their spelled-out equivalents. Because MessageFormatter is locale-aware, it knows what words to use. E.g., "three" in English but "trois" in French. The pattern also includes an argument of type plural. Reusing argument 0, this allows for wholesale different text based on the value of that argument. In English, it outputs item if the argument is 1, but items otherwise. The French construction distinguishes between 0, 1, and everything else to ensure proper grammar.

The plural argument type lets the message formatter make a choice based on the numerical value of an argument. The more general select argument type lets the message formatter make a choice based on arbitrary values. This is useful for choosing different words based on the gender of an argument. Here's how that can work in English:

```php
$message = '{0, select, f {She} m {He} other {It}} went to the store.';

$fmt = new MessageFormatter('en_US', $message);

print $fmt->format(array('f')) . "\n";
print $fmt->format(array('m')) . "\n";
print $fmt->format(array('Unknown')) . "\n";
```

This prints:

```
She went to the store.
He went to the store.
It went to the store.
```

When argument 0 is f, "She" is interpolated into the output. When it's m, then "He" goes into the output. Otherwise, "It" goes into the output.

In PHP 5.5, MessageFormatter supports not just numbered arguments, but named arguments, too. Just make sure that how you refer to the argument in the pattern matches the array key you use when calling format(). For example:

```
$message = 'I like to eat {food} and {drink}.';
$fmt = new MessageFormatter('en_US', $message);
print $fmt->format(array('food' => 'eggs',
                         'drink' => 'water'));
```

This prints:

```
I like to eat eggs and water.
```

If you're using an older version of PHP, you can install version 3.0 (or later) of the intl extension from PECL to get this capability.

See Also

Documentation on the MessageFormatter class (*http://bit.ly/1qapHg7*). Because Mes sageFormatter relies on ICU for its implementation, the ICU documentation on message formatting and arguments is very helpful, in particular the ICU User Guide (*http:// bit.ly/1uzHmOE*) and ICU 53.1 (*http://bit.ly/1mBB6F8*).

19.3 Localizing Dates and Times

Problem

You want to display dates and times in a locale-specific manner.

Solution

Use the date or time argument type, with an optional short, medium, long, or full style inside a MessageFormatter message:

```
$when = 1376943432; // Seconds since epoch
$message = "It is {0,time,short} on {0,date,medium}.";
$fmt = new MessageFormatter('en_US', $message);
print $fmt->format(array($when));
```

This prints:

```
It is 4:17 PM on Aug 19, 2013.
```

Use a formatting pattern with a date or time argument type inside a MessageFormat ter message:

```
$when = 1376943432; // Seconds since epoch
$message = "Maintenant: {0,date,eeee dd MMMM y}";
$fmt = new MessageFormatter('fr_FR', $message);
print $fmt->format(array($when));
```

This prints:

Maintenant: lundi 19 août 2013

Use the `format()` method of an `IntlDateFormatter`:

```
$when = 1376943432; // Seconds since epoch
$fmt = new IntlDateFormatter('en_US', IntlDateFormatter::FULL,
                              IntlDateFormatter::FULL);
print $fmt->format($when);
```

This prints:

Monday, August 19, 2013 at 8:17:12 PM GMT

Discussion

The date and time argument types for `MessageFormatter` make it easy to include appropriate localized representations of dates and times in your output. These "preset" formats not only respect the appropriate settings for a locale by including the right information in the right order (for example, distinguishing between places that list month number before day number and places that list day number before month number), but also translate words for months and days of the week into the appropriate language.

If you want more control over the date and time elements that appear in your message, supply a format pattern. Table 19-1 lists the elements that can appear in a date/time format pattern.

Table 19-1. Date and time format pattern characters

Type	Character	Description	Example
Hour	a	Ante/Post Meridiem designation	PM
Hour	h	Hour, 12-hour clock (1 – 12)	3
Hour	K	Hour, 12-hour clock (0 – 11)	3
Hour	H	Hour, 24-hour clock (0 – 23)	15
Hour	k	Hour, 24-hour clock (1 – 24)	15
Minute	m	Minute (0 – 59)	8
Second	s	Second (0 – 59)	7
Second	S	Decisecond (0 – 9)	0
Second	SS	Centisecond (00 – 99)	00
Second	SSS	Millisecond (000 – 999)	000
Second	A	Milliseconds in day	54487000

Type	Character	Description	Example
Day	d	Day of month (1 – 31)	18
Day	D	Day of year (1 – 366)	78
Day	EEEEE	Day of week, short abbreviation	T
Day	EEE	Day of week, long abbreviation	Thu
Day	EEEE	Day of week, name	Thursday
Day	e	Day of week, number (0 or 1 to 6 or 7, localized)	5
Day	F	Day of week in the month (e.g., 3 for "third Wednesday")	3
Day	g	Modified Julian Day	2453083
Week	w	Week of year, with localized week start (1 – 52)	12
Week	W	Week of month (1 – 5)	3
Month	M	Month (1 – 12)	3
Month	MMMMM	Month, short abbreviation	M
Month	MMM	Month, long abbreviation	Mar
Month	MMMM	Month, name	March
Year	y	Year, 4-digit	2004
Year	yy	Year, 2-digit	04
Time Zone	z	Time zone, including Summer Time, abbreviated	EST
Time Zone	zzzz	Time zone, including Summer Time, full name	Eastern Standard Time
Time Zone	Z	Time zone, RFC-822 format	-0500
Time Zone	ZZZZ	Time zone, as GMT offset	GMT-05:00
Time Zone	ZZZZZ	Time zone, ISO-8601 format	GMT-05:00
Time Zone	v	Time zone, not including Summer Time, abbreviated	ET
Time Zone	vvvv	Time zone, not including Summer Time, full name	Eastern Time
Time Zone	VVVV	Time zone, as location	United States Time (New York)
Other	Q	Quarter, number	1
Other	QQQ	Quarter, number with prefix	Q1
Other	QQQQ	Quarter, as words	1st quarter
Other	G	Era (BC, AD)	AD
Other	''	Two single quotes make one in output	'

PHP's epoch timestamps and `DateTime` objects don't support milliseconds, so the S, SS, and SSS characters are always zeros. Unless a special meaning is listed in the table for a repeating character, most other characters when repeated enable you to include one or more leading zeros. For example, because m represents minute, mm produces 08 for the eighth minute past the hour.

Although a `date` or `time` argument type in a `MessageFormatter` message expects an integer argument representing seconds since epoch, the `IntlDateFormatter` accomodates more ways to specify the time or date you care about. You can provide the value to format as a `DateTime` object or as an array of time parts as returned by `local time()`. For example:

```
$fmt = new IntlDateFormatter('en_US', IntlDateFormatter::FULL,
                             IntlDateFormatter::FULL,
                             'America/Chicago');

// Z for time zone means UTC
$obj = new DateTime('2013-08-20T12:34:56Z');
$parts = array('tm_sec' => 56,
               'tm_min' => 34,
               'tm_hour' => 12,
               'tm_mday' => 20,
               'tm_mon' => 7, /* 0 = January */
               'tm_year' => 113); /* 0 = 1900 */

print $fmt->format($obj) . "\n";
print $fmt->format($parts) . "\n";
```

This prints:

```
Tuesday, August 20, 2013 at 7:34:56 AM Central Daylight Time
Tuesday, August 20, 2013 at 12:34:56 PM Central Daylight Time
```

The values are formatted for output as appropriate for the en_US locale and the America/Chicago time zone. This means that the hour specified in the `DateTime` object—12 P.M. GMT—is adjusted to 7 A.M. Central Daylight Time (the active time zone for August 20, 2013 in Chicago). The time parts provided in the second call to `format()` do not include a time zone, so they are assumed to be the same time zone as specified in the `IntlDateFormatter` constructor.

Starting in PHP 5.5, the `IntlDateFormatter` class also has a helper method to produce localized, formatted date/time strings in one step, rather than having to construct a new `IntlDateFormatter` and then call `format()`. The static `IntlDateFormatter::fromObject()` method takes three arguments: a `DateTime` object, a format, and a locale, and returns the formatted date/time string. Example 19-1 shows how it works.

Example 19-1. DateTime object, format, and locale

```
$obj = new DateTime('2013-08-20T12:34:56');
print IntlDateFormatter::formatObject($obj, 'eeee dd MMMM y', 'es_ES') . "\n";
print IntlDateFormatter::formatObject($obj, IntlDateFormatter::FULL, 'fr_FR') .
                                                                      "\n";
// First element is date format, second is time format
$formats = array(IntlDateFormatter::FULL, IntlDateFormatter::SHORT);
print IntlDateFormatter::formatObject($obj, $formats, 'de_DE') . "\n";
```

This prints:

```
martes 20 agosto 2013
mardi 20 août 2013 12:34:56 UTC
Dienstag, 20. August 2013 12:34
```

As shown, the second argument to formatObject can either be an explicit format pattern string, one of the IntlDateFormatter formatting style constants, or an array of two formatting style constants. If a format pattern string is provided, that is used. If one formatting style constant is provided, that is used for both date and time. If an array of two formatting style constants is provided, the first is used for the date style and the second for the time style.

See Also

Recipe 3.1 discusses localtime(). Documentation on IntlDateFormatter (*http://bit.ly/1kLyRrX*), on IntlDateFormatter::format() (*http://bit.ly/1g7R6pT*), and on IntlDateFormatter::formatObject() (*http://bit.ly/1fOYPOZ*). ICU date and time formatting, including format pattern characters, is explained at the ICU User Guide (*http://bit.ly/1s2v1hU*).

19.4 Localizing Numbers

Problem

You want to display numbers in a locale-specific format.

Solution

Use the number argument type with MessageFormatter:

```
$message = '{0,number} / {1,number} = {2,number}';
$args = array(5327, 98, 5327/98);

$us = new MessageFormatter('en_US',$message);
$fr = new MessageFormatter('fr_FR',$message);
print $us->format($args) . "\n";
print $fr->format($args) . "\n";
```

This prints:

```
5,327 / 98 = 54.357
5 327 / 98 = 54,357
```

Discussion

Notice in the output that the same message produces different output based on what locale the MessageFormatter is set to use. The characters used as the thousands separator and decimal point are locale-specific. What's shown is the default number style output. With an additional style parameter added to the type, you can change that.

For example, there are easy shortcuts for displaying numbers as currency amounts and percentage amounts:

```
$message = '{0,number,currency}, {0,number,percent}';
$us = new MessageFormatter('en_US',$message);
print $us->format(array(3.33333333));
```

This prints:

$3.33, 333%

Instead of the shortcut words currency or percent, you can also specify a format string as understood by the ICU DecimalFormat class. Many of the characters that can go in this format string are listed in Table 19-2.

Table 19-2. DecimalFormat pattern characters

Character	Meaning
0	Digit
1-9	Digit, with rounding
#	Digit, display nothing for zero
@	Significant digit
%	Percent sign, multiplies number by 100
¤	Currency symbol
¤¤	Three-letter currency abbreviation
;	Separator for positive and negative patterns

This code runs through several of these patterns for a few different numbers:

```
$args = array(7,159,-0.3782,6.815574);

$messages = array("0", "00", "1", "11", "222",
                  "#", "##", "@", "@@@",
                  "##%", "¤#", "¤1.11",
                  "¤¤#",
                  "#.##;(#.## !!!)"
                  );

foreach ($messages as $message) {
    $fmt = new MessageFormatter('en_US',"{0,number,$message}\t{1,number,
                                $message}\t"."{2,number,$message}\t
                                {3,number,$message}");
    print "$message:\t" . $fmt->format($args) . "\n";
}
```

And this survey of patterns produces:

0:	7	1590	-0	7
00:	07	159	-00	07
1:	7	159	-0	7
11:	11	154	-00	11
222:	000	222	-000	000
#:	7	159	-0	7
##:	7	159	-0	7
@:	7	200	-0.4	7
@@@:	7.00	159	-0.378	6.82
##%:	700%	15900%	-38%	682%
¤#:	$7	$159	-$0	$7
¤1.11:	$6.66	$158.73	-$0.00	$6.66
¤¤#:	USD7	USD159	-USD0	USD7
#.##;(#.## !!!):	7	159	(0.38 !!!)	6.82

More precise control over number formatting is possible with the separate NumberFormatter class. Its constructor accepts a locale, a formatting style, and an optional pattern string. For example:

```
$args = array(7,159,-0.3782,6.815574);

$sci = new NumberFormatter('en_US', NumberFormatter::SCIENTIFIC);
$dur = new NumberFormatter('en_US', NumberFormatter::DURATION);
$ord = new NumberFormatter('en_US', NumberFormatter::ORDINAL);
$pat = new NumberFormatter('en_US', NumberFormatter::PATTERN_DECIMAL, '@@@@');

print $sci->format(10040)    . "\n";
print $dur->format(64)       . "\n";
print $ord->format(15)       . "\n";
print $pat->format(1.357926) . "\n";
```

This prints:

```
1.004E4
1:04
15th
1.358
```

The first formatter, using the NumberFormatter::SCIENTIFIC style, turns 10040 into appropriate scientific notation: 1.004E4. The second formatter, using NumberFormatter::DURATION, turns 64 seconds into 1:04—one minute and four seconds. The third formatter, using NumberFormatter::ORDINAL, produces "15th" from 15. And the last formatter, using NumberFormatter::PATTERN_DECIMAL, makes use of the same decimal format pattern characters discussed earlier.

The possibilities listed here are only part of what NumberFormatter can do. The PHP manual page for NumberFormatter goes into great detail on additional capabilities.

See Also

Recipe 19.5 shows how to use `NumberFormatter` to localize currency values. Documentation on the `NumberFormatter` class (*http://www.php.net/numberformatter*) and a detailed list of ICU's decimal format pattern characters (*http://bit.ly/1o65kzA*).

19.5 Localizing Currency Values

Problem

You want to display currency amounts in a locale-specific format.

Solution

For default formatting inside a message, use the `currency` style of the `number` argument type:

```
$income = 5549.3;
$debit = -25.95;

$fmt = new MessageFormatter('en_US',
                    '{0,number,currency} in and {1,number,currency} out');

print $fmt->format(array($income,$debit));
```

This prints:

$5,549.30 in and -$25.95 out

For more specific formatting, use the `formatCurrency()` method of a `NumberFormatter`:

```
$income = 5549.3;
$debit = -25.95;

$fmt = new NumberFormatter('en_US', NumberFormatter::CURRENCY);
print $fmt->formatCurrency($income, 'USD') . ' in and ' .
    $fmt->formatCurrency($debit, 'EUR') . ' out';
```

This prints:

$5,549.30 in and -€25.95 out

Discussion

The `currency` style of the `number` argument type in `MessageFormatter` uses the default currency and formatting rules for the locale of the `MessageFormatter` instance. This is certainly a concise and easy way to include local currency amounts in messages you are producing. The code that uses `MessageFormatter` prints:

$5,549.30 in and -$25.95 out

The formatCurrency() method of NumberFormatter makes it easy to specify other currencies. In the example that uses NumberFormatter, because the first call to format Currency() specifies USD (for US dollars) as the currency and the second specifies EUR (for Euro), the code prints:

```
$5,549.30 in and -€25.95 out
```

Although you can construct complex currency formatting rules with the decimal format patterns that MessageFormatter understands, it is often clearer to express those needs via the programmatic interface NumberFormatter provides. For example:

```
$amounts = array( array(152.9, 'USD'),
                  array(328, 'ISK'),
                  array(-1, 'USD'),
                  array(500.53, 'EUR') );

$fmt = new NumberFormatter('en_US', NumberFormatter::CURRENCY);
$fmt->setAttribute(NumberFormatter::PADDING_POSITION,
                   NumberFormatter::PAD_AFTER_PREFIX);
$fmt->setAttribute(NumberFormatter::FORMAT_WIDTH, 15);
$fmt->setTextAttribute(NumberFormatter::PADDING_CHARACTER, ' ');

foreach ($amounts as $amount) {
    print $fmt->formatCurrency($amount[0], $amount[1]) . "\n";
}
```

This prints out a table of four values in different currencies, inserting enough padding between the currency symbol and the value to make each line 15 characters wide. The padding character used is a space, not the default of *. This displays:

```
$        152.90
ISK         328
-$         1.00
€        500.53
```

See Also

Documentation on NumberFormatter::formatCurrency() (*http://bit.ly/1lF2Nu0*) and on the different formatting attributes (*http://bit.ly/1rcdDZk*).

19.6 Localizing Images

Problem

You want to display images that have text in them and have that text in a locale-appropriate language.

Solution

Make an image directory for each locale you want to support, as well as a global image directory for images that have no locale-specific information in them. Create copies of each locale-specific image in the appropriate locale-specific directory. Make sure that the images have the same filename in the different directories. Instead of printing out image URLs directly, treat their paths as localizable strings, either by explicitly storing them in your message catalogs or by computing the right path at runtime.

Discussion

The `img()` wrapper function in Example 19-2 looks for a locale-specific version of an image first, then a global one. If neither are present, it prints a message to the error log.

Example 19-2. Finding locale-specific images

```
function img($locale, $f) {
    static $image_base_path = '/usr/local/www/images';
    static $image_base_url  = '/images';

    if (is_readable("$image_base_path/$locale/$f")) {
        return "$image_base_url/$locale/$f";
    } elseif (is_readable("$image_base_path/global/$f")) {
        return "$image_base_url/global/$f";
    } else {
        error_log("l10n error: locale: $locale, image: '$f'");
    }
}
```

The `img()` function needs to know both the path to the image file in the filesystem (`$image_base_path`) and the path to the image from the base URL of your site (*/images*). It uses the first to test if the file can be read and the second to construct an appropriate URL for the image.

A localized image must have the same filename in each localization directory. For example, an image that says "New!" on a yellow starburst should be called *new.gif* in both the *images/en_US* directory and the *images/es_US* directory, even though the file *images/es_US/new.gif* is a picture of a yellow starburst with "¡Nuevo!" on it.

Don't forget that the `alt` text you display in your image tags also needs to be localized. Example 19-3 prints a complete localized `<img/>` element.

Example 19-3. A localized <img> element

```
print '<img src="' . img($locale, 'cancel.png') . '" ' .
      'alt="' . $messages[$locale]['CANCEL'] . '"/>';
```

If the localized versions of a particular image have varied dimensions, store image height and width in the message catalog as well. Example 19-4 prints a localized `<img/>` element with `height` and `width` attributes.

Example 19-4. A localized <img/> element with height and width

```
print '<img src="' . img($locale, 'cancel.png') . '" ' .
      'alt="' . $messages[$locale]['CANCEL'] . '" ' .
      'height="' . $messages[$locale]['CANCEL_IMG_HEIGHT'] . '" ' .
      'width="' . $messages[$locale]['CANCEL_IMG_WIDTH'] . '"/>';
```

The localized messages for `CANCEL_IMG_HEIGHT` and `CANCEL_IMG_WIDTH` are not text strings, but integers that describe the dimensions of the *cancel.png* image in each locale.

The `img()` function used here is convenient because it inspects the filesystem at runtime to find appropriate files. However, if your image collection rarely changes (or changes in a predictable way, such as when you release a new version of your software) it can be faster to store the paths themselves in the message catalog. This requires you to do some upfront work identifying which locales get a locale-specific image and which get a generic version, however.

See Also

Recipe 19.2 discusses locale-specific message catalogs.

19.7 Localizing Included Files

Problem

You want to include locale-specific files in your pages.

Solution

Modify `include_path` once you've determined the appropriate locale, as shown in Example 19-5.

Example 19-5. Modifying include_path for localization

```
$base = '/usr/local/php-include';
$locale = 'en_US';

$include_path = ini_get('include_path');
ini_set('include_path',"$base/$locale:$base/global:$include_path");
```

Discussion

In Example 19-5, the `$base` variable holds the name of the base directory for your included localized files. Files that are not locale-specific go in the *global* subdirectory of `$base`, and locale-specific files go in a subdirectory named after their locale (e.g., *en_US*). Prepending the locale-specific directory and then the global directory to the include path makes them the first two places PHP looks when you include a file. Putting the locale-specific directory first ensures that nonlocalized information is loaded only if localized information isn't available.

This technique is similar to what the `img()` function does in the Recipe 19.6. Here, however, you can take advantage of PHP's `include_path` feature to have the directory searching happen automatically. For maximum utility, reset `include_path` as early as possible in your code, preferably at the top of a file loaded via `auto_prepend_file` on every request.

See Also

Documentation on `include_path` (*http://bit.ly/1nl0Ks8*) and on `auto_prepend_file` (*http://bit.ly/1l6VcVh*).

19.8 Sorting in a Locale-Aware Order

Problem

You need to sort text in a way that respects a particular locale's rules for character ordering.

Solution

Instantiate a `Collator` object for your locale, and then call its `sort()` method:

```
$words = array('Малина', 'Клубника', 'Огурец');
$collator = new Collator('ru_RU');
// Sorts in-place, just like sort()
$collator->sort($words);
```

Discussion

PHP's normal text-handling routines just treat strings as sequences of bytes. They know nothing about multibyte characters, let alone each locale's rules about which characters go "before" which other ones in that locale's equivalent of alphabetical order. The `Collator` class, however, uses ICU's big database of locale-specific information to do this properly.

The Collator's sort() method corresponds to the PHP sort() function. Collator also has an asort() method which, just like PHP's asort() function, maintains index/value association in the sorted array.

See Also

Documentation on Collator (*http://www.php.net/Collator*).

19.9 Managing Localization Resources

Problem

You need to keep track of your various message catalogs and images.

Solution

Store each message catalog as a serialized PHP array that maps message keys to locale-specific message values. Or, if you need interoperability with ICU-aware tools or other languages, use the ResourceBundle class.

Discussion

At its heart, a message catalog is just a mapping from keys to values. An English message catalog may map HELLO_WORLD to "Hello, World" but a Spanish one maps it to "Hola, Mundo."

A simple way to manage these catalogs is to treat them as PHP arrays and then load them from files (and save them to files) as serialized arrays. Example 19-6 shows a short program that defines some message catalogs and saves them to files.

Example 19-6. Saving message catalogs as serialized arrays

```
$messages = array();
$messages['en_US'] =
    array('FAVORITE_FOODS' => 'My favorite food is {0}.',
          'FRIES' => 'french fries',
          'CANDY' => 'candy',
          'CHIPS' => 'potato chips',
          'EGGPLANT' => 'eggplant');
$messages['en_GB'] =
    array('FAVORITE_FOODS' => 'My favourite food is {0}.',
          'FRIES' => 'chips',
          'CANDY' => 'sweets',
          'CHIPS' => 'crisps',
          'EGGPLANT' => 'aubergine');

foreach ($messages as $locale => $entries) {
```

```
        file_put_contents(__DIR__ . "/$locale.ser", serialize($entries));
    }
```

Given a message catalog saved by Example 19-6, Example 19-7 shows how to load and use it in your program.

Example 19-7. Using message catalogs from serialized arrays

```
/* This might come from user input or the browser */
define('LOCALE', 'en_US');
/* If you can't trust the locale, add some error checking
 * in case the file doesn't exist or can't be
 * unserialized. */
$messages = unserialize(file_get_contents(__DIR__ . '/' . LOCALE . '.ser'));

$candy = new MessageFormatter(LOCALE, $messages['CANDY']);
$favs = new MessageFormatter(LOCALE, $messages['FAVORITE_FOODS']);
print $favs->format(array($candy->format(array()))) . "\n";
```

Treating message catalogs as serialized PHP arrays is straightforward. However, it is a PHP-specific format. ICU defines a generic format, called a "resource bundle" for sharing data such as message catalogs between different programs and tools. If you're working with localization tools or other programming languages that understand ICU resource bundles, use the ResourceBundle class to manage them.

Creating ICU resource bundles involves creating a text file in the proper format, and then running ICU's genrb tool to produce the compiled "binary" version of the bundle. The following examples assume an ICU resource bundle with the following contents:

```
en_US {
    FAVORITE_FOODS { "My favorite food is {0}." }
    FRIES { french fries }
    CANDY { candy }
    CHIPS { potato chips }
    EGGPLANT { eggplant }
}
```

This resource bundle is compiled by genrb to a file named *en_US.res*. The en_US, for the locale, is taken from the top-level table name in the file. The *.res* suffix is the default suffix genrb gives to all compiled resource bundles.

Example 19-8 retrieves message catalog entries from this bundle and prints out the same text as Example 19-7.

Example 19-8. Using message catalogs from resource bundles

```
define('LOCALE', 'en_US');
$bundle = new ResourceBundle(LOCALE, __DIR__);

$candy = new MessageFormatter(LOCALE, $bundle->get('CANDY'));
```

```
$favs = new MessageFormatter(LOCALE, $bundle->get('FAVORITE_FOODS'));
print $favs->format(array($candy->format(array()))) . "\n";
```

In Example 19-8, the two arguments to the ResourceBundle constructor indicate how to find the right compiled resource bundle. The second argument is the directory to look in for the file, and the first argument is the locale name, which is normally the basename of the file. Once the ResourceBundle has been instantiated, you access individual elements in the bundle with the get() method. The code to print out My favorite food is candy. is almost identical to Example 19-7. The only difference is the syntax for retrieving the message strings from the resource bundle, rather then as array elements.

See Also

Recipe 19.2 for a discussion of message catalogs; documentation on ResourceBundle (*http://www.php.net/ResourceBundle*). An overview of ICU resource management, including the syntax for writing resource bundle files (*http://userguide.icu-project.org/ locale/resources*).

19.10 Setting the Character Encoding of Outgoing Data

Problem

You want to make sure that browsers correctly handle the UTF-8 encoded text that your programs emit.

Solution

Set PHP's default_encoding configuration directive to utf-8. This ensures that the Content-Type header PHP emits on HTML responses includes the charset=utf-8 piece, which tells web browsers to interpret the page contents as UTF-8 encoded.

Discussion

Setting default_encoding gives web browsers a heads-up that your page contents should be interpreted as UTF-8 encoded. However, you still have the responsibility of making sure that the page contents really are properly UTF-8 encoded by using string functions appropriately. Recipe 19.12 details how to do that.

If you can't change the default_encoding configuration directive, send the proper Content-Type header yourself with the header() function, as shown in Example 19-9.

Example 19-9. Setting character encoding

```
header('Content-Type: text/html;charset=utf-8');
```

See Also

Recipe 19.12 for information on generating UTF-8-encoded text.

19.11 Setting the Character Encoding of Incoming Data

Problem

You want to make sure that data flowing into your program has a consistent character encoding so you can handle it properly. For example, you want to treat all incoming submitted form data as UTF-8.

Solution

You can't guarantee that browsers will respect the instructions you give them with regard to character encoding, but you can do a number of things that make well-behaved browsers generally follow the rules.

First, follow the instructions in Recipe 19.10 so that your programs tell browsers that they are emitting UTF-8–encoded text. A `Content-Type` header with a `charset` is a good hint to a browser that submitted forms should be encoded using the character encoding the header specifies.

Second, include an `accept-charset="utf-8"` attribute in `<form/>` elements that you output. Although it's not supported by all web browsers, it instructs the browser to encode the user-entered data in the form as UTF-8 before sending it to the server.

Discussion

In general, browsers send back form data with the same encoding used to generate the page containing the form. So if you standardize on UTF-8 output, you can be reasonably sure that you're always getting UTF-8 input. The `accept-charset` `<form/>` attribute is part of the HTML 4.0 specification, but is not implemented everywhere.

See Also

Recipe 19.10 for information about sending UTF-8–encoded output; the `accept-charset` `<form/>` attribute is described at the W3C website (*http://bit.ly/SzxvdB*).

19.12 Manipulating UTF-8 Text

Problem

You want to work with UTF-8–encoded text in your programs. For example, you want to properly calculate the length of multibyte strings and make sure that all text is output as proper UTF-8–encoded characters.

Solution

Use a combination of PHP functions for the variety of tasks that UTF-8 compliance demands.

If the mbstring extension is available, use its string functions for UTF-8–aware string manipulation. Example 19-10 uses the mb_strlen() function to compute the number of characters in each of two UTF-8–encoded strings.

Example 19-10. Using mb_strlen( )

```
// Set the encoding properly
mb_internal_encoding('UTF-8');
// ö is two bytes
$name = 'Kurt Gödel';
// Each of these Hangul characters is three bytes
$dinner = '불고기';

$name_len_bytes = strlen($name);
$name_len_chars = mb_strlen($name);

$dinner_len_bytes = strlen($dinner);
$dinner_len_chars = mb_strlen($dinner);

print "$name is $name_len_bytes bytes and $name_len_chars chars\n";
print "$dinner is $dinner_len_bytes bytes and $dinner_len_chars chars\n";
```

Example 19-10 prints:

```
Kurt Gödel is 11 bytes and 10 chars
불고기 is 9 bytes and 3 chars
```

The iconv extension also offers a few multibyte-aware string manipulation functions, as shown in Example 19-11.

Example 19-11. Using iconv

```
// Set the encoding properly
iconv_set_encoding('internal_encoding','UTF-8');
// ö is two bytes
$name = 'Kurt Gödel';
// Each of these Hangul characters is three bytes
$dinner = '불고기';
```

```
$name_len_bytes = strlen($name);
$name_len_chars = iconv_strlen($name);

$dinner_len_bytes = strlen($dinner);
$dinner_len_chars = iconv_strlen($dinner);

print "$name is $name_len_bytes bytes and $name_len_chars chars\n";
print "$dinner is $dinner_len_bytes bytes and $dinner_len_chars chars\n";

print "The seventh character of $name is " . iconv_substr($name,6,1) . "\n";
print "The last two characters of $dinner are " . iconv_substr($dinner,-2);
```

Use the optional third argument to functions such as htmlentities() and htmlspe
cialchars() that instructs them to treat input as UTF-8 encoded, as shown in
Example 19-12.

Example 19-12. UTF-8 HTML encoding

```
$encoded_name = htmlspecialchars($_POST['name'], ENT_QUOTES, 'UTF-8');
$encoded_dinner = htmlentities($_POST['dinner'], ENT_QUOTES, 'UTF-8');
```

Discussion

Eternal vigilance is the price of proper character encoding. If you've followed the instructions in Recipe 19.10 and Recipe 19.11, data coming into your program should be
UTF-8 encoded and browsers will properly handle data coming out of your program
as UTF-8 encoded. This leaves you with two responsibilities: to operate on strings in a
UTF-8–aware manner and to generate text that is UTF-8 encoded.

Fulfilling the first responsibility is made easier once you have adopted the fundamental
credo of internationalization awareness: a character is not a byte. The PHP-specific
corollary to this axiom is that PHP's string functions only know about bytes, not characters. For example, the strlen() function counts the number of bytes in a string, not
the number of characters. In the prelapsarian days of ISO-8859-1 encoding, this wasn't
a problem—each of the 256 characters in the character set took up one byte. A UTF-8–
encoded character, on the other hand, uses between one and four bytes. The mbstring
and iconv extensions provide alternatives for some string functions that operate on a
character-by-character basis, not a byte-by-byte basis. These functions are listed in
Table 19-3.

Table 19-3. Character-based functions

Regular function	mbstring function	iconv function
strlen()	mb_strlen()	iconv_strlen()
strpos()	mb_strpos()	iconv_strpos()
strrpos()	mb_strrpos()	iconv_strrpos()

Regular function	mbstring function	iconv function
substr()	mb_substr()	iconv_substr()
strtolower()	mb_strtolower()	-
strtoupper()	mb_strtoupper()	-
substr_count()	mb_substr_count()	-
ereg()	mb_ereg()	-
eregi()	mb_eregi()	-
ereg_replace()	mb_ereg_replace()	-
eregi_replace()	mb_eregi_replace()	-
split()	mb_split()	-
mail()	mb_send_mail()	-

For mbstring to work properly, it needs to be told to use the UTF-8 encoding scheme. As in Example 19-10, you can do this in script with the mb_internal_encoding() function. Or to set this value system-wide, set the mbstring.internal_encoding configuration directive to UTF-8.

iconv has similar needs. Use the iconv_set_encoding() function as in Example 19-11 or set the iconv.internal_encoding configuration directive.

mbstring provides alternatives for the ereg family of regular expression functions. However, you can always use UTF-8 strings with the PCRE (preg_*()) regular expression functions. The u modifier tells a preg function that the pattern string is UTF-8 encoded and enables the use of various Unicode properties in patterns. Example 19-13 uses the "lowercase letter" Unicode property to count the number of lowercase letters in each of two strings.

Example 19-13. UTF-8 regular expression matching

```
$name = 'Kurt Gödel';
$dinner = '불고기|';

$name_lower = preg_match_all('/\p{Ll}/u',$name,$match);
$dinner_lower = preg_match_all('/\p{Ll}/u',$dinner,$match);

print "There are $name_lower lowercase letters in $name.\n";
print "There are $dinner_lower lowercase letters in $dinner.\n";
```

Example 19-13 prints:

```
There are 7 lowercase letters in Kurt Gödel.
There are 0 lowercase letters in 불고기|.
```

Other functions help you translate between other character encodings and UTF-8. The utf8_encode() and utf8_decode() functions move strings between the ISO-8859-1 encoding and UTF-8. Because ISO-8859-1 is the default encoding in many situations, these functions are a handy way to bring non-UTF-8–aware data into compliance. For example, the dictionaries that the pspell extension uses often have their entries encoded in ISO-8859-1. In Example 19-14, the utf8_encode() function is necessary to turn the output of pspell_suggest() into a proper UTF-8–encoded string.

Example 19-14. Applying UTF-8 encoding to ISO-8859-1 strings

```
$lang = isset($_GET['lang']) ? $_GET['lang'] : 'en';
$word = isset($_GET['word']) ? $_GET['word'] : 'asparagus';

$ps = pspell_new($lang);
$check = pspell_check($ps, $word);

print htmlspecialchars($word,ENT_QUOTES,'UTF-8');
print $check ? ' is ' : ' is not ';
print ' found in the dictionary.';
print '<hr/>';

if (! $check) {
    $suggestions = pspell_suggest($ps, $word);
    if (count($suggestions)) {
        print 'Suggestions: <ul>';
        foreach ($suggestions as $suggestion) {
            $utf8suggestion = utf8_encode($suggestion);
            $safesuggestion = htmlspecialchars($utf8suggestion,
                                        ENT_QUOTES,'UTF-8');
            print "<li>$safesuggestion</li>";
        }
        print '</ul>';
    }
}
```

It may ease the cognitive burden of proper character encoding to think of it as a task similar to HTML entity encoding. In each case, text must be processed so that it is appropriately formatted for a particular context. With entity encoding, that usually means running data retrieved from an external source through htmlentities() or htmlspecialchars(). With character encoding, it means turning everything into UTF-8 before you process it, using a character-aware function for string operations, and ensuring strings are UTF-8 encoded before outputting them.

See Also

Recipe 19.10 and Recipe 19.11 for setting up your programs for receiving and sending UTF-8–encoded strings; documentation on mbstring (*http://www.php.net/mbstring*), on iconv (*http://www.php.net/iconv*), on htmlentities() (*http://www.php.net/htmlen tities*), on htmlspecialchars() (*http://bit.ly/1qwwOgL*), on PCRE pattern syntax (*http://bit.ly/1ird4Ed*), on `utf8_encode()` (*http://www.php.net/utf8_encode*), and on `utf8_decode()` (*http://www.php.net/utf8_decode*).

Good background resources on managing PHP and character set issues include:

- "Character Sets/Character Encoding Issues" (*http://bit.ly/1mqy5FI*) on the PHP WACT wiki
- "Characters vs. Bytes" (*http://bit.ly/1jiTuM9*) by Tim Bray
- "A Tutorial on Character Code Issues" (*http://bit.ly/1iwlVeR*) by Jukka Korpela

CHAPTER 20

Error Handling

20.0 Introduction

The name *programmer* for those who spend their time developing web applications is misleading: the vast majority of time one spends *programming* is actually spent *debugging*. Whether you're fixing typos or refactoring chunks of code that are performing poorly in a heavily loaded production environment, odds are you'll spend a large amount of your career debugging and testing, and debugging and testing again. And again, and again, and again.

The raucous party that is a frantic, all-night debugging session was probably omitted from your job description—who would sign up for that kind of fun? The fact is that errors, bugs, debugging, and testing are a part of the programmer's life. If you face this head on with good practices and techniques, you can minimize the time you spend debugging and maximize the time you spend on the good stuff.

Unfortunately, many developers don't spend much time building error handling, debugging, and testing skills; don't make the same mistake. If you employ what's affectionately known as pessimistic programming, you'll begin to plan for things to go wrong —and your application will be prepared to handle it gracefully during those moments.

This chapter deals with errors: finding the source of errors, determining what was going on when an error occurred, hiding errors from end users, and logging errors so you can conduct informed debugging sessions after the error occurs. Chapter 21 complements this information with information on using a debugger with PHP and writing tests.

20.1 Finding and Fixing Parse Errors

Problem

Your PHP script fails to run due to fatal parse errors, and you want to find the problem quickly and continue coding.

Solution

Check the line that the PHP interpreter reports as having a problem. If that line is OK, work your way backward in the program until you find the problematic line.

Or use a PHP-aware development environment that will alert you to syntax errors as you code, and that can also help track down parse errors when they occur.

Discussion

Like most programming languages, the PHP interpreter is very picky about the way scripts are written. When things aren't written exactly as they they should be, the PHP interpreter will halt parsing and let you know that things aren't right. This is called a *parse error*.

Take this flawed program:

```
<?php
if isset($user_firstname) {
  print "Howdy, $user_firstname!";
} else {
  print "Howdy!";
}
```

Save that to a file called *howdy.php* and run it, and PHP will display this error message:

```
Parse error: syntax error, unexpected T_ISSET, expecting '(' in ↵
/var/www/howdy.php on line 2
```

Based on this message, we know that there's a problem on line 2—specifically, a syntax error; something about an unexpected T_ISSET.

When PHP parses scripts to convert them into a format that the computer can understand, it breaks down each line into chunks called *tokens*. PHP recognizes dozens of tokens, and it knows the rules about what tokens are allowed to appear in what order in a line of PHP code. In the preceding parse error, the bit about an unexpected T_IS SET means that a T_ISSET token was encountered by the PHP interpreter where it's not supposed to be.

Reading a little further through the parse error, it's suddenly clear that the PHP interpreter was expecting a (where it found the T_ISSET token. Looking back at line 2 of the program, sure enough, the open parenthesis is missing after the `if` and before the `isset()` function.

Some PHP-aware editing tools can alert you to these problems before you get to the stage of running the code and getting the parse error in the first place. Figure 20-1 shows our buggy program in NetBeans IDE, complete with advance warning of the parse error in our future.

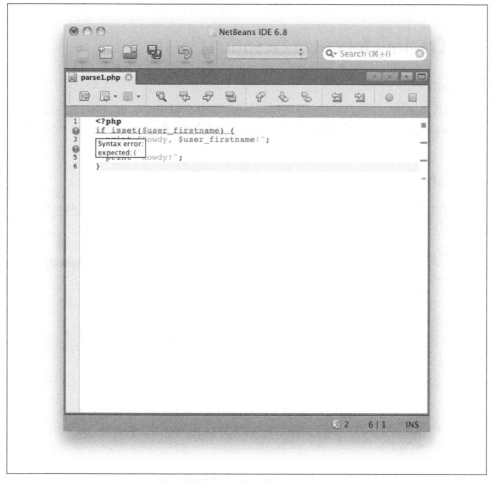

Figure 20-1. NetBeans IDE sees the parse error before it happens

It's not always as easy as going directly to the line that the parse error tells you to go to. Sometimes an error several lines prior to the one reported causes a problem that may not *seem* like a problem when it is encountered, but *is* a problem within the context of what is on the line that the parse error is referring to.

If you have difficulty finding the source of the error and don't have access to a debugging tool to help you root out the cause of the error, remember that when all else fails, commenting is your friend. Start by commenting out blocks of code before the line referred to in the parse error, and then rerunning the offending script. Through the process of elimination, you will eventually find the line causing the problem.

See Also

The PHP parser token cheat sheet (*http://www.php.net/tokens*).

20.2 Creating Your Own Exception Classes

Problem

You want control over how (or if) error messages are displayed to users, even though you're using several third-party libraries that each have their own views on handling errors.

Solution

Take advantage of PHP 5's support for exceptions to create your own exception handler that will do *your* bidding when errors occur in third-party libraries:

```php
class CustomException extends Exception {
    public function __construct($e) {
        // make sure everything is assigned properly
        parent::__construct($e->getMessage(), $e->getCode());

        // log what we know
        $msg = "------------------------------------------------\n";
        $msg .= __CLASS__ . ": [{$this->code}]: {$this->message}\n";
        $msg .= $e->getTraceAsString() . "\n";
        error_log($msg);
    }

    // overload the __toString() method to suppress any "normal" output
    public function __toString() {
        return $this->printMessage();
    }

    // map error codes to output messages or templates
    public function printMessage() {

        $usermsg = '';
        $code = $this->getCode();

        switch ($code) {
        case SOME_DEFINED_ERROR_CODE:
```

```
                $usermsg = 'Ooops! Sorry about that.';
                break;
            case OTHER_DEFINED_ERROR_CODE:
                $usermsg = "Drat!";
                break;
            default:
                $usermsg = file_get_contents('/templates/general_error.html');
                break;
        }
        return $usermsg;
    }

    // static exception_handler for default exception handling
    public static function exception_handler($exception) {
        throw new CustomException($exception);
    }

}

// make sure to catch every exception
set_exception_handler('CustomException::exception_handler');

try {
    $obj = new CoolThirdPartyPackage();
} catch (CustomException $e) {
    echo $e;
}
```

Discussion

PHP 5 introduced the concept of exceptions to PHP. Exceptions are a common construct in many other languages; they're used to deal gracefully with unforeseen error conditions. This is particularly useful when including third-party library code in your scripts when you're not 100 percent confident how that code will behave in unpredictable circumstances, such as loss of database connectivity, an unresponsive remote API server, or similar acts of randomness.

Exceptions provide your scripts with a `try/catch` structure you use to create a sandboxed section of your script where things can go horribly wrong without hurting anything else:

```
try {
  // do something
  $obj = new CoolThing();
} catch (CustomException $e) {
  // at this point, the CoolThing wasn't cool
  print $e;
}
```

So why use a custom exception, when PHP 5 already provides a perfectly functional exception class? The default exception class doesn't exactly fulfill the *graceful* part of handling unpredictable results. It just prints out an error message not much different from regular errors. If you want truly flexible handling of these unfortunate events, a custom exception handler allows you to do what you have determined is the most appropriate given the condition.

In the `CustomException` class in the preceding code, you have two objectives. The first is to log everything you can about what happened; the second is to be as cool as possible from the user's perspective.

The `__construct()` method sets up the exception by calling the `parent`'s constructor (the constructor of the default exception class) to ensure that all possible values are set for use by your custom exception's methods.

Then, you immediately log what you can, using an `error_log()` call that you can replace with a custom error logger of your choice. In keeping with the goal of handling this error gracefully, make sure that your error logger is capable of logging this error without causing another one. For example, if the error you're about to log is related to failed database connectivity, it's probably a good idea if you don't try to log this error to an error log table on that same database server.

From there, the `CustomException` class is written to expect the calling code to print out the error. However, that is not required behavior. You could just as easily have a `try/catch` block like this:

```
try {
  // do something
  $obj = new CoolThing();
} catch (CustomException $e) {
  // at this point, the CoolThing wasn't cool
  $e->redirectToOhNoPage();
}
```

The segment `catch (CustomException $e)` means that an instance of the `CustomException` class will be instantiated and assigned to the variable $e. From there, $e is just an object that has some predefined values and methods relating to the problem that caused the exception, but is otherwise a regular object that can be as simple or as complicated as you want it to be.

One primary difference between a standard error handler and exceptions is the concept of *recovery*. The use case shown in this recipe thus far has a good correlation with the `set_error_handler()` usage you may already be familiar with. The idea is that your custom handler can contain a clean-up routine that checks the state of the application at the time that the custom exception is caught, cleans up as best as it can, and dies gracefully.

Exceptions can also be used to easily recover from an error in the midst of an application's flow. For example, a `try` block can have multiple `catch` blocks that are somewhat neater than a bunch of `if/else/else/else` blocks:

```
try {
    // do something
    $obj = new CoolThing();
} catch (PossibleException $e) {
    // we thought this could possibly happen
    print "<!-- caught exception $e! -->";
    $obj = new PlanB();
} catch (AnotherPossibleException $e) {
    // we knew about this possibility as well
    print "<!-- aha! caught exception $e -->";
    $obj = new PlanC();
} catch (CustomException $e) {
    // if all else fails, go to clean-up
    $e->cleanUp();
    $e->bailOut();
}
```

In this example, we're able to use the `try/catch` structure to check for exception conditions without stepping out of the flow of this chunk of code, unless all else truly fails. If we were unable to recover in any of the ways we knew how to in line with the flow of the application, we still have the option of bailing out to a catchall custom exception. We can even throw a new exception inside the `catch` blocks in order to influence the order in which exceptions bubble up to a `try/catch` block that may be wrapping the chunk of code currently executing.

See Also

Recipe 20.9 for more on logging errors; documentation on exceptions (*http:// www.php.net/exceptions*).

20.3 Printing a Stack Trace

Problem

You want to know what's happening at a specific point in your program, and what happened leading up to that point.

Solution

Use `debug_print_backtrace()`:

```
function stooges() {
    print "woo woo woo!\n";
    larry();
```

```
  }

  function larry() {
    curly();
  }

  function curly() {
    moe();
  }

  function moe() {
    debug_print_backtrace();
  }

  stooges();
```

This will print:

```
woo woo woo!
#0  moe() called at [backtrace.php:12]
#1  curly() called at [backtrace.php:8]
#2  larry() called at [backtrace.php:4]
#3  stooges() called at [backtrace.php:19]
```

Discussion

The handy debug_print_backtrace() function allows you to quickly get a sense of what has been been going on in your application immediately before you called a particular function.

The more complicated your application, the more information you can expect to have returned from the backtrace functions. For debugging larger codebases, you may achieve bug-hunting success more quickly using a full debugging extension, such as Xdebug, or an integrated development environment (IDE), such as NetBeans, that supports setting breakpoints, stepping in and out of blocks of code, watching the evolution of variables, and more.

If all you need is a little more information than you can get from sprinkling print 'Here I am on line ' . *LINE*; statements throughout your code, debug_print_backtrace() will suit your needs well.

The output from debug_print_backtrace() includes, by default, the arguments passed to each function. If those arguments are big arrays or complicated objects, it can make the output unwieldy. You can pass the constant DEBUG_BACKTRACE_IGNORE_ARGS as a first argument to debug_print_backtrace() to have arguments eliminated from the output. If you only need to keep track of the sequence of functions called, this is perfect.

A companion to debug_print_backtrace() is debug_backtrace(). Instead of outputting the backtrace, debug_backtrace() returns it as an array, one element per stack frame. This is useful if you only need to print certain elements of the backtrace, or you want to manipulate it programmatically. Example 20-1 uses the information from de bug_backtrace() to print out a limited trace just showing functions and class names.

Example 20-1. Using debug_backtrace()

```
function print_parsed_backtrace() {
    $backtrace = debug_backtrace();
    for ($i = 1, $j = count($backtrace); $i < $j; $i++) {
        $frame = $backtrace[$i];
        if (isset($frame['class'])) {
            $function = $frame['class'] . $frame['type'] . $frame['function'];
        } else {
            $function = $frame['function'];
        }
        print $function . '()';
        if ($i != ($j - 1)) {
            print ', ';
        }
    }
}

function stooges() {
  print "woo woo woo!\n";
  Fine::larry();
}

class Fine {
    static function larry() {
        $brothers = new Howard;
        $brothers->curly();
    }
}
class Howard {
    function curly() {
        $this->moe();
    }
    function moe() {
        print_parsed_backtrace();
    }
}

stooges();
```

This prints:

```
woo woo woo!
Howard->moe(), Howard->curly(), Fine::larry(), stooges()
```

Example 20-1 causes a chain of functions to be invoked, with one of them calling print_parsed_backtrace(). This function then gets information about the stack frames from debug_backtrace() and then walks through them. The for() loop starts at 1, not 0, because the first frame on the stack (array element 0) is for the call to `print_parsed_backtrace()` itself. If the stack frame is a method call, then the `class` element of the array contains the class name of the method and the `type` element contains `::` for a static method call and `->` for an instance method call. If there's no `class` element, it's just a regular function call.

See Also

Documentation on `debug_backtrace()` (*http://bit.ly/Tx0vm2*) and `debug_print_back trace()` (*http://bit.ly/1qaqoWS*); NetBeans (*https://netbeans.org/*); The Three Stooges (*http://bit.ly/1wxXIHL*).

20.4 Reading Configuration Variables

Problem

You want to get the value of a PHP configuration setting.

Solution

Use `ini_get()`:

```
// find out the include path:
$include_path = ini_get('include_path');
```

Discussion

To get all the configuration variable values in one step, call `ini_get_all()`. It returns the variables in an associative array, and each array element is itself an associative array. The second array has three elements: a global value for the setting, a local value, and an access code:

```
// Put all config values in an associative array
$vars = ini_get_all();
print_r($vars['date.timezone']);
```

This prints:

```
Array
(
    [global_value] => UTC
    [local_value] => UTC
    [access] => 7
)
```

The `global_value` is the value set from the *php.ini* file; the `local_value` is adjusted to account for any changes made in the web server's configuration file, any relevant *.htac-*

cess files, and the current script. The value of `access` is a numeric constant representing the places where this value can be altered. Table 20-1 explains the values for `access`. Note that the name `access` is a little misleading in this respect because the value of the setting can always be checked, but not always adjusted.

Table 20-1. Access values

Value	PHP constant	Meaning
1	PHP_INI_USER	Any script, using `ini_set()`
2	PHP_INI_PERDIR	Directory level, using *.htaccess*
4	PHP_INI_SYSTEM	System level, using *php.ini* or *httpd.conf*
7	PHP_INI_ALL	Everywhere: scripts, directories, and the system

A value of 6 means the setting can be changed in both the directory and system level, as 2 + 4 = 6. In practice, there are no variables modifiable only in PHP_INI_USER or PHP_INI_PERDIR, and all variables are modifiable in PHP_INI_SYSTEM, so everything has a value of 4, 6, or 7.

You can also get variables belonging to a specific extension by passing the extension name to `ini_get_all()`:

```
// return just the session module specific variables
$session = ini_get_all('session');
```

By convention, the variables for an extension are prefixed with the extension name and a period. So all the session variables begin with session. and all the PDO variables begin with pdo, for example.

Because `ini_get()` returns the current value for a configuration directive, if you want to check the original value from the *php.ini* file, use `get_cfg_var()`:

```
$original = get_cfg_var('sendmail_from'); // have we changed our address?
```

The value returned by `get_cfg_var()` is the same as what appears in the `global_val ue` element of the array returned by `ini_get_all()`.

See Also

Recipe 20.5 on setting configuration variables; documentation on `ini_get()` (*http://www.php.net/ini-get*), `ini_get_all()` (*http://www.php.net/ini-get-all*), and `get_cfg_var()` (*http://www.php.net/get-cfg-var*); a complete list of configuration variables, their defaults, and when they can be modified (*http://www.php.net/ini.list*).

20.5 Setting Configuration Variables

Problem

You want to change the value of a PHP configuration setting.

Solution

Use `ini_set()`:

```
// add a directory to the include path
ini_set('include_path', ini_get('include_path') . ':/home/fezzik/php');
```

Discussion

Configuration variables are not permanently changed by `ini_set()`. The new value lasts only for the duration of the request in which `ini_set()` is called. To make a persistent modification, alter the values stored in the *php.ini* file.

It isn't meaningful to alter certain variables, such as `asp_tags`, because by the time you call `ini_set()` to modify the setting, it's too late to change the behavior the setting affects. If a variable can't be changed, `ini_set()` returns `false`.

However, it is useful to alter configuration variables in certain pages. For example, if you're running a script from the command line, set `html_errors` to `off`.

To reset a variable back to its original setting, use `ini_restore()`:

```
ini_restore('sendmail_from'); // go back to the default value
```

See Also

Recipe 20.4 on getting values of configuration variables; documentation on `ini_set()` (*http://www.php.net/ini-set*) and `ini_restore()` (*http://www.php.net/ini-restore*).

20.6 Hiding Error Messages from Users

Problem

You don't want PHP error messages to be visible to users.

Solution

Set the following values in your *php.ini* or web server configuration file:

```
display_errors =off
log_errors     =on
```

You can also set these values using `ini_set()` if you don't have access to edit your server's *php.ini* file:

```
ini_set('display_errors', 'off');
ini_set('log_errors', 'on');
```

These settings tell PHP not to display errors as HTML to the browser but to put them in the server's error log.

Discussion

When `log_errors` is set to on, error messages are written to the server's error log. If you want PHP errors to be written to a separate file, set the `error_log` configuration directive with the name of that file:

```
error_log   = /var/log/php.error.log
```

or:

```
ini_set('error_log', '/var/log/php.error.log');
```

If `error_log` is set to `syslog`, PHP error messages are sent to the system logger using *syslog(3)* on Unix and to the Event Log on Windows. If `error_log` is not set, error messages are sent to a default location, usually your web server's error log file. (For the command-line PHP program, the default error location is the standard error output stream.)

There are lots of error messages you want to show your users, such as telling them they've filled in a form incorrectly, but you should shield your users from internal errors that may reflect a problem with your code. There are two reasons for this. First, these errors appear unprofessional (to expert users) and confusing (to novice users). If something goes wrong when saving form input to a database, check the return code from the database query and display a message to your users apologizing and asking them to come back later. Showing them a cryptic error message straight from PHP doesn't inspire confidence in your website.

Second, displaying these errors to users is a security risk. Depending on your database and the type of error, the error message may contain information about how to log in to your database or server and how it is structured. Malicious users can use this information to mount an attack on your website.

For example, if your database server is down, and you attempt to connect to it with `mysql_connect()`, PHP generates the following warning:

```
<br>
<b>Warning</b>:  Can't connect to MySQL server on 'db.example.com' (111) in
<b>/www/docroot/example.php</b> on line <b>3</b><br>
```

If this warning message is sent to a user's browser, he learns that your database server is called *db.example.com* and can focus his cracking efforts on it.

See Also

Recipe 20.9 for how to log errors; Recipe 20.5 for more about setting configuration values with `ini_set()`; documentation on PHP configuration directives (*http://www.php.net/configuration*).

20.7 Tuning Error Handling

Problem

You want to alter the error-logging sensitivity on a particular page. This lets you control what types of errors are reported.

Solution

To adjust the types of errors PHP complains about, use `error_reporting()`:

```
error_reporting(E_ALL);                 // everything
error_reporting(E_ERROR | E_PARSE);     // only major problems
error_reporting(E_ALL & ~E_NOTICE);     // everything but notices
```

Discussion

Every error generated has an error type associated with it. For example, if you try to `array_pop()` a string, PHP complains that "This argument needs to be an array" because you can only pop arrays. The error type associated with this message is `E_NOTICE`, a nonfatal runtime problem.

By default, the error reporting level is `E_ALL & ~E_NOTICE`, which means all error types except notices. The `&` is a logical `AND`, and the `~` is a logical `NOT`. However, the *php.ini-recommended* configuration file sets the error reporting level to `E_ALL`, which is all error types.

PHP 5.0 introduced a new error level, `E_STRICT`. Enabling `E_STRICT` during development has the benefit of PHP alerting you of ways your code could be improved. You will receive warnings about the use of deprecated functions, along with tips to nudge you in the direction of the latest and greatest suggested methods of coding. For PHP 5.0–5.3, `E_STRICT` is the only error level not included in `E_ALL`; for maximum coverage during development, set the error reporting level to `E_ALL | E_STRICT`. Starting with PHP 5.4, `E_STRICT` is included in `E_ALL`.

Error messages flagged as notices are runtime problems that are less serious than warnings. They're not necessarily wrong, but they indicate a potential problem. One example of an E_NOTICE is "Undefined variable," which occurs if you try to use a variable without previously assigning it a value:

```
// Generates an E_NOTICE
foreach ($array as $value) {
    $html .= $value;
}

// Doesn't generate any error message
$html = '';
foreach ($array as $value) {
    $html .= $value;
}
```

In the first case, the first time through the foreach, $html is undefined. So when you append to it, PHP lets you know you're appending to an undefined variable. In the second case, the empty string is assigned to $html above the loop to avoid the E_NO TICE. The previous two code snippets generate identical code because the default value of a variable is the empty string. The E_NOTICE can be helpful because, for example, you may have misspelled a variable name:

```
foreach ($array as $value) {
    $hmtl .= $value; // oops! that should be $html
}

$html = '';
foreach ($array as $value) {
    $hmtl .= $value; // oops! that should be $html
}
```

A custom error-handling function can parse errors based on their type and take an appropriate action. A complete list of error types is shown in Table 20-2.

Table 20-2. Error types

Value	Constant	Description	Catchable
1	E_ERROR	Nonrecoverable error	No
2	E_WARNING	Recoverable error	Yes
4	E_PARSE	Parser error	No
8	E_NOTICE	Possible error	Yes
16	E_CORE_ERROR	Like E_ERROR but generated by the PHP core	No
32	E_CORE_WARNING	Like E_WARNING but generated by the PHP core	No
64	E_COMPILE_ERROR	Like E_ERROR but generated by the Zend Engine	No
128	E_COMPILE_WARNING	Like E_WARNING but generated by the Zend Engine	No
256	E_USER_ERROR	Like E_ERROR but triggered by calling trigger_error()	Yes

Value	Constant	Description	Catchable
512	E_USER_WARNING	Like E_WARNING but triggered by calling `trigger_error()`	Yes
1024	E_USER_NOTICE	Like E_NOTICE but triggered by calling `trigger_error()`	Yes
2048	E_STRICT	Runtime notices in which PHP suggests changes to improve code quality (since PHP 5)	N/A
4096	E_RECOVERABLE_ERROR	Dangerous error (such as mismatched type hint) but not fatal	Yes
8192	E_DEPRECATED	Warning that you've used a deprecated function or feature	Yes
16384	E_USER_DEPRECATED	Deprecation warning you can trigger in your code	Yes
32767	E_ALL	Everything	No

Errors labeled catchable can be processed by the function registered using `set_er ror_handler()`. The others indicate such a serious problem that they're not safe to be handled by users, and PHP must take care of them.

The E_RECOVERABLE_ERROR type was introduced in PHP 5.2.0. The E_DEPRECATED and E_USER_DEPRECATED types were introduced in PHP 5.3.0.

See Also

Recipe 20.8 shows how to set up a custom error handler; documentation on `error_re porting()` (*http://bit.ly/1qwx7Ih*) and `set_error_handler()` (*http://bit.ly/TjyjT4*); more information about errors (*http://bit.ly/1mqyWpU*).

20.8 Using a Custom Error Handler

Problem

You want to create a custom error handler that lets you control how PHP reports errors.

Solution

To set up your own error function, use `set_error_handler()`:

```
set_error_handler('pc_error_handler');

function pc_error_handler($errno, $error, $file, $line) {
    $message = "[ERROR][$errno][$error][$file:$line]";
    error_log($message);
}
```

Discussion

A custom error handling function can parse errors based on their type and take the appropriate action. See Table 20-2 in Recipe 20.7 for a list of error types.

Pass `set_error_handler()` the name of a function, and PHP forwards all errors to that function. The error handling function can take up to five parameters. The first parameter is the error type, such as 8 for `E_NOTICE`. The second is the message thrown by the error, such as "Undefined variable: html." The third and fourth arguments are the name of the file and the line number in which PHP detected the error. The final parameter is an array holding all the variables defined in the current scope and their values.

For example, in this code, $html is appended to without first being assigned an initial value:

```
error_reporting(E_ALL);
set_error_handler('pc_error_handler');

function pc_error_handler($errno, $error, $file, $line, $context) {
    $message = "[ERROR][$errno][$error][$file:$line]";
    print "$message";
    print_r($context);
}

$form = array('one','two');

foreach ($form as $line) {
    $html .= "<b>$line</b>";
}
```

When the "Undefined variable" error is generated, `pc_error_handler()` prints:

```
[ERROR][8][Undefined variable:  html][err-all.php:16]
```

After the initial error message, `pc_error_handler()` also prints a large array containing all the global, environment, request, and session variables.

Errors labeled catchable in Table 20-2 can be processed by the function registered using `set_error_handler()`. The others indicate such a serious problem that they're not safe to be handled by users and PHP must take care of them.

See Also

Recipe 20.7 lists the different error types; documentation on `set_error_handler()` (*http://www.php.net/set-error-handler*).

20.9 Logging Errors

Problem

You want to save program errors to a log. These errors can include everything from parser errors and files not being found to bad database queries and dropped connections.

Solution

Use `error_log()` to write to the error log:

```
// LDAP error
if (ldap_errno($ldap)) {
    error_log("LDAP Error #" . ldap_errno($ldap) . ": " . ldap_error($ldap));
}
```

Discussion

Logging errors facilitates debugging. Smart error logging makes it easier to fix bugs. Always log information about what caused the error:

```
$r = mysql_query($sql);
if (! $r) {
    $error = mysql_error();
    error_log('[DB: query @'.$_SERVER['REQUEST_URI']."][$sql]: $error");
} else {
    // process results
}
```

You're not getting all the debugging help you could be if you simply log that an error occurred without any supporting information:

```
$r = mysql_query($sql);
if (! $r) {
    error_log("bad query");
} else {
    // process result
}
```

Another useful technique is to include the `__FILE__`, `__LINE__`, `__FUNCTION__`, `__CLASS__`, and `__METHOD__` "magic" constants in your error messages:

```
error_log('['.__FILE__.']['.__LINE__."]: $error");
```

The `__FILE__` constant is the current filename, `__LINE__` is the current line number, `__FUNCTION__` is the current function name, `__METHOD__` is the current method name (if any), and `__CLASS__` is the current class name (if any). Starting with PHP 5.3.0, `__DIR__` is the directory that `__FILE__` is in and `__NAMESPACE__` is the current namespace. Starting in PHP 5.4.0, `__TRAIT__` is the current trait name (if any).

See Also

Recipe 20.6 for hiding error messages from users; documentation on `error_log()` (*http://bit.ly/1sByLfZ*); documentation on magic constants (*http://bit.ly/1lmK9aJ*).

20.10 Eliminating "headers already sent" Errors

Problem

You are trying to send an HTTP header or cookie using `header()` or `setcookie()`, but PHP reports a "headers already sent" error message.

Solution

This error happens when you send nonheader output before calling `header()` or `set cookie()`.

Rewrite your code so any output happens after sending headers:

```php
<?php
// good
setcookie("name", $name);
print "Hello $name!";

// bad
print "Hello $name!";
setcookie("name", $name);

// good
setcookie("name",$name); ?>
<html><title>Hello</title>
```

Discussion

An HTTP message has a header and a body, which are sent to the client in that order. Once you begin sending the body, you can't send any more headers. So if you call `setcookie()` after printing some HTML, PHP can't send the appropriate `Cookie` header.

Also, remove trailing whitespace in any include files. When you include a file with blank lines outside `<?php ?>` tags, the blank lines are sent to the browser. Use `trim()` to remove leading and trailing blank lines from files:

```php
$file = '/path/to/file.php';

// backup
copy($file, "$file.bak") or die("Can't copy $file: $php_errormsg");

// read and trim
$contents = trim(join('',file($file)));

// write
$fh = fopen($file, 'w')  or die("Can't open $file for writing: $php_errormsg");
if (-1 == fwrite($fh, $contents)) { die("Can't write to $file: $php_errormsg");}
fclose($fh)             or die("Can't close $file: $php_errormsg");
```

Instead of processing files on a one-by-one basis, it may be more convenient to do so on a directory-by-directory basis. Recipe 25.7 describes how to process all the files in a directory.

Another perfectly legitimate approach to ensuring included files don't have any trailing whitespace is to just leave off the closing ?> tag. If the included file is purely PHP, this method (*http://bit.ly/1jdiqZ0*) guarantees that you won't have to go back to that file to clean up inadvertent whitespace.

If you don't want to worry about blank lines disrupting the sending of headers, turn on output buffering as shown in Recipe 8.13. Output buffering prevents PHP from immediately sending all output to the client. If you buffer your output, you can intermix headers and body text with abandon. However, it may seem to users that your server takes longer to fulfill their requests because they have to wait slightly longer before the browser displays any output.

See Also

Recipe 8.13 for a discussion of output buffering; Recipe 25.7 for processing all files in a directory; documentation on header() (*http://www.php.net/header*).

20.11 Logging Debugging Information

Problem

You want to make debugging easier by adding statements to print out variables. But you want to be able to switch back and forth easily between production and debug modes.

Solution

Put a function that conditionally prints out messages based on a defined constant in a page included using the auto_prepend_file configuration setting. Save the following code to *debug.php*:

```
// turn debugging on
define('DEBUG',true);

// generic debugging function
function pc_debug($message) {
    if (defined('DEBUG') && DEBUG) {
        error_log($message);
    }
}
```

Set the auto_prepend_file directive in *php.ini* or your site *.htaccess* file:

```
auto_prepend_file=debug.php
```

Now call `pc_debug()` from your code to print out debugging information:

```
$sql = 'SELECT color, shape, smell FROM vegetables';
pc_debug("[sql: $sql]"); // only printed if DEBUG is true
$r = mysql_query($sql);
```

Discussion

Debugging code is a necessary side effect of writing code. There are a variety of techniques to help you quickly locate and squash your bugs. Many of these involve including scaffolding that helps ensure the correctness of your code. The more complicated the program, the more scaffolding needed. Fred Brooks, in *The Mythical Man-Month* (Addison-Wesley), guesses that there's "half as much code in scaffolding as there is in product." Proper planning ahead of time allows you to integrate the scaffolding into your programming logic in a clean and efficient fashion. This requires you to think out beforehand what you want to measure and record and how you plan on sorting through the data gathered by your scaffolding.

One technique for sifting through the information is to assign different priority levels to different types of debugging comments. Then the debug function prints information only if it's higher than the current priority level:

```
define('DEBUG',2);

function pc_debug($message, $level = 0) {
    if (defined('DEBUG') && ($level > DEBUG)) {
        error_log($message);
    }
}

$sql = 'SELECT color, shape, smell FROM vegetables';
pc_debug("[sql: $sql]", 1); // not printed, since 1 < 2
pc_debug("[sql: $sql]", 3); // printed, since 3 > 2
```

Another technique is to write wrapper functions to include additional information to help with performance tuning, such as the time it takes to execute a database query:

```
function db_query($sql) {
    if (defined('DEBUG') && DEBUG) {
        // start timing the query if DEBUG is on
        $DEBUG_STRING = "[sql: $sql]<br>\n";
        $starttime = microtime(true);
    }

    $r = mysql_query($sql);

    if (! $r) {
        $error = mysql_error();
        error_log('[DB: query @'.$_SERVER['REQUEST_URI']."][$sql]: $error");
    } elseif (defined(DEBUG) && DEBUG) {
        // the query didn't fail and DEBUG is turned on, so finish timing it
```

```
            $endtime = microtime(true);
            $elapsedtime = $endtime - $starttime;
            $DEBUG_STRING .= "[time: $elapsedtime]<br>\n";
            error_log($DEBUG_STRING);
        }

        return $r;
    }
```

Here, instead of just printing out the SQL to the error log, you also record the number of seconds it takes MySQL to perform the request. This lets you see if certain queries are taking too long. See Recipe 22.2 for more discussion of timing code execution.

Finally, you may also want to integrate PEAR's Log package, which provides an efficient framework for an abstracted logging system. PEAR Log predefines eight log levels: PEAR_LOG_EMERG, PEAR_LOG_ALERT, PEAR_LOG_CRIT, PEAR_LOG_ERR, PEAR_LOG_WARN ING, PEAR_LOG_NOTICE, PEAR_LOG_INFO, and PEAR_LOG_DEBUG. The Log package provides a robust assortment of options for customizing error logging, including logging errors to SQLite and/or to a pop-up browser window.

See Also

Documentation on define() (*http://www.php.net/define*), defined() (*http://www.php.net/defined*), and error_log() (*http://www.php.net/error-log*); *The Mythical Man-Month* by Frederick P. Brooks (Addison-Wesley); main page for PEAR Log (*http://pear.php.net/package/Log*).

CHAPTER 21

Software Engineering

21.0 Introduction

Typing out the expressions that form your computer program is only the beginning of building a healthy software system. This chapter discusses what should happen after you've written your initial code—tools for debugging and testing your software.

Recipe 21.1 explores the use of Xdebug, an open source PHP extension that allows for line-by-line debugging in real time.

Recipes 21.2, 21.3, and 21.4 explore the world of unit testing in PHP, and show you how to turn your fixed bugs into a test suite that can help you ensure that once a bug is fixed, it stays fixed.

Recipe 21.5 introduces you to easy ways to set up a testing environment on your local computer, so that you can work in a sandbox environment without fear of breaking a production website while you're trying to determine what's gone wrong.

Lastly, Recipe 21.6 explores the built-in web server that's part of PHP 5.4.0 and later.

21.1 Using a Debugger Extension

Problem

You want to debug your scripts interactively during runtime.

Solution

Use the Xdebug extension. When used along with an Xdebug-capable IDE, you can examine data structure; set breakpoints; and step into, out of, or over sections of code interactively.

Discussion

This recipe focuses on Xdebug's interactive debugging capability. To follow along, you need to be able to compile and install a Zend extension, which means permissions to edit *php.ini* on your system. PHP's dl() extension-loading function does not work with Xdebug. Finally, examples in this recipe are intended to work with Xdebug 2.2.

Installing the Xdebug extension is a straightforward procedure. You can build from source, or you can install using the pecl command:

```
% pecl install xdebug
```

After you have the extension compiled and installed, you need to edit your *php.ini* file with the full path to the xdebug.so module, such as zend_extension = /usr/lib/php/extensions/no-debug-non-zts-20050922/xdebug.so. The directory into which pecl installs xdebug.so is the directory specified as the value of the extension_dir configuration directive.

You'll know you've got Xdebug installed correctly when running php -m from the command line lists Xdebug twice—once in the [PHP Modules] section of the output and once in the [Zend Modules] section of the output. If you're trying to install Xdebug with a version of PHP you access via your web browser, check for an "xdebug" section in the output of the phpinfo() function.

In addition, you need to set the xdebug.remote_enable configuration directive to on for remote debugging to function.

Installing the Xdebug extension, however, is only half of what you need for interactive debugging. The other half is a debugging client that can talk to Xdebug and help you inspect your program. In this recipe, we'll use NetBeans IDE as an example—it's free, cross-platform, and easy to operate. Lots and lots of IDEs (*http://xdebug.org/docs/remote*), both free and commercial, support Xdebug and its DBGp debugging protocol.

To set up NetBeans to talk to your Xdebug installation, you need to do a few things. First, in your Project Properties, ensure that your "Project URL" points to the URL of your web server running PHP. Then, in the PHP section of the preferences pane make sure the Debugger Port value matches what PHP is configured to use for xdebug.remote_port (usually 9000).

If everything is set up properly, when you execute the "Debug Project" command in NetBeans, it will fire up a request to the home page of your project in your web browser, and position execution at the first PHP line in your project's home page, displaying the code and a Variables watch pane, as shown in Figure 21-1.

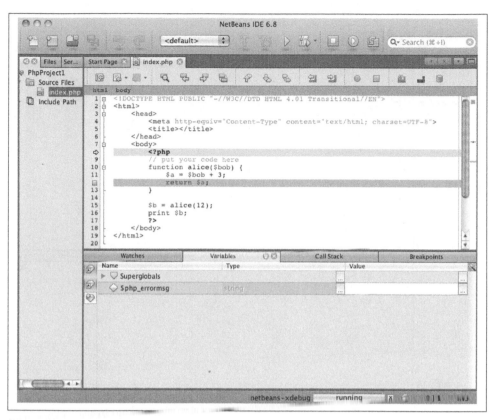

Figure 21-1. Beginning a debug session

In the figure, the red square replacing the line number marker on line 12 is a result of clicking the 12 and inserting a breakpoint. Hitting F5 to continue execution causes PHP to run until the breakpoint is reached, which is shown in Figure 21-2.

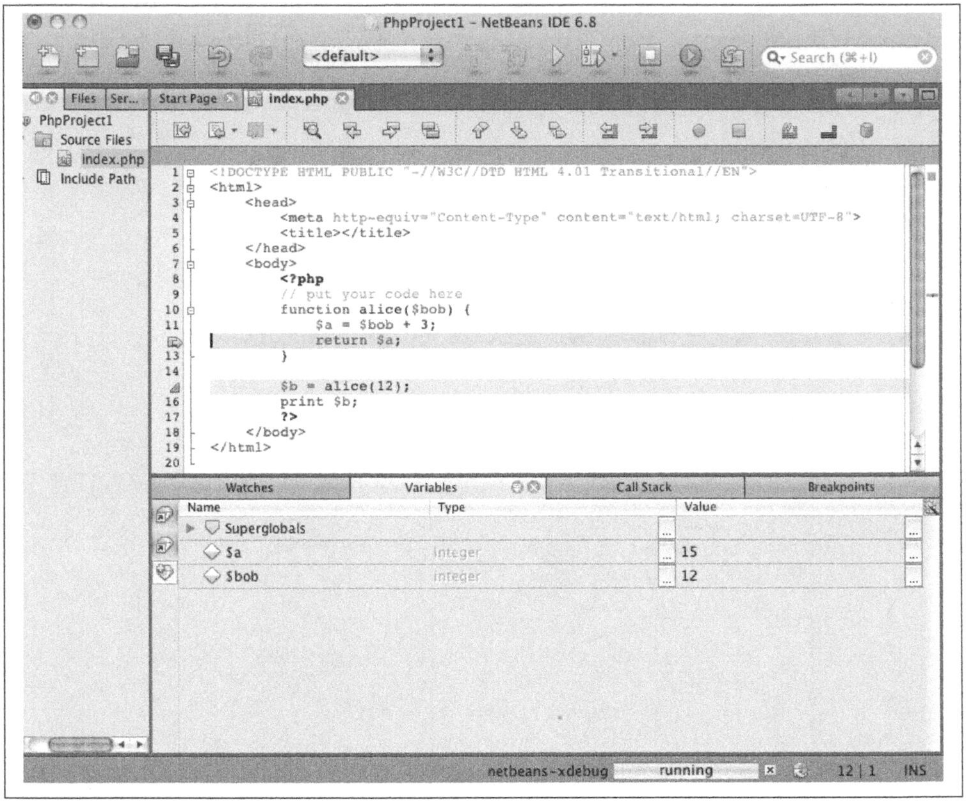

Figure 21-2. Continuing a debug session

At the breakpoint, the Variables watch pane has been updated to include the values of the local variables $a and $bob.

Xdebug supports the wide variety of features you'd expect from an interactive debugger —breakpoints, watchpoints, stack traces, and so forth. Exactly how you access them will depend on your IDE. But when your PHP program is behaving mysteriously, nothing beats being able to set a breakpoint, run exactly to a particular line, and then inspect the values of variables at that point.

See Also

Documentation on Xdebug (*http://www.xdebug.org/*) and on the DBGp protocol (*http://www.xdebug.org/docs-dbgp.php*); NetBeans IDE Xdebug-enabled features for PHP (*http://bit.ly/TrKNIH*).

21.2 Writing a Unit Test

Problem

You're working on a project that extends a set of core functionality, and you want an easy way to make sure everything still works as the project grows.

Solution

Write a unit test that tests the core functionality of a function or class and alerts you if something breaks.

A sample test using PHP-QA's `.phpt` testing system is:

```
--TEST--
str_replace() function
--FILE--

<?php
$str = 'Hello, all!';
var_dump(str_replace('all', 'world', $str));
?>
--EXPECT--
string(13) "Hello, world!"
```

A sample test using the powerful and popular PHPUnit package is:

```
class StrReplaceTest extends PHPUnit_Framework_TestCase
{
    public function testStrReplaceWorks()
    {
        $str = 'Hello, all!';
        $this->assertEquals('Hello, world!', str_replace('all', 'world', $str));
    }
}
```

Discussion

There are a number of ways to write unit tests in PHP. A series of simple `.phpt` tests may be adequate for your needs, or you may benefit from a more structured testing solution such as PHPUnit. We'll discuss each approach, but the first question is: why write a unit test in the first place?

Writing an application from scratch in any language is a lot like peeling an onion, only in reverse. You start with the center of the onion, and build layers on top of layers until you get to the finished product: an onion.

The more layers you build on top of your core, the more important it is for that core to continue functioning as you expect it to. The easiset way to ensure that the core of an application continues functioning as expected, especially after modifications, is through unit tests.

In the earlier example, we're testing that the `str_replace()` function successfully replaces one string with another. The test doesn't care how the `str_replace()` function is written; all that matters is that it works as expected on a recurring basis.

The easiest way to run the `.phpt` test is to save it in a file ending in *.phpt* (str_re place.phpt, for example), and then use PEAR's built-in `.phpt` execution tool, like this:

```
% pear run-tests str_replace.phpt
```

You'll see output like this:

```
Running 1 tests
PASS str_replace() function[str_replace.phpt]
TOTAL TIME: 00:00
1 PASSED TESTS
0 SKIPPED TESTS
```

You can test a number of features of your core functionality by creating multiple *.phpt* files, and executing:

```
% pear run-tests *.phpt
```

For full details on the structure of *.phpt* files, visit *http://qa.php.net/write-test.php*.

You can also write unit tests using the PHPUnit unit testing framework.

If the PHPUnit test from the Solution is in a file named *StrReplaceTest.php*, once PHPUnit is installed, you can run the test like this:

```
% phpunit StrReplaceTest
```

That command will look for the file named *StrReplaceTest.php* and run the test defined within it.

PHPUnit (*http://www.phpunit.de*) is a very powerful unit testing framework that can do much more than run a simple test like in the example.

See Also

Documentation on `.phpt` unit tests (*http://qa.php.net/write-test.php*) and on PHPUnit (*http://www.phpunit.de*).

21.3 Writing a Unit Test Suite

Problem

You want to be able to run more than one unit test conveniently on a regular basis.

Solution

Wrap your unit tests into a group known as a unit test suite.

Discussion

It's rare to have a program simple enough that a single unit test will fulfill all the testing needs that it will have during its lifespan. Over time, as applications grow there is a need to add more and more tests, either to test new functionality or verify that fixed bugs *stay* fixed.

When your library of tests gets larger than a handful, you'll find it much more convenient to group your tests into a unit test suite. A test suite, despite its formal-sounding name, is just a wrapper around a bunch of tests that can all be run by referring to the name of the test suite.

Using the PHPUnit framework, create a test suite to test more than just the `str_re place` function in PHP. A number of tests related to string functions can be put in a single file. For example, in a file named *StringTest.php*, put:

```
class StringTest extends PHPUnit_Framework_TestCase
{
    function testStrReplace()
    {
        $str = 'Hello, all!';
        $this->assertEquals('Hello, world!', str_replace('all', 'world', $str));
    }

    function testSubstr()
    {
        $str = 'Hello, all!';
        $this->assertEquals('e', substr($str, 1, 1));
    }
}
```

Now you have two tests that will be run from the `StringTest` class. Create a similar file called *ArrayTest.php*, with the following tests defined in it:

```
class ArrayTest extends PHPUnit_Framework_TestCase
{
    function testArrayFlip()
    {
        $array = array('foo' => 'bar', 'cheese' => 'hotdog');
        $flipped = array_flip($array);
        $this->assertEquals('foo', reset($flipped));
    }

    function testArrayPop()
    {
        $array = array('foo' => 'bar', 'cheese' => 'hotdog');
        $popped = array_pop($array);
```

```
        $this->assertEquals('hotdog', $popped);
        $this->assertEquals(1, sizeof($array));
    }
}
```

With four tests to run, it's time to put together a suite that will run all of these whenever you want to check to make sure things are working as they should be. By saving both those files in the same directory, you can just point PHPUnit to that directory to run them both:

```
% phpunit testDir
```

Assuming you've saved those two test files in the *testDir* directory, your output will look something like:

```
PHPUnit 3.7.24 by Sebastian Bergmann.

....

Time: 45 ms, Memory: 5.00Mb

OK (4 tests, 5 assertions)
```

whose name matches *Test.php*. PHPUnit will recurse into subdirectories as well.

Using this approach, you can grow your automated testing system to include a large number of tests and still be able to trigger them all through a single command.

See Also

Documentation on organizing test groups in PHPUnit (*http://bit.ly/1pssJM3*).

21.4 Applying a Unit Test to a Web Page

Problem

Your application is not broken down into small testable chunks, or you just want to apply unit testing to the website that your visitors see.

Solution

Use PHPUnit's Selenium Server integration to write tests that make HTTP requests and assert conditions on the responses. These tests make assertions about the structure of *www.example.com*:

```
class ExampleDotComTest extends PHPUnit_Extensions_SeleniumTestCase
{
    function setUp() {
        $this->setBrowser('firefox');
        $this->setBrowserUrl('http://www.example.com');
```

```
        }

        // basic homepage loading
        function testHomepageLoading()
        {
            $this->open('http://www.example.com/');
            $this->assertTitle('Example Domain');
        }

        // test clicking on a link and getting the right page
        function testClick()
        {
            $this->open('http://www.example.com/');
            $this->clickAndWait('link=More information...');
            $this->assertTitle('IANA — IANA-managed Reserved Domains');
        }
    }
}
```

It prints:

```
PHPUnit 3.7.24 by Sebastian Bergmann.

..

Time: 9.05 seconds, Memory: 3.50Mb

OK (2 tests, 2 assertions)
```

Discussion

If you're dealing with a site that's driven in whole or in part by procedural PHP code, it is sometimes difficult to write a smaller unit test that tests encapsulated functionality. Instead, you just want to make sure that the website is working; if it isn't, you'll debug from there. Additionally, running tests against the real web-server output of your code lets you verify UI elements, proper links, and other user-facing features.

The PHPUnit Selenium extension integrates with Selenium Server, a free, cross-platform tool for doing in-browser testing. Once you download and run Selenium Server (just a single Java *.jar* file), PHPUnit test cases that extend from the PHPUnit_Ex tensions_SeleniumTestCase base class can communicate with it via some new methods. In the preceding example, open() retrieves a particular URL, clickAndWait() "clicks" a particular link in the returned page to visit a new page, and assertTitle() makes an assertion about the contents of the <title/> element of a web page.

The Selenium command set is comprehensive, and lets you assert conditions about the contents of web pages, arrangement of elements, links, and much more.

See Also

Documentation on PHPUnit's Selenium integration (*http://phpunit.de/manual/current/en/selenium.html*), on the Selenium Server (*http://seleniumhq.org/*), and on the Selenium command reference (*http://release.seleniumhq.org/selenium-core/1.0.1/reference.html*).

21.5 Setting Up a Test Environment

Problem

You want to test out PHP scripts without worrying about bringing your website down or contaminating your production environment.

Solution

Set up a test environment for your application on your desktop machine, using XAMPP.

Discussion

The complexity of setting up a localized running environment for your web application frequently deters developers from taking that step. The result is often a breakdown in development best practices, such as editing files on the production website as a privileged user—never a good idea!

The XAMPP project provides single-installer solutions for four platforms: Windows 98/NT/2000/XP, Mac OS X, Linux (SuSE/RedHat/Mandrake/Debian), and Solaris. The packages contain synchronized versions of Apache, MySQL, PHP and PEAR, *phpMyAdmin*, and eAccelerator.

With an easy, step-by-step installation procedure, the XAMPP project makes creating a web-application-running environment on your local machine a snap.

Dealing with a large dataset? Unfortunately, developers working with sites that deal extensively with content that changes frequently find that they let best practices development habits slip due to a lack of good test data to work with. Don't let this happen to you! Simply write a script that mirrors your data *structure* locally, and then periodically update your local copy of data with a subset snapshot of the complete dataset. That way you're easily able to pull in a current copy of relevant data that's large enough to be used for real testing and development purposes.

See Also

The XAMPP project home page (*http://www.apachefriends.org/en/xampp.html*).

21.6 Using the Built-in Web Server

Problem

You want to use PHP's built-in web server to quickly spin up a test or simple website.

Solution

With PHP 5.4.0 or later, run the command-line PHP program with an -S argument giving a hostname and a port to listen on and you've got an instant PHP-enabled web server serving up the directory you started it in:

```
% php -S localhost:9876
```

Discussion

With only an -S host:port argument, the built-in web server treats the directory it was started in as the document root directory. If you start it from */home/roger*, then a request to "/files/monkeys.php" corresponds to the file */home/roger/files/monkeys.php*. Requests that map to a directory, rather then to a particular file, cause the built-in web server to first look for *index.php* in that directory, and then *index.html* in that directory.

To use a different document root directory, provide that with a -t argument when starting PHP. For example:

```
% php -S localhost:9876 -t /var/www
```

For more indirect mapping between request URLs and responses, specify a file containing PHP to do request routing as an additional argument:

```
% php -S localhost:9876 router.php
```

Before looking for a path that matches a request URL, PHP executes the code in *router.php*. PHP will only attempt to look for a matching path if that code returns false. This lets you do arbitrary response generation. Example 21-1 shows a request router that will return currency conversion rates between two currency codes provided in the URL.

Example 21-1. Built-in web server request router

```
$parts = explode('/', $_SERVER['REQUEST_URI']);
// Expecting a request URI such as /USD/ISK, so make
// sure there are at least two parts and they are
// each three letters
if (! (isset($parts[1]) &&
        preg_match('/[a-z]{3}/i', $parts[1]) &&
        isset($parts[2]) &&
        preg_match('/[a-z]{3}/i', $parts[2]))) {
    header('Bad Request', true, 400);
```

```
        print "Bad Request";
        exit();
    }

    $quotes = 'http://download.finance.yahoo.com/d/quotes.csv?f=nl1&s=%s%s=X,%s%s=X';
    $url = sprintf($quotes,
                   urlencode($parts[1]), urlencode($parts[2]),
                   urlencode($parts[2]), urlencode($parts[1]));
    $response = file_get_contents($url);
    $lines = explode("\n", trim($response));
    foreach ($lines as $line) {
        list($label, $rate) = str_getcsv($line);
        print "<b>" . htmlentities($label) . "</b>: " .
          htmlentities($rate) . "<br/>";
    }
```

When Example 21-1 is used as a request router by the built-in web server, `$_SERV ER['REQUEST_URI']` contains the request path the client asks for. In this case, we want to make requests such as /USD/EUR return the currency conversion rates between US dollars (USD) and Euro (EUR). So first, the code validates that the request URI contains two three-letter currency codes. Then, it plugs them into a URL that will download the conversion rate info from Yahoo! Finance. The response from that URL is a series of lines, each a set of CSV fields containing what kind of conversion rate it is and the numerical value of the rate. The `foreach` loop at the end of the code prints out the rates with some minimal HTML formatting. Figure 21-3 shows the request URL and the output when asking for conversion between Icelandic krónur and Japanese Yen. In this example, the server has been started on port 9876.

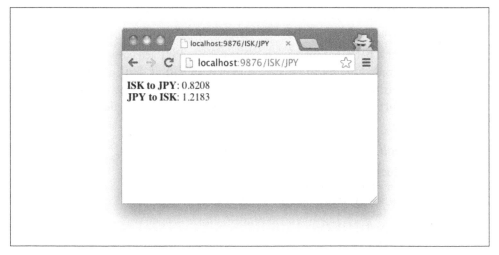

Figure 21-3. Currency conversion request router in action

See Also

Documentation on PHP's built-in web server (*http://bit.ly/1mfjWX5*) and on the Yahoo!
Finance CSV API (*http://bit.ly/1nEe6Ba*).

CHAPTER 22

Performance Tuning

22.0 Introduction

PHP is pretty speedy. Usually, the slow parts of your PHP programs have to do with external resources—waiting for a database query to finish or for the contents of a remote URL to be retrieved. That said, your PHP code itself may not be as efficient as it could be. This chapter is about techniques for finding and fixing performance problems in your code.

There's plenty of debate in the world of software engineering about the best time in the development process to start optimizing. Optimize too early and you'll spend too much time nitpicking over details that may not be important in the big picture; optimize too late and you may find that you have to rewrite large chunks of your application.

Optimization doesn't happen in a vacuum. As you tweak your code, you're not just adjusting raw execution time—you're also affecting code size, readability, and maintainability. There are always circumstances that demand screamingly fast execution time. More frequently, however, programmer time or ease of debugging is a more valuable commodity. Try to balance these concerns as you tackle optimization hurdles in your code.

Installing a code accelerator is the best thing you can do to improve performance of PHP. As of PHP 5.5, PHP bundles and builds the Zend OPcache PHP accelerator, but OPcache works for PHP 5.2 and above. This extension is covered in Recipe 22.1.

If your application is still too slow, get started with integrating some easy analysis methods into your development routine. You want to identify which sections of your application are taking up the largest block of time. It's hard to know in advance what those will be. It can be a section called once that's very slow, or maybe a small function that's quite fast, but is called frequently. The trick is quickly identifying the troublesome area in the code, which can be difficult as your application becomes larger and larger.

Here are five different ways to break apart your application at various levels: Recipe 22.2 shows you how to time the execution of a function, and Recipe 22.3 expands on that to illustrate how to easily time all the function calls in a block of code. See how to profile code by statement in Recipe 22.4 and by self-defined sections in Recipe 22.5. Finally, take these approaches even farther with Recipe 22.6, which covers the use of a debugger extension for application profiling.

An overview of how to stress test your website in Recipe 22.7 reminds you that there's more to performance tuning than the code itself—network latency and hardware also play a big role.

One of the most common bottlenecks in many PHP scripts is misuse of regular expressions; Recipe 22.8 explains a few approaches to solving text-matching problems without incurring the overhead of regular expressions.

22.1 Using an Accelerator

Problem

You want to increase performance of your PHP applications.

Solution

Use the Zend OPcache code-caching PHP accelerator to allow PHP to avoid compiling scripts into opcodes on each request.

Discussion

PHP code accelerators do the bulk of their magic transparently by storing compiled versions of PHP scripts on disk or in shared memory in order to skip the compiling step with each request.

When the PHP engine is told to run a particular program, it reads the source code of the program and compiles it into a compact internal representation. Then, it executes the instructions in that compiled representation. When it's done executing the script, the engine throws away the compiled representation.

An accelerator, by contrast, keeps the compiled instructions around. The next time the PHP engine gets a request to run the same program, the accelerator steps in and checks whether it's saved a compiled version of that program. If so, it tells the PHP engine to skip recompilation and just execute the already compiled version. An accelerator can be configured to update its compiled representations based on different criteria, such as whenever the original program changes or only when you explicitly tell it to.

As of PHP 5.5, Zend OPcache is automatically built and installed. If you're running an earlier version of PHP, install it from GitHub or PECL.

Though PHP 5.5 builds Zend OPcache, you still need to turn it on by editing your *php.ini* file to add a reference to the full path of the extension: `zend_extension=/path/to/php/lib/php/extension/debug-non-zts-20121212/opcache.so`.

Although you should see a large improvement immediately, you can further improve performance with additional tuning. As a start, update your production configuration parameters to:

```
opcache.memory_consumption=128
opcache.interned_strings_buffer=8
opcache.max_accelerated_files=4000
opcache.revalidate_freq=60
opcache.fast_shutdown=1
opcache.enable_cli=1
```

Ultimately, the "right" settings are a balance of factors that depend on the size of the code, how frequently it changes and is called, the amount of memory on your system, and so on. You will need to experiment and use a stress-testing tool to see what's ideal for your specific system. Stress testing is covered in Recipe 22.7.

See Also

Documentation on OPcache (*http://us2.php.net/opcache*).

22.2 Timing Function Execution

Problem

You have a function and you want to see how long it takes to execute.

Solution

Compare time in milliseconds before running the function against the time in milliseconds after running the function to see the elapsed time spent in the function itself:

```php
// create a long nonsense string
$long_str = uniqid(php_uname('a'), true);

// start timing from here
$start = microtime(true);

// function to test
$md5 = md5($long_str);

$elapsed = microtime(true) - $start;
```

```
echo "That took $elapsed seconds.\n";
```

Discussion

To determine how much time a single function takes to execute, you may not need a full benchmarking package. Instead, you can get the information you need from the `microtime()` function.

Here are three ways to produce the exact same MD5 hash in PHP:

```
// PHP's basic md5() function
$hashA = md5('optimize this!');

// MD5 by way of the mhash extension
$hashB = bin2hex(mhash(MHASH_MD5, 'optimize this!'));

// MD5 with the hash() function
$hashC = hash('md5', 'optimize this!');
```

`$hashA`, `$hashB`, and `$hashC` are all `83f0bb25be8de9106700840d66f261cf`. However, the third approach is more than twice as fast as PHP's basic `md5()` function.

The dark side of optimization with head-to-head tests like these, though, is that you need to figure in how frequently the function is called in your code and how readable and maintainable the alternative is.

For example, in choosing hash functions, if you need your code to run on PHP versions earlier than 5.1.2 (Heavens forbid!), you either have to use `md5()` all the time or add a check that, based on PHP's version (and perhaps whether the `mhash` extension is installed), decides which function to use. The absolute time difference between `md5()` and `hash()` is on the order of a tenth of a millisecond. If you're computing thousands or millions of hashes at a time, it makes sense to insert the extra runtime calculations that choose the fastest functions. But the fraction of a fraction of a breath of time saved in a handful of hash computations isn't worth the extra complexity.

See Also

Recipe 3.11 for a discussion on using `microtime()`; documentation on the `microtime()` function (*http://www.php.net/microtime*).

22.3 Timing Program Execution by Function

Problem

You have a block of code and you want to profile it to see how long each function takes to execute.

Solution

Use Xdebug function tracing:

```
xdebug_start_trace('/tmp/factorial-trace');

function factorial($x) {
    return ($x == 1) ? 1 : $x * factorial($x - 1);
}

print factorial(10);

xdebug_stop_trace();
```

Discussion

The Xdebug extension provides a wide range of helpful debugging and profiling features. It's available via PECL or as a prebuilt Windows binary (*http://xdebug.org/docs/install*).

Its function-tracing feature provides insight into what functions are called from where, optionally including the arguments passed and returned. It also records the time and memory taken for each call.

For the factorial example, it generates results such as:

```
TRACE START [2015-01-05 06:32:11]
    0.0005    240136    -> factorial($x = 10) /factorial.php:0
    0.0005    240184     -> factorial($x = 9) /factorial.php:6
    0.0005    240256      -> factorial($x = 8) /factorial.php:6
    0.0006    240304       -> factorial($x = 7) /factorial.php:6
    0.0006    240352        -> factorial($x = 6) /factorial.php:6
    0.0006    240400         -> factorial($x = 5) /factorial.php:6
    0.0007    240448          -> factorial($x = 4) /factorial.php:6
    0.0007    240496           -> factorial($x = 3) /factorial.php:6
    0.0007    240544            -> factorial($x = 2) /factorial.php:6
    0.0008    240592             -> factorial($x = 1) /factorial.php:6
                                  >=> 1
                                 >=> 2
                                >=> 6
                               >=> 24
                              >=> 120
                             >=> 720
                            >=> 5040
                           >=> 40320
                          >=> 362880
                         >=> 3628800
    0.0010    240136    -> xdebug_stop_trace() /factorial.php:12
    0.0010    240176
TRACE END   [2015-01-05 06:32:11]
```

The first column lists the start time in seconds. The next column has the memory usage. Then you see the function called, along with the argument passed. Finally, it lists the filename and line number. As the functions execute, you see the data returned from each one.

Xdebug allows you to format these results in a number of ways. This specific output format uses the following configuration parameters:

```
xdebug.trace_format=0     ; human readable plain text
xdebug.collect_params=4   ; full variable contents and variable name.
xdebug.collect_return=1   ; show return values
```

Xdebug's function profiling provides an easy way to get a detailed overview of everything going on in a section of code. However, there are times when this may be more granular than you need.

See Also

Documentation on Xdebug (*http://www.xdebug.org/*) and function traces (*http:// xdebug.org/docs/execution_trace*); Recipe 21.1 for using Xdebug for debugging and installation instructions.

22.4 Timing Program Execution by Statement

Problem

You have a block of code and you want to profile it to see how long each statement takes to execute.

Solution

Use the `declare` construct and the `ticks` directive:

```
function profile($display = false) {
    static $times;

    switch ($display) {
    case false:
        // add the current time to the list of recorded times
        $times[] = microtime();
        break;
    case true:
        // return elapsed times in microseconds
        $start = array_shift($times);

        $start_mt = explode(' ', $start);
        $start_total = doubleval($start_mt[0]) + $start_mt[1];
```

```
        foreach ($times as $stop) {
            $stop_mt = explode(' ', $stop);
            $stop_total = doubleval($stop_mt[0]) + $stop_mt[1];
            $elapsed[] = $stop_total - $start_total;
        }

        unset($times);
        return $elapsed;
        break;
    }
}

// register tick handler
register_tick_function('profile');

// clock the start time
profile();

// execute code, recording time for every statement execution
declare (ticks = 1) {
    foreach ($_SERVER['argv'] as $arg) {
        print "$arg: " . strlen($arg) ."\n";
    }
}

// print out elapsed times
print "---\n";
$i = 0;
foreach (profile(true) as $time) {
    $i++;
    print "Line $i: $time\n";
}
```

Discussion

The ticks directive allows you to execute a function on a repeatable basis for a block
of code. The number assigned to ticks is how many statements go by before the functions that are registered using register_tick_function() are executed.

In the Solution, we register a single function and have the profile() function execute
for every statement inside the declare block. If there are two elements in $_SERV
ER['argv'], profile() is executed six times: once when the clocks starts; twice for the
two times through the foreach loop; another two when the print strlen($arg) line
is executed; and finally, once when foreach returns false:

```
Line 1: 5.3882598876953E-5
Line 2: 5.6982040405273E-5
Line 3: 6.2942504882812E-5
Line 4: 6.5803527832031E-5
```

```
Line 5: 6.7949295043945E-5
Line 6: 6.9856643676758E-5
```

You can also set things up to call two functions every three statements:

```
register_tick_function('profile');
register_tick_function('backup');

declare (ticks = 3) {
    // code...
}
```

You can also pass additional parameters into the registered functions, which can be object methods instead of regular functions:

```
// pass "parameter" into profile()
register_tick_function('profile', 'parameter');

// call $car->drive();
$car = new Vehicle;
register_tick_function(array($car, 'drive'));
```

If you want to execute an object method, pass the object and the name of the method encapsulated within an array. This lets the `register_tick_function()` know you're referring to an object instead of a function.

Call `unregister_tick_function()` to remove a function from the list of tick functions:

```
unregister_tick_function('profile');
```

See Also

Documentation on `register_tick_function()` (*http://www.php.net/register-tick-function*), `unregister_tick_function()` (*http://www.php.net/unregister-tick-function*), and `declare` (*http://www.php.net/declare*).

22.5 Timing Program Execution by Section

Problem

You have a block of code and you want to profile it to see how long each statement takes to execute.

Solution

Use the PEAR Benchmark module:

```
require_once 'Benchmark/Timer.php';

$timer = new Benchmark_Timer(true);
```

```
$timer->start();
// some setup code here
$timer->setMarker('setup');
// some more code executed here
$timer->setMarker('middle');
// even yet still more code here
$timer->setmarker('done');
// and a last bit of code here
$timer->stop();

$timer->display();
```

Discussion

The PEAR Benchmark package gives you a quick-and-dirty way to set a few markers in your code to identify hotspots at a more macro level. Install it using the PEAR package manager:

```
% pear install Benchmark
```

Calling setMarker() records the time. The display() method prints out a list of markers, the time they were set, and the elapsed time from the previous marker:

marker	time index	ex time	perct
Start	1029433375.42507400	-	0.00%
setup	1029433375.42554800	0.00047397613525391	29.77%
middle	1029433375.42568700	0.00013899803161621	8.73%
done	1029433375.42582000	0.00013303756713867	8.36%
Stop	1029433375.42666600	0.00084602832794189	53.14%
total	-	0.0015920400619507	100.00%

The Benchmark module also includes the Benchmark_Iterate class, which can be used to time many executions of a single function:

```
require 'Benchmark/Iterate.php';

$timer = new Benchmark_Iterate;

// a sample function to time
function use_preg($ar) {
    for ($i = 0, $j = count($ar); $i < $j; $i++) {
        if (preg_match('/gouda/',$ar[$i])) {
            // it's gouda
```

```
        }
      }
    }

    // another sample function to time
    function use_equals($ar) {
        for ($i = 0, $j = count($ar); $i < $j; $i++) {
            if ('gouda' == $ar[$i]) {
                // it's gouda
            }
        }
    }

    // run use_preg() 1000 times
    $timer->run(1000,'use_preg',
                    array('gouda','swiss','gruyere','muenster','whiz'));
    $results = $timer->get();
    print "Mean execution time for use_preg(): $results[mean]\n";

    // run use_equals() 1000 times
    $timer->run(1000,'use_equals',
                    array('gouda','swiss','gruyere','muenster','whiz'));
    $results = $timer->get();
    print "Mean execution time for use_equals(): $results[mean]\n";
```

The `Benchmark_Iterate::get()` method returns an associative array. The `mean` element of this array holds the mean execution time for each iteration of the function. The `iterations` element holds the number of iterations. The execution time of each iteration of the function is stored in an array element with an integer key. For example, the time of the first iteration is in `$results[1]`, and the time of the 37th iteration is in `$re sults[37]`.

See Also

Information on the PEAR `Benchmark` class (*http://pear.php.net/package/Benchmark*).

22.6 Profiling with a Debugger Extension

Problem

You want a robust solution for profiling your applications so that you can continually monitor where the program spends most of its time.

Solution

Use Xdebug, available from PECL. With Xdebug installed, adding `xdebug.profil er_enable=1` to your *php.ini* configuration dumps a trace file to disk. Parsing that trace file with a tool gives you a breakdown of how time was spent during that run of the PHP script.

Discussion

With Xdebug installed, it's a simple matter to start a profiling session that will store reporting information on application runtime.

To generate this for all requests, set the xdebug.profiler_enable configuration variable to 1. To conditionally generate this data, set xdebug.profiler_enable to off and xde bug.profiler_enable_trigger to on. In this configuration, Xdebug will only profile when you pass in a GET, POST, or Cookie variable named XDEBUG_PROFILE set to any value.

Though less simple to activate, conditional generation has benefits because you only save logs for selected requests. For complex applications, profiling dumps can be quite large; this prevents you from running out of disk space. Also, though not ideal, in the event you cannot replicate a problem in your testing environment, you can more safely run Xdebug in production.

The output files generated by Xdebug can be stored anywhere you want them, as long as it's writable by PHP. Set the directory using the xdebug.profiler_output_dir configuration variable and the filename using xdebug.profiler_output_name.

By default, the output filename is cachegrind.out. followed by the process ID. This value makes it difficult to look at the filename and know what was profiled. Fortunately, Xdebug allows you to use a variety of formats. For example, you can use xdebug.pro filer_output_name=cachegrind.out.%R.%t to put the request URI and timestamp. This generates filenames like *cachegrind.out._factorial_php.1388986739*.

Process the output files with an application to more easily view and understand the data. The longest-running functions are good places to start when looking for opportunities to optimize.

A popular tool is KCachegrind, a GUI application used to drill down deeply into applications to determine where hotspots and bottlenecks are occurring. A cross-platform version of this tool, QCachegrind, is available for people not running the KDE Unix desktop environment, such as developers on MacOS X or Windows. QCachegrind requires Qt 4.4 or above.

As a (simplistic) example, this code prints the first 50 factorial numbers:

```
function factorial($x) {
    return ($x == 1) ? 1 : $x * factorial($x - 1);
}

for ($i = 1; $i <= 50; $i++) {
```

```
    print "$i: " . factorial($i) . "\n";
}
```

Loading the Xdebug profile dump into QCachegrind, as shown in Figure 22-1, allows you to see that `factorial()` is called recursively 2,450 times. This takes 13,376 cycles.

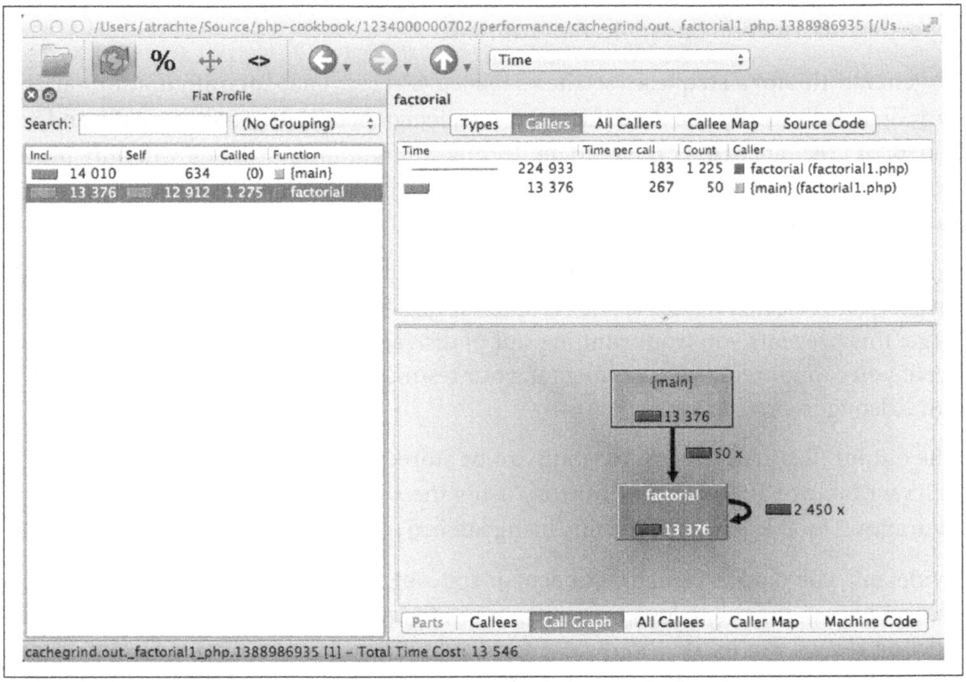

Figure 22-1. Inspecting profiling results in QCachegrind

Looking to reduce the overhead of recursion, you add a quick-and-dirty memoization cache:

```
function factorial($x) {
    static $cache = [];

    if (isset($cache[$x])) return $cache[$x];

    $cache[$x] = (($x == 1) ? 1 : $x * factorial($x - 1));

    return $cache[$x];
}

for ($i = 1; $i <= 50; $i++) {
    print "$i: " . factorial($i) . "\n";
}
```

Now, when you load the profiler output, there are no self-referential calls and there is an order of magnitude decrease in CPU cycles to 643, as shown in Figure 22-2.

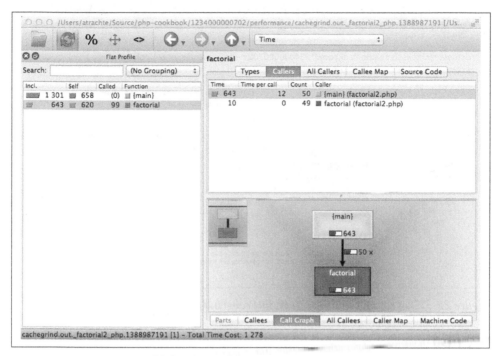

Figure 22-2. Checking for improved results

Depending on your system, QCachegrind can be cumbersome to install because it has a dependency on Qt. Webgrind is an all-PHP application that parses Xdebug output. It's not as full featured, but it does the job for basic exploration, and it's simple to install because it's a PHP script.

Figure 22-3 shows what the results look like.

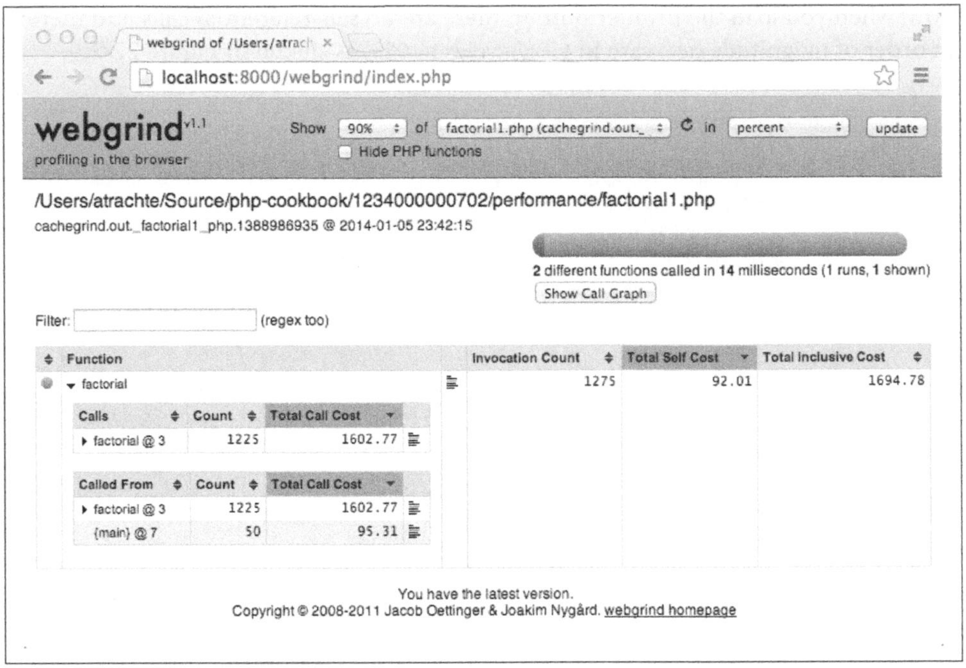

Figure 22-3. Inspecting profiling results in Webgrind

See Also

Documentation on Xdebug (*http://www.xdebug.org/*) and profiling (*http://xdebug.org/docs/profiler*); KCachegrind (*http://kcachegrind.sourceforge.net*); Webgrind (*https://github.com/jokkedk/webgrind*).

22.7 Stress-Testing Your Website

Problem

You want to find out how well your website performs under a heavy load.

Solution

Use a stress-testing and benchmarking tool to simulate a variety of load levels.

Discussion

Stress testing is frequently confused with benchmarking, and it is important to recognize the difference between the two activities.

Benchmarking a website is often a somewhat casual activity when performed by an individual developer. The most commonly used tool is the Apache HTTP server benchmarking tool, *ab*, which is designed to test how many requests per second an HTTP server is capable of serving. For example:

```
% /usr/bin/ab -n 1000 -c 100 -k www.example.com/test.php
```

This test would return a report illustrating the average response time for requests to *http://www.example.com/test.php*, based on 1,000 requests, grouped in batches of 100 concurrent requests.

Though that sort of test has value—it gives you a reasonable estimation of how many requests you can serve per second under normal load—it doesn't tell you much about how your entire web application will behave under heavy load. It only pounds on one URL at a time, after all.

Stress testing is a testing technique whose intent is to *break* your web application. By testing to a breaking point, you can identify and repair weaknesses in your application, or gain a better understanding of when you will need to add additional hardware. When combined with code profiling, you can also get an idea of what part of your application will need to scale first; i.e., will you need to add more servers to your database cluster before you need to add more frontend web server machines?

An excellent open source tool for stress testing is *Siege*. Siege can be configured to read a large number of URLs from a configuration file and run through them in order (regression testing), or it can read a list of URLs and hit them randomly, which better approximates real-world usage of a website. Siege can also pound on a single URL in a similar fashion to *ab*.

If you are unable to install Siege on your system, Lincoln Stein's *torture.pl* script is a good alternative. Many of Siege's design concepts were inspired by *torture.pl*, and the two tools produce similar reports.

See Also

Source and documentation for Siege (*http://www.joedog.org/JoeDog/Siege*); *ab* (*http://bit.ly/Szyw5j*); source and documentation for *torture.pl* (*http://stein.cshl.org/~lstein/torture/*).

22.8 Avoiding Regular Expressions

Problem

You want to improve script performance by optimizing string-matching operations.

Solution

Replace unnecessary regular expression calls with faster string and character type function alternatives.

Discussion

A common source of unnecessary computation is the use of regular expression functions when they are not needed—for example, if you're validating a form submission for a valid username and want to make sure that the username contains only alphanumeric characters.

A common approach to this problem is a regular expression:

```
if (!preg_match('/^[a-z0-9]+$/i', $username)) {
  echo 'please enter a valid username.';
}
```

The same test can be performed much faster with the ctype_alnum() function.

Using code-timing techniques covered in Recipe 22.2, let's compare the preceding test with ctype_alnum():

```
$username = 'foo411';

$start = microtime(true);

if (!preg_match('/^[a-z0-9]+/i', $username)) {
    echo 'please enter a valid username';
}

$regextime = microtime(true) - $start;

$start = microtime(true);

if (!ctype_alnum($username)) {
    echo 'please enter a valid username';
}

$ctypetime = microtime(true) - $start;

echo "preg_match took:  $regextime seconds\n";
echo "ctype_alnum took: $ctypetime seconds\n";
```

This will output results similar to:

```
preg_match took:  0.000163078308105 seconds
ctype_alnum took: 9.05990600586E-06 seconds
```

ctype_alnum() is considerably faster; 9.05990600586E-06 is the same as 0.00000906 seconds, which is *18 times* faster than the preg_match() regular expression, with exactly the same result.

When applied to a complex application, replacing unnecessary regular expressions with equivalent alternatives can add up to a significant performance gain.

A good litmus test for using a regular expression (or not) is to see whether the match you're performing can be explained in a brief sentence. Granted, there are some matches, such as "string is a valid email address," which cannot be adequately verified without a complex regular expression. However, "check if string A contains string B" can be tested with several different approaches, but is ultimately a very simple test that does not require regular expressions:

```
$haystack = 'The quick brown fox jumps over the lazy dog';
$needle = 'lazy dog';

// slowest (and deprecated)
if (ereg($needle, $haystack)) echo 'match!';

// slow
if (preg_match("/$needle/", $haystack)) echo 'match!';

// fast
if (strstr($haystack, $needle)) echo 'match!';

// fastest
if (strpos($haystack, $needle) !== false) echo 'match!';
```

There is certainly a benefit to double-checking the ctype and string functions before making a commitment to a regular expression, particularly if you're working a section of code that will loop repeatedly.

See Also

Documentation on ctype functions (*http://www.php.net/ctype*); string functions (*http://www.php.net/strings*); and regular expression functions (*http://www.php.net/pcre*).

CHAPTER 23

Regular Expressions

23.0 Introduction

Regular expressions are an intricate and powerful tool for matching patterns and manipulating text. Though not as fast as plain-vanilla string matching, regular expressions are extremely flexible. They allow you to construct patterns to match almost any conceivable combination of characters with a simple—albeit terse and punctuation-studded—grammar. If your website relies on data feeds that come in text files—data feeds like sports scores, news articles, or frequently updated headlines—regular expressions can help you make sense of them.

This chapter gives a brief overview of basic regular expression syntax and then focuses on the functions that PHP provides for working with regular expressions. For a bit more detailed information about the ins and outs of regular expressions, check out the PCRE section of the PHP online manual (*http://www.php.net/pcre*) and Appendix B of *Learning PHP 5* by David Sklar (O'Reilly). To start on the path to regular expression wizardry, read the comprehensive *Mastering Regular Expressions* by Jeffrey E.F. Friedl (O'Reilly).

Regular expressions are handy when transforming plain text into HTML, and vice versa. Luckily, because these are such helpful subjects, PHP has many built-in functions to handle these tasks, explained by recipes in other chapters. Recipe 9.10 tells how to escape HTML entities; Recipe 13.6 covers stripping HTML tags; Recipes 13.4 and 13.5 show how to convert plain text to HTML and HTML to plain text, respectively. For information on matching and validating email addresses, see Recipe 9.4.

Over the years, the functionality of regular expressions has grown from its basic roots to incorporate increasingly useful features. As a result, PHP offers two different sets of regular expression functions. The first set includes the traditional (or POSIX) functions, whose names each begin with `ereg` (for *extended* regular expressions; the `ereg` functions themselves are already an extension of the original feature set). The other set includes the Perl-compatible family of functions, prefaced with preg (for Perl-compatible regular expressions).

The preg functions use a library that mimics the regular expression functionality of the Perl programming language. This is a good thing because Perl allows you to do a variety of handy things with regular expressions, including nongreedy matching, forward and backward assertions, and even recursive patterns.

There's no longer any reason to use the ereg functions and they are officially deprecated as of PHP 5.3.0. They offer fewer features, and they're slower than preg functions. However, the ereg functions existed in PHP for many years prior to the introduction of the preg functions, so many programmers still use them because of legacy code or out of habit. Thankfully, the prototypes for the two sets of functions are identical, so it's easy to switch back and forth from one to another without too much confusion. (We list how to do this while avoiding the major gotchas in Recipe 23.1.)

Think of a regular expression as a program in a very restrictive programming language. The only task of a regular expression program is to match a pattern in text. In regular expression patterns, most characters just match themselves. That is, the regular expression rhino matches strings that contain the five-character sequence rhino. The fancy business in regular expressions is due to a handful of punctuation and symbols called *metacharacters*. These symbols don't literally match themselves, but instead give commands to the regular expression matcher.

The most frequently used metacharacters include the period (.), asterisk (*), plus sign (+), and question mark (?). (To match a literal metacharacter in a pattern, precede the character with a backslash.)

- The period means "match any character," so the pattern .at matches bat, cat, and even rat.
- The asterisk means "match 0 or more of the preceding object." (So far, the only objects we know about are characters.)
- The plus is similar to asterisk, but means "match *one* or more of the preceding object." So .+at matches brat, sprat, and even the cat inside of catastrophe, but not plain at. To match at, replace the + with an *.
- The question mark means "the preceding object is optional." That is, it matches 0 or 1 of the object that precedes it. colou?r matches both color and colour.

To apply * and + to objects greater than one character, place the sequence of characters that make up the object inside parentheses. Parentheses allow you to group characters for more complicated matching and also capture the part of the pattern that falls inside them. A captured sequence can be referenced by preg_replace() to alter a string, and all captured matches can be stored in an array that's passed as a third parameter to `preg_match()` and `preg_match_all()`. The `preg_match_all()` function is similar to `preg_match()`, but it finds all possible matches inside a string, instead of stopping at the first match. Example 23-1 shows a few examples of `preg_match()`, `preg_match_all()`, and `preg_replace()` at work.

Example 23-1. Using preg functions

```
if (preg_match('{<title>.+</title>}', $html)) {
    print "The page has a title!\n";
}

if (preg_match_all('/<li>/', $html, $matches)) {
    print 'Page has ' . count($matches[0]) . " list items\n";
}

// turn bold into italic
$italics = preg_replace('/(<\/?)b(>)/', '$1i$2', $bold);
```

Normally, the pattern delimiter character, which starts and ends the pattern string, is /. Because the pattern delimiter character needs to be backslash-escaped if it appears as a literal inside the pattern, this is a clumsy delimiter pattern when matching HTML or XML. The preceding code uses open and close curly braces as delimiters in the first pattern string to avoid this problem. Any nonalphanumeric, nonwhitespace character (except backslash) can be a pattern delimiter character. If you use an open-bracket character as the opening delimiter, you can use a corresponding close bracket as the closing delimiter.

If you want to match strings with a specific set of characters, create a *character class* by putting the characters you want inside square brackets. The character class [aeiou] matches any one of the characters a, e, i, o, and u. You can also put ranges inside of square brackets to form a character class. The class [a-z] matches all lowercase English letters. The class [a-zA-Z0-9] matches digits and English letters. The class [a-zA-Z0-9_] matches digits, English letters, and the underscore.

So far, all the patterns we've seen match anything that contains text that corresponds to the pattern. That is, [a-z0-9]+ matches grapefruit and c3p0, but it also matches grr!!! and *******p. All four of those strings meet the condition that [a-z0-9]+ sets out: "one or more of a digit or lowercase English letter."

Anchoring your pattern enables matching against strings that *only* contain characters that the pattern describes. The caret (^) and the dollar sign ($) anchor the pattern at the beginning and the end of the string, respectively. Without them, a match can occur anywhere in the string. So whereas [a-z0-9]+ means "one or more of a digit or lowercase English letter," ^[a-z0-9]+ means "begins with one or more of a digit or lowercase English letter," [a-z0-9]+$ means "ends with one or more of a digit or lowercase English letter," and ^[a-z0-9]+$ means "contains only one or more of a digit or lowercase English letter." Example 23-2 shows a few character classes at work.

Example 23-2. Matching with character classes and anchors

```
$thisFileContents = file_get_contents(__FILE__);
// http://php.net/language.variables gives a regular expression for
// valid variable names in php. Beginning the pattern with \$ matches
// a literal $
$matchCount = preg_match_all('/\$[a-zA-Z_\x7f-\xff][a-zA-Z0-9_\x7f-\xff]*/',
                             $thisFileContents, $matches);
print "Matches: $matchCount\n";
foreach ($matches[0] as $variableName) {
    print "$variableName\n";
}
```

Example 23-2 prints each variable name it uses:

```
Matches: 8
$thisFileContents
$matchCount
$thisFileContents
$matches
$matchCount
$matches
$variableName
$variableName
```

If it's easier to define what you're looking for by its complement, use that. To make a character class match the complement of what's inside it, begin the class with a caret. A caret outside a character class anchors a pattern at the beginning of a string; a caret inside a character class means "match everything except what's listed in the square brackets." For example, the character class [^aeiou] matches everything but lowercase English vowels.

Note that the opposite of [aeiou] isn't [bcdfghjklmnpqrstvwxyz]. The character class [^aeiou] also matches uppercase vowels such as AEIOU, numbers such as 123, URLs such as http://www.cnpq.br/, and even emoticons such as :).

The vertical bar (|), also known as the pipe, specifies alternatives. Example 23-3 uses the pipe to find various possibilities for image filenames in a block of text.

Example 23-3. Matching with |

```
$text = "The files are cuddly.gif, report.pdf, and cute.jpg.";
if (preg_match_all('/[a-zA-Z0-9]+\.(gif|jpe?g)/',$text,$matches)) {
    print "The image files are: " . implode(',',$matches[0]);
}
```

Example 23-3 prints:

```
The image files are: cuddly.gif,cute.jpg
```

We've covered just a small subset of the world of regular expressions. We provide some additional details in later recipes, but the PHP website also has some very useful information on Perl-compatible regular expressions (*http://www.php.net/pcre*). The links from this last page to Pattern Modifiers and Pattern Syntax are especially detailed and informative.

23.1 Switching from ereg to preg

Problem

You want to convert from using `ereg` functions to `preg` functions.

Solution

First, you have to add delimiters to your patterns:

```
preg_match('/pattern/', 'string');
```

For case-insensitive matching, use the `/i` modifier with `preg_match()` instead:

```
preg_match('/pattern/i', 'string');
```

When using integers instead of strings as patterns or replacement values, convert the number to hexadecimal and specify it using an escape sequence:

```
$hex = dechex($number);
preg_match("/\x$hex/", 'string');
```

Discussion

There are a few major differences between `ereg` and `preg`. First, when you use `preg` functions, the pattern isn't just the string `pattern`; it also needs delimiters, as in Perl, so it's `/pattern/` instead.[1] So:

```
ereg('pattern', 'string');
```

becomes:

```
preg_match('/pattern/', 'string');
```

When choosing your pattern delimiters, don't put your delimiter character inside the regular expression pattern, or you'll close the pattern early. If you can't find a way to

---

1. Or {pattern}, <pattern>, |pattern|, #pattern#, or just about whatever your favorite delimiters are. If you use an opening pair character such as (, <, [, or { as the starting delimiter, PHP expects the corresponding closing pair character as the ending delimiter ((), >,], or }). If you use another character as the starting delimiter, PHP expects the same character as the ending delimiter.

avoid this problem, you need to escape any instances of your delimiters using the back-slash. Instead of doing this by hand, call addcslashes().

For example, if you use / as your delimiter:

```
$ereg_pattern = '<b>.+</b>';
$preg_pattern = addcslashes($ereg_pattern, '/');
```

the value of $preg_pattern is now <b>.+<\/b>.

The preg functions don't have a parallel series of case-insensitive functions. They have a case-insensitive modifier instead. To convert, change:

```
eregi('pattern', 'string');
```

to:

```
preg_match('/pattern/i', 'string');
```

Adding the i after the closing delimiter makes the change.

Finally, there is one last obscure difference. If you use a number (not a string) as a pattern or replacement value in ereg_replace(), it's assumed you are referring to the ASCII value of a character. Therefore, because 9 is the ASCII representation of tab (i.e., \t), this code inserts tabs at the beginning of each line:

```
$tab = 9;
$replaced = ereg_replace('^', $tab, $string);
```

Here's how to convert linefeed endings:

```
$converted = ereg_replace(10, 12, $text);
```

To avoid this feature in ereg functions, use this instead:

```
$tab = '9';
```

On the other hand, preg_replace() treats the number 9 as the one-character string '9', not as a tab substitute. To convert these character codes for use in preg_re place(), convert them to hexadecimal and prefix them with \x. For example, 9 becomes \x9 or \x09, and 12 becomes \x0c. Alternatively, you can use \t , \r, and \n for tabs, carriage returns, and linefeeds, respectively.

See Also

Documentation on ereg() (*http://www.php.net/ereg*), preg_match() (*http://www.php.net/preg-match*), and addcslashes() (*http://www.php.net/addcslashes*).

23.2 Matching Words

Problem

You want to pull out all words from a string.

Solution

The simplest way to do this is to use the PCRE "word character" character type escape sequence, \w:

```
$text = "Knock, knock. Who's there? r2d2!";
$words = preg_match_all('/\w+/', $text, $matches);
var_dump($matches[0]);
```

Discussion

The \w escape sequence matches letters, digits, and underscores. It does not include other punctuation. So the output from the preceding code is:

```
array(6) {
  [0]=>
  string(5) "Knock"
  [1]=>
  string(5) "knock"
  [2]=>
  string(3) "Who"
  [3]=>
  string(1) "s"
  [4]=>
  string(5) "there"
  [5]=>
  string(4) "r2d2"
}
```

This is mostly correct except that Who's is broken up into Who and s. To extend this pattern to handle English contractions properly, we can match against either a word character or an apostrophe sandwiched by word characters:

```
$text = "Knock, knock. Who's there? r2d2!";
$pattern = "/(?:\w'\w|\w)+/";
$words = preg_match_all($pattern, $text, $matches);
var_dump($matches[0]);
```

(The ?: syntax in this pattern prevents the text that matches the parenthesized subpattern from being "captured." This is explained in more detail in Recipe 23.7.)

With the addition of the u modifier, a pattern becomes Unicode-aware and will handle words properly in non-ASCII character sets. For example:

```
$fr = 'Toc, toc. Qui est là? R2D2!';
$fr_words = preg_match_all('/\w+/u', $fr, $matches);
print "The French words are:\n\t";
print implode(', ', $matches[0]) . "\n";

$kr = '노크, 노크. 거기 누구입니까? R2D2!';
$kr_words = preg_match_all('/\w+/u', $kr, $matches);
print "The Korean words are:\n\t";
print implode(', ', $matches[0]) . "\n";
```

This prints:

```
The French words are:
        Toc, toc, Qui, est, là, R2D2
The Korean words are:
        노크, 노크, 거기, 누구입니까, R2D2
```

Without that u at the end of each pattern, the non-ASCII characters would be stripped out of the matches, producing incorrect results.

See Also

Documentation on `preg` escape sequences (*http://php.net/regexp.reference.escape*); Recipe 19.12 for information about using UTF-8–encoded strings with the PCRE regex functions.

23.3 Finding the nth Occurrence of a Match

Problem

You want to find the *n*th word match instead of the first one.

Solution

Use `preg_match_all()` to pull all the matches into an array; then pick out the specific matches in which you're interested, as shown in Example 23-4.

Example 23-4. Finding the nth match

```
$todo = "1. Get Dressed 2. Eat Jelly 3. Squash every week into a day";

preg_match_all("/\d\. ([^\d]+)/", $todo, $matches);

print "The second item on the todo list is: ";
// $matches[1] is an array of each substring captured by ([^\d]+)
print $matches[1][1] . "\n";

print "The entire todo list is: ";
foreach($matches[1] as $match) {
```

```
    print "$match\n";
}
```

Discussion

Because the preg_match() function stops after it finds one match, you need to use preg_match_all() instead if you're looking for additional matches. The preg_match_all() function returns the number of full pattern matches it finds. If it finds no matches, it returns 0. If it encounters an error, such as a syntax problem in the pattern, it returns false.

The third argument to preg_match_all() is populated with an array holding information about the various substrings that the pattern has matched. The first element holds an array of matches of the complete pattern. For Example 23-4, this means that $match es[0] holds the parts of $todo that match /\d\. ([^\d]+)/: 1. Get Dressed, 2. Eat Jelly, and 3. Squash every week into a day.

Subsequent elements of the $matches array hold arrays of text matched by each parenthesized subpattern. The pattern in Example 23-4 has just one subpattern ([^\d\]+). So $matches[1] is an array of strings that match that subpattern: Get Dressed, Eat Jelly, and Squash every week into a day.

If there were a second subpattern, the substrings that it matched would be in $match es[2], a third subpattern's matches would be in $matches[3], and so on.

Instead of returning an array divided into full matches and then submatches, preg_match_all() can return an array divided by matches, with each submatch inside. To trigger this, pass PREG_SET_ORDER in as the fourth argument. This is particularly useful when you've got multiple captured subpatterns and you want to iterate through the subpattern groups one group at a time, as shown in Example 23-5.

Example 23-5. Grouping captured subpatterns

```
$todo = "
first=Get Dressed
next=Eat Jelly
last=Squash every week into a day
";

preg_match_all("/([a-zA-Z]+)=(.*)/", $todo, $matches, PREG_SET_ORDER);

foreach ($matches as $match) {
    print "The {$match[1]} action is {$match[2]}\n";
}
```

Example 23-5 prints:

```
The first action is Get Dressed
The next action is Eat Jelly
The last action is Squash every week into a day
```

With PREG_SET_ORDER, each value of $match in the foreach loop contains all the sub-patterns: $match[0] is the entire matched string, $match[1] the bit before the =, and $match[2] the bit after the =.

See Also

Documentation on preg_match_all() (*http://www.php.net/preg-match-all*).

23.4 Choosing Greedy or Nongreedy Matches

Problem

You want your pattern to match the smallest possible string instead of the largest.

Solution

Place a ? after a quantifier to alter that portion of the pattern, as in Example 23-6.

Example 23-6. Making a quantifier match as few characters as possible

```
// find all <em>emphasized</em> sections
preg_match_all('@<em>.+?</em>@', $html, $matches);
```

Or use the U pattern-modifier ending to invert all quantifiers from greedy ("match as many characters as possible") to nongreedy ("match as few characters as possible"). The code in Example 23-7 does the same thing as the code in Example 23-6.

Example 23-7. Making a quantifier match as few characters as possible

```
// find all <em>emphasized</em> sections
preg_match_all('@<em>.+</em>@U', $html, $matches);
```

Discussion

By default, all regular expression quantifiers in PHP are *greedy*. For example, consider the pattern ., which matches ", one or more characters, ," matching against the string I simply love your work. A greedy regular expression finds one match, because after it matches the opening , its .+ slurps up as much as possible, finally grinding to a halt at the final . The .+ matches love your work.

A nongreedy regular expression, on the other hand, finds a pair of matches. The first `<em>` is matched as before, but then `.+` stops as soon as it can, only matching love. A second match then goes ahead: the next `.+` matches work.

Example 23-8 shows the greedy and nongreedy patterns at work.

Example 23-8. Greedy versus nongreedy matching

```
$html = 'I simply <em>love</em> your <em>work</em>';
// Greedy
$matchCount = preg_match_all('@<em>.+</em>@', $html, $matches);
print "Greedy count: " . $matchCount . "\n";
// Nongreedy
$matchCount = preg_match_all('@<em>.+?</em>@', $html, $matches);
print "First non-greedy count: " . $matchCount . "\n";
// Nongreedy
$matchCount = preg_match_all('@<em>.+</em>@U', $html, $matches);
print "Second non-greedy count: " . $matchCount . "\n";
```

Example 23-8 prints:

```
Greedy count: 1
First non-greedy count: 2
Second non-greedy count: 2
```

Greedy matching is also known as *maximal matching* and nongreedy matching can be called *minimal matching*, because these methods match either the maximum or minimum number of characters possible.

The `ereg()` and `ereg_replace()` functions are always greedy. Being able to choose between greedy and nongreedy matching is another reason to use the PCRE functions instead.

Although nongreedy matching is useful for simplistic HTML parsing, it can break down if your markup isn't 100 percent valid and there are, for example, stray `<em>` tags lying around.[2] If your goal is just to remove all (or some) HTML tags from a block of text, you're better off not using a regular expression. Instead, use the built-in function `strip_tags()`; it's faster and it works correctly. See Recipe 13.6 for more details.

Finally, even though the idea of nongreedy matching comes from Perl, the U modifier is incompatible with Perl and is unique to PHP's Perl-compatible regular expressions. It inverts all quantifiers, turning them from greedy to nongreedy and also the reverse. So to get a greedy quantifier inside of a pattern operating under a trailing /U, just add a ? to the end, the same way you would normally turn a greedy quantifier into a nongreedy one.

---

2. It's possible to have valid HTML and still get into trouble; for instance, if you have bold tags inside a comment. A true HTML parser would ignore them, but our pattern won't.

See Also

Recipe 23.6 for more on capturing text inside HTML tags; Recipe 13.6 for more on stripping HTML tags; documentation on `preg_match_all()` (*http://www.php.net/preg-match-all*).

23.5 Finding All Lines in a File That Match a Pattern

Problem

You want to find all the lines in a file that match a pattern.

Solution

Read the file into an array and use `preg_grep()`.

Discussion

There are two ways to do this. Example 23-9 is faster, but uses more memory. It uses the `file()` function to put each line of the file into an array and `preg_grep()` to filter out the nonmatching lines.

Example 23-9. Quickly finding lines that match a pattern

```
$pattern = "/\bo'reilly\b/i"; // only O'Reilly books
$ora_books = preg_grep($pattern, file('/path/to/your/file.txt'));
```

Example 23-10 is slower, but more memory efficient. It reads the file a line at a time and uses `preg_match()` to check each line after it's read.

Example 23-10. Efficiently finding lines that match a pattern

```
$fh = fopen('/path/to/your/file.txt', 'r') or die($php_errormsg);
while (!feof($fh)) {
    $line = fgets($fh);
    if (preg_match($pattern, $line)) { $ora_books[ ] = $line; }
}
fclose($fh);
```

Because the code in Example 23-9 reads in everything all at once, it's about three times faster than the code in Example 23-10, which parses the file line by line but uses less memory. Keep in mind that because both methods operate on individual lines of the file, they can't successfully use patterns that match text that spans multiple lines.

See Also

Recipe 24.5 on reading files into strings; documentation on `preg_grep()` (*http://www.php.net/preg-grep*).

23.6 Capturing Text Inside HTML Tags

Problem

You want to capture text inside HTML tags. For example, you want to find all the heading tags in an HTML document.

Solution

Read the HTML file into a string and use nongreedy matching in your pattern, as shown in Example 23-11.

Example 23-11. Capturing HTML headings

```
$html = file_get_contents(__DIR__ . '/example.html');
preg_match_all('@<h([1-6])>(.+?)</h\1>@is', $html, $matches);
foreach ($matches[2] as $text) {
    print "Heading: $text\n";
}
```

Discussion

Robust parsing of HTML is difficult using a simple regular expression. This is one advantage of using XHTML; it's significantly easier to validate and parse.

For instance, the pattern in Example 23-11 can't deal with attributes inside the heading tags and is only smart enough to find matching headings, so `<h1>Dr. Strangelove</h1>` is OK, because it's wrapped inside `<h1></h1>` tags, but not `<h2>How I Learned to Stop Worrying and Love the Bomb</h3>`, because the opening tag is `<h2>`, whereas the closing tag is not.

This technique also works for finding all text inside reasonably well constructed `<strong>` and `<em>` tags, as in Example 23-12.

Example 23-12. Extracting text from HTML tags

```
$html = file_get_contents(__DIR__.'/example.html');
preg_match_all('@<(strong|em)>(.+?)</\1>@is', $html, $matches);
foreach ($matches[2] as $text) {
    print "Text: $text\n";
}
```

However, Example 23-12 breaks on nested headings. If *example.html* contains `<strong>Dr. Strangelove or: <em>How I Learned to Stop Worrying and Love the Bomb</em></strong>`, Example 23-12 doesn't capture the text inside the `<em></em>` tags as a separate item.

This isn't a problem in Example 23-11: because headings are block-level elements, it's illegal to nest them. However, as inline elements, nested `<strong>` and `<em>` tags are valid.

Regular expressions can be moderately useful for parsing small amounts of HTML, especially if the structure of that HTML is reasonably constrained (or you're generating it yourself). For more generalized and robust HTML parsing, use the Tidy extension. It provides an interface to the popular libtidy HTML cleanup library. After Tidy has cleaned up your HTML, you can use its methods for getting at parts of the document. Or if you've told Tidy to convert your HTML to XHTML, you can use all of the XML manipulation power of SimpleXML or the DOM extension to slice and dice your HTML document.

See Also

Recipe 13.1 for information on marking up a web page and Recipe 13.3 for extracting links from an HTML file; documentation on `preg_match()` (*http://www.php.net/preg-match*) and Tidy (*http://www.php.net/tidy*).

23.7 Preventing Parentheses from Capturing Text

Problem

You've used parentheses for grouping in a pattern, but you don't want the text that matches what's in the parentheses to show up in your array of captured matches.

Solution

Put `?:` just after the opening parenthesis, as in Example 23-13.

Example 23-13. Preventing text capture

```
$html = '<link rel="icon" href="http://www.example.com/icon.gif"/>
<link rel="prev" href="http://www.example.com/prev.xml"/>
<link rel="next" href="http://www.example.com/next.xml"/>';

preg_match_all('/rel="(prev|next)" href="([^"]*?)"/', $html, $bothMatches);
preg_match_all('/rel="(?:prev|next)" href="([^"]*?)"/', $html, $linkMatches);

print '$bothMatches is: '; var_dump($bothMatches);
print '$linkMatches is: '; var_dump($linkMatches);
```

In Example 23-13, $bothMatches contains the values of the rel and the href attributes. $linkMatches, however, just contains the values of the href attributes. The code prints:

```
$bothMatches is: array(3) {
  [0]=>
  array(2) {
    [0]=>
    string(49) "rel="prev" href="http://www.example.com/prev.xml""
    [1]=>
    string(49) "rel="next" href="http://www.example.com/next.xml""
  }
  [1]=>
  array(2) {
    [0]=>
    string(4) "prev"
    [1]=>
    string(4) "next"
  }
  [2]=>
  array(2) {
    [0]=>
    string(31) "http://www.example.com/prev.xml"
    [1]=>
    string(31) "http://www.example.com/next.xml"
  }
}
$linkMatches is: array(2) {
  [0]=>
  array(1) [
    [0]=>
    string(49) "rel="prev" href="http://www.example.com/prev.xml""
    [1]=>
    string(49) "rel="next" href="http://www.example.com/next.xml""
  }
  [1]=>
  array(2) {
    [0]=>
    string(31) "http://www.example.com/prev.xml"
    [1]=>
    string(31) "http://www.example.com/next.xml"
  }
}
```

Discussion

Preventing capturing is particularly useful when a subpattern is optional. Because it might not show up in the array of captured text, an optional subpattern can change the number of pieces of captured text. This makes it hard to reference a particular matched piece of text at a given index. Making optional subpatterns noncapturing prevents this problem. Example 23-14 illustrates this distinction.

Example 23-14. A noncapturing optional subpattern

```
$html = '<link rel="icon" href="http://www.example.com/icon.gif"/>
<link rel="prev" title="Previous" href="http://www.example.com/prev.xml"/>
<link rel="next" href="http://www.example.com/next.xml"/>';

preg_match_all('/rel="(?:prev|next)"(?: title="[^"]+?")? href="([^"]*?)"/',
               $html, $linkMatches);

print '$bothMatches is: '; var_dump($linkMatches);
```

See Also

The PCRE Pattern Syntax documentation (*http://php.net/refer
ence.pcre.pattern.syntax*).

23.8 Escaping Special Characters in a Regular Expression

Problem

You want to have characters such as * or + treated as literals, not as metacharacters, inside a regular expression. This is useful when allowing users to type in search strings you want to use inside a regular expression.

Solution

Use `preg_quote()` to escape PCRE metacharacters:

```
$pattern = preg_quote('The Education of H*Y*M*A*N K*A*P*L*A*N').'.':(\d+)';
if (preg_match("/$pattern/",$book_rank,$matches)) {
    print "Leo Rosten's book ranked: ".$matches[1];
}
```

Discussion

Here are the characters that `preg_quote()` escapes:

. \ + * ? ^ $ [ ] ( ) { } < > = ! | :

It escapes the metacharacters with a backslash.

You can also pass `preg_quote()` an additional character to escape as a second argument. It's useful to pass your pattern delimiter (usually /) as this argument so it also gets escaped. This is important if you incorporate user input into a regular expression pattern. The following code expects `$_GET['search_term']` from a web form and searches for words beginning with `$_GET['search_term']` in a string `$s`:

```
$search_term = preg_quote($_GET['search_term'],'/');
if (preg_match("/\b$search_term/i",$s)) {
```

```
    print 'match!';
}
```

Using `preg_quote()` ensures the regular expression is interpreted properly if, for example, a *Magnum, P.I.* fan enters `t.c` as a search term. Without `preg_quote()`, this matches `tic`, `tucker`, and any other words whose first letter is `t` and third letter is `c`. Passing the pattern delimiter to `preg_quote()` as well makes sure that user input with forward slashes in it, such as `CP/M`, is also handled correctly.

See Also

Documentation on `preg_quote()` (*http://www.php.net/preg-quote*).

23.9 Reading Records with a Pattern Separator

Problem

You want to read in records from a file, in which each record is separated by a pattern you can match with a regular expression.

Solution

Read the entire file into a string and then split on the regular expression:

```
$contents = file_get_contents('/path/to/your/file.txt');
$records = preg_split('/[0-9]+\) /', $contents);
```

Discussion

This breaks apart a numbered list and places the individual list items into array elements. So if you have a list like this:

```
1) Gödel
2) Escher
3) Bach
```

you end up with a four-element array, with an empty opening element. That's because `preg_split()` assumes the delimiters are between items, but in this case, the numbers are before items:

```
array(4) {
  [0]=>
  string(0) ""
  [1]=>
  string(7) "Gödel
"
  [2]=>
  string(7) "Escher
```

```
"
  [3]=>
  string(5) "Bach
"
}
```

From one point of view, this can be a feature, not a bug, because the *n*th element holds the *n*th item. But, to compact the array, you can eliminate the first element:

```
$records = preg_split('/[0-9]+\) /', $contents);
array_shift($records);
```

Another modification you might want is to strip newlines from the elements and substitute the empty string instead:

```
$records = preg_split('/[0-9]+\) /', str_replace("\n",'',$contents));
array_shift($records);
```

PHP doesn't allow you to change the input record separator to anything other than a newline, so this technique is also useful for breaking apart records divided by strings. However, if you find yourself splitting on a string instead of a regular expression, substitute explode() for preg_split() for a more efficient operation.

See Also

Recipe 24.5 for reading from a file; Recipe 1.12 for parsing CSV files.

23.10 Using a PHP Function in a Regular Expression

Problem

You want to process matched text with a PHP function. For example, you want to decode all HTML entities in captured subpatterns.

Solution

Use preg_replace_callback(). Instead of a replacement pattern, give it a callback function. This callback function is passed an array of matched subpatterns and should return an appropriate replacement string. Example 23-15 decodes entities between <code></code> tags.

Example 23-15. Generating replacement strings with a callback function

```
$h = 'The &lt;b&gt; tag makes text bold: <code>&lt;b&gt;bold&lt;/b&gt;</code>';
print preg_replace_callback('@<code>(.*?)</code>@','decode', $h);

// $matches[0] is the entire matched string
// $matches[1] is the first captured subpattern
function decode($matches) {
```

```
        return html_entity_decode($matches[1]);
    }
```

Example 23-15 prints:

```
The <b> tag makes text bold: <b>bold</b>
```

Discussion

The second argument to `preg_replace_callback()` specifies the function that is to be called to calculate replacement strings. Like everywhere the PHP "callable" pseudotype is used, this argument can be a string or an array. Use a string to specify a function name. To use an object instance method as a callback, pass an array whose first element is the object and whose second element is a string containing the method name. To use a static class method as a callback, pass an array of two strings: the class name and the method name. In PHP 5.4.0 and later, you can pass a variable containing an anonymous function, or define the function inline with the call to `preg_replace_callback()`.

The callback function is passed one argument: an array of matches. Element 0 of this array is always the text that matched the entire pattern. If the pattern given to `preg_re` `place_callback()` has any parenthesized subpatterns, these are present in subsequent elements of the `$matches` array. The keys of the `$matches` array are numeric, even if there are named subpatterns in the pattern.

If you are providing an anonymous function as a callback, it can be memory intensive if the function creation is inline with the call to `preg_replace_callback()` and inside a loop. If you want to use an anonymous function with `preg_replace_callback()`, store the anonymous function callback in a variable. Then, provide the variable to `preg_replace_callback()` as the callback function. Example 23-16 uses an anonymous function to apply the transformation in Example 23-15 to every line in a file.

Example 23-16. Generating replacement strings with an anonymous function

```
$callbackFunction = function($matches) {
    return html_entity_decode($matches[1]);
};

$fp = fopen(__DIR__ . '/html-to-decode.html','r');
while (! feof($fp)) {
    $line = fgets($fp);
    print preg_replace_callback('@<code>(.*?)</code>@',$callbackFunction, $line);
}
fclose($fp);
```

Example 23-16 uses the anonymous function declaration syntax introduced in PHP 5.3.0. If you're using an older version of PHP, you can use `create_function()` to build your callback, as follows:

```
$callbackFunction = create_function('$matches',
                            'return html_entity_decode($matches[1]);');
$fp = fopen(__DIR__ . '/html-to-decode.html','r');
while (! feof($fp)) {
    $line = fgets($fp);
    print preg_replace_callback('@<code>(.*?)</code>@',$callbackFunction, $line);
}
fclose($fp);
```

So you can avoid using it, you should be aware of the e pattern modifier. This causes the replacement string to be evaluated as PHP code. This pattern modifier is deprecated as of PHP 5.5.0. Using the e modifier opens up remote code execution security vulnerabilities when user input is part of the text that `preg_replace()` operates on. If you encounter code using `preg_replace()` with the e modifier, convert it to use `preg_replace_callback()` instead.

See Also

Documentation on `preg_replace_callback()` (*http://www.php.net/preg_replace_call back*), on `preg_replace()` (*http://www.php.net/preg_replace*), on `create_func tion()` (*http://www.php.net/create_function*), and on the callable pseudotype (*http:// www.php.net/language.types.callable*).

CHAPTER 24

Files

24.0 Introduction

The input and output in a web application usually flow between browser, server, and database, but there are many circumstances in which files are involved too. Files are useful for retrieving remote web pages for local processing, storing data without a database, and saving information to which other programs need access. Plus, as PHP becomes a tool for more than just pumping out web pages, the file I/O functions are even more useful.

PHP's interface for file I/O is similar to that of C, although less complicated. The fundamental unit of identifying a file to read from or write to is a filehandle. This handle identifies your connection to a specific file, and you use it for operations on the file. This chapter focuses on opening and closing files and manipulating filehandles in PHP, as well as what you can do with the file contents once you've opened a file. Chapter 25 deals with directories and file metadata such as permissions.

This example opens */tmp/cookie-data* and writes the contents of a specific cookie to the file:

```
$fh = fopen('/tmp/cookie-data','w')      or die("can't open file");
if (-1 == fwrite($fh,$_COOKIE['flavor'])) { die("can't write data"); }
fclose($fh)                              or die("can't close file");
```

The function fopen() returns a filehandle if its attempt to open the file is successful. If it can't open the file (because of incorrect permissions, for example), it returns false and generates an E_WARNING-type error. Recipes 24.1 through 24.3 cover ways to open files.

In the example, fwrite() writes the value of the flavor cookie to the filehandle. It returns the number of bytes written. If it can't write the string (not enough disk space, for example), it returns -1.

Last, `fclose()` closes the filehandle. This is done automatically at the end of a request, but it's a good idea to explicitly close all files you open anyway. It prevents problems when using the code in a command-line context and frees up system resources. It also allows you to check the return code from `fclose()`. Buffered data might not actually be written to disk until `fclose()` is called, so it's here that "disk full" errors are sometimes reported.

As with other processes, PHP must have the correct permissions to read from and write to a file. This is usually straightforward in a command-line context but can cause confusion when running scripts within a web server. Your web server (and consequently your PHP script) probably runs as a specific user dedicated to web serving (or perhaps as user `nobody`). For good security reasons, this user often has restricted permissions on what files it can access. If your script is having trouble with a file operation, make sure the web server's user or group—not yours—has permission to perform that file operation. Some web-serving setups may run your script as you, though, in which case you need to make sure that your scripts can't accidentally read or write personal files that aren't part of your website.

Because most file-handling functions just return `false` on error, you have to do some additional work to find more details about that error. When the `track_errors` configuration directive is `on`, each error message is put in the global variable `$php_errormsg`. Including this variable as part of your error output makes debugging easier, as shown:

```
$fh = fopen('/tmp/cookie-data','w')      or die("can't open: $php_errormsg");
if (-1 == fwrite($fh,$_COOKIE['flavor'])) { die("can't write: $php_errormsg"); }
fclose($fh)                              or die("can't close: $php_errormsg");
```

If you don't have permission to write to *tmp/cookie-data*, it dies with this error output:

```
can't open: fopen(/tmp/cookie-data): failed to open stream: Permission denied
```

Windows and Unix treat files differently. To ensure your file access code works appropriately on Unix and Windows, take care to handle line-delimiter characters and pathnames correctly.

A line delimiter on Windows is two characters: ASCII 13 (carriage return) followed by ASCII 10 (line feed or newline). On Unix, it's just ASCII 10. The typewriter-era names for these characters explain why you can get "stair-stepped" text when printing out a Unix-delimited file. Imagine these character names as commands to the platen in a typewriter or character-at-a-time printer. A carriage return sends the platen back to the beginning of the line it's on, and a line feed advances the paper by one line. A misconfigured printer encountering a Unix-delimited file dutifully follows instructions and does a line feed at the end of each line. This advances to the next line but doesn't move the horizontal printing position back to the left margin. The next stair-stepped line of text begins (horizontally) where the previous line left off.

PHP functions that use a newline as a line-ending delimiter (for example, `fgets()`) work on both Windows and Unix because a newline is the character at the end of the line on either platform.

To remove any line-delimiter characters, use the PHP function `rtrim()`:

```
$fh = fopen('/tmp/lines-of-data.txt','r') or die($php_errormsg);
while(false !== ($s = fgets($fh))) {
    $s = rtrim($s);
    // do something with $s ...
}
fclose($fh)                            or die($php_errormsg);
```

This function removes any trailing whitespace in the line, including ASCII 13 and ASCII 10 (as well as tab and space). If there's whitespace at the end of a line that you want to preserve, but you still want to remove carriage returns and line feeds, provide `rtrim()` with a string containing the characters that it should remove. Other characters are left untouched, as shown:

```
$fh = fopen('/tmp/lines-of-data.txt','r') or die($php_errormsg);
while(false !== ($s = fgets($fh))) {
    $s = rtrim($s, "\r\n");
    // do something with $s ...
}
fclose($fh)                            or die($php_errormsg);
```

Unix and Windows also differ on the character used to separate directories in pathnames. Unix uses a slash (/), and Windows uses a backslash (\). PHP makes sorting this out easy, however, because the Windows version of PHP also understands / as a directory separator. For example, this successfully prints the contents of *C:\Alligator\Crocodile Menu.txt*:

```
$fh = fopen('c:/alligator/crocodile menu.txt','r') or die($php_errormsg);
while(false !== ($s = fgets($fh))) {
    print $s;
}
fclose($fh)                            or die($php_errormsg);
```

It also takes advantage of the fact that Windows filenames aren't case sensitive. However, Unix filenames are.

Sorting out line-break confusion isn't only a problem in your code that reads and writes files, but in your source code files as well. If you have multiple people working on a project, make sure all developers configure their editors to use the same kind of line breaks.

Once you've opened a file, PHP gives you many tools to process its data. In keeping with PHP's C-like I/O interface, the two basic functions to read data from a file are `fread()`, which reads a specified number of bytes, and `fgets()`, which reads a line at a time (up to an optional specified number of bytes). This example handles lines up to 256 bytes long:

```
$fh = fopen('orders.txt','r') or die($php_errormsg);
while (! feof($fh)) {
    $s = fgets($fh,256);
    process_order($s);
}
fclose($fh)                        or die($php_errormsg);
```

If *orders.txt* has a 300-byte line, `fgets()` returns only the first 256 bytes. The next `fgets()` returns the next 44 bytes and stops when it finds the newline. The next `fgets()` after that moves to the next line of the file. Without the second argument, `fgets()` reads until it reaches the end of the line.

Many operations on file contents, such as picking a line at random (see Recipe 24.8) are conceptually simpler (and require less code) if the entire file is read into a string or array. The `file_get_contents()` function reads an entire file into a string, and the `file()` function puts each line of a file into an array. The trade-off for simplicity, however, is memory consumption. This can be especially harmful when you are using PHP as a server module.

Generally, when a process (such as a web server process with PHP embedded in it) allocates memory (as PHP does to read an entire file into a string or array), it can't return that memory to the operating system until it dies. This means that calling `file_get_con tents()` on a 1 MB file from PHP running as an Apache module increases the size of that Apache process by 1 MB until the process dies. Repeated a few times, this decreases server efficiency. There are certainly good reasons for processing an entire file at once, but be conscious of the memory-use implications when you do.

If you are able to avoid loading the entire file into memory, generators are an elegant way to encapsulate file-iteration logic. Recipe 4.24 shows how to loop over the the lines of a file as if they are stored in an array, while only loading into memory one line at a time.

Recipes 24.17 through 24.19 deal with running other programs from within a PHP program. Some program execution operators or functions offer ways to run a program and read its output all at once (backticks) or read its last line of output (`system()`). PHP can use pipes to run a program, pass it input, or read its output. Because a pipe is read with standard I/O functions (`fgets()` and `fread()`), you decide how you want the input and you can do other tasks between reading chunks of input. Similarly, writing to a pipe is done with `fputs()` and `fwrite()`, so you can pass input to a program in arbitrary increments.

Pipes have the same permission issues as regular files. The PHP process must have execute permission on the program being opened as a pipe. If you have trouble opening a pipe, especially if PHP is running as a special web server user, make sure the user is allowed to execute the program to which you are opening a pipe.

24.1 Creating or Opening a Local File

Problem

You want to open a local file to read data from it or write data to it.

Solution

Use fopen():

```
$fh = fopen('file.txt','r') or die("can't open file.txt: $php_errormsg");
```

Discussion

The first argument to fopen() is the file to open; the second argument is the mode in which to open the file. The mode specifies what operations can be performed on the file (reading and/or writing), where the file pointer is placed after the file is opened (at the beginning or end of the file), whether the file is truncated to zero length after opening, and whether the file is created if it doesn't exist, as shown in Table 24-1.

Table 24-1. fopen() file modes

Mode	Readable?	Writable?	File pointer	Truncate?	Create?
r	Yes	No	Beginning	No	No
r+	Yes	Yes	Beginning	No	No
w	No	Yes	Beginning	Yes	Yes
w+	Yes	Yes	Beginning	Yes	Yes
a	No	Yes	End	No	Yes
a+	Yes	Yes	End	No	Yes
x	No	Yes	Beginning	No	Yes
x+	Yes	Yes	Beginning	No	Yes

The x and x+ modes return **false** and generate a warning if the file already exists.

On non-POSIX systems, such as Windows, you need to add a b to the mode when opening a binary file, or reads and writes get tripped up on NUL (ASCII 0) characters. For instance:

```
$fh = fopen('c:/images/logo.gif','rb');
```

Even though Unix systems handle binary files fine without the b in the mode, it's a good idea to use it always. That way, your code is maximally portable and runs well on both Unix and Windows.

To operate on a file, pass the filehandle returned from fopen() to other I/O functions such as fgets(), fputs(), and fclose().

If the file given to fopen() doesn't have a pathname, the file is opened in the directory of the running script (web context) or in the current directory (command-line context).

You can also tell fopen() to search for the file to open in the include_path specified in your *php.ini* file by passing true as a third argument. This example searches for *file.inc* in the include_path:

```
$fh = fopen('file.inc','r',true) or die("can't open file.inc: $php_errormsg");
```

See Also

Documentation on fopen() (*http://www.php.net/fopen*).

24.2 Creating a Temporary File

Problem

You need a file to temporarily hold some data.

Solution

If the file needs to last only the duration of the running script, use tmpfile():

```
$temp_fh = tmpfile();
// write some data to the temp file
fputs($temp_fh,"The current time is ".strftime('%c'));
// the file goes away when the script ends
exit(1);
```

If the file needs to last longer, generate a filename with tempnam(), and then use fopen():

```
$tempfilename = tempnam('/tmp', 'data-');
$temp_fh = fopen($tempfilename, 'w') or die($php_errormsg);
fputs($temp_fh, "The current time is ".strftime('%c'));
fclose($temp_fh)                    or die($php_errormsg);
```

Discussion

The tmpfile() function creates a file with a unique name and returns a filehandle. The file is removed when fclose() is called on that filehandle, or the script ends.

Alternatively, `tempnam()` generates a filename. It takes two arguments: the first is a directory, and the second is a prefix for the filename. If the directory doesn't exist or isn't writable, `tempnam()` uses the system temporary directory—the `TMPDIR` environment variable in Unix or the `TMP` environment variable in Windows. This example shows what `tempnam()` generates:

```
$tempfilename = tempnam('/tmp','data-');
print "Temporary data will be stored in $tempfilename";
```

This prints:

Temporary data will be stored in /tmp/data-GawVoL

Because of the way PHP generates temporary filenames, a file with the filename that `tempnam()` returns is actually created but left empty, even if your script never explicitly opens the file. This ensures another program won't create a file with the same name between the time that you call `tempnam()` and the time you call `fopen()` with the filename.

See Also

Documentation on `tmpfile()` (*http://www.php.net/tmpfile*) and `tempnam()` (*http://www.php.net/tempnam*).

24.3 Opening a Remote File

Problem

You want to open a file that's accessible to you via HTTP or FTP.

Solution

Pass the file's URL to `fopen()`:

```
$fh = fopen('http://www.example.com/robots.txt','r') or die($php_errormsg);
```

Discussion

When `fopen()` is passed a filename that begins with *http://*, it retrieves the given page with an HTTP/1.0 GET request (although a `Host:` header is also passed along to work with virtual hosts). Only the body of the reply can be accessed using the filehandle, not the headers. Files can be read, but not written, via HTTP.

When `fopen()` is passed a filename that begins with *ftp://*, it returns a pointer to the specified file, obtained via passive-mode FTP. You can open files via FTP for either reading or writing, but not both.

To open URLs that require a username and a password with `fopen()`, embed the authentication information in the URL as shown:

```
$fh = fopen('ftp://username:password@ftp.example.com/pub/Index','r');
$fh = fopen('http://username:password@www.example.com/robots.txt','r');
```

Opening remote files with `fopen()` is implemented via a PHP feature called the stream wrapper. It's enabled by default but is disabled by setting `allow_url_fopen` to `off` in your *php.ini* or web server configuration file. If you can't open remote files with `fopen()`, check your server configuration.

See Also

Recipe 14.1 through Recipe 14.7, which discuss retrieving URLs; documentation on `fopen()` (*http://www.php.net/fopen*), remote files (*http://www.php.net/features.remote-files*) and stream wrappers (*http://www.php.net/wrappers*).

24.4 Reading from Standard Input

Problem

You want to read from standard input in a command-line context—for example, to get user input from the keyboard or data piped to your PHP program.

Solution

Use `fopen()` to open *php://stdin*:

```
$fh = fopen('php://stdin','r') or die($php_errormsg);
while($s = fgets($fh)) {
    print "You typed: $s";
}
```

Discussion

Recipe 26.3 discusses reading data from the keyboard in a command-line context in more detail. Reading data from standard input isn't very useful in a web context, because information doesn't arrive via standard input. The bodies of HTTP POST and file-upload requests are parsed by PHP and put into special variables. Non–file-upload POST request bodies can also be read with the `php://input` stream, as discussed in Recipe 8.5.

See Also

Recipe 26.3 for reading from the keyboard in a command-line context; Recipe 8.5 for reading POST request bodies; documentation on `fopen()` (*http://www.php.net/fopen*).

24.5 Reading a File into a String

Problem

You want to load the entire contents of a file into a variable. For example, you want to determine if the text in a file matches a regular expression.

Solution

Use `file_get_contents()`:

```
$people = file_get_contents('people.txt');
if (preg_match('/Names:.*(David|Susannah)/i',$people)) {
    print "people.txt matches.";
}
```

Discussion

If you want the contents of a file in a string to manipulate, `file_get_contents()` is great, but if you just want to print the entire contents of a file, there are easier (and more efficient) ways than reading it into a string and then printing the string. PHP provides two functions for this. The first is `fpassthru($fh)`, which prints everything left on the filehandle `$fh` and then closes it. The second, `readfile($filename)`, prints the entire contents of `$filename`.

You can use `readfile()` to implement a wrapper around images that shouldn't always be displayed. This program makes sure a requested image is less than a week old:

```
$image_directory = '/usr/local/images';

if (preg_match('/^[a-zA-Z0-9]+\.(gif|jpe?g)$/',$image,$matches) &&
    is_readable($image_directory."/$image") &&
    (filemtime($image_directory."/$image") >= (time() - 86400 * 7))) {

  header('Content-Type: image/'.$matches[1]);
  header('Content-Length: '.filesize($image_directory."/$image"));

  readfile($image_directory."/$image");

} else {
  error_log("Can't serve image: $image");
}
```

The directory in which the images are stored, `$image_directory`, needs to be outside the web server's document root for the wrapper to be effective. Otherwise, users can just access the image files directly. The code tests the image file for three things. First, that the filename passed in `$image` is just alphanumeric with an ending of either *.gif*, *.jpg*, or *.jpeg*. You need to ensure that characters such as .. or / are not in the filename; this prevents malicious users from retrieving files outside the specified directory. Second, use `is_readable()` to make sure the program can read the file. Finally, get the file's modification time with `filemtime()` and make sure the time is after 86,400 × 7 seconds ago. There are 86,400 seconds in a day, so 86,400 × 7 is a week.[1]

If all of these conditions are met, you're ready to send the image. First, send two headers to tell the browser the image's MIME type and file size. Then use `readfile()` to send the entire contents of the file to the user.

See Also

Documentation on `filesize()` (*http://www.php.net/filesize*), `fread()` (*http://www.php.net/fread*), `fpassthru()` (*http://www.php.net/fpassthru*), and `readfile()` (*http://www.php.net/readfile*).

24.6 Counting Lines, Paragraphs, or Records in a File

Problem

You want to count the number of lines, paragraphs, or records in a file.

Solution

To count lines, use `fgets()`:

```
$lines = 0;

if ($fh = fopen('orders.txt','r')) {
  while (! feof($fh)) {
    if (fgets($fh)) {
      $lines++;
    }
  }
}

print $lines;
```

Because `fgets()` reads a line at a time, you can count the number of times it's called before reaching the end of a file.

To count paragraphs, increment the counter only when you read a blank line:

```
$paragraphs = 0;
```

---

1. When switching between standard time and daylight saving time, there are not 86,400 seconds in a day. See Recipe 3.10 for details.

```
if ($fh = fopen('great-american-novel.txt','r')) {
  while (! feof($fh)) {
    $s = fgets($fh);
    if (("\n" == $s) || ("\r\n" == $s)) {
      $paragraphs++;
    }
  }
}

print $paragraphs;
```

To count records, increment the counter only when the line read contains just the record separator and whitespace. Here the record separator is stored in `$record_separator`:

```
$records = 0;
$record_separator = '--end--';

if ($fh = fopen('great-american-textfile-database.txt','r')) {
  while (! feof($fh)) {
    $s = rtrim(fgets($fh));
    if ($s == $record_separator) {
      $records++;
    }
  }
}

print $records;
```

Discussion

When counting lines, $lines is incremented only if `fgets()` returns a true value. As `fgets()` moves through the file, it returns each line it retrieves. When it reaches the last line, it returns `false`, so $lines isn't incremented incorrectly. Because EOF has been reached on the file, `feof()` returns `true`, and the `while` loop ends.

When counting paragraphs, the solution works properly on simple text but may produce unexpected results when presented with a long string of blank lines or a file without two consecutive line breaks. These problems can be remedied with functions based on `preg_split()`. If the file is small and can be read into memory, use the `split_para graphs()` function. This function returns an array containing each paragraph in the file. For example:

```
function split_paragraphs($file,$rs="\r?\n") {
    $text = file_get_contents($file);
    $matches = preg_split("/(.*?$rs)(?:$rs)+/s",$text,-1,
                        PREG_SPLIT_DELIM_CAPTURE|PREG_SPLIT_NO_EMPTY);
    return $matches;
}
```

The contents of the file are broken on two or more consecutive newlines and returned in the $matches array. The default record-separation regular expression, \r?\n, matches both Windows and Unix line breaks.

If the file is too big to read into memory at once, use the split_paragraphs_large file() function, which reads the file in 16 KB chunks:

```
function split_paragraphs_largefile($file,$rs="\r?\n") {
    global $php_errormsg;

    $unmatched_text = '';
    $paragraphs = array();

    $fh = fopen($file,'r') or die($php_errormsg);

    while(! feof($fh)) {
        $s = fread($fh,16384) or die($php_errormsg);
        $text_to_split = $unmatched_text . $s;

        $matches = preg_split("/(.*?$rs)(?:$rs)+/s",$text_to_split,-1,
                        PREG_SPLIT_DELIM_CAPTURE|PREG_SPLIT_NO_EMPTY);

        // if the last chunk doesn't end with two record separators, save it
        // to prepend to the next section that gets read
        $last_match = $matches[count($matches)-1];
        if (! preg_match("/$rs$rs\$/",$last_match)) {
            $unmatched_text = $last_match;
            array_pop($matches);
        } else {
            $unmatched_text = '';
        }

        $paragraphs = array_merge($paragraphs,$matches);
    }

    // after reading all sections, if there is a final chunk that doesn't
    // end with the record separator, count it as a paragraph
    if ($unmatched_text) {
        $paragraphs[] = $unmatched_text;
    }
    return $paragraphs;
}
```

This function uses the same regular expression as split_paragraphs() to split the file into paragraphs. When it finds a paragraph end in a chunk read from the file, it saves the rest of the text in the chunk in $unmatched_text and prepends it to the next chunk read. This includes the unmatched text as the beginning of the next paragraph in the file.

The record-counting function at the end of the Solution lets fgets() figure out how long each line is. If you can supply a reasonable upper bound on line length, `stream_get_line()` provides a more concise way to count records. This function reads a line until it reaches a certain number of bytes or it sees a particular delimiter. Supply it with the record separator as the delimiter, as shown:

```
$records = 0;
$record_separator = '--end--';

if ($fh = fopen('great-american-textfile-database.txt','r')) {
    $done = false;
    while (! $done) {
        $s = stream_get_line($fh, 65536, $record_separator);
        if (feof($fh)) {
            $done = true;
        } else {
            $records++;
        }
    }
}

print $records;
```

This example assumes that each record is no more that 64 KB (65,536 bytes) long. Each call to `stream_get_line()` returns one record, not including the record separator. When `stream_get_line()` has advanced past the last record separator, it reaches the end of the file, so $done is set to true to stop counting records.

See Also

Documentation on `fgets()` (*http://www.php.net/fgets*), `feof()` (*http://www.php.net/feof*), `preg_split()` (*http://www.php.net/preg-split*), and `stream_get_line()` (*http://www.php.net/stream_get_line*).

24.7 Processing Every Word in a File

Problem

You want to do something with every word in a file. For example, you want to build a concordance of how many times each word is used to compute similarities between documents.

Solution

Read in each line with `fgets()`, separate the line into words, and process each word:

```
$fh = fopen('great-american-novel.txt','r') or die($php_errormsg);
while (! feof($fh)) {
    if ($s = fgets($fh)) {
        $words = preg_split('/\s+/',$s,-1,PREG_SPLIT_NO_EMPTY);
```

```
        // process words
    }
}
fclose($fh) or die($php_errormsg);
```

Discussion

This example calculates the average word length in a file:

```
$word_count = $word_length = 0;

if ($fh = fopen('great-american-novel.txt','r')) {
  while (! feof($fh)) {
    if ($s = fgets($fh)) {
      $words = preg_split('/\s+/',$s,-1,PREG_SPLIT_NO_EMPTY);
      foreach ($words as $word) {
        $word_count++;
        $word_length += strlen($word);
      }
    }
  }
}

print sprintf("The average word length over %d words is %.02f characters.",
              $word_count,
              $word_length/$word_count);
```

Processing every word proceeds differently depending on how "word" is defined. The code in this recipe uses the Perl-compatible regular expression engine's \s whitespace metacharacter, which includes space, tab, newline, carriage return, and formfeed.

Recipe 1.5 breaks apart a line into words by splitting on a space, which is useful in that recipe because the words have to be rejoined with spaces. The Perl-compatible engine also has a word-boundary assertion (\b) that matches between a word character (alphanumeric) and a nonword character (anything else). Using \b instead of \s to delimit words most noticeably treats words with embedded punctuation differently. The term 6 o'clock is two words when split by whitespace (6 and o'clock); it's four words when split by word boundaries (6, o, ', and clock).

See Also

Recipe 23.2 for using regular expressions to match words; Recipe 1.5 for breaking apart a line by words; documentation on fgets() (*http://www.php.net/fgets*), preg_split() (*http://www.php.net/preg-split*), and on the Perl-compatible regular expression extension (*http://www.php.net/pcre*).

24.8 Picking a Random Line from a File

Problem

You want to pick a line at random from a file; for example, you want to display a selection from a file of sayings.

Solution

Spread the selection odds evenly over all lines in a file:

```php
$line_number = 0;

$fh = fopen(__DIR__ . '/sayings.txt','r') or die($php_errormsg);
while (! feof($fh)) {
    if ($s = fgets($fh)) {
        $line_number++;
        if (mt_rand(0, $line_number - 1) == 0) {
            $line = $s;
        }
    }
}
fclose($fh) or die($php_errormsg);
```

Discussion

As each line is read, a line counter is incremented, and this example generates a random integer between 0 and $line_number - 1. If the number is 0, the current line is selected as the randomly chosen line. After all lines have been read, the last line that was selected as the randomly chosen line is left in $line.

This algorithm neatly ensures that each line in an n line file has a $1/n$ chance of being chosen without having to store all n lines into memory.

See Also

Documentation on mt_rand() (*http://www.php.net/mt-rand*).

24.9 Randomizing All Lines in a File

Problem

You want to randomly reorder all lines in a file. You have a file of funny quotes, for example, and you want to pick out one at random.

Solution

Read all the lines in the file into an array with `file()` and then shuffle the elements of the array:

```
$lines = file(__DIR__ . '/quotes-of-the-day.txt');

if (shuffle($lines)) {
    // okay
} else {
    die("Failed to shuffle");
}
```

Discussion

The `shuffle()` function randomly reorders the array elements, so after shuffling, you can pick out `$lines[0]` as a quote to display.

See Also

Recipe 4.20 for `shuffle()`; documentation on `shuffle()` (*http://www.php.net/shuffle*).

24.10 Processing Variable-Length Text Fields

Problem

You want to read delimited text fields from a file. You might, for example, have a database program that prints records one per line, with tabs between each field in the record, and you want to parse this data into an array.

Solution

Use `fgetcsv()` to read in each line and then split the fields based on their delimiter:

```
$delim = '|';

$fh = fopen('books.txt','r') or die("can't open: $php_errormsg");
while (! feof($fh)) {
    $fields = fgetcsv($fh, 1000, $delim);
    // ... do something with the data ...
    print_r($fields);
}
fclose($fh) or die("can't close: $php_errormsg");
```

Discussion

To parse the following data in *books.txt*:

```
Elmer Gantry|Sinclair Lewis|1927
The Scarlatti Inheritance|Robert Ludlum|1971
The Parsifal Mosaic|Robert Ludlum|1982
Sophie's Choice|William Styron|1979
```

process each record as shown:

```
$fh = fopen('books.txt','r') or die("can't open: $php_errormsg");
while (! feof($fh)) {
    list($title,$author,$publication_year) = fgetcsv($fh, 1000, '|');
    // ... do something with the data ...
}
fclose($fh) or die("can't close: $php_errormsg");
```

The fgetcsv() function reads in lines from a file, like fgets(), but it also parses them into individual fields. As the name suggests, its default delimiter is a comma, but the function accepts any field. In this example, it's a pipe.

The line-length argument to fgetcsv() needs to be at least as long as the longest record, so that a record doesn't get truncated.

If any of your records contain your delimiter, fgetcsv() can parse these properly if the data is enclosed or escaped. By default, this is the double quote and backslash characters, respectively. You can change this:

```
$fh = fopen('books.txt','r') or die("can't open: $php_errormsg");
while (! feof($fh)) {
    list($title,$author,$publication_year) = fgetcsv($fh, 1000, '|', "'", '*');
    // ... do something with the data ...
}
fclose($fh) or die("can't close: $php_errormsg");
```

Here, records are wrapped in single quotes and the single-quote character is escaped using an asterisk.

If lines are not properly detected, enable the auto_detect_line_endings configuration option prior to opening the file:

```
ini_set('auto_detect_line_endings', true);

$fh = fopen('books.txt','r') or die("can't open: $php_errormsg");
// rest of processing
```

See Also

Recipe 1.15 discusses ways to break strings into pieces; Recipes 1.12 and 1.14 cover parsing comma-separated and fixed-width data; documentation on fgetcsv() (*http://www.php.net/fgetcsv*).

24.11 Reading Configuration Files

Problem

You want to use configuration files to initialize settings in your programs.

Solution

Use `parse_ini_file()`:

```
$config = parse_ini_file('/etc/myapp.ini');
```

Discussion

The function `parse_ini_file()` reads configuration files structured like PHP's main *php.ini* file. Instead of applying the settings in the configuration file to PHP's configuration, however, `parse_ini_file()` returns the values from the file in an array.

For example, when `parse_ini_file()` is given a file with these contents:

```
; physical features
eyes=brown
hair=brown
glasses=yes

; other features
name=Susannah
likes=monkeys,ice cream,reading
```

the array it returns is:

```
Array
(
    [eyes] => brown
    [hair] => brown
    [glasses] => 1
    [name] => Susannah
    [likes] => monkeys,ice cream,reading
)
```

Blank lines and lines that begin with ; in the configuration file are ignored. Other lines with name=value pairs are put into an array with the name as the key and the value, appropriately, as the value. Words such as on and yes as values are returned as 1, and words such as off and no are returned as the empty string.

To parse sections from the configuration file, pass 1 as a second argument to `parse_ini_file()`. Sections are set off by words in square brackets in the file:

```
[physical]
eyes=brown
```

```
hair=brown
glasses=yes

[other]
name=Susannah
likes=monkeys,ice cream,reading
```

If this file is in */etc/myapp.ini*, then:

```
$conf = parse_ini_file('/etc/myapp.ini',1);
```

puts the array in `$conf`:

```
Array
(
    [physical] => Array
        (
            [eyes] => brown
            [hair] => brown
            [glasses] => 1
        )

    [other] => Array
        (
            [name] => Susannah
            [likes] => monkeys,ice cream,reading
        )

)
```

Another approach to configuration is to make your configuration file a valid PHP file that you load with `require` instead of `parse_ini_file()`. If the file *config.php* contains:

```
<?php
// physical features
$eyes = 'brown';
$hair = 'brown';
$glasses = 'yes';

// other features
$name = 'Susannah';
$likes = array('monkeys','ice cream','reading');
```

you can set the variables `$eyes`, `$hair`, `$glasses`, `$name`, and `$likes` with a simple `require 'config.php';`.

The configuration file loaded by `require` needs to be valid PHP—including the `<?php` start tag. The variables named in *config.php* are set explicitly, not inside an array, as in `parse_ini_file()`. For simple configuration files, this technique may not be worth the extra attention to syntax, but it is useful for embedding logic in the configuration file, such as this statement:

```
$time_of_day = (date('a') == 'am') ? 'early' : 'late';
```

See Also

Documentation on `parse_ini_file()` (*http://www.php.net/parse-ini-file*).

24.12 Modifying a File in Place Without a Temporary File

Problem

You want to change a file without using a temporary file to hold the changes.

Solution

Read the file with `file_get_contents()`, make the changes, and rewrite the file with `file_put_contents()`:

```
$contents = file_get_contents('pickles.txt');
$contents = strtoupper($contents);
file_put_contents('pickles.txt', $contents);
```

Discussion

This example turns text emphasized with asterisks or slashes into text with HTML <b> or <i> tags:

```
$contents = file_get_contents('message.txt');
// convert *word* to <b>word</b>
$contents = preg_replace('@\*(.*?)\*@i','<b>$1</b>',$contents);
// convert /word/ to <i>word</i>
$contents = preg_replace('@/(.*?)/@i','<i>$1</i>',$contents);
file_put_contents('message.txt', $contents);
```

Because adding HTML tags makes the file grow, the entire file has to be read into memory and then processed. If the changes to a file make each line shrink (or stay the same size), the file can be processed line by line, saving memory.

For example, this converts text marked with <b> and <i> to text marked with asterisks and slashes:

```
$fh = fopen('message.txt','r+')          or die($php_errormsg);

// figure out how many bytes to read
$bytes_to_read = filesize('message.txt');

// initialize variables that hold file positions
$next_read = $last_write = 0;

// keep going while there are still bytes to read
while ($next_read < $bytes_to_read) {
```

```
    /* move to the position of the next read, read a line, and save
     * the position of the next read */
    fseek($fh,$next_read);
    $s = fgets($fh)                        or die($php_errormsg);
    $next_read = ftell($fh);

    // convert <b>word</b> to *word*
    $s = preg_replace('@<b[^>]*>(.*?)</b>@i','*$1*',$s);
    // convert <i>word</i> to /word/
    $s = preg_replace('@<i[^>]*>(.*?)</i>@i','/$1/',$s);

    /* move to the position where the last write ended, write the
     * converted line, and save the position for the next write */
    fseek($fh,$last_write);
    if (-1 == fwrite($fh,$s))              { die($php_errormsg); }
    $last_write = ftell($fh);
}

// truncate the file length to what we've already written
ftruncate($fh,$last_write)              or die($php_errormsg);

// close the file
fclose($fh)                            or die($php_errormsg);
```

See Also

Recipes 13.4 and 13.5 for additional information on converting between plain text and HTML; documentation on `fseek()` (*http://www.php.net/fseek*), `rewind()` (*http://www.php.net/rewind*), `ftruncate()` (*http://www.php.net/ftruncate*), `file_get_contents()` (*http://www.php.net/file_get_contents*), and `file_put_contents()` (*http://www.php.net/file_put_contents*).

24.13 Flushing Output to a File

Problem

You want to force all buffered data to be written to a filehandle.

Solution

Use `fflush()`:

```
fwrite($fh,'There are twelve pumpkins in my house.');
fflush($fh);
```

This ensures that `There are twelve pumpkins in my house.` is written to `$fh`.

Discussion

To be more efficient, system I/O libraries generally don't write something to a file when you tell them to. Instead, they batch the writes together in a buffer and save all of them to disk at the same time. Using `fflush()` forces anything pending in the write buffer to be actually written to disk.

Flushing output can be particularly helpful when generating an access or activity log. Calling `fflush()` after each message to the logfile makes sure that any person or program monitoring the logfile sees the message as soon as possible.

See Also

Documentation on `fflush()` (*http://www.php.net/fflush*).

24.14 Writing to Standard Output

Problem

You want to write to standard output.

Solution

Use echo or `print()`:

```
print "Where did my pastrami sandwich go?";
echo  "It went into my stomach.";
```

Discussion

Whereas `print()` is a function, echo is a language construct. This means that `print()` returns a value, and echo doesn't. You can include `print()` but not echo in larger expressions, as shown:

```
// this is OK
(12 == $status) ? print 'Status is good' : error_log('Problem with status!');

// this gives a parse error
(12 == $status) ? echo 'Status is good' : error_log('Problem with status!');
```

Use *php://stdout* as the filename if you're using the file functions `$fh = fopen('php://stdout','w') or die($php_errormsg);`.

Writing to standard output via a filehandle instead of simply with `print()` or echo is useful if you need to abstract where your output goes, or if you need to print to standard output at the same time as writing to a file. See Recipe 24.15 for details.

You can write to standard error by opening *php://stderr*: `$fh = fopen('php://stderr','w');`.

See Also

Recipe 24.15 for writing to many filehandles simultaneously; documentation on `echo` (*http://www.php.net/echo*) and on `print()` (*http://www.php.net/print*).

24.15 Writing to Many Filehandles Simultaneously

Problem

You want to send output to more than one filehandle; for example, you want to log messages to the screen and to a file.

Solution

Wrap your output with a loop that iterates through your filehandles:

```
function multi_fwrite($fhs,$s,$length=NULL) {
  if (is_array($fhs)) {
    if (is_null($length)) {
      foreach($fhs as $fh) {
        fwrite($fh,$s);
      }
    } else {
      foreach($fhs as $fh) {
        fwrite($fh,$s,$length);
      }
    }
  }
}

$fhs = array();
$fhs['file'] = fopen('log.txt','w') or die($php_errormsg);
$fhs['screen'] = fopen('php://stdout','w') or die($php_errormsg);

multi_fwrite($fhs,'The space shuttle has landed.');
```

Discussion

If you don't want to pass a length argument to `fwrite()` (or you always want to), you can eliminate that check from your `multi_fwrite()`. This version doesn't contain a `$length` argument:

```
function multi_fwrite($fhs,$s) {
  if (is_array($fhs)) {
    foreach($fhs as $fh) {
```

```
        fwrite($fh,$s);
      }
    }
  }
```

See Also

Documentation on `fwrite()` (*http://www.php.net/fwrite*).

24.16 Escaping Shell Metacharacters

Problem

You need to incorporate external data in a command line, but you want to escape special characters so nothing unexpected happens; for example, you want to pass user input as an argument to a program.

Solution

Use `escapeshellarg()` to handle arguments and `escapeshellcmd()` to handle program names:

```
system('ls -al '.escapeshellarg($directory));
system(escapeshellcmd($ls_program).' -al');
```

Discussion

The command line is a dangerous place for unescaped characters. Never pass unmodified user input to one of PHP's shell-execution functions. Always escape the appropriate characters in the command and the arguments. This is crucial. It is unusual to execute command lines that are coming from web forms and not something we recommend lightly. However, sometimes you need to run an external program, so escaping commands and arguments is useful.

`escapeshellarg()` surrounds arguments with single quotes (and escapes any existing single quotes). This example uses `escapeshellarg()` in printing the process status for a particular process:

```
system('/bin/ps '.escapeshellarg($process_id));
```

Using `escapeshellarg()` ensures that the right process is displayed even if its ID has an unexpected character (e.g., a space) in it. It also prevents unintended commands from being run. If `$process_id` contains `1; rm -rf /`, then `system("/bin/ps $process_id")` not only displays the status of process 1, but also executes the command *rm -rf /*.

However, `system('/bin/ps'.escapeshellarg($process_id))` runs the command /bin/ps 1; rm -rf, which produces an error because *1-semicolon-space-rm-space-hyphen-rf* isn't a valid process ID.

Similarly, `escapeshellcmd()` prevents unintended command lines from executing. The command `system("/usr/local/bin/formatter-$which_program");` runs a different program depending on the value of $which_program.

For example, if $which_program is pdf 12, the script runs */usr/local/bin/formatter-pdf* with an argument of 12. But if $which_program is pdf 12; 56, the script runs */usr/local/bin/formatter-pdf* with an argument of 12, but then also runs the program *56*, which is an error.

To successfully pass the arguments to *formatter-pdf*, you need `escapeshellcmd()`: `system(escapeshellcmd("/usr/local/bin/formatter-$which_program"));`. This runs */usr/local/bin/formatter-pdf* and passes it two arguments: 12; and 56.

See Also

Documentation on `system()` (*http://www.php.net/system*), `escapeshellarg()` (*http://www.php.net/escapeshellarg*), and `escapeshellcmd()` (*http://www.php.net/escapeshellcmd*).

24.17 Passing Input to a Program

Problem

You want to pass input to an external program run from inside a PHP script. For example, your database requires you to run an external program to index text and you want to pass text to that program.

Solution

Open a pipe to the program with `popen()`, write to the pipe with `fputs()` or `fwrite()`, and then close the pipe with `pclose()`:

```
$ph = popen('/usr/bin/indexer --category=dinner','w') or die($php_errormsg);
if (-1 == fputs($ph,"red-cooked chicken\n"))    { die($php_errormsg); }
if (-1 == fputs($ph,"chicken and dumplings\n")) { die($php_errormsg); }
pclose($ph)                                     or die($php_errormsg);
```

Discussion

This example uses `popen()` to call the *nsupdate* command, which submits Dynamic DNS Update requests to name servers:

```
$ph = popen('/usr/bin/nsupdate -k keyfile')              or die($php_errormsg);
if (-1 == fputs($ph,"update delete test.example.com A\n")) { die($php_errormsg);}
if (-1 == fputs($ph,"update add test.example.com 5 A 192.168.1.1\n"))
                                                        { die($php_errormsg);}
pclose($ph)                                             or die($php_errormsg);
```

Two commands are sent to *nsupdate* via popen(). The first deletes the *test.example.com* A record, and the second adds a new A record for *test.example.com* with the address 192.168.1.1.

See Also

Documentation on popen() (*http://www.php.net/popen*) and pclose() (*http://www.php.net/pclose*); Dynamic DNS is described in RFC 2136 (*http://www.faqs.org/rfcs/rfc2136.html*).

24.18 Reading Standard Output from a Program

Problem

You want to read the output from a program. For example, you want the output of a system utility, such as *route(8)*, that provides network information.

Solution

To read the entire contents of a program's output, use the backtick (`` ` ``) operator:

```
$routing_table = `/sbin/route`;
```

To read the output incrementally, open a pipe with popen():

```
$ph = popen('/sbin/route','r') or die($php_errormsg);
while (! feof($ph)) {
    $s = fgets($ph)             or die($php_errormsg);
}
pclose($ph)                     or die($php_errormsg);
```

Discussion

The backtick operator executes a program and returns all its output as a single string. On a Linux system with 1.6 GB of RAM, the command $s = /usr/bin/free; puts the following multiline string in $s:

```
                total       used       free     shared    buffers     cached
Mem:         16471704   15488260     983444          0     627820   12076120
-/+ buffers/cache:       2784320   13687384
Swap:               0          0          0
```

If a program generates a lot of output, it is more memory efficient to read from a pipe one line at a time. If you're printing formatted data to the browser based on the output of the pipe, you can print it as you get it.

This example prints information about recent Unix system logins formatted as an HTML table. It uses the */usr/bin/last* command:

```
// print table header
print<<<_HTML_
<table>
<tr>
 <td>user</td><td>login port</td><td>login from</td><td>login time</td>
 <td>time spent logged in</td>
</tr>
_HTML_;

// open the pipe to /usr/bin/last
$ph = popen('/usr/bin/last','r') or die($php_errormsg);
while (! feof($ph)) {
    $line = fgets($ph) or die($php_errormsg);

    // don't process blank lines or the info line at the end
    if (trim($line) && (! preg_match('/^wtmp begins/',$line))) {
        $user = trim(substr($line,0,8));
        $port = trim(substr($line,9,12));
        $host = trim(substr($line,22,16));
        $date = trim(substr($line,38,25));
        $elapsed = trim(substr($line,67,10),' ()'),

        if ('logged in' == $elapsed) {
            $elapsed = 'still logged in';
            $date = substr_replace($date,'',-5);
        }

        print "<tr><td>$user</td><td>$port</td><td>$host</td>";
        print "<td>$date</td><td>$elapsed</td></tr>\n";
    }
}
pclose($ph) or die($php_errormsg);

print '</table>';
```

See Also

Documentation on popen() (*http://www.php.net/popen*), pclose() (*http://www.php.net/pclose*), and the backtick operator (*http://bit.ly/1qJnCrJ*).

24.19 Reading Standard Error from a Program

Problem

You want to read the error output from a program. For example, you want to capture the system calls displayed by *strace(1)*.

Solution

Redirect standard error to standard output by adding 2>&1 to the command line passed to popen( ). Read standard output by opening the pipe in r mode:

```
$ph = popen('strace ls 2>&1','r') or die($php_errormsg);
while (!feof($ph)) {
    $s = fgets($ph)            or die($php_errormsg);
}
pclose($ph)                    or die($php_errormsg);
```

Discussion

In both the Unix *sh* and the Windows *cmd.exe* shells, standard error is file descriptor 2, and standard output is file descriptor 1. Appending 2>&1 to a command tells the shell to redirect what's normally sent to file descriptor 2 (standard error) over to file descriptor 1 (standard output). fgets( ) then reads both standard error and standard output.

This technique reads in standard error but doesn't provide a way to distinguish it from standard output. To read just standard error, you need to prevent standard output from being returned through the pipe. You do this by redirecting it to */dev/null* on Unix and *NUL* on Windows:

```
// Unix: only read standard error
$ph = popen('strace ls 2>&1 1>/dev/null','r') or die($php_errormsg);

// Windows: only read standard error
$ph = popen('ipxroute.exe 2>&1 1>NUL','r') or die($php_errormsg);
```

See Also

Documentation on popen( ) (*http://www.php.net/popen*); see your *popen(3)* manpage for details about the shell your system uses with popen( ); for information about shell redirection, see the Redirection section of the *sh(1)* manpage on Unix systems; on Windows, see the entry on redirection in the Command Reference section of your system help.

24.20 Locking a File

Problem

You want to have exclusive access to a file to prevent it from being changed while you read or update it. For example, if you are saving guestbook information in a file, two users should be able to add guestbook entries at the same time without clobbering each other's entries.

Solution

Use flock() to provide advisory locking:

```
$fh = fopen('guestbook.txt','a')        or die($php_errormsg);
flock($fh,LOCK_EX)                       or die($php_errormsg);
fwrite($fh,$_POST['guestbook_entry']) or die($php_errormsg);
fflush($fh)                              or die($php_errormsg);
flock($fh,LOCK_UN)                       or die($php_errormsg);
fclose($fh)                              or die($php_errormsg);
```

Discussion

In general, if you find yourself needing to lock a file, it's best to see if there's an alternative way to solve your problem. Often you can (and should!) use a database (or SQLite, if you don't have access to a standalone database) instead.

The file locking flock() provides is called advisory file locking because flock() doesn't actually prevent other processes from opening a locked file; it just provides a way for processes to voluntarily cooperate on file access. All programs that need to access files being locked with flock() need to set and release locks to make the file locking effective.

You can set two kinds of locks with flock(): exclusive locks and shared locks. An exclusive lock, specified by LOCK_EX as the second argument to flock(), can be held only by one process at one time for a particular file. A shared lock, specified by LOCK_SH, can be held by more than one process at one time for a particular file. Before writing to a file, you should get an exclusive lock. Before reading from a file, you should get a shared lock.

If any of your code uses flock() to lock a file, then all of your code should. For example, if one part of your program uses LOCK_EX to get an exclusive lock when writing to a file, then in any place where you must read the file, be sure to use LOCK_SH to get a shared lock on the file. If you don't do that, a process trying to read a file can see the contents of the file while another process is writing to it.

To unlock a file, call `flock()` with `LOCK_UN` as the second argument. It's important to flush any buffered data to be written to the file with `fflush()` before you unlock the file. Other processes shouldn't be able to get a lock until that data is written.

By default, `flock()` blocks until it can obtain a lock. To tell it not to block, add `LOCK_NB` to the second argument, as shown:

```
$fh = fopen('guestbook.txt','a')                 or die($php_errormsg);
$tries = 3;
while ($tries > 0) {
    $locked = flock($fh,LOCK_EX | LOCK_NB);
    if (! $locked) {
        sleep(5);
        $tries--;
    } else {
        // don't go through the loop again
        $tries = 0;
    }
}
if ($locked) {
    fwrite($fh,$_POST['guestbook_entry'])        or die($php_errormsg);
    fflush($fh)                                  or die($php_errormsg);
    flock($fh,LOCK_UN)                           or die($php_errormsg);
    fclose($fh)                                  or die($php_errormsg);
} else {
    print "Can't get lock.";
}
```

When the lock is nonblocking, `flock()` returns right away even if it couldn't get a lock. The previous example tries three times to get a lock on *guestbook.txt*, sleeping five seconds between each try.

Locking with `flock()` doesn't work in all circumstances, such as on some NFS implementations and older versions of Windows. To simulate file locking in these cases, use a directory as an exclusive lock indicator. This is a separate, empty directory whose presence indicates that the datafile is locked. Before opening a datafile, create a lock directory and then delete the lock directory when you're finished working with the datafile. Otherwise, the file access code is the same:

```
// loop until we can successfully make the lock directory
$locked = 0;
while (! $locked) {
    if (@mkdir('guestbook.txt.lock',0777)) {
        $locked = 1;
    } else {
        sleep(1);
    }
}
$fh = fopen('guestbook.txt','a')         or die($php_errormsg);

if (-1 == fwrite($fh,$_POST['guestbook_entry'])) {
```

```
    rmdir('guestbook.txt.lock');
    die($php_errormsg);
}
if (! fclose($fh)) {
    rmdir('guestbook.txt.lock');
    die($php_errormsg);
}
rmdir('guestbook.txt.lock')                    or die($php_errormsg);
```

A directory is used instead of a file to indicate a lock because the `mkdir()` function fails to create a directory if it already exists. This gives you a way, in one operation, to check if the lock indicator exists and create it if it doesn't. Any error trapping after the directory is created, however, needs to clean up by removing the directory before exiting. If the directory is left in place, no future processes can get a lock by creating the directory.

If you use a file instead of a directory as a lock indicator, the code to create it looks something like this:

```
$locked = 0;
while (! $locked) {
    if (! file_exists('guestbook.txt.lock')) {
        touch('guestbook.txt.lock');
        $locked = 1;
    } else {
        sleep(1);
    }
}
```

This code fails under heavy load because it checks for the lock's existence with `file_ex ists()` and then creates the lock with `touch()`. After one process calls `file_ex ists()`, another might call `touch()` before the first calls `touch()`. Both processes would then think they've got exclusive access to the file when neither really does. With `mkdir()` there's no gap between checking for existence and creation, so the process that makes the directory is ensured exclusive access.

See Also

Documentation on `flock()` (*http://www.php.net/flock*).

24.21 Reading and Writing Custom File Types

Problem

You want to use PHP's standard file access functions to provide access to data that might not be in a file. For example, you want to use file access functions to read from and write to shared memory. Or you want to process file contents when they are read before they reach PHP.

Solution

Use the PEAR Stream_SHM module, which implements a stream wrapper that reads from and writes to shared memory:

```
require_once 'Stream/SHM.php';
stream_register_wrapper('shm','Stream_SHM') or die("can't register shm");
$shm = fopen('shm://0xabcd','c');
fwrite($shm, "Current time is: " . time());
fclose($shm);
```

Discussion

Stream wrappers handle the details of moving data back and forth between PHP and your custom location or your custom format. This class implements the methods PHP needs to access your custom data stream: opening, closing, reading, writing, and so on. A particular wrapper is registered with a particular prefix. You use that prefix when passing a filename to `fopen()`, `include()`, or any other PHP file-handling function to ensure that your wrapper is invoked.

Stream wrappers are handy for nonfile data sources, but they can also be used to pre-process file contents on their way into PHP. Mike Naberezny demonstrates a clever example of this as applied to templating. With `short_open_tags` turned off, printing an object instance variable in a template requires the comparatively verbose `<?php echo $this->property; ?>`. Mike's solution uses a stream wrapper that allows the @ character to stand in for `echo $this->`.

Here's the stream wrapper code:

```php
<?php
/**
 * Stream wrapper to convert markup of mostly PHP templates into PHP prior
 * to include().
 *
 * Based in large part on the example at
 * http://www.php.net/manual/en/function.stream-wrapper-register.php
 *
 * @author Mike Naberezny (@link http://mikenaberezny.com)
 * @author Paul M. Jones  (@link http://paul-m-jones.com)
 */
class ViewStream {
    /**
     * Current stream position.
     *
     * @var int
     */
    private $pos = 0;

    /**
     * Data for streaming.
```

```
 *
 * @var string
 */
private $data;

/**
 * Stream stats.
 *
 * @var array
 */
private $stat;


/**
 * Opens the script file and converts markup.
 */
public function stream_open($path, $mode, $options, &$opened_path) {

    // get the view script source
    $path = str_replace('view://', '', $path);
    $this->data = file_get_contents($path);

    /**
     * If reading the file failed, update our local stat store
     * to reflect the real stat of the file, then return on failure
     */
    if ($this->data===false) {
        $this->stat = stat($path);
        return false;
    }

    /**
     * Convert <?= ?> to long-form <?php echo ?>
     *
     * We could also convert <%= like the real T_OPEN_TAG_WITH_ECHO
     * but that's not necessary.
     *
     * It might be nice to also convert PHP code blocks <? ?> but
     * let's quit while we're ahead.  It's probably better to keep
     * the <?php for larger code blocks but that's your choice.  If
     * you do go for it, explicitly check for <?xml as this will
     * probably be the biggest headache.
     */
    if (! ini_get('short_open_tag')) {
        $find = '/\<\?\= (.*)? \?>/';
        $replace = "<?php echo \$1 ?>";
        $this->data = preg_replace($find, $replace, $this->data);
    }

    /**
     * Convert @$ to $this->
     *
```

```
     * We could make a better effort at only finding @$ between <?php ?>
     * but that's probably not necessary as @$ doesn't occur much in the wild
     * and there's a significant performance gain by using str_replace().
     */
    $this->data = str_replace('@$', '$this->', $this->data);

    /**
     * file_get_contents() won't update PHP's stat cache, so performing
     * another stat() on it will hit the filesystem again.  Since the file
     * has been successfully read, avoid this and just fake the stat
     * so include() is happy.
     */
    $this->stat = array('mode' => 0100777,
                        'size' => strlen($this->data));

    return true;
}


/**
 * Reads from the stream.
 */
public function stream_read($count) {
    $ret = substr($this->data, $this->pos, $count);
    $this->pos += strlen($ret);
    return $ret;
}


/**
 * Tells the current position in the stream.
 */
public function stream_tell() {
    return $this->pos;
}


/**
 * Tells if we are at the end of the stream.
 */
public function stream_eof() {
    return $this->pos >= strlen($this->data);
}


/**
 * Stream statistics.
 */
public function stream_stat() {
    return $this->stat;
}
```

```
/**
 * Seek to a specific point in the stream.
 */
public function stream_seek($offset, $whence) {
    switch ($whence) {
        case SEEK_SET:
            if ($offset < strlen($this->data) && $offset >= 0) {
                $this->pos = $offset;
                return true;
            } else {
                return false;
            }
            break;

        case SEEK_CUR:
            if ($offset >= 0) {
                $this->pos += $offset;
                return true;
            } else {
                return false;
            }
            break;

        case SEEK_END:
            if (strlen($this->data) + $offset >= 0) {
                $this->pos = strlen($this->data) + $offset;
                return true;
            } else {
                return false;
            }
            break;

        default:
            return false;
    }
}
```

And a sample template:

```
<html> <?= @$hello ?> </html>
```

They work together as so:

```
/** Stream wrapper */
require_once dirname(__FILE__) . DIRECTORY_SEPARATOR . 'ViewStream.php';

/**
 * A very dumb template class just to demonstrate the concept.
 *
 * @author Mike Naberezny
 * @link    http://mikenaberezny.com/archives/40
 * @link    http://phpsavant.com
```

```
    */
    class IdiotSavant {
        public function __construct() {
            if (!in_array('view', stream_get_wrappers())) {
                stream_wrapper_register('view', 'ViewStream');
            }
        }

        public function render($filename) {
            include 'view://' . dirname(__FILE__) . DIRECTORY_SEPARATOR .
            $filename . '.html';
        }
    }

    // Create a new view
    $view = new IdiotSavant();

    // Assign the variable "hello" to the scope of the view
    $view->hello = 'Hello, World!';

    // Render the view from a template.  Outputs "<html> Hello, World! </html>"
    $view->render('ExampleTemplate');
```

The stream wrapper code is saved as *ViewStream.php* and the sample template is named *ExampleTemplate.html*.

See Also

Documentation on `stream_register_wrapper()` (*http://bit.ly/1nEepf4*); the PEAR Stream_SHM module (*http://bit.ly/1pOG9kz*); Mike Naberezny's blog post "Symfony Templates and Ruby's ERb." (*http://bit.ly/Vo5bvS*)

24.22 Reading and Writing Compressed Files

Problem

You want to read or write compressed files.

Solution

Use the `compress.zlib` or `compress.bzip2` stream wrapper with the standard file functions.

To read data from a gzip-compressed file:

```
    $file = __DIR__ . '/lots-of-data.gz';
    $fh = fopen("compress.zlib://$file",'r') or die("can't open: $php_errormsg");
    if ($fh) {
        while ($line = fgets($fh)) {
```

```
            // $line is the next line of uncompressed data
        }
        fclose($fh) or die("can't close: $php_errormsg");
    }
```

Discussion

The `compress.zlib` stream wrapper provides access to files that have been compressed with the gzip algorithm. The `compress.bzip2` stream wrapper provides access to files that have been compressed with the bzip2 algorithm. Both stream wrappers allow reading, writing, and appending with compressed files. To enable the zlib and bzip2 compression streams, build PHP with `--with-zlib` and `--with-bz2`, respectively.

In addition to the stream wrappers, which allow access to compressed local files, there are stream filters that compress (or uncompress) arbitrary streams on the fly. The `zlib.deflate` and `zlib.inflate` filters compress and uncompress data according to the zlib "deflate" algorithm. The `bzip2.compress` and `bzip2.uncompress` filters do the same for the bzip2 algorithm.

Each stream filter must be applied to a stream after it is created. This example uses the `bzip2` stream filters to read compressed data from a URL:

```
$fp = fopen('http://www.example.com/something-compressed.bz2','r');
if ($fp) {
    stream_filter_append($fp, 'bzip2.uncompress');
    while (! feof($fp)) {
        $data = fread($fp);
        // do something with $data;
    }
    fclose($fp);
}
```

See Also

Documentation on compression stream wrappers (*http://www.php.net/wrappers.compression*), on compression filters (*http://www.php.net/filters.compression*), and on `stream_filter_append()` (*http://www.php.net/stream_filter_append*); the *zlib* algorithm is detailed in RFCs 1950 (*http://www.faqs.org/rfcs/rfc1950.html*) and 1951 (*http://www.faqs.org/rfcs/rfc1951.html*).

CHAPTER 25

Directories

25.0 Introduction

A filesystem stores a lot of additional information about files aside from their actual contents. This information includes such particulars as the file size, directory, and access permissions. If you're working with files, you may also need to manipulate this metadata. PHP gives you a variety of functions to read and manipulate directories, directory entries, and file attributes. Like other file-related parts of PHP, the functions are similar to the C functions that accomplish the same tasks, with some simplifications.

Files are organized with *inodes*. Each file (and other parts of the filesystem, such as directories, devices, and links) has its own inode. That inode contains a pointer to where the file's data blocks are as well as all the metadata about the file. The data blocks for a directory hold the names of the files in that directory and the inode of each file.

PHP provides a few ways to look in a directory to see what files it holds. The `Directory-Iterator` class provides a comprehensive object-oriented interface for directory traversal. This example uses `DirectoryIterator` to print out the name of each file in a directory:

```
foreach (new DirectoryIterator('/usr/local/images') as $file) {
    print $file->getPathname() . "\n";
}
```

The `opendir()`, `readdir()`, and `closedir()` functions offer a procedural approach to the same task. Use `opendir()` to get a directory handle, `readdir()` to iterate through the files, and `closedir()` to close the directory handle. For example:[1]

---

1. PHP also has a `dir()` class that mirrors the procedural approach (open, read, close) in its methods. Because `DirectoryIterator` is so much more capable, use that if you want an OO interface.

```
$d = opendir('/usr/local/images') or die($php_errormsg);
while (false !== ($f = readdir($d))) {
    print $f . "\n";
}
closedir($d);
```

In this chapter, we generally use `DirectoryIterator` for examples.

The filesystem holds more than just files and directories. On Unix, it can also hold symbolic links. These are special files whose contents are a pointer to another file. You can delete the link without affecting the file it points to. To create a symbolic link, use `symlink()`:

```
symlink('/usr/local/images','/www/docroot/images') or die($php_errormsg);
```

This code creates a symbolic link called *images* in */www/docroot* that points to */usr/local/ images*.

To find information about a file, directory, or link you must examine its inode. The function `stat()` retrieves the metadata in an inode for you. Recipe 25.2 discusses `stat()`. PHP also has many functions that use `stat()` internally to give you a specific piece of information about a file. These are listed in Table 25-1.

Table 25-1. File information functions

Function name	What file information does the function provide?
file_exists()	Does the file exist?
fileatime()	Last access time
filectime()	Last metadata change time
filegroup()	Group (numeric)
fileinode()	Inode number
filemtime()	Last change time of contents
fileowner()	Owner (numeric)
fileperms()	Permissions (decimal, numeric)
filesize()	Size
filetype()	Type (fifo, char, dir, block, link, file, unknown)
is_dir()	Is it a directory?
is_executable()	Is it executable?
is_file()	Is it a regular file?
is_link()	Is it a symbolic link?
is_readable()	Is it readable?
is_writable()	Is it writable?

On Unix, the file permissions indicate what operations the file's owner, users in the file's group, and all users can perform on the file. The operations are reading, writing, and executing. For programs, executing means the ability to run the program; for directories, executing is the ability to search through the directory and see the files in it.

Unix permissions can also contain a setuid bit, a setgid bit, and a sticky bit. The setuid bit means that when a program is run, it runs with the user ID of its owner. The setgid bit means that a program runs with the group ID of its group. For a directory, the setgid bit means that new files in the directory are created by default in the same group as the directory. The sticky bit is useful for directories in which people share files because it prevents nonsuperusers with write permission in a directory from deleting files in that directory unless they own the file or the directory.

When setting permissions with chmod() (see Recipe 25.3), they must be expressed as an octal number. This number has four digits. The first digit is any special setting for the file (such as setuid or setgid). The second digit is the user permissions—what the file's owner can do. The third digit is the group permissions—what users in the file's group can do. The fourth digit is the world permissions—what all other users can do. To compute the appropriate value for each digit, add together the permissions you want for that digit using the values in Table 25-2. For example, a permission value of 0644 means that there are no special settings (the 0), the file's owner can read and write the file (the 6, which is 4 + 2, for read and write, respectively), users in the file's group can read the file (the first 4), and all other users can also read the file (the second 4). A permission value of 4644 is the same, except that the file is also setuid.

Table 25-2. File permission values

Value	Permission meaning	Special setting meaning
4	Read	setuid
2	Write	setgid
1	Execute	sticky

The permissions of newly created files and directories are affected by a setting called the *umask*, which is a permission value that is removed or masked out from the initial permissions of a file (0666) or directory (0777). For example, if the umask is 0022, the default permissions for a new file created with touch() or fopen() are 0644 and the default permissions for a new directory created with mkdir() are 0755. You can get and set the umask with the function umask(). It returns the current umask and, if an argument is supplied to it, changes the umask to the value of that argument. This example shows how to make the permissions on newly created files prevent anyone but the file's owner (and the superuser) from accessing the file:

```
$old_umask = umask(0077);
touch('secret-file.txt');
umask($old_umask);
```

The first call to umask() masks out all permissions for group and world. After the file is created, the second call to umask() restores the umask to the previous setting. When PHP is run as a server module, it restores the umask to its default value at the end of each request. Windows has a different (and more powerful) system for organizing file permissions and ownership, so PHP's umask() function (like every other permissions-related function) isn't available on Windows.

25.1 Getting and Setting File Timestamps

Problem

You want to know when a file was last accessed or changed, or you want to update a file's access or change time; for example, you want each page on your website to display when it was last modified.

Solution

The fileatime(), filemtime(), and filectime() functions return the time of last access, modification, and metadata change of a file, as shown:

```
$last_access = fileatime('larry.php');
$last_modification = filemtime('moe.php');
$last_change = filectime('curly.php');
```

Update a file's modification time with touch(). Without a second argument, touch() sets the modification time to the current date and time. To set a file's modification time to a specific value, pass that value as an epoch timestamp to touch() as a second argument. This example changes the modification time of two files without changing their contents:

```
touch('shemp.php');          // set modification time to now
touch('joe.php',$timestamp); // set modification time to $timestamp
```

Discussion

The fileatime() function returns the last time a file was opened for reading or writing. The filemtime() function returns the last time a file's contents were changed. The filectime() function returns the last time a file's contents or metadata (such as owner or permissions) were changed. Each function returns the time as an epoch timestamp.

This code prints the time a page on your website was last updated:

```
print "Last Modified: ".strftime('%c',filemtime($_SERVER['SCRIPT_FILENAME']));
```

See Also

Documentation on `fileatime()` (*http://www.php.net/fileatime*), `filemtime()` (*http://www.php.net/filemtime*), and `filectime()` (*http://www.php.net/filectime*).

25.2 Getting File Information

Problem

You want to read a file's metadata—for example, permissions and ownership.

Solution

Use `stat()`, which returns an array of information about a file:

```
$info = stat('harpo.php');
```

Discussion

`stat()` returns an array with both numeric and string indexes with information about a file. The elements of this array are in Table 25-3.

Table 25-3. Information returned by stat()

Numeric index	String index	Value
0	dev	Device
1	ino	Inode
2	mode	Permissions
3	nlink	Link count
4	uid	Owner's user ID
5	gid	Group's group ID
6	rdev	Device type for inode devices (−1 on Windows)
7	size	Size (in bytes)
8	atime	Last access time (epoch timestamp)
9	mtime	Last change time of contents (epoch timestamp)
10	ctime	Last change time of contents or metadata (epoch timestamp)
11	blksize	Block size for I/O (−1 on Windows)
12	blocks	Number of blocks allocated to this file

The mode element of the returned array contains the permissions expressed as a base 10 integer. This is confusing because permissions are usually either expressed symbolically (e.g., *ls*'s `-rw-r—r--` output) or as an octal integer (e.g., `0644`). To convert the permissions to the more understandable octal format, use `base_convert()`:

```
$file_info = stat('/tmp/session.txt');
$permissions = base_convert($file_info['mode'],10,8);
```

Here, $permissions is a six-digit octal number. For example, if *ls* displays the following about */tmp/session.txt*:

```
-rw-rw-r--   1 sklar   sklar        12 Oct 23 17:55 /tmp/session.txt
```

then $file_info['mode'] is 33204 and $permissions is 100664. The last three digits (664) are the user (read and write), group (read and write), and other (read) permissions for the file. The third digit, 0, means that the file is not setuid or setgid. The leftmost 10 means that the file is a regular file (and not a socket, symbolic link, or other special file).

Because stat() returns an array with both numeric and string indexes, using fore ach to iterate through the returned array produces two copies of each value. Instead, use a for loop from element 0 to element 12 of the returned array.

Calling stat() on a symbolic link returns information about the file the symbolic link points to. To get information about the symbolic link itself, use lstat().

Similar to stat() is fstat(), which takes a filehandle (returned from fopen() or pop en()) as an argument.

PHP's stat() function uses the underlying *stat(2)* system call, which is expensive. To minimize overhead, PHP caches the result of calling *stat(2)*. So if you call stat() on a file, change its permissions, and call stat() on the same file again, you get the same results. To force PHP to reload the file's metadata, call clearstatcache(), which flushes PHP's cached information. PHP also uses this cache for the other functions that return file metadata: file_exists(), fileatime(), filectime(), filegroup(), filei node(), filemtime(), fileowner(), fileperms(), filesize(), filetype(), fstat(), is_dir(), is_executable(), is_file(), is_link(), is_readable(), is_writable(), and lstat().

See Also

Documentation on stat() (*http://www.php.net/stat*), lstat() (*http://www.php.net/ lstat*), fstat() (*http://www.php.net/fstat*), and clearstatcache() (*http:// www.php.net/clearstatcache*).

25.3 Changing File Permissions or Ownership

Problem

You want to change a file's permissions or ownership; for example, you want to prevent other users from being able to look at a file of sensitive data.

Solution

Use `chmod()` to change the permissions of a file:

```
chmod('/home/user/secrets.txt', 0400);
```

Use `chown()` to change a file's owner and `chgrp()` to change a file's group:

```
chown('/tmp/myfile.txt','sklar');            // specify user by name
chgrp('/home/sklar/schedule.txt','soccer');  // specify group by name

chown('/tmp/myfile.txt',5001);               // specify user by uid
chgrp('/home/sklar/schedule.txt',102);       // specify group by gid
```

Discussion

The permissions passed to `chmod()` must be specified as an octal number.

The superuser can change the permissions, owner, and group of any file. Other users are restricted. They can change only the permissions and group of files that they own, and can't change the owner at all. A nonsuperuser can also change only the group of a file to a group to which the user belongs.

The functions `chmod()`, `chgrp()`, and `chown()` don't work on Windows.

See Also

Documentation on `chmod()` (*http://www.php.net/chmod*), `chown()` (*http://www.php.net/chown*), and `chgrp()` (*http://www.php.net/chgrp*).

25.4 Splitting a Filename into Its Component Parts

Problem

You want to find a file's path and filename; for example, you want to create a file in the same directory as an existing file.

Solution

Use `basename()` to get the filename and `dirname()` to get the path:

```
$full_name = '/usr/local/php/php.ini';
$base = basename($full_name);  // $base is "php.ini"
$dir  = dirname($full_name);   // $dir is "/usr/local/php"
```

Use `pathinfo()` to get the directory name, base name, and extension in an associative array:

```
$info = pathinfo('/usr/local/php/php.ini');
// $info['dirname'] is "/usr/local/php"
// $info['basename'] is "php.ini"
// $info['extension'] is "ini"
```

Discussion

To create a temporary file in the same directory as an existing file, use `dirname()` to find the directory, and pass that directory to `tempnam()`. For instance:

```
$dir = dirname($existing_file);
$temp = tempnam($dir,'temp');
$temp_fh = fopen($temp,'w');
```

The `dirname()` function is particularly useful in combination with the special constant `__FILE__`, which contains the full pathname of the current file. This is not the same as the currently executing PHP script. If */usr/local/alice.php* includes */usr/local/bob.php*, then `__FILE__` in *bob.php* is `/usr/local/bob.php`.

This makes `__FILE__` useful when you want to include or require scripts in the same directory as a particular file, but you don't know what that directory is and it isn't necessarily in the include path. For example:

```
$currentDir = dirname(__FILE__);
include $currentDir . '/functions.php';
include $currentDir . '/classes.php';
```

If this code is in the */usr/local* directory, then it includes */usr/local/functions.php* and */usr/local/classes.php*. This technique is particularly useful when you're distributing code for others to use. With it, you don't have to require any configuration or include path modification for your code to work properly. As of PHP 5.3, you use the constant `__DIR__` instead of `dirname(__FILE__)`.

Using functions such as `basename()`, `dirname()`, and `pathinfo()` is more portable than just splitting up full filenames on the / character because the functions use an operating system–appropriate separator. On Windows, these functions treat both / and \ as file and directory separators. On other platforms, only / is used.

There's no built-in PHP function to combine the parts produced by `basename()`, `dirname()`, and `pathinfo()` back into a full filename. To do this, combine the parts with . and the built-in `DIRECTORY_SEPARATOR` constant, which is / on Unix and \ on Windows.

See Also

Documentation on `basename()` (*http://www.php.net/basename*), `dirname()` (*http://www.php.net/dirname*), `pathinfo()` (*http://www.php.net/pathinfo*), and `__FILE__` (*http://www.php.net/language.constants.predefined*).

25.5 Deleting a File

Problem

You want to delete a file.

Solution

Use unlink():

```
$file = '/tmp/junk.txt';
unlink($file) or die ("can't delete $file: $php_errormsg");
```

Discussion

The unlink() function is only able to delete files that the user of the PHP process is able to delete. If you're having trouble getting unlink() to work, check the permissions on the file and how you're running PHP.

See Also

Documentation on unlink() (*http://www.php.net/unlink*).

25.6 Copying or Moving a File

Problem

You want to copy or move a file.

Solution

Use copy() to copy a file:

```
$old = '/tmp/yesterday.txt';
$new = '/tmp/today.txt';
copy($old,$new) or die("couldn't copy $old to $new: $php_errormsg");
```

Use rename() to move a file:

```
$old = '/tmp/today.txt';
$new = '/tmp/tomorrow.txt';
rename($old,$new) or die("couldn't move $old to $new: $php_errormsg");
```

Discussion

If you have multiple files to copy or move, call copy() or rename() in a loop. You can operate only on one file each time you call these functions.

See Also

Documentation on `copy()` (*http://www.php.net/copy*) and `rename()` (*http://www.php.net/rename*).

25.7 Processing All Files in a Directory

Problem

You want to iterate over all files in a directory. For example, you want to create a `<select/>` box in a form that lists all the files in a directory.

Solution

Use a `DirectoryIterator` to get each file in the directory:

```
echo "<select name='file'>\n";
foreach (new DirectoryIterator('/usr/local/images') as $file) {
    echo '<option>' . htmlentities($file) . "</option>\n";
}
echo '</select>';
```

Discussion

The `DirectoryIterator` yields one value for each element in the directory. That value is an object with some handy characteristics. The object's string representation is the filename (with no leading path) of the directory element. For example, if */usr/local/images* contains the files *cucumber.gif* and *eggplant.png*, the code in the Solution prints:

```
<select name='file'>
<option>.</option>
<option>..</option>
<option>cucumber.gif</option>
<option>eggplant.png</option>
</select>
```

A `DirectoryIterator` yields an object for *all* directory elements, including . (current directory) and .. (parent directory). Fortunately, that object has some methods that help us identify what it is. The `isDot()` method returns `true` if it's either . or ... This example uses `isDot()` to prevent those two entries from showing up in the output:

```
echo "<select name='file'>\n";
foreach (new DirectoryIterator('/usr/local/images') as $file) {
    if (! $file->isDot()) {
        echo '<option>' . htmlentities($file) . "</option>\n";
    }
}
echo '</select>';
```

Table 25-4 lists the other methods available on the objects that a `DirectoryIterator` yields.

Table 25-4. DirectoryIterator object information methods

Method Name	Return value	Example
isDir()	Is the element a directory?	false
isDot()	Is the element either . or ..?	false
isFile()	Is the element a regular file?	true
isLink()	Is the element a link?	false
isReadable()	Is the element readable?	true
isWritable()	Is the element writable?	true
isExecutable()	Is the element executable?	false
getATime()	The last access time of the element	1144509622
getCTime()	The creation time of the element	1144509600
getMTime()	The last modification time of the element	1144509620
getFilename()	The filename (without leading path) of the element	*eggplant.png*
getPathname()	The full pathname of the element	*/usr/local/images/eggplant.png*
getPath()	The leading path of the element	*/usr/local/images*
getGroup()	The group ID of the element	500
getOwner()	The owner ID of the element	1000
getPerms()	The permissions of the element, as an octal value	16895
getSize()	The size of the element	328742
getType()	The type of the element (dir, file, link, etc.)	file
getInode()	The inode number of the element	28720

The data that the functions in Table 25-4 report come from the same underlying system calls as the data that the functions in Table 25-1 report, so the same cautions on differences between Unix and Windows apply.

See Also

Documentation on `DirectoryIterator` (*http://www.php.net/DirectoryIterator*).

25.8 Getting a List of Filenames Matching a Pattern

Problem

You want to find all filenames that match a pattern.

Solution

Use a `FilterIterator` subclass with `DirectoryIterator`. The `FilterIterator` subclass needs its own `accept()` method that decides whether or not a particular value is acceptable.

To only accept filenames that end with common extensions for images:

```
class ImageFilter extends FilterIterator {
    public function accept() {
        return preg_match('@\.(gif|jpe?g|png)$@i',$this->current());
    }
}
foreach (new ImageFilter(new DirectoryIterator('/usr/local/images')) as $img) {
    print "<img src='".htmlentities($img)."'/>\n";
}
```

Discussion

The `FilterIterator` encloses a `DirectoryIterator` and only allows certain elements to emerge. It's up to the `accept()` method to return `true` or `false` to indicate whether a particular element (accessed with `$this->current()`) is OK. In the Solution, `accept()` uses a regular expression to make that determination, but your code can use any logic you like.

If your pattern can be expressed as a simple shell *glob* (e.g., `*.*`), use the `glob()` function to get the matching filenames. For example, to find all the text files in a particular directory:

```
foreach (glob('/usr/local/docs/*.txt') as $file) {
    $contents = file_get_contents($file);
    print "$file contains $contents\n";
}
```

The `glob()` function returns an array of matching full pathnames. If no files match the pattern, `glob()` returns `false`.

See Also

Recipe 25.9 for details on iterating through each file in a directory recursively; documentation on `FilterIterator` (*http://bit.ly/1rceARt*) and on `glob()` (*http://www.php.net/glob*); information about shell pattern matching (*http://bit.ly/1qdMh8j*).

25.9 Processing All Files in a Directory Recursively

Problem

You want to do something to all the files in a directory and in any subdirectories. For example, you want to see how much disk space is consumed by all the files under a directory.

Solution

Use a RecursiveDirectoryIterator and a RecursiveIteratorIterator. The RecursiveDirectoryIterator extends the DirectoryIterator with a getChildren() method that provides access to the elements in a subdirectory. The RecursiveIteratorIterator flattens the hierarchy that the RecursiveDirectoryIterator returns into one list. This example counts the total size of files under a directory:

```
$dir = new RecursiveDirectoryIterator('/usr/local');
$totalSize = 0;
foreach (new RecursiveIteratorIterator($dir) as $file) {
    $totalSize += $file->getSize();
}
print "The total size is $totalSize.\n";
```

Discussion

The objects that the RecursiveDirectoryIterator spits out (and therefore that the RecursiveIteratorIterator passes along) are the same as what you get from DirectoryIterator, so all the methods mentioned in Table 25-4 are available.

See Also

Documentation on RecursiveDirectoryIterator (*http://bit.ly/1j2uPKc*) and RecursiveIteratorIterator (*http://bit.ly/1fP2qN4*).

25.10 Making New Directories

Problem

You want to create a directory.

Solution

Use mkdir():

```
mkdir('/tmp/apples',0777) or die($php_errormsg);
```

Discussion

The second argument to `mkdir()` is the permission mode for the new directory, which must be an octal number. The current umask is taken away from this permission value to create the permissions for the new directory. So, if the current umask is `0002`, calling `mkdir(/tmp/apples,0777)` sets the permissions on the resulting directory to `0775` (user and group can read, write, and execute; others can only read and execute).

By default, `mkdir()` only creates a directory if its parent exists. For example, if */usr/local/images* doesn't exist, you can't create */usr/local/images/puppies*. To create a directory and its parents, pass `true` as a third argument to `mkdir()`. This makes the function act recursively to create any missing parent directories.

See Also

Documentation on `mkdir()` (*http://www.php.net/mkdir*).

25.11 Removing a Directory and Its Contents

Problem

You want to remove a directory and all of its contents, including subdirectories and their contents.

Solution

Use `RecursiveDirectoryIterator` and `RecursiveIteratorIterator`, specifying that children (files and subdirectories) should be listed before their parents:

```
function obliterate_directory($dir) {
    $iter = new RecursiveDirectoryIterator($dir);
    foreach (new RecursiveIteratorIterator($iter,
                RecursiveIteratorIterator::CHILD_FIRST) as $f) {
        if ($f->isDir()) {
            rmdir($f->getPathname());
        } else {
            unlink($f->getPathname());
        }
    }
    rmdir($dir);
}

obliterate_directory('/tmp/junk');
```

Discussion

Removing files, obviously, can be dangerous. Because PHP's built-in directory removal function, `rmdir()`, works only on empty directories, and `unlink()` can't accept shell wildcards, the `RecursiveIteratorIterator` must be told to provide children before parents with its `CHILD_FIRST` constant.

See Also

Documentation on `rmdir()` (*http://www.php.net/rmdir*) and on `RecursiveIterator Iterator` (*http://bit.ly/1fP2qN4*).

25.12 Program: Web Server Directory Listing

The *web-ls.php* program shown in Example 25-1 provides a view of the files inside your web server's document root, formatted like the output of the Unix command *ls*. Filenames are linked so that you can download each file, and directory names are linked so that you can browse in each directory, as shown in Figure 25-1.

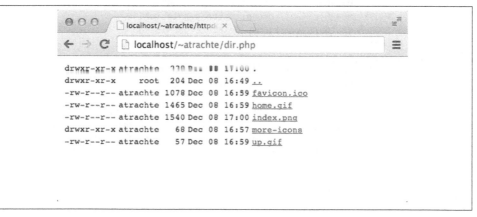

Figure 25-1. Web listing

Most lines in Example 25-1 are devoted to building an easy-to-read representation of the file's permissions, but the guts of the program are in the `foreach` loop at the end. The `DirectoryIterator` yields an element for each entry in the directory. Then, various methods on the element's object provide information about that file, and `printf()` prints out the formatted information about that file.

The `mode_string()` functions and the constants it uses turn the octal representation of a file's mode (e.g., 35316) into an easier-to-read string (e.g., `-rwsrw-r--`).

Example 25-1. web-ls.php

```
/* Bit masks for determining file permissions and type. The names and values
 * listed below are POSIX-compliant; individual systems may have their own
 * extensions.
 */

define('S_IFMT',0170000);    // mask for all types
define('S_IFSOCK',0140000);  // type: socket
define('S_IFLNK',0120000);   // type: symbolic link
define('S_IFREG',0100000);   // type: regular file
define('S_IFBLK',0060000);   // type: block device
define('S_IFDIR',0040000);   // type: directory
define('S_IFCHR',0020000);   // type: character device
define('S_IFIFO',0010000);   // type: fifo
define('S_ISUID',0004000);   // set-uid bit
define('S_ISGID',0002000);   // set-gid bit
define('S_ISVTX',0001000);   // sticky bit
define('S_IRWXU',00700);     // mask for owner permissions
define('S_IRUSR',00400);     // owner: read permission
define('S_IWUSR',00200);     // owner: write permission
define('S_IXUSR',00100);     // owner: execute permission
define('S_IRWXG',00070);     // mask for group permissions
define('S_IRGRP',00040);     // group: read permission
define('S_IWGRP',00020);     // group: write permission
define('S_IXGRP',00010);     // group: execute permission
define('S_IRWXO',00007);     // mask for others permissions
define('S_IROTH',00004);     // others: read permission
define('S_IWOTH',00002);     // others: write permission
define('S_IXOTH',00001);     // others: execute permission

/* mode_string() is a helper function that takes an octal mode and returns
 * a 10-character string representing the file type and permissions that
 * correspond to the octal mode. This is a PHP version of the mode_string()
 * function in the GNU fileutils package.
 */
$mode_type_map = array(S_IFBLK => 'b', S_IFCHR => 'c',
                       S_IFDIR => 'd', S_IFREG => '-',
                       S_IFIFO => 'p', S_IFLNK => 'l',
                       S_IFSOCK => 's');
function mode_string($mode) {
    global $mode_type_map;
    $s = '';
    $mode_type = $mode & S_IFMT;
    // Add the type character
    $s .= isset($mode_type_map[$mode_type]) ?
          $mode_type_map[$mode_type] : '?';

    // set user permissions
    $s .= $mode & S_IRUSR ? 'r' : '-';
    $s .= $mode & S_IWUSR ? 'w' : '-';
    $s .= $mode & S_IXUSR ? 'x' : '-';
```

```php
    // set group permissions
    $s .= $mode & S_IRGRP ? 'r' : '-';
    $s .= $mode & S_IWGRP ? 'w' : '-';
    $s .= $mode & S_IXGRP ? 'x' : '-';

    // set other permissions
    $s .= $mode & S_IROTH ? 'r' : '-';
    $s .= $mode & S_IWOTH ? 'w' : '-';
    $s .= $mode & S_IXOTH ? 'x' : '-';

    // adjust execute letters for set-uid, set-gid, and sticky
    if ($mode & S_ISUID) {
        // 'S' for set-uid but not executable by owner
        $s[3] = ($s[3] == 'x') ? 's' : 'S';
    }

    if ($mode & S_ISGID) {
        // 'S' for set-gid but not executable by group
        $s[6] = ($s[6] == 'x') ? 's' : 'S';
    }

    if ($mode & S_ISVTX) {
        // 'T' for sticky but not executable by others
        $s[9] = ($s[9] == 'x') ? 't' : 'T';
    }

    return $s;
}

// start at the document root if not specified
$dir = isset($_GET['dir']) ? $_GET['dir'] : '';

// locate $dir in the filesystem
$real_dir = realpath($_SERVER['DOCUMENT_ROOT'].$dir);
// Passing document root through realpath resolves any
// forward-slash vs. backslash issues
$real_docroot = realpath($_SERVER['DOCUMENT_ROOT']);

// make sure $real_dir is inside document root
if (! (($real_dir == $real_docroot) ||
        ((strlen($real_dir) > strlen($real_docroot)) &&
         (strncasecmp($real_dir,$real_docroot.DIRECTORY_SEPARATOR,
          strlen($real_docroot.DIRECTORY_SEPARATOR)) == 0)))) {
    die("$dir is not inside the document root");
}

// canonicalize $dir by removing the document root from its beginning
$dir = substr($real_dir,strlen($real_docroot)+1);

// are we opening a directory?
if (! is_dir($real_dir)) {
    die("$real_dir is not a directory");
```

```
    }

    print '<pre><table>';

    // read each entry in the directory
    foreach (new DirectoryIterator($real_dir) as $file) {
        // translate uid into user name
        if (function_exists('posix_getpwuid')) {
            $user_info = posix_getpwuid($file->getOwner());
        } else {
            $user_info = $file->getOwner();
        }

        // translate gid into group name
        if (function_exists('posix_getgrid')) {
            $group_info = $file->getGroup();
        } else {
            $group_info = $file->getGroup();
        }

        // format the date for readability
        $date = date('M d H:i',$file->getMTime());

        // translate the octal mode into a readable string
        $mode = mode_string($file->getPerms());

        $mode_type = substr($mode,0,1);
        if (($mode_type == 'c') || ($mode_type == 'b')) {
            /* if it's a block or character device, print out the major and
             * minor device type instead of the file size */
            $statInfo = lstat($file->getPathname());
            $major = ($statInfo['rdev'] >> 8) & 0xff;
            $minor = $statInfo['rdev'] & 0xff;
            $size = sprintf('%3u, %3u',$major,$minor);
        } else {
            $size = $file->getSize();
        }

        // format the <a href=""> around the filename
        // no link for the current directory
        if ('.' == $file->getFilename()) {
            $href = $file->getFilename();
        } else {
            // don't include the ".." in the parent directory link
            if ('..' == $file->getFilename()) {
                $href = urlencode(dirname($dir));
            } else {
                $href = urlencode($dir) . '/' . urlencode($file);
            }

            /* everything but "/" should be urlencoded */
            $href = str_replace('%2F','/',$href);
```

```php
        // browse other directories with web-ls
        if ($file->isDir()) {
            $href = sprintf('<a href="%s?dir=/%s">%s</a>',
                            $_SERVER['PHP_SELF'],$href,$file);
        } else {
            // link to files to download them
            $href= sprintf('<a href="%s">%s</a>',$href,$file);
        }

        // if it's a link, show the link target, too
        if ('l' == $mode_type) {
            $href .= ' -&gt; ' . readlink($file->getPathname());
        }
    }

    // print out the appropriate info for this file
    printf('<tr><td>%s</td><td align="right">%s</td>
            <td align="right">%s</td><td align="right">%s</td>
            <td align="right">%s</td><td>%s</td></tr>',
            $mode,                 // formatted mode string
            $user_info['name'],    // owner's user name
            $group_info['name'],   // group name
            $size,                 // file size (or device numbers)
            $date,                 // last modified date and time
            $href);                // link to browse or download
}

print '</table></pre>';
```

25.13 Program: Site Search

You can use *site-search.php* as a search engine for a small-to-medium, file-based, site:

```php
class SiteSearch {
    public $bodyRegex = '';
    protected $seen = array();

    public function searchDir($dir) {
        // array to hold pages that match
        $pages = array();

        // array to hold directories to recurse into
        $dirs = array();

        // mark this directory as seen so we don't look in it again
        $this->seen[realpath($dir)] = true;

        try {
            foreach (new RecursiveIteratorIterator(
            new RecursiveDirectoryIterator($dir)) as $file) {
                if ($file->isFile() && $file->isReadable() &&
```

```
                    (! isset($this->seen[$file->getPathname()])))) {
                        // mark this as seen so we skip it
                        // if we come to it again
                        $this->seen[$file->getPathname()] = true;

                        // load the contents of the file into $text
                        $text = file_get_contents($file->getPathname());

                        // if the search term is inside the body delimiters
                        if (preg_match($this->bodyRegex,$text)) {

                            // construct the relative URI of the file by removing
                            // the document root from the full path
                            $uri = substr_replace($file->getPathname(),'',0,strlen
                            ($_SERVER['DOCUMENT_ROOT']));

                            // if the page has a title, find it
                            if (preg_match('#<title>(.*?)</title>#Sis',$text,$match)) {
                                // and add the title and URI to $pages
                                array_push($pages,array($uri,$match[1]));
                            } else {
                                // otherwise use the URI as the title
                                array_push($pages,array($uri,$uri));
                            }
                        }
                    }
                }
            } catch (Exception $e) {
                // There was a problem opening the directory
            }
            return $pages;
        }
    }

    // helper function to sort matched pages alphabetically by title
    function by_title($a,$b) {
            return ($a[1] == $b[1]) ?
                    strcmp($a[0],$b[0]) :
                    ($a[1] > $b[1]);
    }

    // SiteSearch object to do the searching
    $search = new SiteSearch();

    // array to hold the pages that match the search term
    $matching_pages = array();
    // directories underneath the document root to search
    $search_dirs = array('sports','movies','food');
    // regular expression to use in searching files. The "S" pattern
    // modifier tells the PCRE engine to "study" the regex for greater
    // efficiency.
    $search->bodyRegex = '#<body>(.*' . preg_quote($_GET['term'],'#').
```

```
                    '.*)</body>#Sis';

// add the files that match in each directory to $matching pages
foreach ($search_dirs as $dir) {
    $matching_pages = array_merge($matching_pages,
                  $search->searchDir($_SERVER['DOCUMENT_ROOT'].'/'.$dir));
}

if (count($matching_pages)) {
    // sort the matching pages by title
    usort($matching_pages,'by_title');
    print '<ul>';
    // print out each title with a link to the page
    foreach ($matching_pages as $k => $v) {
        print sprintf('<li> <a href="%s">%s</a>',$v[0],$v[1]);
    }
    print '</ul>';
} else {
    print 'No pages found.';
}
```

The program looks for a search term (in $\_GET['term']$) in all files within a specified set of directories under the document root. Those directories are set in $search_dirs. It also recurses into subdirectories and follows symbolic links but keeps track of which files and directories it has seen so that it doesn't get caught in an endless loop.

If any pages are found that contain the search term, it prints a list of links to those pages, alphabetically ordered by each page's title. If a page doesn't have a title (between the <title> and </title> tags), the page's relative URI from the document root is used.

The program looks for the search term between the <body> and </body> tags in each file. If you have a lot of text in your pages inside <body> tags that you want to exclude from the search, surround the text that should be searched with specific HTML comments and then modify $body_regex to look for those tags instead. If your page looks like what is shown here:

```
<html>
<head>
        <title>Your Title</title>
</head>
<body>

// Some HTML for menus, headers, etc.

<!-- search-start -->

<h1>Aliens Invade Earth</h1>

<h3>by H.G. Wells</h3>

<p>Aliens invaded earth today. Uh Oh.</p>
```

```
// More of the story

<!-- search-end -->

// Some HTML for footers, etc.

</body>
</html>
```

to match the search term against just the title, author, and story inside the HTML comments, change `$search->bodyRegex` to this:

```
$search->bodyRegex = '#<!-- search-start -->(.*' . preg_quote($_GET['term'],'#').
            '.*)<!-- search-end -->#Sis';
```

If you don't want the search term to match text that's inside HTML or PHP tags in your pages, add a call to `strip_tags()` to the code that loads the contents of the file for searching, as shown:

```
// load the contents of the file into $text
$text = strip_tags(file_get_contents($file->getPathname()));
```

CHAPTER 26

Command-Line PHP

26.0 Introduction

PHP was created for web programming and is still used mostly for that purpose. However, PHP is also capable as a general-purpose scripting language. Using PHP for scripts you run from the command line is especially helpful when they share code with your web applications. If you have a discussion board on your website, you might want to run a program every few minutes or hours to scan new postings and alert you to any messages that contain certain keywords. Writing this scanning program in PHP lets you share relevant discussion-board code with the main discussion-board application. Not only does this save you time, but it also helps avoid maintenance overhead down the road.

PHP builds include a command-line interface (CLI) version. The CLI binary is similar to web server modules and the CGI binary but has some important differences that make it more shell friendly. Some configuration directives have hardcoded values with CLI; for example, the html_errors directive is set to false, and implicit_flush is set to true. The max_execution_time directive is set to 0, allowing unlimited program runtime. Finally, register_argc_argv is set to true. This means you can look for argument information in $argv and $argc instead of in $_SERVER['argv'] and $_SERVER['argc']. Argument processing is discussed in Recipe 26.1 and Recipe 26.2.

To run a script, pass the script filename as an argument:

```
% php scan-discussions.php
```

On Unix, you can also use the *hash-bang* syntax at the top of your scripts to run the PHP interpreter automatically. If the PHP binary is in */usr/local/bin*, make the first line of your script:

```
#!/usr/local/bin/php
```

You can then run the script just by typing its name on the command line, as long as the file has execute permission.

If it's likely that you'll use some of your classes and functions both for the Web and for the command line, abstract the code that needs to react differently in those different circumstances, such as HTML versus plain-text output or access to environment variables that a web server sets up. A useful tactic is to check if the return value of php_sapi_name() is cli. You can then branch your scripts' behavior as follows:

```
if ('cli' == php_sapi_name()) {
  print "Database error: ".mysql_error()."\n";
} else {
  print "Database error.<br/>";
  error_log(mysql_error());
}
```

This code not only adjusts the output formatting based on the context it's executing in (\n versus <br>), but also where the information goes. On the command line, it's helpful to the person running the program to see the error message from MySQL, but on the Web, you don't want your users to see potentially sensitive data. Instead, the code outputs a generic error message and stores the details in the server's error log for private review.

One helpful option on the command line is the -d flag, which lets you specify custom INI entries without modifying your *php.ini* file. For example, here's how to turn on output buffering:

```
% php -d output_buffering=1 scan-discussions.php
```

The CLI binary also takes an -r argument. When followed by some PHP code without <?php and ?> script tags, the CLI binary runs the code. For example, here's how to print the current time:

```
% php -r 'print strftime("%c");'
```

For a list of complete CLI binary options, pass the -h command:

```
% php -h
```

Finally, the CLI binary defines handles to the standard I/O streams as the constants STDIN, STDOUT, and STDERR. You can use these instead of creating your own filehandles with fopen():

```
// read from standard in
$input = fgets(STDIN,1024);

// write to standard out
fwrite(STDOUT,$jokebook);

// write to standard error
fwrite(STDERR,$error_code);
```

26.1 Parsing Program Arguments

Problem

You want to process arguments passed on the command line.

Solution

Look in `$argc` for the number of arguments and `$argv` for their values. The first argument, `$argv[0]`, is the name of script that is being run:

```
if ($argc != 2) {
    die("Wrong number of arguments: I expect only 1.");
}

$size = filesize($argv[1]);

print "I am $argv[0] and report that the size of ";
print "$argv[1] is $size bytes.";
```

Discussion

To set options based on flags passed from the command line, loop through `$argv` from 1 to `$argc`, as shown in Example 26-1.

Example 26-1. Parsing command-line arguments

```
for ($i = 1; $i < $argc; $i++) {
    switch ($argv[$i]) {
    case '-v':
        // set a flag
        $verbose = true;
        break;
    case '-c':
        // advance to the next argument
        $i++;
        // if it's set, save the value
        if (isset($argv[$i])) {
            $config_file = $argv[$i];
        } else {
            // quit if no filename specified
            die("Must specify a filename after -c");
        }
        break;
    case '-q':
        $quiet = true;
        break;
    default:
        die('Unknown argument: '.$argv[$i]);
        break;
```

```
        }
    }
```

In this example, the -v and -q arguments are flags that set $verbose and $quiet, but the -c argument is expected to be followed by a string. This string is assigned to $con fig_file.

The $argc and $argv variables are concise, but they are not populated if the regis ter_argc_argv config directive is turned off. However, $_SERVER['argc'] and $_SERV ER['argv'] always contain the argument count and argument values. Those are good places to look for argument information if you want maximally portable code.

See Also

Recipe 26.2 for more on parsing arguments with *getopt*; documentation on $argc (*http:// bit.ly/1sFlzqk*), $argv (*http://bit.ly/1rz6sud*), and $_SERVER (*http://bit.ly/1mqGJDX*).

26.2 Parsing Program Arguments with getopt

Problem

You want to parse program options that may be specified as short or long options, or they may be grouped.

Solution

Use the built-in getopt() function. As of PHP 5.3.0, it supports long options, optional values, and other convenient features:

```
// accepts -a, -b, and -c
$opts1 = getopt('abc');

// accepts --alice and --bob
$opts2 = getopt('', array('alice','bob'));
```

Discussion

To parse short-style options, pass getopt() the array of command-line arguments and a string specifying valid options. This example allows -a, -b, or -c as arguments, alone or in groups:

```
$opts = getopt('abc');
```

For the previous option string abc, these are valid sets of options to pass:

```
% program.php -a -b -c
% program.php -abc
% program.php -ab -c
```

The getopt() method returns an array. For each option specified on the command line, there is one element in the array. The key of the array element is the option name and the value of the array element is the option value. Counterintuitively, for flag-style options that don't take a value (such as a, b and c in the preceding), the value in the corresponding array element is false. For example, if the preceding program is run as:

```
% program.php -a -b sneeze
```

This makes $opts:

```
array(2) {
  ["a"]=>
  bool(false)
  ["b"]=>
  bool(false)
}
```

Put a colon after an option in the specification string to indicate that it requires a value. Two colons means the value is optional. So ab:c:: means that a can't have a value, b must, and c can take a value if specified. With this specification string, running the program as:

```
% program.php -a -b sneeze
```

This makes $opts:

```
array(2) {
  ["a"]=>
  bool(false)
  ["b"]=>
  string(6) "sneeze"
}
```

Instead of being ignored as an unspecified option, sneeze is now set as the value of b.

To parse long-style arguments, supply a second argument to getopt() containing an array that describes your desired arguments. Put each argument in an array element (leave off the leading --) and follow it with : to indicate a mandatory argument or :: to indicate an optional argument. The first argument to getopt() (the string for short-style arguments) can be left blank or not, depending on whether you also want to parse short-style arguments. This example allows debug as an argument with no value, name with a mandatory value, and size with an optional value:

```
$opts = getopt('',array('debug','name:','size::'));
```

These are valid ways to run this program:

```
% program.php --debug
% program.php --name=Susannah
% program.php --name Susannah
% program.php --debug --size
% program.php --size=56 --name=Susannah
% program.php --name --debug
```

The last example is valid (if counterproductive) because it treats --debug as the value of the name argument and doesn't consider the debug argument to be set. Values can be separated from their arguments on the command line by either an = or a space.

Note that for long-style arguments, getopt() does not include the leading -- in the array of parsed arguments. An argument specified as --name on the command line results in a key of name in the parsed argument array.

See Also

Recipe 26.1 for parsing of program options without *getopt*; documentation on ge topt() (*http://php.net/getopt*).

26.3 Reading from the Keyboard

Problem

You need to read in some typed user input.

Solution

Read from the special filehandle STDIN:

```
print "Type your message. Type '.' on a line by itself when you're done.\n";

$last_line = false;  $message = '';
while (! $last_line) {
    $next_line = fgets(STDIN,1024);
    if (".\n" == $next_line) {
      $last_line = true;
    } else {
      $message .= $next_line;
    }
}

print "\nYour message is:\n$message\n";
```

If the Readline extension is installed, use readline():

```
$last_line = false; $message = '';
while (! $last_line) {
    $next_line = readline();
```

```
        if ('.' == $next_line) {
            $last_line = true;
        } else {
            $message .= $next_line."\n";
        }
    }

    print "\nYour message is:\n$message\n";
```

If the ncurses extension is installed, use `ncurses_getch()`:

```
$line = '';
ncurses_init();
ncurses_addstr("Type a message, ending with !\n");
/* Display the keystrokes as they are typed */
ncurses_echo();
while (($c = ncurses_getch()) != ord("!")) {
    $line .= chr($c);
}
ncurses_end();
print "You typed: [$line]\n";
```

Discussion

With the special filehandle STDIN, you can use all the standard file-reading functions to process input (`fread()`, `fgets()`, etc.). The Solution uses `fgets()`, which returns input a line at a time. If you use `fread()`, the input still needs to be newline terminated to make `fread()` return. For example, if you run:

```
$msg = fread(STDIN,4);
print "[$msg]";
```

and type in tomato and then a newline, the output is [toma]. The `fread()` grabs only four characters from STDIN, as directed, but still needs the newline as a signal to return from waiting for keyboard input.

The Readline extension provides an interface to the GNU Readline library. The `readline()` function returns a line at a time, without the ending newline. Readline allows Emacs- and vi-style line editing by users. You can also use it to keep a history of previously entered commands:

```
$command_count = 1;
while (true) {
    $line = readline("[$command_count]--> ");
    readline_add_history($line);
    if (is_readable($line)) {
        print "$line is a readable file.\n";
    }
    $command_count++;
}
```

This example displays a prompt with an incrementing count before each line. Because each line is added to the Readline history with `readline_add_history()`, pressing the up and down arrows at a prompt scrolls through the previously entered lines.

The ncurses extension is an interface to the GNU ncurses library, which provides comprehensive control over keyboard events, mouse events, and screen output in text mode. The primary way to read keyboard input with ncurses is the `ncurses_getch()` function, which returns the ASCII code for the key pressed. A key difference between ncurses and the other two methods described here is that no newline is required before the keystroke is processed. The `ncurses_getch()` function returns right away after one keypress. In the example in the Solution, the code loops, repeatedly calling `ncurses_getch()` (and appending the typed character to `$line`) until ! is typed.

See Also

Documentation on `fopen()` (*http://www.php.net/fopen*), `fgets()` (*http://www.php.net/fgets*), `fread()` (*http://www.php.net/fread*), the Readline extension (*http://www.php.net/readline*), and the Readline library (*http://bit.ly/1g59HTw*); the ncurses extension (*http://pecl.php.net/ncurses*), and the ncurses library (*http://www.gnu.org/software/ncurses/*). Recipe 26.5 also discusses ncurses.

26.4 Running PHP Code on Every Line of an Input File

Problem

You want to read an entire file and execute PHP code on every line. For example, you want to create a command-line version of grep that uses PHP's Perl-compatible regular expression engine.

Solution

Use the `-R` command-line flag to process standard input:

```
% php -R 'if (preg_match("/$argv[1]/", $argn)) print "$argn\n";'
    php
    < /usr/share/dict/words
```

ephphatha

To execute a block of code before or after processing the lines, use the `-B` and `-E` options, respectively:

```
% php -B '$count = 0;'
    -R 'if (preg_match("/$argv[1]/", $argn)) $count++;'
    -E 'print "$count\n";'
    php
```

```
< /usr/share/dict/words
```

ι

Discussion

Sometimes you want to quickly process a file using PHP via the command line, either as a standalone project or within a sequence of piped commands. This lets you whip up a quick-and-dirty script to transform data.

PHP makes that easy using three command-line flags and two special variables: -R, -B, -E, $argn, and $argi.

The -R flag specifies the PHP code you want to execute for every line in the file. Within that block of code, you can access the line's text in the $argn variable.

As a basic example, here's a PHP script that takes HTML input, strips the tags, and prints out the result:

```
php -R 'print strip_tags($argn) . "\n"; ' < index.html
```

Because PHP automatically strips the newline from the end of the input, this code not only displays the results of strip_tags($argn), but also echos a newline.

It operates on the file *index.html*, which is passed in as standard input. There is no mechanism for specifying the file that you want processed.

This slightly more complicated example, which is a simple version of grep, shows how to accept input arguments via the $argv array:

```
% php -R 'if (preg_match("/$argv[1]/", $argn)) print "$argn\n";'
    php
    < /usr/share/dict/words

ephphatha
```

The first value passed to preg_match() is /$argv[1]/, which is the first argument passed to the script. In this example, it's php, so this code is searching for all the words in the */usr/share/dict/words* file containing php.

For what it's worth, ephphatha is an Aramaic word meaning *be opened*.

Beyond the individual lines, you sometimes need to execute initialization or clean-up code. Specify this using the -B and -E flags.

Building on the grep example, this code counts the total number of matching lines:

```
% php -B '$count = 0;'
    -R 'if (preg_match("/$argv[1]/", $argn)) $count++;'
    -E 'print "$count\n";'
    php
    < /usr/share/dict/words
```

1

Inside the -B block, you initialize the $count to 0. It's then incremented in the -R block whenever there's a match. Finally, the total number is printed out in the -E block.

To find out the percentage of matching lines, in addition to the total, use $argi:

```
% php -B '$count = 0;'
       -R 'if (preg_match("/$argv[1]/", $argn)) $count++;'
       -E 'print "$count/$argi\n";'
       php
       < /usr/share/dict/words
```

1/234937

The $argi variable contains the current line number of the file, so inside the -E block, it's set to the total number of lines.

See Also

Documentation on using PHP from the command line (*http://bit.ly/1my8axL*).

26.5 Reading Passwords

Problem

You need to read a string from the command line without it being echoed as it's typed —for example, when entering passwords.

Solution

If the ncurses extension is available, use ncurses_getch() to read each character, making sure "noecho" mode is turned on:

```
$password = '';
ncurses_init();
ncurses_addstr("Enter your password:\n");
/* Do not display the keystrokes as they are typed */
ncurses_noecho();
while (true) {
    // get a character from the keyboard
    $c = chr(ncurses_getch());
    if ( "\r" == $c || "\n" == $c ) {
        // if it's a newline, break out of the loop, we've got our password
        break;
    } elseif ("\x08" == $c) {
        /* if it's a backspace, delete the previous char from $password */
        $password = substr_replace($password,'',-1,1);
    } elseif ("\x03" == $c) {
```

```
        // if it's Control-C, clear $password and break out of the loop
        $password = NULL;
        break;
    } else {
        // otherwise, add the character to the password
        $password .= $c;
    }

}
ncurses_end();
```

Otherwise, on Unix systems, use */bin/stty* to toggle echoing of typed characters:

```
// turn off echo
`/bin/stty -echo`;

// read password
$password = trim(fgets(STDIN));

// turn echo back on
`/bin/stty echo`;
```

Neither ncurses nor stty is available on Windows platforms.

Discussion

Because ncurses gives character-by-character control over input (and because it's easy to toggle whether input is echoed to the screen), it makes it a great solution for reading passwords. The ncurses_getch() function reads a character without echoing it to the screen. It returns the ASCII code of the character read, so you convert it to a character using chr(). You then take action based on the character typed. If it's a newline or carriage return, you break out of the loop because the password has been entered. If it's a backspace, you delete a character from the end of the password. If it's a Ctrl-C interrupt, you set the password to NULL and break out of the loop. If none of these things are true, the character is concatenated to $password. When you exit the loop, $password holds the entered password.

If you're using a Unix system but don't have the ncurses extension available, use */bin/ stty* to control the terminal characteristics so that typed characters aren't echoed to the screen while you read a password.

The following code displays Login: and Password: prompts, and compares the entered password to the corresponding encrypted password stored in */etc/passwd*. This requires that the system not use shadow passwords:

```
print "Login: ";
$username = rtrim(fgets(STDIN)) or die($php_errormsg);

preg_match('/^[a-zA-Z0-9]+$/',$username)
    or die("Invalid username: only letters and numbers allowed");
```

```
print 'Password: ';
`/bin/stty -echo`;
$password = rtrim(fgets(STDIN)) or die($php_errormsg);
`/bin/stty echo`;
print "\n";

// find corresponding line in /etc/passwd
$fh = fopen('/etc/passwd','r')   or die($php_errormsg);
$found_user = 0;
$pattern = '/^' . preg_quote($username) . ':/';
while (! ($found_user || feof($fh))) {
    $passwd_line = fgets($fh,256);
    if (preg_match($pattern,$passwd_line)) {
        $found_user = 1;
    }
}
fclose($fh);

$found_user or die ("Can't find user \"$username\"");

// parse the correct line from /etc/passwd
$passwd_parts = split(':',$passwd_line);

/* encrypt the entered password and compare it to the password in
   /etc/passwd */
$encrypted_password = crypt($password, $password_parts[1]);
if ($encrypted_password == $passwd_parts[1]) {
    print "login successful";
} else {
    print "login unsuccessful";
}
```

See Also

Documentation on readline() (*http://www.php.net/readline*), chr() (*http://www.php.net/chr*), the ncurses extension (*http://pecl.php.net/ncurses*), and the ncurses library (*http://www.gnu.org/software/ncurses/*); on Unix, see your system's *stty(1)* man-page.

26.6 Colorizing Console Output

Problem

You want to display console output in different colors.

Solution

Use PEAR's Console_Color2 class:

```
$color = new Console_Color2();

$ok = $color->color('green');
$fail = $color->color('red');
$reset = $color->color('reset');

print $ok . "OK   " . $reset . "Something succeeded!\n";
print $fail . "FAIL " . $reset . "Something failed!\n";
```

If you're already using ncurses, incorporate colors by using the appropriate functions:

```
ncurses_init();
ncurses_start_color();

ncurses_init_pair(1, NCURSES_COLOR_GREEN, NCURSES_COLOR_BLACK);
ncurses_init_pair(2, NCURSES_COLOR_RED, NCURSES_COLOR_BLACK);
ncurses_init_pair(3, NCURSES_COLOR_WHITE, NCURSES_COLOR_BLACK);

ncurses_color_set(1);
ncurses_addstr("OK   ");
ncurses_color_set(3);
ncurses_addstr("Something succeeded!\n");
ncurses_color_set(2);
ncurses_addstr("FAIL ");
ncurses_color_set(3);
ncurses_addstr("Something succeeded!\n");
```

Discussion

By including special escape sequences in console output, you can instruct the console to display text in different colors. Instead of having to remember the magical numbers of the different special characters that make up these escape sequences, use PEAR's Console_Color2. Its color() method returns a string containing the right escape sequence to change colors. When one of those strings is included in the output stream, it changes the color of all subsequent text (until another escape sequence alters the active color). In addition to the special "color" reset (which resets the active color to the default), the color() method understands the following color names: black, red, green, brown, blue, purple, cyan, grey, and yellow.

The ncurses extension also offers its own functions for manipulating color. Although the syntax is different, logically it behaves the same way. Color values are defined, and then function calls (to ncurses_color_set()) that alter the "active" color can be interspersed with functions that output text.

See Also

The Console_Color2 class (*http://pear.php.net/Console_Color2*); documentation on ncurses_init_pair() (*http://www.php.net/ncurses_init_pair*) and ncurses_col or_set() (*http://www.php.net/ncurses_color_set*). More information about ncurses color programming (*http://bit.ly/1kSvDpt*) and about color escape sequences (*http://bit.ly/RnTN0G*).

26.7 Program: DOM Explorer

The *dom-explorer.php* program shown in Example 26-2 provides a shell-like prompt to let you explore an HTML document interactively. It reads an HTML document from a provided URL, parses it into a DOMDocument, and then gives you a prompt at which you can enter commands to see the node structure and contents of the documents.

Additionally, *dom-explorer.php* uses the Readline word-completion features to more easily enter node locations. Enter a few characters and hit Tab to see a list of nodes that match the characters you've typed:

```
% php dom-explorer.php http://www.php.net
/html > ls
head body
/html > ls head
title style[1] comment()[1] style[2] comment()[2] meta link[1] link[2] link[3] ↵
script[1] link[4] script[2]
/html > cat head/title
PHP: Hypertext Preprocessor
/html > cd body
/html/body > ls
text()[1] div[1] text()[2] div[2] text()[3] div[3] text()[4] div[4] text()[5] ↵
div[5] text()[6] div[6] text()[7] script comment()
/html/body > cd div[2]
/html/body/div[2] > ls
a text()[1] div text()[2]
/html/body/div[2] > cat a

/html/body/div[2] > cat div
downloads |
documentation | faq
| getting help | mailing lists | licenses | wiki
| reporting bugs | php.net sites | conferences | my
php.net
/html/body/div[2] > exit
```

The code for *dom-explorer.php* is in Example 26-2.

Example 26-2. dom-explorer.php

```
/* Need to specify a URL on the commandline */
isset($argv[1]) or die("No URL specified");

/* Load the HTML and start the command loop */
$explorer = new DomExplorer($argv[1]);
$explorer->loop();

class DomExplorer {
```

```php
public function __construct($url) {
    $html = file_get_contents($url);
    if (false === $html) {
        throw new Exception("Can't retrieve $url");
    }
    /* Turn the HTML into valid XHTML */
    $clean = tidy_repair_string($html, array('output-xhtml' => true));

    /* Load it into a DOMDocument, hiding any libxml
     * warnings */
    $this->doc = new DOMDocument();
    libxml_use_internal_errors(true);
    if (false === $this->doc->loadHtml($clean)) {
        throw new Exception("Can't parse {$url} as HTML");
    }
    libxml_use_internal_errors(false);
    $this->currentNode = $this->doc->documentElement;
    $this->x = new DOMXPath($this->doc);
}

public function loop() {
    /* The "completion" function will provide tab-completion at the prompt */
    readline_completion_function(array($this, 'completion'));
    while (true) {
        /* Use the current node as part of the prompt */
        $line = readline($this->currentNode->getNodePath() . ' > ');
        readline_add_history($line);

        /* The first word typed in is the command, the rest are arguments */
        $parts = explode(' ', $line);
        $cmd = array_shift($parts);

        /* Each command is a method, so call it if it exists */
        $cmd_function_name = "cmd_$cmd";
        if (is_callable(array($this, $cmd_function_name))) {
            try {
                $this->$cmd_function_name($parts);
            } catch (Exception $e) {
                print $e->getMessage() . "\n";
            }
        }
        else {
            print "Unknown Command: $line\n";
        }
    }
}

/**
 * Command: exit the program
 */
protected function cmd_exit($args) {
```

```php
        exit();
    }

    /**
     * Command: list all nodes under the current node or
     * a specified node
     */
    protected function cmd_ls($args) {
        if (isset($args[0]) && strlen($args[0])) {
            $node = $this->resolvePath($args[0]);
        }
        else {
            $node = $this->currentNode;
        }
        print implode(' ' , $this->getChildNodePaths($node)) . "\n";
    }

    /**
     * Command: change to a new current node
     */
    protected function cmd_cd($args) {
        /* If an argument is provided, use it */
        if (isset($args[0]) && strlen($args[0])) {
            $this->currentNode = $this->resolvePath($args[0]);
        }
        /* Otherwise go back to the "root" */
        else {
            $this->currentNode = $this->doc->documentElement;
        }
    }

    /**
     * Command: print the text content of a node
     */
    protected function cmd_cat($args) {
        if (isset($args[0]) && strlen($args[0])) {
            $node = $this->resolvePath($args[0]);
            print $node->textContent . "\n";
        }
        else {
            throw new Exception("cat requires an argument");
        }
    }

    /**
     * Get all the paths of the nodes under the provided
     * node, trimming off the path of the current node from
     * the paths of the child nodes
     */
    protected function getChildNodePaths($node) {
        $children = array();
        $curdir = $node->getNodePath();
```

```
        foreach ($node->childNodes as $node) {
            $path = $node->getNodePath();
            $sub = substr($path, strlen($curdir) + 1);
            $children[] = $sub;
        }
        return $children;
    }

    /**
     * When tab is pressed, return an array of child
     * node paths as possible completion targets
     */
    protected function completion($str, $index) {
        return $this->getChildNodePaths($this->currentNode);
    }

    /**
     * Resolve an xpath expression relative to the current
     * node, and make sure it only matches 1 target node
     */
    protected function resolvePath($arg) {
        $matches = $this->x->query($arg, $this->currentNode);
        if ($matches === false) {
            throw new Exception("Bad expresion: $arg");
        }
        if ($matches->length == 0) {
            throw new Exception("No match for $arg");
        }
        if ($matches->length > 1) {
            throw new Exception("{$matches->length} matches for arg");
        }
        return $matches->item(0);
    }

}
```

CHAPTER 27

Packages

27.0 Introduction

Packages and libraries allow you to not reinvent the wheel. Instead, you're able to use the wheels created by others in your projects. This chapter shows you how to use three collections of packages: Composer, PEAR, and PECL. Each provides a set of tools for you to easily incorporate packages into your own code, and even contribute packages of your own back to the common collective.

Composer is a dependency manager. Use it to install the code, including any external packages, needed by the libraries you want use. Composer makes it simple to wrangle the proper versions of code into your projects, both when you begin the project and when you decide to upgrade a package to a newer release. Packagist, the primary place to find Composer packages, has tens of thousands PHP packages.

PEAR is the PHP Extension and Application Repository, a collection of open source classes that work together. Developers can use PEAR classes to parse XML, implement authentication systems, generate CAPTCHAs, send MIME mail with attachments, and a wide variety of other common (and not so common) tasks. A pear is also a tasty fruit.

PECL is the PHP Extension Community Library. PECL, pronounced "pickle," is a series of extensions to PHP written in C. These extensions are just like the ones distributed with the main PHP release, but they're of more specialized interest—such as a MongoDB database driver or an OAuth 1.0 extension.

Each of these three collections fills a different need. Composer accepts all contributions. Anyone can register their package for use by anyone. There are often multiple packages that all solve similar problems, and quality can be anywhere from first class to highly buggy. In contrast, PEAR is a vetted set of code with one best implementation of any area, each working in conjunction with another. It's like *The Cathedral and the Ba-*

zaar. And where Composer and PEAR both handle code written in PHP, PECL covers the C extension side of PHP's world.

PEAR and PECL also install one version of a library to be used across all projects. In theory, this simplifies management because there's only one set of files to keep up-to-date. However, in practice, it's common to need two different versions of the same package at the same time. Two libraries often use the same underlying package, such as an HTTP request utility.

But whereas the first library requires features from HTTP version 2.0, the second library is still on version 1.8. Even worse, version 2.0 is backwards incompatible with 1.8. So, by upgrading the HTTP package to solve one dependency, you've broken another package in the process. And without any obvious way to foresee or workaround the problem when it comes up.

Composer takes a more limited approach. It installs separate copies of packages for every single project. This allows fine-grained control over the specific versions in use at any time, allows you to upgrade multiple projects at your own schedule, and makes it easy for you to bundle up your code and its dependencies into a self-contained unit. Many people have found this to take less time to manage, despite its duplicative nature.

Composer is not bundled with PHP, so the first step is to download and install it onto your computer. Installing and using Composer is the topic of Recipe 27.1. Information about Composer, including the documentation, the latest version of the software, and its issue tracker is at the Composer website (*https://getcomposer.org/*).

After Composer is running, you need to find packages to use. Recipe 27.2 covers searching and browsing Packagist. After you locate the packages and versions you want, ask Composer to add them.

For example, to install the latest 2.x version of the PHP_CodeCoverage library from PHPUnit:

```
% php composer.phar require phpunit/php-code-coverage:2.*
```

This downloads and installs the package into your project. Then, to let your scripts know where to find PHP_CodeCoverage, or any other package installed by Composer, add this to the top of your script:

```
require 'vendor/autoload.php';
```

That's it! One single file handles the work to discover where each package and its related classes live. Full details on installing Composer packages is covered in Recipe 27.3.

To find general information on PEAR, read the PEAR manual; to discover the latest PEAR packages, go to *http://pear.php.net*. The PEAR website also provides links to mailing list archives, as well as RSS feeds that allow easy monitoring of new package releases.

Part of PEAR is a program called *pyrus* that makes it easy for you to download and install additional PEAR packages. This program is also known as the PEAR installer for PHP 5.3+.[1] Recipe 27.4 shows how to use the PEAR installer.

Any developer can use the PEAR class management infrastructure with her projects. When developers create their own packages using the PEAR format, you can use *pyrus* to download and install the files from each project's website. This is called creating a PEAR channel. The PEAR installer supports a wide variety of channel-specific features that are covered in recipes throughout this chapter.

This chapter explains how to find a PEAR package that you may want to use and how to install it on your machine. Because PEAR and PEAR channels offer many packages, you need an easy way to browse them. Recipe 27.5 covers different ways to find PEAR packages. When you've found a package's name and determined which channel server it is on, Recipe 27.6 shows how to view package details and information.

After you locate a package you want to use, you need to run *pyrus* to transfer the package to your machine and install it in the correct location. Installing PEAR packages and PECL extensions are the subjects of Recipes 27.7 and 27.10, respectively. Recipe 27.8 shows how to discover if any upgrades are available to packages on your machine and how to install the latest versions. If you want to remove a package, see Recipe 27.9.

To view instructions and examples of how to use a particular PEAR package, check the PEAR website (*http://pear.php.net/packages.php*). Many packages have end-user documentation complete with examples. The rest typically include at least a set of generated API documentation that provides examples of usage. If all else fails, read the top section of the package's PHP files; most contain an example of usage there as well.

Documentation for PECL extensions is not always as easy to find. Some PECL extensions are very well documented within the main PHP manual; the APC extension (*http://www.php.net/apc*) is an excellent example. Other PECL extensions are not documented at all, and usage must be gleaned by reading PHP test scripts included with the source bundles from the PECL website. In extreme cases, you can only get the full idea of what an extension does by reading the extension source code.

The combination of Composer, PEAR, and PECL provides a vast collection of high-quality reusable code that make these projects tremendous assets to the PHP community at large.

---

1. There is an older PEAR installer named *pear*, which you may come across. This works with earlier versions of PHP, which is helpful for people using legacy systems.

27.1 Defining and Installing Composer Dependencies

Problem

You want to use Composer. This allows you to install new packages, upgrade, and get information about your existing packages.

Solution

Install Composer:

```
% curl -sS https://getcomposer.org/installer | php
```

To execute a command, type the command name as the first argument on the command line:

```
% php composer.phar command
```

Discussion

To install Composer, you download the installer file and send it to PHP. Composer uses PHP to ensure your system is set up as it requires, handle any configuration settings, and complete the installation process. When it's done, you have a file called *composer.phar* in the current directory.

Composer is a PHP script, so you can ask PHP to run it:

```
% php composer.phar command
```

Or, run it directly by putting *composer.phar* in the same location as PHP:

```
% mv composer.phar /usr/local/bin/composer
% composer command
```

If you have problems, make sure you have permission to write to that directory and that the file is executable:

```
% sudo mv composer.phar /usr/local/bin/composer
% sudo chmod +x /usr/local/bin/composer
```

Your copy of PHP may be in a different place. To find it, run:

```
% which php
/usr/bin/php
```

With Composer up and running, pass it commands to execute. For example, to install a package:

```
% composer install
```

For a list of all valid Composer commands, use list.

Composer has commands for both using and developing packages; as a result, there are some commands that you may not need. The `archive` command, for example, creates a new package. If you only run other people's packages, you can safely ignore this command. See Table 27-1 for a list of frequently used commands.

Table 27-1. Common Composer commands

Command name	Description
search	Searches for packages
init	Creates a basic *composer.json* file
install	Installs the project dependencies
update	Updates your dependencies to the latest version
self-update	Updates Composer to the latest version

See Also

The Composer site (*https://getcomposer.org*) and documentation on installation (*https://getcomposer.org/doc/00-intro.md*).

27.2 Finding Composer Packages

Problem

You want to find packages you can install using Composer.

Solution

Check Packagist (*https://packagist.org/*) or ask Composer to list or search packages.

Discussion

Packagist is the primary collection of Composer packages. Anyone can add their package to its directory, so others can find it by browsing or searching.

After you find a package, Packagist provides you with a terse overview, as shown in Figure 27-1.

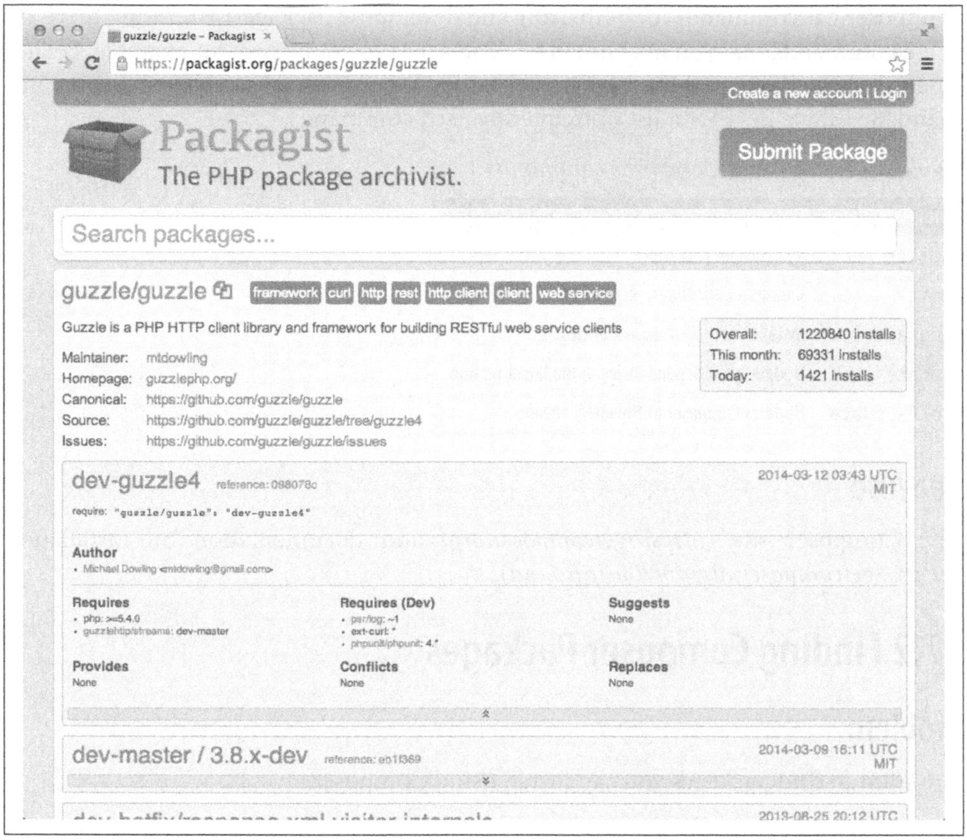

Figure 27-1. Guzzle Package Information page on the Packagist website

Packagist doesn't host any source code or documentation. For that, you need to visit the project's repository and home page.

Composer can list all the packages known by Packagist with the show command:

```
% php composer.phar show
No composer.json found in the current directory, showing available packages ↵
from packagist

platform:
  composer-plugin-api 1.0.0     The Composer Plugin API
  ext-bcmath          0         The bcmath PHP extension

...

  lib-xsl             1.1.26    The xsl PHP library
  php                 5.3.26    The PHP interpreter
  php-64bit           5.3.26    The PHP interpreter (64bit)
```

```
available:
  0k/php-oe-json
  0s1r1s/dev-shortcuts-bundle
  0x20h/monoconf

...

  zz/zz
  zzal/cakephp-hash
```

However, this list is tens of thousands of lines long. So, it's better to search instead using the search command:

```
% php composer.phar search http
No composer.json found in the current directory, showing packages from packagist
guzzle/http HTTP libraries used by Guzzle
illuminate/http
symfony/http-foundation Symfony HttpFoundation Component
symfony/http-kernel Symfony HttpKernel Component
net/http A basic HTTP client
minfraud/http MaxMind minFraud HTTP API
react/http Library for building an evented http server.
techdivision/http HTTP protocol implementation for usage in server context
vinelab/http An http library developed for the laravel framework. aliases
    itself as HttpClient
joomla/http Joomla HTTP Package
minond/http Http helpers
icanboogie/http Provides an API to handle HTTP requests.
aura/http The Aura HTTP package provides objects to build and send HTTP ↵
requests and responses.
orno/http A wrapper for Symfony\HttpFoundation with some encapsulation and ↵
convenience methods.
zendframework/zend-http provides an easy interface for performing Hyper-Text ↵
Transfer Protocol (HTTP) requests
```

See Also

Packagist (*https://packagist.org/*).

27.3 Installing Composer Packages

Problem

You want to install packages using Composer.

Solution

Use Composer's `require` command:

```
% php composer.phar require vendor/package:version
```

For example, to install the latest 2.x version of the PHP_CodeCoverage library from PHPUnit:

```
% php composer.phar require phpunit/php-code-coverage:2.*
```

Or use a *composer.json* file:

```
{
    "require" : {
        "phpunit/php-code-coverage": "2.*"
    }
}
```

with Composer's `install` command:

```
% php composer.phar install
```

Discussion

Composer reads instructions from a file, *composer.json*, to calculate a set of packages you want it to install.

This file is a simple JSON document. The most important element is the `require` key. This tells Composer which packages you need to have. For example:

```
{
    "require": {
        "phpunit/php-code-coverage": "2.1.*"
    }
}
```

This says you require the package `php-code-coverage` published by `phpunit`, and you're willing to take any version, as long as it's somewhere in the 2.1s.

Create this file using any text editor, or use Composer itself with the `require` command:

```
% php composer.phar require vendor/package:version
```

This creates (or edits) the file and adds the necessary JSON.

Composer uses a combination of `vendor` and `package` as a simple way to namespace packages. Many people have created packages with the same basic names, such as `log` or `json` or `db`. This lets you specify exactly which one.

In some cases, the vendor and the package have the same name. For example, `guzzle/guzzle`. That's okay.

The *composer.json* file can contain multiple packages with more sophisticated instructions:

```
{
    "require": {
        "phpunit/php-code-coverage": "2.1.*",
```

```
            "guzzle/guzzle": ">=3.7.0",
            "monolog/monolog": "1.7.0"
        }
    }
```

This asks for any 2.1.x version of phpunit/php-code-coverage (but less than 2.2.0), any version of guzzle/guzzle 3.7.0 or higher (including 3.8 and 4.0), and only version 1.7.0 of monolog/monolog (and nothing else).

To trigger the install, use the install command:

```
% php composer.phar install
```

These packages may have their own dependencies, which the vendor specifies in its own *composer.json* file. This includes a version of PHP, specific PHP extensions (such as cURL), and other packages (such as a basic logging class).

During installation, Composer automatically checks your system for these requirements. If you don't meet them, it will attempt to fix this (by downloading packages) or complain (if you need to upgrade PHP).

By convention, Composer places all installed packages inside a *vendor* folder in the current working directory. This keeps everything in one place and allows you to easily add this folder to your *.gitignore* file.

After installation, Composer writes out a file named *composer.lock* with the exact set of packages and version it installed. This allows you to "lock in" the particular set of packages that work for your application. That way, in case you encounter some unexpected change in one of the packages when you upgrade, you can always recover to a "known good" set.

To use a package, require Composer's standard autoloader code at the top, then declare the namespace of your package, and instantiate the object. This is the beginning of a script that uses the Guzzle HTTP Client:

```
require 'vendor/autoload.php';

use Guzzle\Http\Client;

// Create a client to work with the LinkedIn API
$client = new Client('https://api.linkedin.com/{version}', array(
    'version' => 'v1'
));
```

The mystery of how Composer can have a short autoloader class, yet still manage to find all the packages, is solved through standards.

Two separate packages found on Packagist don't promise any form of similar design or architecture. However, many packages do commit to various levels of interoperability.

They do so by implementing a set of standards defined by a working group of developers of PHP Frameworks.

PSRs, for PHP Standards Recommendation, lets you know how two packages will behave with each other. The most critical one is PSR-0, the autoloading standard. When you have many packages, each with its own file naming and directory syntax, it's not easy to know how to properly `require` them into your code.

Packages that implement PSR-0 agree to a common set of conventions for namespaces and how their PHP files, and the directories they're located in, are named and organized. This allows any PSR-0–compatible package to safely live alongside every other PSR-0 package and to be loaded using one common `autoload` function.

All packages managed by Composer follow this standard. This allows Composer to make it easy for you to use them.

See Also

Documentation on using Composer (*https://getcomposer.org/doc/01-basic-usage.md*); the PSR-0 Autoloading Standard (*https://github.com/php-fig/fig-standards/blob/master/accepted/PSR-0.md*); the PHP_CodeCoverage package (*https://github.com/sebastianbergmann/php-code-coverage*); the Guzzle project (*http://guzzlephp.org/*); and Monolog (*https://github.com/Seldaek/monolog*).

27.4 Using the PEAR Installer

Problem

You want to use the PEAR installer, *pyrus*. This allows you to install new packages, upgrade, and get information about your existing PEAR packages.

Solution

Install Pyrus. (*http://pear2.php.net/pyrus.phar*)

To execute a command, type the command name as the first argument on the command line:

```
% php pyrus.phar command
```

Discussion

Pyrus is a tool to manage PEAR packages. It's not bundled with PHP, so you need to install it yourself. Fortunately, Pyrus is distributed as a self-contained PHP Archive (aka a `phar`). So, all that's necessary is to download the file (*http://pear2.php.net/pyrus.phar*).

Then use PHP to run it:

```
% php pyrus.phar --version
Pyrus version 2.0.0a4 SHA-1: 72271D92C3AA1FA96DF9606CD538868544609A52
Using PEAR installation found at /Users/rasmus/lib
php pyrus.phar version 2.0.0a4.
```

Here's how to list all installed PEAR packages with the list-packages command:

```
% php pyrus.phar list-packages
Pyrus version 2.0.0a4 SHA-1: 72271D92C3AA1FA96DF9606CD538868544609A52
Using PEAR installation found at /Users/rasmus/lib
Listing installed packages [/Users/rasmus/lib]:
[channel pecl.php.net]:
(no packages installed in channel pecl.php.net)
[channel doc.php.net]:
(no packages installed in channel doc.php.net)
[channel __uri]:
(no packages installed in channel __uri)
[channel pear.php.net]:
Archive_Tar 1.3.7 stable
Console_Getopt 1.3.0 stable
PEAR 1.9.4 stable
Structures_Graph 1.0.4 stable
XML_Util 1.2.1 stable
```

For a list of all valid PEAR commands, use help.

pyrus has commands for both using and developing PEAR packages; as a result, there are many commands that you may not need. The package command, for example, creates a new PEAR package. If you only run other people's packages, you can safely ignore this command. See Table 27-2 for a list of frequently used commands.

Table 27-2. Common PEAR installer commands

Command name	Shortcut	Description
install	i	Download and install packages
upgrade	up	Upgrade installed packages
uninstall	un	Remove installed packages
list-packages	l	List installed packages
list-upgrades	lu	List all available upgrades for installed packages
channel-discover	di	Initialize an alternate PEAR Channel from its server
list-channels	lc	List all locally configured PEAR Channels
search	s	Search for packages

To find where your PEAR packages are located, run the get php_dir PEAR command. You can check the value of the include_path by calling ini_get('include_path') from within PHP or by looking at your *php.ini* file. If you can't alter *php.ini* because you're in a shared hosting environment, add the directory to the `include_path` at the top of your script before including any PEAR files. See Recipe 20.5 for more on setting configuration variables from within PHP.

You can configure Pyrus settings using:

```
% php pyrus.phar set setting value
```

Here *setting* is the name of the parameter to modify and *value* is the new value. To see all your current settings, use the `get` command:

```
% php pyrus.phar get
Pyrus version 2.0.0a4 SHA-1: 72271D92C3AA1FA96DF9606CD538868544609A52
Using PEAR installation found at /Users/rasmus/lib
System paths:
  php_dir => /Users/rasmus/lib/php
  ext_dir => /usr/lib/php/extensions/no-debug-non-zts-20121212
  cfg_dir => /Users/rasmus/lib/cfg
  doc_dir => /Users/rasmus/lib/docs
  bin_dir => /usr/bin
  data_dir => /Users/rasmus/lib/data
  www_dir => /Users/rasmus/lib/www
  test_dir => /Users/rasmus/lib/tests
  src_dir => /Users/rasmus/lib/src
  php_bin => /usr/bin/php
  php_ini => /private/etc/php.ini
  php_prefix =>
  php_suffix =>
Custom System paths:
User config (from /Users/rasmus/.pear/pearconfig.xml):
  default_channel => pear2.php.net
  auto_discover => 0
  http_proxy =>
  cache_dir => /Users/rasmus/lib/cache
  temp_dir => /Users/rasmus/lib/temp
  verbose => 1
  preferred_state => stable
  umask => 0022
  cache_ttl => 3600
  my_pear_path => /Users/rasmus/lib
  plugins_dir => /Users/rasmus/.pear
(variables specific to pear2.php.net):
  username =>
  password =>
  preferred_mirror => pear2.php.net
  download_dir => /Users/rasmus/lib/downloads
  openssl_cert =>
  handle =>
  paranoia => 2
Custom User config (from /Users/rasmus/.pear/pearconfig.xml):
(variables specific to pear2.php.net):
```

See Also

Pyrus documentation on installation (*http://bit.ly/Vo5xmn*).

27.5 Finding PEAR Packages

Problem

You want a listing of PEAR packages. From this list you want to learn more about each package and decide if you want to install it.

Solution

Browse PEAR 2 packages (*http://pear2.php.net/categories*) and PEAR packages (*http://bit.ly/1sFiJ4E*), or search for packages (*http://pear.php.net/search.php*). Use pear's remote-list command to get a listing of PEAR packages. Explore listings of PEAR channel servers (*http://pear.php.net/channels*).

Discussion

There are a few ways to review available PEAR and PEAR-compatible packages. First, to browse the listings of official PEAR packages in a directory-style fashion, go to *http://pear2.php.net/categories/* and *http://pear.php.net/packages.php?php=5*. From there you can burrow into each individual PEAR category.

Alternatively, you can search through the listings at the following address: *http://pear.php.net/search.php*. The search page allows you to search by package name, author, category, and release date.

You can also ask Pyrus to provide you with a listing of packages in the PEAR channel using the remote-list command:

```
% php pyrus.phar remote-list pear
Pyrus version 2.0.0a4 SHA-1: 72271D92C3AA1FA96DF9606CD538868544609A52
Using PEAR installation found at /Users/rasmus/lib
Remote packages for channel pear:
Audio:
Key: * = installed, ! = upgrades available
Authentication:
    Auth                        1.6.4     Creating an authentication system.
    Auth_HTTP                   2.1.8     HTTP authentication
    Auth_PrefManager            1.2.2     Preferences management class
    Auth_PrefManager2           2.0.0dev\ Preferences management class
                                1

...

    XML_XPath2                  n/a       The PEAR::XML_XPath2 package provided
                                          an XPath/DOM XML manipulation,
```

```
                                      maneuvering and query interface.
       XML_XRD                0.3.0   PHP library to parse and generate
                                      "Extensible Resource Descriptor"
                                      (XRD + JRD) files
       XML_XSLT_Wrapper       0.2.2   Provides a single interface to the
                                      different XSLT interface or commands
       XML_XUL                0.9.1   Class to build Mozilla XUL applications.
    Key: * = installed, ! = upgrades available
```

You can also query compatible PEAR Channel servers for available packages using the remote-list command. To do so, you must first make Pyrus aware of the alternate channel server. For example:

```
% php pyrus.phar channel-discover pear.drush.org
Pyrus version 2.0.0a4 SHA-1: 72271D92C3AA1FA96DF9606CD538868544609A52
Using PEAR installation found at /Users/rasmus/lib
Discovery of channel pear.drush.org successful

% php pyrus.phar list-channels
Pyrus version 2.0.0a4 SHA-1: 72271D92C3AA1FA96DF9606CD538868544609A52
Using PEAR installation found at /Users/rasmus/lib
Listing channels [/Users/rasmus/lib]:
__uri (__uri)
doc.php.net (phpdocs)
pear.drush.org (drush)
pear.php.net (pear)
pecl.php.net (pecl)

% php pyrus.phar remote-list drush
Pyrus version 2.0.0a4 SHA-1: 72271D92C3AA1FA96DF9606CD538868544609A52
Using PEAR installation found at /Users/rasmus/lib
Remote packages for channel drush:
Default:
    drush                     6.2.0.0   command line shell and Unix scripting
                                        interface for Drupal
    Key: * = installed, ! = upgrades available
```

To install a file from a remote channel, prepend the channel name and a slash before the package name. For example, to install the drush package from the drush channel:

```
% php pyrus.phar install drush/drush
Using PEAR installation found at /Users/rasmus/lib
Downloading pear.drush.org/drush
Mime-type: application/x-tar
[=======================================================>] 100% (494/494 kb)
Installed pear.drush.org/drush-6.2.0.0
```

See Also

Recipe 27.6 to find more information about a package.

27.6 Finding Information About a Package

Problem

You want to gather information about a package, such as a description of what it does, who maintains it, what version you have installed, and which license it's released under.

Solution

Use Pyrus's `info` command:

```
% php pyrus.phar info pear/HTTP2
```

You can also view the package's home page (*http://pear.php.net*).

Discussion

The `info` command provides summary information about a package:

```
% php pyrus.phar info pear/HTTP2
Pyrus version 2.0.0a4 SHA-1: 72271D92C3AA1FA96DF9606CD538868544609A52
Using PEAR installation found at /Users/rasmus/lib
HTTP2 (pear.php.net Channel)
-----------------------------------------------------------------------------
Package type: Version:    1.1.1 (API 1.1.0), Stability:    stable (API stable)
Release Date: 2013-10-23 15:33:41
Package Summary: Miscellaneous HTTP utilities
Package Description Excerpt:
   The HTTP class is a class with static methods for doing
   miscellaneous HTTP related stuff like date formatting,
   language negotiation or HTTP redirection....
(`php pyrus.phar info pear/HTTP2 description` for full description)
Release Notes Excerpt:

   - Fix parsing arguments values without quotes...
(`php pyrus.phar info pear/HTTP2 notes` for full release notes)
```

If you don't have the package installed, it will ask the remote server for a description.

For further details about the package description or release notes, append `descrip tion` or `notes` to your request.

The package home page provides a more complete view and also provides links to earlier releases, a change log, and browsable access to the package's repository. You can also view package download statistics. Figure 27-2 shows a sample package information page.

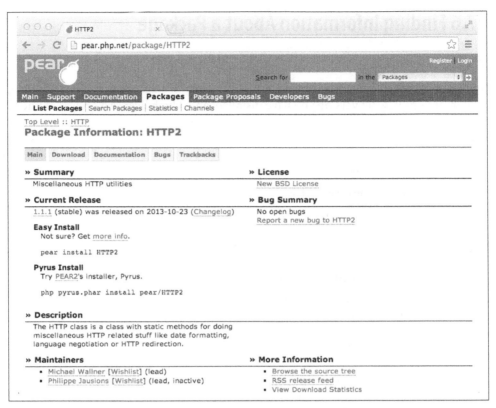

Figure 27-2. HTTP2 Package Information page on the PEAR website

See Also

Recipe 27.5 to search for packages.

27.7 Installing PEAR Packages

Problem

You want to install a PEAR package.

Solution

Download and install the package from the PEAR Channel server using Pryus:

```
% php pyrus.phar install pear/Package_Name
```

You can also install from another PEAR Channel:

```
% php pyrus.phar install channel/Package_Name
```

You can also install from any location on the Internet:

```
% php pyrus.phar install http://pear.example.com/Package_Name-1.0.0.tgz
```

Here's how to install if you have a local copy of a package:

```
% php pyrus.phar install Package_Name-1.0.0.tgz
```

Discussion

To install PEAR packages, you need write permission where the packages are stored; this defaults to */usr/local/lib/php/*.

You can also request multiple packages at the same time:

```
% php pyrus.phar install pear/XML_RSS pear/XML_SVG
Pyrus version 2.0.0a4 SHA-1: 72271D92C3AA1FA96DF9606CD538868544609A52
Using PEAR installation found at /Users/rasmus/lib
Downloading pear.php.net/XML_RSS
Mime-type: application/octet-stream
Downloading pear.php.net/XML_SVG===============================>] 100% ( 6/ 6 kb)
Mime-type: application/octet-stream
Installed pear.php.net/XML_RSS-1.0.2==========================>] 100% ( 7/ 7 kb)
Installed pear.php.net/XML_SVG-1.1.0
```

When installing a package, Pyrus checks that you have all the necessary PHP functions and PEAR packages that the new package depends on. If this check fails, it installs all required PEAR dependencies:

```
% php pyrus.phar install pear/XML_XUL-alpha
Pyrus version 2.0.0a4 SHA-1: 72271D92C3AA1FA96DF9606CD538868544609A52
Using PEAR installation found at /Users/rasmus/lib
Downloading pear.php.net/XML_XUL
Mime-type: application/octet-stream
Downloading pear.php.net/XML_Util2===========================>] 100% (26/26 kb)
Mime-type: application/octet-stream
Downloading pear.php.net/XML_Parser2=========================>] 100% (16/16 kb)
Mime-type: application/octet-stream
Installed pear.php.net/XML_XUL-0.9.1=========================>] 100% (11/11 kb)
Installed pear.php.net/XML_Util2-0.1.0
Installed pear.php.net/XML_Parser2-0.1.0
```

Once a PEAR package is installed, use it in your PHP scripts by calling require_once. For example, here's how to include the HTTP_Request2 package:

```
require_once 'HTTP/Request2.php';
```

Generally, if a package name contains an underscore, replace it with a slash, and add *.php* to the end.

Because PEAR packages are included as regular PHP files, make sure the directory containing the PEAR packages is in your include_path. If it isn't, include_once and require_once can't find PEAR class files.

See Also

Recipe 27.10 for information on installing PECL packages; Recipe 27.8 for more on upgrading an existing package; Recipe 27.9 to uninstall a package.

27.8 Upgrading PEAR Packages

Problem

You want to upgrade a package on your system to the latest version for additional functionality and bug fixes.

Solution

Find out if any upgrades are available and then tell Pyrus to upgrade the packages you want:

```
% php pyrus.phar list-upgrades
% pear upgrade  pear/Package_Name
```

Discussion

Upgrading to a new version of a package is a simple task with Pyrus. If you know a specific package is out of date, you can upgrade it directly. However, you may also just want to check periodically to see if any new releases are available.

To do this, use the list-upgrades command, which prints out a table showing the channel server of the package, package name, local version number and state, version number and state of the remote upgrade, and size of the download of the upgrade:

```
% php pyrus.phar  list-upgrades
Pyrus version 2.0.0a4 SHA-1: 72271D92C3AA1FA96DF9606CD538868544609A52
Using PEAR installation found at /Users/rasmus/lib
(no packages installed in channel __uri)
(no packages installed in channel doc.php.net)
(no upgrades for packages installed in channel pear.drush.org)
Upgrades for channel pear.php.net:
  XML_Beautifier 1.2.2 (stable, released 2010-10-25)
  Console_Getopt 1.3.1 (stable, released 2011-03-08)
  Archive_Tar 1.3.11 (stable, released 2013-02-09)
(no packages installed in channel pecl.php.net)
```

To upgrade a particular package, use the upgrade command. For example:

```
% php pyrus.phar upgrade pear/XML_Beautifier-1.2.2
Pyrus version 2.0.0a4 SHA-1: 72271D92C3AA1FA96DF9606CD538868544609A52
Using PEAR installation found at /Users/rasmus/lib
Downloading pear.php.net/XML_Beautifier
```

```
Mime-type: application/octet-stream
Installed pear.php.net/XML_Beautifier-1.2.2=======>] 100% (14/14 kb)
```

The short command for `list-upgrades` is `lu`; for `upgrade` it's `up`.

PEAR also has an RSS feed listing new and upgraded packages (*http://pear.php.net/feeds/latest.rss*).

See Also

Recipes 27.7 and 27.10 for information on installing PEAR and PECL packages; Recipe 27.9 to uninstall a package; Recipe 12.12 for more on parsing RSS feeds.

27.9 Uninstalling PEAR Packages

Problem

You wish to remove a PEAR package from your system.

Solution

The `uninstall` command tells the PEAR installer to delete packages:

```
% php pyrus.phar uninstall pear/XML_Beautifier
Pyrus version 2.0.0a4 SHA-1: 72271D92C3AA1FA96DF9606CD538868544609A52
Using PEAR installation found at /Users/rasmus/lib
Uninstalled pear.php.net/XML_Beautifier
```

Discussion

Uninstalling a package removes it completely from your system. If you want to reinstall it, you must begin as if the package was never installed.

If you try to remove a package that another package depends on, Pyrus will warn you and halt the uninstall process. For example, take a look at a sample PEAR installation:

```
% sudo php pyrus.phar list-packages
Pyrus version 2.0.0a4 SHA-1: 72271D92C3AA1FA96DF9606CD538868544609A52
Using PEAR installation found at /Users/rasmus/lib
Listing installed packages [/Users/rasmus/lib]:
[channel pear.php.net]:
Archive_Tar 1.3.7 stable
Console_Getopt 1.3.0 stable
HTTP2 1.1.1 stable
PEAR 1.9.4 stable
Structures_Graph 1.0.4 stable
XML_Beautifier 1.2.1 stable
XML_Parser 1.3.4 stable
XML_Parser2 0.1.0 beta
```

```
XML_RSS 1.0.2 stable
XML_SVG 1.1.0 stable
XML_Util 1.2.1 stable
XML_Util2 0.1.0 alpha
```

Now, try to uninstall the XML_Parser package:

```
% php pyrus.phar uninstall pear/XML_Parser
Pyrus version 2.0.0a4 SHA-1: 72271D92C3AA1FA96DF9606CD538868544609A52
Using PEAR installation found at /Users/rasmus/lib
Pyrus\Installer\Exception: Dependency validation failed for some installed
    packages, installation aborted
 Pyrus\Dependency\Exception: channel://pear.php.net/XML_Parser (version >=
     1.0.1, excluded versions: 1.0.1) is required by installed package
     "channel://pear.php.net/XML_RSS"
```

You can still force a package that has dependencies to uninstall by using the -f flag or
--force flag to instruct Pyrus to ignore dependencies and uninstall anyway. Use this
capability with caution.

There is no way to automatically roll back an upgrade to an earlier version of a package
by using uninstall.

The short command for uninstall is un.

See Also

Recipes 27.7 and 27.10 for information on installing PEAR and PECL packages.

27.10 Installing PECL Packages

Problem

You want to install a PECL package; this builds a PHP extension written in C to use
inside PHP.

Solution

Make sure you have all the necessary extension libraries and then use the bundled installer *pecl*:

```
% pecl install mailparse
```

To use the extension from PHP, add the appropriate line to your *php.ini* file:

```
extension=mailparse.so
```

Discussion

The frontend process for installing PECL packages is just like installing PEAR packages for code written in PHP. However, the behind-the-scenes tasks are very different. Because PECL extensions are written in C, the installer needs to compile the extension and configure it to work with the installed version of PHP. As a result, at present, you can build PECL packages on Unix machines if you have the necessary development tools installed.

Unlike PHP-based PEAR packages, PECL extensions don't automatically inform you when you lack a library necessary to compile the extension. Instead, you are responsible for correctly preinstalling these files. If you are having trouble getting a PECL extension to build, check the *README* file and the other documentation that comes with the package. The installer puts these files inside the *docs* directory under your PEAR hierarchy.

When you install a PECL extension, the *pecl* command downloads the distribution file, extracts it, runs *phpize* to configure the extension for the version of PHP installed on the machine, and then makes and installs the extension. It may also prompt you for the location of libraries:

```
% pecl install memcached
downloading memcached-2.1.0.tgz ...
Starting to download memcached-2.1.0.tgz (39,095 bytes)
.........done: 39,095 bytes
11 source files, building
running: phpize
Configuring for:
PHP Api Version:        20100412
Zend Module Api No:     20100525
Zend Extension Api No:  220100525

...

Build complete.

...

install ok: channel://pecl.php.net/memcached-2.1.0
You should add "extension=memoize.so" to php.ini
```

PECL extensions are stored in different places than PEAR packages written in PHP. If you want to run *pecl*, you must be able to write inside the PHP *extensions* directory. Because of this, you may want to install these packages while running as the same user you used to install PHP. Also, check the execute permissions of these files; because most PEAR files aren't executable, your umask may not provide those executable files with the correct set of permissions.

If you're running PHP and PECL in a Windows environment, you may prefer to download precompiled DLLs for the PECL extensions you need by browsing the extension's page (*http://pecl.php.net/*).

See Also

Recipe 27.7 for information on installing PEAR packages; Recipe 27.8 for more on upgrading an existing package; Recipe 27.9 to uninstall a package.

Index

Symbols

!== (not-identity operator), 5, 116
"" (double quotes), 1, 311
$ (dollar sign), 142
$argc, 733
$argv, 733
$GLOBALS, 177
$_COOKIE array
  PHP page processing and, 277
  preventing global variable injection and, 303
  reading cookie values and, 240
  using cookie authentication and, 249
$_ENV array, 258, 277
$_FILES array, 277, 294
$_GET array
  building dynamic images and, 530
  escaping special characters and, 668
  exposing clean resource paths, 473
  exposing/routing to a resource and, 470
  handling remote variables and, 305
  in Site Search program, 731
  PHP page processing and, 277
  preventing global variable injection and, 303
$_POST array
  cookie authentication and, 248
  creating a resource and, 479
  handling remote variables and, 305
  PHP page processing and, 237, 277
  preventing global variable injection and, 303

required fields and, 242
using form elements with multiple options and, 306
validating form input and, 283, 290
verifying data with hashes and, 558
$_REQUEST array, 278
$_SERVER array
  argument processing and, 733, 736
  creating a resource and, 479
  detecting SSL and, 566
  exposing/routing to a resource and, 470
  generating high-precision time and, 83
  PHP page processing and, 277
  processing form input and, 279
  reading an HTTP header and, 250
  removing passwords from source code and, 551
  setting environment variables and, 259
  supporting multiple formats and, 487
  using cookie authentication and, 248
  using HTTP basic/digest authentication and, 243
  validating form input and, 281
$_SERVER[HTTPS], 566
$_SESSION array, 298, 356
% (percent sign), 328
& (ampersand symbol), 242
& operator, 163, 169
-> (arrow), 184, 220

We'd like to hear your suggestions for improving our indexes. Send email to index@oreilly.com.

. (dot)
    concatenation operator, 16
    in remote variables, 305
:: (double colon), 184, 213, 217
; (semicolon), using heredoc formats, 3
<<< (heredoc format), 3
= (assignment operator), 199, 200
= (equals), 139
    cloning objects, 200
    object references, assigning, 199
=& (assignment operator), 169
    object references, assigning, 199
== (equality operator), 114, 139
=== (identity operator), 5
=== (strict equality check), 114
? (question mark), 662
?: operator, 659, 666
[ ] (square brackets)
    creating a character class with, 655
    form elements with multiple options and,
       306
    parsing configuration files and, 690
    referencing individual bytes with, 5
\ (backslash), 1, 654, 675
\b (word-boundary assertion), 686
\n (newline), 2, 18, 27
\r (carriage return), 2, 27
\s (whitespace metacharacter), 686
\t (tab), 2
\w (word character), 659
^ (caret), 656
_ (SQL wildcard), 328
_ (underscore), 186
_getch(), 739
__autoload(), 231
__call(), 209, 214
__callStatic(), 209, 214
__CLASS__ constant, 221, 616
__clone method, 202
__construct, 183, 186, 211, 604
__destruct(), 187
__DIR__ constant, 281
__FILE__ constant, 148, 616, 718
__FUNCTION__ constant, 616
__get(), 203
__isset(), 203
__LINE__ constant, 616
__METHOD__ constant, 616
__set(), 203

__sleep(), 222
__toString(), 192, 602
__unset(), 203
__wakeUp(), 153, 222
{} (curly braces)
    dynamic variable names and, 142
    interpolating strings and, 17
| (vertical bar), 656

A

abstract classes, 195
abstract methods, 198
accelerators, 636
Accept-Encoding header, 257
Accept-Language header, 573
access control, 188
access values, 609
accessor functions, 190
acos(), 52
addcslashes(), 658
addresses, looking up with LDAP, 502
Ajax requests, 430
allow_url_fopen, 443
ampersand symbol (&), 242
anonymous FTP, 500
Apache
    communicating within, 259
    mod_rewrite, 473
    rogue scripts and, 551
APC extension, data store functionality, 145,
    364
arcs, drawing, 519
$argc, 733
arguments
    argument list, 167
    controlling cookies with, 238
    ensuring value types, 165
    long-style, 736
    method polymorphism and, 215
    passing by reference, 163
    specifying by name, 164
    variable numbers of, 166
$argv, 733
arithmetic functions, 53
array(), 96, 141
ArrayAccess interface, 133
arrays
    accessing objects using array syntax, 133
    anonymous, 100

applying functions to each element in, 127
assigning integer series to, 101
assigning multiple values to, 96
associating multiple elements per key, 99
auto-global, 278
combining, 108
converting to strings, 110
definition of, 95
deleting elements from, 104
eliminating duplicates in, 126
finding differences in pairs of, 129
finding elements in, 113
finding intersection in pairs of, 129
finding keys in, 113
finding largest/smallest elements in, 117
finding specific elements in, 116
finding unions in pairs of, 129
finding value positions in, 115
in PHP, 95
initializing empty, 549
iterating over large, 131
iterating through, 101
modifying size of, 106
multidimensional, 307
printing with commas, 111
randomizing element order in, 125
reversing element order in, 118
sorting, 119
sorting by computable fields, 120
sorting multiple, 123
sorting with methods, 124
specifying first element index, 98
types of, 95
array_intersect(), 290
array_key_exists(), 113, 287
array_merge(), 108, 164
array_multisort(), 123
array_pad(), 106
array_push(), 96
array_reverse(), 118
array_search(), 115
array_splice(), 104
array_to_comma_string(), 111
array_unique(), 126
array_walk(), 127
arrow (->), 184, 220
asin(), 52
asort(), 118, 119, 122, 589

assignment operators
=, 169, 199, 200
=&, 169
associative arrays, 95
atan(), 51
atan2(), 52
Atom feeds
reading, 403
writing, 409
attributes (XML), 371
authentication
benefits of, 237
cookie, 247
Digest, 244
HTTP basic, 243
LDAP, 504
session, 249
auto-global arrays, 278

B

backslash (\), 1, 654, 675
bar charts, 516, 541
base classes, 182, 197
base e (natural log), 46
Base64 encoding, 244, 566
basename(), 717
bases
converting between, 55
using numbers in, 56
base_convert(), 55
BCMath library, handling large and small numbers, 53
bcrypt, 552
bearer tokens, 462
Benchmark (PEAR), 642
binary data
escaping quotes for queries, 327
storing in strings, 29
bindColumn(), 320
bindec(), 55
bindParam(), 325
blanks, removing from strings, 17
Blowfish, 555
bound parameters, 324, 550
browsers
buffering output to, 255, 618
download interruptions, 267
flushing output to, 255
redirecting to mobile optimized sites, 260

static declaration, 143, 219
status codes, 252
STDIN, 738
stream-based parsers, 384
streams feature, 443
Stream_SHM module, 704
stress testing, 648
strftime(), 62
strict equality check (===), 114
string.strip_tags, 427
strings
    accessing substrings, 5
    altering with regular expressions, 655
    concatenation of, 16
    controlling case in, 14
    converting arrays to, 110
    double-quoted, 2, 16
    downloadable CSV files, 31
    dumping variable contents as, 153
    encapsulating complex data types, 152
    escape sequences, 2
    expanding/compressing tabs in, 12
    extracting substrings, 6
    generating comma-separated data, 19
    generating fixed-width field data, 21
    generating random, 11
    generating replacement, 670
    generating XML as, 374
    initializing, 1
    interpolating functions/expressions in, 16
    matching words with regular expressions,
        659
    optimizing string-matching operations, 649
    parsing comma-separated data, 20
    parsing dates/times from, 77
    parsing fixed-width field data, 22
    printing with commas, 111
    processing bytes individually, 9
    reading files into, 681
    reading without echoes, 742
    removing HTML/PHP tags from, 426
    replacing substrings, 7
    reversing by word or byte, 10
    single-quoted, 1
    storing binary data in, 29
    taking apart, 25
    trimming blanks from, 17
    wrapping text lines in, 27
strip_tags(), 427

strpos(), 5
strrev(), 10
strtolower(), 16
strtotime(), 77
strtoupper(), 16
str_rand(), 11
str_replace(), 12, 417
subclassing, 182, 191
substr(), 6, 22
substrings
    accessing, 5
    extracting, 6
    replacing, 7
substr_replace(), 7
summary tables, 367
symmetric difference, 129
syntactic validation, 293
System V shared memory extension, 145

T

tabs, expanding/compressing, 12
tab_expand(), 13
tab_unexpand(), 13
tags, removing HTML/PHP, 426
tangent, 51
tempfile(), 678
tempnam(), 678, 718
test environments, creating, 630
text
    aligning with tab stops, 12
    avoiding stair-stepped, 674
    building dynamic images based on, 528
    capturing inside HTML tags, 665
    controlling case of, 14
    drawing as a graphic, 522
    drawing centered, 525
    escaping quotes for queries, 327
    localization of images containing, 585
    manipulating UTF-8, 593
    preventing capture with regular expressions,
        666
    processing variable-length fields, 688
    reversing words in a string, 10
    sorting in locale-aware order, 588
    wrapping lines of, 27
text messages, localizing, 574
text nodes
    appending in DOM method, 376

website account deactivators, 261
WEEK(), 75
WEEKDAY(), 75
well-formed XML, 373, 376
whereis program, 233
whitespace
    in XML, 372
    removing, 17, 618, 675
whitespace metacharacter (\s), 686
Whois servers, 511
wikis, Tiny Wiki program, 264
word character (\w), 659
word-boundary assertion (\b), 686
words, processing every, 686
wordwrap(), 27

X

XAMPP project, 630
Xdebug, 606, 621, 638, 644
XHTML documents, generating, 423
XML
    document restrictions, 372
    extracting information using XPath, 389
    generating as a string, 374
    generating with DOM, 375
    handling content encoding, 374, 402
    overview of, 371
    parsing basic douments, 378
    parsing complex documents, 378
    parsing large documents, 383
    PHP extensions for, 372

reading RSS/Atom feeds, 403
setting XSLT parameters from PHP, 394
SimpleXML extension, 378
transforming with XSLT, 392
validation of, 373, 400
vs. HTML, 371
well-formed, 373, 376
writing Atom feeds, 409
writing RSS feeds, 406
XML Reader extension, 383
XML Schema, 401
XMLHTTPRequest, 430
XMLReader extension, 383
XPath, 390
XSL (eXtensible Stylesheet Language), 393
XSLT (eXtensible Stylesheet Language Transformations)
    calling PHP functions, 396
    setting parameters from PHP, 394
    transforming XML documents with, 393
XSLTProcessor::registerPHPFunctions(), 396
XSLTProcessor::setParameter(), 394

Y

Y2K issues, 62

Z

Zend Engine 2 (ZE2), 181
Zend OPcache accelerator, 636
Zetacomponent excMailComposer, 492

About the Authors

David Sklar is an independent technology consultant. In addition to *PHP Cookbook*, he is the author of *Learning PHP 5* (O'Reilly), *Essential PHP Tools* (Apress), and a scintillating blog (*http://www.sklar.com/blog/*). David lives in New York City and has a degree in Computer Science from Yale University.

Adam Trachtenberg is the Director of the LinkedIn Developer Network. He's the author of *Upgrading to PHP 5* and *PHP Cookbook* (O'Reilly). He was previously the Director for Platform and Services for eBay. Adam lives in Mountain View, California, and has a BA in mathematics and an MBA from Columbia University.

Colophon

The animal on the cover of *PHP Cookbook*, Third Edition, is a Galapagos land iguana (*Conolophus subcristatus*). Once abundant in the Galapagos Islands, this iguana proved tasty to the settlers of the early 1800s, and domestic animals later introduced on the islands played further havoc with the reptile's home and food supply. Today there are no iguanas left on Santiago Island and very few left on the other islands.

Distantly related to the green iguana of the South American continent, Galapagos land iguanas can be over three feet long, with males weighing up to 30 pounds. Their tough, scaly skin is yellow with scattered patches of white, black, brown, and rust. These lizards resemble mythical creatures of the past-dragons with long tails, clawed feet, and spiny crests. In reality, however, they are harmless.

Land iguanas live in the drier areas of the islands and in the morning are found basking in the sun. During midday, however, they seek the shade of cactus, rocks, and trees. To conserve body heat at night, they sleep in burrows dug in the ground.

These reptiles are omnivores, but they generally depend on low-growing plants and shrubs, as well as the fallen fruits and pads of cactus trees. These plants provide most of the moisture they need; however, they will drink fresh water whenever it's available.

Depending on their size, land iguanas reach maturity between 8 and 15 years of age. They congregate and mate during specific periods, which vary from island to island. The females then migrate to suitable areas to nest. After digging a burrow, the female lays 2 to 20 eggs in the nest. She then defends the covered nest site to prevent other females from nesting in the same spot.

Young iguanas hatch 85 to 110 days later and take about a week to dig their way out of the nest. Normally, if hatchlings survive the first year when food is often scarce and native predators such as hawks, egrets, herons, and snakes are a danger, they can live for more than 60 years. In reality, predation by feral cats is far worse because the young must survive and grow for at least three to four years before becoming large enough that cats can't kill them.

The cover image is a 19th-century engraving from the Dover Pictorial Archive. The cover fonts are URW Typewriter and Guardian Sans. The text font is Adobe Minion Pro; the heading font is Adobe Myriad Condensed; and the code font is Dalton Maag's Ubuntu Mono.

CPSIA information can be obtained at www.ICGtesting.com
Printed in the USA
BVOW09s0937080714

357868BV00002B/1/P